# A REBEL BORN

# ✺ THE LOCHLAINN SEABROOK COLLECTION ✺

*Five-Star Books & Gifts With Five-Star Service!*

# SeaRavenPress.com

# DEDICATION

*To All That Forest Stood, Fought, and Lived For:*

God, family, home, tradition, ancestors,
hard work, racial tolerance, integration,
and harmony, the land, the great
outdoors, sports, animals, strict
Constitutionalism, the original
Confederate Republic, liberty, the
South, states' rights, state sovereignty,
a small weak constitutionally limited
central government, free trade, a
voluntary union, entrepreneurship,
individualism, capitalism, self reliance,
and above all personal freedom and
self-determination.

# EPIGRAPH

Lord Garnet J. Wolseley, commanding general of the British armies: "Who do you think was the greatest military genius developed by the War?"

General Robert E. Lee: "General Nathan Bedford Forrest, of Tennessee, whom I have never met. He accomplished more with fewer troops than any other officer on either side."

# CONTENTS

# Notes to the Reader

☛ In any study of America's antebellum, bellum, and postbellum periods, it is vitally important to understand that in 1860 the two major political parties—the Democrats and the newly formed Republicans—were the opposite of what they are today. In other words, the Democrats of the mid 19th Century were Conservatives, akin to the Republican Party of today, while the Republicans of the mid 19th Century were Liberals, akin to the Democratic Party of today.

Thus the Confederacy's Democratic president, Jefferson Davis, was a Conservative (with libertarian leanings); the Union's Republican president, Abraham Lincoln, was a Liberal (with socialistic leanings). This is why, in the mid 1800s, the conservative wing of the Democratic Party was known as "the States' Rights Party."[1] Hence, the Democrats of the Civil War period referred to themselves as "conservatives," while the Republicans called themselves "liberals."[2]

Since this idea is new to most of my readers, let us further demystify it by viewing it from the perspective of the American Revolutionary War. If Davis and his conservative Southern constituents (the Democrats of 1861) had been alive in 1775, they would have sided with George Washington and the American colonists, who sought to secede from the tyrannical government of Great Britain; if Lincoln and his Liberal Northern constituents (the Republicans of 1861) had been alive at that time, they would have sided with King George III and the English monarchy, who sought to maintain the American colonies as possessions of the British Empire. It is due to this very comparison that Southerners often refer to the "Civil War" as the Second American Revolutionary War.

☛ As I heartily dislike the phrase "Civil War," its use throughout this book (as well as in my other works) is worthy of an explanation.

---

1. See J. W. Jones, TDMV, pp. 144, 200-201, 273.
2. See e.g., Pollard, LC, p. 178; J. H. Franklin, pp. 101, 111, 130, 149; Nicolay and Hay, ALCW, Vol. 1, p. 627.

Today America's entire literary system refers to the conflict of 1861 using the Northern term the "Civil War," whether we in the South like it or not. Thus, as all book searches by readers, libraries, and retail outlets are now performed online, and as all bookstores categorize works from this period under the heading "Civil War," book publishers and authors who deal with this particular topic have little choice but to use this term themselves. If I were to refuse to use it, as some of my Southern colleagues have suggested, few people would ever find or read my books.

Add to this the fact that scarcely any non-Southerners have ever heard of the names we in the South use for the conflict, such as the "War for Southern Independence"—or my personal preference, "Lincoln's War." It only makes sense then to use the term "Civil War" in most commercial situations.

We should also bear in mind that while today educated persons, particularly educated Southerners, all share an abhorrence for the phrase "Civil War," it was not always so. Confederates who lived through and even fought in the conflict regularly used the term throughout the 1860s, and even long after. Among them were Confederate generals such as Nathan Bedford Forrest, Richard Taylor, and Joseph E. Johnston, not to mention the Confederacy's vice president, Alexander H. Stephens. Even the Confederacy's highest leader, President Jefferson Davis, used the term "Civil War,"[3] and in one case at least, as late as 1881—the year he wrote his brilliant exposition, *The Rise and Fall of the Confederate Government*.[4]

☛ Lincoln's War on the American people and the Constitution can never be fully understood without a thorough knowledge of the South's perspective of the conflict. As *A Rebel Born* only briefly touches on this complex topic, one cannot hope to learn the whole truth about the "Civil War" here. For those who are interested in a more in-depth study, please see my other more scholarly books, listed on page 2.

---

**3**. See e.g., Seabrook, TQJD, pp. 30, 38, 76.
**4**. Seabrook, EYWTATCWIW, p. 13.

# FOREWORD

There is a story that a year or two after the great American war of 1861–1865, a visiting Englishman asked Gen. R.E. Lee, "Who is the greatest soldier produced by the war?" It is reported that Lee without hesitation replied: "A gentleman in Tennessee whom I have never met. His name is Forrest."

There can be no doubt that Bedford Forrest was one of the great captains of history.

Time and time again he defeated much larger forces in battle. Other enemy forces he regularly dispersed, captured, and deprived of their supplies. By bold and quick movement, accompanied by a genius for terrain and for surprising his opponents, he tied down or diverted large opposing armies. Time and again he raised new forces and equipped them from the enemy.

General J.E.B. Stuart is justly celebrated for his ride around the Union army in Virginia in 1862. More than once Forrest rode around Union armies into occupied Kentucky and Tennessee, eluding or thwarting every cavalry expedition sent against him and returning home with vast booty of horses, provisions and equipment, prisoners, and recruits. Beyond his accomplishments as a soldier, Forrest was and remains a hero to the people of the mid-South that he led in resistance to a vicious invasion.

Forrest's record is even more impressive when we remember that the armies he opposed were the biggest ever mustered in the century between Napoleon and World War I. It is no wonder that General William T. Sherman called Forrest "that devil" and said that no resources should be spared to find Forrest and murder him. It is a plain fact, whatever efforts are made to deceive us, that the labels "war criminal" and "terrorist" fit General Sherman well, but do not fit General Forrest at all. Even so, when he was finished shooting and burning, Sherman said that Forrest was "the most remarkable man the Civil War produced on either side."

There was a long period in the earlier twentieth century when the Confederacy and its heroes were considered an honoured part of American history, when the War was viewed as a great national tragedy with good and bad on both sides. That was the spirit of the centennial in the 1960s. As we enter the sesquicentennial observance, it is clear that the times are changed mightily, and that interpretation of history is to be dominated by people who will use every sort of falsehood, distortion, and emotional fury they can perpetrate to banish the Confederacy into one dark little corner labelled "slavery and treason."

It is clear also that this hate campaign is directed not just at the Confederacy but at the entire South and its people, past, present, and future. It is equally evident that the campaign I am referring to does not rest upon any special knowledge or understanding of history or any concern about the truth of history. The first axiom of a real historian is that history—the acts of our predecessors of the human race and the times in which they acted—are complicated and should be approached with open mind and with the intent to understand rather than to hasten to condemnation. For instance, the present authorities do not know that hundreds of black Americans paid their respects to General Forrest at his funeral, while black people were not allowed at Lincoln's funeral. (Indeed, most of them had been banished from Springfield by mobs before the war of "emancipation," at the time Lincoln was a prominent citizen of the city.) If the present authorities were confronted with these facts, they would scream loudly that it's not true and make sure that as few people as possible heard about it. A few of the more honest might make up elaborate excuses why the facts don't really mean what they say. But any true history is a living thing, always open to debate, new evidence, and different perspectives.

Instead of wholesaling a phony image of Forrest as a unique monster, a writer who really understands American history would note his strong resemblance to Andrew Jackson. Though of different generations, both were Tennesseans, raised on the Southern frontier. Both survived difficult early years to emerge as men of indomitable courage, inspired leadership, fierce personal pride, and decisive action and few words. Both were self-made men without much formal schooling. Neither was a professional military man, but both learned to lead Southern volunteers to victory over the forces of imperial governments. Only their times were different. Jackson came along when a Southern spirit was large in the guidance of the United States, Forrest when new forces were seeking domination and suppressing the old. That is history as life rather than mere material for propaganda labels.

The hatred of the South does not rest upon historical judgment. It is the result of an ideological will to power in which propaganda slogans are repeated again and again to stop independent thought and discussion and impose an official party line of historical interpretation. V.I. Lenin wrote this play book for his disciples. One also wonders about the quality of the American patriotism shown by the haters of Forrest. Could it match that of Forrest's grandson, General Nathan Bedford Forrest, U.S. Army, who died in 1943 when his flying fortress was shot down during a raid over Germany?

One recent would-be historian of the War, who regards every thing positive that can be said about the Confederacy as a "Lost Cause Myth," wonders in print how anyone today can admire such an awful character as Forrest. The proper question to ask is, rather, how can any normal human being not admire a hero who defended his people with tremendous courage and skill against a superior enemy intent on conquest? Horatio at the Bridge, Roland at Ronscevalles, the defenders of the Alamo, Forrest belongs in that great pantheon of heroes.

He is also a great American, and American history cannot be understood without Forrest in his proper place. That is why Mr. Seabrook's accounting of the truth of Forrest and his enemies that is presented here is so welcome and has appeared with such perfect timing.

Dr. Clyde N. Wilson
Distinguished Professor Emeritus of History
University of South Carolina
June 2010

(Photo © Lochlainn Seabrook)

# PREFACE

Ilive and work in Middle Tennessee just thirty miles from where Forrest was born,[5] and at the center of where he rode, fought, and lived during the War for Southern Independence. Even 130 years after his death it is impossible not to be aware of him in these parts, for this is Forrest country.

At last count Tennessee has erected some thirty-two statues of Forrest (and at least one of his favorite horse, Roderick—in Thompson's Station, Tennessee). This is more statues than Illinois has erected for Abraham Lincoln, or Virginia for George Washington.[6] In our area specifically Forrest's name is everywhere, from street signs and the names of schools, to the names of businesses, stores, golf courses, and modern subdivisions. There is even a large statue of him, surrounded by all of the Confederate state flags, situated in plain view along our busiest interstate.[7]

My interest in Forrest and Dixie is more than just historical, however. It is also personal. My entire family is from the South and over a dozen of my ancestors fought proudly for the Confederacy. One of these was my third great-grandfather, Private Elias Jent, Sr. Elias served in "Caudill's Army" under my second cousin, the noted Confederate colonel, Benjamin Everage Caudill, in the First Company of the Thirteenth Kentucky Cavalry. The Thirteenth fought at such engagements as Saltville, Poor Fork, Mill Cliff, Whitesburg, Gladsville, and Leatherwood.

As the story has been handed down to us through several generations, Elias was home on furlough sometime in 1864. He and his wife, my third great-grandmother, Rachel Cornett, were out one day walking from Hindman to Lott's Creek, Perry County (now Knott

---

5. Forrest was born in Chapel Hill, Bedford (now Marshall) County, Tennessee.

6. Ashdown and Caudill, p. 177.

7. The statue sits on a private Confederate park located on the east side of I-65 near the border between Brentwood and Nashville. The park is presently owned by Sir William Dorris. The Forrest statue there was created by Nashville attorney Jack Kershaw, the grandson of one of Forrest's cavalrymen.

County), Kentucky, and had stopped at the home of a "Mrs. Cornett," one of Rachel's relatives. Some Union soldiers happened by and searched the house, discovering that Elias was a Confederate soldier. He and Rachel were then forcibly taken outside. Shots were heard.

After the soldiers left and it was felt to be safe again, the others in the house ran outside only to find that Elias and Rachel had been hanged from a tree in the yard.[8] This Yankee war crime against my family has reverberated down into the present day, nearly 150 years later, the emotion, pain, and drama little diminished by time.[9]

I have happier personal associations with, and connections to, Forrest himself: he and I are cousins through mutual European ancestors, some of them of royal blood. Then there are my cousins Colonel Edmund Winchester Rucker, who led Rucker's Brigade,[10] and Lieutenant General Richard Taylor, both who rode and fought with Forrest through many of his engagements, including John Bell Hood's disastrous Tennessee Campaign in late 1864.[11]

Rucker's and Forrest's relationship, in particular, developed into a strong friendship that lasted many years. During the War, in September 1864, Forrest gave Rucker permanent command of the newly reorganized Rucker's Brigade, bypassing a senior officer who had been

---

8. It is very probable that some of my family members actually witnessed the murder of Elias and Rachel from inside the house.

9. I am not the only Forrest biographer who had innocent Southern ancestors (many of them noncombatants) attacked by Yankee soldiers. Another was Andrew Nelson Lytle, author of *Bedford Forrest and His Critter Company*. As a little girl Lytle's grandmother was unaccountably shot in the neck by a Union soldier while she was playing in the street. As blood poured from her wound and imminent death drew near, her terrified family called for a doctor. Their request was denied by Yankee authorities, however: the girl's father had not yet signed Lincoln's ridiculous and illegal "Oath of Allegiance" (not an oath to God at all, but a threat of violence upon anyone who did not publically side with Lincoln and the North). Fortunately, a kindly Kentucky officer was able to procure a doctor, and Lytle's grandmother was saved, living into old age (her father was later arrested anyway and forced to sign "Honest Abe's" oath).

10. I am a direct descendant of the Ruckers of Virginia and West Virginia. My 4th great-grandmother was Phoebe Rucker (a 1st cousin of Colonel Rucker), who married Henry Allen. Colonel Rucker is my 3rd cousin. John Allan Wyeth, who penned *Life of General Nathan Bedford Forrest*, one of the best biographies on Forrest, knew Rucker well and consulted with him on various details for his book. See Wyeth, LGNBF, p. 398. Another Rucker cousin of mine, G. W. Rucker, fought with the Confederate Third Kentucky Regiment, which was associated with Forrest during Lincoln's War. Jordan and Pryor, p. 700.

11. Forrest, Taylor, and I all descend from the royal English family the Plantagenets, one of whose most famous members is King Edward I "Longshanks." Considered the greatest of England's Medieval rulers, Longshanks is my 21st great-grandfather.

in line for promotion ahead of Rucker. Naturally this created a good deal of rancor, and several officers (Major Phil Allen and Colonels W. L. Duckworth, J. U. Green, and J. J. Neely) refused to acknowledge Forrest's order or recognize Rucker's new rank. Forrest would not stand for this kind of behavior and immediately had the five officers arrested for insubordination and sent to Mobile, Alabama, where they faced trial by court martial.[12]

One of Forrest's men, Private John Milton Hubbard, later said of my 3rd cousin:

> A man of great physical force and a fine horseman, [Edmund W. Rucker] impressed men with his prowess in battle. Recklessly brave, he did not mind riding down an enemy, or engaging him in single combat. He helped to make the reputation of his old brigade as a body of fast and furious fighters.[13]

After the War, in September 1869, as president of the Selma, Marion, and Memphis Railroad, Forrest hired the now one-armed Rucker to serve as superintendent of his "road."[14] Just as they had done on the battlefield, the two former Confederate officers worked closely together as civilian business partners for many years, until Forrest resigned his presidency in 1874.[15]

Taylor, one of the few Confederate officers Forrest genuinely admired and respected,[16] was the brother of my cousin Sarah Knox Taylor, the first wife of the Confederacy's only president, Jefferson Davis. Richard and Sarah were, of course, the children of the 12th President of the U.S., Zachary Taylor.[17]

Another cousin of mine, 1st Lieutenant Nathan Boone—a

---

12. Mathes, pp. 282-283.

13. Hubbard, p. 154.

14. Rucker's arm was seriously wounded during Hood's inglorious retreat from Nashville in December 1864, and he had to have it amputated. Note: Rucker also served with distinction under Forrest at the General's most brilliant victory, Brice's Cross Roads.

15. The exact date of Forrest's resignation from the Selma, Marion, and Memphis Railroad was April 1, 1874. Rucker stayed on with the company as superintendent after Forrest left.

16. See e.g., Forrest's warm letter of friendship to Taylor in Wyeth, LGNBF, p. 533.

17. President Taylor is my 11th cousin.

relative of American pioneer Daniel Boone[18]—rode with (and at times officered) Forrest's famous band of elite horsemen known as Forrest's Escort.[19] Forrest himself fought under the command of my cousin Lieutenant General Stephen Dill Lee,[20] who is related to another cousin of mine, Confederate hero General Robert E. Lee. It was General Lee who called Forrest "the greatest soldier produced on either side during the war."[21]

Stephen Dill Lee fought at Franklin II, as did my cousin John Byars Womack, who served with the Tennessee Rebels in Company E, Sixteenth Infantry Regiment.[22] Unlike Lee, who survived Franklin II, John (from Warren County, Tennessee) was killed during the battle and is buried in the McGavock Confederate Cemetery. His fading moss-covered headstone can still be see in Section 61, Grave 147. We visit the site often to pay our respects.[23]

Just before the Battle of Franklin II, November 30, 1864, Forrest stood on the upper deck of Carnton Mansion, Franklin, Williamson County, Tennessee, to survey the situation.[24] Carnton Plantation was built by my cousins the McGavocks, one of whom was Randal McGavock, the 11th mayor of Nashville. His grandnephew and namesake, and also my cousin, Lieutenant Colonel Randal William McGavock, of the Tenth Tennessee, was captured by the Yanks at Fort Donelson in February 1862, where Forrest futilely tried to talk his

---

18. The modern singers Pat Boone and his daughter Debbie are also related to Nathan and Daniel.

19. Dr. Michael R. Bradley, personal correspondence. Several of my other Boone cousins also rode in Forrest's Escort: A. B. Boone, Alfred H. Boone, and Hugh L. W. Boone, as did my cousins Thomas Gorum Cheairs and Jordan H. Womack. See Bradley, pp. 191, 195, 197, 199, 200, 206.

20. Like Rucker, Lieutenant General Stephen Dill Lee also personally communicated with Wyeth while he was writing *The Life of General Nathan Bedford Forrest*. Wyeth, LGNBF, p. 399.

21. See my books on Lee: *The Old Rebel: Robert E. Lee as Seen by His Contemporaries* and *The Quotable Robert E. Lee: Selections From the Writings and Speeches of the South's Most Beloved Civil War General*.

22. Both John and myself are related to country artist Lee Ann Womack.

23. My 7th great-grandmother was Martha Womack. Her husband (my 7th great-grandfather) was John Mosby, Sr., the 3rd great-granduncle of Confederate icon John Singleton Mosby, my 5th cousin.

24. After studying the countryside's topography from Carnton's upper portico, Forrest told Hood that a full frontal attack across the open plain at Franklin, as Hood proposed, would be suicidal, and suggested a flanking movement. As we will see, Hood ignored Forrest's advice and proceeded to lead the Army of Tennessee into the "Valley of Death," the Battle of Franklin II, one of the War's most needless and bloodiest conflicts. For more on 2nd Franklin, see my book *The McGavocks of Carnton Plantation: A Southern History*.

superiors out of surrendering.[25]

Randal William McGavock (of the Deery Family Home, Allisona, Tennessee), who later died at the Battle of Raymond, Mississippi, was a first cousin of another one of my relations, Harriet Young "Hattie" McGavock, who married Lieutenant George Limerick Cowan, one of the officers in Forrest's Escort. Hattie grew up at Carnton,[26] and she and George later moved into their own house, Windermere, at the foot of Carnton's driveway.[27]

The McGavocks' home, beautiful Carnton Plantation, was one of forty-four sites in Franklin used as field hospital during the Battle of Franklin II. Hundreds of wounded and dying Rebel soldiers were brought to the house and grounds that night, where many perished and were later laid to rest in what became known as the McGavock Confederate Cemetery, the largest privately owned military cemetery in the U.S.

Well-known then as today as perhaps the Confederacy's greatest debacle of the entire War, Franklin II has justifiably gone down in history as only one of the many conflicts in which Forrest was misused, his innate military genius squandered, his talents ignored, by his superiors. The Southern gentleman at the head of this particular disaster was my cousin General John Bell Hood.

The McGavocks married into the Cheathams, another family with which I am related and that was linked to Forrest. One of its most

---

25. Forrest's superiors should have listened to him. By surrendering Fort Donelson to the Yanks, Grant, who was on the verge of being removed from his command, and arrested and imprisoned, was instead promoted, allowing him to go on and win at Shiloh, one of the South's most decisive defeats. The loss, as we will discuss, helped seal the fate of the Confederacy, launched Grant into worldwide celebrity, and even helped put him in the White House as our 18th president. Wyeth, LGNBF, pp. 39-42.

26. Seabrook, CPGS, p. 19.

27. Hattie's and George's little brown house in Franklin, Tennessee, still exists but is currently privately owned. The couple are buried together at Mount Hope Cemetery in Franklin, only a few miles from where they lived. A side note: Hattie's father, my cousin Confederate Colonel John W. McGavock, son of Mayor Randal McGavock, who owned Carnton during Lincoln's War (at which time it was used as a Confederate field hospital), was married to Caroline Elizabeth "Carrie" Winder, a woman known as the "Good Samaritan of Williamson County (Tennessee)." The Winders (the *wind* element in this surname is pronounced as in "windy," not as in "whine") are another family I am closely related to. Carrie's and my cousin, Confederate Brigadier General John H. Winder, was inspector general of military camps in the Richmond area. Winder died on February 6, 1865, during an inspection of the prison camp in Florence, South Carolina.

famous members was General Benjamin Franklin "Frank" Cheatham, an outstanding Rebel officer, but one who Forrest disliked and with whom he clashed on occasion.[28]

The McGavocks were a large, wealthy, well-liked, and influential Confederate family in Middle Tennessee, and so it is not surprising that one of them would eventually cross paths with Forrest. In Memphis, in the summer of 1867, Forrest began working with a company, Hopper and Montgomery, whose project at the time was to improve the city's image, and thereby increase its commercial viability, by paving its muddy roads. One of the business partners in this firm was my cousin Dr. Felix Grundy McGavock, whose company contracts bore the heading: "N. B. Forrest, F. G. McGavock, and Joseph Mitchell."

As a professional genealogist, over the years I have found—besides those mentioned above—a vast array of notable Confederates in my family tree. Among them: John Hunt Morgan,[29] Thomas "Stonewall" Jackson, (as mentioned) John Singleton Mosby,[30] John W. McGavock (of Carnton Plantation, Franklin, Tennessee), Lysander McGavock (of Midway Plantation, Brentwood, Tennessee), States Rights Gist, George Washington Gordon, Arthur Middleton Manigault, James Longstreet, John Henry Winder, Gideon Johnson Pillow, John Cabell Breckinridge, James Randal McGavock (of Riverside Plantation, Franklin, Tennessee), Leonidas Polk, Lucius Eugene Polk, Charles Sidney Winder, Pierre G. T. Beauregard, David Harding McGavock (of Two Rivers Plantation, Nashville, Tennessee), Zebulon Vance, James Ewell Brown "Jeb" Stuart, George Washington Custis Lee, George Wythe Randolph (Thomas Jefferson's grandson), Felix Kirk Zollicoffer,[31] Fitzhugh Lee, William Henry Fitzhugh Lee, Benjamin E.

---

28. As we will see, the famous pair once came close to bloodshed when an irate Forrest drew his pistol on Cheatham. Disaster was averted only because General Stephen Dill Lee arrived on the scene.

29. I am a Morgan descendant.

30. As mentioned, I am a Mosby descendant.

31. After my cousin General Zollicoffer was killed at the Battle of Fishing Creek, Kentucky (also known as the Battle of Mill Springs or Logan's Cross Roads), on January 19, 1862, the Cincinnati *Commercial* printed the following statement from a Yankee soldier who was on the scene. Note his cruelty, arrogance, and callousness, not to mention his complete lack of understanding of the purpose of Lincoln's War: "The corpse lay by the side of the road along which we all passed, and all had a fair view of what was once Zollicoffer.

Caudill,[32] Robert Brank Vance, Jesse James, Alexander "Frank" James, William Giles Harding (of Belle Meade Plantation, Nashville, Tennessee),[33] Carrie (Winder) McGavock (of Ducros Plantation, Houma, Louisiana), Louisa Minor Meriwether (wife of William Andrew Charles, who fought at the Battle of Franklin II), Ellen Bourne Tynes (the wife of Forrest's Chief of Artillery, Captain John W. Morton),[34] and famed South Carolinian diarist Mary Chesnut.

Two other interesting personal Forrest connections: I am cousins with Confederate Major Nathaniel Francis Cheairs, who built Rippavilla Plantation in Spring Hill, Tennessee, in the early 1850s.[35] Rippavilla served as an overnight encampment site for some of Hood's men on the evening of November 29, 1864, after the disastrous Battle of Spring Hill. The next morning at breakfast Forrest and Hood argued here, this time because Hood, as he often did, unfairly placed the blame for the fiasco on the shoulders of his subordinates, including Forrest.[36] Earlier, in the spring of 1863, Forrest's command itself also camped at Rippavalla, fighting in, and winning, the Battle of Thompson's Station on March 5.[37]

Nathaniel Cheair's brother, Martin Ternell Cheairs, another cousin of mine, once owned Ferguson Hall in Spring Hill, which served as the headquarters of General Earl Van Dorn during the spring of 1863. Forrest had an acrimonious relationship with Van Dorn as well, and the two almost came to blows.[38]

Wisely, however, Forrest always restrained himself, on one

---

I saw the lifeless body as it lay in a fence-corner by the side of the road, but Zollicoffer himself is now in hell. Hell is a fitting abode for all such arch-traitors. May all the other chief conspirators in this rebellion soon share Zollicoffer's fate—shot dead through the instrumentality of an avenging God—their spirits sent straightway to hell, and their lifeless bodies lie in a fence-corner, their faces spattered with mud, and their garments divided up, and even the hair of their head cut off and pulled out by an unsympathizing soldiery of a conquering army, battling for the right." Pollard, LC, p. 201.

32. I am a Caudill descendant (twice).
33. I am a Harding descendant.
34. Mrs. Morton descends from the English Bourne family and the Scottish Maxwell family, both from which I also descend. See Morton, pp. 348-349.
35. Major Cheairs and his residence are mentioned in Morton, p. 80.
36. McDonough and Connelly, pp. 53-55.
37. Logsdon, TATG, pp. 65-66.
38. Mathes, pp. 106-107; Wyeth, LGNBF, pp. 176-177.

occasion saying to Van
Dorn: "General, I think
there are Yankees enough
for you and me to fight
without fighting each
other." Finally parting as
friends, they shook hands,
never to set eyes on one
another again. Why?

One month later, at Ferguson Hall, Van Dorn was murdered by an angry and jealous Dr. George B. Peters for an alleged affair with his wife and cousin, Jessie (McKissack) Peters.[39] After Van Dorn's death, at General Braxton Bragg's orders, Forrest took over Van Dorn's command of the cavalry on the left wing of the Army of Tennessee.[40]

I am also related to Forrest's wife, Mary Ann Montgomery, and the list goes on.[41]

Suffice it to say that I have numerous links to the General, Lincoln's War, and the South, personally, emotionally, historically, even genetically, for all are part of my DNA. In short, I wrote this book because Dixie is home and Forrest is family.

LOCHLAINN SEABROOK
Nashville, Tennessee
June 2010

THE NORTH IS STILL LYING ABOUT LINCOLN'S WAR

---

39. *Blue and Gray Magazine*, "The General's Tour: The Mysteries of Spring Hill, Tennessee," Volume 2, Issue 2, pp. 12-20.

40. Wyeth, LGNBF, p. 177; Mathes, p. 127.

41. I am a direct descendant of the royal Montgomery clan of Scotland, whose descendants settled in North Carolina and Kentucky, where at least half of my American ancestors are from.

# Acknowledgments

I would like to thank my wife Cassidy, Dr. Clyde N. Wilson, Dr. Michael R. Bradley, Gene Ingram, John Paul Strain, Ronny Mangrum, Kate Barger, Elizabeth Scott-Whipkey, Fiona, and Dixie for their generosity and support. Special thanks to the United Daughters of the Confederacy for awarding me the Jefferson Davis Historical Gold Medal for this book.

## A UNIQUE LOOK AT A UNIQUE INDIVIDUAL

Forrest's admirers understandably focus their books on his military career—for which he is most famous, while his critics focus their works on his imperfections and faults—for which he is most infamous. While touching on his martial period, my book, *A Rebel Born*, concentrates more on what I feel are actually the most interesting aspects of Forrest's life: his amazing emotional growth, material achievements, and spiritual transformation, all which occurred in a mere fifty-six years.

Forrest's metamorphosis from dirt-poor farmer to multimillionaire, from rough-hewn frontiersman to refined urban gentleman, from agnostic to born-again Christian, from slave owner to civil rights worker, from violent warrior to gentle pacifist, is nothing short of astonishing, and certainly must earn him a place as one of history's most intriguing and uncommon individuals.

The telling of this story makes up the very heart of my book, a story that allows me to correct the misinformation *and* disinformation that has grown up around Forrest over the past century and a half.

As such, *A Rebel Born* is devoted almost exclusively to the positive aspects of Forrest's deeds, personality, and life, revealing how his fatherless childhood, his boyhood on America's Western frontier, near total lack of formal education, and fiery personality shaped his destiny and sculpted events throughout his life. This work then is my unabashed and unapologetic memorial to a great American spirit.

## THE ANTI-FORREST CROWD

Forrest's enemies see him as a simpleminded Southern redneck, a violent sadist, and an intolerant racist. One of his worst contemporary critics, General William Tecumseh Sherman, called him "that Devil Forrest," a name that stuck and is still used to this day.

Like millions of others around the world, I see him quite the opposite. While I do not ignore Forrest's faults, it is also clear that he was a man of astonishing intelligence, strength, and character, prone to kindness, loyalty, open-mindedness, forgiveness, perseverance, and even tenderness (all of these traits, and more, were on display throughout his life, but have been almost completely ignored by a majority of writers).

Though Forrest is known the world over as a "racist," for instance, objective research reveals that he was more a humanitarian than a bigot. As we will see, he often went out of his way for people of color, both bonded and free. If Forrest was truly a racist (and a cruel slaver), one must wonder why forty-five of his slaves proudly fought by his side during the War Against Northern Aggression (a number of them serving as his personal armed guards), and why so many lined up eagerly asking to be purchased by him at the slave markets.

More revealing, many of his slaves, though freed even before the War, chose to stay on with their former master, working for Forrest as paid employees, while after the War many voluntarily returned from other states to continue working for him. In the latter years of his life Forrest fought vigorously for social equality for blacks and enthusiastically campaigned to repopulate the devastated South with new African immigrants. And at his funeral on Halloween Day in Memphis in 1877, fully one-third of the grieving attendees were black. Forrest was no racist, certainly not by the standards of his day.

It must be one of history's most incredible ironies that Lincoln, the "Great Emancipator," who publically promoted extreme white supremacist views his entire adult life—such as his plan to establish American apartheid and ship all blacks back to Africa—has never once been labeled a racist by the same individuals who call Forrest one. It is this very type of ignorance and misunderstanding that we will confront and address.

Forrest, a slave trader and owner who fought for black civil rights? An unschooled farm boy who was considered a "military genius"? An impetuous and aggressive man (he killed thirty Yanks with his bare hands during the War) who was gentle toward women and loved children? A man's man who neither smoked or drank? An undying Confederate who was a "strong Union man" and loved the U.S. flag? A born Southron who was against secession and who did business with Yanks after the War? The face of today's pro-South Movement, but a man who was considered the epitome of the reconstructed Rebel by the North? All of this is true!

He was without question a walking contradiction. And it is this very complexity, this very polarity that, in part, makes him so captivating and worthy of an in-depth study.

THE PRO-NORTH VERSUS THE ANTI-SOUTHERN PERSPECTIVE
Only a few books on Forrest have been written by so-called "neutral" historians, their very "objectivity" usually making them of uncertain value. Some are by non-Southerners, whose works are, by nature, often factually inaccurate and insensitive to Southern sensibilities.

By far most books on the General, however, are penned by Northerners and New South Southerners (Northernized Southerners, or turncoats, known in Dixie as scallywags), whose books are highly prejudicial toward Forrest specifically and Southern culture in general. Unfortunately, instead of being decried, this anti-Forrest approach is actually praised, and it has become, as have all things Yankee pertaining to the "Civil War," the accepted politically correct view.

Indeed, it is a sad commentary on the depth of the anti-South mindset that has permeated America: Northern books on the War are considered "objective history," while Southern books on the War are labeled "slanted," "cherry-picked," "biased," and "subjective." Books written from a wholly Northern perspective are held up as paragons of impartial historical research and the standard to which all other works must be measured, while books written from a purely Southern view are attacked and dismissed as "partisan," "one sided," and "skewed toward the Confederacy." This is anti-South bias and political correctness gone mad, for Southerners are now "criminalized" for defending their own region, and for writing honestly and accurately about their own history.

Tragically, *political correctness always disguises truth*, in particular Southern truth. Since our aim is to uncover the truth about Forrest, this book will necessarily be politically incorrect.

Many of us, such as myself, take the biblical injunction to honor our ancestors quite seriously.[42] As mine are Southern all the way back to the settling of Jamestown, Virginia, in 1607 (thirteen generations), the first North American colony settled by Europeans, it is only natural that I see things from the Southern point of view. And so this book will offer a Southern perspective, not only on Forrest, but on everything connected with the world in which he lived.

---

42. See e.g., Exodus 20:12; Matthew 15:4.

## WHY *A REBEL BORN* IS IMPORTANT

Today Southern pride is reemerging, accompanied by a powerful, renewed interest in the War for Southern Independence and the individuals who played a role in it.[43] As a former docent for a Civil War museum and the author of (currently) eleven other books on the War, I have experienced this growing fascination first-hand.

To many of us no figure associated with Lincoln's War is more important and intriguing than Forrest, and with good reason. He greatly delayed the Confederacy's surrender at Appomattox. Yet, had he been given command of larger forces (such as the Army of Tennessee), as President Jefferson Davis and many others later lamented, it is quite probable that the tide would have turned in favor of Dixie. Pro-South sympathizers will never tire of reading about and discussing what could have been—which is why my book touches on all aspects of Forrest the warrior, the imposing Tennessean who Sherman called "the greatest cavalryman America ever produced."

More importantly, however, *A Rebel Born* is about Forrest the man, and how he grew from a rugged, non-believing pioneer to a sophisticated Christian urbanite during his brief life. In that time he survived the loss of his father at an early age; the death (from disease) of his twin sister Fanny and four of his other siblings; his own death-defying bouts with illness; numerous stressful moves across the South; the early death of his only daughter; four unnecessary years of danger, blood, and violence (including four serious wounds and the death of one of his brothers—not to mention numerous friends and business partners), fighting against the tyrannical Northern invasion of his homeland; countless failed businesses and bankruptcy; the slings and arrows of his lifelong critics; numerous attempts on his life (before, during, and after the War); innumerable lawsuits; a grilling before Congress (pertaining to his time allegedly heading the KKK); the loss of nearly his entire estate due to the War; and finally, at war's end, the double humiliation of Reconstruction (for many years he was not allowed to vote and was subject to impromptu arrest as a former Confederate officer) and starting his life over from scratch under post-war

---

43. As I write this, for example, Virginia Governor Bob McDonnell has declared April "Confederate History Month." In his statement the governor said that the nation's Confederate history "should not be forgotten, but instead should be studied, understood and remembered," for millions of Southerners "fought for their homes and communities and Commonwealth in a time very different than ours today."

Yankee military rule and a carpetbag-scallywag government made up of South-hating whites and illiterate blacks.

Through all of this Forrest fought and conquered, never giving in, never giving up.

No matter what one thinks of Forrest personally the fact is that he was an extraordinary man, one whose life epitomizes the triumph of the human spirit. In the amazing transfiguration that he underwent there are many valuable life lessons to be learned, making him an exceptional role model for the modern era.

Forrest's life teaches other lessons as well—about the insanity and futility of war, the dangers of tyranny and despotism, and the perennial issues of culture and race. Most significantly Forrest teaches us about spiritual growth, the very essence of the Christian life. These things and more can all be gleaned from a better understanding of this great American light. For these reasons *A Rebel Born* is both topical and important.

## CELEBRATING A SOUTHERN HERO

Like thousands of others around the world, I have an unabashed admiration for Nathan Bedford Forrest. But it is not a blind admiration. I am aware of his imperfections, and we will be discussing these both honestly and factually as we journey through his life story.

Forrest himself was cognizant of his shortcomings and knew full well that he was disliked by some. But, as he was quick to point out, this dislike of him was based largely on a lack of knowledge about his true character. When one studies the actual facts of his life, there is no question that he was correct in this, and that he has been completely and unfairly portrayed and pilloried by enemies of the South. Indeed, nowhere is the old axiom that "the less you know about him the less you like him" more true than it is with Forrest. Conversely, the more one learns about him, the more human and likeable he becomes.

To a great extent the entire anti-Forrest movement has been founded on this sandy soil: the wholesale misunderstanding of who Forrest really was; a Yankee mind-set that has invented lies about him in an attempt to tarnish his reputation and diminish the South; an anti-Dixie agenda that has promoted obvious wartime propaganda about him as "fact"; a progressive New South cult that has unfairly judged the 19th-Century Forrest—as the politically correct always do—through the lens of the present (known as presentism).

For many of us in the South this equates to nothing short of the desecration of the name of one of our greatest and most celebrated heroes. All of this vitriol, of course, comes from those who are least acquainted with Forrest—and with Dixie.

There are those who see Forrest as the Devil incarnate and will never think any differently; there are those who dislike him and who will never be swayed by fact or logic; there are those who will never give up their preconceived notions about him; there are those who will simply never "get" Forrest.

But for those who have a negative opinion of "old Bedford" *and* have an open mind, this book will be a revelation. For those who love Forrest, this book will be a celebration.

Ever since the last of the great pro-Forrest biographies were written by his wartime contemporaries (Jordan and Pryor, 1868; Wyeth, 1899; and Mathes, 1902), a new, modernized and updated defense of Forrest has been begging to be told.

*A Rebel Born: A Defense of Nathan Bedford Forrest - Confederate General, American Legend*, attempts to be that book; a one-of-a-kind tribute to a one-of-a-kind man.

LOCHLAINN SEABROOK
Nashville, Tennessee
June 2010

# A Rebel Born

## A Defense of Nathan Bedford Forrest

*Confederate General, American Legend*

# Part 1

# ORIGINS OF THE ANTI-FORREST MOVEMENT

# PREJUDICE, FEAR, JEALOUSY, & IGNORANCE: DISLIKE OF FORREST IS DISLIKE OF THE SOUTH

"Come on boys, if you want a heap o' fun and to kill some Yankees!" — From one of Forrest's wartime recruitment posters

## THE JOHN WAYNE OF DIXIE

NATHAN BEDFORD FORREST. HIS VERY name evokes images of humble log cabins, the heat-drenched South, the hardscrabble life of the frontiersman, paddle-wheeled steamboats plying the Mississippi River, the devastating War of 1861, and the European expansion into the new Western territories of the Chickasaw, the Choctaw, and the Creek. He was Americana personified, and one of the most fascinating, remarkable, romantic, complicated, and provocative individuals to have ever lived.

In the conservative traditional South, where countless statues and monuments of him dot the land and where he is compared to the great Revolutionary War fathers George Washington (1732-1799) and Thomas Jefferson (1743-1826), every detail of Forrest's life has been, and continues to be, lovingly studied, discussed, and revered. He is, in a word, a real-life hero, the John Wayne of Dixie, a role he has held for six generations across the South.

36 ∞ A REBEL BORN

## THE SIMON LEGREE OF TENNESSEE

In today's more liberal progressive North, however, Forrest's name is shunned and he is treated as a loathsome symbol of Southern racism and ignorance, an embarrassment to the American people. Here he has been branded the Simon Legree of Tennessee, the fictitious "cruel and godless" slave master of *Uncle Tom's Cabin*, who humiliates, abuses, and finally kills his long-suffering black chattel.

The North has never forgiven Forrest for his alleged atrocities on the battlefield either, a memory only hinted at by Yankee General Sherman, who once referred to Forrest as "the devil." The title has stuck, becoming the favored moniker of Forrest's critics.[44]

## SAINT OR DEMON?

In fact, just as the Pagan deities of Old Europe were demoted to "devils" by the modern Christian Church,[45] the Confederate deities of the Old South have indeed been demonized by the modern Liberal Left. With his reputation as a slave trader preceding him into battle, "that Devil Forrest" was naturally the very first Rebel to be transformed into a hellish fiend by Northern partisans: finding it impossible to sully the names of either the non-slave owning Robert E. Lee or the saintlike Stonewall Jackson, they turned to the South's third most beloved hero, General Forrest, who was more easily mischaracterized.

That Forrest is seen as either a deity or a devil is just part of what makes him so intriguing. But it is also what makes him so divisive, and so difficult for many to understand. To this day the mere mention of his name is sure to elicit a strong reaction, positive or negative.

Who then was the real Nathan Bedford Forrest, saint or demon?

Many trees have died and much ink has been spilled trying to explain this intensely complex, powerfully charismatic man of contradictions, ironies, and extremes. Unfortunately, most of it has been penned from the "Forrest the devil" point of view. What is worse, it is this unfavorable image of Forrest, one first created by Victorian Yankees, that is today gaining ground both in the North and in the South,

---

44. Sherman, of course, was using the word devil for Forrest to mean "pesky," or "troublesome," while today's politically correct wrongly use the word literally, as if Forrest were truly an evil monster.
45. For more on this syncretistic process, see my book *Christmas Before Christianity*.

further diluting the truth about this singular man.

PALEOCONSERVATISM & THE ANTI-FORREST AGENDA
Mid 19th-Century Northern attacks on Forrest were for the express purpose of whipping up, and maintaining, hatred toward the South, typical wartime propaganda. This is why Yankees who met Forrest in person nearly always changed their minds about him, finding him to be quite unlike the cartoon character villain portrayed in Northern newspapers.

But the 20th- and 21st-Centuries brought something new: an authentic anti-Forrest movement, complete with hate-mongering slander and outrageous lies meant to humiliate, not only Forrest, but all those who admire him; that is, those who belong to the pro-Forrest movement.

There is something deeply sinister behind the "we hate Forrest" agenda, however. Generally, at its foundation is a left-wing abhorrence and liberal prejudice toward what Forrest symbolizes, namely the South, a region that has long embraced the ideas of strict constitutionalism (as originally laid down by the Founding Fathers), states' rights, a small limited (decentralized) government (a republic), a non-interventionist foreign policy (isolationism), free trade, Old World ideals and traditions, localism, agrarianism, military neutrality, and cultural regionalism. These concepts are, of course, embodied in the modern-day movement that parallels the beliefs and goals of the Confederacy: libertarianism (and to a great extent, paleoconservatism and Tea Partyism), the near opposite of modern liberalism, with its nationalistic, socialistic, and even communistic leanings.

POLITICAL CORRECTNESS
And herein we discover why there has been a change in attitude toward Nathan Bedford Forrest between the 19th and 21st Centuries. It is the modern phenomenon of political correctness, or what some call cultural Marxism. This fanatical leftist movement, mainly comprised of self-deluded, self-righteous fanatics, who utilize discriminatory relativism,[46] exaggerates the weaknesses and wrongdoings of others—almost always

---

46. See L. Johnson, pp. xiv-xv.

conservatives, like Forrest—to support its own radical social, economic, and political views. When no offense can be found, members of this group will often fabricate one. The more odious the enemy is to them the more outrageously they lie and the stronger they attack.

Rewriting and distorting, even completely inventing, history to match their political and cultural ideas of "truth," the politically correct then go on to pronounce their fairy tales "authentic history." This false data often ends up in college courses and even textbooks, which is happily printed by liberal, cultural Marxist publishers. Generally, these nefarious pseudo historians like to focus on the topic of traditional Western history, which they view as a weapon of the "white male establishment" to oppress the powerless. Hence, one of their favorite targets is the traditional South and its conservative inhabitants.

WHY THE POLITICALLY CORRECT HAVE TARGETED FORREST
It was inevitable then that Forrest, who today would be most accurately called a paleoconservative, and who has long been stereotyped as the archetypal "racist hillbilly" and "Southern redneck," would draw fire from the politically correct crowd. It is this left-wing group which has angrily marked him as an illiterate hayseed, psychopathic racist, brutal sadist, homicidal soldier, arrogant military officer, underhanded businessman, crooked politician, and even an unfaithful husband.

Such preconceived and erroneous notions of him, along with the movement's unscientific, subjective, and thus unjust, evaluation of him by today's standards (presentism), their intentional perversion of Southern (and Northern) history for political purposes, and their lack of familiarity with life on the southwestern frontier of 19th-Century America, have turned Forrest into one of the most despised and misunderstood men in U.S. history.

Just as often, dislike of Forrest stems from a dislike of the South, a sentiment that is usually Northern in origin. But surprisingly and increasingly, this loathing is self-loathing and springs from Dixie herself, where the "New South" (that is, the Northernized South) movement is increasing in membership each year, as more and more Northerners move into the region and more and more Southerners adopt Northern views.

## DETESTATION OF THE SOUTH

This phenomenon is not new. Northern repugnance toward the South can be traced back to the early era of the United States when Southerners began resisting the efforts of Northerners to raise tariffs in the South,[47] centralize the government, and overturn and rewrite the original Constitution.[48]

The Old South was particularly attached to the Founding Fathers, most of whom were Southerners, and to the South-centric Constitution they had created. She did not want to see it destroyed for any reason, and certainly not because of Northern greed. As Forrest himself said in 1868:

> I loved the old [pre-Civil War, conservative] Government of 1861; I love the old [pre-Lincoln, Jeffersonian] Constitution yet. I think it the best government in the world if administered as it was before the war. I do not hate it; I am opposing now only the radical [i.e., liberal, Northern] revolutionaries who are trying to destroy it. I believe that party to be composed . . . of the worst men on God's earth—men who would hesitate at no crime, and who have only one object in view, to enrich themselves.[49]

Along with economic and political differences, religious, cultural, philosophical, ethnic, and social differences also began to emphasize a sharp line of demarcation between the industrial North and the agricultural South,[50] one that would later lead even postwar Northerners to admit that: "The North and the South are simply convenient names for two distinct, hostile and irreconcilable ideas."[51]

As time passed the gap between these two "irreconcilable" regions grew ever wider, finally held together only by a mutually beneficial economic link: the South depended on the North to purchase its raw products, while the North depended on the South's products for manufacturing.

But trouble continued to brew when the liberal North wanted

---

47. C. Adams, p. 80.
48. DiLorenzo, RL, pp. 2, 233-256.
49. *Report of the Joint Select Committee to Inquire into the Condition of Affairs in the Late Insurrectionary States*, p. 33.
50. McWhiney and Jamieson, pp. 171-173.
51. Tourgée, p. 300.

to make radical changes to this system, while the conservative South preferred the stability and continuity of the existing order. Northerners simply could not understand the seemingly strange, inflexible traditionalism of Dixie,[52] her opposition to any kind of change,[53] a Southern trait W. J. Cash defines as a stalwart resistance to every new invention, a mind-set that immediately rejects all new ideas while clinging to the old with obsessive resolve.[54]

In the eyes of the North then, the South was clearly standing in the way of progress; Northern progress, that is. And so the North labeled Southerners ignorant hillbillies, uncivilized morons, and misguided barbarians.[55]

The final bond of civility had been broken. With its enormous financial, manufacturing,[56] and numerical advantage (20,000,000 white Northerners to 7,500,000 white Southerners),[57] Northern cultural imperialism began in earnest—that is, the Northern movement to destroy the South and bring her round to the Yankee way of seeing things.[58]

A physical war between the two regions, waged with saber, shot, and shell, would come later. The first battles between South and North were intellectual, fought with pen, paper, and pulpit.

## NOTED EARLY SOUTH-HATERS SPEAK OUT

Among the North's 20 million whites, there were plenty of enthusiastic and articulate members of the anti-South movement. One of the more outspoken of these was Yankee journalist, Henry Louis Mencken, who saw Dixie as an intellectual wasteland inhabited by backwoods buffoons and illiterate imbeciles. To Mencken the typical Southerner was little more than a downtrodden halfwit, deceived by infantile religious beliefs, and a neurotic revulsion toward anything related to education, beauty, or sophistication.[59]

---

52. Catton, Vol. 2, p. 438.
53. Sword, SI, p. 16.
54. Cash, p. 101.
55. See Kennedy and Kennedy, pp. 274, 305.
56. E. M. Thomas, p. 105.
57. Katcher, CWSB, pp. 46, 225.
58. DiLorenzo, LU, p. 43.
59. Mencken, p. 68.

In 1858 New Yorker William Henry Seward, who was to shortly become President Lincoln's secretary of state, campaigned on the idea that the South was a backward region and that its population was illiterate.[60]

Arch Negrophobe and Southerner-turned-Northerner, Hinton Rowan Helper (1829-1909)—soon to become Lincoln's U.S. Consul to Argentina—spread the gospel of "the shame, poverty, ignorance, tyranny and imbecility of the South."[61] According to his book, *The Impending Crisis of the South: How to Meet It*,

> the South, woefully inert and inventionless, has lagged behind the North, and is now weltering in the cesspool of ignorance and degradation.[62]

Helper's book, which threatened the "degenerate South" with death and destruction, was Lincoln's primary campaign document during the 1860 election.[63] An abridged 1859-version—funded by Lincoln and his party—added new, insulting, and malicious captions to the work, such as "The Stupid Masses of the South."[64]

New Englander and liberal Transcendentalist Ralph Waldo Emerson regarded the South as a primitive dark land, awash in cruelty and sin, populated by inbred hicks and savage rednecks. To Emerson the average Southerner was a

> spoiled child, with graceful manners, excellent self-command, very good to be spoiled more, but good for nothing else,—a mere parader. He has conversed so much with rifles, horses and dogs that he has become himself a rifle, a horse and a dog, and in civil, educated company, where anything human is going forward, he is dumb and unhappy, like an Indian in a church. Treat them with great deference, as we often do, and they accept it all as their due without misgiving. Give them an inch and they take a mile. They are mere bladders of conceit. Each snipper-snapper of them all undertakes to speak for the entire Southern States. . . . They are

---

60. J. M. McPherson, BCF, p. 198.
61. Helper, IC, p. 153.
62. Helper, IC, p. 45.
63. Lytle, p. 32.
64. Potter, p. 387.

more civilized than the Seminoles, however, in my opinion; a little more.[65]

Writing in 1910, William Witherspoon, one of Forrest's cavalrymen, confirms Emerson's Yankee notions of Southerners. The Northern soldiers who came South in 1861, noted Witherspoon, clearly "regarded us as barbarians, one type removed from the wild horde of Aborigines that once roamed our country . . ."[66]

One of the most outspoken South-haters was the lionized New England Congressman Charles Sumner, after whom Boston's well-known Sumner Tunnel was named. Sumner, like many other Northerners, enjoyed emphasizing the differences between South and North, with the latter always in the superior position, the former in the inferior. On the one side there were the moral, diligent, Christian people of the North, while on the other, there were the perverted, beastly, illiterate, bullies of the South,[67] "hirelings picked from the drunken spew and vomit of an uneasy civilization," as Sumner so indelicately phrased it.[68] (For his intolerance and South-hating views, Sumner was caned, and crippled for several years, in the Senate chamber by a Southerner, South Carolina Representative, Preston S. Brooks.)[69]

Though ridiculous, mean-spirited, biased, and false, these stereotypes, coming from men of such influence and stature, were widely believed and accepted across the North.

## SHERMAN: THE ARCHETYPAL SOUTH-HATER

One of the more vocal of the Northern South-haters was, of course, Yankee general and strong pro-Unionist William T. Sherman, who, during the conflict of 1861, took his dislike of the Southland to its ultimate extreme by using total war to crush the remnants of the Confederacy, scattering her people and laying waste the Southern landscape.

Lincoln's War gave Sherman full justification to wage this type

65. R. W. Emerson, JRWE, Vol. 4, pp. 312-313.
66. Witherspoon, p. 88.
67. See L. Johnson, p. 34.
68. Sumner, p. 30.
69. J. S. Bowman, CWDD, s.v. "May 1856"; Grissom, pp. 160-161; Annunzio, p. 18.

of combat on his hated fellow Americans in the South: though they were innocent victims of Northern tyranny who were merely defending themselves against his invasion, Sherman referred to all Southerners as "belligerents." He believed, like so many other Northerners, that Southerners were a wicked people. How else can one explain the fact that "they had intentionally initiated the War"?[70] Therefore in order to humble them, force them to repent, and bring them back into the fold, they must be punished, Sherman bluntly maintained.[71]

According to the cold-blooded Ohioan, there is only one way to subdue an "immoral population" like Dixie, and that is by using a scorched-earth policy of total war:[72]

> I would banish all minor questions, assert the broad doctrine that as a nation the United States has the right, and also the physical power, to penetrate to every part of our national domain, and that we will do it—that we will do it in our own time and in our own way; that it makes no difference whether it be in one year, or two, or ten, or twenty; that we will remove and destroy every obstacle, if need be, take every life, every acre of land, every particle of property, every thing that to us seems proper; that we will not cease till the end is attained; that all who do not aid us are enemies, and that we will not account to them for our acts. If the people of the South oppose, they do so at their peril; and if they stand by, mere lookers-on in this domestic tragedy, they have no right to immunity, protection, or share in the final results.
>     . . . In accepting war, *it* should be 'pure and simple' as applied to the belligerents. I would keep it so, till all traces of the war are effaced; till those who appealed to it are sick and tired of it, and come to the emblem of our nation, and sue for peace. I would not coax them, or even meet them half-way, but make them so sick of war that generations would pass away before they would again appeal to it.[73]

When Sherman ordered all of the residents of Atlanta, Georgia, to evacuate the city, Confederate General John Bell Hood (1831-1879),

---

70. See Sherman's scathing letter in reply to General John Bell Hood, dated September 10, 1864, in which he castigates the South, "who, in the midst of peace and prosperity, have plunged a nation into war—dark and cruel war—who dared and badgered us to battle, insulted our flag . . ." Sherman, Vol. 2, p. 120.
71. L. Johnson, p. 187.
72. DiLorenzo, RL, pp. 173-174, 178-199.
73. Sherman, Vol. 1, pp. 339-340.

commander of the Army of Tennessee, beseeched him "in the name of God and humanity" to allow them to remain, for "you are expelling from their homes and firesides the wives and children of a brave people."[74] Sherman's reply was icy and predictable:

> If the people raise a howl against my barbarity and cruelty, I will answer that war is war, and not popularity-seeking. If they want peace, they and their relatives must stop the war.[75]

It would be difficult to find a more hateful, arrogant, and ignorant Yankee attitude toward the South.

Though only military resources were supposed to have been destroyed, Sherman and his minions also went after private homes and businesses, gutting, in fact, most of the town.[76] After more than a month of bombardment, the once magnificent city was turned to rubble.[77] Some 1,600 people (mostly seniors, women, and children) were evicted from their Atlanta homes before Sherman was through.[78] Here was inhumanity at its peak.

After his Meridian Expedition, at which time he literally wiped the city of Meridian, Mississippi, off the map,[79] Sherman made official his policy of waging war on noncombatants, an obvious admission that the North was losing and that Yankee armies could not win on the battlefield against "bold and enterprising" Confederate officers like Forrest.[80]

From then on, Sherman robbed, burned, and bombed his way through the rest of the Magnolia state, cutting, as he boasted, "a swath of desolation fifty miles broad across the state of Mississippi, which the present generation will not forget."[81] In Savannah, Georgia, he bragged that 80 percent of the devastation he had caused was "simple waste and

---

74. Sherman, Vol. 2, p. 119.
75. Sherman, Vol. 2, pp. 96-136.
76. Gragg, p. 173.
77. In all fairness to the Yanks, some of this devastation was caused by retreating Confederate forces. But this was done only to prevent supplies from being captured by Union soldiers, an illegal military force that should not have been there in the first place. Civil War Society, p. 16.
78. E. M. Thomas, p. 276.
79. DiLorenzo, RL, p. 185.
80. Wyeth, LGNBF, p. 634; Lytle, p. 271.
81. ORA, Ser. 1, Vol. 32, Pt. 2, p. 498.

destruction."[82] In late 1864, after subduing and occupying the city, a cocky Sherman sent a telegram to Lincoln, offering the defeated town to the president as a Christmas present.  It read:

> SAVANNAH, GEORGIA, December 22, 1864.
> To His Excellency President LINCOLN, Washington, D.C.:
> I beg to present you as a Christmas-gift the city of Savannah, with one hundred and fifty heavy guns and plenty of ammunition, also about twenty-five thousand bales of cotton.
> W. T. Sherman, Major-General.[83]

Lincoln's December 26 reply to this missive deserves mention since it reveals his complicity in Sherman's war crimes:

> My Dear General Sherman,—Many, many thanks for your Christmas gift,—the capture of Savannah.  When you were about to leave Atlanta for the Atlantic, I was anxious, if not fearful; but feeling that you were the better judge, and remembering that 'nothing risked, nothing, gained,' I did not interfere.  Now, this undertaking being a success, the honor is all yours; for I believe that none of us went further than to acquiesce.  And taking the work of General [George H.] Thomas into the count, as it should be taken, it is indeed a great success.
>
> Not only does it afford the obvious and immediate military advantages, but in showing to the world that your army could be divided, putting the stronger part to an important new service, and yet leaving enough to vanquish the old opposing forces of the whole,—Hood's army,—it brings those who sat in darkness to see a great light.
>
> But what next?  I suppose it will be safe, if I leave General Grant and yourself to decide.  Please make my grateful acknowledgments to your whole army,—officers and men.
> Yours very truly, A. Lincoln.[84]

Like Lincoln, Sherman held special loathing for South Carolina: it was the first Southern state to secede and the home of numerous and fiercely anti-North fire-eaters.  As he approached the Palmetto State,

---

82. ORA, Ser. 1, Vol. 44, p. 13.
83. Sherman, Vol. 2, p. 231.
84. Nicolay and Hay, ALCW, Vol. 2, p. 622.

Sherman's army was "burning with an insatiable desire to wreak vengeance" on it, a sentiment with which the Yankee officer concurred, ominously promising: "She deserves all that is in store for her."[85] Sherman then rubbed salt into the wound by joking that he would bring every wealthy, white Southern woman to the washtub. The insult did not go unnoticed by the Carolina aristocracy, further inflaming South-North animosities.[86]

In all, Sherman, by his own admission, had inflicted some $100,000,000 (the equivalent of $2,130,000,000 today) worth of damage during his "March to the Sea" across the South, much of it leveled against civilians, and with the full knowledge and approval of Lincoln. Private residences, barns, servants' quarters, mansions, granaries, plantations, ginhouses, even churches, were looted then burned to the ground, along with countless other "pointless acts of vandalism and destruction."[87]

And Sherman had the gall to call Forrest the "Devil"!

For those who still doubt this Yankee officer's innate criminality as well as his murderous intentions toward Dixie, below we offer just one example of his many official field reports. As he so often did, Sherman calls not only for the destruction of non-military property, but also for the murder of unarmed Southern civilians:

> HDQRS. MILITARY DIVISION OF THE MISSISSIPPI,
> In the Field, Rome, Ga., October 29, 1864.
> Brigadier-General WATKINS, Calhoun, Ga.:
> Cannot you send over about Fairmount and Adairsville, burn ten or twelve houses of known secessionists, kill a few at random, and let them know that it will be repeated every time a train is fired on from Resaca to Kingston?
> W. T. SHERMAN, Major. General, Commanding.[88]

In November 1864, Sherman ordered the burning of the town of Columbus, Kentucky, rather than let it fall into Forrest's hands. Sherman's official report:

---

85. Sherman, Vol. 2, pp. 227-228.
86. Daugherty, p. 208.
87. Civil War Society, pp. 80-81; Wyeth, LGNBF, pp. 430-431.
88. ORA, Ser. 1, Vol. 39, Pt. 3, p. 494.

HDQRS. MILITARY DIVISION OF THE MISSISSIPPI,
In the Field, Kingston, Ga., November 5, 1864.
Col. J. N. McARTHUR,
Commanding Post, Columbus, Ky.:
Dispatch received. Eight hundred men are plenty. When I refer
to Columbus I refer to the forts and guns, not the town. I don't
care a cent about the town. If the enemy approaches Columbus the
guns of large caliber must be defended to the death and the town
should be burned by you rather than that Forrest should get a
pound of provisions or forage. Any attack on Columbus will be a
mere dash, and Forrest will not attack men, no matter what their
number, who show a determination to fight.
W. T. SHERMAN, Major-General.[89]

Sherman's violent loathing of the South has been returned to him
a thousand times over by traditional Southerners, who to this day, 150
years on, wince in disgust at the very mention of his name.[90]

## NEW ENGLAND'S HATRED OF THE SOUTH

Some Victorian Northerners despised the South more than others. New
Englanders, like Emerson, in particular, stand out in this regard.
Sometimes, however, their attacks on the South were more indirect than
his.

Such was the case of Emerson's friend, Henry David Thoreau,
the author of *Walden*, a man who evinced a deep sympathy for the
robber, kidnapper, and murderer, New England abolitionist John
Brown. After Brown's death, though he had been widely known as a
true enemy of the South, one whose stated mission was the
indiscriminate murder of Southern women and children,[91] Thoreau
proclaimed him an unfairly executed saint.[92] This was the same man
Southerners considered a demented zealot.[93]

But Brown was not Dixie's opponent because he opposed slavery
(the overwhelming majority of Southerners, 94 percent, did not own

---

89. ORA, Ser. 1, Vol. 39, Pt. 3, p. 656.
90. Civil War Society, pp. 80, 81.
91. Wiley, LJR, p. 15.
92. J. M. McPherson, BCF, p. 210.
93. Daugherty, p. 95.

slaves, had no connection to it, and cared nothing about it).[94] It was because he intended to start up a massive slave insurrection across Dixie, an act that would have put all Southerners (including blacks) in great peril.[95]

Unfortunately for Brown, his plan backfired: he was captured and not a single slave revolt occurred in the South during the entire "Civil War."[96] This did not prevent Yankees from apotheosizing Brown, who was arrested at Harper's Ferry, Virginia, October 17, 1859, and later tried (for treason)[97] and hanged, along with six of his henchmen.[98]

On December 2, 1859, the day of Brown's execution, New Englander Thoreau wrote his famous *Plea for Captain John Brown*, which contained the following remarkable statements:

> Some eighteen hundred years ago Christ was crucified; this morning, perchance, Captain Brown was hung. These are the two ends of a chain which is not without its links. He is not Old Brown any longer; he is an angel of light.[99]

Thoreau's literal worship of the South-loathing Brown did not end there. That same day the famed nonconformist asked that he be allowed to ring the bells of the First Parish Church in Concord, Massachusetts, in honor of "Old Ossawatomie," as Brown was popularly known.[100] Wisely, the town's selectmen turned down his request,[101] no doubt because Negrophobia and white racism were the ruling sentiments (abolitionists were a tiny and much hated minority)[102] in New England at the time, and they did not want to stir up trouble.[103] Despite Thoreau's experience in Concord, however, in a number of Northern towns, guns were fired in salute and church bells rang in honor of the

94. Seabrook, AL, pp. 212-215.
95. Woods, pp. 58-59.
96. Pollard, SHW, Vol. 1, p. 364.
97. Catton, Vol. 1, p. 335.
98. Pollard, SHW, Vol. 1, pp. 32-33.
99. Rhodes, Vol. 2, p. 414.
100. Shenkman and Reiger, p. 99. Brown was also called "Old Brown of Osawatomie." Neilson, s.v. "Brown, John."
101. Farrow, Lang, and Frank, p. 176.
102. L. Johnson, pp. 33, 34, 129; Farrow, Lang, and Frank, pp. 155-177.
103. Kennedy and Kennedy, pp. 53-58.

deceased criminal-turned-divinity.[104]

In countless other Northern places of worship Brown was reverently called the first martyr for slavery, God's servant, one comparable to Saint Stephen, and a man who had certainly gone straight to Heaven.[105] Referring to the fanatic from the Constitution State as a true hero whose execution had been "cowardly," other Northerners cried that he should have been allowed to live, and that America was in desperate need of "the religion of John Brown." After all, they claimed, his goals were truly noble: to abolish slavery and humiliate the South, for her people were arrogant, tyrannical, and low-born, and thus needed to be humbled.[106] Here was a sentiment that, at the time, the majority of Northerners could agree with.

Brown's demise had indeed deified him in the North, where he was celebrated in countless songs, poems, and speeches.[107] Clearly, to Yankee antislavery advocates, psychopath Brown had died with the halo of martyrdom and was nothing less than a crucified god, one who deserved to be worshiped in the Church of Liberty.[108]

Another Yankee friend of Thoreau's and Emerson's, Louisa May Alcott, the celebrated author of *Little Women*, asserted that the late John Brown was now to be known as "St. John the Just."[109]

Emerson himself, who called John Brown "a saint . . . whose martyrdom . . . will make the gallows as glorious as the cross,"[110] must have heartily applauded when one of his own protégés, American journalist Franklin Benjamin Sanborn, became a member of the Secret Six, a group that financially supported Brown's Lincolnesque plan to start a slave revolt in the South,[111] beginning with the seizure of Harper's Ferry.[112]

---

104. Catton, Vol. 1, p. 216; J. M. McPherson, BCF, p. 209.
105. J. M. McPherson, MFO, pp. 14-15.
106. See J. M. McPherson, MFO, pp. 16-18.
107. Sword, SI, p. 23.
108. Daugherty, p. 95.
109. Stanford, p. 76.
110. Carpenter, p. 69.
111. J. M. McPherson, BCF, p. 204.
112. Sanborn eventually fled to Canada, ostensibly to avoid appearing at Brown's trial, then returned after the abolitionist's one-way trip to the gallows on December 2, 1859. When an investigative committee was formed to look into the Secret Six, Sanborn again escaped northward to avoid testifying, even resisting arrest in the interim. He was only spared the pain and humiliation of imprisonment because Massachusetts Chief

Another New Englander who belonged to the Secret Six was fanatical abolitionist Samuel Gridley Howe,[113] whose wife, Julia Ward, later composed the words to *The Battle Hymn of the Republic*.[114] The original song, however, had been called *John Brown's Body Lies A-mouldering in the Grave*, a tune very popular with Lincoln's troops during his illegal War on the South.[115]

Emerson must have loved both versions of this song, in particular the former, which euphemistically called for the North to "trample out the vintage [i.e., the Old South] where the grapes of wrath [the fruits of secession] are stored." Though Brown had butchered innocent non-slave owning families and had been a fugitive on the run from the law, the Transcendentalist and Boston Brahmin described his fellow Yankee as

> a fair specimen of the best stock of New England . . . a romantic character absolutely without any vulgar trait . . . All women are drawn to him by their predominance of sentiment. All gentlemen, of course, are on his side.[116]

Another member of the Secret Six, New England liberal Theodore Parker,[117] held that Brown was "not only a martyr . . . but also a saint,"[118] while New England poet Henry Wadsworth Longfellow vowed that the day of Brown's execution "will be a great day in our history; the date of a new Revolution, quite as much needed as the old one."[119]

Of Brown, New England poet William Cullen Bryant said: "History . . . will record his name among those of its martyrs and

---

Justice, Lemuel Shaw, canceled the criminal's arrest warrant. Emerson would have supported the various illicit shenanigans of his student Sanborn, a talented writer who would later go on to write biographies of not only his abolitionist mentor (in 1901) and of Thoreau (in 1882), but also of Brown himself (in 1885). Neilson, s.v. "Sanborn, Franklin Benjamin."

113. L. Johnson, p. 58.

114. Neilson, s.v. "Howe, Samuel Gridley."

115. Parry, s.v. "Brown, John." The original words and music for *John Brown's Body Lies A-mouldering in the Grave* are traditionally attributed to Thomas B. Bishop (1835-1905), who penned the song to commemorate Brown's raid on Harper's Ferry. Parry, s.v. "Brown, John."

116. R. W. Emerson, CWRWE, Vol. 11, pp. 279, 280.

117. Neilson, s.v. "Parker, Theodore."

118. *The Liberator*, February 3, 1860.

119. Rhodes, p. 410.

heroes,"[120] while New England journalist and founder of the New York *Tribune* newspaper, Horace Greeley, eulogized Brown's "grandeur and nobility."[121]

Some New Englanders not only supported Brown's insane plot to destroy the South through inciting a slave insurrection, but were also involved in equally preposterous plans to break him out of prison after he was captured. One of these was Reverend Thomas Wentworth Higginson, who was active in devising several schemes to rescue and free Brown. Among the plots was a raid by sea; the kidnaping of Virginia Governor Henry A. Wise (who was to be held hostage in exchange for Brown); and an overland charge of German refugees who would release Brown from prison and escape on the cavalry horses used by his guards.[122]

After Brown's death, Higginson publically stated that he loved, admired, and defended Brown.[123] Later, as a Union colonel in the War for Southern Independence, Higginson would go on to command the first all black force in Lincoln's highly segregated U.S. Army,[124] a "slave regiment" known as the First Regiment of the South Carolina Volunteers.[125]

A complete list of the names of New Englanders who adored Brown and despised the South would require dozens of pages, but among them must also be mentioned the noted poet, essayist, and diplomat, James Russell Lowell (1819-1891), and also Massachusetts Governor John Albion Andrew (1818-1867), who said of Brown, his murder spree, and his attempt to wreck the South with a slave revolt: John Brown was right, and I know it.[126]

Support from such luminaries did nothing to discourage Brown from viewing himself, as he did, as an "instrument of God,"[127] even one comparable to Christ, believing that his own death would bring salvation

---

120. Nevins, p. 258.
121. *The Great Issue*, p. 14.
122. Page Smith, pp. 308-309.
123. O. J. Scott, p. 302.
124. Neilson, s.v. "Higginson, Thomas Wentworth Storrow."
125. Eaton, HSC, p. 263. As we will see, despite Higginson's seemingly non-racist views, his command of a black-only troop actually turned out to be a product of the North's deeply held racism.
126. L. Johnson, pp. 59, 60.
127. Boatner, s.v. "Brown, John."

to millions.[128]

## YANKEE BITTERNESS TOWARD THE SOUTH
All of this, of course, was calculated to hurt and infuriate the South. And it did.

In her diary, on November 27, 1861, a confused and angry Southern belle, Mary Chesnut (1823-1886), wrote of the strange animosity Yankees feel toward the South, in particular those self-righteous New Englanders, like Thoreau and Emerson,[129] who helped encourage John Brown to travel down to Dixie to kill Southerners in the name of Christianity.[130]

While it is clear that New Englanders felt they were superior to the "inferior" South, what Chesnut may not have fully realized was that much of this invective originated in the region's profound racism toward blacks, as we will see.[131]

## NORTHERN ADMIRATION FOR ENEMIES OF THE SOUTH
New Englanders were not the only Northerners who loved the South-hating Brown.[132] While a fugitive on the run for numerous heinous crimes, Brown was given money, food, and supplies, and treated like a hero in countless Northern states, including Iowa and Illinois. In Cleveland, Ohio, where Brown was virtually deified by his admirers,[133] Allan Pinkerton (1819-1884), famed founder of the U.S. detective agency (and soon to become Lincoln's chief of intelligence),[134] gave the

128. Warren, JB, pp. 428-429.
129. It is exceedingly strange and contradictory that Emerson, an abolitionist and racist, a staunch individualist, a rebel toward authority, imitation, and conformance, the author of the famed essay "Self Reliance," and the man who admonished 19th-Century Americans to buck conformity (see Donald, LR, p. 226), would be so violently against the independent-thinking South, which was attempting to follow this very advice. It is tempting to think that if Emerson had been born in the South, and was still living there in the mid 1800s, he would have been a pro-secessionist *and* an abolitionist, like so many other "rebellious" and individualistic Southerners. (The same could be said for the South-hating Yankee Thoreau, who was what we would today call a libertarian.)
130. Chesnut, MCCW, p. 245. Not all New Englanders idolized psychopath John Brown. Some were more well informed than others, such as Massachusetts novelist Nathaniel Hawthorne (1804-1864), who flatly said of Brown: "Nobody was ever more justly hanged." N. Hawthorne, Vol. 12, p. 327.
131. DiLorenzo, LU, pp. 40-41; Current, LNK, p. 234.
132. Eaton, HSC, p. 13.
133. Shenkman and Reiger, p. 100.
134. Donald, L, p. 385.

gangster $500 he had raised, the equivalent of nearly $12,000 today.[135] Even Lincoln himself contributed financially to Brown, money that eventually went to fund his attack on Harper's Ferry.[136]

It was New York, however, that rivaled New England in its support of the madman. In the city of Rochester, for example, Brown was allowed to give public lectures,[137] while New Yorkers, such as Seward (Lincoln's future secretary of state), said of him that his utter sense of morality allowed him to rise above his critics to the point where his crimes would be all but forgotten.[138]

Sometimes Northern hatred of the South was even more subtle, such as with Emerson's and Thoreau's friend, Long Islander Walt Whitman (1819-1892), author of the infamous *Leaves of Grass*, and whose brother, George Whitman, was a Yankee officer.

Walt—who during his walks often saw the mysterious, sad-faced president riding with his cavalry escort to and from the Soldiers' Home in Washington, D.C.—was particularly drawn to Lincoln,[139] even stating publically that he "loved" him.[140] After the president's assassination, the bard, a long-standing member of the antislavery Free-Soil party, over-glorified Lincoln in flowery prose in his famous poems, "O Captain! My Captain!" and "When Lilacs Last in the Dooryard Bloom'd."[141] It was Lincoln, of course, who shared Brown's vision,[142] and who later adopted the lunatic's deranged plan to destroy the South.

## THE NORTH'S NEGATIVE MYTHS ABOUT THE SOUTH

Nineteenth-Century hatred of the South was often much more overt and direct, and intentionally so. In *Cracker Culture: Celtic Ways in the Old South*, Grady McWhiney cites an Englishman who visited the North before the War. The Brit reported that there was nothing Northerners deplore with such an intense odium as Southerners, while Yankee journalists referred to the South as the home of the crude, the

---

135. Shenkman and Reiger, p. 100.
136. Lincoln is said to have given Brown $100, today's equivalent of about $2,500. Oates, AL, p. 19.
137. Shenkman and Reiger, p. 100.
138. Van Deusen, p. 214.
139. W. B. Garrison, CWTFB, p. 76.
140. Daugherty, p. 246. See also Oates, AL, pp. 8-9.
141. Whitman, LG, pp. 278, 286.
142. Oates, AL, p. 118.

unschooled, and the primitive, a land that had already retraced its steps toward civilization back 300 years to a time of savagery and animal-like cruelty.[143]

Anti-South propaganda, enthusiastically taken up by Northern abolitionists and Republicans (at the time what we would now call Democrats), was spread far and wide in an effort to brand the South as a belligerent, inhumane, benighted, immoral society that needed to be chastised, punished, then Northernized.[144]

During the 1860 election these same stereotypes were used by Lincoln and his liberal Republican (today the Democratic) party to cast dispersions upon the South in an effort to gain votes nationwide, discourage European support, and create political, social, and psychological distance between the two regions. The South's fellow Americans to the North, Yankee liberals and abolitionists, then began circulating the news that:

> . . . the South was an inferior part of the country; that she was a spotted and degraded section; that the national fame [of America] abroad was compromised by the association of the South in the Union; and that a New England traveller in Europe blushed to confess himself an American, because half of the nation of that name were slaveholders.[145]

These kinds of anti-South myths persisted and took root, despite the overt facts that both the American slave trade and slavery began in the North;[146] that the American abolition movement started in the South;[147] that only a tiny fraction of Southerners actually owned slaves;[148] that most Southern slaves did not work on large, impersonal, prison-like plantations, but on small, informal, open-gated farms;[149] and that a sizeable percentage of the South's slave owners were black and Native-American.[150]

143. Kennedy and Kennedy, p. 239.
144. L. Johnson, p. 191.
145. Pollard, SHW, Vol. 1, p. 32.
146. Farrow, Lang, and Frank, p. xii.
147. Seabrook, AL, pp. 194-200.
148. Seabrook, AL, pp. 212-215.
149. Genovese, p. 7.
150. Seabrook, AL, pp. 389-394.

So successful was the North's slanderous propagandizing and mythologizing, that it transformed countless everyday Yankee soldiers, many with kin in Dixie, into South-loathing, Confederate-hating militants. Their dislike of the South and its demonized citizens was allegedly backed by Divine Ordination. Thus, some Yankees called for the complete and utter eradication of all Confederates, men, women, and children. Shortly after Lee's surrender, T. R. Kennan, a Yank with the 17th Massachusetts Volunteers, wrote the following to his sister:

> If I should speak my real feelings, I should say that I am sorry the war is ended. Pray do not think me murderous. No; but all the punishment we could inflict on the rebels would not atone for one drop of the blood so cruelly spilled. I would exterminate them, root and branch. They have often said they preferred it before subjugation, and, with the good help of God, I would give it them. I am only saying what thousands [of other Yanks] say every day. Our army is sorry that they have done their work; they have a deep-seated love for Abraham Lincoln, and when they see no chance for further chastisement of our enemy, they give vent to their feelings in other ways. I do hope you won't think me violent. I cannot help it.[151]

Amazingly, even after Dixie and her people were invaded, blockaded, starved, run off, looted, pillaged, knifed, shot, raped, tortured, burned, and bombed into surrendering, anti-South polemics, filled with outworn stereotypes, continued to pour forth from a relentlessly cruel North. "Confederate soldiers had committed countless atrocities," so the propaganda went, "butchering and torturing Yankee prisoners." "The Rebels," Northern newspapers cried, "know nothing but brutality and savagery," even cutting up the bodies of Union soldiers to make drum sticks out of their shin bones, drinking cups out of their skulls, and baskets out of their rib cages.[152] According to the influential *Harper's Weekly Magazine*, the latest fashion in Dixie was for Southern women to wear necklaces made from the teeth of dead Yanks.[153] These and thousands of other fanciful horrors titillated Victorian Northern

---

151. Post, p. 468.
152. L. Johnson, pp. 191-192.
153. Bailyn, Dallek, Davis, Donald, Thomas, and Wood, p. 5.

readers and strengthened Lincoln's liberal party, while sustaining Yankee hatred of the South.

## YANKEE PROPAGANDA CREATED THE "NEW SOUTH"

So thoroughly entrenched have these Northern Civil War myths become that not only have they have survived into the 21st Century, but they are now stronger than ever. Some are so cartoonishly simplistic and patently ridiculous that it is obvious they are fallacious, yet they continue to be taken seriously by millions.

In *Trial by Fire: A People's History of the Civil War and Reconstruction* (1982), for instance, Yankee historian, Page Smith, takes up where 19th-Century Northern writers left off by reminding us of what he believes is the innate sickness of the Southern mind. According to Smith, in the 1800s this "pathology" created a plantation society in which violence against black slaves was an everyday occurrence. There is nothing shocking in this, he states, since 19th-Century Southerners were raised in a culture of violence, one specific to the American South.[154] These and other pieces of anti-South nonsense, all of which go against known and well established data to the contrary, continue to be paraded around the world as fact.[155]

Some 20th-Century South-haters, like Italian-American Eugene D. Genovese, actually attribute the South's world famous Southern hospitality to the inborn primitive temperament of Southerners! In his book *Roll, Jordan, Roll: The World the Slaves Made* (1974)—certainly one of the most malevolent anti-South works ever penned—the much admired "objective" scholar suggests that the only reason 19th-Century Southerners developed a polite society was because it prevented them from killing each other in the overly violent environment of Dixie. Furthermore, Genovese claims, Southern hospitality itself only flourished as a means for racist whites to communicate with blacks.[156]

For nearly a thousand pages the ultra liberal, race-conscious,

---

154. Page Smith, p. 852. Smith also gleefully attacks the intelligence of European-American Southerners, in particular female Southerners, with statements like: a white upper-class Southern woman of the day could not cook a simple meal or even do basic housework. Page Smith, p. 853.

155. For positive examinations of Southern society, see all of the author's "Civil War" books, and also C. Johnson, passim.

156. Genovese, p. 116. Actually, Southern hospitality was a natural outgrowth of the South's love and embrace of Old European culture, ancient European history, and classical education.

Marxist author uses nearly every page as an opportunity to slander white Southern culture, which he repeatedly calls the "regime," despite the fact that less than 6 percent of white Southerners owned slaves in 1860. He goes on to make derogatory remarks about nearly everything connected with white Southerners, including their European heritage, their cooking, their educational system, their religion, their sexuality, and even their personal hygiene.[157]

In Genovese's eyes, 19th-Century white Southerners could do no right, while 19th-Century black Southerners could do no wrong, a point of view not supported by the evidence, and not held by any rational person—whatever their racial heritage. Reading *Roll, Jordan, Roll*, one would never know that, as noted, both the American slave trade and American slavery got their start in the North; that the author's birthplace, New York City, was the center of America's slave trade for a century or more; or that tens of thousands of African-Americans and Native-Americans also owned slaves.[158]

With its subjective presentism and sharp Northern liberal slant, Genovese's seminal work on slavery appears to be more a sledgehammer wielded to hurt the South than a rational and enlightened discussion of the institution of American slavery, as the title suggests.

In *The Confederate Nation: 1861-1865* (1979), author Emory M. Thomas picks up the same banner, insisting that the people of the South are inherently violent, stupid, and racist. Southerners, Thomas asserts, have a well-earned reputation as a vain, bloodthirsty people, all stemming from the unfortunate fact that they are not so much thinkers as they are doers. In nearly every situation the Southerner falls back on physical action over intellectual thought. This alleged aberration has created a region-wide mental immaturity in Southerners, one in which the Self asserts its individualism in the form of violence.[159]

The conclusion Thomas draws from this bizarre, biased theory is predictable: the South's slave owning planter class was inherently

---

157. See Genovese, pp. 616, 777, 561-566, 161-284, 458-475, 553.

158. To his credit, Genovese does mention black slave owners, though only briefly, in the main text (pp. 406-408). A few other references to this all-important topic are relegated to endnotes at the back of the book (see pp. 747-749).

159. E. M. Thomas, pp. 19, 20.

violent and, as such, routinely and unhesitatingly beat its black slaves.[160] Though there is no evidence for this—and in fact, the record indicates the opposite[161]—this false image, of cruel white Southern masters constantly whipping and beating their long-suffering black chattel, has survived into the present day, thanks in great part to books like Thomas'.

But Thomas does not stop there. Dixie is also a land of laziness and sexual perversion, he avows. Speaking of the ubiquitous "drinkin' and sinnin'" mentality of Southerners, Thomas contends that the Old South earned the contempt given to it by Northern critics because it was indeed a land of sloth and sin. These traits derive, no doubt, from the South's deep passion for Protestantism, which acted as a kind of counterweight to the South's native hedonism. Thus, in antebellum Dixie the unbridled pursuit of physical pleasure and religious fundamentalism coexisted in the souls of all Southerners. This was the same conservative belief system, Thomas opines, which not only motivated John Brown to murder innocent, non-slave owning Southerners, but which helped justify Dixie's obsession with slavery.[162]

Thomas fires a parting shot at the South for daring to become an independent nation, speaking of the very idea of secession in the negative, as a disease; in fact, as a contagious virus[163] (even though the right of secession was thought of as the cornerstone of the Constitution by the Founding Fathers). And when the Confederacy finally decided to emancipate its slaves, Thomas sees it, not as the inevitable act of the region where the American abolition movement got its start,[164] but as the final, desperate act of a dwindling and decaying society. For from the beginning the Confederacy was destined for failure due to its outworn traditions, its hillbilly mind-set, and its "peculiar institution."[165]

We would strongly beg to differ.


## SOUTHERN SLAVERY: CORRECTING THE NORTHERN VERSION

To begin with, there was nothing "peculiar" about Southern slavery. Not

---

160. E. M. Thomas, p. 20.
161. Fogel and Engerman, pp. 144-147.
162. E. M. Thomas, p. 22.
163. E. M. Thomas, p. 54.
164. See L. Johnson, p. 179; Tocqueville, Vol. 1, pp. 403-405.
165. E. M. Thomas, p. 299.

only did American slavery begin in the North (in 1641 Massachusetts became the first state to officially legalize it),[166] but slavery is one of humanity's oldest and most enduring institutions, dating back to the mists of prehistory. As such, it has been known among every people, every race, every religion, every culture, and every society, from time immemorial.[167]

Africa herself was enslaving her own people for thousands of years before the arrival of Arab and later European slave traders,[168] and although Columbus brought European slavery to the Americas,[169] Native-Americans were already practicing slavery on one another millennia before his arrival.[170]

So ubiquitous is slavery that it continues to be a well entrenched worldwide institution, nowhere more so than in modern-day America, where untold thousands are sold into various forms of bondage each year.[171] Indeed, there are more slaves in the world today than at any other time in history,[172] hardly what one would call a "peculiar institution of the South."

## LINCOLN: WAR CRIMINAL

Smith's, Genovese's, and Thomas' biting criticisms of Dixie are undeserved for another reason. For four long years the South defended herself against her meddlesome, aggressive Northern neighbor, one possessed of superior numbers, superior economics, superior industry, superior weapons, an already existing navy, superior rail systems,[173] largely superior military tactics,[174] and, some would argue, a superior political administration.[175]

It was this same nation that, under Lincoln's direct orders, also suppressed and shut down hundreds of Northern newspapers,[176]

---

166. G. H. Moore, pp. 5, 11, 17-19.
167. Meltzer, Vol. 1, pp. 1-6.
168. Davidson, pp. 30, 32; Rozwenc, p. 253.
169. Meltzer, Vol. 2, p. 4.
170. Meltzer, Vol. 2, pp. 61-73.
171. Website: www.pbs.org/newshour/bb/law/jan-june01/slavery_3-8.html.
172. CNN News, June 10, 2008.
173. L. Johnson, pp. 163-182.
174. McWhiney and Jamieson, passim.
175. Eaton, HSC, pp. 56, 67.
176. DiLorenzo, RL, pp. 132, 145-148, 160.

unlawfully imprisoned between 13,000[177] and 38,000 Yankee civilians,[178] and arrested and deported Northern peace advocates like Ohio congressman Clement Laird Vallandigham,[179] for speaking out against the War.[180]

Some of Lincoln's other crimes include calling up militia into federal service, instituting reconstruction measures in seceded states occupied by Yankee troops,[181] introducing the idea of forced conscription,[182] initiating a war, and spending $2,000,000—all without congressional approval; seizing rail and telegraph lines leading to the capital, ordering a naval blockade of the Southern ports, illegally suspending the writ of *habeas corpus*,[183] censoring telegraph communications, intimidating judges, and rigging Northern elections. By subverting the Constitution, all of these crimes, and others, greatly aided him in securing a victory in his war against Southern self-determination.[184]

During the 1863 elections, under Lincoln's direct and indirect approval, his Republican aides were ordered to do whatever was necessary to guarantee a win at the polls. This included furloughing government employees and soldiers known to be Lincoln supporters so they could return home to vote. He also sanctioned the establishment of martial law in the border state of Kentucky, then ordered that Democratic candidates and voters be imprisoned. This easily handed the governorship to Lincoln's favored man, Colonel Thomas E. Bramlette (1817-1875), a pro-Union Democrat.[185]

The Confederacy did not involve itself in such illegalities. Nonetheless, it is safe to say that if the South had matched the North in population, and in economic, industrial, political, and military might (even without cheating, lying, poll-rigging, horse-trading, and breaking the law as Lincoln did), she would have easily won the War for Southern

---

177. Neely, p. 23.
178. Donald, LR, p. 189.
179. DiLorenzo, LU, pp. 163-166.
180. DiLorenzo, RL, pp. 132, 134-142, 150, 151.
181. Rosenbaum and Brinkley, s.v. "Lincoln Administration."
182. Mirabello, p. 164.
183. Ingersoll and O'Connor, p. 22.
184. See Seabrook, AL, passim.
185. Donald, L, pp. 454-455.

Independence. After all, she had both the Constitution and the Founding Fathers on her side.

EARLY SOUTH-BASHING
The above anti-South authors are not the first, nor will they be the last, to smear Dixie with venomous stereotypes.

As early as 1831, as chronicled in his book *Democracy in America*, French aristocrat Alexis de Tocqueville (1805-1859),[186] dwells with some frequency on the "innate indolence" of Southerners. He no doubt picked up this bromide during his travels through the Northeastern states, where hatred of the South was the deepest. According to the French civil servant, the typical Kentuckian, for example,

> scorns not only labour, but all the undertakings which labour promotes; as he lives in an idle independence, his tastes are those of an idle man; money loses a portion of its value in his eyes; he covets wealth much less than pleasure and excitement; and the energy which his neighbour devotes to gain turns with him to a passionate love of field sports and military exercises; . . . [Among Southern aristocratic whites] whose leisure was hereditary . . . [they] maintained the honour of inactive life. . . . As we advance toward the South, the prejudice which sanctions idleness increases in power. [Clearly, the south is a region] in which labour has not yet been reinstated in its rightful honours.[187]

Here we have the 1831-version of the "moonlight and magnolias" stereotype, of lounging white planters, "lords of the lash," who sit idly by while their army of cruelly treated, barebacked slaves thanklessly toil upon their vast plantations under the remorseless Southern sun.

SOME SOUTHERNERS AIDED IN THE CREATION OF THE NEW SOUTH
Tragically, even many in Dixie have come to embrace this kind of anti-South falderal, turning countless Southerners—who now call themselves the "New South" (i.e., good) as opposed to the "Old South" (i.e.,

---

186. Of noble birth, Tocqueville's full name was Count de Alexis Charles Henri Clerel Tocqueville.
187. Tocqueville, Vol. 1, pp. 388-389, 390, 396, 397.

bad)—against their own people, culture, and history.[188] Across Dixie such individuals are universally known as scallywags, turncoats who have betrayed their own region, people, ancestors, and heritage.

Among the most vociferous of New South advocates is author W. J. Cash, a South Carolinian, whose book *The Mind of the South* (1941) paints a bleak portrait of his homeland, one filled with strong animus, wanton prejudice, and wholesale untruths. For Cash the Old South was a grim region of hedonism, native paganism, primitive naivete, useless leisure time, and white supremacy, all values supposedly near and dear to the heart of every Southerner. Here is a land, Cash claims, where the innate cruelty, brutality, and sadism of Southerners turned the Confederacy into a nation of "nigger-killers," where the black man was seen as little more than a prey animal for sport hunting.[189]

The repugnant and baleful Southerner was to be all the more despised for the pleasure he or she took in violence, including the torture, burning, shooting, roasting, and hanging of blacks, a trait Cash believes sprang from the South's alleged inbred predilection for sadism.[190]

In a book where nearly every page is filled with absurd South-hating comments (each more outrageous than its predecessor), Cash ends part one by earnestly quoting, not a Southerner, but a Yankee, Henry Adams (1838-1918),[191] a Harvard professor who declared the following:

> Strictly, the [19th-Century] Southerner had no mind; he had temperament. He was not a scholar; he had no intellectual training; he could not analyze an idea, and he could not even conceive of admitting two . . .[192]

Penned shortly after the start of World War II, Cash's work epitomizes New South thinking; that is, a Southern school of thought based on Northern anti-South propaganda and Yankee anti-South

---

188. Confederate monuments and symbols, as well as the homes and property of those who support the modern Confederate, pro-South movement, are regularly vandalized all across the South, incredibly mainly by Southerners, most who have been inculcated by Yankee propaganda and myth to despise their own past.
189. Cash, pp. 46-55, 56, 126, 51, 362, 125.
190. Cash, p. 125.
191. Cash, p. 102.
192. H. Adams, EHA, pp. 57-58.

mythology, rather than on Southern reality.

The phrase "New South" itself was popularized by a Southerner. In 1886, Georgia-born, Atlanta newspaper editor, Henry Woodfin Grady, used the term to describe a reconciled South, one ready for Northern settlement and investment;[193] that is, for remaking the South into the political, social, and economic image of the North (Northernization), one of Lincoln's stated major goals.[194]

Confirming this point was T. J. Barnett, of the U.S. Interior Department, who recorded that Lincoln personally told him that the Southern states were to be exterminated and supplanted by new businessmen and new concepts.[195] (Naturally this view, which has its roots in 17th-Century New England,[196] was backed up by the Radicals in Lincoln's party, who held that after the War, during so-called "Reconstruction," the Southern states first needed to be completely and permanently altered, remodeled, and improved.)[197]

As we have seen with examples like W. J. Cash and Henry Woodfin Grady, Southerners themselves have greatly aided in the process of their own Northernization. Not only was Lincoln himself a Southerner, but his modern compatriots are the ones primarily responsible for banning the playing of the song Dixie at sporting events; for having the Confederate flag removed from government buildings; for changing the names of streets bearing the names of Confederate officers; for trying to stop the celebration of Confederate holidays; and for having statues and monuments of famed Confederate heroes removed from public spaces.[198]

Indeed, as I was writing this book I was notified by a friend that a bust of Forrest, that had long sat in Tennessee's state capitol building in Nashville, is being removed.

The Yankee anti-South propaganda machine has been so

---

193. Horwitz, p. 285. Today Atlanta, Georgia, is considered the most "Northern of the Southern cities," a thoroughly reconstructed town whose "disloyalty to Dixie" prompted Southerner John Shelton Reed to note: To me Atlanta represents what hundreds of thousands of Confederates gave their lives trying to prevent. N. Thompson, p. 23.

194. Oates, AL, p. 141.

195. Catton, Vol. 2, p. 443.

196. DiLorenzo, LU, p. 38.

197. Current, LNK, p. 254.

198. Grissom, pp. iv, 69.

successful in the New South that many Southerners no longer care about, or are even aware of, their Confederate heritage. A 1990s survey of young Southerners tested their knowledge of the "Civil War." Among eighteen to twenty-four year-olds, 50 percent of them could only name one battle, while only one in eight were aware that they had a Confederate ancestor.[199] Just as appalling, in 1979 students from a large, popular Southern college were asked whether they had ever heard of Forrest. Three-fourths of the respondents answered "no."[200]

Little wonder that one can drive all the way across Dixie today without ever once seeing a Confederate flag,[201] or that this same emblem is now held to be a symbol of white racism by the uninformed. How far it has come from its original intended meaning as a symbol of the time-honored, Jeffersonian concepts of states' rights and a small, limited central government.[202] Forrest, a stalwart son of the South and valiant defender of Dixie, would not be pleased.

## SOUTHERN STEREOTYPING IN TV & FILM

Today, in the 21st-Century, it is considered politically incorrect to ridicule the South openly in mainstream public forums. So the anti-South movement has shifted into the realm of TV and film (where South-bashing remains politically correct), just two more pieces in the arsenal of weapons in the North's continuing war on the South's dignity, reputation, people, symbols, culture, and heritage.[203]

Despite their clever scripts and high ratings, old television shows like *The Beverly Hillbillies*, *The Real McCoys*, and *The Dukes of Hazzard* did little to forward the cause of Southern heritage. Many would say they reversed it.

But even if these are dismissed as "fluff" and "entertainment," what are we to say about more scholarly television productions like Ken

---

199. Horwitz, p. 376.
200. Ashdown and Caudill, p. xx.
201. Grissom, p. 63.
202. Kennedy, pp. 195-209.
203. I use the phrase "the North" generically here, to indicate any region outside the South that continues to attack, slander, and deprecate Dixie and her people. Actually, today one of the foremost enemies of the South is not anywhere near the North. I speak here of the West Coast Elite, many of whose members, like their Eastern compatriots, the Northeast Coast Elite, seem to believe that anyone living outside Los Angeles and New York are poor uneducated bumpkins.

Burns' wildly popular eleven-hour documentary, *The Civil War*? As can be seen from the title, a golden opportunity to set the record straight was squandered, for the moniker itself merely reinforces many of the banal Northern myths about the War for Southern Independence. While this earned Burns numerous accolades and awards from unenlightened Northerners (many who labeled his documentary "brilliant"), New South scallywags, and the Western culture-loathing, European-American-hating, politically correct crowd, it won him the eternal condemnation of traditional Southerners.

The South has fared far worse in the arena of film. Scriptwriters, film makers, and producers (mainly from New York and Los Angeles, and mostly non-Southern) continue to affront the South with movies brimming with negative Southern stereotypes. This process began almost as soon as motion picture cameras were invented.

In the 1930s, for example, films depicting the South in a poor light (compared to the "superior" North, that is), such as those about Tom Sawyer and Huckleberry Finn, were already being made. In more recent times, a largely liberal, South-detesting Hollywood has offered up movies like *Deliverance*, *Sommersby*, *The Texas Chainsaw Massacre*, *Cape Fear*, *Cold Mountain*, *O Brother Where Art Thou?*, *Venom*, *The Reaping*, *The Skeleton Key*, *Songcatcher*, *Fried Green Tomatoes*, and *Talladega Nights: The Ballad of Ricky Bobby*, just to name a few.

Each of these films includes a Southerner portraying one or more of the following anti-South stereotypical characteristics: moronic, violent, lazy, racist, conniving, dopey, selfish, inbred, simple-minded, uneducated, corn-fed, gun-crazy, moonshinin', alcohol-lovin', sex-obsessed, shallow, illiterate, red-necky, and psychopathic. And let us not forget the six-Oscar winning blockbuster *Forrest Gump*, whose main character is named after General Forrest—but for reasons that seem favorable to neither the South or to Forrest.

In these and hundreds of other films that could be named, Southerners are portrayed as the lowest and worst type of American.

Of course, as we speak, ever new anti-South films are being written, cast, produced, directed, scored, edited, and released to the public, in the seemingly never-ending, bewilderingly hateful, widely accepted tradition of South-bashing.

What does all of this have to do with Forrest?

Though spurious and negative, these simplistic and mean-spirited depictions of Dixie and her people have provided ample justification for the North's irrational hostility toward both the South and toward the politically correct's most convenient scapegoat: "slaver, racist, and butcher," Nathan Bedford Forrest.

# THE DEMONIZATION OF FORREST: NORTHERN PROPAGANDA, YANKEE MYTHOLOGY, & POLITICAL CORRECTNESS

"Never stand and take a charge. Charge them too!" — Nathan Bedford Forrest

## FORREST'S CRITICS UTILIZE FALSE & BIASED INFORMATION

WHAT FORREST'S CRITICS, ENEMIES, AND detractors do not realize is that their views of him are based on information that is inaccurate, outdated, or just plain false. Forrest was definitely *not* the monster the general public seems to think he was, as Southern historian Shelby Foote once rightly noted.[204] For while what little the average person knows of him seems current, objective, and factual, it has actually been derived from scathing, highly biased sources, primarily Northern newspaper articles, written during the "Civil War" period a century and a half ago.

Forrest, himself an avid newspaper reader,[205] was highly cognizant of what the media was printing about him. In 1866, in a letter to President Andrew Johnson, he stated that he was aware that many Yankees viewed him with repugnance and antipathy, as a merciless killer who was responsible for countless crimes. This upsets and torments me

---

204. Wills, p. 381.
205. Wyeth, LGNBF, pp. 626-627.

terribly, for none of it is true, he noted with obvious anguish.[206]

Articles espousing such sentiments were penned by prejudicial Yanks trying to incite slave riots in the South while whipping up Northern support for Lincoln's War.[207] This type of politically slanted, propagandist journalism—wholly endorsed and promoted by Lincoln and his cabinet—was noticed in the South even as it was occurring.

In postwar 1866, for instance, in his brilliant work *Southern History of the War*, Edward A. Pollard notes that:

> The Lincoln government had not hesitated to keep up the spirits of the people of the North by the most audacious and flaming falsehoods . . . which have always been found to be, in nations using this expedient in war, evidences of not only imperfect civilization, but of natural cowardice.[208]

Northern journalists, of course, were happy to oblige Lincoln's predilection for fabrication, misrepresentation, libel, and defamation. For they too detested the South, even though most of them had never been to Dixie, and were completely ignorant of the dazzling physical wonders of the South and the grace, warmth, generosity, beauty, humor, talent, and intelligence of her people. As we will see, actually much of the Northern citizenry disliked the South, a fact that is as true today as it was in Forrest's time. Michael Andrew Grissom, author of *Southern by the Grace of God*, got it right when he said that the Yankee intellect has never comprehended the Southern soul.[209]

There was another motivation for writing and publishing articles that made Confederate officers like Forrest look bad, however: pure sensationalism for the purpose of increasing Northern newspaper sales. Some saw through this form of highly biased journalism, even in Europe. In 1892 famed British military man General Garnet Joseph Wolseley wrote that Northern press accounts written during the War must always be treated with suspicion, for they are nothing but a

---

206. Bedwell, p. 68.
207. Ashe, p. 35.
208. Pollard, SHW, Vol. 1, p. 313.
209. Grissom, p. 164.

skillful seasoning of horrors which only those can equal who are accustomed to prepare these sort of repasts for the public, or who have some party object to accomplish.[210]

Simply put, the North's "party object" was slander, partisan politics, and commercialism, all which they "accomplished" by printing falsehoods about the Confederacy and its finest officers.

## FORREST BECOMES THE TARGET OF THE NORTHERN PRESS

When it came to such men, there is no doubt that the Confederacy's most obvious bull's-eye was Forrest, the favored whipping post for Northern anger, prejudice, and jealousy toward the South. This is why, after all, the Northern media targeted him as the satanic fiend of the Confederacy. Piling one fiction on top of another, he finally became an abomination to both Northerners and pro-Union Southerners.

Of these periodicals, Forrest's earliest biographers, Thomas Jordan and J. P. Pryor, wrote:

> . . . the highly wrought narratives with which the Northern newspapers of the day abound . . . are mean, extravagant fictions . . . set afloat in the like channels . . . to infuriate the Northern people.[211]

Between 1861 and 1865, while Southern newspapers were portraying Forrest in an accurate light—as a kindly, honorable, brilliant, brave, and patriotic Southerner fighting for home and country—the Northern media was busy printing hundreds of stories and articles containing preposterous lies, absurd fables, outlandish canards, and slanderous insults about him and the South. The more outrageous the better.

To their credit, some Northern newspapers admitted as much. The *Chicago Tribune* noted with distaste that there was so much exaggeration and lying about Forrest going on, that it was now impossible to tell fact from fiction:

---

210. *The United Service Magazine*, April/May 1892, London, UK.
211. Jordan and Pryor, p. 413.

> The wildest and most absurd rumors continually prevail, respecting Forrest . . . At any time to-day a score of persons were willing to swear he had invaded our State with 20,000 cavalry, accompanied by eighteen pieces of artillery. It is very difficult to arrive at the truth among so many excited rumors.[212]

And what "wild and absurd rumors" they were. Forrest never commanded a force of over 15,000 men (usually considerably less, between 300 and 5,000)[213] and he never stepped foot in Illinois.

Nonetheless, a naive Northern populace, already indoctrinated with Lincoln's own personal anti-South biases and myths, eagerly gobbled it all up, trusting that their president and their media would not lie to them. But lie they did, and repeatedly.

Behind all of this was Lincoln himself. At one time a newspaper agent and journalist (for the Springfield, Illinois, *Sangamo Journal*) and a newspaper owner (of the *Illinois Staats-Anzeiger*), he was highly aware of the power of the press in shaping public opinion. Little wonder then that newspaperman Lincoln often used and manipulated the media, not only to assist with his own political aspirations,[214] but in aiding and abetting the creation of what is now a large corpus of spurious anti-Forrest myths.

As the sensationalist but wholly counterfeit legend of Forrest as a "racist butcher," "demonic sociopath," "cruel slaver," and "Negro killer" spread across the North during this period of South-bashing hysteria, vast fortunes were made for those newspapers and magazines involved.

One Illinois newspaper, for example, regaled its Northern audience with the following extremely tall tale about Forrest and his troops. According to the unenlightened writer, as evidence of the barbarity of Southerners, one of Forrest's men had recently been captured carrying the bloody scalp of a Yankee soldier. Are we up against human beings or savage animals?, the Northern slanted article asked. Fraudulent and ludicrous as this story obviously was, things did not stop there. Furthermore, the writer proclaimed, Forrest used women as human shields, forcing them in front of his charging troops to

---

212. *Chicago Tribune*, March 31, 1864.
213. Henry, ATSF, pp. ix, x; Browning, p. 106.
214. Mitgang, pp. 8-12.

prevent Union soldiers from firing on them.[215]

How different this portrayal is from the real Forrest, who adored women[216] and considered himself their personal protector.[217]

Another newspaper at the time, the New York *Tribune*, called Forrest a malicious, unforgiving, sadist; an amoral butcher with snake-like eyes, who worked in the "nigger trade" and tortured his slaves to death by whipping them with chains. Though the General is painted here as a white racist who hated blacks, strangely, the article goes on to say that he fell in love with one of his colored slave women ("Catharine") and had two out-of-wedlock children with her.[218] The writer reports one outlandish invention after another, finally attributing Forrest's behavior to the fact that he was born in the misogynist, child-thieving South. Southerners rightly called the April 18, 1864, article a classic piece of anti-South disinformation.[219]

These kinds of fictions, which portray Forrest as diametrically opposite of who he really was, would be laughable if it were not for the serious damage they have inflicted. Indeed, 150 years later, the North's 19th-Century myths, prejudices, hatred, and misunderstandings of the Confederacy and Southern culture, continue to be passed down from generation to generation as "fact," perpetuating the unhistorical legend of Forrest as the "devil from Dixie." For demonizing both Forrest and the South is integral to the North's effort to prevent the world from knowing the truth about the General and the War for Southern Independence.

Yankee war criminal Sherman called him "that devil Forrest." Is this how Forrest, one of America's greatest military figures, a veritable "legend in gray," should be recorded for posterity? Is this how an individual, known far and wide across the South at the time as a "charming," "friendly," "courteous," "engaging,"[220] "tender-hearted, kindly man,"[221] should be remembered?

---

215. Ashdown and Caudill, pp. 77-78.
216. See e.g., Mathes, p. 30.
217. Hurst, pp. 216, 365.
218. Davison and Foxx, pp. 253-254.
219. Lytle, p. 281.
220. Gragg, pp. 200-201.
221. R. Taylor, p. 200.

## HOW THE INTERNET IS DAMAGING FORREST

In recent decades the politically correct assault on Forrest has been aided by a new and powerful weapon: the Internet. With the convenience of the home computer, many, especially the young, now consider the local library an archaic institution from the past.

As such, in many cases reference books like encyclopedias and dictionaries are being replaced by on-line virtual "encyclopedias" and "dictionaries" (many of extremely dubious value), and real books in general are being replaced by Websites that can be created and filled with material by anyone on any topic for any purpose.

Though commercially published books and articles must often go through an intense editing process—and often rigorous peer-review and approval—before they are made available to the public, virtual books and articles require no such thing. Actually, the Internet has no restrictions, editors, or censors of any kind. This makes it the perfect medium for the politically correct to attack their enemies and mislead their own followers.

For these types of writers, proper research, accuracy, and citation of sources are unnecessary, and even unwanted. This allows them to write whatever they please, unchallenged and unimpeded by facts. Why? Because facts might interfere with their personal agenda: to destroy an individual's reputation in order to further their own goals.

But the politically correct do not just seek out and attack specifically targeted victims. They will also often go after the followers of their targets.

## FORREST-BASHING IN THE NAME OF POLITICAL CORRECTNESS

The politically correct and other liberal groups often accuse Forrest's admirers and apologists of creating false myths about him, which, over time, have turned into "accepted historical fact." Those who are pro-Forrest are then treated like imbeciles because they embrace these "myths."

Actually, this is exactly what Forrest's critics have done, only from the opposing (negative) point of view. Untold numbers of hostile and patently false tales have been invented by Forrest-haters and Dixie-loathers over the years, most from outside the South. But many of the latest contributors to the anti-Forrest mythology are Southerners themselves, uninformed "New South" scallywags who have been indoctrinated by both the perverted history of the politically correct and the contrived fictions of anti-South Yankee propaganda.

Because this highly vocal group far outnumbers those of us who are pro-Forrest, this is the perspective of him that has been the most widely disseminated, read, and accepted by the general public, and even by scholars. Additionally, because Forrest and the South "lost the War," there is the added incentive to "kick the enemy while he is down." Certainly no Confederate has been kicked around as much as Forrest.

## FORREST DEBASED & DISMISSED AS MYTHOLOGY

Anti-Forrest sentiment is found not only in the writings of 19th-Century Northern journalists and newspaper reporters, however, but also more recently among modern-day authors, where it is laced with generous lashings of 21st-Century political correctness.

In *The Myth of Nathan Bedford Forrest*, authors Paul Ashdown and Edward Caudill enthusiastically tear Forrest apart piece by piece, dismissing nearly everything known about him as a fairy tale, reducing his figure to little more than that of a fictional character in a children's story book, or a mythological figure from ancient classical folklore.[222]

Then, after asserting that Forrest was an ignorant and illiterate yokel, a primitive ruffian, and a Southern hayseed, we are told that he was also quite probably a murderer. To drive their point home, they intimate that the General was a piece of white trash who strong-armed his way through life, operating in much the same fashion as a modern drug dealer. Forrest was, according to the authors, Dixie's equivalent of a Nazi-styled super hero, one who represented the Confederacy's most sinister attributes.[223]

Those who knew Forrest personally would have been outraged by such senseless and libelous remarks.

Historically accurate biographies that show Forrest in a positive light fare no better under Ashdown and Caudill's distorted magnifying glass.[224] These are labeled moral theatrics, revisionist propaganda

---

222. Ashdown and Caudill, p. 5.
223. Ashdown and Caudill, pp. 5, xvii, xvi, xviii, 9, 117, xvii.
224. For more on this issue from a pro-South point of view, see Bradley, p. 211.

written by naive and uncritical authors whose sole purpose is to hide Forrest's flaws and sins under a cloak of fairy tales, while at the same time turning him into an impossibly perfect symbol of Southern manliness, heroism, and chivalry. The two authors accept Yankee mythology at face value, while dismissing the factual history of the South as nothing more than fabricated redneck folklore.[225]

Is this what "the myth of Nathan Bedford Forrest" is really all about? Only if you dislike the South and are inclined to believe the wartime propaganda invented by Lincoln and his followers a century and a half ago. We are all entitled to our opinions, but should not our opinions be based on reality rather than fantasy?

## THE TRUE BEAUTY, MEANING, & FUNCTION OF MYTH

Just as they misunderstand Forrest and Southern culture most of these same individuals also misunderstand mythology itself.

In *The Power of Myth* distinguished scholar Joseph Campbell reminds us that mythology serves four vital functions in human society:

1. *The Mystical Function*: myth allows us to experience a reality that is beyond the five physical senses, beyond the material; a place full of wonder, mystery, and holiness, unexplainable by science.
2. *The Cosmological Function*: myth explains this mysterious reality, giving order, meaning, and purpose to our lives, from a spiritual point of view.
3. *The Sociological Function*: myth provides instructions on how to behave socially, how to get by in the world, and how to maintain an orderly society.
4. *The Pedagogical Function*: myth educates us as to what it means to be human, and teaches us ethical and moral lessons integral to attaining our full potential as individuals.[226]

Myths serve other functions as well. They act as vehicles that transmit impulses, messages, and knowledge from the deepest part of our souls, our subconscious, to the outer world of the conscious mind.

---

225. See e.g., Ashdown and Caudill, pp. 3-6, 109-113, 117.
226. Campbell, pp. 31, 70, 91, 143, 155.

As the Swiss psychoanalyst Carl Jung (1875-1961) noted, myths employ archetypes (that is, inherent psychic tendencies) that are part of our "collective unconscious."[227] Archetypes often take the form of universal motifs and themes that are common to tribal myths and even individual dreams, representing humanity's quest for self-realization, or oneness, with the universe and with God.[228]

Myths then instruct, explain, and bring order to a chaotic, changing, and inexplicable world. Using symbols, metaphor, parables, and allegory, they teach us about the universal human condition and predicament; about how to come to terms with our biology, our psychology, and our spirituality. To this end, myths glorify a particular person, community, tribe, or country, and infuse them with adventure and gallantry.[229] In other words, they help define us as individuals, along with our families, cultures, religions, and nations.[230]

To transmit these important ideas to us down through the generations, myths give us heros and heroines who teach through example, and who provide an ideal for each person to strive for. This explains why, for many people—especially in the South where fighters and soldiers are highly honored[231]—Forrest is at the top of the list of the great mythic heros.

EVERYMAN FORREST IS PART OF OUR COMMON HERITAGE
But "mythic" does not necessarily mean imaginary, false, or fictitious, as is commonly believed. As noted, the primary definition of myth is *a tradition that embodies the ideals and institutions of a society*; in particular, one based on a historical person (or event) that serves to illustrate or explain an aspect (or aspects) of the world view of a people.[232]

By this definition Forrest was indeed a mythic historical Southern figure, an extraordinary but real flesh and blood man, who lived and died in the 19th Century; a period in American history when the U.S. was transformed by Lincoln and his Yankee cohorts from a

---

227. Rosenbaum, s.v. "Jung, Carl Gustav."
228. Leeming, p. 5.
229. Grant and Hazel, p. vii.
230. Leeming, p. 4.
231. McWhiney and Jamieson, p. 171.
232. Mish, s.v. "myth."

conservative confederate republic to a liberal federate nation. This makes the conservative-libertarian ideals and virtues Forrest represents all the more important for those of us today, living in an age when the U.S. government is becoming larger, more complex, more powerful, and more intrusive than ever before.[233]

Even if Forrest were nothing more than a fanciful symbol of Southern Culture, however, and his life story was nothing more than a fable fabricated by pro-South storytellers, there are those of us who would still embrace him, still believe in him. For he personifies the romantic Southern myth of the cavalier, the courtly horseman, who fights and destroys evil and rescues damsels in distress. In short, he is real to us because we believe in him, and we believe in him because he is real.[234]

Forrest's life truly instructs and explains, gives meaning, purpose, and structure, providing a healthy and positive paradigm by which to live. He is, in a sense, an everyman who represents the human quest for self-fulfillment, identity, security, and perfection in a world of entropy, inequality, mystery, and disorder. Forrest's life story then is true both literally and mythically, for it is, as mythologist Campbell might have called it, the eternal anthem of the soul's incredible journey.[235]

Though Forrest is physically dead, his spirit and the ideals he stood for and symbolized, live on. For Forrest mirrored human life, our attitudes, opinions, virtues, weaknesses, aspirations, follies, dreams, successes, failures, and yes, also our dark sides. His story is the eternal narrative of the human psyche itself, and thus is the common heritage of each and every one of us.[236]

## AUTHORS WHO SMEAR FORREST
Some authors, while admitting that Forrest had admirable qualities, seem

---

233. In his three short years in office, for example, our current president, liberal-socialist Barack Hussein Obama, has created hundreds of new governmental bureaucracies, agencies, departments, and positions. At the same time he has racked up more debt than all of the former U.S. presidents combined. "America Live," FOX News, October 8, 2011.

234. For more on the topic of the Southern mind and myth (though from an anti-South point of view), see E. M. Thomas, pp. 23-24.

235. Leeming, pp. 6, 8.

236. Carlyon, p. x.

to retain a subtle distaste for him. This distaste is, again, usually born of a skewed politically correct point of view, one based both on modern conditioning and on a gross misunderstanding of Victorian Southern culture and life on America's 19th-Century Western frontier.

In *The Confederacy's Greatest Cavalryman: Nathan Bedford Forrest* (1992), Brian Steel Wills literally leads off his biography by saying that there are many reasons to detest Forrest. According to Wills, Forrest is a contaminated individual, an impure paragon, the archetypal Southern racist, the mastermind of the "massacre" at the Battle of Fort Pillow—for which he was solely responsible. Apparently psychic, Wills tells us that in Forrest's eyes, the surrendering blacks at the fort no doubt got what they deserved, for, deeply prejudiced, Forrest did not respect blacks or even see them as people; to him they were only objects of commercial interest. Furthermore, we are told, Forrest did indeed personify many of the negative character traits described by Dixie-hating men like New Englander Emerson,[237] who as we saw earlier, believed that Southerners are dumb, unhappy, "good for nothing," and "bladders of conceit."[238]

In Kenneth C. Davis' *Don't Know Much About the Civil War* (1996), we are informed that Forrest was a nasty, illiterate brute whose financial success came primarily from exploiting blacks,[239] while in Robert M. Browning's *Forrest: The Confederacy's Relentless Warrior* (2004), the author, speaking of Fort Pillow, asserts that the responsibility for the alleged "massacre" there lies with and only with Forrest.[240] In John S. Bowman's Northern-slanted *The Civil War Day by Day* (1989), we are told that the abominations committed by Forrest and his men at Fort Pillow will one day surely be upheld by history.[241]

In *A Stillness at Appomattox* (1953), Bruce Catton describes Fort Pillow as a conflict in which Forrest and his men intentionally formed themselves into a lynch mob. Under "Fort Pillow" in Catton's index, one finds the indicting and presumptive sentence: "massacre of captured Negro soldiers at."[242] Likewise, in *The Great Republic: A History of the*

---

237. Wills, pp. xix, 2, 323, 196, 180, 7, 4-5.
238. R. W. Emerson, JRWE, Vol. 4, pp. 312-313.
239. K. C. Davis, pp. 344-345.
240. Browning, p. 57.
241. J. S. Bowman, CWDD, p. 150.
242. Catton, Vol. 3, p. 263.

*American People* (1977), author David Herbert Donald solemnly relates that trustworthy Yankee newspapers described how, in April 1864, Forrest and his cavalry intentionally beat, shot, and burned surrendering Union soldiers and prisoners at Fort Pillow.[243]

As we will see, not a single word of the above statements is true. Many of us have carefully studied the details of the Battle of Fort Pillow, along with the actions of Forrest and his men, and have come to quite different conclusions.

Some authors, particularly Northern ones, insist on disseminating the same old hackneyed falsehoods about Forrest, keeping his reputation as a "racist hillbilly-redneck" alive generation after generation. In their Northern-biased book *Civil War Battlefields and Landmarks* (2003), Carol M. Highsmith and Ted Landphair once again assure us (as if we have not been told enough) that Forrest was the founder of the Ku Klux Klan,[244] while in *A Concise Encyclopedia of the Civil War* (1965), Henry E. Simmons states that Forrest had a questionable history concerning his dealing with blacks, who he murdered in disproportionate numbers during the notorious massacre at Fort Pillow. None of this should surprise us, claims Simmons, since Forrest was both the originator and the head of the KKK.[245]

In *The Fiery Cross: The Klu Klux Klan in America* (1987), author Wyn Craig Wade treats his readers to even less objectivity concerning Forrest and the "massacre," referring to him as the commanding Rebel officer at Fort Pillow who had all of the Yankee unit's black soldiers killed on the spot. Wade then quotes a Union soldier who calls Forrest a filthy demon disguised as a human, one well-known for his homicidal tendencies, inhumanity, and shocking outrages.[246]

While this type of hyperbole is now known to be patently erroneous, such statements, masquerading as fact, continue to spread. In *Battle Cry of Freedom: The Civil War Era* (2003), James M. McPherson, renowned pro-North Civil War scholar, maintains that it has by now been well established *and* accepted that—contrary to Southern history—Yankee officer Major William F. Bradford, along with dozens

---

243. Bailyn, Dallek, Davis, Donald, Thomas, and Wood, p. 5.
244. Highsmith and Landphair, p. 28.
245. Simmons, s.v. "Forrest, Nathan Bedford."
246. Wade, pp. 16-17.

of black and white Federal soldiers, were shot down in cold blood at Fort Pillow while trying to flee.[247]

Though the opinions of many others—including those who were actually at the Battle of Fort Pillow and those of modern-day traditional Southern scholars—contradict such statements completely, it is views like McPherson's that have been the most widely adopted and accepted, both in the North and in the New South.

Then there are those authors who are fascinated with the South and who even seem to have a grudging respect for Forrest, but who continue to wantonly perpetuate negative images of him. In *Confederates in the Attic* (1998), Pulitzer prize-winner Tony Horwitz characterizes Forrest as a simple primitive, maintaining that his great equestrian monument in Memphis, Tennessee, with its nefarious looking eyes, drawn face and sharpened goatee, indeed matches Sherman's description of Forrest as "the Devil."[248]

## HOW REFERENCE BOOKS DEPICT FORREST

Without question, among the most egregious anti-South propagandists are the so-called "Civil War" reference books, the many dictionaries, encyclopedias, atlases, guides, and handbooks that are allegedly written to enlighten the public about Lincoln's War. Nearly every one of these books is written by a pro-North author, none who come close to being able to conceal their detestation of 19th-Century Dixie and her people.

Naturally, one of their favorite whipping posts is Forrest, who they excoriate with undisguised relish. In *Brassey's Almanac: The American Civil War* (2003), for example, author Philip Katcher describes Forrest as an illiterate raider whose military record was tainted by his cavalry's slaughter of surrendered "loyal" Tennesseans (that is, whites from Tennessee who sided with the Union) and blacks at Fort Pillow. Furthermore, the author tells us, Forrest literally ruined his military reputation by founding, and becoming the grand wizard of, the Ku Klux Klan.[249]

In *The Confederacy* (1993), one of the most pro-North

---

247. J. M. McPherson, BCF, p. 748.
248. Horwitz, pp. 155, 156.
249. Katcher, BAACW, pp. 101-102.

encyclopedias ever written about the wartime South, we are told that Forrest lost control at Fort Pillow, allowing the murder of innocent black soldiers, and that he was the first grand wizard of the KKK, part of his attempt to reestablish white supremacy throughout Dixie.[250]

In Simmons' *A Concise Encyclopedia of the Civil War*, the author relates that Forrest was one of the most feared individuals during the time period, no doubt because of his violent temperament, questionable history, slaughter of blacks at Fort Pillow, and the fact that he was the founder and leader of the KKK.[251]

John S. Bowman's *Encyclopedia of the Civil War* (1992) offers nothing new; merely a repetition of the usual anti-Forrest propaganda: the General was a violent, pro-slavery racist, and the grand wizard of the KKK.[252]

In the Civil War Society's *Encyclopedia of the Civil War* (1997), Forrest is depicted as a man with a killer instinct, who became the KKK's first grand wizard; a cunning and fearless Rebel chieftain who encouraged his soldiers to murder unarmed black Yankee soldiers during the wicked drama that unfolded at Fort Pillow.[253]

All of this is old news, and false at that; all of it, as we will show, nothing more than lies, slander, and fiction created about Forrest by anti-South Northerners during Lincoln's War. The tragedy is that this misinformation, *and* disinformation, is merely being repeated generation after generation (now by New South Southerners as well), all without a thorough investigation of their sources.

EXTREME FORREST-HATING
While such books make only passing shots at the General, some authors have chosen to devote entire books to the practice of Forrest-bashing.

One of the more egregious of these is Andrew Ward's *River Run Red: The Fort Pillow Massacre in the American Civil War* (2005), which could be best described as 500 pages of contempt, unadulterated hostility, personal animus, and venomous loathing of Forrest and his homeland.

Brimming with slanted revisionism, the villain of the book is

---

250. Current, TC, s.v. "Forrest, Nathan Bedford."
251. Simmons, s.v. "Forrest, Nathan Bedford."
252. J. S. Bowman, ECW, s.v. "Forrest, Nathan Bedford."
253. Civil War Society, CWSECW, s.v. "Forrest, Nathan Bedford."

repeatedly, disrespectfully, and sarcastically referred to throughout, not as Nathan Bedford Forrest, Bedford Forrest, General Forrest, or even Forrest, but as "the Wizard." This appears to be a play, not on his uncanny abilities as the Wizard in the Saddle, but more maliciously on his alleged role as the grand wizard of the KKK.[254]

Though oddly, Ward states that he wrote his book because of an insalubrious enthrallment with Victorian mass murders,[255] many would argue that it seems more an excuse to denounce Forrest, anger his admirers, and further shame and punish the South.

Numerous other works of this ilk could be cited, such as Richard L. Fuchs' *An Unerring Fire: The Massacre at Fort Pillow* (1994); John Gauss' *Black Flag! Black Flag! The Battle at Fort Pillow* (2003); and John Cimprich's *Fort Pillow, A Civil War Massacre, and Public Memory* (2005).

## THE PROBLEM WITH ANTI-FORREST WORKS

In going out on the limb of fiction in order to assail and degrade Forrest, such authors dilute, and even wholly disregard, Forrest's achievements and the many warm reports of his contemporaries. At the same time they focus on his fiascos and the words of his enemies, which anti-Forrest authors seem to regard as Gospel truth. Even more troubling, they take Northern war propaganda at face value, obvious disinformation and laughable slurs that were not even believed by most Northerners at the time.

Such authors also conveniently ignore, abbreviate, or downplay the Confederate view of Forrest's battles, such as Fort Pillow, while focusing on, magnifying, and accentuating the Union's. Thus, while adding much heat but little light to the discussion, they are merely repeating the same timeworn Northern myths about "Forrest, the Butcher of Fort Pillow."

Among their many offences, the greatest made by anti-Forrest authors is interpreting the General, his life, actions, words, thoughts, and beliefs, through the lens of the 21st Century; and a politically correct 21st-Century lens at that.

---

254. See e.g., A. Ward, pp. 110, 142, 143, 144, 186, 187, 194, 228, 236, 247, 257, 283, 284, 320, 336, 357, 381.
255. A. Ward, p. xiii.

As just one example of this type of presentism, Forrest was born in an America where the ideas of white superiority and slavery were nearly fully accepted (even by many Quakers)[256] until the 1830s. Why then should Forrest be pilloried for embracing the beliefs and customs of his day, social mores he was taught by his parents, his school, his religion, his community, his region, indeed, his nation, the United States?

The U.S. Constitution itself upheld and protected slavery until December 6, 1865, eight months after the War ended and Lincoln died. One can only imagine how we will be seen by the politically correct 150 years from now. As of 2010, for example, women are still not paid the same as men for the same job.

As is true of so many of the works of Forrest's critics, what we have here are highly biased and sadistic diatribes; denunciations not based on facts, evidence, or reason; excoriations devoted not to education, ennoblement, and enlightenment. Merely one-sided criticisms whose sole intent seems to be the humiliation of an individual and his modern day blood relations, and an attempt to finally and totally destroy his reputation and name across the region of his birth.

None of this is meant to personally denigrate any of the authors mentioned above. It is only to point out how 20th- and 21st-Century political correctness has influenced and augmented the anti-Forrest trend today, and how this trend has permeated the literary world of modern-day historians, authors, and scholars, and even Forrest biographers.

---

256. See e.g., Litwack, NS, pp. 204-207.

# Part 2

# CHARGES AGAINST FORREST

# WHITE RACISM, BLACK SLAVERY: COMPARING FORREST WITH LINCOLN

*"There is no doubt we could soon wipe old Sherman off the face of the earth . . . if they'd give me enough men and . . . enough guns." —* Nathan Bedford Forrest

### THE BIG THREE

THERE ARE THREE PRIMARY REASONS typically cited as to why Forrest is detested by some. We can gain a better understanding of both his detractors and Forrest himself by briefly examining these. For as it turns out none have any basis in fact. All are fables that began as Northern anti-South war propaganda. Truly, as the authors of *The South Was Right!*, James R. Kennedy and Walter D. Kennedy, point out, Northern folklore and Southern fact are not even remotely related.[257]

The basis for the entire anti-Forrest movement can be encapsulated in three Northern/New South beliefs:

1. Forrest was not only a slave owner and a slave trader, he was a cruel and racist slave owner and slave trader.
2. Forrest and his troops slaughtered Yanks, mainly black Yanks, in disproportionate numbers at the Battle of Fort Pillow.

---

257. Kennedy and Kennedy, p. 119.

3. Forrest founded the Klu Klux Klan and was its first leader.

A fourth reason can be appended to this list, as well: hatred of the South, one of whose primary symbols is Forrest.

Before beginning both a realistic and a compassionate look at the life of the General, let us briefly examine these one by one.

FORREST & SLAVE OWNERSHIP

Forrest was indeed a slave owner. But does this make him a racist? If so, then Yankee war hero and America's eighteenth president, Ulysses S. Grant, was also a racist, for he too owned numerous slaves,[258] individuals he did not free until *after* the War,[259] several years *after* Lincoln's unconstitutional Emancipation Proclamation was issued.[260]

Many other men of note owned slaves as well, among them other American presidents. A partial list of this illustrous group includes: Greek philosopher, Aristotle; Greek moralist, Plutarch; Italian theologian, Saint Thomas Aquinas; Italian navigator, Christopher Columbus; German Reformation leader, Martin Luther; Spanish conqueror of Mexico, Hernando Cortes; French Protestant reformer, John Calvin; English explorer, Sir Francis Drake; empress of Russia, Catherine the Great; 1st U.S. president, George Washington (owned 216 slaves); American political leader, Patrick Henry (owned 65 slaves); 3rd U.S. president, Thomas Jefferson (owned 185 slaves); 4th U.S. president, James Madison (owned 116 slaves); American statesman, Alexander Hamilton; 7th U.S. president, Andrew Jackson (owned 160 slaves while president); U.S. vice president, John C. Calhoun; 10th U.S. president, John Tyler; 11th U.S. president, James K. Polk (owned 18 slaves); 12th U.S. president, Zachary Taylor (owned 300 slaves while in office); first and only president of the Confederate States of America, Jefferson Davis; and 17th U.S. president, Andrew Johnson.[261]

Were these men racists merely because they owned African slaves? The C.S. Constitution protected domestic Southern slavery until April 9, 1865 (though it banned foreign slavery almost five years before

---

258. Wallechinsky, Wallace, and Wallace, p. 11.
259. Woods, p. 67.
260. Kennedy and Kennedy, p. 27.
261. Wallechinsky, Wallace, and Wallace, pp. 10-11.

the U.S. Constitution did), while the U.S. Constitution protected it eight months longer, until December 6, 1865 (when the Thirteenth Amendment was ratified). Thus, until that date all white Americans could be considered racists. But if not then neither was Forrest.[262]

## FORREST & THE SLAVE TRADE

It is also true that Forrest was involved in the slave trade. But if this makes him a racist then nearly the entire North at that time must be considered racist as well. Not only did thousands of Northerners own slaves (in the 1700s, for example, one-fifth of the New York City's population were slaves),[263] but the American slave trade itself began in the North where the institution was fueled by New Englanders and New Yorkers right up until Lincoln (very reluctantly) abolished it in 1863.[264]

Indeed, the North's entire industrial and commercial strength during the 19th Century was based on the buying, trading, and selling of Africans,[265] with the Yankee cities of Newport and Bristol, Rhode Island, being America's busiest slaving ports.[266] Abolitionist Harriet Beecher Stowe (1811-1896) observed that this was the way Northerners preferred their slavery: with all of the gains and none of the pain.[267]

Many Northern antislavery advocates were fully aware of their region's integral role in the institution of slavery, and they were not at all happy about it. In his 1870 essay, "No Treason," New England abolitionist Lysander Spooner (1808-1887) angrily attacked the "lenders of blood money": Northern bankers, Northern manufacturers, and Northern railroad companies. All had, Spooner affirmed, "for a long series of years previous to the war, been the willing accomplices of the slaveholders in perverting the government from the purpose of liberty and justice" for the sole purpose of prospering off the slave trade and its cotton.[268]

It is clear then that while the South did indeed own slaves, it was

---

262. We will discuss the often ignored topic of African-American and Native-American slave owners shortly.
263. Farrow, Frank, and Lang, p. xxvii.
264. Kennedy and Kennedy, pp. 59-80, 145-146.
265. Kennedy and Kennedy, p. 72.
266. Garraty, p. 77.
267. Farrow, Frank, and Lang, p. xxvi.
268. Spooner, NT, No. 6, p. 54.

the North who sold her these slaves, and it was the Northern textile mills that made clothing from Southern slave-grown cotton.[269] And what a profit the North derived: *all* of the cotton used by Yankee industry came from Dixie. Not only this, the North's cotton industry was by far its biggest and most profitable business.[270]

New York City is today America's wealthiest and largest metropolis, in large part, because in the 1800s it was both the hub and the literal capital of the extremely lucrative American slave industry.[271] In contrast, even at the peak of the slavery business in 1860, slightly less than 6 percent of Southerners actually owned slaves.[272] Let us look at this topic in more detail for a moment.

AUTHENTIC SLAVERY STATISTICS
In 1861 exactly 96.73 percent of small landholders (known as yeoman farmers) in the South operated without labor assistance (other than their wives and children).[273] These were men who never owned slaves[274] and who, for the most part, cared nothing for the institution and wanted to see it eradicated. They were, in other words, typical Southerners, the "plain folk,"[275] small non-slave owning farmers.[276]

Take Rowan County, North Carolina, for example. In 1860, of the county's 14,589 people, only one individual owned as many as 100 slaves, while only 37 owned more than 20.[277]

These facts reveal, if nothing else, that slavery truly was expendable and not at all necessary to the life of the South, as was made patently clear near the end of the War: when the Confederacy was finally faced with the choice of emancipation in order to enlist blacks or the destruction of the South by Lincoln, she chose to enlist blacks.[278]

What about the other 3.27 percent of Southerners? Contrary to

269. Kennedy and Kennedy, p. 117.
270. Owsley, KCD, pp. 2-3.
271. Farrow, Frank, and Lang, pp. 4-5, 13-25.
272. Kennedy and Kennedy, p. 83. The actual number of Southern slaveholders in 1850 was 5.8 percent.
273. Stampp, p. 29.
274. White, Foscue, and McKnight, p. 209.
275. Brinkley, p. 319.
276. Stampp, p. 30.
277. H. C. Bailey, p. 4.
278. Barrow, Segars, and Rosenburg, BC, p. 26.

"Northern history," which maintains that most or even *all* Southerners owned black chattel, this tiny group, just fifty out of 1,000 people, made up the entire slave owning population of Dixie.[279] Faced with such facts, even slavery's fiercest 19th-Century opponents had to acknowledge that Southern slaveholders comprised "an insignificant fraction of the population."[280]

To put this number in perspective, the South's 300,000 white slave owners made up only 1 percent of the total U.S. white population of 30,000,000 people in 1861, and only 3 percent of the South's 9,150,000 whites.[281] If America's 4,000,000 black slaves (North and South) are added to this figure, the South's white slave owners comprised only 0.8 percent of the total white and black population of America in 1861.[282]

The reality is that land and black servants were extraordinarily costly in the 1800s, so invariably slavery was a rich man's business. Yet nearly all 19th-Century Southerners were poor farmers. This fact alone proves that in all actuality very few Southerners owned black servants, and thus it was not, and could not have been, the "cornerstone of the Confederacy," as so many have claimed.[283] There was no "slave owning majority," as Northern myth consistently maintains. Quite the opposite. The large slaveholding families of the South numbered only about 10,000, this out of literally millions of Southern families.[284] They were so rare that most Southerners, being poor rural farmers, probably did not even personally know a slave owning family.

Indeed, according to the U.S. Census, in 1860 only 4.8 percent (or 385,000) of all Southerners owned slaves, the other 95.2 percent did

---

279. To arrive at these numbers I used Hacker's figure of 9,150,000 Southern whites in 1861 (Hacker, p. 581) and the Kennedy brothers' figure of 300,000 Southern white slave owners in 1860 (Kennedy and Kennedy, p. 83).

280. Hacker, p. 542.

281. See Foner, FSFLFM, pp. 87-88.

282. In 1861 there were 20,750,000 million whites in the North, and 9,150,000 whites in the South (Hacker, p. 581), making the total American white population 29,900,000; or rounded off, 30,000,000. In 1861 there were 3,500,000 black slaves in the South ( Quarles, p. xiii; Weintraub, p. 70; Cooper, JDA, p. 378; Rosenbaum and Brinkley, s.v. "Civil War"), and 500,000 black slaves in the North (Eaton, HSC, p. 93), making a total of 4,000,000 slaves nationwide. (Some estimates indicate that there were as many as 1,000,000 slaves in the North in the 1860s. See Hinkle, p. 125.)

283. Stampp, pp. 402-403. For the facts about Confederate Vice President Alexander H. Stephens' "Cornerstone Speech," see Seabrook, EYWTAACIW, pp. 260-269.

284. Long and Long, p. 702.

not.[285] Of those that did, most owned less than five.[286] Correcting for the mistakes of Census takers—which would include counting slave-hirers as slave owners and counting more than once those thousands of slave owners who annually moved the same slaves back and forth across multiple states—this figure, 4.8 percent, is no doubt much smaller. Either way, the average Southerner himself believed that only 5 percent of his number owned slaves, which is slightly high, but roughly accurate.[287]

Going back in time, the number of Southern slave owners decreases precipitously. In 1850, for example, of the 8,039,000 whites living in the Southern states, only 186,551 were slave owners, a mere 2.3 percent of the total white population. Thus, 97.7 percent of Southern whites that year were non-slave owners.[288] Of these same

---

285. M. M. Smith, pp. 4-5.

286. Gragg, p. 84; DiLorenzo, LU, p. 174.

287. Parker, p. 343. Important note: in an attempt to tarnish the South, anti-South proponents like to artificially inflate the numbers of white Southern slave owners (they completely ignore black, brown, and red slave owners) by calculating using the number of *households* ("families") instead of the *total number of white Southerners*. Using the lower number of households as opposed to the higher number of total whites, of course, gives a higher number of slave owners, which is why they use this method: it puts the South in the worst light possible, and gives further justification for Lincoln's unjustifiable War. For example, the socialist, anti-South, Yankee historian Kenneth M. Stampp, who Northerners and scallywags consider the "authority" on slavery figures, states that in 1860 there were 385,000 Southern slave owners, about 1,500,000 free Southern families, and a total of 8,000,000 whites. Stampp, pp. 29-30. All of this is true, up to this point. Enemies of the South, however, compute the number of Southern slave owners by calculating what percentage 385,000 (the number of Southern slave owners) is of 1,500,000 (the number of Southern households). This gives a result of about 25 percent, the pro-North claim being then that "25 percent of all Southern whites were slave owners in 1860." This indeed is the exact figure and calculation formula Stampp and his ilk use (see e.g., Stampp, p. 30). Unfortunately, as "households," women, and children did not (and could not) own slaves, this formula is not only disingenuous and misleading, it is mathematically incorrect. The correct calculation, the one I and other traditional Southern folks use, is to compute the number of Southern slave owners by calculating what percentage 385,000 is of 8,000,000 (the total number of Southern whites). This gives a result of 4.8 percent. When we correct for enumeration errors (see the following footnote), this number comes down to about 4 percent or less. Hence, we can safely *and* accurately say that only about 4 percent of Southern whites were slave owners in 1860. The other 96 percent were not. Be aware of this cowardly and treacherous pro-North trick, one found in nearly every anti-South book.

288. For the number of Southern whites in 1850, see Wilson and Ferris, s.v. "Plantations"; Bradley, p. 33. For the number of slave owners in 1850, see Helper, ICS, p. 148. How the total number of slave owners was arrived at: while "official" records state that there were 347,525 slave owners in the South in 1850, this is a gross error. Famed publisher and statistician Professor James D. B. DeBow, Superintendent of the Census at the time, stated that this number wrongly includes slave hirers, a profession entirely different than that of a slave owner. Additionally, when slaveholders owned slaves in different states, or moved the same ones from state to state, they were erroneously counted more than once. Adjusting for these mistakes, we find the following: from 347,525 we must subtract 158,974 (the number of Southern slave-hirers) and 2,000 (the number of multi-state slave owners who were entered more than once). Thus the total number of slave owners in the South in 1850 was 186,551. See Helper, ICS, pp. 146-148.

whites only 46,274 owned twenty or more servants (0.5 percent), only 2,500 owned thirty or more (0.03 percent), and a mere handful (0.02 percent) owned 100 or more.[289]

This last group, the so-called "Aristocratic Planters" (hated by 19th-Century Northerners more than they hated slavery),[290] eventually numbered about 150,000,[291] but still comprised only 1.6 percent of the total number of white Southerners (9,000,000) in the 1860s. In fact, the extremely wealthy planters, and thus those who owned the most servants, made up only one-half of 1 percent of the total population of the South.[292] According to the 1860 Census only fifteen slave owners across the entire South owned more than 500 slaves.[293] In 1859 Lincoln himself acknowledged that

> in all our slave States except South Carolina, a majority of the whole people of all colors are neither slaves nor masters.[294]

Let us compare these statistics with those for Northern slave owners. In the early 1700s, 42 percent of New York households owned slaves, and the share of slaves in both New York and New Jersey was larger than that of North Carolina.[295] By 1690, in Perth Amboy, New Jersey, as just one example, nearly every white inhabitant owned one or more black slaves.[296] Based on mathematics alone it is clear that Yankees were far more enthusiastic slavers than Southerners ever were.

There were so few Southern slave owners that the minority proslavery leaders were at a loss as to how to promote their cause. After trying everything from offering financial inducements to racist scare tactics, they eventually gave up.[297] The American abolition movement had gotten its start in the South and Southern antislavery sentiment was by now several centuries old.

Slave trading then began as, and always was, an exclusively

289. Wilson and Ferris, s.v. "Plantations"; Bradley, p. 33.
290. Foner, FSFLFM, p. 68.
291. Kennedy and Kennedy, p. 83.
292. Channing, p. 8; Grissom, p. 131.
293. J. C. Perry, p. 99.
294. Nicolay and Hay, ALCW, Vol. 1, p. 581.
295. Fogel, pp. 203-204.
296. McManus, BBN, p. 5.
297. Stampp, pp. 425-426.

Northern enterprise, not a Southern one; which is why slave ships sailed only under the United States flag, never under the Confederate flag.[298]

Was Forrest a racist solely because he traded in slaves? The answer is obvious.

## RACISM: FORREST VS. LINCOLN

Much more will be said about Abraham Lincoln in Chapters 4 and 9. But since we are on the topics of race and Forrest's attitudes towards blacks, and since most of Forrest's critics are also admirers of Lincoln, it is instructive to compare the two in detail. For when it comes to racism Forrest could never hold a candle to the man whose followers curiously call the "Great Emancipator."

## LINCOLN & THE EMANCIPATION PROCLAMATION

To begin with Lincoln did not issue his unconstitutional Emancipation Proclamation in 1863 for humanitarian reasons, for racial equality for blacks, as has been taught by Yankee mythologists.[299] Indeed, this is why, when he started his War in 1861, though many Northern blacks turned out at recruiting offices to sign up, they were "thanked for their troubles and sent home." At the time Lincoln had no intention whatsoever of using blacks in his military, and neither did any of the governors of the Northern states.[300]

What changed Lincoln's mind two years later was, in great part, the problem of manpower: white enlistments were down and his all-white army was sharply dwindling in numbers.[301] Though he was still against enlisting blacks in the U.S. Army, thinking them inferior to whites,[302] he eventually gave in to military expediency, for it was obvious by then that their numbers would be needed by the Union in order to subdue the South.[303]

There was also the inevitable racist motivation. As Lincoln later

---

298. Ashe, p. 10.
299. Donald, LR, p. 203.
300. Mullen, p. 19. Racist Lincoln at first also prohibited Native-Americans from serving in the U.S. Army, even though many volunteered. D. Brown, p. 179.
301. Mullen, p. 19.
302. L. Johnson, p. 131.
303. Mullen, pp. 19-21.

asserted:

> I thought that whatever negroes could be got to do as soldiers, leaves just so much less for white soldiers to do in saving the Union.[304]

This would have included, of course, taking Confederate steel and dying for Lincoln's cause, purportedly "preserving the Union." (As we will see, Lincoln actually destroyed the voluntary Union envisioned and created by the Founding Fathers, turning individual allegiance from the state to the nation, one whose capital in Washington, D.C. became the head of an all-powerful, monolithic empire—Thomas Jefferson's worst nightmare.)[305]

The problem was that slaves could not be made soldiers as long as they were considered "property."[306] The resolution to this difficulty was the Emancipation Proclamation,[307] which is why Lincoln later admitted that without the added numbers of black soldiers in the Union Army the North would not have won the war.[308]

Tellingly, Lincoln's enrollment of African-Americans did not stop deeply entrenched European-American racism among his troops, or at the White House. White U.S. soldiers hissed and booed when they were told of Lincoln's new policy and finally only accepted black soldiers in their midst under penalty of arrest. Even then this did not put an end to subtler forms of racism.

Eventually the Yankee Army had to not only ban the word "nigger," but also "demeaning punishment" of black soldiers and "insulting language" directed at black soldiers.[309] Yankee General Lorenzo Thomas, for example, promised white soldiers a quick dismissal from the army if they persisted in abusing and tormenting black soldiers. The threat had little impact and Thomas ended up removing a number of white Union officers who refused to treat blacks equitably.[310] It was

---

304. Nicolay and Hay, ALCW, Vol. 2, p. 398.
305. DiLorenzo, LU, pp. 138, 139, 147, 159.
306. W. B. Garrison, LNOK, pp. 174-177.
307. L. Johnson, p. 133.
308. Mullen, p. 22.
309. Page Smith, p. 308, 309.
310. Cornish, pp. 118-119.

this "bitterly hostile" white racism in the North, in fact, that was behind Lincoln's decision to segregate his troops, with all-black troops to be led by white officers.[311]

White racism among Lincoln's soldiery was not just strongly ingrained, it was also pervasive, for any black wearing a Yankee uniform inevitably stirred up the prejudices of white soldiers, men who hailed from an American society where racism was known to be both widespread and deeply rooted: the North.[312] As one Pennsylvania soldier said of "them damn nigger Regiments:" Lincoln would be wise not to put any of them in our department. We detest the nigger way worse than any Confederate soldier, and we will kill more of them than Johnny Reb.[313] This Pennsylvanian was not exaggerating. In fact, Northern white racism among Lincoln's military forces also included officers.

Shortly after Lincoln issued his document illegally "liberating" Southern slaves while permitting slavery to continue in the North, his army, which was "strongly anti-abolition," was described as severely "demoralized." One of the most demoralized of Lincoln's commanders was Union General Joseph "Fighting Joe" Hooker,[314] who sent the president a scathing letter concerning his Emancipation Proclamation. It read, in part:

> A large element of the army had taken sides against it, declaring that they would never have embarked in the war had they anticipated this action of the government.[315]

Another U.S. officer was even more to the point: if the Union army ever comes to believe that this war is for the abolition of slavery, at least 75 percent of our men will give up their weapons and refuse to fight, he declared.[316]

In the summer of 1862, the staff of Yankee General George Brinton McClellan "seriously discussed" marching to Washington to

---

311. Eaton, HSC, p. 263.
312. Wills, p. 191.
313. Robertson, p. 32.
314. C. Adams, p. 134.
315. Henderson, Vol. 2, p. 411.
316. C. Adams, p. 134.

"intimidate the president," in the hopes that he would refrain from interfering with slavery and simply bring the War to a quick and peaceful close. Union General John Pope noted that among the Army of the Potomac there were frequent comments made about Lincoln's flaws and the possibility of replacing him with someone more able.[317]

Another disgruntled Yankee general, the infamous Fitz John Porter,[318] wrote that Lincoln's Emancipation Proclamation was widely jeered throughout the Union army, inducing revulsion, dissatisfaction, and words of infidelity toward the U.S. president that were very close to treasonous. Our soldiers, Porter complained, are worn out, sick of the violence; they want the war to come to a moral and fair end, not because of the ridiculous edict of a sissy.[319]

Porter, of course, was referring here to Lincoln.

## EVIDENCE THAT LINCOLN WAS OPPOSED TO RACIAL EQUALITY

Unlike Forrest, there is abundant evidence showing that "Honest Abe" was not only not interested in complete racial equality, he was aggressively opposed to it throughout his life, as the following examples reveal.

• First and foremost, Lincoln was no abolitionist. He was scrupulous in avoiding being called an abolitionist[320] and regarded the entire abolition movement as a nuisance and its doctrines as pernicious. At first he repeatedly blocked efforts to end slavery, and finally only relented because, eventually, he had no choice, for the pressure from the Radicals (that is, abolitionists) in his party grew unbearable.

Indeed, it was Lincoln who said that the "evils of immediate emancipation" should be avoided "as far as possible,"[321] and that "the promulgation of abolition doctrines tends rather to increase than to abate

---

317. Donald, L, p. 385.

318. Lincoln formally dismissed Porter from military service in January 1863 over problems at the Battle of Manassas II, on August 29, 1862. As usual, Lincoln acted incorrectly. In 1879, fourteen years after his death, more intelligent individuals prevailed: Porter's dismissal was revoked and he was reinstated in the Federal army. J. S. Bowman, CWDD, s.v. "10 January 1863"; "21 January 1863."

319. J. M. Perry, p. 103; Catton, Vol. 2, pp. 440-441.

320. W. B. Garrison, LNOK, p. 41.

321. Tarbell, Vol. 2, p. 212.

its evils."[322]    When asked if he minded having abolitionists in the Republican party, Lincoln snapped back: "As long as I am not painted with the Abolitionist brush."[323]

In truth, Lincoln was not against slavery.  He was against the spread of slavery, and this only for racist and economic reasons, as we will see.[324]

• By his own repeated admissions, some subtle, some overt, Lincoln's number one interest was always politics (that is, money and power), not humanitarian concerns.

For example, being truly forthright for once he called his Emancipation Proclamation, not a racial, or even a social, measure, but simply a "military necessity,"[325] a "fit and necessary war measure for suppressing said rebellion," as he so succinctly put it.[326]  It was, at its very heart, nothing more than a pragmatic means to ending his war.[327] Lincoln's secretary of state, Seward, went even further, saying that *all* of the measures Lincoln had taken to end slavery were "war measures," and that these were only issued to "preserve the Union."[328]

The blatant political expediency behind Lincoln's Emancipation Proclamation aroused the ire of every true abolitionist.  One of these, Spooner, wrote that Lincoln and his party had not abolished slavery

> as an act of justice to the black man himself, but only . . . because they wanted his assistance . . . in carrying on the war they had undertaken for maintaining and intensifying that political, commercial, and industrial slavery.[329]

Proof of this comes from the bold fact that Lincoln's black soldiers were usually used as shock troops, advance units who took the brunt of enemy fire in order to spare white lives, usually in engagements

---

322. Nicolay and Hay, ALCW, Vol. 1, p. 15.
323. C. Adams, p. 135; DiLorenzo, GC, p. 255; Johannsen, p. 55.
324. Rosenbaum and Brinkley, s.v. "Lincoln Administration."
325. Nicolay and Hay, ALCW, Vol. 2, p. 296.
326. Nicolay and Hay, ALCW, Vol. 2, p. 287.
327. Neely, p. 221.
328. L. Johnson, pp. 140-141.
329. Spooner, NT, No. 6, pp. 56-57.

where the outcome was in doubt.[330]

• Lincoln also conceded that his proclamation was political not racial when he called it a "civil necessity,"[331] one he hoped would "prevent the Radicals from openly embarrassing the government in the conduct of the war."[332]

• Winning the support of Europe, by then a vigorously anti-slavery region, was paramount to Lincoln, yet another reason for issuing the Emancipation Proclamation. Unfortunately for "Honest Abe" this particular ploy did not work, as most of Europe, in particular England and France, did not believe that the object of the War was to abolish slavery, thus they sided with the Confederacy. The true objective, they held, was domination and acquisition on the part of the North and self-determination on the part of the South (Europe was correct). As the London *Times* put it on November 7, 1861:

> . . . the contest is really for empire on the side of the North, and for independence on that of the South, and in this respect we recognize an exact analogy between the North and the Government of George III, and the South and the [original] Thirteen Revolted Provinces. These opinions . . . are the general opinions of the English nation.[333]

The idea that the War was over slavery was known to be a lie because of Lincoln himself.[334] During his first Inaugural Address, March 4, 1861, Lincoln clearly and emphatically promised not to disturb the system of slavery. Even if he did, the president affirmed, it would be illegal.[335]

The text of Lincoln's First Inaugural Address, widely published in newspapers across Europe, was eagerly read by millions. It said, in part:

---

330. Cornish, pp. 87, 269.
331. L. Johnson, p. 131.
332. Rice, RAL, p. 533.
333. Rhodes, Vol. 3, p. 545.
334. Owsley, KCD, pp. 187-191.
335. Pollard, SHW, Vol. 2, pp. 372-373; Woods, p. 66.

Apprehension seems to exist among the people of the Southern States that by the accession of a Republican administration their property and their peace and personal security are to be endangered.[336] There has never been any reasonable cause for such apprehension. Indeed, the most ample evidence to the contrary has all the while existed and been open to their inspection. It is found in nearly all the published speeches of him who now addresses you. I do but quote from one of those speeches when I declare that 'I have no purpose, directly or indirectly, to interfere with the institution of slavery in the States where it exists. I believe I have no lawful right to do so, and I have no inclination to do so.' Those who nominated and elected me did so with full knowledge that I had made this and many similar declarations, and had never recanted them.[337]

• Another reason for issuing the Emancipation Proclamation, again one that had nothing to do with black civil rights, was to procure votes. Midway through his War Lincoln's "approval ratings" (along with re-enlistments) were decreasing rapidly, causing great consternation throughout his party.[338] A pessimistic Lincoln even wrote a memorandum to his cabinet stating that "it seems exceedingly probable that this Administration will not be re-elected."[339]

Freeing Southern slaves and enrolling them in the U.S. Army at the beginning of 1863, however, added some 100,000 new soldiers. These, along with about 100,000 Northern blacks, gave him a total of 205,000 new recruits (186,000 blacks joined the U.S. army; about 19,000 enlisted in the U.S. navy),[340] an enormous pool of fresh potential Republican voters for the upcoming 1864 election. Lincoln then sent out "directives" to his commanders in the field strongly suggesting that they allow their soldiers to "go home to vote at the State election." His order to Yankee General William T. Sherman in September 1864 read:

> Any thing you can safely do to let your soldiers, or any part of them, go home to vote at the State election, will be greatly in

---

336. As a reminder: the Republicans of Forrest's day were what we would now call Democrats (liberals), while the Democrats of that time period were what we would today refer to as Republicans (conservatives).
337. Nicolay and Hay, ALCW, Vol. 2, p. 1.
338. Mullen, p. 19.
339. Tarbell, Vol. 2, p. 201.
340. Greenberg and Waugh, p. xi.

point.[341]

Lincoln's "point" was well understood.

As a result, tens of thousands of Yankee soldiers were furloughed "just in time to return home and vote." Lincoln would not have been reelected in 1864 without the army vote, one only made possible by his politically motivated enlistment of nearly a quarter of a million blacks,[342] half who were "freed" Southern slaves[343]—many of these who were violently coerced into the Union military at gunpoint.[344]

• But Lincoln, America's most calculating president, was not one to leave things to chance. To make sure newly freed enlisted blacks (as well as whites) voted, and voted for him specifically, Lincoln cunningly waited to issue his proclamation until the U.S. army achieved a momentous victory. If the plot worked it would renew public support and revitalize his image among both black and white troops.[345]

Lincoln did not have to wait long. In Maryland on September 17, 1862, the devastating Battle of Sharpsburg (Antietam to Yanks) was fought, marking the bloodiest day in the War up to that time.[346] Though according to military standards the conflict was a draw,[347] Lincoln observed that Confederate General Robert E. Lee had retreated the next day.[348] In the Yankee president's eyes this seemed to be as close to a real victory as he could expect.[349]

Though completely non-religious,[350] Lincoln then declared that the "South's defeat" at Sharpsburg was an omen, an expression of "Divine will,"[351] a veritable message from God that it was time to issue his Preliminary Emancipation Proclamation, which he did on September 22,

341. McClure, AL, p. 83.
342. Donald, LR, p. 80; Simmons, s.v. "Lincoln, Abraham."
343. C. Johnson, p. 170.
344. Wiley, SN, pp. 241, 309-310, 317.
345. W. B. Garrison, LNOK, p. 169.
346. Long and Long, p. 267.
347. W. B. Garrison, LNOK, p. 169.
348. Civil War Society, p. 8.
349. Current, LNK, p. 224.
350. Seabrook, AL, pp. 482-489.
351. Nicolay and Hay, ALCW, Vol. 2, pp. 243-244.

1862.[352] Here is an example of some of the most brazen political scheming in the history of the presidency, a plot involving not the protection of African-Americans, but one involving their exploitation.

We will further note here that as added reinforcement in his bid to be reelected, Lincoln also rigged Northern elections,[353] inaugurated the first national conscription program in U.S. history,[354] shut down over 300 opposition newspapers in the North,[355] illegally suspended *habeas corpus*[356] across the entire U.S. for the first time in the nation's history,[357] imprisoned thousands of political dissidents and peace advocates,[358] spent $2,000,000 without congressional approval,[359] threatened judges, recruited thousands of foreigners into the U.S. army, censored telegraphs, and arrested, silenced, and deported his critics, such as Congressman Vallandigham.[360]

Whatever sins Forrest may have committed (and only he and God truly know what these might have been), he never even began to approach the level of guileful criminality achieved by Lincoln in the four years between 1861 and 1865.

• There is other evidence that Lincoln's Emancipation Proclamation was not about racial equality. The edict was also both unconstitutional and illegal, and could only be issued—according to Lincoln's distorted and self-serving view of the Constitution—as a necessity of the war he had created. Indeed, Lincoln openly confessed that his proclamation was illegal.[361]

In a September 2, 1863, letter to Secretary of the Treasury Salmon P. Chase, for example, he stated that: "The original proclamation has no constitutional or legal justification, except as a military measure."[362] A year earlier, on September 22, 1862, he told a group of

352. Nicolay and Hay, ALCW, Vol. 2, pp. 237-238.
353. DiLorenzo, LU, p. 52.
354. Donald, LR, pp. 79-80.
355. L. Johnson, p. 125.
356. Current, LNK, pp. 183-184.
357. W. B. Garrison, LNOK, p. 104.
358. Kennedy and Kennedy, pp. 28-29.
359. Ingersoll and O'Connor, p. 22.
360. Napolitano, p. 69.
361. Donald, LR, p. 203.
362. Nicolay and Hay, ALCW, Vol. 2, pp. 402-403.

abolitionist ministers that it was pointless to issue a proclamation of emancipation, for it would "necessarily be inoperative, like the Pope's bull against the comet."[363]

• Even after allowing blacks into the U.S. Army, Lincoln's bigotry—along with the North's ubiquitous white racism—toward his new dark-skinned combatants continued to resurface in a myriad of ways.

For one thing, the idea that they were now "free" must have been treated with some suspicion by many newly emancipated blacks, who were immediately assigned slave-like duties around camp, such as laundry, cooking, cleaning, animal tending, and working as personal valets (body slaves) for Union officers.[364]

In addition, black Yankee soldiers were paid almost half that of whites;[365] they were officered by whites rather than blacks (according to Lincoln and other Northerners, blacks could not lead themselves);[366] and they remained sequestered from white soldiers through the use of all-white troops and separate all-black troops.[367] (We will note here that while the U.S. Army segregated its men by race and paid blacks less than whites, when the Confederacy also later officially recruited blacks, on March 13, 1865, whites and blacks fought side by side, in integrated troops, and blacks were given equal pay, equal rations, and equal clothing.)[368]

• Lincoln's actions and beliefs show that he delayed issuing the Emancipation Proclamation for several years, even saying: "We didn't go into the war to put down slavery . . ."[369] When he finally did issue it, it was against his own wishes.[370] For this lassitude he was roundly criticized by abolitionists, one, Wendell Phillips (1811-1884)—soon to become the president of the Anti-Slavery Society—who angrily

---

363. Nicolay and Hay, ALCW, Vol. 2, p. 234.
364. DiLorenzo, RL, p. 34.
365. Oates, AL, p. 113.
366. L. Johnson, p. 134.
367. Mullen, p. 31.
368. J. C. Perry, pp. 218, 223.
369. Lester, pp. 359-360.
370. W. B. Garrison, LNOK, p. 192.

denounced him as "the slavehound of Illinois."[371]

So unmistakably clear was Lincoln's procrastination toward emancipation that some of the more vociferous antislavery groups saw it as a sign of traitorousness. Lincoln, they complained, is not only a Southerner by birth, he has a brother-in-law who fights for the Confederacy. Obviously, his sympathies lie with the South and with slavery, for he could end the War tomorrow if he would only go after the slave owners, they cried.[372]

• Lincoln consistently voted against black suffrage[373] and never advocated social or political equality for African-Americans.[374]

• Making a mockery of what would become his infamous nickname, the "Great Emancipator," lawyer Lincoln is well-known to have defended, not abolitionists, but slaveholders.[375]

• As late as 1862 Lincoln was still supporting the Fugitive Slave Act of 1850[376] (in which the government, and citizens, were obligated to return runaway slaves to their owners, with fines imposed on those who interfered),[377] promising that he would enforce it.[378] This despite increased public opposition to the law after the publication, in 1852, of *Uncle Tom's Cabin*, a fictitious (and highly embellished) attack on slavery by Stowe[379] (a Northerner who had never seen a Southern plantation or a Southern slave).

• On February 27, 1860, Lincoln gave his famous Cooper Union pre-nomination speech in New York, in which he stated that he held the view of slavery of Jefferson and the other Founding Fathers. Said Lincoln:

---

371. McGehee, p. 81; Meriwether, p. 159.
372. Donald, LR, pp. 19-20.
373. Woods, p. 67.
374. Rosenbaum and Brinkley, s.v. "Lincoln Administration."
375. Current, LNK, pp. 218-219; W. B. Garrison, LNOK, pp. 35-37; Greenberg and Waugh, p. 355.
376. Daugherty, p. 122.
377. K. L. Hall, s.v. "Fugitive Slaves."
378. L. Johnson, p. 54.
379. K. L. Hall, s.v. "Fugitive Slaves."

This is all Republicans ask—all Republicans desire—in relation to slavery. As those fathers marked it, so let it be again marked, as an evil not to be extended, but to be tolerated and protected only because of and so far as its actual presence among us makes that toleration and protection a necessity. Let all the guaranties those fathers gave it be not grudgingly, but fully and fairly, maintained.[380]

Lincoln then quoted Jefferson, emphasizing his own desire that the slaves should be gradually liberated and then shipped out of the country:

It is still in our power to direct the process of emancipation and deportation peaceably, and in such slow degrees, as that the evil will wear off sensibly; and their places be, *pari passu* ["of equal step"], filled up by free white laborers. If, on the contrary, it is left to force itself on, human nature must shudder at the prospect held up.[381]

• Lincoln disregarded and delayed the emancipation ideas of others, in part, because he had his own emancipation plan, one that he relentlessly embraced until the last day of his life. Because of his premature death, however, this plan was never initiated: the Radical members of his party believed it was too generous, and replaced it with their own far more severe scheme. Thus, Lincoln's is little known today.

In our search for the truth about how Lincoln and Forrest compare in their views of blacks and slavery, it is beneficial to briefly examine Lincoln's emancipation plan, which was comprised of five-parts:

1) Lincoln held that slavery was a domestic concern and that therefore the states themselves must take whatever action they deemed necessary on the issue.

2) Slave owners must be compensated if their slaves are

---

380. Nicolay and Hay, ALCW, Vol. 1, p. 605.
381. Nicolay and Hay, ALCW, Vol. 1, p. 608. Jefferson's words are from his autobiography, written in 1821, when he was seventy-seven years old. See Foley, p. 816.

freed.

3) This compensation should come from the Federal government in the form of grants-in-aid bonds to the states.

4) The abolition of slavery must occur gradually, so as to allow whites, blacks, and society itself, time to adjust; the states, in fact, would have until the year 1900 to free their last slave.[382]

5) All freed blacks must be deported and settled outside the U.S., though this must be done on a voluntary basis.

Not surprisingly, no one liked every aspect of this plan and it never got off the ground. But Lincoln never gave up promoting it.[383]

• Even after nearly two years as president Lincoln permitted slavery to continue in the nation's capital city, Washington, D.C., admitting that he was not interested in abolishing slavery there.[384] As he himself said just a few months prior to his inauguration:

> I have no thought of recommending the abolition of slavery in the District of Columbia, nor the slave-trade among the slave States.[385]

Indeed, citizens of Washington, D.C. were allowed to own slaves and trade in slaves until the passage of the District of Columbia Bill, approved on April 16, 1862, which effectively prohibited the practices.[386] Incidentally, this was one year *after* the Confederacy banned

---

382. See e.g., Nicolay and Hay, ALCW, Vol. 2, p. 270.

383. Current, LNK, pp. 221-222. See also Delbanco, pp. 260-263.

384. Delbanco, p. 234; Basler, CWAL, Vol. 5, p. 169.

385. Nicolay and Hay, ALCW, Vol. 1, p. 659. Lincoln made this statement in a "strictly confidential" letter to North Carolinian John A. Gilmer, on December 15, 1860. The president-elect was interested in appointing Gilmer secretary of the treasury. Desperate to have a Southerner in his cabinet (a futile attempt to garner support across the South), in his letter Lincoln laid out his position on slavery, hoping to allay any fears Gilmer might have about the future of the institution. Gilmer saw through it and the ploy failed, after which New Englander Salmon P. Chase became Lincoln's first secretary of the treasury.

386. J. C. Perry, p. 191.

the foreign slave trade.[387]

• Lincoln blocked the extension of slavery into the new Western territories for several reasons, none of them out of concern for blacks. First, he prohibited it because it would have artificially magnified the congressional power of his opposing party, the Democrats.[388]

Second, Lincoln opposed the spread of slavery into the new Western territories, not because he was against the institution, but because he did not want whites in those areas to have to live among blacks or compete with blacks for jobs. As he noted in a speech on October 16, 1854:

> Whether slavery shall go into Nebraska, or other new Territories, is not a matter of exclusive concern to the people who may go there. The whole nation is interested that the best use shall be made of the Territories. We want them for homes of free white people. This cannot be, to any considerable extent, if slavery shall be planted within them.[389]

On this topic Lincoln had the "almost unanimous" support of the North, whose inhabitants agreed with the President that the territories should remain as white as New England.[390] If there is any doubt as to Lincoln's stand on the matter, one of his own senators, Lyman Trumbull (1813-1896), referred to their Republican party as "the white man's party."[391]

• More than once Lincoln suggested that he might not issue any proclamation to free the slaves,[392] and he even backed the Corwin Amendment, a constitutional clause which promised that the Federal government would never interfere with the domestic institutions of the states—including slavery. "I have no objection to its being made express and irrevocable," he said in his First Inaugural Address on March 4,

387. Kennedy, p. 184.
388. DiLorenzo, RL, pp. 23-34.
389. Nicolay and Hay, ALCW, Vol. 1, p. 197.
390. See DiLorenzo, LU, p. 101.
391. *The Congressional Globe*, 36th Congress, 1st Session, p. 58; Carey, p. 181.
392. Current, LNK, p. 225.

1861.[393]

• Lincoln routinely prevented U.S. officials and military officers possessed of abolitionist leanings, such as John Charles Frémont,[394] Simon Cameron,[395] and David Hunter,[396] from freeing Southern slaves,[397] actions for which, again, he was angrily denounced by antislavery advocates.[398]

• In the summers of 1861 and 1862 respectively, the U.S. Congress passed two confiscation acts, the first which automatically freed Southern slaves who were serving in the Confederacy, the second which freed slaves whose owners were serving in the Confederacy. Lincoln showed no enthusiasm for either law, never followed up on them, never made sure they were carried out, and almost vetoed the second, considering it unconstitutional.[399]

• On August 22, 1862, in a famous letter to Free-Soiler Horace Greeley, Lincoln publically asserted that if he could save the Union without freeing a single slave he would:

> If there be those who would not save the Union unless they could at the same time save slavery, I do not agree with them. If there be those who would not save the Union unless they could at the same time destroy slavery, I do not agree with them. My paramount object in this struggle is to save the Union, and is not either to save or destroy slavery. . . . If I could save the Union without freeing any slave, I would do it . . . What I do about slavery and the colored race, I do because I believe it helps save the Union . . .[400]

As we will see, however, even the idea of "saving the Union" turned out to be one of Lincoln's great political scams. The above

393. Seabrook, EYWTAASIW, p. 706.
394. L. Johnson, p. 129; C. Adams, pp. 134-135; Foote, Vol. 1, pp. 95-97.
395. Foote, Vol. 1, pp. 242-243.
396. W. B. Garrison, LNOK, 136-141; Foote, Vol. 1, p. 535.
397. Katcher, CWSB, p. 158.
398. Neely, p. 35.
399. Current, LNK, p. 221.
400. Nicolay and Hay, ALCW, Vol. 2, pp. 227-228.

statements do reveal two important items, however: Lincoln's War was not over slavery and he was not interested in racial equality, both points emphatically made by the president himself.

• In 1858, when the Republican senatorial candidate's party was accused of favoring racial equality (taboo in the North at the time), Lincoln snapped back: "[you] know that we advocate no such doctrines as those."[401]

• Originally, by Lincoln's orders, the Emancipation Proclamation was supposed to be temporary, not permanent; he said it would cease when the South (or individual states) surrendered,[402] then offered "liberal terms on . . . substantial and collateral points."[403] What were these points?

At least one of them was allowing any Southern state returning to the Union to continue practicing slavery within its borders. Lincoln demanded only one thing: slaves who were already free could not be reenslaved (for eventually he wanted to be able to deport them to Liberia). As for those still under slavery, he said he would leave their fate to their individual state governments,[404] a states' right he had been defending for many years prior to the War.[405]

In essence, in the summer and fall of 1864, complete and full emancipation was not absolutely necessary to Lincoln if a Confederate state would simply surrender peacefully, rejoin the Union,[406] and pay its taxes.[407]

Seward confirmed this, stating that the effect of the Emancipation Proclamation and other "war measures" would end with the fighting. It is patently clear then that Lincoln originally intended that the institution of slavery would be reestablished after the South's defeat, or if and when it capitulated.[408]

401. Nicolay and Hay, CWAL, Vol. 3, p. 354.
402. W. B. Garrison, LNOK, p. 181.
403. Nicolay and Hay, ALCW, Vol. 2, p. 550.
404. Current, LNK, p. 245.
405. Litwack, NS, p. 277.
406. Current, LNK, pp. 239-240.
407. DiLorenzo, LU, pp. 24, 25.
408. L. Johnson, p. 141.

• Further evidence of this is supplied by Lincoln's Ten Percent Plan, issued in December 1863.[409] Here a Confederate state could be "readmitted" to the Union if just 10 percent of its citizens took an oath of allegiance to the U.S. Afterward that state could reestablish slavery if it so desired.[410]

In 1864, according to Confederate Secretary of State Judah Benjamin, far from demanding complete and immediate abolition, Lincoln let it be known that he was willing to let the issue be decided on by a general vote in both the South and the North.[411]

The president backed up such views and laws with numerous public statements. For example, in July 1864 he responded to an attack charging him with demanding complete emancipation in all Southern states. This is incorrect, he pointed out:

> To me it seems plain that saying reunion and abandonment of slavery would be considered, if offered, is not saying that nothing *else* or *less* would be considered, if offered. . . . If Jefferson Davis wishes, for himself, or for the benefit of his friends at the North, to know what I would do if he were to offer peace and reunion, saying nothing about slavery, let him try me.[412]

• As late as February 3, 1865, only two months before his death, Lincoln was still of the same mind. On this day he attended a peace conference on board the presidential steamer *River Queen*, anchored at Fort Monroe, at Hampton Roads (Hampton, Virginia). A Southern committee, headed by Confederate Vice President Alexander Hamilton Stephens, had come to the Yankee garrison to negotiate for peace.

As with all of the Confederate peace commissions, the Hampton Roads Peace Conference accomplished nothing, Lincoln being unwilling to yield or compromise on any important points. However, it did reveal how the president felt about slavery at the time.

Stephens asked about the Emancipation Proclamation. "Would it be held to emancipate the whole, or only those who had, at the time the war ended, become actually free under it?" Stephens recollected

---

409. W. S. Powell, p. 144.
410. See Current, LNK, pp. 223, 239, 240, 241.
411. Harwell, p. 307.
412. Nicolay and Hay, ALCW, Vol. 2, pp. 563-564.

later that Lincoln's

> own opinion was, that as the Proclamation was a *war measure*, and
> would have effect only from its being an exercise of the war power,
> as soon as the war ceased, it would be inoperative for the future.
> It would be held to apply only to such slaves as had come under its
> operation while it was in active exercise.[413]

• Most importantly, we know that Lincoln did not care about the welfare of blacks or about racial equality because he was an outspoken white supremacist throughout his entire life.[414] In September 1859, for example, just a year before he was elected president, he said:

> Negro equality. Fudge! How long in the Government of a God
> great enough to make and maintain this universe, shall there
> continue to be knaves to vend and fools to gulp, so low a piece of
> demagoguism as this?[415]

## LINCOLN & HIS COLONIZATION SCHEME

How could freed black slaves ever merge and assimilate into a European-American dominant nation that, like Lincoln, saw them as inherently inferior? This was a problem that had been plaguing the lanky Kentuckian since at least 1852, some eight years before he became president. Fortunately for him a solution was at hand.

Lincoln—who held that whites were intellectually and physically superior to blacks,[416] that whites and blacks should not intermarry, and that blacks should not be allowed to vote, hold office, or serve on juries[417]—did not see blacks as future permanent citizens of the U.S.[418] Their very presence in America was thus a thorny issue. The only way

---

413. Nicolay and Hay, ALAH, Vol. 10, p. 123.

414. Kennedy and Kennedy, p. 27; DiLorenzo, RL, p. 204.

415. U.S. gov. Website: www.nps.gov/gett/forteachers/upload/7%20Lincoln%20on%20Race.pdf.

416. See e.g., Nicolay and Hay, ALCW, Vol. 1, p. 289.

417. On September 18, 1858, in his fourth debate with Stephen Douglas, before a *Northern* audience, Lincoln said: ". . . I am not, nor ever have been, in favor of bringing about in any way the social and political equality of the white and black races, [applause] . . . I am not nor ever have been in favor of making voters or jurors of negroes, nor of qualifying them to hold office, nor to intermarry with white people . . . I give him [Douglas] the most solemn pledge that I will to the very last stand by the law of this State, which forbids the marrying of white people with negroes [continued laughter and applause]." Nicolay and Hay, ALCW, Vol. 1, p. 370.

418. Oates, AL, p. 63.

to solve the "Negro problem," he came to believe, was to simply ship all blacks "back to Africa."[419]

Though Radicals (that is, abolitionists) like John Parker Hale (1806-1873)—the first antislavery advocate elected to the U.S. senate[420]—felt that colonization was one of the most ridiculous and impossible notions ever conceived by the mind of man,[421] Lincoln embraced it with a burning passion, fostering it at every opportunity. "What I would most desire," he told a Springfield, Illinois, audience on July 17, 1858, "would be the separation of the white and black races."[422] If deportation proved unfeasible, then Lincoln wanted American blacks to be set up in their own all-black state, preferably far from his adopted home state, Illinois.[423]

In 1862, midway through his War, one of the bargaining chips he used to pressure the border states into siding with the Union (and freeing their slaves) was his assurance that after emancipation freed blacks could all be quickly gotten rid of by shipping them out of the country. As he solemnly promised:

> Room in South America for colonization [of blacks] can be obtained cheaply and in abundance, and when numbers shall be large enough to be company and encouragement for one another, the freed people will not be so reluctant to go.[424]

For Lincoln, it was all about skin color, and politics.

In August 1862 Lincoln invited a black delegation to the White House, the first one ever to step foot in the Oval Office. But the purpose of the visit was not to inform them of his emancipation plans or his goals to establish black civil rights. It was to discuss the issue of colonization, of deporting all blacks out of the U.S. When he met with some resistance from his obviously disappointed audience, he replied stonily that "it is better for us both . . . to be separated." Why?, they asked incredulously. He was ready with an answer:

---

419. Nicolay and Hay, ALCW, Vol. 1, p. 288.
420. Neilson, s.v. "Hale, John Parker."
421. Sewell, p. 211.
422. Nicolay and Hay, ALCW, Vol. 1, p. 273.
423. Nicolay and Hay, ALCW, Vol. 1, p. 355.
424. Nicolay and Hay, ALCW, Vol. 2, p. 205.

You and we are different races. We have between us a broader difference than exists between almost any other two races. Whether it is right or wrong I need not discuss; but this physical difference is a great disadvantage to us both, as I think. Your race suffer very greatly, many of them, by living among us, while ours suffer from your presence. In a word, we suffer on each side. If this is admitted, it affords a reason, at least, why we should be separated. . . . The aspiration of men is to enjoy equality with the best when free, but on this broad continent not a single man of your race is made the equal of a single man of ours. Go where you are treated the best, and the ban is still upon you. . . . This is (I speak in no unkind sense) an extremely selfish view of the case. You ought to do something to help those who are not so fortunate as yourselves. There is an unwillingness on the part of our people, harsh as it may be, for you free colored people to remain with us. Now, if you could give a start to the white people, you would open a wide door for many to be made free. If we deal with those who are not free at the beginning, and whose intellects are clouded by slavery, we have very poor material to start with. If intelligent colored men, such as are before me, would move in this matter, much might be accomplished. It is exceedingly important that we have men at the beginning capable of thinking as white men, and not those who have been systematically oppressed. There is much to encourage you. For the sake of your race you should sacrifice something of your present comfort for the purpose of being as grand in that respect as the white people. . . . The colony of Liberia has been in existence a long time. In a certain sense it is a success. The old President of Liberia, Roberts, has just been with me—the first time I ever saw him. He says they have within the bounds of that colony between three and four hundred thousand people, or more than in some of our old States, such as Rhode Island or Delaware, or in some of our newer States, and less than in some of our larger ones. They are not all American colonists or their descendants. Something less than 12,000 have been sent thither from this country. Many of the original settlers have died; yet, like people elsewhere, their offspring outnumber those deceased. The question is, if the colored people are persuaded to go anywhere, why not there?[425]

Obviously, thanks to the "Great Emancipator," the scene was anything but warm and welcoming for the first free blacks ever to be invited into

---

425. Nicolay and Hay, ALCW, Vol. 2, pp. 222-224.

the White House.

When news of the meeting got out blacks nationwide were outraged. One angrily penned the following to the president: why is our right to live in the United States of America any less than yours?[426] Lincoln, of course, did not reply. As we have seen, he had absolutely no intention of allowing blacks to become permanent citizens.[427]

## NORTHERN WHITE RACISM
Some may be surprised at the depth of Lincoln's racism, his obsession with the idea of deporting freed blacks (known as "Lincoln's white dream"),[428] and his lack of interest in welcoming blacks into the North, or anywhere else in America, as equals. But he was not alone. In fact, he was well within the Northern mainstream, a populace referred to by some as the "Negrophobe masses" of the North.[429]

While most Northern white Americans were in favor of colonization both as a way to emancipate blacks and rid the country of them (by the 1830s fourteen states had passed resolutions favoring the plan), New England in particular—in 1641, the birthplace of legalized American slavery[430]—was actually a bastion of vehement racist sentiment, among non-abolitionists and abolitionists alike.

In 1834 a Southern visitor to the Northeast, who remarked that the idea of deporting blacks is extremely popular here, must have also observed the overt fact that "racial mixing" was still considered taboo by Yankee abolitionists, who would not allow blacks to attend their meetings or become members of their societies. Even early Yankee Quakers, long held by Northern myth to have been ardent abolitionists, often treated African-Americans with appalling prejudice.[431] This kind of racist guile was practically unknown in the Old South.

Tocqueville pointed out as early as 1831 that racism toward blacks was worse in the North than it was in the South,[432] which explains

---

426. Randall and Current, p. 317; Quarles, p. 150; Current, LNK, p. 223.
427. Oates, AL, p. 63.
428. See Bennett, passim.
429. H. C. Bailey, p. 139.
430. G. H. Moore, pp. 5, 11, 17-19.
431. Litwack, NS, pp. 24, 216, 205-207.
432. Tocqueville, Vol. 1, pp. 383-385.

why the infamous Black Codes (which restricted the advancement of black civil rights) of the South actually originated in the North, not in Dixie—as the world has been falsely taught.[433]

Indeed, Negrophobia was the prevailing sentiment of white Northern society at the time,[434] the great majority of which had never accepted the abolitionist idea of "racial brotherhood."[435] Uncompromisingly opposed to emancipation,[436] their real fear was that the "Negro menace"[437] would swarm northward and mix with their females,[438] dilute and corrupt the white race, add an "unwholesome colored population" to the region, endanger racial purity, spread disease, threaten prosperity, lower moral standards, scare off visitors and tourists, frighten away potential new students of local colleges, encourage further Negro immigration, drive down property values and wages, instigate a massive crime wave, thwart colonization, "abolitionize" and "Africanize" the local white populace,[439] and most important of all, take away jobs from whites.[440]

In essence, most Northern whites believed that the continued presence of blacks on U.S. soil would endanger, if not completely demolish, the very framework of American society, inevitably producing disorder and violence.[441] This is why Yankee politicians nearly always merged demands for social regulations that restricted blacks with the idea of black colonization (deportation).[442]

Thus, concerning the extent of white racism in the "abolitionist North," it has been rightly said that even the most vociferous critics of slavery played a role in sustaining it.[443]

During the New York City Draft riots, which began on July 11,

---

433. DiLorenzo, LU, pp. 44-45.

434. L. Johnson, pp. 33, 34, 129.

435. Page Smith, p. 975.

436. Oates, AL, p. 100.

437. H. C. Bailey, p. 134.

438. The rape of white women by blacks was a major issue after emancipation, but it was a crime not generally known because Southern women were too proud to disclose the attacks. There was also the problem of the Northern press, which refused to print stories that hurt the abolitionist cause. H. C. Bailey, pp. 148-149.

439. Garraty and McCaughey, p. 254; Litwack, NS, pp. 113-152.

440. H. C. Bailey, p. 155.

441. Seabrook, EYWTACWW, pp. 63-70.

442. Litwack, NS, p. 22.

443. Catton, Vol. 1, p. 86.

1863, for example, whites did not take their frustrations out on Lincoln and the U.S. Congress, those responsible for issuing the Draft Act to begin with. Instead, for three days they targeted blacks,[444] who they "literally hunted down like wild beasts," beating, lynching, and shooting them, both adults and children. African-American homes were robbed and laid waste, as well. Such was the intensity of white racism in the North at this time that even black babies were murdered. Black adult females meanwhile were viciously assaulted, while black adult males were "burnt by slow fires."[445]

That July Northern whites also senselessly plundered, then torched, the building of the Colored Orphan Asylum and Association for the Benefit of Colored Children in the City of New York. The orphanage, founded by two Quaker women, was valued at $80,000, the equivalent of nearly $2,000,000 today. When New York whites got done with it the building was nothing but a charred ruin, leaving the association's 233 black orphans homeless.[446]

Although Lincoln did not support open violence against blacks (as we will see, however, he condoned *clandestine* violence against them), he did embrace the Northern idea of white superiority. This is why early on, believing that neither he or the rest of the North would ever accept blacks as equals,[447] and that the two races were so different they could never live in harmony together,[448] he became a leading proponent of Henry Clay's idea of colonization.[449]

This idea was, in essence, the racial cleansing of America of its blacks by resettling them in Liberia (a colony founded in 1822 by the American Colonization Society for the express purpose of settling "liberated" American slaves there),[450] Haiti, Honduras, Ecuador, or the

---

444. Daugherty, p. 184.
445. J. C. Perry, p. 198.
446. Quarles, pp. 241-244.
447. C. Adams, p. 159.
448. Lincoln's exact words on this point were: "There is a physical difference between the two [races], which, in my judgement, will probably forever forbid their living together upon the footing of perfect equality . . . I have never said anything to the contrary . . ." Nicolay and Hay, ALCW, Vol. 1, p. 539.
449. Oates, AL, p. 64.
450. Brunner, p. 252, s.v. "Liberia." To this day five percent of Liberia's population is made up of Americo-Liberians, English-speaking descendants of former American slaves.

Amazon,[451] anywhere but America.[452] So strongly did Lincoln support the idea of racially cleansing the U.S. that he himself became a leader of the Illinois chapter of the American Colonization Society, a state whose legislature he convinced to finance the deportation of free blacks.[453]

For the record let us note here that the American Colonization Society was not a Southern organization, but a Northern one, founded by New Jerseyan Reverend Robert Finley in Washington, D.C. in December 1816.[454] Among its early leaders, officers, and supporters were such famed Northerners as New England statesman Daniel Webster (after whom the town of Webster, Massachusetts, was named), New Yorker William H. Seward (Lincoln's secretary of state), and Marylander Francis Scott Key, author of the U.S. National Anthem, *The Star-Spangled Banner*.[455]

Abolitionist-racist Hinton Rowan Helper, one of Lincoln's most passionate supporters,[456] summed up the chief goal of the ACS this way: America will only have peace after the "country shall have been thoroughly cleansed of the vulgar and disgusting negroes and their next of kin . . ."[457]

Lincoln's postmaster general, lawyer Montgomery Blair, agreed, insisting that the forced deportation of Negroes was vital, for after emancipation "it would be necessary to rid the country of its black population, and some place must be found for them."[458] Helper's notorious anti-black pro-colonization book, *The Impending Crisis of the South*, was not only endorsed by Lincoln's party, Lincoln himself used it as his chief campaign document during the 1860 election,[459] greatly assisting him in his presidential win that year.[460]

To his credit Lincoln was against compulsory deportation. He hoped instead that freed blacks would go voluntarily, or that "Great

451. Woods, p. 67.
452. W. B. Garrison, LNOK, pp. 185-192.
453. DiLorenzo, LU, p. 28; W. B. Garrison, LNOK, p. 186.
454. Litwack, NS, p. 20.
455. Website: www.slavenorth.com/colonize.htm.
456. H. C. Bailey, p. 139.
457. Helper, NQC, p. 281.
458. Welles, Vol. 1, p. 152.
459. Lytle, p. 32.
460. H. C. Bailey, pp. 61-81, 195.

Britain, Denmark, and perhaps other powers would take them."[461]

In Lincoln's mind, either way they had to go, and the reason was simple enough, as we will now explore.

---

461. Woodson, Vol. 4, p. 16.

# EMANCIPATION & COLONIZATION: THE TRUTH BEHIND LINCOLN & THE NORTHERN ABOLITION MOVEMENT

"If you surrender, you shall be treated as prisoners of war, but if I have to storm your works, you may expect no quarter." — Nathan Bedford Forrest to the enemy

## HOW ABOLITIONISM & RACISM WENT HAND IN HAND

NORTHERN WHITE RACISM WAS INTENSE and deeply entrenched, the very idea of race mixing of any kind, even merely socializing, being both repugnant and feared by the average Northerner. Whites and blacks were just too different, in too many ways, to ever live in harmony with one another, it was widely believed. This is why, while slavery was considered morally wrong, segregation was considered morally right.[462] And here we discover one of the primary roots of the Northern abolition movement.

In the North slavery was seen as an evil, not so much because it hurt blacks, but because it hurt whites, who by nature of the institution were unnaturally forced into personal, even intimate, contact with blacks. We will recall that Lincoln told blacks to their faces that "we

---

462. Ellis, AS, p. 174.

whites suffer from your presence."[463] Why did Lincoln and most other Yankees feel this way?

At the time Northern whites considered people of African descent to be a creature somewhere between an ape and a human, lower, coarser, less evolved, than Europeans. Respected Yankee historian James Ford Rhodes, for instance, described slaves as "indolent and filthy," "stupid" and "duplicitous," with "brute-like countenances."[464]

Other Northerners were less kind. Famed Harvard scientist Louis Agassiz declared that "the negro race groped in barbarism and never originated a regular organization among themselves."[465] Agassiz, like his English associate, Charles Darwin (who originated the idea of natural selection, or "survival of the fittest"),[466] believed that blacks were so evolutionarily feeble that once freed from slavery they would eventually "die out" in the U.S.[467]

Thus, it was widely believed, the slavery relationship degraded whites while elevating blacks. Indeed, it was this very belief which, for many, justified slavery. Did not the relationship between slave and master help to civilize the African, by inculcating him with the ideas of cleanliness, morals, a work ethic, culture, and religion? For most Northern whites though, these few "benefits" which blacks received under slavery far outweighed the detrimental impact on their white owners, who were daily exposed to the base behavior, "ugly" appearance, gross depravity, "proverbial dishonesty," "malodorous exhalations," "apathetic indifference," and the mental "puerility" of their black chattel.[468]

In short, it was held that slavery ought to be abolished and whites and blacks then separated. To think otherwise was "racial treason," as many whites saw it, a crime considered to be greater than treason against the state.[469]

463. Nicolay and Hay, ALCW, Vol. 2, p. 223.
464. Rhodes, Vol. 1, pp. 307, 309.
465. Seligmann, p. 9.
466. See Darwin, p. 91.
467. Bailyn, Dallek, Davis, Donald, Thomas, and Wood, p. 29.
468. Helper, NN, p. x.
469. H. C. Bailey, p. 149.

THE ABOLITIONIST-RACIST

This curious combination of beliefs created the *abolitionist-racist* of the North, one who was against both slavery and black equality. As pure authentic abolitionism was extremely rare in the North,[470] it was the abolitionist-racist who made up the great majority of what we think of today as "Yankee abolitionists."

One of the better known of the traditional Yankee abolitionists was Ralph Waldo Emerson, a true abolitionist-racist who, though he worshiped antislavery advocate John Brown, was a Negrophobe who felt that blacks were so "inferior" that they would eventually become as extinct as the Dodo bird.[471] As such, the Massachusetts Transcendentalist understood the true motivation behind the Northern abolition movement. According to Emerson, the abolitionist's authentic goal was to abolish, not slavery, but the black man,[472] for what New England really wanted was not racial equality, but a mono-racial, purely Caucasian society.[473]

One of Emerson's friends, New Englander, pacifist, and Unitarian theologian, William Ellery Channing, was, like most Northerners, also an abolitionist-racist, one who could preach heartily for the abolition of slavery while adding the following:

> I should expect from the African race, if civilized, less energy, less courage, less intellectual originality than our race, but more amiableness, tranquility, gentleness, and content. They might not rise to an equality in outward condition, but would probably be a much happier race. There is no reason for holding such a race in chains; they need no chains to make themselves harmless.[474]

Racial mixing and social intercourse between whites and blacks was rare and frowned upon in New England in the early 1800s. After several blacks had been allowed to attend an abolition meeting, Channing angrily spoke out against them. This in turn elicited a strong response from staunch antislavery advocate William Lloyd Garrison, who

---

470. By "authentic abolitionist" I mean one who was for both abolition *and* racial equality.
471. R. W. Emerson, JMNRWE, Vol. 13, p. 286.
472. R. W. Emerson, JMNRWE, Vol. 13, p. 198.
473. Melish, p. 164
474. J. A. Collins, p. 58.

lambasted abolitionist Channing for saying that white abolitionists should have never allowed blacks to associate with them in the first place.[475]

But Garrison was not as unprejudiced as he appeared to be. In fact, he too was an abolitionist-racist and, at one time, was even a proponent of black colonization.[476] In his influential abolitionist journal, *The Liberator*, which he published from 1831 to 1865, one could often find the following types of remarks:

> The black color of the body, the wooly hair, the thick lips, and other peculiarities of the African forms so striking a contrast to the Caucasian race, that they may be distinguished at a glance . . . are branded by the hand of nature with a perpetual mark of disgrace.[477]

If the literal leader of the entire Northern abolitionist movement himself was an overt abolitionist-racist, we can be sure that nearly every white Northerner at the time was as well.

While the notion of an abolitionist who is also a racist may seem like an oxymoron to us in the 21st Century, in the 19th Century a majority of the Northern white populace felt as Emerson did: they detested slavery while favoring voluntary, and even forced, deportation of all blacks out of the U.S. To the Northern abolitionist-racist there was nothing contradictory about this belief. In fact right up to the beginning of Lincoln's War the white dislike of slavery, combined with the white dislike of the black race, was the norm in the North, a region where white supremacist ideas and practices were the rule rather than the exception. At the head of the abolitionist-racist movement was, of course, President Lincoln.[478]

Not surprisingly, blacks universally condemned the double standard expressed by white Northern abolitionists, who claimed to hate slavery but had no love whatsoever toward those who were enslaved. Northern blacks had good cause for their anger.

Yankee abolitionists often referred to blacks, as Lincoln

---

475. Litwack, NS, p. 216.
476. Fogel, p. 254.
477. *The Liberator*, January 22, 1831.
478. DiLorenzo, LU, pp. 44-45.

sometimes did, as "niggers,"[479] and comments about their "niggerly odour"[480] and "woolly heads" were not uncommon at antislavery meetings.[481] Such attitudes led one black teacher to remark that there are numerous Yankees ready and eager to take up the cross of abolition, but few who are able to bear it.[482] The constitution of the American Anti-Slavery Society, a Yankee group founded in Philadelphia in 1833, did not even mention social equality as its goal.[483]

The truth is that it was far easier for Northern whites to simply support the idea of deporting all blacks out of the country than have to confront the issue of their own prejudice and learn to live in a multiracial, multicultural society, as Forrest and 8,000,000 other white Southerners were well on their way to accomplishing.

Clearly, in America's Northeast the word abolition had a double meaning. Here, for whites the idea of abolishing slavery was part and parcel of the idea of abolishing all blacks from their population as well. By 1861 New Englanders had already shipped some 12,000 African-Americans "back to Africa" under the auspices of Lincoln's favorite organization, the American Colonization Society.[484]

It is little wonder that the non-racist South Carolinian Mary Chesnut could never fully understand either New England or the region's animosity toward the South.[485] This animus, in fact, was far more complex than most Southerners realized. For the North's dislike of the South resulted not just from a hatred of Dixie, but also from a hatred of both slavery and of blacks. As New England abolitionist Henry Wilson noted,[486] when Northerners voted overwhelmingly for the

---

479. See e.g., Nicolay and Hay, CWAL, Vol. 11, pp. 105-106; Nicolay and Hay, ALCW, Vol. 1, p. 483; Holzer, pp. 22-23, 67, 318, 361.

480. Litwack, NS, p. 226.

481. Garrison and Garrison, Vol. 1, p. 327.

482. Barnes and Dumond, p. 380.

483. Litwack, NS, p. 227.

484. DiLorenzo, LU, pp. 40-41.

485. Chesnut, MCCW, p. 245.

486. Wilson, whose birth name was Jeremiah Jones Colbath, was an industrious antislavery politician from New Hampshire. The Whig convention he called at Buffalo, New York, in 1848, led to the formation of the Free-Soil party, after which he became editor of its periodical, "The Free-Soil Party Journal," and the Boston *Republican*. After chairing the 1852 Free-Soil convention he joined the American (Know-Nothing) party in 1854, becoming a Massachusetts senator in 1855. Wilson was also one of the founders of the Republican party and chairman of the Senate committee on military affairs during the War for Southern Independence. He ended his political career, and life, as vice president of the U.S. under Ulysses S. Grant in 1873. Neilson,

Thirteenth Amendment (which finally freed all slaves eight months after Lincoln's death), their votes were more an effort to hurt white slaveholders than to liberate their black servants.[487]

Like their constituents, most Northern politicians (mainly Republicans, the equivalent of today's Democrats) were also abolitionist-racists as well.[488] All agreed that after their emancipation former slaves would need to be removed from the U.S. and colonized in their own all-black region. This idea was vigorously championed by everyone from Northern educated President James Madison[489] to President Lincoln[490] and his cabinet members, which included abolitionist-racist Hinton Rowan Helper, Lincoln's Consul to Argentina.[491]

Even many Europeans, like Tocqueville, were abolitionist-racists, individuals who detested slavery but saw merit in the idea of colonization. During his nine-month tour of eastern America in 1831, the Frenchman was horrified by the plight of both black slaves and the whites who owned them. Speaking for most 19th-Century Europeans and European-Americans alike, Tocqueville wrote of the African-American:

> . . . we scarcely acknowledge the common features of mankind in this child of debasement whom slavery has brought among us. His physiognomy is to our eyes hideous, his understanding weak, his tastes low; and we are almost inclined to look upon him as a being intermediate between man and the brutes.[492]

This is why, Tocqueville continued:

> You may set the negro free, but you can not make him otherwise than an alien to the European. . . . Those who hope that the Europeans will ever mix with the negroes appear to me to delude themselves; and I am not led to any such conclusion by my own

s.v. "Wilson, Henry."
487. Current, LNK, p. 234.
488. H. C. Bailey, p. 147.
489. Peterson, JM, pp. 371-377.
490. Nicolay and Hay, ALCW, Vol. 1, p. 288.
491. H. C. Bailey, pp. 31, 134, 142, 151, 154, 155, 156.
492. Tocqueville, Vol. 1, p. 382.

reason or by the evidence of facts.[493]

Interbreeding of the races was especially troubling to whites like Tocqueville, who echoed the conviction of millions of white Northern Americans when he said:

> The most formidable of all the ills which threaten the future existence of the [American] Union arises from the presence of a black population upon its territory.[494]

A little over a decade earlier, in 1819, Madison wrote:

> To be consistent with existing and probably unalterable prejudices in the United States, the freed blacks ought to be permanently removed beyond the region occupied by, or allotted to, a white population. The objections to a thorough incorporation of the two people are, with most of the whites, insuperable; and are admitted by all of them to be very powerful. If the blacks, strongly marked as they are by physical aud lasting peculiarities, be retained amid the whites, under the degrading privation of equal rights, political or social, they must be always dissatisfied with their condition, as a change only from one to another species of oppression; always secretly confederated against the ruling and privileged class; and always uncontrolled by some of the most cogent motives to moral and respectable conduct. The character of the free blacks, even where their legal condition is least affected by their colour, seems to put these truths beyond question. It is material, also, that the removal of the blacks be to a distance precluding the jealousies and hostilities to be apprehended from a neighbouring people, stimulated by the contempt known to be entertained for their peculiar features; to say nothing of their vindictive recollections, or the predatory propensities which their state of society might foster. . . . The [American Colonization] Society proposes to transport to the African Coast all free and freed blacks who may be willing to remove thither; . . . The measure implies, also, the practicability of procuring in Africa an enlargement of the district or districts for receiving the exiles sufficient for so great an augmentation of their numbers.[495]

---

493. Tocqueville, Vol. 1, pp. 382-383.
494. Tocqueville, Vol. 1, p. 380.
495. Madison, pp. 134, 138.

Like most slave owners Madison felt he was an innocent pawn in the game of slavery, for the institution had been created before he was born, then forced on him involuntarily by way of inheritance. Disliking not only the idea of enslaving humans, but also the notion of close association between whites and blacks, he would have preferred that slavery had never come to America. Colonization, however, was a way for whites to expiate the sins of their slave owning ancestors. Said Madison:

> And if in any instances wrong has been done by our forefathers to people of one colour, by dispossessing them of their soil, what better atonement is now in our power than that of making what is rightfully acquired a source of justice and of blessings to a people of another colour?[496]

Decades later Lincoln was of the same mind as Madison and Tocqueville, and he never tried to hide his feelings on the matter. Believing whites to be superior to blacks in color, physique, morals, and intellect, he too greatly abhorred and feared the idea of interracial relationships and marriage (known as miscegenation), along with what he perceived as the potential horrors of allowing blacks to vote and serve on juries.[497] "We cannot make them equals," Lincoln consistently maintained.[498]

There was only one solution: blacks could not remain in the U.S. It was thus that Lincoln came to advocate the idea of black colonization outside North America. The Yankees' American Colonization Society would soon found Liberia, Africa, the colony where freed black slaves were to be sent after they were "liberated" in America.[499]

Lincoln loved the idea. On August 21, 1858, he appeared before a large *Northern* crowd (in Ottawa, Illinois) where he was asked what he would like to do about slavery: "My first impulse would be to free all of the slaves," he replied unhesitatingly, "and send them to

---

496. Madison, p. 136.
497. Nicolay and Hay, Vol. 1, pp. 257, 291, 292, 539.
498. Nicolay and Hay, Vol. 1, p. 288.
499. Brunner, p. 252.

Liberia—to their own native land."[500]

To back up his words, Lincoln's Preliminary Emancipation Proclamation, issued on September 22, 1862, included the following stunning statement:

> I, Abraham Lincoln . . . do hereby proclaim and declare . . . that it is my purpose . . . to again recommend [to Congress] . . . the immediate or gradual abolishment of slavery . . . and that the effort to colonize persons of African descent with their consent upon the Continent or elsewhere, with the previously obtained consent of the governments existing there, will be continued.[501]

This clause was only pulled from the Final Emancipation Proclamation (issued January 1, 1863), the one popularly known today, because Lincoln's cabinet advised him that it might alienate abolitionist voters in the upcoming 1864 election.

Abolitionist-racists, like Lincoln devotee Helper, were quick to praise the document for its message favoring "the deportation of all the Negroes from the United States." Declaring that it was second in importance only to the Declaration of Independence, Helper suggested acting upon it "earnestly, fully, and speedily,"[502] a recommendation that had the full backing of nearly all white Northerners.[503]

The Yankee abolitionist war cry? It was not, "Death to slavery! Integrate the Negroes!" It was: "Death to slavery! Away with the Negroes! . . . Universal, supreme and exclusive dominion of the white races!"[504]

## ANGER OVER LINCOLN'S RACIAL DECEPTION

Not all Yankees followed in Lincoln's white racist, white separatist footsteps, however. Some, in fact, were just as discerning as their Southern counterparts, easily seeing through the "Great Emancipator's" duplicity in the area of race. One of these was Massachusetts-born Lysander Spooner, who was infuriated over the president's handling of

---

500. Nicolay and Hay, ALCW, Vol. 1, p. 288.
501. Nicolay and Hay, ALCW, Vol. 2, p. 237.
502. Helper, NQC, p. 255.
503. See Litwack, NS, p. 22; DiLorenzo, LU, pp. 44, 45, 101, 176; Tocqueville, Vol. 1, pp. 383, 400.
504. Helper, NQC, pp. 253, 254.

the slavery issue. And for good reason.

While Lincoln preached against slavery in public, behind closed doors he was busy thinking up laws, like his proposed 1861 amendment to the Constitution, that would have allowed slavery to continue in perpetuity without any interference from the federal government (Lincoln's pro-slavery amendment was passed by the U.S. House of Representatives on February 28, 1861, and by the U.S. Senate on March 2, 1861, two days before his presidential inauguration).[505]

With a "forked tongue" Lincoln was condemning slavery while at the same time using the Constitution to make slavery "irrevocable"—permitting it, in fact, to persist as long as the Southern states remained in the Union and paid their taxes.[506] It was just such cynical politics that prompted Spooner to call Lincoln and his cabinet "double-faced demagogues" who were trying to "ride into power on the two horses Liberty and Slavery."[507]

Black civil rights leaders, who were particularly incensed by Lincoln's colonization scheme, were not fooled by the president's ambiguous double-talk either. One of them, abolitionist and former slave, Frederick Douglass (1817-1895), publically denounced Lincoln's white racial pride, disdain for blacks, and rank dishonesty.[508]

If only the brilliant African-American orator could have known that Lincoln's ludicrous and racist colonization plans would eventually be watered down and turned into the final, and as yet unreleased, version of the Emancipation Proclamation.[509] He would have been even more furious.


LINCOLN ONLY FREED THE SLAVES IN THE CONFEDERACY
More duplicity, double-dealing, and double-talk was to come out of the White House, and in short order, revealing a vigorous and insidious racism that was completely unknown to Southerners like Forrest.

When Lincoln did finally officially "free" the slaves on January 1, 1863, it was not in the North, in the United States of America

505. Beard and Beard, Vol. 2, p. 65.
506. DiLorenzo, LU, pp. 24, 25.
507. Website: www.lysanderspooner.org/letters/SESP012260.htm.
508. Oates, AL, p. 103.
509. J. C. Perry, p. 190.

(U.S.A.), but only in the South, in the Confederate States of America (C.S.A.), where he had no legal power or control.[510] (Let us note here that the complete abolition of slavery across the entire U.S. was not accomplished until nearly a year after the end of the War and Lincoln's assassination, when the Thirteenth Amendment was ratified on December 6, 1865.[511] This important constitutional amendment had begun in 1864 as a resolution introduced by one of Lincoln's most racist supporters and party members, Illinois Senator and black colonizationist Lyman Trumbull, a Yankee originally from Connecticut.)[512]

Even then Lincoln's proclamation only had effect in Rebel areas that were *not* occupied by Union troops.[513] All of the Northern states and all of the Federally-held areas in Dixie, such as Yankee-occupied regions in Tennessee, Virginia, West Virginia, Kentucky, and Louisiana, were exempt. Slavery was still legal in these places,[514] or as Lincoln put it, the exempted "parts are for the present left precisely as if this proclamation were not issued."[515] This left the 500,000 to 1 million slaves still in the North to serve out their lives in bondage,[516] while their Yankee president meddled unconstitutionally with those in the South.

In short, Lincoln the lawyer had guilefully constructed his proclamation so that *no* slaves would be freed—North or South.[517] Little wonder that even pro-North Civil War scholars have called it a remarkably insipid decree.[518]

Here is the full text in Lincoln's own words:

> Now, therefore I, Abraham Lincoln President of the United States, by virtue of the power in me vested as Commander-in-Chief, of the Army and Navy of the United States in time of actual armed rebellion against the authority and government of the United States, and as a fit and necessary war measure for suppressing said rebellion, do on this first day of January, in the year of our Lord

---

510. W. B. Garrison, LNOK, p. 181.
511. Kane, s.v. "Abraham Lincoln," p. 179.
512. Neilson, s.v. "Trumbull, Benjamin."
513. E. M. Thomas, p. 180.
514. L. Johnson, p. 133.
515. Nicolay and Hay, ALCW, Vol. 2, p. 288.
516. Eaton, HSC, p. 93; Hinkle, p. 125.
517. DiLorenzo, RL, pp. 37-38.
518. Catton, Vol. 2, p. 348.

one thousand eight hundred and sixty-three, and in accordance with my purpose so to do publicly proclaimed for the full period of one hundred days, from the day first above mentioned, order and designate as the States and parts of States wherein the people thereof, respectively, are this day in rebellion against the United States, the following, to wit: Arkansas, Texas, Louisiana (except the parishes of St. Bernard, Plaquemines, Jefferson, St. John, St. Charles, St. James, Ascension, Assumption, Terrebonne, Lafourche, St. Mary, St. Martin, and Orleans, including the City of New Orleans), Mississippi, Alabama, Florida, Georgia, South Carolina, North Carolina, and Virginia (except the forty-eight counties designated as West Virginia, and also the counties of Berkeley, Accomac, Northampton, Elizabeth City, York, Princess Ann, and Norfolk, including the cities of Norfolk and Portsmouth); and which excepted parts are for the present left precisely as if this proclamation were not issued.[519]

The question is why would Lincoln intentionally craft a largely impotent proclamation? The answer, of course, is power, politics, and money—the same reasons that motivate most corrupt liberal politicians.

If Lincoln were to have freed the slaves in the ultra-racist and largely anti-abolitionist North,[520] where the idea of "nigger equality" was causing great fear, among the working class in particular,[521] the money market and general morale could have been adversely affected. Additionally, his party might have lost both the upcoming midterm fall elections of 1862[522] and the crucial 1863 elections,[523] and he himself might have forfeited potential white votes for his upcoming bid for re-election in 1864. Not only this, there was the possibility that the U.S. army could suffer huge losses due to desertion (most Northern soldiers had no interest whatsoever in risking their lives to abolish slavery).[524]

Then there were the border states. Lincoln had promised their

519. Nicolay and Hay, ALCW, Vol. 2, pp. 287-288.
520. Numerous 19th-Century European (see e.g., Tocqueville, Vol. 1, p. 383) and Northern (Yankee) eyewitnesses report that racism was far more intense and widespread in the North than in the South. Seabrook, EYWTACWW, pp. 63-108.
521. J. M. McPherson, BCF, p. 200.
522. Catton, Vol. 2, p. 349.
523. Donald, L, pp. 454-455.
524. Lincoln's fear was justifiable. After he issued his Final Emancipation Proclamation, Yankee soldiers deserted by the hundreds of thousands (DiLorenzo, RL, p. 45), while recruitment levels dropped off precipitously. Daugherty, p. 169.

citizens that he would not interfere with slavery. If he did so now they might decide to join the Confederacy.[525] Why issue the Emancipation Proclamation at all then?, he must have often asked himself.

## THE REAL PURPOSE OF THE EMANCIPATION PROCLAMATION

Besides his desire to increase the ever declining numbers of Yankee soldiers[526] and acquire more potential Republican voters,[527] the main reason Lincoln issued the Emancipation Proclamation, and then one with no teeth, was because, like murderer and abolitionist John Brown,[528] he was hoping to incite a slave insurrection in Dixie.[529]

As mentioned, Lincoln also wanted to retain European support while preventing Europe from recognizing the Confederacy as a legitimate nation[530] (Europeans, he assumed, would not side with the South as long as he could persuade them that the Confederacy was merely a "belligerent" region rather than a legally formed country)[531] and dissuade Britain from aiding the South in breaking up his illegal naval blockade.[532] This is certainly how Southerners regarded his issuance of the Emancipation Proclamation in January 1863, and they were right.[533] (Lincoln's plan to provoke a Southern slave revolt utterly failed,[534] while his scheme to discourage Europe from aligning itself with the

---

525. Foote, Vol. 1, pp. 537-538.
526. L. Johnson, pp. 133-134.
527. Donald, LR, pp. 79-80.
528. Horwitz, p. 219.
529. Ashe, pp. 35, 57-58.
530. Pollard, SHW, Vol. 2, p. 195; Donald, L, p. 379.
531. Great Britain and France in particular had strong motivations for wanting to side with the South. Lincoln's blockade of Southern ports was beginning to produce hardships among the two nations' textile manufacturers, who depended on Dixie's cotton, while French and English shipbuilders stood to earn enormous profits from providing vessels to the Rebel navy. Donald, L, p. 413. Lincoln battled against Europe's desire to join hands with the Confederacy throughout the entire War, finally succeeding; but only through the use of outrageous falsehoods, prevarication, secrecy, his famous ambiguous double-talk, and finally, an all-out threat of war against any European nation that dared aid the South. See Owsley, KCD, pp. 401-412. All of this was illegal, of course, for the Confederacy, properly known as the Confederate States of America, was indeed an independent nation, one legally formed from tenets laid down in the Constitution by the Founding Fathers, most of whom were Southerners. If Lincoln had not threatened and lied to Europe she would have supported the Confederacy; not only politically, but also financially and perhaps even militarily, changing the outcome of the War in favor of the South.
532. P. J. Buchanan, p. 128.
533. L. Johnson, p. 177.
534. In fact, there was not a single case of slave insurrection in the South either during the War (Pollard, SHW, Vol. 2, p. 201; E. M. Thomas, p. 237), or after it—even though at the time millions of blacks were free and carrying weapons. Bailyn, Dallek, Davis, Donald, Thomas, and Wood, p. 7.

Confederacy largely succeeded.[535] The result was that Europe never officially intervened, mediated, or recognized the legitimacy of the South).[536]

In the end, by Lincoln's own estimate, only 200,000 slaves out of the nation's 4,000,000[537]—a mere 5 percent—were freed by his Emancipation Proclamation.[538] While this figure is doubtful (being optimistically high) and not supported by outside evidence, even if it were true it means that 95 percent of all "enslaved" Southern blacks remained in bondage for two more years, despite his alleged best efforts.

Lincoln, "the Great Emancipator"? A humanitarian who loved all races and abolished slavery to create equal rights for blacks? As Shelby Foote states, Lincoln would go down in history, not as the restorer of the union—which he was, but as the Great Emancipator—which he clearly was not.[539]

## WHY DID LINCOLN USE PHYSICAL VIOLENCE TO TRY & END SLAVERY?

While the final abolition of slavery was right, moral, and just, Lincoln's method of emancipation left much to be desired. In fact, it was both irrational and counterproductive, revealing a striking lack of humanity toward blacks coming from one who would become known as "the greatest friend the Negro ever had."

For one thing Lincoln disregarded numerous intelligent and time-tested emancipation programs previously used by other nations, setting back black civil rights and race relations in America for decades. While nearly all other civilized countries had abolished slavery peacefully in the courts—typically using gradual and compensated emancipation (wherein slave owners were financially reimbursed and blacks were liberated by degrees and given an education and jobs), Lincoln abolished slavery in America through the use of full-scale warfare (a conflict in

---

535. Kennedy and Kennedy, p. 26.
536. Owsley, KCD, pp. 542-558.
537. In 1861 there were 3,500,000 black slaves in the South ( Quarles, p. xiii; Weintraub, p. 70; Cooper, JDA, p. 378; Rosenbaum and Brinkley, s.v. "Civil War"), and 500,000 black slaves in the North (Eaton, HSC, p. 93), making a total of 4,000,000 slaves nationwide. (As noted previously, some estimates state that there were as many as 1,000,000 slaves in the North in the 1860s. See Hinkle, p. 125.)
538. Current, LNK, p. 228. See also Barney, p. 141.
539. Foote, Vol. 1, p. 708.

which Southern historians estimate as many as 3 million soldiers and citizens died),[540] only compensated a tiny minority of slave owners for their loss of revenue (by this method he liberated a mere 3,100 slaves, a mere 0.0775 percent,[541] out of 4,000,000),[542] and then suddenly set slaves free without any time for adjustment (for blacks or whites), and without funds, homes, schooling, job training, or occupations.[543]

Where was the plan for a smooth transition from captivity to freedom? There was not one. As a former female slave later recollected of those times: We had no idea what to do. There was no place to go after we were freed. We were just turned loose with no direction and no assistance, she bemoaned.[544]

How odd that Lincoln did this. Today whenever possible, America even provides rehabilitation, therapy, job training, education, and money, for its convicted felons before they are released back into free society. Lincoln, however, "liberated" 3,500,000 Southern blacks with literally nothing. Why?

In his defense Lincoln apologists maintain that their idol believed it was the job of the local and state authorities to supervise the postwar transition of freed blacks from servitude to liberty, not the national government.[545] But with Lincoln's bleak lifelong record of white supremacist beliefs, white separatist goals, white racist statements, his continuous and flagrant disregard for constitutional law, and his often repeated pledge that his war was not about freeing the slaves, we cannot accept this statement as valid.

---

540. Timothy Manning, personal correspondence.
541. The exact number of slaves freed by Lincoln under his compensated emancipation plan was .089 percent, a mere fraction of the total amount.
542. J. C. Perry, p. 191.
543. DiLorenzo, RL, pp. 33-53. In fairness to Lincoln it should be noted that he did embrace and promote the idea of compensated emancipation, in which slaveholders would be reimbursed for the loss of their slaves at the time of emancipation. On February 5, 1865, in a draft message to Congress, he proposed setting aside some $400,000,000 to be paid to those slave states who abandoned slavery and returned to the Union. Unfortunately for Northern and Southern slaves at the time, the Yankee Congress "unanimously disapproved" of the proposal, believing that Southern slave owners (no mention of Northern slave owners) needed to be "punished" not "rewarded" for owning slaves. See Nicolay and Hay, ALCW, Vol. 2, pp. 635-636. This rejection of Lincoln's somewhat more "generous" plan spelled social and economic disaster for the South, precisely the intention of the Radicals (i.e., the abolitionists) in Lincoln's party. The ultimate demagogue, Lincoln, of course, caved into Radical pressure in order to maintain financial support for his administration and his War.
544. Bailyn, Dallek, Davis, Donald, Thomas, and Wood, p. 11.
545. Bailyn, Dallek, Davis, Donald, Thomas, and Wood, pp. 8-11.

Indeed, the notion that Lincoln would initiate a conflict in which 3 million of his own citizens would perish[546] and one half of his nation would be gutted, burned, and bombed into rubble—all for the alleged purpose of ending an institution comprised of a race he considered inferior[547] and which he wanted to deport as quickly as possible[548]—is illogical in the extreme. Particularly when we consider that all around him every other nation was abolishing slavery gradually, rationally, and amicably, without a drop of blood being shed. Lincoln was many things: utterly non-religious, deceptive, secretive, opportunistic, vulgar, passive, overly pragmatic, ambiguous, and wholly governed by political expediency. But he was not stupid.

If he was, as his followers assert, a civil rights advocate whose main goal was black equality through the destruction of slavery, why not do it peacefully? Lincoln was a lawyer. Why not abolish slavery reasonably and safely through the court system?

## THE SOUTHERN ABOLITION MOVEMENT

There is also the bold fact that the American abolition movement began in the South, in Virginia specifically.[549] Virginians such as Thomas Jefferson and James Madison, for instance, strove mightily to find the means by which to rid the early states of the wicked institution, for they understood that it was morally incompatible with the principles of the American Revolution.[550]

As this fact was known by nearly all Americans in 1860, including Lincoln, why then try to bomb the South into rubble? It was obvious that slavery would eventually die out in Dixie just as it had in the North. Likewise, nearly all citizens of the Confederacy, including their president, Jefferson Davis, knew that slavery was doomed from the very beginning, even if the South were to win Lincoln's War.

Even many Northerners, like the Dixie-loathing Daniel Webster, predicted years before the Lincoln's War that eventually the Southern abolition movement would help end the institution once and

---

546. Timothy Manning, personal correspondence.
547. See e.g., Nicolay and Hay, ALCW, Vol. 1, pp. 289, 370.
548. See e.g., Nicolay and Hay, ALCW, Vol. 1, p. 288; Vol. 2, p. 237.
549. Seabrook, TQJD, p. 68.
550. Ellis, AS, p. 102.

for all. And indeed, antislavery sentiment was alive and well in antebellum Dixie,[551] as Tocqueville observed in 1831.[552] But records of the movement date back long before the 1830s. Southerner, St. George Tucker (1752-1827), one of the earliest abolitionists in the U.S.,[553] was formulating ideas for ending slavery in Virginia in 1796.[554]

Of the 130 abolition societies established before 1827 by Northern abolitionist Benjamin Lundy (1789-1839), over 100, comprising four-fifths of the total membership, were in the South.[555] Early North Carolina, as another state example, had a number of well-known "forceful" antislavery leaders, such as Benjamin Sherwood Hedrick (1827-1886) and Daniel Reaves Goodlow.[556]

As mentioned, in the early 1800s Madison[557] and Jefferson were discussing, and fully expecting, their home state of Virginia to move toward terminating slavery,[558] and by mid 1863 white Southerners everywhere were adopting ever more liberal reforms that, along with the forces of industrialization, urbanization, and the Enlightenment, would have inevitably led to eventual abolition and emancipation.[559]

Plainly, warfare was not needed to end slavery in the South, or anywhere else in America.

## PEACE COMMISSIONS & COLONIZATION
And what of the many Confederate peace commissions President Davis sent to see Lincoln before and during the War, hoping to resolve the North-South conflict on paper? Lincoln ignored nearly all of them, and in most cases would not even acknowledge their presence.[560]

His four long years of warmongering are all the more strange

---

551. L. Johnson, p. 179; E. M. Thomas, p. 242; Eaton, HSC, pp. 237-238.
552. Tocqueville, Vol. 1, p. 405.
553. Though Tucker was born in Bermuda, he moved to the South while still a child, becoming a Virginian. It was in the Old Dominion that he married, raised a family, became a lawyer and a judge, served in the Revolutionary War, and prepared and annotated an edition of *Blackstone's Commentaries* (in 1803). Neilson, s.v. "Tucker, St. George."
554. DiLorenzo, LU, p. 76.
555. Cash, p. 63.
556. H. C. Bailey, p. 197.
557. Peterson, JM, p. 371.
558. Ellis, AS, pp. 102, 173.
559. E. M. Thomas, p. 242.
560. DiLorenzo, RL, p. 121.

when we consider that he himself knew that the South would eventually abolish slavery on her own. At a speech he gave on July 10, 1858, in Chicago, for example, he said of the institution:

> I always believed . . . that it was in course of ultimate extinction.[561]

Indeed, had not Virginia, far earlier in 1832 (the year Lincoln entered politics), publically declared that it was already considering black emancipation?[562] And had not antebellum Southerners, like Senator Preston S. Brooks of South Carolina, repeatedly stated, as even Lincoln himself admitted in 1858, that

> when this government was originally established, nobody expected that the institution of slavery would last until this day. [563]

Clearly, the idea that Lincoln went to war with the South to end slavery is as false as it is absurd. In 1862, midway through the conflict, Lincoln himself said that the one and only purpose of the War had always been, and would always remain, to restore and maintain "the constitutional relation between the general government and each and all of the states wherein that relation is now suspended or disturbed."[564] No mention of a fight over slavery.

A year earlier, in the summer of 1861, after angrily revoking an attempt by one of his officers to emancipate slaves in Missouri, Lincoln had a conversation with abolitionist Reverend Charles Edward Lester. The President expressed his impatience with Lester and other Northern abolitionists who were pushing for the destruction of slavery.[565] Said Lincoln:

> I think [Massachusetts Senator Charles] Sumner, and the rest of you, would upset our apple-cart altogether, if you had your way. . . . We didn't go into the war to put down Slavery, but to put the flag back, and to act differently at this moment, would, I have no

---

561. Nicolay and Hay, ALCW, Vol. 1, p. 252.
562. Cash, p. 63; Oates, AL, p. 64.
563. Nicolay and Hay, ALCW, Vol. 1, p. 347.
564. Nicolay and Hay, ALCW, Vol. 2, p. 213.
565. Oates, AL, p. 100.

doubt, not only weaken our cause, but smack of bad faith; for I never should have had votes enough to send me here, if the people had supposed I should try to use my power to upset Slavery. Why, the first thing you'd see, would be a mutiny in the army. No! We must wait until every other means has been exhausted. This thunderbolt will keep.[566]

We will note that Lincoln admits here that the Northern people would never have elected him and that Northern soldiers would have mutinied if he had tried to "use his power to upset slavery." In other words, neither Northern citizens or Northern soldiers were interested in black civil rights in the summer of 1861.[567]

For those who still believe the War was over slavery, consider the following two points.

Compensated emancipation (buying every Southern slave from their owners at market value and then freeing them) would have cost the nation ten times less than what it cost to go to war. In other words, it cost Americans ten times more to fight and kill each other for four years than if they would have simply ended slavery. If abolishing slavery had been Lincoln's one and only true goal, not even he could have been so foolish, dense, and irrational as to disregard this obvious fact, one well-known to all thinking people on the eve of his War.[568]

Finally, as Patrick J. Buchanan notes, at the time Lincoln declared war on the South, the vast majority of slave owners and their slaves were still part of the U.S. On April 12, 1861, the day the Battle of Fort Sumter began, Virginia, for example, one of the largest slave-holding states, had not yet seceded and was still in the Union. This fact alone destroy's the Northern/New South view that Lincoln's attack on the South was an attack on slavery, and that he inaugurated the War for the express purpose of abolition.[569]

So why did he issue the Emancipation Proclamation? Aside from the reasons already given, we can be sure it was not for humanitarian reasons. For if Lincoln had truly been interested in ending slavery in an effort to establish racial equality for blacks, he would have done so

---

566. Lester, pp. 359-360.
567. Seabrook, TMCP, p. 121.
568. Rutland, p. 226. See also C. Johnson, p. 200.
569. Website: http://buchanan.org/blog/the-new-intolerance-3878.

peacefully and efficiently, using the U.S. court system and the vast judicial acumen possessed by he and his cabinet members. The fact is that he did not. This tells us that for the Yankee president the Emancipation Proclamation was neither an abolitionary or a civil rights document.

How else can one explain the fact that by the middle of the War he still had not given up on his colonization plan to ship blacks out of the country? Strangely, for one who was supposed to be "the Negro's best friend," on the release of his emancipation he had $100,000 set aside (the equivalent of about $2,130,000 today) that was to be used by any newly liberated slaves willing to leave America permanently for Africa or Haiti.[570]

## FREED BLACKS REFUSED TO ALLOW LINCOLN TO DEPORT THEM

Thoroughly Americanized, and viewing the U.S. as not only their home, but also the home of all their known ancestors, few if any blacks took the president up on his overtly racist offer.[571] Most American blacks at the time were fourth and fifth generation Americans[572]—some were even as much as sixth and seventh generation Americans. A great many whites, however, were not more than first, second, or third generation Americans. In light of this, which race was more American, the European one or the African one, blacks asked? After all, by 1860, 99 percent of all blacks were native born Americans, a larger percentage than for whites.[573]

Said one white Northern journalist of America's huge black population: They are no longer Africans. They have become Americans, just as happened with Europeans who came to this land.[574] How true.

But Lincoln never grasped this elemental concept. Or perhaps he did, but did not care. Either way, these are not the traits of a

---

570. J. C. Perry, p. 191.
571. Greenberg and Waugh, pp. 374-375.
572. Fogel, pp. 31-32.
573. Fogel and Engerman, pp. 23-24. Contrary to Northern mythology, of the South's 3,500,000 black servants, only 14 percent (or about 500,000 individuals) were imported from Africa—*by Yankee slavers*—between the early 1600s and 1861. The other 3,000,000 (86 percent), all American-born, were the result of natural reproduction. Garraty and McCaughey, p. 214.
574. Foner, FSFLFM, p. 274.

humanitarian interested in equal rights for all races.

As for Lincoln's freed Africans themselves, they were now indeed Americans in every sense of the word and they would not be going anywhere. Not "back to Africa," not to Central America, not to the Carribean, as Lincoln so desired.[575] Quite the opposite, in fact. Most were horrified at the idea of being expelled to Africa[576] and angrily denounced Lincoln's harebrained idea, suggesting that he deport slaveholders instead.[577] After all, they correctly asked, was there not a link between colonization and slavery?[578] For abolitionist-racists like Lincoln, there certainly was. But again he played deaf and dumb while continuing his quest to remove all people of African descent from the U.S.

To make sure he did not succeed, blacks repeatedly issued their "vigorous opposition" to African colonization in newspapers, national and state conventions, leaflets, anywhere their voice could be heard. Their outright rejection of Lincoln's racist scheme was as clear as it could be. Wrote one black American:

> This is our home, and this is our country. Beneath its sod lie the bones of our fathers; for it some of them fought, bled, and died. Here we were born, and here we will die.[579]

Little wonder that after Lincoln played his trump card (issuing the Final Emancipation Proclamation), absolutely nothing happened. No slave revolts occurred in the South and not a single Southern slave voluntarily left their plantation and headed North.[580]

FREED SLAVES WERE NOT REALLY FREE
There were other signs that Lincoln was far more racist than Forrest could ever be, and that his emancipation had been a hollow and self-serving political tool.

Lincoln had promised freed blacks "forty acres and a mule." But

---

575. Catton, Vol. 2, pp. 352-353.
576. Peterson, JM, p. 378.
577. Oates, AL, p. 113.
578. Quarles, p. 148.
579. W. L. Garrison, Pt. 2, p. 17.
580. Daugherty, p. 169.

it was an outright political ploy and a lie,[581] and the promise never materialized:[582] there were no mules,[583] the land giveaways were only meant to be temporary,[584] and nearly all those that were issued in the South were handed over to rich Northerners.[585]

When former slaves did manage to make economic progress, they found themselves blocked at every turn by a hostile racist Northern government, the very body that had "emancipated" them. This blockage was accomplished mainly through the North's implementation of Black Codes (racist anti-Negro laws),[586] Jim Crow laws, and public segregation laws. Trade unions and a highly discriminatory legal system further undermined black efforts to merge into Northern society.[587] All of this was done under the auspices of President Lincoln, and later, after his assassination, with the authorization of his cabinet, all of whom he had carefully hand-picked.[588]

It is little wonder that some freed blacks soon came to believe that they had been better off under slavery as opposed to the "quasi-freedom" they were now experiencing under Lincoln's "emancipation." For he had hurled them unprepared, uneducated, and untrained into a "precarious existence,"[589] a world dominated by white supremacy, where they had to compete for jobs with whites who were nearly always far more skilled.[590] In regard to blacks Lincoln's real agenda has now finally been exposed.

## LINCOLN'S TRUE GOAL

The result of all of this in the South was, of course, a chaos that initiated the erosion of Southern society through the destruction of the secession movement, one of Lincoln's stated goals.[591]

This was only a small part of his much larger plan to overturn

581. Mullen, p. 33; Rosenbaum and Brinkley, s.v. "Forty Acres and a Mule."
582. J. C. Perry, p. 230.
583. J. H. Franklin, p. 37.
584. Foner, R, pp. 70-71.
585. Thornton and Ekelund, p. 96.
586. H. C. Bailey, p. 155; DiLorenzo, RL, pp. 26-27, 257-258.
587. Thornton and Ekelund, pp. 95-98.
588. Donald, L., pp. 261-267.
589. Fogel and Engerman, pp. 243-244.
590. Kennedy and Kennedy, pp. 53-58.
591. Napolitano, p. 61.

the Founding Fathers' conservative (Southern) form of government,[592] the republic,[593] and in its place install the liberal (Northern) mercantilist American System form of government,[594] the federation,[595] as advanced by Lincoln's political idol Henry Clay.[596]

It must be said that only a thoroughly politically motivated individual who detested the South, possessed little humanity, and had no interest in racial equality (or American constitutional tradition), could even entertain such a monstrous thing, let alone actually seek to achieve it. According to Mary Chesnut, as one newly freed slave accurately put it after being read Lincoln's proclamation: he has removed the chains

---

592. DiLorenzo, LU, pp. 139, 150.

593. A republic (or by the modern definition, a confederacy) is a weak decentralized government with a loose union of powerful sovereign states; or as Webster defines a republic: "a government in which supreme power resides in a body of citizens entitled to vote and is exercised by elected officers and representatives responsible to them and governing according to law." Mish, s.v. "republic." The true definition of a Republican then is one who favors "a restricted governmental role in social and economic life." Mish, s.v. "republican." Thus, the Republican party of Lincoln's day was actually more closely aligned with what we now call the Democratic party. In other words, if Lincoln were alive today we would refer to him as a member of the Democratic party, not the Republican party, the party to which he actually belonged. Many more changes have taken place in the two parties since Lincoln's day. Unfortunately, as the two parties have moved ever closer to the center, by the above definitions and standards the Republican party of the 20th and 21st Centuries has almost nothing in common with the original idea of a republic as envisioned by the Founding Fathers. One might say then, with good reason, that today there is little difference between America's Republican party and the Democratic party, both which lean toward socialism, and in some ways, even toward imperialism—the opposite intent of the original Republic formed by the Founding Generation in 1776. The political groups that are now closest in sentiment to the Founders are the National Tea Party, the Libertarian party, and the Paleoconservative party (also known as the "classical conservatives"), the latter whose most well-known member is currently my cousin Patrick J. Buchanan. Libertarian Thomas Jefferson, a type of early "Paleo," would be horrified at what Lincoln and later generations of Americans, such as President Barack Hussein Obama, have done to the Republic he so carefully and passionately helped create. For more on the topics of confederation and federation, see the "Notes to the Reader" section in my book *Abraham Lincoln: The Southern View*.

594. DiLorenzo, RL, pp. 54-84.

595. A federation is a strong centralized government with a tightly bound coalition of weak dependent states; or as Webster defines a federation: a union formed by a compact between political units (such as several states) who retain limited residuary powers of government, but who surrender their individual sovereignty to a strongly centralized authority (such as a government). A federation then is a "federal government with strong centralized powers." See Mish, s.v. "federal"; s.v. "federation." A Federalist is one who favors a strong centralized government. Mish, s.v. "federalist." Thus, a Federalist in Jefferson's time period would be most closely aligned to what we would today term a Democrat. The same could be said for those who were called Republicans during Lincoln's reign. These would now be most closely aligned with what we call the Democratic party. In essence, Republican Lincoln would be considered a (liberal, social) Democrat today. On this topic Dr. Thomas E. Woods, Jr. writes that in the 1790s, when the first American party system was launched, it pitted the small-government, states' rights Republicans against the big-government Federalists. Our nation's second party system arose as a result of divisions surrounding Andrew Jackson's presidency (1829-1837). It was similar to the first, but in this case the Whigs took over the Federalist tradition while the Democrats took over the Republican tradition. Woods, p. 47.

596. Nicolay and Hay, ALCW, Vol. 1, p. 299.

from our feet, but left them on our wrists.[597] Things, however, were about to get much worse than this freedman could have ever imagined.

## INITIALLY EMANCIPATION HURT BLACKS

In truth, Lincoln's form of "emancipation" at first actually brutalized blacks rather than helped them. For example, in-depth studies by modern day economic historians, called cliometricians, reveal that there was an enormous decline in the material condition of blacks "freed" by Lincoln's Emancipation Proclamation, including a substantial decrease in life expectancy, health, diet, and work opportunities. At the same time there was an increase both in sickness among former slaves and in the wage gap between whites and blacks.[598]

Thousands of freed slaves ended up living in fetid shanty town camps, many literally starving to death in conditions that would have killed even farm animals (which are used to rough treatment).[599] During slavery blacks had been allowed to live anywhere in any state. After Lincoln's liberation, however, laws were passed that greatly restricted their movement, and in fact, they were completely prohibited from entering new rural regions, such as the Southwest territories.[600]

## A MOST RACIST STATE: "THE LAND OF LINCOLN"

The fear of a mass immigration of Lincoln's newly freed Southern blacks into Northern white enclaves was very real. Clearly, whites, particularly in the North where racism was the deepest,[601] did not want blacks living among them.[602]

Illinois, Lincoln's adopted state, expressed this fear to the lawyer-president, who then advised them on how to solve the problem: simply amend their state constitution to include a passage that read, "no negro or mulatto shall immigrate or settle in this state." In 1862, in the middle of Lincoln's War to "free the slaves," the vast majority of citizens of the "Land of Lincoln" voted in this new amendment. The dread of a

---

597. See Chesnut, MCCW, p. 829.
598. Fogel and Engerman, p. 261.
599. J. C. Perry, p. 229.
600. Fogel and Engerman, p. 262.
601. Tocqueville, Vol. 1, pp. 383-385.
602. Oates, AL, p. 63.

flood of freed blacks had been stemmed, temporarily at least, in Illinois, all with the direct aid and encouragement of the "Great Emancipator."[603]

Little wonder that before the War the Prairie State—where white bigotry was intense and where white citizens refused to put the issue of black suffrage to the vote[604]—had been the only contiguous state that did not pass some type of personal-liberty law;[605] or that after the War it had one of the lowest percentages of blacks (1.1 percent) living within its borders of any state.[606] Well into the mid 1800s, though considered a "free state," Illinois possessed laws that permitted "Negro servitude." According to these laws slave labor was legal, but only under one condition: the slaves were not allowed to be kept permanently in the state.[607]

Illinois' white prejudice was already in full bloom by the time Lincoln was four years-old. In 1813, for example, Negrophobia there was being fueled by numerous black crime waves, which included house break-ins, robbery, and the burning down of farms. Most disturbing to white Illinoisans was the innate "moral laxity" of Africans, which promised to result in a growing mulatto population and the "inevitable decline of white society." This belief, along with the accompanying illegal activities, led the state's whites to adopt a law that required justices of the peace to instruct any incoming "free Negro or mulatto" to immediately depart from the region. Offenders were whipped thirty-nine times for failure to obey, a punishment that was to be repeated every fifteen days until the "sable-colored criminal" exited the state.[608]

Years later, this same racism was helped along by President Lincoln, who assisted white Illinoisans by opposing the immigration of blacks into the state and by supporting the Illinois Black Codes.[609] These included prohibiting blacks from voting, along with the deprivation of numerous other rights, which is why Illinois was then known as one of the most virulent of the Jim Crow states.[610]

---

603. Kennedy, p. 165.
604. Page Smith, p. 974.
605. Neely, p. xvi.
606. Page Smith, p. 974.
607. Current, LNK, p. 218.
608. Berwanger, pp. 23-24.
609. DiLorenzo, LU, pp. 27-28.
610. Current, LNK, p. 235.

## ABOLISHING SLAVERY WAS FOR WHITES, NOT BLACKS

Illinois was not alone of course, nor was it the first Northern state in which whites sought to curtail the rights and movements of blacks. Indeed, throughout the first half of the 19<sup>th</sup> Century *all* of the Northern states had discriminatory laws on the books that were aimed at blacks.[611] This is why, long before slavery ended, free blacks faced a daily waking nightmare throughout the North: though they were physically free, they continued to be socially enslaved by white racism. In Ohio, for example, slavery was prohibited, but freed blacks were not allowed to enter the state or buy land.[612]

Tocqueville was discomforted, but not surprised, when he observed this phenomenon in 1831:

> The States in which slavery is abolished [i.e., the Northern states] usually do what they can to render their territory disagreeable to the negroes as a place of residence; and as a kind of emulation exists between the different States in this respect, the unhappy blacks can only choose the least of the evils which beset them.[613] . . . The emancipated negroes, and those born after the abolition of slavery, do not, indeed, migrate from the North to the South; but their situation with regard to the Europeans is not unlike that of the aborigines of America [i.e., Native-Americans]; they remain half civilized, and deprived of their rights in the midst of a population which is far superior to them in wealth and in knowledge; where they are exposed to the tyranny of the laws and the intolerance of the people. On some accounts they are still more to be pitied than the Indians, since they are haunted by the reminiscence of slavery, and they can not claim possession of a single portion of the soil: many of them perish miserably, and the rest congregate in the great towns, where they perform the meanest offices, and lead a wretched and precarious existence.[614]

Though Tocqueville is describing the Northern states in the early 1830s, as we have seen, African-Americans in the North faced exactly the same situation immediately both after Lincoln abolished slavery in 1863 and after the passage of the Thirteenth Amendment in 1865.

---

611. Greenberg and Waugh, p. 375.
612. Tocqueville, Vol. 1, p. 415.
613. Tocqueville, Vol. 1, p. 416.
614. Tocqueville, Vol. 1, pp. 392-393.

What does this tell us about America's sixteenth president? Is this a defense of slavery? Should slavery have been continued rather than abolished? Of course not. Today the very idea of enslaving a human being is contrary to our American concept of individual freedom and innate civil and natural rights. It is, in fact, an evil that goes contrary to all of our 21st-Century religious, social, and philosophical mores.

What it tells us is that Lincoln was not concerned with racial equality. His main concern was politics, and more to the point, *white* politics. Indeed, Lincoln's Emancipation Proclamation, which he always said was nothing more than a "war measure"[615] and a "military necessity,"[616] was simply an extension of his original colonization plans, to have all blacks loaded on ships and removed from the United States as soon as they were set free.[617] This is why his soulless and emotionless proclamation[618] was utterly devoid of any emphasis on racial justice or equity,[619] and why it contained no resounding request for black liberty.[620]

This is also why, as Tocqueville remarked in 1831, white racism in 19th-Century America increased in proportion to the emancipation of blacks. For, as the young French aristocrat unflinchingly noted:

> It is not for the good of the negroes, but for that of the whites, that measures are taken to abolish slavery in the United States.[621]

## THE SPECIAL RELATIONSHIP BETWEEN BLACK SLAVES & THEIR WHITE OWNERS

Emancipation wreaked havoc on other aspects of African-American, and European-American, society.

Most black slaves never came to hate whites because of slavery.[622] Instead, they hated slavery itself.[623] Likewise, most white

---

615. Nicolay and Hay, Vol. 2, pp. 235, 285, 287.
616. Nicolay and Hay, Vol. 2, pp. 216, 288, 296.
617. J. C. Perry, p. 190.
618. Current, LNK, p. 228.
619. W. B. Garrison, LNOK, p. 192.
620. Current, LNK, p. 228.
621. Tocqueville, Vol. 1, p. 385.
622. Catton, Vol. 3, p. 263.
623. L. Johnson, p. 181.

slave owners did not hate their black slaves. Instead, they hated Northern interference, which had been intruding into their lives and businesses for decades,[624] long even before Lincoln's War.[625]

After Lincoln officially abolished the absurdly nicknamed "peculiar institution" in the South in January 1863, however, both white and black racism escalated to a level there completely unknown prior to the conflict.[626]

During slavery white and black Southerners lived in informal friendship, in close proximity to one another.[627] This was far more than just a simple owner-slave dynamic. For centuries the two races often worked together, ate, farmed, and hunted together. During the War they fought side-by-side, solidly united against Lincoln's invading bluecoats.[628] As we will see, Forrest took forty-five of his own slaves into the army with him,[629] where they enthusiastically and faithfully served as teamsters, cooks, body servants, and even soldiers in the General's cavalry for the duration of the War.[630] Seven of them functioned as Forrest's personal armed guard.[631]

Even in death white master and black servant often ended up near each other, as slave cemeteries were usually located close to, or even next to, their white owners' family cemeteries. This intimate intermingling of whites and blacks bred a friendly, even loving, familiarity that naturally banished stereotypes and eradicated the very possibility of racism.[632]

In most cases the result was a unique, warm, and special relationship[633] of authentic fondness and loving concern between whites and blacks, one that often began in childhood,[634] and which was much commented on in letters, journals, diaries, and books by Victorian Southerners—both European and African. It was said that owners and

---

624. Catton, Vol. 1, pp. 21, 105.
625. Grissom, pp. 94-95.
626. L. Johnson, pp. 181-182.
627. Catton, Vol. 1, p. 88.
628. Barrow, Segars, and Rosenburg, BC, p. 41.
629. Henry, FWMF, p. 14.
630. Wiley, SN, p. 111; Horn, IE, p. 414; Henry, ATSF, p. 105; Bradley, pp. 22, 215-219.
631. Ashdown and Caudill, pp. 184-185.
632. Kennedy, pp. 117-125.
633. Kennedy and Kennedy, pp. 87-88.
634. Wiley, LJR, p. 328.

slaves had two families each: a black one and a white one,[635] which is why many white Confederate soldiers included lines like the following in their letters home: please say hello to the black members of our family.[636]

This was not true just among average Southerners. The Southern elite also viewed their African servants with familial warmth. America's third president, Virginian Thomas Jefferson, warmly referred to his slaves as members of "my family,"[637] and in fact, listed them as such in his *Farm Book* (begun in 1774).[638]

Black "mammys" in particular were much loved, as they spent nearly all of their time in the "big house" with the white family, literally raising generations of European-American children.[639] Indeed, white infants—who were often suckled by, and even mentored into adulthood, by their black mammies, often spent more time with them than with their biological mothers.[640]

As Margaret Mitchell's novel *Gone With the Wind* comes to a close, the narrator describes Scarlett O'Hara as she reminisces of earlier happier times at her beloved plantation "Tara": Scarlett paused, recalling the many little things, the boulevard of pines winding up to the mansion, the jessamine shrubs, the green of the trees against Tara's white walls, the pale sheer drapes as they fluttered in the wind. And, of course, there was Mammy. How she wanted to be back with her, just as she had been as a youngster, with her comforting dark hand on her head. Here, wrote Mitchell, in her black surrogate mother, was Scarlett's last connection with the Old South, one that she loved so dearly.[641]

In the fields a similar phenomenon took place between white and black. White plantation owners quickly learned that some of their black servants were better leaders, organizers, and mathematicians than many whites, and thus promoted them to positions of power and prestige. Contrary to Yankee myth, black overseers and black drivers, who

635. J. C. Perry, p. 145.
636. Wiley, LJR, p. 211.
637. Ellis, AS, p. 175.
638. Jefferson, TJFB, p. 18.
639. J. C. Perry, pp. 145-146.
640. Cash, p. 51.
641. Mitchell, p. 1024.

possessed numerous and important responsibilities, were a common sight on Southern plantations. In fact, the vast majority, 70 percent, of Southern plantations were managed by blacks, who would often administer the entire estate for weeks at a time when the owner was off on business.[642]

It has been rightfully said that without the efforts of millions of loyal slaves, who aided in holding together the homes, farms, businesses, and families of their white male owners while they were away fighting for the Confederacy, European-American Southern Culture itself might have disappeared entirely between 1861 and 1865. Esteemed African-American historian Benjamin Quarles affirms that the Southern black's contributions to the Confederate Cause were beyond counting,[643] for the support of countless Southern slaves (and also free Southern blacks) who served in the Confederate Army as teamsters, construction workers, drivers, cooks, nurses, body servants, and orderlies,[644] not to mention the hundreds of thousands who served as soldiers,[645] helped prolong the South's military efforts against Lincoln and his illegal invasion of Dixie.[646]

Southern blacks supported the Confederacy in a myriad of other ways as well. Financial contributions, for example, came from thousands of African-Americans who held bake sales, raffles, and yard sales, eagerly donating all of the proceeds to local Confederate military units, garrisons, and officers' quarters. In Talladega, Alabama, a group of slaves took up a collection amounting to $53.20, an effort to alleviate the suffering of Rebel soldiers.[647] Such endeavors were repeated thousands of times by thousands of blacks across Dixie between 1861 and 1865.

The cross-racial relationships that were formed in Dixie during slavery, and later during the War, were so strong that they often lasted long after the fighting ceased. Contrary to Northern anti-South propaganda, among many white and black Southerners loyalty and friendship only grew more enduring with time. In her diary Mary Chesnut noted the words of a freed black slave to his former white

642. Fogel and Engerman, pp. 210-215.
643. Quarles, p. 273.
644. E. M. Thomas, p. 236.
645. Barrow, Segars, and Rosenburg, BC, passim.
646. Kennedy and Kennedy, p. 89.
647. Quarles, pp. 49-50, 263-264.

owner after the War:

> When you all had de power you was good to me, and I'll protect
> you now. No niggers nor Yankees shall tech [touch] you. If you
> want anything call for Sambo. I mean, call for Mr. Samuel; dat my
> name now.[648]

Naturally all Southern blacks were happy to see slavery come to
an end. But this did not mean that they turned on their former owners.
In nearly every case during the so-called "Reconstruction" period, freed
blacks had the opposite reaction. An early black political convention in
Alabama, for instance, called for a policy of peace and friendship toward
all people, in particular the white race. Likewise, in numerous states
African-Americans were the first to try and repeal laws that hurt,
penalized, or disenfranchised former Confederates, or prevented them
from holding political office.[649]

As after, so before. Throughout the antebellum and War
periods the records are replete with stories of warm relations between
Southern whites and Southern blacks,[650] and of free blacks and slaves
providing various forms of support for both the war effort[651] and for
those former white overlords who had been made indigent by Lincoln's
War. Noted Virginia slave and educator, Booker T. Washington (1856-
1915), wrote:

> As a rule, not only did the members of my race entertain no
> feelings of bitterness against . . . [Southern] whites before and
> during the war, but there are many instances of Negroes tenderly
> caring for their former masters and mistresses who for some reason
> have become poor and dependent since the war. I know of
> instances where the former masters of slaves have for years been
> supplied with money by their former slaves to keep them from
> suffering. I have known of still other cases in which the former
> slaves have assisted in the education of the descendants of their
> former owners. I know of a case on a large plantation in the South
> in which a young white man, the son of the former owner of the

648. Chesnut, DD, p. 389.
649. Bailyn, Dallek, Davis, Donald, Thomas, and Wood, p. 7.
650. Kennedy and Kennedy, p. 112.
651. Barrow, Segars, and Rosenburg, BC, pp. 12-13, 94.

estate, has become so reduced in purse and self control by reason of drink that he is a pitiable creature; and yet, notwithstanding the poverty of the coloured people themselves on this plantation, they have for years supplied this young white man with the necessities of life. One sends him a little coffee or sugar, another a little meat, and so on. Nothing that the coloured people possess is too good for the son of 'old Mars Tom,' who will perhaps never be permitted to suffer while any remain on the place who knew directly or indirectly of 'old Mars Tom.'[652]

## EMANCIPATION DAMAGED RACE RELATIONS IN THE SOUTH

Southern interracial harmony was greatly disrupted, however, by Lincoln's Emancipation Proclamation. As Ludwell Johnson sees it, freedom caused a physical division between blacks and whites as the two races went their separate ways. The old personal relationships decayed and the gap between European-Americans and African-Americans widened evermore rapidly. Thus, with freedom racial tension in the South grew rather than diminished.[653]

One of Lincoln's many legacies is the remnant of deep mistrust between some whites and blacks that continues in the South to this day, one that was almost nonexistent before the start of Northern agitation against slavery in the early 1830s. By 1865 this bond of trust was greatly weakened (though not completely destroyed), thanks to Lincoln's devastating War and his barbaric emancipation scheme.

## EMANCIPATION DIVIDED BLACK FAMILIES & CONTINUED SLAVE-LIKE CONDITIONS

Lincoln's proclamation of "freedom" had other dire consequences, these within the black community itself. For one thing it divided African-American families and even continued to perpetuate the institution of slavery in various forms, such as serfdom.[654]

After being freed from the bonds of slavery, for example, males were taken by Yankee soldiers at gunpoint from a peaceful, healthy, and safe life of service and domesticity on the plantation, to the filth, hardships, and dangers of life on the battlefield, where at least 50 percent

---

652. B. T. Washington, pp. 13-14.
653. L. Johnson, pp. 181-182.
654. Hurst, p. 10.

of them died alone in muddy ditches fighting against their own native homeland: the South.[655] Those Southern blacks who refused enlistment in Lincoln's armies (most did) were executed on the spot.[656] Those who were not put to death were turned into common U.S. army laborers, doing work little different than what they had experienced as slaves,[657] and at almost half the pay of white soldiers.[658]

Female slaves and their children, meanwhile, were driven off in cattle-like droves and set to work on U.S. "government plantations," so-called "abandoned" Southern farms.[659] In reality these were Confederate plantations whose original owners had been chased off or killed, replaced by Yankee bosses who often withheld food, clothing, bedding, and medicine from their new black charges, resulting in an appalling number of deaths.[660]

## FORREST'S ATTITUDE TOWARD HIS SLAVES
All of this is in the starkest contrast to how Forrest and the majority of other Southern slave owners treated their slaves. Eyewitnesses report that Forrest approached his bondsmen with extreme kindness and humanity, taught them to read and write, kept them well-fed, bathed, and well-dressed, and even protected them by refusing to divide slave families or sell them to cruel slavers.[661]

## THE WHITE SUPREMACY BEHIND LINCOLN'S EMANCIPATION
In short, the Emancipation Proclamation was a shrewd and audacious political move by a white separatist, a "vindictive war measure" (as Britain accurately called it),[662] one steeped in "hollow pretensions for the negro,"[663] rampant racism, political prostitution, the raw realities of war, and unconstitutional illegalities.[664] The white supremacist behind all this

---

655. Pollard, SHW, Vol. 2, pp. 196-198.
656. Wiley, SN, pp. 306-310.
657. DiLorenzo, RL, p. 34.
658. J. M. McPherson, BCF, pp. 788-789.
659. L. Johnson, p. 135.
660. Pollard, SHW, Vol. 2, p. 198.
661. Sheppard, p. 25.
662. Owsley, KCD, p. 190.
663. Pollard, SHW, Vol. 2, p. 196.
664. Kennedy and Kennedy, pp. 26-32.

was none other than Abraham Lincoln, a man Southerners referred to as "stinkin' Lincoln" and an "obscene animal,"[665] one they regarded as a non-religious,[666] coarse,[667] low, brutish,[668] anti-South vulgarian.[669]

In point of fact the sixteenth president of the U.S. was an overt bigot, a Negrophobe who publically spoke in favor of apartheid, but who much preferred black colonization, and whose party openly declared itself the "white man's party" during the 1860 presidential election.[670] This is why Lincoln was widely known by both non-racist white and black Southerners as the "Yankee monster of inhumanity and falsehood,"[671] and why he became a Christ-like hero to various early 20th-Century white supremacists like Thomas Dixon, Jr. and D. W. Griffith.[672]

No "Negro-baiter" admired Lincoln more or "praised him oftener," however, than Mississippi governor, senator, white supremacist, and Democrat, James Kimble Vardaman (1861-1930). According to Vardaman, right up until the day Lincoln died he continued his attempts at prohibiting blacks from participating in the running of the government. In fact, the Mississippian correctly states, Lincoln preferred that blacks vacate the U.S. as soon as possible after emancipation via his colonization plan. Why? Because "Honest Abe" believed that deporting the black race was the only solution to America's "race problem."[673]

## WHY SO MANY BLACKS SUPPORTED THE CONFEDERACY

With a virulent white supremacist heading not only the U.S. government but also the Union army and navy (Lincoln had illegally "assumed

---

665. J. M. McPherson, BCF, p. 790.
666. Foote, Vol. 1, p. 709.
667. Page Smith, p. 576.
668. Wiley, LJR, p. 312.
669. Pollard, SHW, Vol. 1, pp. 40, 48. Mary Chesnut, who likened Lincoln to an "ape," too noted his well-known proclivity for vulgarity and for telling "nasty jokes." Chesnut, DD, pp. 12, 19, 203, 270. She was not alone. Many others criticized the inappropriateness of Lincoln's humor (Page Smith, p. 576), considering him the embodiment of loathsomeness and offensiveness. Wiley, LJR, p. 16. According to Rebel soldiers, however, the trait of vulgarity was common among all Yankees. Wiley, LJR, p. 309.
670. *The Congressional Globe*, 36th Congress, 1st Session, p. 58; Carey, p. 181.
671. Pollard, SHW, Vol. 2, p. 194.
672. Oates, AL, pp. 21-23.
673. Current, LNK, pp. 231, 233.

command" of the U.S. military March 11, 1862),[674] and the inhumanity, racism, and destructiveness of so many of Lincoln's troops,[675] it is not surprising that between 93,000[676] and 300,000 (mostly undocumented) free and enslaved blacks fought valiantly against Lincoln on the side of the Confederacy;[677] or that over 300,000 non-military blacks supported the Confederacy (far more than those who supported the Union);[678] that thousands of black Confederate soldiers who were captured and taken North during the War returned to their Southern homes as soon as they were able to;[679] that many Southern slaves faked illness to prevent Yanks from forcing them off their owners' plantations;[680] that thousands of Southern slaves who had been "freed" by the Yanks fled back South at their first opportunity;[681] or that the huge majority of slaves—95 percent—simply chose to stay at home[682] on their Southern farms and plantations during the War,[683] even though they had been offered "freedom forever" by Lincoln.[684]

## COMPARING FORREST WITH LINCOLN: THE RESULTS

In summary, Lincoln hated the institution of slavery primarily because it both brought blacks into close contact with whites[685] and because it created job competition.[686] (That it was a social atrocity that exploited blacks was of far less concern to him; in fact, he often claimed that promoting abolition only increased its evils.)[687] Also believing blacks to be inferior to whites[688] and their presence degrading to white society,[689] he vigorously and ceaselessly campaigned to deport them by sending

674. Kane, s.v. "Abraham Lincoln," p. 170.
675. Gragg, p. 84.
676. Shenkman and Reiger, pp. 105-106.
677. Barrow, Segars, and Rosenburg, BC, p. 176.
678. Barrow, Segars, and Rosenburg, BC, p. 97. Over 3,000 blacks fought as soldiers in Stonewall Jackson's Army alone. Seabrook, EYWTACWW, p. 158.
679. Barrow, Segars, and Rosenburg, BC, p. 23; Greenberg and Waugh, p. 374.
680. Page Smith, p. 363.
681. Grissom, p. 162; Pollard, SHW, Vol. 2, p. 201; Barrow, Segars, and Rosenburg, BC, pp. 13-16.
682. Gragg, pp. 84, 88.
683. L. Johnson, p. 135.
684. Kennedy and Kennedy, p. 90.
685. See e.g., Nicolay and Hay, ALCW, Vol. 1, p. 234.
686. See e.g., Nicolay and Hay, ALCW, Vol. 1, p. 197.
687. See e.g., Nicolay and Hay, ALCW, Vol. 1, p. 15.
688. See e.g., Nicolay and Hay, ALCW, Vol. 1, pp. 289, 370.
689. See e.g., Nicolay and Hay, ALCW, Vol. 2, p. 223.

them "to Liberia—to their own native land."[690]

Forrest was the opposite. He at first he accepted slavery as a necessary evil. But, like a majority of other Southerners, he was never completely comfortable with it. Thus, even before the War he came to the happy realization that slavery was a dying institution, closing down his slave trading business and emancipating nearly every one of his servants.[691]

During the War, while Lincoln was stalling black enlistment for as long as possible, Forrest enthusiastically enlisted, trained, and armed forty-five of his own servants. Midway through the conflict he freed all forty-five of them, only months after Lincoln issued his fake Emancipation Proclamation,[692] and over two years before the U.S. finally ended slavery all across America with the ratification of the Thirteenth Amendment on December 6, 1865.[693]

After the War, now believing that whites and blacks were truly equals, Forrest recommended opening up the job market to them, while using freedmen, as well as black African immigrants, to share in the rebuilding of the South.[694] Why? Because he felt that their work ethic was superior to that of whites. He then went on to fight for black civil rights and racial harmony.[695]

Lincoln, in contrast, never did any of these things. Actually, while he was in the White House, he was the primary obstacle to black social and political advancement, prompting many to correctly note that abolition would have come much sooner had he not become president.[696]

Yes, Forrest was a slaver for a short period of time while Lincoln was never a slaver. But Lincoln was a white separatist and black colonizationist right up to the day he was assassinated, while Forrest was never a white separatist or a black colonizationist—and both men died at the exact same age: fifty-six.

Forrest spent the entire postwar period of his life (1865-1877)

---

**690**. See e.g., Nicolay and Hay, ALCW, Vol. 1, p. 288.

**691**. Henry, FWMF, p. 27.

**692**. See the *Report of the Joint Select Committee to Inquire into the Condition of Affairs in the Late Insurrectionary States*, p. 20.

**693**. Wyeth, TDF, p. xxi.

**694**. Wills, p. 359; Ashdown and Caudill, pp. 63, 84.

**695**. See e.g., Hurst, pp. 4, 11, 365-367, 330, 332.

**696**. Ashe, p. 58.

promoting racial peace and black civil rights. Lincoln spent his entire political career (1832-1865) creating racial strife and blocking black civil rights.

In the end, who was the true racist monster? The answer is obvious.

The irony becomes more absurd when we consider that while Forrest is often compared to the Devil,[697] Lincoln is routinely compared to Jesus.[698] According to the Bible, however, unlike Lincoln, Jesus was "no respecter of persons." Red, white, black, and brown, all were equal in his eyes,[699] the same view that Forrest eventually came to hold.

## BLACK & NATIVE-AMERICAN SLAVE OWNERS

It is even more difficult to single out Forrest as being racist toward blacks when we consider the well-documented fact that tens of thousands of both Native-Americans[700] and African-Americans themselves also owned black slaves. Some blacks even owned white slaves.[701] Should not these black and red slave holders then also be considered racists?

In 1830, thirty-one years before Lincoln's War, 2 percent (or 3,690) of all free American blacks owned 12,601 black slaves.[702] That same year, 186,000 whites,[703] or about 4 percent of all Southern whites (4,000,000)[704] owned slaves. Thus only 2 percent separated the number of black slave owners and white slave owners in 1830. In the deep South, just one specific region of Dixie, nearly 25 percent of free blacks owned black slaves during that same period.[705]

Thirty years later the number of black slave owners had decreased, but only slightly. Despite the aggressive actions of abolitionists (a tiny minority at the time), in 1860, near the start of the War, the Census shows that some 10,000 American black slaves were

---

697. Lytle, p. 304.
698. DiLorenzo, LU, p. 12.
699. Acts 10:34.
700. Jahoda, pp. 85, 148, 154, 225, 241, 246, 247, 249; J. C. Perry, pp. 96, 99, 101; Grissom, p. 182.
701. J. C. Perry, pp. 96, 174.
702. Grissom, p. 131.
703. Hartzell, p. 37.
704. Tocqueville, Vol. 1, p. 417.
705. Greenberg and Waugh, pp. 376-377.

still owned by other blacks.[706]

In Charleston, South Carolina, alone between 1820 and 1840, 75 percent of the city's free blacks owned slaves.[707] Wealthy blacks purchased and peddled slaves as vigorously as any white slaver, two examples being African-American John Stanley of South Carolina, who owned 163 black slaves, and the black Metoyer family of Louisiana, who owned some 400 black slaves.[708] At an average price of about $2,000 a piece their servants were worth a total of $20,000,000 in today's currency, making the Metoyers one of the most affluent families in all of American history, black or white.[709]

Lincoln's white soldiers, being more racist than their white Southern counterparts,[710] did not believe blacks were intelligent enough to own and run their own businesses, or that Southern whites would allow them to. Thus, as they invaded Dixie, they were shocked, and sometimes reacted violently, as they came across plantation after plantation without any white residents. Both the owners and their slaves were black.[711]

While it is true that some of the slaves belonging to blacks were family members that had been bought back, most were not.[712] And in fact, many black slave owners had two sets of slaves: their recently purchased family members and a pool of actual black slave laborers.[713]

If African-Americans themselves were owners of enslaved blacks,[714] how then is it possible to call Forrest a racist because he too owned them? If so, then thousands of black slavers must also be considered black racists—toward their own kind.

If Lincoln, a publically avowed white supremacist who never worked or fought along side blacks,[715] who consistently hampered the

---

**706.** Kennedy and Kennedy, pp. 64-65.

**707.** J. C. Perry, p. 175.

**708.** Greenberg and Waugh, p. 376.

**709.** Greenberg and Waugh, p. 376.

**710.** Tocqueville, Vol. 1, pp. 383-385.

**711.** J. C. Perry, pp. 175-176.

**712.** Greenberg and Waugh, p. 376.

**713.** J. C. Perry, p. 176.

**714.** Kennedy and Kennedy, pp. 133-134; Greenberg and Waugh, pp. 376-377; J. C. Perry, pp. 96, 173-179.

**715.** See e.g., Nicolay and Hay, ALCW, Vol. 1, pp. 291-292, 370, 539-540. Nicolay and Hay, CWAL, Vol. 5, pp. 87-89.

civil and social progress of blacks,[716] segregated white and black troops,[717] paid black soldiers far less than whites,[718] and campaigned to have all blacks shipped back to Africa,[719] is considered the "Great Savior of African-Americans," then Forrest, who actually worked and fought side-by-side with blacks his entire life,[720] freed all of his slaves before and during the War,[721] labored industriously for racial equality, and who wanted to bring over more blacks from Africa after the War,[722] should be considered the epitome of non-racist, white egalitarianism.

Is it not the height of irony that racist Lincoln, like a Roman emperor, has been apotheosized, and that his giant Zeus-like statue at his "temple" (the Lincoln Memorial) in Washington, D.C.[723] is eagerly visited by tens of thousands of devout "believers" every year,[724] while non-racist Forrest has been demonized and his monuments, which are regularly vandalized, are under constant attack by the self-appointed but wholly uninformed PC police?[725]

## SLAVING DID NOT EQUAL RACISM

The existence of black and red slave owners proves that being a slave owner or a slave trader in the 1800s clearly did not mean that one was also a racist. Indeed, the 19th-Century white Southerner's involvement in slavery was not motivated by evil (which has its roots in psychopathy), bigotry (which has its roots in cultural protectionism), or racism (which has its roots in xenophobia and in economic strife).[726] Just like his Yankee counterparts to the North, who launched both the American

---

716. Woods, p. 67.

717. J. C. Perry, pp. 218, 223.

718. W. B. Garrison, LNOK, p. 176.

719. Donald, L, pp. 165-167; W. B. Garrison, LNOK, pp. 172-182.

720. Horn, IE, p. 414.

721. Wyeth, TDF, pp. xxi; Wyeth LGNBF, p. 616.

722. Hurst, pp. 365-367, 330; Ashdown and Caudill, pp. 63, 84.

723. There are indeed numerous similarities between the now missing statue of Zeus at his ancient temple in Olympia, Greece, and Lincoln's statue at the Lincoln Memorial in Washington, D.C. Like the 40-foot Zeus, a giant Lincoln sits on a throne-like chair in a Greek, Pagan-styled "temple," staring into the distance with a penetrating gaze. At his feet countless "worshipers" gather daily to offer praise and thanks. Wallechinsky, Wallace, and Wallace, p. 256. What his devotees praise and thank him for remains baffling, insulting, and hurtful to many Southerners.

724. Kennedy, p. 163.

725. Horwitz, p. 155.

726. Bultman, p. 285.

slave trade (in Massachusetts in 1638)[727] and American slavery (in Massachusetts in 1641),[728] Forrest was motivated to own and trade in slaves purely out of monetary self-interest.[729]

As we have seen it was mainly Northern antislavery advocates (like Lincoln), not Southern slave owners (like Forrest), who were racist. To white separatists like Lincoln slavery was to be detested, not merely because it is immoral to enslave human beings, but more importantly because it prevented the U.S. from being a racially pure, all-white country.[730]

This is why Lincoln and millions of other white Northerners supported the absurd, impractical, bigoted, and ultimately physically, socially, and financially impossible idea of colonization: in order to restore white hegemony, America had to be purged of all blacks, they maintained. Unfortunately for Lincoln and the thousands of other Yankee colonizationists, very few blacks—now seeing themselves, not as Africans, but as African-Americans—were willing to accept his offer of deportation.[731]

At first Forrest was not an abolitionist either. But he was also not a racist as the term is defined today. This is why, after the Confederates' indecisive victory at the Battle of Chickamauga, Georgia (September 18-20, 1863), he so easily gave up the idea of slavery and freed his forty-five slaves-turned-soldiers,[732] and this is why he so readily became a civil rights proponent after the War.[733]

In contrast Lincoln and thousands of other Northerners continued to promote the concept of black colonization (shipping all African-Americans out of the country), even after the Emancipation Proclamation had been issued (in 1863) and the War had ended (in 1865).[734] Some, like Union general and politician Benjamin Franklin "the Beast" Butler (1818-1893), testified that Lincoln continued to favor

---

727. Meltzer, Vol. 2, p. 139; Cartmell, p. 26; Norwood, p. 31.
728. G. H. Moore, pp. 5, 11, 17-19.
729. Garraty, p. 305.
730. Barrow, Segars, and Rosenburg, BC, pp. 154-155.
731. Donald, L, pp. 165-167; W. B. Garrison, LNOK, pp. 172-182; Oates, AL, p. 113.
732. Wyeth, TDF, p. xxi.
733. Hurst, pp. 365-367.
734. J. C. Perry, p. 191.

the idea of black colonization right up until the very last day of his life.[735] According to the postwar officer,[736] in March 1865, just weeks before Lincoln's assassination, he was summoned to the White House by the president, at which time Lincoln discussed with him his plan for expatriating American blacks.[737]

Why, some may now be asking, is white supremacist Lincoln continually voted the number one "greatest" American president year after year,[738] and why, in 1972, was he voted the second "most beloved hero of all time"?[739] The answers to these questions will be revealed as our story of Forrest's life unfolds.

---

**735**. W. P. Pickett, p. 326; M. Davis, pp. 147-148; Adams and Sanders, p. 192.

**736**. In 1866 Republican Butler was elected to Congress, and in 1883 he became the governor of Massachusetts—the state that launched both American slavery and the American slave trade. Boatner, s.v. "Butler, Benjamin Franklin."

**737**. B. F. Butler, p. 903.

**738**. Ellis, AS, p. 5; Wallechinsky, Wallace, and Wallace, pp. 30-31.

**739**. Wallechinsky, Wallace, and Wallace, p. 2.

# FORT PILLOW & THE KKK: OVERTURNING NORTHERN FOLKLORE

*"I'm . . . aware that at this moment I am regarded in large communities, in the North, with great abhorrence, as a detestable monster, ruthless and swift to take life." — Nathan Bedford Forrest*

## FORT PILLOW: CORRECTING THE LIES

ON NOW TO THE SECOND reason Forrest is persecuted and slandered by so many: the "incident" at Fort Pillow. An entire chapter will later be devoted to this infamous battle.

As we will see the facts clearly show, as Forrest himself stated, that the so-called "massacre" said to have taken place during this engagement on April 12, 1864, was entirely fabricated by "dastardly Yankee reporters."[740] Under oath Forrest and his men would later testify that no atrocities occurred, and that

> all allegations to the contrary are mere malicious inventions, started, nurtured, and accredited at a time, and through a sentiment of strong sectional animosity.[741]

These statements were later corroborated by both Union and

---

740. Wyeth, LGNBF, p. 428.
741. Jordan and Pryor, p. 440.

Confederate witnesses. After all, it was widely understood and accepted, at least in the South, that, as Forrest asserted, nearly everything reported about him in the newspapers were "gotten up merely to affect the elections in the North."[742] "I have been vilified and abused in the papers," he honestly noted, "and accused of things I never did while in the army . . ."[743]

## FORREST & THE KKK

We come now to the third reason the anti-Forrest movement is growing: his involvement with the Ku Klux Klan.

To begin with, the idea that Forrest started the KKK is pure Yankee mythology. The names of the six founders were long ago recorded and are well-known,[744] and Forrest himself was not even aware of the group until at least one year after it was formed,[745] and he did not begin to openly support it until two years after was formed.[746]

Additionally, he did not become involved with the KKK for racist reasons as his critics charge, for at the time it was not a racist organization.[747] Actually, it began as a type of self-protective police and social aid society, made up of both thousands of white *and* thousands of black members[748] (we even have evidence of an all-black KKK that operated for some time in Nashville), its original purpose being to help war widows and their children and to maintain law and order across the South[749] during the rise of pre-Reconstruction tensions and escalating crime (remnants of Lincoln's illegal invasion, which had damaged much of the South's infrastructure).[750]

Indeed, in the genuine original KKK, which lasted only a little over three years (1865-1869) and which is completely unconnected to today's KKK (which began in 1915), the main focus was on unscrupulous

---

**742.** *Report of the Joint Select Committee to Inquire into the Condition of Affairs in the Late Insurrectionary States*, p. 13.

**743.** *Report of the Joint Select Committee to Inquire into the Condition of Affairs in the Late Insurrectionary States*, p. 30.

**744.** Horn, IE, p. 9.

**745.** Horn, IE, pp. 312-314.

**746.** Henry, FWMF, pp. 442-443. The Klan formed in late 1865; Forrest began to support it in 1867.

**747.** Horn, IE, p. 436.

**748.** Lester and Wilson, p. 26; Rogers, KKS, p. 34; Hurst, p. 305.

**749.** Horn, IE, pp. 362-363, 38.

**750.** Browning, p. 98.

Northern whites—known as "carpetbaggers," and on nefarious anti-South Southern whites—known as "scallywags," not on blacks.[751]

It was only later, when carpetbaggers and scallywags encouraged the formation of the black Loyal Leagues—which were used to inculcate freed slaves in Northern anti-South propaganda and train them to use weapons and military tactics to taunt, punish, and even murder their former owners—that the KKK began to understandably turn their attention toward African-Americans.[752]

Again, this was only for self-protection, not for racist purposes. Proof of this is that when carpetbag rule ended (about 1869), the original KKK immediately came to an end as well all across the "Invisible Empire" (i.e., the Southern states). In essence, when Southerners were allowed to take back political control of their own states there was no longer any need for an organization like the KKK.[753]

Today's South-haters also delight in emphasizing "Forrest's role as grand wizard of the Klan." Sadly, this fiction has become so thoroughly entrenched that it was even believed by some Confederate soldiers into the early 1900s.[754]

But in fact there is no irrefutable or even documentary evidence of this, as every klansman took an oath of secrecy,[755] and none ever publically named their leader in print.[756] It was George W. Gordon (the man who some say introduced Forrest to the KKK)[757] who was grand wizard during the 1860s, not Forrest. Gordon's own wife, Ora Susan Paine, later testified to this fact.[758]

Some speculate that at most Forrest may have been the founder of the Tennessee chapter of the KKK.[759] But again, since nothing was ever written down there is no proof even of this theory,[760] and indeed, there is evidence that a man named Minor Meriwether started the

---

751. Horn, IE, pp. 426-439, 365-367, 369.
752. Horn, IE, pp. 3, 26-30.
753. Horn, IE, pp. 376-377.
754. See e.g., Robuck, pp. 118-119.
755. Horn, IE, pp. 312, 36.
756. Henry, FWMF, p. 443.
757. Gordon, a cousin of mine, was captured at Fort Donelson in February 1862. See Morton, p. 363.
758. Wills, p. 336.
759. Page Smith, p. 844.
760. Horn, IE, p. 37.

Tennessee chapter.[761]

In his excellent 655-page Forrest biography, *Life of General Nathan Bedford Forrest* (1899) author John Allan Wyeth—who believed the General was too shrewd to associate himself with an "illegal" organization like the KKK[762]—devotes a mere single paragraph to Forrest's involvement with the group, with no mention of his being grand wizard.[763]

Likewise, Captain John W. Morton (another candidate for the man who introduced Forrest to the organization),[764] a noted Klan member and one who knew more about Forrest and this secret society than anyone else,[765] also wrote a book on the General without mentioning the KKK.[766]

In 1905, Thomas Dixon, Jr. penned a novel called *The Clansman* (the basis for the 1915 film *Birth of a Nation*). A fictionalized account of the development and life of the KKK, neither Forrest's name or even a hint of his personality, appear anywhere in the book.[767]

In 1871 and 1872, under oath, Forrest himself swore that he had not taken an active role in the organization,[768] and in fact had never even been a member, and only knew of it "from information from others."[769]

Whatever the actual facts it is safe to say that he played an important role of some type (most likely as simply a recruiter-advisor and a charismatic symbolic figurehead), for in March 1869, when various splinter groups began to grow racist and violent, a disappointed Forrest, the Klan's most well-respected, best known, and most influential associate, issued a "proclamation of dissolution," ordering the entire KKK to disband.[770]

From that moment on he forever disassociated himself from the

761. Page Smith, p. 844.
762. Horn, IE, p. 313.
763. Wyeth, LGNBF, p. 619.
764. Sheppard, p. 289.
765. Horn, IE, pp. 315-316.
766. Morton, passim.
767. Bradley, pp. 211-212.
768. Wyeth, LGNBF, p. 619.
769. *Report of the Joint Select Committee to Inquire into the Condition of Affairs in the Late Insurrectionary States*, p. 6.
770. Sheppard, p. 291.

organization.[771] Again, a South-loathing U.S. governmental committee later questioned Forrest, but found him innocent of any wrongdoing in connection with the Klan.[772]

## DISLIKE OF FORREST BASED ON YANKEE MYTH

We have now briefly covered and dismantled the three main reasons Forrest is disliked by so many groups and individuals: his ownership of and trade in slaves; his actions at Fort Pillow; and his role in the KKK.

What this plainly illustrates is that for the most part the reasons people detest Forrest are not based on fact, but on "myths" invented by anti-Forrest and anti-South partisans. This is unconscionable, for the truth is there for anyone to study. Thus, it is time for those of us who know the facts, who admire Forrest, who are his blood relations, or who have Southern roots, to speak out in his defense.

## FORREST THE EXEMPLAR

We are not making excuses for him. God knows Forrest was no choirboy. For example, he was literally fearless and was known to have a "killer instinct," a ferocious temperament, and a penchant for violence. Foote rightly called him a slender, fierce giant of a man with a propensity for conflict,[773] while in his memoirs Sherman described Forrest as one of the most dangerous types of men "that this war has turned loose upon the world."[774]

Forrest's own soldiers said he was only afraid of one man in the entire world: his brother, the often frightening five foot, eleven inch, 200-pound, William Hezekiah Forrest.[775] But the General himself was most feared by his enemies. Of his Yankee foes it was said that "Forrest was not a soldier whom they were willing to meet in the dark . . ."[776]

These descriptions perfectly befit the General, who walked about armed with either a knife or a pistol, often both, and who was not

---

771. Wyeth, LGNBF, pp. 619-620.
772. Henry, FWMF, p. 448.
773. Foote, Vol. 1, p. 172.
774. Sherman, Vol. 1, p. 337.
775. A powerfully built reckless man who loved to fight as much as his famous older brother Nathan, it was said that William, though he would give his last penny to someone in need, would shoot a man dead without hesitation for the smallest incitation. Henry, ATSF, p. 257.
776. Jordan and Pryor, p. 643.

afraid to use them, or any other weapon at hand when necessary.[777]

Once, in March 1866, when he was savagely attacked with an ax by a truculent employee named Thomas ("Tom") Edwards (Forrest had simply asked the man to stop beating his wife), the quick-thinking General grabbed the weapon and buried it in Edward's skull, escaping his own bloody demise by less than a hair's breadth.[778] Asked by an acquaintance if he was ever able to reign in his terrible temper, Forrest replied: No sir. I've tried plenty a' times. But I'll be damned if I could do it![779]

He had less hazardous, but still discomforting, traits: he could be rude, insolent, bull-headed, overly sensitive, intimidating, conniving, reckless, and confrontational. And he swore like a sailor and was addicted to gambling.[780]

But are these truly legitimate reasons to dislike Forrest? Hardly.

In the era of the "lynch-law," nearly every citizen of the Old South walked about fully armed.[781] More importantly, most of the above "negative" behaviors ascribed to the General were considered both socially acceptable and even essential for survival on the masculine frontier of America's early Wild West where violence, by necessity, had to be met with violence.[782]

Here, pioneering self-reliance, raw individualism,[783] deadly force,[784] brawny machismo, provincial pride, defensive confrontation,[785] and personal and family honor were the everyday codes that men of the Old South lived by.[786] Frontiersmen like Forrest simply did what they deemed right at the moment, whether it was lawful or not. While sometimes what we would now consider brutal, it was nonetheless an

---

777. Henry, ATSF, p. 26.

778. Browning, p. 97.

779. Bedwell, p. 69.

780. In the spring of 1861 the Grand Jury of Coahoma County, Mississippi, indicted Forrest for gambling. Up for arrest and trial, he was off fighting Yankees in Lincoln's War at the time and could not be found. The court wisely dropped the charges.

781. Here in the South, where guns and hunting have always been a way of life and the Second Amendment is regarded as something akin to a biblical commandment, a large percentage of the population proudly walks about fully armed to this day. The safest American cities remain those with the most legally owned guns.

782. Sheppard, p. 309.

783. Garraty, pp. 66-67.

784. Eckert, p. 212.

785. E. M. Thomas, p. 20.

786. Wills, pp. 15-17.

even-handed form of justice.

Thus the cardboard portrayal of Forrest as the one-dimensional "bad boy" of the South is both unfair and inaccurate, for despite his very real flaws, as we will see, there is much about Forrest that is commendable. In fact, one could say with justification that Forrest, a complex and contradictory man by any definition, possessed many traits that embody the loftiest qualities of humanity.

This is extremely important, for today, in our modern, impersonal, urbanized, high-tech mass society, we have few healthy role models, either for children or adults. Forrest is one of those rare individuals who fills this missing gap, for he is an exemplar whose life inspires and motivates, whatever one's age, color, religion, culture, or nationality. He is truly a man for all ages, people, and times, as will be plainly illustrated throughout this book.

Since Forrest can no longer defend or explain himself, and since the anti-Forrest crowd no longer regards anything positive written about him as factual, I will attempt to speak for him in a new and modern appraisal. To do this we will examine his traits and character in the context of his astonishing life story, one set against the backdrop of the rough-and-tumble life of the 19th-Century pioneer and Lincoln's needless and illicit War.

## A LITERARY MONUMENT TO THE EMBODIMENT OF THE SOUTH

During our exploration to uncover the real Forrest we will build a literary monument to him, one that corrects old falsehoods, polishes his tarnished image, and restores his reputation to its rightful place of glory and honor on the stage of American history. For in Forrest's memory the positive and enriching Old European traditions, beliefs, rituals, and qualities that once made the Old South itself great, live on: love of God, country, family, the Constitution, liberty, the land, one's ancestors, tradition, animals, sports, and hard work.

In this day and age, when the North continues to grow in influence over nearly every aspect of American life (how often do we hear a Southern voice compared to a Northern one on national TV?), and as our Southern heros, symbols, and traditions continue to be mocked, attacked, and eroded by the politically correct, the South is in danger of losing its singular identity altogether.

This nefarious process to obliterate the South—rightly referred to by some as the Yankee/New South campaign of "cultural genocide"[787]—can be slowed down, and even possibly reversed, by a true understanding of Nathan Bedford Forrest. For he naturally functions as a curative and cohesive force, a symbol that binds and preserves one of the world's most unique, fascinating, wondrous, fragile, and quickly disappearing cultures in the world: the American South.

Not the negative stereotyped South created by the North, of cruel, ignorant, aristocratic white slackers, living off slavery on their sprawling plantations, lounging about under magnolia blossoms and Spanish moss by the side of a lazy moonlit river, sipping mint-juleps with one hand, while wielding a whip in the other. But the real South, the one all Southerners love and understand; and the one known by non-Southerners who have visited or come to live and work in Dixie.[788]

As we will see, no one is better suited to the role of national healer than Forrest, who remains, and will always remain, a knight in shining armor to those Southerners (and enlightened non-Southerners) who truly know and understand him. For he is the manly personification of all that it means to be Southern: direct but polite, powerful but merciful, assertive but gentle, a fierce warrior in the face of evil, but a protector of the innocent,[789] women,[790] and family.[791]

More than this he was the great defender of the Confederacy, of states' rights, the agrarian life, the Constitution and government (as they were originally created by the Founding Fathers), and conservative family values. In other words, Forrest was the guardian of the Southern Way, of the South's principles, the very ones that some 2 million Southerners died for[792] during what Robert Penn Warren calls Dixie's "Homeric Period": the War for Southern Independence.[793]

And yet with his courage, ambition, work ethic, individualism,

---

787. See Kennedy and Kennedy, pp. 271-303.

788. For more on the slanderization of the South and the Confederacy from a black perspective, see e.g., Hervey, pp. 11-13, passim.

789. Henry, FWMF, p. 18.

790. Hurst, pp. 216, 365.

791. Wills, p. 334.

792. Timothy Manning, personal correspondence. See also Gragg, p. 240.

793. Horwitz, p. 385.

and pride, he was more than just a great and true Southerner. Forrest was, in essence, the very incarnation of all that it means to be American.

It is these two ideals, being a great Southerner *and* a great American, that make Forrest so special and so interesting. More importantly this is also what makes him the ideal ambassador between South and North in a nation still deeply divided a century and a half after Lincoln's War.

To gain an authentic understanding of this complex and fascinating man, we will begin our journey in 1821, in the wilderness of what was then America's Wild West: my home, Middle Tennessee.

# Part 3

# FROM RURAL FARMER TO URBAN MILLIONAIRE

# - 1821 TO 1844 -
# ANGLO-CELTIC YEOMAN ROOTS:
# FORREST'S BIRTH & CHILDHOOD ON
# AMERICA'S WESTERN FRONTIER

"No one knows the embarrassment I labor under
when I'm thrown into the company of educated
persons." — Nathan Bedford Forrest

## TENNESSEE BIRTH

ORIGINALLY NATIVE-AMERICAN TERRITORY, TENNESSEE takes its name from the Cherokee word *Tanasi*, the name of a Cherokee village on the Little Tennessee River. Tennessee's Native-American name is a fitting one for the birthplace of the energetic, quick-tempered, and impulsive boy who came into the world in that state, along with a fragile twin sister, Fanny, on July 13, 1821.

For this child of Nature, born in dire poverty in a dirt-floored log cabin in the Duck River region near Chapel Hill, Bedford County, spent his early years on the unbridled edge of civilization, living little different than the Cherokee themselves. His very surname, Forrest, personifies the natural world in which he grew, lived, played, and toiled during his first decade and a half.

His parents' humble home with a fenced-in yard, situated on the roughly rutted public road, was so primitive that daylight could be seen through the chinks between the logs. Through these gapping holes blew both the sizzling hot breezes of summer and the numbing icy winds of winter. The floor was made of logs cut in half, the split side up, while massive beams, held together with wooden pegs, supported the roof.

This crudely built, single-room cedar-log structure, with ill-fitting doors and an enormous fireplace at one end, was a mere 18 by 20 feet (360 square feet). The large common room was used during the day, while at night the entire family slept in a small "sleeping loft" built into the rafters. The rude abode, located on the edge of what was then America's most westerly and civilized boundary, and surrounded by endless miles of virgin woodlands, housed the Forrests for the next nine years, from 1821 to 1830.[794]

FORREST'S PARENTS

The man of the house, William Forrest (1798-1837), was a tall, well-built, English-Irish-American mule-trader and blacksmith from North Carolina. His wife, Mariam Beck (1802-1887),[795] also tall and robust, was a Scots-Irish-American pioneer whose parents emigrated from South Carolina to Caney Springs, Tennessee, in 1796, the year the Volunteer State was admitted to the Union. William and Mariam married in Bedford County, Tennessee, in 1820, the year of the Missouri Compromise, for the South an ill omen of things to come.

As is still true in many Southern homes today the Forrest household was more matriarchal than patriarchal, with Mariam ruling the family with a stern but loving hand. She was a strict Victorian mother who expected her children to mind her, and to work hard and keep themselves neat and clean. In return she provided a warm and safe household for her loved ones. Like most Victorian children, Forrest both worshiped and feared his mother until his dying day, calling her "the best woman I ever knew."

William and Mariam were intrepid pioneers who descended from plain, honest, straightforward, restless, robust, thrifty, independent, temperate, fearless, vigorous, active, bright, self-reliant, hard-working European stock, characteristics they passed on to their

---

794. This was indeed early America: the year Forrest was born, the U.S. was a mere forty-three years old, Thomas Jefferson was still alive, there were only twenty-three states, and the total U.S. population numbered about 7,480,000 people (the population of New York City today). James Monroe, America's fifth president, was in the White House.

795. Some records spell her first name Miriam.

first-born son, a boy they named Nathan Bedford Forrest. To his credit, Forrest would never stray far from the Southern agrarian life he loved, remaining loyal to his plebeian, yeoman roots until the day he died.

## FORREST'S THREE NAMES

Forrest's character, and indeed his entire life story, can be understood, in part, through an understanding of his three names.

His first derives from his paternal grandfather, Nathan Forrest (1776-1827),[796] a tough English-American pioneer[797] who moved his family westward from Orange County, North Carolina, to the wilds of Tennessee in 1806, buying 150 acres on Caney Spring Creek in 1810—where Forrest would be born eleven years later.

Forrest's middle name, Bedford,[798] comes from the Middle Tennessee county he was born in.[799] Naming children after grandparents and localities (especially Southern towns, counties, and states) were part of the naming tradition in the Old South, and it continues among proud and true Southerners to this day.

I have not been able to trace Forrest's paternal ancestors back past 17th-Century America, to their European origins. But it is my opinion, despite the oft repeated phrase by some of his other biographers that "the Forrests are of Celtic origins," that the earliest members of this family were English, a view I base on etymology.

The Forrest family crest (which displays a large tree) and the Forrest family's Latin motto, *Vivunt dum Virent* ("they live as long as they [the trees] are green"), only reinforces this view: the surname Forrest is English and derives from the Old English *forest*, meaning "woods," or in Medieval times, "an enclosed forest (usually set aside for hunting) owned

---

796. Nathan is a Jewish (Hebrew) name, meaning "a gift," or "given of God." This biblical name was usually given to a child for religious reasons; to remind him or her of their spiritual duties on earth and the promised heavenly rewards to come. However, in Forrest's case, in one of the many great ironies of his life, he was a man who wavered between agnosticism and faith up until his last days.

797. Forrest's paternal grandmother was Jane Ledbetter, of English heritage. Ledbetter is the modern spelling of the Old English words, *lēad bēatere*, a "lead beater"; one who worked in lead. Reaney and Wilson, s.v. "Leadbeater."

798. Bedford is English and derives from the Old English man's first name *Bīeda* and the Old English word *ford* (a river-crossing). Thus *Bīedaford* means "Bieda's river-crossing." As early as the year 880 the name was written *Bedanford*, and in 1086 it was spelled *Bedeford* in William the Conqueror's *Doomsday Book*. Over time this became corrupted and modernized to Bedford. Mills, s.v. "Bedford."

799. The part of Bedford County in which Forrest was born (in what is now the city of Chapel Hill) is today part of Marshall County.

by a royal family or wealthy individual." The surname can thus be either a toponym for "one who lived in or near a forest," or a metonymic occupational name for "one who works in a forest," or who is a "keeper of a forest."[800]

## SCOTTISH ORIGINS?

While Forrest is normally considered an English surname with deep Anglo-Saxon roots, it was also found in early Scotland where it appears in Medieval records as an occupational name for Scottish-born forest workers.

For example, in 14th-Century Scotland, a name like "William de Forrest" would not have been unknown, particularly in the area of Dumfriesshire where we have chronicles of Scots with the surname *de Forrest* living and working in the royal woods at the time.[801] Some of these Scottish *de Forrest* families may have eventually made their way to America's South, where they dropped the preposition "de" and became Scottish-Americans known by the surname Forrest.

While this theory cannot be ruled out for Nathan Bedford Forrest's own origins, I consider it highly unlikely. Until ironclad proof emerges either way, however, it is best to keep an open mind.

We can say then that Forrest's paternal line at least was almost certainly of English derivation, for the General himself is a direct descendant of royal English ancestors (Edward I "Longshanks" King of England, for example, is Forrest's twenty-first great-grandfather).[802] And indeed early biographies describe his earliest known ancestors as of "English parentage."

No doubt his oft-discussed Celtic heritage came through his mother's side of the family, which was Scots-Irish. It is safest to say then, as Jordan and Pryor assert, that he is "of pure, though mixed, British stock."[803]

---

800. Reaney and Wilson, s.v. "Forrest." The English word forest derives from the Old French word *forestier*, which derives from the Late Latin word *forestis*, a derivative of *foris*, meaning "outside." Mish, s.v. "forest."
801. Dorward, s.v. "Forrest."
802. I discovered this fact during my genealogical research on the Forrest family.
803. Jordan and Pryor, p. 18.

OCCUPATION: FORRESTER

Despite the spelling used by Forrest and his own family, it would appear that originally, many centuries ago, their surname was Forrester, as some of his earlier ancestors spelled the name in this fashion.[804] Nonetheless, the surname Forrester is also English, with the same etymology as Forrest, but with the specific meaning, "an officer in charge of the forest" (Forrester can also sometimes mean "a worker in the forest").[805]

From this we can be quite certain that one of Nathan Bedford Forrest's earliest English ancestors was either a forest worker or a watchman over a royal family's private forest,[806] and that this individual probably spelled the name *Le Forester* or *DeForest*. (One very early English timberman, living in Hitcham, Suffolk County, is listed in the year 1277 as Robertus *forestarius*, the latter word being Middle Latin for "forester.")[807]

A probable paternal ancestor of Forrest's was Sir Thomas Forrest,[808] an Englishman of royal blood, who settled at Jamestown,

---

804. See Forrest's family tree, Appendix E.

805. Reaney and Wilson, s.v. "Forester."

806. In ancient and Medieval times the forester who guarded a private woods was sometimes not paid. Instead he was given special privileges, such as the right to keep his farm animals (e.g., pigs) in the woods, or gather up any trees or branches (for firewood) that had been knocked down during inclement weather. The Medieval forester was also allowed a single log for his Christmas fire. Reaney and Wilson, s.v. "Forester."

807. Other early spellings were: *le Forestier* ("the forester"), *ate Forest* (one who works "at the forest"), and *del fforest* (a shortening of *de le forest*, meaning one "of the forest"; that is, one who lives or works in the forest). Beginning in the modern period (1500s), the preposition (de, le, del, la, etc.) was usually dropped from one's surname. Modern spellings of this surname include: Forrest, Forester, Forrester, Forestier, and Forrestor. Reaney and Wilson, s.v. "Forester."

808. There are other noted individuals associated with this line. Thomas Forrest's wife, Mrs. Forrest (her first and maiden names are unknown), is often referred to as "America's First Lady," since, in 1608, she was the first recorded European woman to step foot ashore at Jamestown—thirteen years before the Pilgrims landed at Plymouth Rock, Massachusetts. National Park Service Website, Colonial National Historical Park, Jamestown Historic Briefs: "The Indispensable Role of Women in Virginia." Website: www.nps.gov/archive/colo/Jthanout/Women.html. See also the Website of the Association for the Preservation of Virginia Antiquities: "Jamestown Rediscovery: Burial 2, JR156C." Website: www.apva.org/finding/jr156c.html. Mrs. Forrest's title discounts the fact that the Vikings, led by the Scandinavian explorer Leif Eriksson, actually landed in North America nearly six centuries earlier; for the Viking settlement at *L'Anse aux Meadows*, Newfoundland, founded about the year 1,000—some 500 years before Columbus—has been proven authentic. See the official Website of "L'Anse aux Meadows National Historic Site of Canada": www.pc.gc.ca/lhn-nhs/nl/meadows/index_e.asp. There was also Mrs. Forrest's maid, Englishwoman Anne Burras, said to have been "the first European woman to marry in North America," when she wed Jamestown settler John Laydon in December 1608. *Archaeology*, Vol. 52, No. 2, March/April 1999; Newsbriefs: "Jamestown's First Lady," Elizabeth J. Himelfarb. Website: www.archaeology.org/9903/newsbriefs/jamestown.html. However, since the Pagan Vikings preceded Anne by 600 years (and doubtless celebrated numerous marriages on North American soil), it would be more

Virginia, in 1607,[809] while on the maternal side Forrest could claim
Celtic blood through his mother's many Irish and Scottish forebears.[810]

Names are destiny, and as such, for all eternity Forrest's three
names will deeply connect him with family pride, manly honor,
Tennessee, early America, Southern roots, pioneer ancestry, the great
outdoors, and royal European (Anglo-Saxon and Celtic) heritage.

## THE AGRARIAN LIFE AT FORREST'S BOYHOOD HOME

In 1830, when Forrest was just nine years old, his father William
obtained a parcel of land from Mr. W. S. Mayfield, of Chapel Hill,
Tennessee, who had constructed a log cabin on the property about 1825.     .
It was into this log and frame house that the Forrests moved in 1830, a
home ideally suited to their way of life.

William had made a utilitarian real estate deal. Besides the log
home, the acreage included a double crib log barn, a log corn crib, and
a frame smokehouse. These additions were important because like a
majority of Southern families at the time, the Forrests were small
landowners, yeoman farmers who lived primarily from planting and
harvesting corn, wheat, oats, and cotton.

Also on the farmstead was a stone-lined well, a limestone fence,
and several barbeque pits (local oral tradition has it that Forrest later
returned here during Lincoln's War to hold "recruiting barbeques," an
ingenious method of military enrollment if there ever was one).

A tiny piece of cleared land supplied flowers and garden

---

historically correct to say that Anne and John were the first Europeans to hold a *Christian* wedding in the
Americas.

**809.** See B. F. Johnson, pp. 334-338. The General also has Celtic blood on his father's side; in this case,
Welsh, through his paternal grandmother Nancy Shepherd Baugh (b. 1781). Baugh is an anglicization of the
Welsh word *bach*, meaning "little" (probably at first indicating one of small stature, or conversely, a tall or
large person). Reaney and Wilson, s.v. "Baugh."

**810.** Forrest's mother, Mariam Beck, who is said to come from Irish and Scottish stock, actually possesses
what would ordinarily be considered an English surname. While Beck has a number of different possible
etymologies, the most common one derives from the Middle English word *bekke*, meaning a brook, thus
indicating "one who dwells by the stream." Reaney and Wilson, s.v. "Beck." Like many English surnames,
however, Beck is not uncommon in Ireland (particularly in Ulster), either due to English immigration or to
the forced adoption of English surnames by the Irish under various periods of Anglo domination.
MacLysaght, s.v. "Beck." There is another possible explanation for why Mariam is said to be of Irish origins
but has an English-like surname: it may simply be an anglicized form of the Irish surname *Ó Béice*, from the
Irish word *béice*, meaning "weeping" (thus, *Ó Béice* indicates "one from the clan of the weeping one"). The
name, also sometimes anglicized in Ireland as the surnames Beakey and Bakey, is found predominately in
Counties Clare and Wicklow. MacLysaght, s.v. "Beck" and "Beakey."

vegetables (and seed for the following year), while an orchard of small apple, peach, and pear trees provided fresh fruit. These may have been be canned and then stored through the long winter months in the house's cellar, or perhaps in a cool limestone cavern that can still be seen on the property.

Wild game supplemented the family's diet, with William's meager earnings as a smithy rounding out their impoverished lifestyle. Like all rural farming families, the Forrests awoke before sunrise and retired after sundown, eating their breakfast and dinner by candlelight.

The pioneer family owned livestock as well, cattle, mules, and chickens, but mainly horses, which the young Forrest was particularly adept at riding and caring for.[811] It is said that as a child he "practically lived upon the backs of these noble animals," which he rode "with the skill . . . of Comanches."[812]

The Forrests would live at the 1825 Mayfield house, in this bucolic Eden in Middle Tennessee, for three and a half years.[813]

## FORREST'S CHILDHOOD

Forrest led an extremely active life as a young boy, the nearly limitless expanse of the great outdoors being his personal playground. His family's log home was located near the farm of his uncle Orrin Beck (1803-1868), whose large, loud, Celtic clan provided the young Forrest with numerous playmates.[814]

With his Beck cousins[815] he spent countless hours climbing trees, cooling off in the local swimming hole, fishing, hunting with their dogs, and racing horses. One of his favorite pastimes was "brag and bluff," a game he would use to great benefit—and one for which he would

---

811. Along with horses, Forrest also had a profound love for dogs.

812. Wyeth, LGNBF, p. 14.

813. The rustic house, known as "the Nathan Bedford Forrest Boyhood Home," is now being preserved and restored by the Sons of Confederate Veterans' "Forrest Boyhood Home Committee," at Chapel Hill, Tennessee. See *Confederate Veteran*, July/August, 2006, "SCV Mechanized Cavalry Visits Elm Springs," p. 48.

814. Orrin Beck was Forrest's mother's brother. Decades later, on June 11, 1864, Forrest and his staff and escort would spend the night at Orrin's house during the Battle of Brice's Cross Roads (Jordan and Pryor, p. 481)—widely considered to be Forrest's greatest military achievement. Mathes, p. 247.

815. I do not know the names of Orrin Beck's children with any certainty, but some of their names may have been: William, John, Joshua, Fredonia, Darthula, Morning, Orrin, Jr., and James. Orrin's wife may have been Nancy Ann Mourning Davis.

become famous—on the battlefields of Lincoln's War some forty odd years later.

Known for his undaunted spirit and for possessing "excellent lungs," a neighbor, Mrs. Putnam, later recalled that while playing, Forrest could make more noise, and while being whipped by his mother, could yell louder, than any of the other children in Chapel Hill.[816] (His boisterous voice too would later come in handy during Lincoln's War, where he would use it to excellent effect to cut through the noise while leading his men amidst the din of battle.)

The entire Forrest family was distinguished for its intense high energy, but this trait was most strongly manifested in the oldest son, whose blue-grey eyes burned strangely with a fiery, piercing light—particularly during the heat of battle—until the day he died. At the Battle of Sacramento, Kentucky, for example, one fellow officer, Major David C. Kelley, later described Forrest's eyes as "blazing with the intense glare of a panther's springing upon its prey."[817] Eyewitnesses recount that even when deathly ill or wounded, his eyes continued to emit an unearthly glow.

This characteristic, a brilliant, indomitable energy that shone through the eyes, was one of the most commented on by those who encountered Forrest. Even his enemies on the field of action could not help but notice it.[818] Forrest was fortunate indeed to possess such a mysterious driving inner force, for it sustained him from the very beginning of his difficult and eventful life, one he would later accurately refer to as a "battle from the start."[819]

EDUCATION

Born into rural impoverishment with little time and no funds for formal education, Forrest did not experience childhood as we know it today.[820] Instead, he entered adulthood almost as soon as he could walk, for education was practically an inessential luxury at the time, while child

---

816. Wyeth, LGNBF, p. 13.
817. Jordan and Pryor, pp. 53-54.
818. N. Bradford, p. 521.
819. Wyeth, LGNBF, p. 622.
820. Jordan and Pryor, p. 34.

labor was an absolute necessity among early pioneer families.[821] Indeed, Forrest was already a seasoned frontiersman before reaching his teens.

While his childhood peers in the big, wealthy Eastern cities were learning the "three R's" at public school, Forrest was being "home-schooled" by life on the frontier, with Mother-Nature as his "teacher." His "classroom" was the wilderness, his "lessons" were clearing land, farming, hunting, and buying and selling livestock. In this way Forrest's education was largely one of hands-on personal experience rather than one derived from books.[822]

But Forrest, though largely self-taught, was not completely deprived of a proper English education, nor was he illiterate, as his critics assert. At the time (1820s through the 1830s), public schools in Tennessee (and also in Mississippi) met once a year for three-month terms during the winter.[823] This allowed children of these largely rural states to be at home on their farms during the all-important planting (spring), cultivating (summer), and harvest (fall) seasons, when they were needed most by their families.[824] Thus it was during the winter of 1833, while still living in Middle Tennessee, that the twelve year-old Forrest got his first three months of a six-month education.[825]

Here he was taught the rudimentary skills of "readin', writin,' and 'rithmetic" at the town's local schoolhouse, a crude log structure about the size of his own family's home, with a large fireplace at one end and a split-log floor. As was the tradition in the 1830s, Forrest, being one of the older children, sat in the back of the room, with the youngest sitting in front.

Despite even this modest education, Forrest grew up with less book learning than most of the children he attended school with, which was his own doing. Like most Southern boys at the time, he hated sitting in class and would have much preferred to be outdoors hunting with his dogs, or horse-racing with his cousins and brothers (as a teen, these were

---

821. Early American families normally had as many children as possible, for the sole purpose of creating a large free work force. That children were considered an economic asset can be seen in one of the common wedding toasts of the day: "Health to the groom, not forgetting myself; and here's to the bride, thumping luck and big children." Doddridge, p. 156.
822. Wills, p. 11; Lytle, p. 17.
823. Mathes, p. 4.
824. Sheppard, p. 16.
825. Henry, FWMF, p. 23.

his main forms of recreation). As such, the overly energetic child seldom studied or listened to his teachers, making the small amount of education he did receive of questionable value at times.

A natural-born outdoorsman who disliked being idle, young Forrest was described by one of his teachers, Colonel John Laws, as having an abundance of common sense, but at the same time, as one who would not apply himself to his studies. An innate athlete, he was much more interested in wrestlin' than studyin', Laws observed. Forrest remembered his teacher Mr. Laws as well, but only for the number of whippings he had received from him.[826]

Forrest's distaste for the art of learning endured throughout his life and, as we will discover, both helped and hindered him, even playing a small role in the Confederacy's downfall.[827] Though outwardly he pretended not to care, he certainly, at times, became defensive about his limited schooling, and often felt uncomfortable around the more educated. "I never see a pen," he once bristled, "but what I think of a snake."[828]

In early 19ᵗʰ-Century Tennessee, however, there was something even more important than education to the Western pioneer: survival.

In the "rude and reckless society" Forrest lived in, where life was cheap, where one's honor was sacred, where lawlessness was the law,

---

826. Parks, p. 78; Lytle, p. 14.

827. It was not Forrest's lack of education itself that helped bring down the Confederacy. (Indeed, his brilliance as a commander might have helped the South win, as a postwar President Davis later opined, had he been given command of larger forces.) Rather, it was, in part, his lack of education that provoked prejudice against him. Not only that, it created a distrust in Forrest against those who had attended military school, which included nearly all of his superiors. Was it sour grapes? Or did his astonishing innate grasp of warfare justify his feelings of superiority? No doubt it was some of both. In any event, Forrest found it difficult, and in many instances impossible, to get along with his fellow officers, whose orders he sometimes ignored or actually overrode. In particular he detested West Pointers ("West Pinters," he called them), believing that he knew more about the art of war than could ever be taught at that or any other military school. This was certainly true in many cases, but acting superior to his college educated peers did not help his career, or the Rebel Cause. Instead, it gave him the reputation among the Confederate top brass as being little more than a plucky but insubordinate raider, which delayed and prevented promotion. His insubordination was sometimes taken to extremes, such as when he threatened the lives of other Confederate officers. One of them, General Earl Van Dorn, was only saved from certain death because another officer came upon the scene at the last moment. Forrest's arguments with generals like John Bell Hood, and in particular, Braxton Bragg, are legendary, and as we will see, had profound consequences for the South. There can be little question that this type of behavior hindered Forrest's military career, and in doing so changed the outcome of the War. It is just one of this complex man's many contradictions: he was a great leader who could not be led.

828. Wyeth, LGNBF, p. 580.

where "steel and bullet" ruled, and where even the ordinary citizen went about armed, the athletic farm boy learned how to survive through determination, grit, self-reliance, confidence, fortitude, bluff and bluster, sheer will power, self defense, and even violence.[829] By necessity Forrest thus became a crack shot, an expert horseman, and a formidable fighter at a very tender age, traits that would come back to both reward and haunt him later in life.

### FORREST & AN UNLUCKY PANTHER

An event that typified these characteristics occurred in 1837, when he was just 16.

One evening his mother Mariam and her sister Fanny Beck were riding home after visiting a distant neighbor, when they were attacked by a panther at the creek near the Forrest cabin.[830] No doubt drawn by the smell and sound of a basket of baby chickens Mrs. Forrest had been carrying, the big cat had sprung from the bushes, sinking its claws into her and her terrified horse.

Though seriously mauled, being a frontierswoman Mariam was not only tough and smart, she was also an excellent rider, and she and Fanny managed to spur themselves up the creek bank to safety. Spooked, the panther ran off and was seen no more.

Hearing the nearby screams of the big cat and the shouts of the two women, Forrest and his younger siblings raced outside to investigate. The quick thinking son carried his mother, now covered in blood from deep lacerations in her neck and shoulder, into their log cabin where he adroitly dressed her wounds with turpentine.

Always intensely protective of kinfolk, the youngster listened with rapt excitement to every detail of the story, deciding there and then to track the panther down and avenge his family. "Mother," he said, "I am going to kill that beast if it stays on the earth."[831] Against her earnest protestations, the rash boy flew out the door with his beloved dogs, Nero, Plunger, and Gammon, to go in search of his quarry.

It was not long before his hounds caught the cat's scent and

---

829. Henry, ATSF, p. 26.
830. In some versions of the story the animal is also referred to as a mountain lion or puma.
831. Wyeth, LGNBF, p. 10.

chased it up a tree. Forrest, a born hunter, settled in for the night at its base, patiently waiting for morning to come. In the pitch blackness of the woods he could not afford to wound the animal with an ill-aimed shot. He would only have one opportunity to make a clean kill, otherwise he himself might be attacked and injured, or worse.

At dawn's first light he put fresh powder in his flintlock and leveled the weapon at his prey, who was laid out on a limb hissing and spitting at the dogs. The crackling report of the gun was shortly followed by the dull thud of the panther falling limply to the ground, expertly shot through the heart.

The proud teenaged rifleman cut off the scalp and ears of the huge feline as trophies to show his family and friends. In a few years, Forrest would be tracking and hunting Yankees with the same fearlessness and determination.

HARD WORK & ILLNESS
Forrest's father William spent most of his days in his log blacksmith shop, the smithy, located across the road from their log cabin home. Here his skillful usage of bellows, anvil, tongs, and hammer helped the family scrap out a meager living. Forrest often labored by his father's side in the smithy as helper and metallurgical apprentice, deftly learning the ferric arts of casting, welding, forging, and shoeing.

Despite the father-and-son team's efforts the blacksmith trade never earned enough money to raise the Forrest family up and out of indigence. Thus shopping outings to the "big city" were out of the question. Instead, nearly everything was either grown or handmade on their farm. Only occasionally could basic staples, such as coffee, sugar, salt, and flour, be purchased from the country general store, located miles away from the Forrest farmstead.

While Bedford County, Tennessee, was becoming rich from its slave economy (by 1818, one-fourth of the county was made up of African-American servants),[832] and while William's own grandfather (Forrest's great-grandfather), Shadrack Forrest (born about 1755), had been a slave owner, William himself was far too poor to afford

---

832. Lytle, p. 15.

indentured servants.[833] For this reason, this period of his son's life was one of brutal privation and unending menial labor, the typical daily fight for survival inherent to the lower classes.

One reason for this was that, though still a lad, Forrest was the oldest male. Thus, the bulk of labor fell on his young shoulders. Yet, no matter how long and how hard he worked each day for his family, there was never enough money. In this way he was brought up, as Napoleon taught, in the best of all military schools: "poverty," an academy that prepared the young Forrest well for the road ahead, one he could not have imagined at the time.

Surviving his first ten years was a feat in and of itself. While details are obscure, we know that all three of Forrest's sisters (including his twin, Fanny) and two of his eight brothers all perished from disease (typhoid fever) while still in their youth.[834] The area they lived in being "insalubrious" and "bug infested," young Forrest himself almost died from the same malady (later, some even attributed his death in 1877, in part, to "malarial fever").

Indeed, at the time he fell ill, so desperately poor was his health that he was not even aware that Fanny had passed away; he only learned of the tragedy later. Unlike his twin sister he managed to recover. But only after a long rehabilitation. This experience imbued him, at an early age, with genuine fortitude and with a true appreciation for life.

As the Forrest family struggled to carve a living out of the western wilds of Middle Tennessee, an event was taking place in the North that would forever alter the face of the United States. In the process, young Forrest's own fortunes, and future, would change dramatically.

---

833. Curiously, during Lincoln's War, Forrest told one of his commanders, Gen. Richard Taylor, that his father William had been a "trader in negroes and mules." R. Taylor, p. 200. Whether Forrest was embellishing the truth to create a more interesting story, or whether his father actually was a slave trader in the early 1830s, is unknown. Currently, however, there is no evidence to support Forrest's statement. The fact is that even an inexpensive slave, one costing under $400 (Foote, Vol. 1, p. 536)—the equivalent of $9,000 today, would have been well beyond William's means, even at the peak of his money-earning period as a smithy in Middle Tennessee. And there are no records, letters, reports, or censuses mentioning William as either a slave owner or a slave trader. Another Forrest mystery.

834. Many of the important dates in Forrest's life are today unknown. This is chiefly because the Forrest Family Bible, along with numerous private documents and papers pertaining to his family and relations, were lost when his temporary home on President's Island (near Memphis, Tennessee), burned down sometime around September 1877. Mathes, p. 22.

## THE NEW ENGLAND "ENGINE"

Twenty-eight years before Forrest's birth, in 1793, New Englander Eli Whitney invented the cotton gin (a word derived from "engine"),[835] a machine that could clean cotton at a greatly improved rate of speed.[836] But rather than diminish the need for slavery, as one might expect, it helped to increase and perpetuate it, as even Lincoln admitted on October 13, 1858:

> Mr. [Preston Smith] Brooks, of South Carolina, once said, and truly said, that when this government was established, no one expected the institution of slavery to last until this day; and that the men who formed this government were wiser and better than the men of these days; but the men of these days had experience which the fathers had not, and that experience had taught them the invention of the cotton-gin, and this had made the perpetuation of the institution of slavery a necessity in this country.[837]

Before 1793 a single slave had to work an entire day to clean a pound of cotton, which entailed removing thirty to forty green, sticky seeds—embedded inside each fluffy boll of upland cotton—by hand. The gin, however, expedited this slow, cumbersome process through mechanization. Inside the hand-cranked machine, a roller with wire teeth caught the pesky seeds, separating them from the highly prized white cotton fibers.[838]

Now, with Whitney's newfangled contraption, one person could clean fifty pounds of cotton a day. Since more cotton could be cleaned more quickly, more human laborers were needed. Not only did this aid in increasing an already burgeoning slave trade, it also made growing the fibrous plant extremely lucrative.

Business-savvy farmers quickly changed their main crop (typically tobacco) over to cotton and bought more slaves, transforming the institution from a largely family-run patriarchal system into a highly

---

835. Unfortunately for Whitney his invention was stolen, and he ended up spending most of the profits he earned from the ingenious machine on lawsuits and legal defense. Parry, s.v. "Whitney, Eli." The perspicacious inventor died thirty-six years before Lincoln's War, a conflict to which he indirectly and unknowingly contributed.

836. See Wilson and Ferris, s.v. "Cotton Culture."

837. Nicolay and Hay, ALCW, Vol. 1, p. 480.

838. R. S. Phillips, s.v. "Whitney, Eli."

dynamic commercial one.[839] Thus Yankee Whitney and his gin were largely responsible for keeping an institution alive, which, as we have seen, the abolitionist South never wanted to begin with.

From this moment forward, slavery became ever more profitable, an irresistible lure for large Southern land owners.[840]

For those pursuing the cotton dream, however, there was one thing still standing in the way of complete success. Native-Americans.

## NATIVE-AMERICANS & KING COTTON

European-Americans had broken away from King George III (1738-1820),[841] but had put a new royal in his place: cotton. One of King Cotton's first edicts was to obtain as much new land in rural areas as possible so that more and bigger cotton plantations could be built. The "problem" was that Native-Americans—who were by and large nomadic hunters—were still living across, and owned,[842] great swaths of America's most fertile crop lands,[843] lands needed by the new large cotton planters. Clearly the hunting lifestyle was impeding the progress of the farming lifestyle, now dedicated to King Cotton. The "red hunters" would have to be relocated.

In 1830, with the approval of President Andrew Jackson, the U.S. Congress passed the Indian Removal Bill, which forever sealed the fate of the hunting natives. Jackson, who already had a long history warring with and conquering Indians, had campaigned on the idea of Indian removal, illustrating its immense popularity with white America at the time.[844]

---

839. Curti, Thorp, and Baker, p. 507.

840. Fogel and Engerman, pp. 89, 93.

841. George III (my eighth cousin), whose full name was George William Frederick, was king of Great Britain and Ireland from 1760-1820, and also elector (1760-1815), then king of Hanover from 1815-1820. He supported a policy that led to war and the eventual loss of the American colonies, a conflict known as the Revolutionary War in what was to become the U.S. Toward the end of his life George became blind, then went insane, his son, George IV—full name George Augustus Frederick (1762-1830)—acting as regent until his father's death in 1820. Neilson, s.v. "George III," s.v. "George IV." At the onset of the War for Southern Independence in 1861, Southerners came to consider their fight against Northern tyranny the "Second Revolutionary War" and compared Lincoln with King George III.

842. It is a myth that Native-Americans did not buy, own, and sell land. See e.g., Deloria, p. 15.

843. In Tennessee, Forrest's home state, the main Native-American tribes were the Cherokee, Chickasaw, and the Shawnee. The Creek and Choctaw were also found across various parts of the South. All were eventually pushed off their lands, or bought out, by emigrating Europeans. Jahoda, pp. 50, 162.

844. Jahoda, pp. 39-41.

And so, as ordained by Providence,[845] under the banner of America's Manifest Destiny[846] (which made the eradication of Native-American society permissible[847] and the establishment of European-American rule absolute[848]), began the forced relocation of thousands of Indians from their aboriginal lands onto reservations.[849]

U.S. imperialism, the unavoidable path of Manifest Destiny, had begun in earnest,[850] a trend that would have appalled the Founding Fathers. In 1867 Yankee William H. Seward, once Lincoln's secretary of state, summed up the new way of thinking:

> Give me fifty, forty, thirty more years of life, and I will engage to give you the possession of the American continent and the control of the world.[851]

Untold numbers of Native-Americans were disenfranchised, imprisoned, killed, and pushed from America's Southland by Union soldiers during this unfortunate but inevitable period in American history,[852] a period which the Indians have aptly called "the Trail of Tears."[853] In the 1830s alone some 85,000 Cherokee, Choctaw, Creek, Seminole, and Chickasaw were forcibly removed from the southeastern states to reservations located just west of Arkansas.[854] During the Cherokee Trail of Tears, in the winter of 1838-1839, one out of every four individuals perished from disease, cold, or hunger,[855] about 4,000 in total.[856]

So that European society could expand, Native society had to diminish; and they would do so voluntarily or at the end of a rifle. "Assimilation or extermination" became the slogan of the U.S.

---

845. P. J. Buchanan, p. 141.
846. D. Brown, p. 8.
847. J. W. Ward, p. 145.
848. J. M. McPherson, BCF, pp. 45-46.
849. Lytle, p. 15.
850. P. J. Buchanan, p. 167.
851. Farrar, p. 113.
852. Tocqueville marvelously chronicled this dark chapter in American history through the eyes of a European. See Tocqueville, Vol. 1, pp. 364-380.
853. Jahoda, passim.
854. J. M. McPherson, BCF, p. 45.
855. D. Brown, p. 7.
856. K. L. Hall, s.v. "Native Americans."

government,[857] a nation whose ruling policy was that "any power" that presented a barrier to European expansion into the American West was to be expelled, peacefully or violently.[858]

Between 1840 and 1850 whites purchased some 20,000,000 acres from the Indians at a cost of about fifteen cents an acre (for a total cost of about $3,000,000, or some $85,000,000 in today's currency). In return, Native-Americans were shuttled onto a mere 4,000,000 acres of land that had already been rejected by whites and was unsuitable for human occupation.[859] By 1860 two-thirds of the original Native-American population was gone.[860] A European-American song of the day captured the mood of the land-hungry cotton planters:

> All I want in this creation
> Is a pretty little wife and a big plantation
> Away up yonder in the Cherokee nation.[861]

## THE UNION'S WAR AGAINST NATIVE-AMERICANS

Building a "big plantation in the Cherokee nation," however, was not as easy as this simple tune suggests.

Under the "genocidal policy" of the U.S.,[862] countless treaties broken by the government had made Native-Americans distrustful of nearly all whites. Indian resistance to the European "invasion" escalated, along with violence and death.[863]

The U.S. government's reaction was immediate and severe. Faced with a crusade of ethnic cleansing,[864] Indians had but two choices: become part of European-American society, or perish.[865] Most reluctantly opted for the former, but many decided on neither, and fought white encroachment well into the 1890s. White frontier families grew up with the doctrine "there ain't no game like Injuns,"[866] for

---

857. Bailyn, Dallek, Davis, Donald, Thomas, and Wood, p. 106.
858. P. J. Buchanan, p. 60.
859. Jahoda, p. 312.
860. D. Brown, p. 9.
861. J. C. Harris, p. 216.
862. K. L. Hall, s.v. "Native Americans."
863. Jahoda, p. 135.
864. DiLorenzo, LU, p. 114.
865. Ellis, AS, p. 240.
866. Jahoda, p. 135.

dehumanizing the enemy made it easier for the military to eliminate them.

The motto "the only good Indian is a dead Indian," later famously reiterated by the likes of Yankee officers General Philip Henry Sheridan[867] and General William Tecumseh Sherman,[868] now became the official policy of the U.S. Government,[869] shades of things to come. In a few short decades this same political body, and these very same men, would turn their violent, imperialistic attentions on the Southern States, with similar tragic results.

Indeed, the parallels between the antebellum Indian War and Lincoln's ensuing War of 1861 are striking. Ever since the 16th Century, thousands of former black slaves had escaped into the non-American Western territories, only to become slaves of Native-Americans.[870] Their original white owners wanted them back, and the U.S. government, operating under the Constitution and the Fugitive Slave

---

867. Thomas C. Leonard, "The Reluctant Conqueror: How the Generals Viewed the Indians," *American Heritage*, August 1979, p. 36.

868. D. Brown, p. 170. After Appomattox, Sherman would indeed be sent West to do what he did best during Lincoln's War: wipe out entire populations of Americans. In this case, Sherman was ordered to rid the nation's best lands of Native-Americans. His "final solution" to the "Indian problem" was simply to slaughter them all, or as he put it: "We must act with vindictive earnestness against the Sioux, even to their extermination, men, women, and children. Nothing less will reach the root of this case." Custer, p. 119. Yankee General John Pope held similar sentiments, stating that "it is my purpose to utterly exterminate the Sioux." Kennedy and Kennedy, pp. 291-292. Sherman and Pope were not the only Northern racists to despise Native-Americans. Lincoln, well-known, as we have seen, for his extreme white supremacist views (see e.g., Berwanger, pp. 136-137), not only prohibited Native-Americans from military enlistment during his War, in 1862 he had thirty-eight Indians hanged, allegedly for causing an uprising (actually he was trying to curry favor, and thus win votes, in Minnesota for his upcoming bid for reelection). Lincoln thus became the only president in American history to order a mass execution—and that of his own citizens. See Nicolay and Hay, ALCW, Vol. 2, p. 267; Seabrook, EYWTACWW, p. 118; Donald, L, 392-395; W. B. Garrison, CWTFB, p. 62; C. Adams, p. 210.

869. In postbellum America both Sheridan and Sherman would become deeply feared and hated by Native-Americans for the cruelty, deception, inhumanity, hostility, and soulless violence they displayed toward Indians and their way of life—the same traits they had shown the South only a few years earlier. Sherman's appearance had a particular impact on Native peoples, a man they described as "fierce and hairy with a cruel mouth." D. Brown, p. 34. As for Sheridan, with his "short legs and thick neck and long swinging arms," Indians said he reminded them of a "bad-tempered bear." D. Brown, p. 163. Ironically, Sherman was named after an Indian: Tecumseh (1768-1813), chief of the Shawnee. Neilson, s.v. "Tecumseh." It was Chief Tecumseh who said: "Where today are the Pequot? Where are the Narragansett, the Mohican, the Pokanoket, and many other once powerful tribes of our people? They have vanished before the avarice and the oppression of the White Man, as snow before a summer sun." Cushman, p. 311. Fifty-two years after Chief Tecumseh's death, similar thoughts would be uttered by white and black Southerners alike about the "Great White War Chief" Tecumseh Sherman and his fellow Yankee invaders. By 1865 the imperialistic North had conquered Southern civilization; by 1900 it had conquered Native-American civilization. The Yankee goal of the white Northernization of the entire U.S. was well on its way to completion.

870. Jahoda, pp. 246, 276.

Law of 1793 (both which supported the rights of slave owners to have their "property" returned), was responsible for obliging them .[871] Thus the Union's war to obtain the lands of the Indians also became, in part, a war to return escaped Southern slaves.

Southern and Northern abolitionists cried out in bitter protest, angering Southern and Northern slave owners, further fracturing the already tenuous connection between South and North. By the 1850s, as the two regions lurched ever closer to a bloody conflict of unimaginable proportions (the largest and bloodiest ever held on American soil), perceptive Southerners, like Forrest, could not have helped but notice the correlation between the plight of Native-Americans and their own.[872]

## DEATH OF THE SOUTHERN AGRARIAN LIFESTYLE

There were other serious consequences of King Cotton's reign. Native-American culture at the time was a barometer culture, one that could be used to track and record the condition of European-American culture. For as native peoples disappeared, so did the pioneer lifestyle, and along with it the European-American dream of accumulating land so that one might live independently, close to God and Mother Nature. Thanks to the Northern creation of the American slave trade, and the South's growing embrace of Northern extremist anti-Negro prejudices,[873] Southern pioneers and farmers were fast being transformed into planters and slavers, while the original goal of accumulating land was now simply to become wealthy.[874]

The remaining Native peoples were urged to settle, take up farming, and assimilate into white American society,[875] but most refused. Why? Because for millennia they had lived off the land as hunter-gatherers, worshiping the earth as the Great Mother, creator and provider of all life.[876] As the red man assimilated into the white man's culture, gradually the native nomadic hunting lifestyle vanished, replaced

871. J. C. Perry, p. 79.
872. Jahoda, p. 276.
873. Tocqueville, Vol. 1, p. 383. See also Litwack, NS, passim; Berwanger, passim; J. C. Perry, passim; Lott, passim; Farrow, Lang, and Frank, passim; Melish, passim; G. H. Moore, passim.
874. Lytle, pp. 15-16.
875. Ellis, AS, p. 239.
876. Deloria, p. 107. For more on Mother-Goddess worship see my books, *Britannia Rules*, *The Book of Kelle*, *Christmas Before Christianity*, *Aphrodite's Trade*, and *The Goddess Dictionary of Words and Phrases*.

by the European farming lifestyle, one now tied to newly invented machinery, like Whitney's cotton gin.

The Industrial Revolution had begun, and with it the purely agrarian lifestyle—the only one Forrest and his ancestors had ever known—was coming to an end.[877] Behind all of this was the once lowly Southern cotton plant, whose central importance had by now earned it a new title: King Cotton.[878]

## THE COTTON TRIANGLE

With cotton as the new monarch the South was fast becoming inseparably tied to the North,[879] the birthplace of both American slavery and the American slave trade.[880]

This was no accident. The industrial North, climatologically and topographically unsuited to large-scale farming,[881] was the home of the great business magnates who owned the ships, banks, insurance companies, and textile mills required to fuel and maintain slavery. In turn, it needed the agrarian South, whose rural farmers owned broad, expansive, fertile lands in a sub-tropical climate, both vital for growing cotton.[882] Thus was created the infamous politically and economically symbiotic "Cotton Triangle."

Here, Northerners shipped supplies (mainly clothing and food)

---

877. By 1890 the American frontier itself had vanished, and with it the "first period of American history." Ellis, AS, p. 352.

878. Owsley, KCD, p. 2.

879. Farrow, Lang, and Frank, p. 25.

880. Ashe, pp. 9-10. Contrary to accepted wisdom, though the first Africans were brought—unrequested, it should be noted—to the English colony at Jamestown, Virginia, in 1620 (by the Dutch), these were indentured servants, not true slaves. Thus, the real start of the slave trade and its massive growth must be attributed to the North. For it was from a Massachusetts harbor that America's first slave ship, *Desire*, sailed in 1637, only seventeen years later. It was not long before the slave trade became the veritable cornerstone of Northern society. This was only natural, for the money that fueled slavery came from the North. Thus, this is where America's slave ships and their captains and crews were to be found as well. The distilleries that made rum (used to trade for slaves in Africa) were all in the North, and the ports from which the slave ships sailed to Africa (laden with rum) were based in Northern harbors. In addition, nearly all of the textile mills that made cloth from cotton were in the North. For fifty years prior to Lincoln's War the North ruled both the slave and the cotton industries, with New York City as their capital. In contrast, the original Southern colonies did not own slave ships and were not involved in the slave trade, which is one reason the Confederacy banned the foreign slave trade in 1861, several years before the North. And yet, in a tragic irony based solely on topography and climate, it was the South who suffered most because of slavery, a topic we will be exploring in greater detail. These facts have been cleverly and tragically disguised by Northern propagandists and Yankee mythologists for a century and a half. But no more.

881. W. Davis, LA, p. 8.

882. Sword, SI, p. 18.

to Southern ports for the slaves working on Dixie's 75,000 cotton plantations. These same ships would return north with holds full of raw cotton prepared by the slaves. New England's thousands of mills then transformed the cotton into textiles, which were sold around the world. Finally, this money was used to buy more supplies to ship back down south to the cotton plantations, completing the Triangle.[883]  As James Madison noted in 1813:

> The great road of profitable intercourse for New England . . . lies through the . . . cotton . . . fields of her Southern and Western confederates.[884]

## THE POWER OF KING COTTON

As exploitive and cruel as it was for those on the lower rungs of the social ladder, the Cotton Triangle worked magnificently for the wealthy and powerful who controlled it from the top, mainly Northern bankers and ship owners. But Southern plantation owners also profited.

In 1855 the South produced 2,982,634 bales of cotton. Four years later, in 1859, that number had almost doubled.[885] Between 1857 and 1860 alone the production of cotton rose by 1,500,000 bales, an increase greater than the forty years between the invention of the cotton gin in 1793 and the end of Andrew Jackson's presidency in 1836.[886] By 1860 cotton made up 50 percent of all U.S. exports, and was the number one American product.[887] Indeed, the South's production of cotton had doubled each decade since 1800, making it the supplier of three-fourths of the world's supply in 1860.[888]

This staggering increase was partially due to the development of steam-powered spinning and weaving machines, improvements in the varieties of cotton seeds, the invention of the steamboat (which reduced transportation and additional marketing costs), the expansion of railroads, and the relocation of cotton plantations to land (generally westward) more conducive to growing cotton, such as the fertile, alluvial

---

883. Farrow, Lang, and Frank, pp. 10, 14, 18, 25-26.
884. Madison, pp. 561-562.
885. Wilson and Ferris, s.v. "Cotton Culture," p. 55.
886. Fogel and Engerman, p. 89.
887. J. C. Perry, p. 56.
888. Sword, SI, p. 18.

flood plain of Mississippi.[889]

New cotton plantations also opened in Alabama and Louisiana. By 1834 these three states were producing more than half of all America's cotton crop. This increase was aided by the nearly 1,000,000 slaves who took part in the western and southern cotton migration between 1790 and 1860, as farmers moved their plantations to more cotton-friendly soils.[890]

The main reasons the production of cotton exploded in the early 1800s, however, were Whitney's gin and the accompanying need for more slaves,[891] spurned on by a worldwide increase in the demand for U.S. cotton. It was simple supply and demand.[892]

In 1790, three years before the invention of the gin, there were slightly less than 700,000 black slaves in the U.S. By the start of the War for Southern Independence in 1861, just seventy-one years later, there were nearly 3,500,000 slaves in the South alone,[893] a majority of them (some 2,250,000) involved in the cotton industry.[894] Between 1820 and 1860 alone there was an increase of 160 percent in the total slave population.[895]

Cotton was big business now, and so was Southern plantation slavery, a system that, contrary to Northern myth, was proving to be much more lucrative and efficient than free labor farms.[896] Along with Southern planters and slavers, Northern industrialists profited heavily too, as the Cotton Triangle swept an entire generation into new levels of indescribable wealth, for cotton was now the North's largest and most lucrative industry.[897] Naturally, the allure of cotton spread across the nation, both South and North, like a prairie wildfire, attracting both the rich and the poor.

---

889. Fogel and Engerman, pp. 44, 93, 199.
890. J. C. Perry, p. 56.
891. Wyeth, LGNBF, p. 20.
892. Fogel and Engerman, p. 94.
893. Cooper, JDA, p. 378; Quarles, p. xiii; Stephenson, ALU, p. 168.
894. Farrow, Lang, and Frank, p. 26.
895. Fogel and Engerman, p. 98.
896. E. M. Thomas, pp. 14-15; Fogel and Engerman, pp. 158-257.
897. Owsley, KCD, p. 3.

MISSISSIPPI

Many millionaires were created, and many souls were lost, during those heady seductive times, as countless aristocratic country gentlemen were transformed into materialistic cotton capitalists, ruthless men who placed profits above humanity.[898]

Despite the hazards, Forrest's father, frontiersman and smithy William, like so many of his fellow Southerners, could not resist the temptation to try his own hand at becoming a planter, for all around him friends and neighbors were becoming wealthy planting cotton, using slaves to prepare it.[899]

And so with an eye toward advancing his family's station in life, in 1833 (some say 1834)[900] William gave up blacksmithing[901] and followed the westward flow of emigration,[902] moving his struggling family from Middle Tennessee to the heart of cotton country in northwestern Mississippi.[903] Native-Americans in the area had recently been moved westward by the U.S. government, leaving vast tracts of "good cotton land," an irresistible temptation for men like William who wanted to try their hand at cotton farming.[904]

The energetic young Nathan, who was just twelve years-old, must have been saddened to leave behind both his friends and the natural wonderland of seemingly endless woods, fields, streams, and limestone caves of Chapel Hill. He would have been even unhappier had he known that the move would bring about a sudden end to what little childhood he had left.

The small Mississippi farm William leased in 1833 was located in Indian Territory on the Mississippi-Tennessee border in a rugged hilly wilderness area not far from what used to be the village of Salem in

---

898. E. M. Thomas, pp. 7-8.
899. Lytle, pp. 15-16.
900. The exact year of the Forrest family's move to Mississippi is debated. See e.g., Jordan and Pryor, p. 18; Wills, p. 10; Parks, p. 115.
901. Grissom, p. 345.
902. Mathes, p. 3.
903. Browning, p. 4.
904. Parks, pp. 98, 113.

Tippah County,[905] land recently purchased from the Chickasaw.[906] As was the custom of the day, the Forrests moved to an area that was close to kinfolk; again, William's wife's family, the Becks, who owned land nearby.

The Forrest's little rented cabin stood on a clearing next to a cool stream, the "Victorian refrigerator," the perfect place for keeping milk, eggs, cheese, and various produce fresh during the long hot sub-tropical Mississippi summers.

It was here, in the winter of 1836-1837, that Forrest, now fifteen, began his second term as a student at the local primary school. This session, in Mississippi, combined with his three-months of schooling in Tennessee, gave the youngster a total of six months of proper education.[907] He could never have imagined that nearly two centuries into the future, thousands of people would still be discussing these 180 days, and how they impacted both his life and the War for Southern Independence.

## DEATH & FAMILY RESPONSIBILITIES

In 1837, as young Forrest was finishing up his last term of school, he was unexpectedly ushered into an entirely new world: adulthood.

That year, before he had had time to find true success as a cotton planter, his father William died suddenly.[908] Forrest, though not yet sixteen, was the eldest son, automatically making him head of the family. And so was laid another stone in the foundation of Forrest's often difficult but eventful future.[909]

Literally overnight he became the father-figure of a thirteen-person clan,[910] one that included himself, his three sisters, six brothers,[911] his mother Mariam (who was five months pregnant with her

---

905. Jordan and Pryor, p. 34. The town of Salem, Mississippi, no longer exists and the area is now called "Old Salem." Today it is near Ashland, Benton County, Mississippi. Thus the area of Tippah County William Forrest originally moved his family to is now part of Benton County.

906. Jordan and Pryor, p. 18. The Indians who once lived on what became the Mississippi land leased by the Forrests, had been only recently removed to reservations. Wyeth, LGNBF, p. 5.

907. Jordan and Pryor, p. 19.

908. The cause of William's death is unknown.

909. Morton, p. 11.

910. Jordan and Pryor, p. 34.

911. Morton, p. 151.

and William's eleventh, and last, child, Jeffrey[912]—later to become Forrest's favorite sibling),[913] and Mariam's sister, the unmarried Fanny Beck, who had come to live with them in Mississippi.[914]

Though this would have overwhelmed most young teens, Forrest was anything but a typical boy.[915] In fact, he took to his new role with surprising enthusiasm and maturity.[916]

Pledging to care for his mother and siblings, he worked long hours as a menial laborer and supervised both their rented farm and his mother's affairs, all of this while attending his final three months of school.[917] (So family-oriented, kind-hearted, and generous was Forrest that for the rest of his life he would continue to look after his family members.)[918]

Under Forrest's direction, he and his brothers (four of whom would later go on to serve in the Confederate military with him)[919] spent their days in the fields clearing land, planting cotton, and speculating on horses and cattle,[920] while their nights were spent making buckskin clothes, leggings, shoes (moccasins), and hats (coonskin caps) for themselves and their family by candle and firelight. His sisters were in charge of the spinning wheel, and other household duties such as sewing, washing, and mending clothing. It was also their job tend to the farm's ducks, chickens, rabbits, and other small animals. Again, Forrest put family and home before school, sacrificing the furtherance of his education in order to care for his loved ones.[921]

Due to the youngster's "robust constitution," "resolute soul,"[922] "unflinching industry, clear, good sense, and thrifty management,"[923] all attributed to his Scots-Irish blood,[924] the Forrest homestead began

912. R. Taylor, p. 200.
913. Mathes, p. 9.
914. Parks, p. 123.
915. Boatner, s.v. "Forrest, Nathan Bedford."
916. Jordan and Pryor, pp. 18-19.
917. Henry, FWMF, p. 23.
918. Wills, p. 20.
919. Morton, p. 152.
920. Wyeth, LGNBF, p. 17.
921. Mathes, pp. 10-11, 5.
922. Morton, p. 11.
923. Jordan and Pryor, p. 19.
924. Grissom, p. 345.

turning a profit for the first time, something his father had never been able to accomplish.[925] This gave the entire family a level of financial security and comfort previously unknown to them. Finally, under the young Forrest's imperious will, his innate horse sense, and ambitious but unerring guiding hand, all were well provided for.

## FORREST'S TEXAS SOJOURN

With his mother's family now taken care of, and he no longer a teenager, Forrest felt that he could afford to begin to explore the world outside Mississippi. As such, in February 1841, with trouble brewing in America's Southwest, the excitable twenty year-old outdoorsman eagerly answered the call to help Texas win her independence from Mexico.

Enrolling as a volunteer in a militia under Captain Wallace Wilson in Holly Springs, Mississippi, he headed for New Orleans, where he planned to take a steamer on to Galveston. Upon arriving in the Crescent City, however, money and transportation problems caused the company to disband.[926]

Undaunted, the ever persistent Forrest pressed on to Texas with what was now a much smaller group of tired but still keen tenderfeet. But by the time the band arrived in Houston, the conflict had dissipated and soldiers were no longer needed. Disappointed after having spent his last penny, he had little choice but to go to work on a Texas plantation splitting rails (for fifty cents per 100) for four months to earn enough money for his trip home to Tippah County.

The "Texas volunteer" did not return to his mother's house with what he had expected: military fame. Instead, he brought back something he had not intended: a severe illness, one that kept him flat on his back for a full winter.

The malady turned out to be more of a blessing than a curse, for as he laid on his sick-bed recovering over the next several months, he had plenty of time to mull over the sights he had seen traveling to and from New Orleans. And what sights they were to the wide-eyed young man

---

925. Jordan and Pryor, p. 19.

926. These problems stemmed from the company's mismanagement of funds, which left Forrest and the other volunteers without the means to hire a steamer to take them the rest of the way to Texas. Jordan and Pryor, p. 21.

from the backwoods of Tennessee.

During the weeks he had spent journeying up and down the Mississippi River, Forrest could not help but notice the innumerable cotton plantations dotting its banks. On them he saw planters and their servants toiling away, working side-by-side, cutting down trees and clearing the fields of stumps and brush, preparing the land for growing cotton.[927]

There was also his time on the Texas plantation splitting rails, where for 120 days he got an inside view of plantation life. Perhaps, Forrest no doubt pondered, he could one day find financial stability in the same profession his father had dreamed of following. Fascinated, these were scenes Forrest would never forget, and in fact, they would resurface shortly to dramatically alter his life.[928]

After making a full recovery from the Lone Star fever he had protracted, Forrest worked for another year at his mother's farm,[929] dreaming of the day when he would own and operate his own spread. In preparation for that day, and to bring in extra income, he began to focus more specifically on dealing in horses and cattle.[930]

FORREST LEAVES HOME

By autumn 1842, Forrest, being a thrifty Celt and an excellent judge of horse flesh, soon became highly successful at his new found occupation. In fact, he had amassed a small fortune, more than enough to move out and start a life of his own.[931]

As some of his family members were moving again, this time westward to DeSoto County, Mississippi, Forrest, now twenty-one, decided to leave home for good to settle in the same region to pursue what he had discovered was his true passion: livestock trading.

BUSINESS PARTNERSHIP & A NEW STEP-FATHER

There was another worthwhile reason for his move to DeSoto County. His uncle, Jonathan Forrest (1803-1845), noting his nephew's

927. Lytle, p. 19.
928. Lytle, p. 19.
929. Wyeth, LGNBF, p. 17.
930. Mathes, p. 11.
931. Henry, ATSF, p. 29.

accomplishments with horses and cattle, his head for figures,[932] his frugality, and his boundless energy, offered him a junior partnership in his mercantile, livery stable, and livestock-trading business in Hernando, twenty-five miles south of Memphis.[933] Forrest happily accepted, making the move to the northwestern Mississippi town where he would spend the next nine years of his life.

Jonathan's choice for his new junior partner was a good one. Forrest quickly developed a reputation for being energetic, honest, professional, and enthusiastic.[934] The naturally shrewd and mentally acute lad made an excellent business associate, and as their business grew, so did their bank accounts.[935]

A year later, in 1843, Forrest's widowed mother Mariam remarried, to Joseph Luxton, Sr. (born about 1798), and had four more children, three sons and a daughter, Forrest's half-siblings.[936] Two of these boys, like Forrest and four of his full brothers, would go on to fight for the Confederacy, making seven children in all that Mariam contributed to the Southern Cause. This earned her the honorific title, "Mother of the Gracchi."[937] Forrest was no doubt somewhat relieved that the responsibility of heading the family was now turned over to his new step-father Joseph, allowing him greater freedom than he had ever known.[938]

A KILLING IN THE FAMILY

Sadly, Forrest's successful and prosperous equine venture with his uncle would be all too brief. Just three years after it began, on March 10, 1845,[939] a long-running dispute came to a head between Jonathan and a

---

932. Parks, p. 161.

933. Mathes, p. 11.

934. R. Taylor, p. 237.

935. Simmons, s.v. "Forrest, Nathan Bedford."

936. Wyeth, LGNBF, pp. 6, 11.

937. The Gracchi were one of the famed noble families of ancient Rome, coming to power in the 2nd Century BC. Two of the sons of this family, Tiberius Sempronius Gracchus (the Younger) and Gaius Sempronius Gracchus, are known for fighting to the death during a period of Roman social reform. Hence, Mariam (Beck) Forrest, whose seven Confederate sons also fought for reform, though some 2,000 years later, is sometimes poetically referred to as the "Mother of the Gracchi."

938. Mathes, p. 10.

939. Some say the date was March 11, 1845; others March 20, 1845. The confusion probably derives from the various newspaper accounts of the incident, which appeared on different dates in different parts of the country.

man named William Matlock, Esquire, his two brothers, Jefferson and James Matlock, and an overseer named Bean.[940]  Not used to mincing words, and always one ready and able to defend his kin, the young hot-headed Forrest inevitably found his way into the middle of the argument, staunchly standing up for his uncle.[941]

Voices and fists were raised that cool spring day in the public square of Hernando, and soon guns emerged.  In the ensuing unequal melee (four against two), a bullet intended for Forrest struck his unarmed uncle, who was killed instantly.[942]  In response Forrest unflinchingly shot down two of the Matlocks with his double-barrel pistol, and wounded the third Matlock with a large Bowie knife tossed to him by a quick-thinking and sympathetic bystander.  Bean, meanwhile, after seeing his compatriots cut down by the agile twenty-four year-old, wisely fled the scene, ducking into a nearby building.

Few, however, could escape Forrest, who had the perilous senses of both a psychic and a bloodhound.  He quickly discovered the homicidal overseer cowering under a bed and summarily dragged him out.  According to an eyewitness, one F. W. Chamberlain, Forrest then told his stunned captive:

> You deserve death at my hands, but I am too brave a man to murder one so completely in my power; I give you your life.[943]

SHERIFF FORREST

While his two surviving attackers (Bean and one of the Matlock brothers) were promptly imprisoned without bail (and later tried and found guilty of murder), Forrest, though also arrested, was immediately released, since he had acted in self-defense while trying to help his uncle.[944]

His pluck and magnetism did not go unnoticed by the grateful people of Mississippi.  Besieged with thanks and adulation by the townsfolk, the courageous young man who had taken on, and beaten,

---

940. Jordan and Pryor, p. 23.

941. Wyeth, LGNBF, p. 18.

942. Though he had dodged numerous bullets meant for him, Forrest did receive a minor wound during the fight, one from which he soon recovered. Jordan and Pryor, p. 23.

943. Mathes, p. 12.

944. Bean and the one surviving Matlock, both who suffered through a long court trial and an even longer imprisonment, were eventually released after paying heavy fines and court costs.

four armed thugs by himself, was promptly elected constable of Hernando and coroner of DeSoto County.

## THE BEGINNING OF AN AMERICAN LEGEND

It was early 1845 and Forrest was only twenty-four years old. Nevertheless, inklings of what he would one day become were already manifesting. Indeed, in just a few years this formidable "young blood of the South," as an awed Sherman later referred to him,[945] would be hailed for a stunning variety of virtues, talents, and heroic qualities.

Among them Forrest would one day become known as a self-made success-story, a devout family man, a man of action, a self-reliant tough guy, a skillful hunter, a devil-may-care Tennessee mountaineer, an inflexible and tireless frontiersman, a ubiquitous daredevil, a superlative horseman, a well-respected citizen, an influential and well-connected businessman, a modest and retiring Victorian gentleman, an ambitious military gambler, a splendid cavalry officer, a first-rate shooter, a natural-born orator, a hot-blooded individualist, an aggressive combatant, a tough taskmaster, an able and exacting soldier, a man of great courage, a dynamic leader, a great Southern chieftain, a battlefield adventurer, a dangerous raider, a dreaded rebel leader, the War's most fearsome cavalry officer, one of the South's most hard-driving commanders, a self-taught soldier without peer, a diamond in the rough, a beloved commander of men, an innovator in the field of military science, an audacious wartime general, the ablest Confederate military man, a fearless warrior, an ingenious military tactician, and, above all, the "spiritual comforter" of the Southern people.

Lincoln's War was still sixteen years away, and the fantastic but true legend of Nathan Bedford Forrest had just begun. Ahead there awaited a life of incredible contrasts that few have ever experienced; a life of passion and high drama, love and hate, fortune and ruin, fame and infamy, health and sickness, celebrity and loneliness, praise and slander, tranquility and fury.

For the young intense mountaineer of humble origins, it was to be a life he could have scarcely imagined at the time, one he had read about only in picture books.

---

945. Sherman, Vol. 1, p. 337.

# - 1845 TO 1858 -
# SETTLER, POLITICIAN,
# HUSBAND, & FATHER:
# A NEW LIFE ON THE MISSISSIPPI

"Whenever you meet the enemy, no matter how
few there are of you or how many of them,
show fight." – Nathan Bedford Forrest

## MARRIAGE

A S WAS TO BE THE pattern in Forrest's life, only six weeks after his uncle Jonathan's death, his life took another abrupt turn, forcing him in an entirely new direction.

It was at this time that the rough-hewn Tennessean began courting his future wife, Mary Ann Montgomery, a sophisticated high society girl who was related to both Sam Houston the celebrated Texan,[946] and Richard Montgomery,[947] hero of the American

---

946. Mary Ann and Sam Houston were 2nd cousins, twice removed (from my personal family tree). Born in Virginia on March 2, 1793, Houston later spent his youth in Tennessee, where he was raised by his widowed mother and became fascinated with Cherokee culture. After serving in the Creek Wars under Andrew Jackson, he was elected attorney general for Nashville, and later, governor of Tennessee. Houston's first marriage to Eliza Allen (in 1829) ended suddenly, and he returned to the wilderness to live with the Cherokee for six years. Here he married a Cherokee woman, Tiana Rogers, and became a member of the Cherokee nation. Given the Indian name the "Blackbird," or the "Raven," he set up a trading post, but later abandoned both his post and his Indian wife, probably due to his alcoholism. This affliction prompted the Cherokee to give him another name: *Ootsetee Ardeetahskee*, "Big Drunk." In 1833 Houston moved to Texas where, during the Texas Revolution, he helped the region secure independence from Mexico, becoming the first president of the new nation, the Republic of Texas. Later, when Texas became a state, he was elected its governor. In 1840 Houston married a third time, to Margaret Moffette Lea, with whom he had eight

Revolution[948]— and a direct descendant of numerous royals,[949] including the Norman earl, Roger de Mundegumbrie, who fought under William the Conqueror at the Battle of Hastings in 1066.[950]

Forrest's first meeting with the pretty teenage Southern belle was to be as romantic as her family's ancient Norman and Scottish heritage.

Riding slowly along a country road near Hernando one spring Sunday morning in 1845, he came across a horse and buggy stuck in a mudhole along a swollen creek. Just yards away he noticed two men sitting idly by on their horses, watching, but offering no assistance.

The carriage contained two elegantly dressed women: Elizabeth (Cowan) Montgomery and her nineteen year-old daughter Mary Ann. After courteously receiving their permission, he carried them back to the safety of terra firma, then waded back into the water. Putting his shoulder to one of the buggy's wheels, he encouraged the horses forward, muscling the vehicle free and back onto dry land.

The two refined ladies, new residents of nearby upper-crust Horn Lake, Mississippi, were both thankful, but leery, for Forrest had neglected to help them back into their wagon. In his anger at the two slackers sitting on their horses nearby he had forgotten about the two women momentarily.

Turning to the men, he said angrily: "Why didn't y'all help these ladies?" Getting no response from the startled ne'er-do-wells, he yelled: "I suggest that you remove yerselves from this vicinity at once, or I'll give you a thrashin' you won't soon fergit!" Seeing that Forrest was not a man to be trifled with, the two turned and quickly rode off.[951]

Right about then Elizabeth and Mary Ann must have been asking

---

children.  Margaret was instrumental in inspiring Houston to become a member of the Baptist Church and gain control over his addiction to liquor.  At the start of the War for Southern Independence Houston openly opposed Texas' secession from the Union, an unpopular stance with the largely anti-Northern Texan populace.  Removed from office, he retired in Huntsville, Texas, passing away there on July 26, 1863, midway through Lincoln's War.  The city of Houston, Texas, is named after him.

**947.** Mary Ann was also related to the famous Tennessee family, the Cowans, through her mother Elizabeth McCroskey Cowan.  The city of Cowan, Franklin Co., Tennessee, takes its name from them.

**948.** Irish-born General Richard Montgomery died in the American Revolutionary War on December 31, 1775, during the Quebec Campaign.

**949.** Burke, s.v. "Montgomery," pp. 1749-1750.

**950.** Way and Squire, s.v. "Montgomery," p. 278.

**951.** Wyeth, LGNBF, pp. 18-19.

themselves: "Who is this pushy and coarse but chivalrous backwoodsman?" They thanked Forrest exuberantly, after which he asked for—and was granted—permission to pay them a visit.[952] An assertive opportunist, Forrest wasted no time in pursuing the young Montgomery girl, still fresh from the famous school, the Nashville Female Academy.[953]

A few days later he called on Mary Ann at home to ask her hand in marriage. Naturally she turned him down (she hardly knew him and they were, after all, from opposite ends of the socioeconomic spectrum). He came a second time (their third meeting), repeating his proposal, at which time she accepted.[954]

Forrest had not won a complete victory yet, however. Mary Ann's uncle and legal guardian,[955] the noted influential clergyman of the Cumberland Presbyterian Church, Reverend Samuel Montgomery Cowan, was strongly against any marriage between his highly cultivated niece and the rough-and-tumble frontiersman. Forrest, fearing no man, confronted him.

"Why Bedford, I couldn't consent," replied the formidable pastor. "You cuss and gamble and Mary Ann is a Christian girl."

"That's very true sir. And that is exactly why I want to marry her," Forrest replied unhesitatingly. There was only one response possible to this bullet-proof rejoinder.

On September 25, 1845,[956] just months after they first met at the country mudhole, Reverend Cowan married the young couple in

---

952. Mathes, p. 14.
953. The Nashville Female Academy, founded in 1816, was a well respected, extremely popular school for Southern girls. Located on Church Street in downtown Nashville, it educated the South's young women right up until the city was captured by the Union army in 1862. The faculty and students had all sided with the Confederacy, of course, but there was no logical reason for what happened next: Yankee soldiers immediately set about pillaging and despoiling the school. Even her beautiful pianos were stolen and shipped North. By 1866 there was nothing left of the academy and her empty buildings were turned into a seedy boarding house. When this business too failed, the entire dilapidated campus was finally torn down to make way for new construction. Blandin, pp. 273-281.
954. One of Forrest's strongest traits was perseverance, a quality that brought him much success, both on the domestic front and on the military front.
955. Mary Ann's father, War of 1812 veteran William H. Montgomery, died at age 37 in 1829, leaving her mother, Elizabeth Cowan, a widow at age 27 (note: William and Elizabeth were 1ˢᵗ cousins). Mary Ann was only three years old at the time. As Elizabeth was now alone and struggling with four young children, her brother Sam took over for William, becoming the family's foster father.
956. Forrest was twenty-four years old and Mary Ann was nineteen years old at the time of their marriage in 1845.

Hernando, the local newspaper announcing that the wedding had been accompanied by "a good sweet morsel of cake and a bottle of the best wine."[957]

## CHILDREN

The next few years would be the happiest of Forrest's short but amazing life. Settling in with his new bride, their family began to grow with the birth of their first child, William Montgomery "Willie" Forrest, September 26, 1846[958] (during Lincoln's War Willie would become his father's aid-de-camp, and later a captain on his staff).[959] Three years later, 1849, brought more hope for a bright future with the arrival of their second and last child, Frances Ann "Fanny" Forrest.[960]

According to the 1850 Census, the Forrest family home consisted of Forrest, Mary Ann, son Willie, and daughter Fanny, along with three additional individuals, two of them kin: Ann Cowan, a relative of Mary Ann's (probably her aunt), and Joseph F. Forrest (a relative of Forrest's), and also a boarder named James Patton Anderson, later to become a Confederate general of some note.[961] It is also highly probable that at this time Forrest was supporting and caring for his younger brother John Nathaniel Forrest, who had come home from the Mexican War partly paralyzed from a shot through his spine. Here again we see both Forrest's dedication to family life and his innate compassion and generosity.

## MEMPHIS, TENNESSEE

In 1851 Forrest closed the mercantile business he had shared with his Uncle Jonathan and moved his new little family to the thriving river port of Memphis, Tennessee,[962] a move that would have profound repercussions.

---

957. *Confederate Veteran*, Vol. 20, p. 210.
958. Young William was no doubt named after Forrest's father, William Forrest (naming children after their grandparents was a traditional part of the naming system in early North America), though the name could have served the dual purpose of honoring Mary Ann's father, William H. Montgomery, as well.
959. Mathes, p. 170.
960. Forrest's daughter, Frances "Fanny" Forrest, seems to have been named after his twin sister Fanny, or perhaps his aunt, Fanny Beck.
961. Warner, s.v. "James Patton Anderson."
962. Wyeth, LGNBF, p. 20.

Despite his lack of proper schooling (he had a total of only six months of public education), Forrest evinced an amazing proclivity for making both money and friends. Throughout the 1850s he started numerous businesses in rapid succession, including a stage line, a brickyard, a construction company, and a livery and stable operation.[963] He also dabbled in railroads, insurance, real estate, and farming supplies, and by 1852, he had entered into the occupation that would change his life: slave trading.[964]

A year later, in 1853, so it would later be claimed, Forrest had a torrid affair with one of his slave girls ("Catharine"), resulting in several children.[965] How strange for one who, as anti-South Northern writers assert, hated the very sight of blacks. Not surprisingly, the "evidence" for this story is pure Yankee mythology: a mean-spirited newspaper article fabricated years later by Northerners who wished to harm Forrest's reputation.[966]

The following year brought personal tragedy into Forrest's world. On June 26, 1854, his six year-old daughter Frances Ann died of "flux" (dysentery). This could have been nothing short of devastating for the thirty-three year-old father, who was known for his deep love of family and children.

## POLITICS & REAL ESTATE

Not content to be merely a businessman, Forrest got into politics as well. His powerful, 6 foot 2 inch, 185-pound frame, wide shoulders, broad chest, muscular arms and legs, delicately formed hands and feet, his intense steel-blue eyes, high cheek-bones, trimmed moustache and beard, fine white teeth, sun-tanned features (from practically living outside), and his long, wavy, dark brown hair worn in the then popular

---

963. Lytle, p. 23.
964. According to Lafcadio Hearn, Forrest's Memphis slave market was a standard four-story yellow building, located at the corner of Adams and Third Streets. Henry, FWMF, p. 26.
965. Davison and Foxx, p. 253.
966. As this book will clearly show, the Northern press was obsessed with Forrest, taking sinister delight in running highly prejudicial stories on him (nearly all invented or based on mere rumor), and cunningly calculated to inflict the most damage. Forrest became, in essence, a convenient symbol of all that the North hated about the South. It could be truthfully said that nearly all of today's abhorrence of and racism toward Forrest can be directly traced to Yankee newspaper articles from 150 years ago. The newsmen who wrote and printed them no doubt knew that their slanted fables would continue to haunt the figure of Nathan Bedford Forrest well into the future.

Cavalier style, set him very much apart from the crowd. One of the most charismatic figures in American history, Forrest naturally gravitated to positions of power and leadership.

As such, in 1858 the Memphis townspeople eagerly elected the magnetic charmer to the office of alderman (without opposition),[967] where he energetically pushed through new legislation,[968] even setting up the town's first commercially viable fire department.[969]

In the meantime Forrest was fast becoming a real estate mogul of unprecedented proportions, buying up every piece of available land in the surrounding region. On one occasion, for instance, he purchased 1,900 acres of prime cotton-growing land for $47,500, today's equivalent of $1,200,000. Just a few months later he sold this same land for three times what he paid originally.

It was at this time that Forrest bought several plantations in Mississippi. The first was a small farm in Tunica County. The second, called Green Grove, was an enormous 3,000 acre farm possessing a six-room house and twelve servants' cabins (that housed thirty-six of Forrest's slaves), located at Sunflower Landing, in Coahoma County.[970] In 1859 Forrest shut down his real estate and slave business in Memphis, turning his attention solely to his plantations.[971]

Forrest's hard work, native intelligence, endearing social graces, and well earned business connections paid off. In 1858 the thirty-seven year-old Forrest earned a staggering $96,000 from slave trading alone, the equivalent of about $2,500,000 today. And his wealth only continued to increase. In 1859, after selling approximately 1,000 servants at $1,100 each (today worth about $30,000 each),[972] he earned $1,100,000, or by today's standards, nearly $30,000,000.

His cotton sales were bringing in untold millions more. Green

---

967. Jordan and Pryor, p. 33.

968. Forrest was reelected to Memphis' Board of Aldermen several times, only retiring from that office just prior to the War when his enormous real estate holdings (mainly cotton plantations along or near the Mississippi River) began to demand his daily attention. This would prove to be the only political office Forrest ever held. Wyeth, LGNBF, p. 22.

969. Hurst, p. 56.

970. Wills, p. 35.

971. Wyeth, LGNBF, p. 22.

972. Hurst, p. 58.

Grove by itself was producing some 1,000 bales of cotton a year,[973] earning Forrest $30,000 annually,[974] today's equivalent of $800,000. By 1860, the Mississippi plantation became so productive that some 200 field servants were needed to run it.[975]

According to Forrest's own statements, he was worth $1,500,000 at the start of Lincoln's War, or what today would be about $40,000,000. Considering that he owned thousands of acres of real estate, numerous homes and plantations, and hundreds of slaves, and dabbled in dozens of other businesses, this figure is no doubt quite conservative.

This impressive achievement was due in no small measure to the efforts of his huge slave force, which helped Forrest become not only the most successful slave trader in Tennessee, but one of the wealthiest men and largest plantation owners in the South.[976]

## A GENEROUS & CONTRADICTORY CELEBRITY

The poverty-stricken young man had become a self-made millionaire by the age of forty—and a generous one at that. He not only supported his own wife and children in what would today be considered an upperclass lifestyle, but he also took care of his mother's every need and paid for his younger brothers' college educations, a privilege that he himself had been denied.[977] In addition, he financially supported a wide assortment of family members, boarders, and distant kin, including his mother's sister, the unmarried Fanny Beck.[978]

Even prior to the War Forrest was already a celebrity: his rags-to-riches story, which led to stunning material success, fascinated the public. Here was a young unschooled farm boy who had come from nothing, and yet who now owned millions of dollars in real estate and servants, lived on a handsome, sprawling Victorian plantation, married to an aristocratic Southern belle with whom he had two lovely children.

But just as intriguing to people was Forrest's unusual and

---

973. Jordan and Pryor, p. 26.
974. Wyeth, LGNBF, p. 22.
975. Wills, p. 35.
976. Katcher, CWSB, p. 271.
977. R. Taylor, p. 237; Lytle, p. 183; Mathes, p. 9.
978. Parks, p. 123.

seemingly contradictory personality. Combining a mere six months of schooling with a heavy Tennessee accent,[979] at the same time he had both a genius IQ and what some would consider psychic abilities,[980] a strange mixture that mesmerizes the world to this day.

A tall, imposing, powerfully built man, he was tender toward children and polite toward women, and considered himself their personal defender and protector. He was somewhat shy and quiet, and detested womanizing and carousing.[981] Born in the tobacco-growing, whiskey-making state of Tennessee, he eschewed both cigarettes and alcohol, though he did drink once—and regretted it. Of this experience he once told a friend:

> I was never drunk but once in my life. I had observed the antics of a drunken man, and a strange fancy to try a spell of it took possession of me. I got the liquor and drank it one afternoon. What happened as a consequence I do not know, but when I got over the spree I found myself with a burning case of typhoid fever. I promised 'Old Master' that if he would let me up from that bed I would never get drunk again. And I never broke that pledge.[982]

Probably as a result of this incident, during Lincoln's War, whenever the teetotaling Forrest was invited to imbibe, he always gave the same answer: "My staff does all my drinking for me."[983]

One we would today call a Right-wing traditionalist

---

**979.** According to one of Forrest's biographers, John Allan Wyeth (1845-1922), Forrest typically dropped the "g" from the end of words; hence, he said "walkin'" instead of "walking." He also used the word "betwixt" instead of "between," "fetch" instead of "bring," "fit" instead of "fought," and "mout" instead of "might." Forrest's spelling, often phonetic, was of a similar caliber. For instance, he wrote "hir" for "her," "know" for "no," and "hed" for "head." Though his speaking and spelling did improve with time, he kept most of these habits, ingrained in boyhood, throughout his entire life. Forrest's devotees at the time found his home-spun ways endearing, while his critics found them irritating, branding him "uncivilized." Wyeth, LGNBF, pp. 625-626. Along with most other Southerners, I see nothin' uncivilized about droppin' one's "g's." The custom derives from America's early British founders, who brought it over in the 1600s. To this day many Britons (including the Scots, Irish, and Welsh)—among them even the most well educated—continue to drop their "g's." Thus, Forrest was merely practicin' a long and accepted British tradition, one still cherished, and practiced, in the American South.
**980.** Mathes, p. 101.
**981.** Wyeth, LGNBF, p. 632; Sheppard, p. 308.
**982.** Mathes, p. 357. One other time Forrest drank alcohol was in September 1863, and it was certainly not for pleasure. After receiving a wound during his stand at Tunnel Hill (Battle of Chickamauga), his doctor ordered him to drink whiskey to ease the pain.
**983.** Wyeth, LGNBF, p. 629.

Republican,[984] or more specifically a Libertarian, Forrest was a lover of Dixie and a constitutional conservative; and yet he at first voted against secession from the United States.[985] Though a true Southern gentleman brimming with old-fashioned chivalrous values, before the War he was not religious, and was addicted to gambling, had a short fuse, a violent temper, and cursed constantly.[986] It was said, however, that while he did indeed take the Lord's name on many an occasion, it was never in vain.[987]

During the South's fight for home rule, this singular combination of traits, along with his infernal harass-and-destroy maneuvers, diabolic bluffs, and fiendish surrender-or-die tactics, earned him the Yankee sobriquet, "the Devil." It is not known what Forrest personally thought of this title. But we can be certain that during the War he enjoyed the dread it caused in the North and the elation it caused in the South.

Though he transformed himself into a well-quaffed, well-dressed multimillionaire who lived in a mansion surrounded by servants, during his earlier years he was the epitome of the rough-and-tumble frontiersman. As such, the irascible rebel was involved in countless shouting matches, fisticuffs, lawsuits, death threats, knife and gunfights, and gentlemanly duels.[988]

Some of his brawls ended in murder, and he lived much of his life in courtrooms. He never spent a night in jail, however, and he was always exonerated, for Forrest was a fair fighter who seldom, if ever, aggressed. Instead, he simply sought justice when he or his own had been wronged, the accepted custom on early America's western frontier.

---

984. At the time Forrest was actually a conservative Democrat: the names of the two parties, Republicans and Democrats, were reversed in the 1800s. Hence, Lincoln, who belonged to the Republican Party, was what we would call today a left-wing liberal Democrat. Even into the present, the South remains primarily conservative and Republican, while the North remains mainly liberal and Democrat. This was just one of the many factors that split the nation in two by 1861.

985. Forrest was not the only Confederate officer who originally loved the Union and disagreed with the idea of secession. Among others were Gideon Johnson Pillow, Jubal Anderson Early, Robert E. Lee, and even President Jefferson Davis. In fact, contrary to Yankee myth, in 1860 most Southerners were against the notion of breaking up the Union. It was the election of the anti-South, big government liberal Abraham Lincoln that November which made secession seem a reasonable, even imperative, option.

986. Henry, ATSF, pp. 107, 120. Unlike many Yanks at the time, Forrest's swearing never included obscene or vulgar language.

987. Lytle, p. 159.

988. As one example, see Wyeth, LGNBF, pp. 617-619. Fortunately for all involved, this particular duel ended peacefully, without a shot being fired.

# - 1859 TO 1860 -
# PLANTATIONS, COTTON, & WEALTH: FORREST AS SLAVE OWNER & SLAVE TRADER

"We can't hold 'em, but we can run over 'em." —
Nathan Bedford Forrest to his superiors at the
Battle of Fort Donelson

## FORREST THE SLAVER

THOUGH THE GENERAL LIVED A short life, it was packed to the brim from start to finish with adventure and drama, the equivalent of one-hundred everyday lives. Of his time here on Earth, only a small fraction of it was devoted to slave ownership, however—a mere seven years. And yet it is his work as a plantation owner and slave trader for which he is best known by anti-Forrest proponents, occupations which have naturally brought forth charges of "racism" from the ignorant and politically correct. Since this is one of the main indictments against him, his slaving days are worthy of detailed analysis.

As we have thoroughly shown, calling Forrest a racist because he owned slaves is quite absurd, for at the start of the War (and beyond) tens of thousands of Northerners did as well,[989] including Yankee hero

---

989. Some estimate that there were as many as between 500,000 and 1,000,000 slaves in the North in 1860. See e.g., Eaton, HSC, p. 93; Hinkle, p. 125.

Ulysses S. Grant.[990] Yet Grant is never called a racist. We have seen too that thousands of blacks and Native-Americans also bought, sold and owned black slaves. But they are never called racists.

Forrest has also been taken to task for using the "n" word, but the word was common enough at the time, and was regularly used by both 19th- and 20th-Century blacks when referring to their own kind.[991] Among those African-Americans who were known to use this word were famous former servants, such as Harriet Tubman. Some 19th-Century blacks even occasionally referred to whites as "niggers."[992]

What will be more surprising to many is that the "n" word was also used in public by the so-called "Great Emancipator," Abraham Lincoln[993]—a man who also strongly opposed marriage between whites and blacks and who, throughout his administration, vigorously campaigned to have all blacks shipped "back to their native land" (Africa),[994] or at least corralled into their own all-black state.[995]

A hint of Lincoln's true feelings about blacks and slavery can be found in the fact that his Final Emancipation Proclamation only freed slaves in the South where he had no legal control (by 1861, the Confederate States of America, or C.S.A., was an independent sovereign nation), but not in the North where he had full legal control. Why would he do this when, as a lifelong lawyer, he knew full well that this rendered his edict completely ineffectual?

The abolition of slavery was simply not an important issue to Lincoln. He used it merely as a political tool to stir up Northern hatred of the South and as an attempt to disrupt the Southern economy.

Indeed, at first, not wanting to injure the Northern economy, he left slavery in place in that region. This explains the words of Lincoln's own secretary of state, William H. Seward, who called the Emancipation

---

990. Grant continued to keep his slaves (as slaves) even after the War, since Lincoln's Emancipation Proclamation did not free slaves in the North, only in the Confederates States. And because the Confederate States were an independent nation at the time, the Emancipation Proclamation had no affect in the South either. Wallechinsky, Wallace, and Wallace, p. 11; Woods, p. 67.
991. See e.g., Gragg, pp. 84-88.
992. Genovese, p. 438.
993. See e.g., Nicolay and Hay, CWAL, Vol. 11, pp. 105-106; Nicolay and Hay, ALCW, Vol. 1, pp. 292, 298; Holzer, pp. 22-23, 67, 318, 361.
994. Seabrook, EYWTACWW, pp. 116-131, 146-56.
995. Nicolay and Hay, ALCW, Vol. 1, p. 355. For more on Lincoln's racist politics and language, see Seabrook, TUAL, passim.

Proclamation an empty, purposeless document, one "that emancipates the slaves where we cannot reach them and holds them in bondage where we can set them free."[996]

If allowing the practice of slavery to continue and promoting the idea of black deportation are considered racism by many, why is Lincoln also not known as a racist, for he was both an opponent of true civil rights for blacks[997] and an arch supporter of black colonization?[998]

Whatever Lincoln's motivations were, Forrest never supported any of the Yankee president's white supremacist policies, and in fact, after the War, as he told the Louisville *Courier-Journal*, he wanted to repopulate and revitalize the devastated South with both freedmen and new immigrant blacks from Africa.[999] How different this was from Lincoln who, right up until his death, campaigned incessantly to rid the country of blacks altogether, as one of his own generals (Benjamin F. Butler) attested.[1000]

It is, of course, not right to judge our 19th-Century predecessors using 21st-Century values. Presentism—judging the past based on the values of today—is always unfair and misleading. Though a slave trader and owner, Forrest was, after all, a product of his times, just as we are.

Today we cringe at the mere thought of slavery. But it was perfectly legal across the United States from 1776 to 1865 (again, we will note that the Confederacy banned the foreign slave trade in 1861, three years earlier than the U.S.). Protected by the U.S. Constitution, slave ownership and slave trading were accepted and even integral aspects of everyday society, one also enthusiastically practiced by African-Americans and Native-Americans, not just European-Americans.

We must also consider that both American slavery and the American slave trade got their start in the North, and that Yankees only finally abolished slavery, not out of concern for black civil rights, but because it became unprofitable.[1001]

996. Piatt, p. 150.
997. See e.g., Lincoln and Douglas, p. 187.
998. See e.g., Nicolay and Hay, ALCW, Vol. 2, p. 237.
999. Hurst, p. 330; Wills, p. 359; Ashdown and Caudill, pp. 63, 84.
1000. See e.g., B. F. Butler, p. 903. Many other famous Northerners also did not believe in abolition or equality of the races, such as General William T. Sherman. See e.g., Seabrook, EYWTACWW, p. 175.
1001. Roberts, p. 198; Garraty and McCaughey, p. 81; Rosenbaum and Brinkley, s.v. "Slavery"; "Slave States."

With such facts at hand, why should Forrest and only Forrest be selected out and targeted as a racist?[1002]

In Forrest's beloved South, where less than 6 percent of the population actually owned slaves and where 94 percent did not,[1003] and where slave trading was considered an honest (if not the most desirable) way to make a living, Forrest approached it simply as an occupation, a way to feed and clothe his family. This is not to say that he treated his human property like livestock. Quite the opposite.

First-hand accounts from those who purchased slaves from Forrest reveal that his slaves were regularly bathed, exceedingly well-groomed, and were daily dressed in clean, freshly starched, stiff clothing.[1004] One of Forrest's advertisements noted that his rules regarding "cleanliness, neatness and comfort . . . [are] strictly observed and enforced."[1005]

He also encouraged his servants to learn to read and write (quite unlike typical slave treatment in the North), always handled them with respect and dignity, and went out of his way to make sure he did not divide families—even though there was no law against this in Mississippi or Tennessee at the time.[1006] Indeed, it was his routine practice to purchase all members of a slave household if need be, in order to keep husbands, wives, and children together.[1007]

In cases where the male heads of slave families had been sold away from their wives and children, Forrest would go in search of them, no matter how widely scattered they happened to be, then purchase them on the spot.[1008] Thus in countless instances he was instrumental in reuniting slave families who had been separated. As Jordan and Pryor

---

1002. It should be noted that most whites were perfectly content to work their own fields, and only took on slaves because of the belief at the time that those of African descent had a greater tolerance of the malarial diseases that were then so common across the hot, humid Southern states. Wyeth, LGNBF, p. 20.

1003. M. M. Smith, pp. 4-5. Slaves were extremely expensive and were often more valuable than the farms they worked on or the homes they worked in. In the 1850s the average cost for one healthy slave was about $1,500, the equivalent of nearly $40,000 today. This put them out of reach of all but the absolute wealthiest individuals, who comprised but a small minority of early American society (most of which consisted of poor farming families).

1004. Sheppard, p. 25.

1005. Bancroft, STOS, p. 258.

1006. Contrary to Yankee anti-South propaganda, some Southern states, such as Louisiana, had laws against dividing slave families. U. B. Phillips, p. 493.

1007. Henry, ATSF, p. 29.

1008. Lytle, p. 28.

write, he was a slaver of "admitted probity and humanity" who never split slave families up, even if he had to take a loss.[1009]

He also refused to do trade with inhumane slavers:[1010] according to journalist Lafcadio Hearn, Forrest possessed a list of especially vicious Memphis slave traders that he refused to sell to.[1011] Forrest also made sure that his servants were well housed and well fed.[1012] Little wonder that they were "strongly attached to him."[1013]

## A NOTE ON WHIPPING

According to Yankee myth, "Forrest mercilessly whipped his slaves on a daily basis." This is a ludicrous lie, however, for the simple fact that the General was not the type of man to wantonly abuse others, especially servants, whom he considered valuable property—and in some cases even comrades and friends.

Obviously, the truth about the whip, slaves, and plantation discipline has been completely distorted by South-hating advocates, authors, and scholars, particularly in regards to Forrest. Therefore, let us pause for a moment to establish the facts.[1014]

When a Southern slave owner was put in a position where force was needed (such as with a violent servant), which for the average slaver was seldom if at all, it was not motivated by "the innate cruelty" or "sadistic tendencies of Southern whites," as Yankee myth ridiculously promotes. It was motivated by the same thing that motivates modern, free labor bosses: the desire for maximum profits.

While today's supervisors use the threat of demotion and termination for inferior work or bad behavior, Victorian slavers used the threat of force, for this was then the accepted approach to discipline. One of the instruments of force sometimes resorted to was the infamous whip.

But whipping was not a corrective tool created specifically for

---

1009. Jordan and Pryor, p. 26.
1010. Wyeth, LGNBF, pp. 20-21.
1011. Henry, FWMF, p. 14.
1012. Mathes, p. 16.
1013. Jordan and Pryor, p. 26.
1014. Some of the material in this particular subsection was taken from my book, *The McGavocks of Carnton Plantation: A Southern History*.

the institution of Southern slavery, as the North and New South teaches. Actually, from the 1600s to the 1800s it was the standard form of punishment in the U.S. for misdemeanors; and it was applied to lawbreakers of every kind, whether male or female, whether black, white, brown, or red.[1015] As such, there can little doubt that far more American whites were whipped by the local sheriff than American blacks.[1016]

The custom of whipping was a gift of the English, who left us records of "rogues" being "graciously whipped" from as early as the late 1500s. The practice was then brought to America with the very first wave of Anglo immigrants.[1017]

As early as 1698, for example, Pennsylvanian Gabriel Thomas was writing that:

> Thieves of all sorts, are oblig'd to restore four fold after they have been Whipt and Imprison'd, according to the Nature of their Crime; and if they be not of Ability to restore four fold, they must be in Servitude till 'tis satisfied.[1018]

Here we see that at the time criminals were not only whipped for their misdeeds, but were also sentenced to a form of mild bondage known as servitude, the exact same type that millions of black "slaves" would later serve under in the American South.

## WHIPPING WAS UNIVERSAL

The truth, contrary to Northern anti-South folklore, is that from New England to the Deep South, the whipping post was the centerpiece of the village green in hundreds of towns and cities across early America. The standard punishment for horse thieves, for example, nearly all who were white, was "three good whippings," each one consisting of thirty-nine lashes.[1019]

Whipping was a standard military punishment at the time as well. During the Revolutionary War, while the "father of the nation,"

---

1015. Fogel and Engerman, p. 146.
1016. Ashe, p. 64.
1017. Hacker, pp. 29, 35.
1018. G. Thomas, p. 47.
1019. Coit, pp. 37, 48.

George Washington, served as General of the Continental Army, he regularly whipped his white soldiers for a host of offences ranging from drunkenness to desertion.[1020] His floggings were so brutal that Congress had to create a rule regulating the amount of times a whip could be applied to one's bare back.[1021]

In 1812 an enlightened and more humane Congress made courts-martial whippings entirely unlawful (in one of the more outrageous cases a white soldier had been branded, had his head shaved, and was given fifty lashes). Military officers, however, believed it was the only sure means of enforcing discipline. Congress later lifted its ban and whipping was reinstated in 1833.[1022] Aboard navy ships whipping was so common as a form of punishment that even abolitionists protested against the practice on humanitarian terms.[1023]

During Lincoln's War, white farmers in the South risked being whipped for violating the governmental ban on growing cotton instead of food.[1024] And it is well-known that both white and black Yankee soldiers used the whip on "stubborn" captured Southern blacks between 1861 and 1865.[1025] "Insubordinate" black Yankee soldiers were sometimes whipped by their white superiors as well.[1026] Black Union soldiers were known to whip white civilians during the War.[1027]

JUST WHO USED THE WHIP?
The whip then was the normal American penalty for bad behavior. Thus it was only natural that it was also used to enforce authority on plantations. In fact, black slaves themselves, such as those who worked in positions of power (e.g., mammies, overseers, and drivers), regularly used the whip on other black slaves when the situation warranted it.[1028] And we will note that *black* slave owners—of which there were tens of thousands across the South—occasionally used it on their black chattel

1020. Collier and Collier, p. 51.
1021. Jensen, NN, p. 33.
1022. Alotta, p. 3.
1023. Stampp, p. 410.
1024. Channing, p. 29.
1025. Wiley, SN, pp. 213, 244, 245.
1026. See Quarles, pp. 208-209; Wiley, SN, pp. 316-317.
1027. Henry, ASTF, p. 246.
1028. See Fogel, p. 26; Genovese, pp. 356, 368, 371, 374, 378-380, 385, 386, 542.

as well.[1029]

Such intimidation was not imposed to create submissive and docile slaves, as Northern mythologists have long claimed. Rather it was used to create the largest and best product at the lowest cost in the most efficient manner.

We must keep in mind that while today even shoving a person can result in arrest for "assault and battery," in the 1800s physical punishment of all kinds was regarded as the norm. As late as the mid 1800s the English were still whipping child factory workers (all of them white) who underperformed. In America black slave parents routinely whipped their unruly offspring (with switches), while black male slaves were known to whip their wives when they felt it was warranted.[1030] Lincoln's wife Mary Todd Lincoln often whipped their children, as the Yankee president unabashedly acknowledged in a letter dated October 22, 1846.[1031] In most Western nations this approach to discipline lasted well into the 20th Century, and there are no doubt people reading this book who will recall being "whipped" with a belt or spanked with a paddle as a youngster.

In the 18th-Century America then, the whipping of a slave was considered no more exceptional or barbaric than the whipping of a disobedient child by its parents.[1032] Forrest himself, like most Victorian Southern children, was regularly whipped on the behind for bad behavior as a schoolboy,[1033] so it was only natural that later in life, as a slave trader and slave owner, he saw nothing wrong with occasionally applying the lash to the backside of disobedient servants.

THE ECONOMICS OF DISCIPLINE

Does this shock and repulse us today? Of course. But perhaps not quite as much when we learn that as a military officer in the Confederate army Forrest also whipped his white soldiers for insubordination.[1034]

We must also bear in mind that the U.S. judicial system

---

1029. Drescher and Engerman, pp. 214, 215.
1030. Genovese, pp. 470, 482, 504, 508-511.
1031. Nicolay and Hay, ALCW, Vol. 1, p. 89.
1032. Horn, IE, p. 68.
1033. Lytle, p. 14; Parks, p. 82.
1034. Morton, pp. 148-149; Wyeth, LGNBF, p. 302.

expected slave owners (Northern and Southern) to attend to disciplinary matters themselves, and not clog up the courts with petty grievances concerning contumacious slaves.[1035] Additionally, as there were far worse penalties, such as being shot before a firing squad, the use of the whip was an accepted and recognized form of penalizing not only black servants, but criminals of all colors and social statuses.

In the end physical discipline on Southern plantations was about pure economics. Too much force would have increased rather than decreased the cost of labor, which is just one of the many reasons why African-American, Native-American, and European-American slave owners did not use physical coercion on their human chattel unless absolutely necessary.[1036]

Yes, threat of punishment was also important in sustaining the power hierarchy on the early plantation. But it is for this very same reason that it is also vital today in the modern office. Obviously the balance between a superior and his or her subordinates cannot be achieved, however, if the former resorts to brute violence.

Slave owners, most who were experienced, professional, and highly intelligent businessmen, understood this, as did the authors of a variety of Victorian plantation books, all which strongly discouraged farm managers from using any kind of corporal punishment.

Here is what one such work, the popular 19th-Century *Instructions to Managers*, had to say on the subject: the most important thing is the manner in which a manager approaches his black servants. Yes, he must be strict at times. But he must balance this with fair and humane treatment, offering kindness and even indulgences for good work, behavior, and attitude. For rewards are nearly always more effective than punishments.[1037]

---

1035. Horn, IE, p. 68.
1036. Fogel and Engerman, pp. 232, 238-239.
1037. Fogel and Engerman, p. 240.

# FORREST FREED MANY OF HIS SLAVES BEFORE THE WAR

Forrest went as far as to free many of his slaves even before Lincoln's War,[1038] and in 1859 he shut down his slave business in Memphis and sold his last servant.[1039] This was five years before Lincoln himself issued his fake Emancipation Proclamation (January 1, 1863) and seven years before the Thirteenth Amendment finally ended slavery all across the United States (December 6, 1865).

What many do not realize, however, is that Forrest got out of the slave trading business in great part because of his slaves themselves. While the North finally abolished its slave trade only when it became unprofitable, Forrest abolished his at the height of its profitability in 1859.[1040] Why? Because his servants had come to him "in a body" with the idea of closing his slave trading business and opening up a plantation, where they could continue to work for him without fear of being sold to someone else.[1041]

While Forrest was emancipating his African-American servants, here is what Lincoln was saying about slavery, blacks, abolition, and racial equality:

> If all earthly power were given me, I should not know what to do as to the existing institution. My first impulse would be to free all the slaves, and send them to Liberia [Africa]—to their own native land. But a moment's reflection would convince me, that whatever of high hope (as I think there is) there may be in this, in the long run, its sudden execution is impossible. If they were all landed there in a day, they would all perish in the next ten days; and there are not surplus shipping and surplus money enough in the world to carry them there in many times ten days. What then? Free them all, and keep them among us as underlings? Is it quite certain that this betters their condition? I think I would not hold one in slavery at any rate; yet the point is not clear enough to me to denounce people upon. What next? Free them, and make them politically and socially our equals? My own feelings will not admit of this; and if mine would, we well know that those of the great mass of white

---

1038. *Report of the Joint Select Committee to Inquire into the Condition of Affairs in the Late Insurrectionary States*, p. 20.

1039. Wyeth, LGNBF, p. 22.

1040. Slavery in the South was at its peak profitability in 1859 and 1860. Fogel and Engermann, pp. 38-106.

1041. Lytle, p. 28.

people will not.[1042]

Forrest's attitude toward both free and enslaved blacks could not have been more different than that of the Yankee president from Illinois. Confederate Colonel George W. Adair, an intimate friend of the General, had this to say on the topic:

> Forrest was kind, humane, and extremely considerate of his slaves. He was overwhelmed with applications from a great many of this class, who begged him to purchase them. He seemed to exercise the same influence over these creatures that in a greater degree he exercised over the soldiers who in later years served him as devotedly as if there was between them a strong personal attachment. When a slave was purchased for him his first act was to turn him over to his negro valet, Jerry, with instructions to wash him thoroughly and put clean clothes on him from head to foot. Forrest applied the rule of cleanliness and neatness to the slaves which he practised for himself. In his appearance, in those ante-bellum days, he was extremely neat and scrupulously clean. In fact, so particular was he in regard to his personal appearance that some were almost inclined to call him foppish. The slaves who were thus transformed were proud of belonging to him. He was always very careful when he purchased a married slave to use every effort to secure also the husband or wife, as the case might be, and unite them, and in handling children he would not permit the separation of a family.[1043]

Compare this with Lincoln's treatment of blacks during the War. Contrary to popular belief, Lincoln's idea of "humane treatment" was not to issue freedmen "forty acres and a mule" as he had falsely promised,[1044] but rather to pen them up like livestock in "government corrals," and withhold food, clothing, and medical care from them.

On September 26, 1864, at the Brown Farm at Elkton,

---

1042. Nicolay and Hay, ALCW, Vol. 1, p. 288.

1043. Wyeth, LGNBF, pp. 20-21.

1044. Lincoln's promise of "forty acres and a mule" for freedmen was an outright lie, one he never intended to uphold. It turned out to be nothing but a lure to draw blacks off their plantations in an effort to destroy the South's infrastructure. There were never any mules, and most of his so-called "black land giveaways" ultimately went to rich white Northerners. See Seabrook, EYWTACWW, p. 128; Mullen, p. 33; Rosenbaum and Brinkley, s.v. "Forty Acres and a Mule"; J. H. Franklin, p. 37; Thornton and Ekelund, p. 96.

Tennessee (near Pulaski), Forrest came across one of these squalid U.S. black camps[1045] and described it like this:

> From Elkton I directed my course toward a Government corral at Brown's plantation, toward Pulaski. At this place I found about 2,000 negroes, consisting mostly of old men, women, and children, besides a large amount of commissary stores and medical supplies. General Buford having completed his work at Elk River joined me at this place, where I issued to my entire command several days' rations, distributing among the troops as much sugar and coffee as they needed. The negroes were all ragged and dirty, and many seemed in absolute want. I ordered them to remove their clothing and bed clothes from the miserable hovels in which they lived and then burnt up this den of wretchedness. Near 200 houses were consumed.[1046]

Forrest's absolute disgust at the way Yankees treated the blacks they had "freed" is evident here. He carried this sense of humanity with him into the treatment of his own servants. The result? Not a single one of his slaves ever tried to run away. In fact, so favorable was his reputation among blacks, that anytime he went to the local market, dozens blocked his way "begging" to be purchased by him, as Colonel Adair intimated above.[1047]

Was Forrest motivated solely by altruism? Of course not. Whatever the trade, the cool-headed businessman always kept profitability foremost in mind.[1048] On the other hand it is clear that, compared to his Yankee enemies, he was a nonracist equal opportunity employer, as we will see from his service in the Confederate Army.

---

1045. Henry, ATSF, pp. 200-201.

1046. ORA, Ser. 1, Vol. 39, Pt. 1, p. 545.

1047. Sheppard, p. 25.

1048. Forrest was a stickler for cleanliness himself, and always made great effort to be neat and hygienic, hence he expected the same from his slaves. But more importantly, clean, healthy, educated servants were worth more than unkempt, sickly, and illiterate ones. Beyond his humanitarian concerns, for a slaver like Forrest this was also good business practice. See Wills, pp. 31-32.

# Part 4

# FORREST & THE WAR FOR SOUTHERN INDEPENDENCE

# - 1861, PART 1 -
# ELECTION, SECESSION, INVASION

*"When you hear the guns, and the bugle sounds, every man must charge, and we will give 'em hell!"* — Nathan Bedford Forrest at the Battle of Brice's Cross Roads

## FORREST'S FIGHT AGAINST LINCOLN

THE YEAR 1861 MARKED THE boiling point for the South, and on a more personal level, a major turning point for the distinguished looking 185-pound Tennessean. It was in that year that the Southerner-turned-Northern dictator from Illinois violated the Constitution and illicitly ordered his invaders to march on the legally-formed Confederate States of America.

The question is why? What would cause the leader of a free democracy to willingly kill nearly three million of his own citizens (both military and civilian),[1049] bankrupt the treasury, drive a knife through the heart of the Constitution, overturn and destroy the original confederate republic established by the Founding Fathers, utilize total war and a scorched earth policy to obliterate half his country, create a wound that

---

1049. Timothy Manning, personal correspondence. Some Southern historians, like Manning, estimate that Lincoln's War took the lives of as many as 1 million Northerners and 2 million Southerners. These figures include all races and both noncombatants and black slaves (both genders, all ages). Additionally, it is important to note that nearly *all* civilian deaths occurred in the South. While the exact Southern death toll is not known, and will never be known, Jefferson Davis estimated that Lincoln killed at least half of the South's Negro population, or about 1,750,000 black men, women, and children, free and bonded. See F. Moore, pp. 278-279.

will never heal between North and South, and initiate laws meant to create hatred between the races? And what would motivate this leader to engage in overt illegal activity and war crimes to accomplish all of this?

How did Forrest respond to Lincoln's outrageous acts, and in what ways did this conflict alter his life?

To answer these questions, let us pause from Forrest's life for a moment and look at the initial causes of this conflict. While this may seem like a digression, understanding Lincoln and his War from a *Southern* point of view is vital in helping us to better understand Forrest, the world he grew up in, and the man he eventually became.

## A WAR OF TARIFFS

The War for Southern Independence, America's Second Revolutionary War of secession, was no accident. It was not initiated by the South, nor was it about slavery, as we have been taught by Northern-printed history books and Yankee mythology. As with all wars, it was about money and politics.

This economic-political conflict did not erupt suddenly, in 1861. The division between North and South began almost as soon as the U.S. was formed, in the late 18th Century. In fact, arguments between the South and the North could be seen as early the Constitutional Convention in Philadelphia, Pennsylvania, in 1787,[1050] where sectional friction actually stalled the creation of the U.S. Constitution.[1051]

Two years later the U.S. Congress passed the Tariff Act of 1789, which imposed an 8 percent tax on the importation of foreign goods, an attempt to raise revenue for the new government. This was one of the earliest financial hardships imposed on Dixie. For unlike the North, whose economy was based chiefly on manufacturing, the South's economy was based mainly on agriculture, which meant that it was dependent on imports from the North and from Europe. Thus, the 1789 Tariff placed an undue burden on Dixie, raising the hackles of Southerners everywhere. This was just the beginning, however.

Just twenty-seven years later the Tariff of 1816 was pushed through. This, the nation's first authentic protective (importation-

1050. Collier and Collier, p. 202.
1051. Napolitano, pp. 4-5.

exportation) tax, raised rates to 20 percent, temporarily ending the concept of a revenue-generating tariff (as found in the Tariff of 1789). Protectionist tariffs hinder free trade, one of the holy grails of the South, which is why this particular tariff was much hated by Southern cotton growers.

Eight years later the "Sectional" Tariff of 1824 was passed, raising rates to 30 percent. It was called "sectional" because it was legislated primarily by Northern and Western interests, and because it once again imposed an undue financial burden on the South, whose products were sold primarily to Europe. As usual, the North, whose products were sold mainly in the U.S., suffered little by the introduction of this tariff.

A mere four years later Lincoln's political idol, militant Whig and Kentucky slave owner, Henry Clay (1777-1852), sponsored the Tariff of 1828, nicknamed the "Tariff of Abominations" because it raised rates much higher, to nearly 50 percent, a staggering increase. It became, in fact, the highest tariff ever levied on the South. With cotton prices now exorbitantly high, Britain began to look for other markets, threatening the Southern economy.

Naturally the South was infuriated. But things were about to get even worse.

Four years later, in a modest attempt to appease Dixie, the U.S. Congress passed the Tariff of 1832, an ineffectual reform that promised to lower rates to their 1824 levels. One Southern state, South Carolina, was not amused. Threatening to secede from the Union, it refused to collect the tax at Charleston Harbor, sparking the Nullification Crisis of 1832 (in which a South Carolina state convention voted to nullify the tariffs of 1828 and 1832).[1052]

An angry President Andrew Jackson, though himself a native South Carolinian, believed that the state's repeal of U.S. tariff acts was treasonous. And so, with Jackson's blessing, Congress passed the Force Bill in early 1833, allowing the president to use military force, if necessary, to implement the collection of tariffs.

South Carolina backed down and rescinded nullification, but, still infuriated, nullified the Force Bill. The War for Southern

---

1052. Thornton and Ekelund, p. 10.

Independence (the "Civil War" to Yanks) would have started then and there, in early 1833, had Jackson not disregarded the state's act of rebellion against the U.S. government. All of this was an ill omen of things to come.

One year later, under continuing pressure, the U.S. government passed the Tariff of 1833. This tax, which was meant to slowly reduce the rates back to 1816 levels, passed, but just barely—and with great reluctance by Northern politicians. In fact, anti-Dixie senator Clay, speaking in the House of Representatives, pledged that he would eventually "defy the South" and raise the tariff rates back up again.[1053]

By the 1840s, the reduced tariffs put in place by the Tariff of 1833, while appeasing the South, now began to agitate the North. And so the Tariff of 1842 was inaugurated, canceling the rate reductions of the Tariff of 1833, allowing rates to climb back up. Tempers in the South inevitably began to simmer again.

Under the new Democratic (i.e., conservative) president, James K. Polk (1795-1849), the tariff see-saw reversed direction once more. Now with a Democratically-held Congress (that sympathized with the South),[1054] Northerners were outvoted and the Tariff of 1846 (also known as the "Walker Tariff") was passed, once again lowering the rates. While this tariff benefitted the South by galvanizing trade with Britain (which had formerly threatened to buy their cotton elsewhere), tensions, of course, increased in the North.

Eleven years later the Tariff of 1857 was enacted, lowering taxes to 20 percent, their 1816 level. The South was overjoyed. The North sulked, and began plotting its revenge. The conflict between the protectionist North and the free-trade South was coming to a head.[1055]

By early 1861, with the anti-South dictator Lincoln on the sure-to-win Republican (i.e., liberal) ticket, seven Southern states had seen the writing on the wall and had already seceded from the Union. With almost no Southern representation now in the U.S. Congress, Northerner and Republican senator Justin Smith Morrill had no trouble

---

1053. DiLorenzo, RL, pp. 63-64.
1054. Let us bear in mind that the Democrats during Forrest's day were what we would now call Conservatives (or Republicans), while the Republicans of that period were what we would think of today as Liberals (or Democrats).
1055. DiLorenzo, RL, p. 128.

introducing the Morrill Tariff of 1861. The act, implemented two days before Lincoln's inauguration (on March 4, 1861), would send rates soaring once again.

Over the next few years, to the South's horror (but not to its surprise), the U.S. government would implement protectionist tariffs that would eventually reach 47 percent, nearly the same rate as the despised Tariff of Abominations in 1828.

## LINCOLN'S PSYCHOLOGICAL WAR ON THE SOUTH

Under the laws of the Constitution (in particular the Tenth Amendment), additional Southern states quickly and legally seceded, forming an independent nation, the Confederate States of America (C.S.A.). Lincoln bristled and threatened to make war on the South.

The Confederate States, however, assumed the president was bluffing. To begin with, what national leader would send the government's military forces against his own people?

Second, the C.S.A. knew it was fully justified in leaving the Union: for almost as long as the U.S. had existed, the South had been taxed more heavily than the North, while most of the revenues from these taxes had been spent in the North. This was indeed a recipe for war. But war was not yet inevitable.

Lincoln proclaimed that if the South left the Union the Union would crumble and anarchy would reign, setting off further secessions.[1056] This, however, was nothing but a clever political ploy. Nations do not fall apart when they divide. When Norway seceded from Sweden in 1905, for example, no other secessions occurred and anarchy did not arise. Instead, stability and prosperity only increased for both nations.[1057]

Lincoln's concept of "preserving the Union" was actually a euphemism for his true agenda: to create a vast and all-powerful centralized government based on Clay's American System, which promoted a nationalized banking system, modern industrialization, a market-oriented economy, protective tariffs, and internal improvements (or as we refer to it today, corporate welfare).

---

1056. See e.g., Nicolay and Hay, ALCW, Vol. 2, pp. 4, 5, 62, 93, 439.
1057. DiLorenzo, RL, p. 117.

To achieve this Lincoln would need to ignore the Constitution, destroy the concept of states' rights, completely reverse the structure of the original form of government (a confederate republic, a "voluntary association of friendly states," as Jefferson Davis called it)[1058] created by the Founding Fathers,[1059] and force the South to remain within the Union—with deadly force if necessary. We will note here that for his efforts Lincoln would later be lovingly cited by another socialist dictator, Adolf Hitler,[1060] who wrote admiringly of "Honest Abe's" anti-states' rights views in his book *Mein Kampf* ("My Struggle").[1061]

Lincoln's hatred of the U.S. Constitution (which next to the Bible was the most beloved document in the South) was evident even before he was inaugurated. In February 1861, at Willard's Hotel in Washington, D.C., the president-elect was asked by New York businessman William E. Dodge what he was going to do, if anything, to try and prevent war with the South. Lincoln's response was both dire and appalling. When I get to the Oval Office, he said,

> I shall take an oath to the best of my ability to preserve, protect, and defend the Constitution. This is a great and solemn duty. With the support of the people and the assistance of the Almighty I shall undertake to perform it. I have full faith that I shall perform it. It is not the Constitution as I would like to have it, but as it *is* that is to be defended.[1062]

Such sentiments did not last long, indicating that from the beginning he had every intention of rewriting the Constitution to suit his own big government liberal agenda as soon as possible after entering the White House.

In altering the Constitution and the form of the U.S. government, Lincoln intended to change the latter from one that was created to simply protect the lives, liberties, and property of its citizens to one that focused on empire building; from the original weak,

---

1058. Seabrook, TQJD, pp. 20, 21.
1059. See Stephens, CV, Vol. 1, pp. 504-505.
1060. DiLorenzo, LU, pp. 81-84.
1061. See Hitler, Vol. 2, pp. 830-831.
1062. Coffin, p. 235. Lincoln-worshiper President Barack Hussein Obama recently made a similar statement, calling the U.S. Constitution "an imperfect document." "Glenn Beck," FOX News, September, 17, 2009 (Constitution Day, 222nd anniversary).

decentralized government with a loose coalition of sovereign states (a Confederation), to a new strong, centralized government with a strictly controlled consolidation of dependent, nearly powerless states (a Federation).

All of this, of course, was solidly and even violently opposed in the South, a constitutionally conservative, Old European, agrarian society, made up of fiercely independent thinking, freedom loving men and women, who still believed in the confederate government their Southern ancestors had created, and had fought and died for, in 1776.[1063]

Lincoln was not worried about resistance in the South. He had military might on his side and was not afraid to use it in order to accomplish his political goals.

He began by disregarding American tradition, the Constitution, the rules of the land, the innate laws of civilized society, and even the will of the American people. For up until 1860, the right of secession was considered a God-given prerogative in both the North and the South: it was after all, clearly spelled out in both the Declaration of Independence and the U.S. Constitution (Ninth and Tenth Amendments).[1064] Thousands of Yanks and hundreds of Northern newspapers supported the South's right to peaceful secession and were outraged at Lincoln's idea of forcing the Confederacy to remain in the Union at gunpoint.

If Lincoln were to succeed, however, the American public would have to be convinced that the existence of a free and independent South would be detrimental to the Union. This he did by fabricating the concept of "preserving the Union," a classic example of Lincoln's political doublespeak (i.e., saying one thing while meaning another).[1065]

As for the thousands of peace advocates and pro-South sympathizers in the North, Lincoln had a cunning plan for dealing with

---

1063. We will note here that the U.S. was actually first known as "the Confederacy," or more specifically as "the Confederate States of America." See Seabrook, C101, passim. The original U.S. Confederacy lasted from 1781 to 1789, after which its constitution, the Articles of Confederation, were replaced with the U.S. Constitution. See Jensen, NN, passim; Jensen, AC, passim. The idea that the U.S. was still a confederacy, a "Confederate Republic," as Alexander Hamilton called it, continued right up until Lincoln's election, however. In a March 6, 1860, speech at New Haven, Connecticut, for example, Lincoln himself referred to the United States as "this great Confederacy." Nicolay and Hay, ALCW, Vol. 1, p. 628.

1064. Napolitano, pp. 62-63.

1065. Seabrook, TUAL, pp. 8-9.

them. He simply suspended the right of *habeas corpus* and began arresting and jailing anyone who disagreed with his policies, or even questioned them.

Thus it was that throughout the duration of the War, thousands of Northerners were incarcerated at "Lincoln's Prison," Fort Lafayette, New York, and hundreds of Northern newspapers were either shut down, or their owners were forced to sell their papers to individuals who supported Lincoln and his War. In this way the American public was hoodwinked and his critics in the North were silenced.

## LINCOLN PLAYS THE SLAVERY CARD

Though, as we have proven, the War was clearly not about slavery, Lincoln was helped in his goal to turn North against South by the North's late-blooming abolition movement, which had been stirring up Yankee hatred toward Dixie for some thirty years. Painting Northerners as righteous humanitarians while portraying Southerners as inhumane slavers was of course an outrageous fallacy.

One, the American slave trade began in the North: every slave brought into America came aboard a Yankee ship sailing under a U.S. flag. In other words, all "Southern" slaves were purchased from the North.[1066]

Two, since the slave trade got its start in the North, in early America the North had far more slaves and far more slave owners than the South.

Three, abolition was not as popular as the North wanted the South to believe. In fact, Lincoln did not support abolition at the beginning of the War, and considered the abolitionists a nuisance ("don't tar me with the abolitionist brush," he had once emphatically stated);[1067] though later the crafty politician used this group to his benefit, as a political tool against the South.

Four, it is well-known that slaves were treated far more equitably in the South (where they were protected by numerous laws, treated as family members, and called "servants") than they were in the North (where they were more typically treated as chattel and called

---

1066. Kennedy and Kennedy, pp. 59-80.
1067. C. Adams, p. 135; DiLorenzo, GC, p. 255; Johannsen, p. 55.

"slaves"). First-hand accounts, like those of a British correspondent who visited America, noted that: "The North dislikes the negro even more than the South does . . ."[1068]

In the early 1800s Northern landscape architect Frederick Law Olmsted (1822-1903) journeyed to Virginia and was astounded to see whites and slaves freely and warmly intermingling, a sight unknown in the North. On a train, for example, Olmsted witnessed a white woman and a black woman comfortably seated next to one another, their children happily sharing candy from the same container.[1069] This type of familiarity between Europeans and Africans, naturally accepted in the South, would have heartily offended Northerners, Olmsted noted.[1070]

Tocqueville, who also visited America in the early 1800s (in 1831), noted that Northerners were much less tolerant and less compassionate toward blacks than Southerners, and that in the South white and blacks interacted more openly and warmly than in the North.[1071] In his book *Democracy in America*,[1072] Tocqueville had this to say about how Northerners viewed blacks:

> Whosoever has inhabited the United States must have perceived that in those parts of the Union in which the negroes are no longer slaves, they have in nowise drawn nearer to the whites. On the contrary, the prejudice of the race appears to be stronger in the States which have abolished slavery than in those where it still exists; and nowhere is it so intolerant as in those States where servitude never has been known.[1073]

In 1842, after visiting America, English abolitionist and author James S. Buckingham noted that:

> This is only one among the many proofs I had witnessed of the fact, that the prejudice of colour is not nearly so strong in the South as in the North. [In the South] it is not at all uncommon to see the black slaves of both sexes, shake hands with white people when

---

1068. Dicey, Vol. 2, p. 301.
1069. Olmsted, CK, Vol. 1, p. 39.
1070. Kennedy and Kennedy, p. 87.
1071. C. Adams, p. 132.
1072. Volume One of Tocqueville's book *Democracy in America* was published in 1834, Volume Two in 1840.
1073. Tocqueville, Vol. 1, p. 383.

they meet, and interchange friendly personal inquiries; but at the North I do not remember to have witnessed this once; and neither in Boston, New York, or Philadelphia would white persons generally like to be seen shaking hands and talking familiarly with blacks in the streets.[1074]

How then was Lincoln able to persuade the North that Southerners were "cruel and heartless slavers"?  Through rhetorical doublespeak, disinformation, and Northern mythology.

One of Lincoln's primary weapons was the book *Uncle Tom's Cabin*, by New England abolitionist Harriet Beecher Stowe.  First published (in serial form) in 1851, Stowe attempted to depict the life of a Southern slave, even though she knew nothing about Southern culture or the Southern people, had never seen a Southern plantation, and had never even stepped foot in the South.  Thus she knew virtually nothing about Southern blacks, Southern slavery, or African-American culture in the South.  As a result, *Uncle Tom's Cabin* is filled with absurd racist stereotypes of both blacks and Southern whites, false and harmful images that linger to this day.

Actually, Stowe's highly imaginative fiction was inspired by the book, *Truth Is Stranger Than Fiction*, the autobiography of Josiah Henson (1789-1883), a *Northern* slave.[1075]  In her appeal to end slavery Stowe tried to incite Northern hatred toward the South by denigrating the people of Dixie.  But in fact she revealingly based most of her story on the behavior of *Northern* slave owners from Maryland, Henson's birthplace.

All of this was lost on the North, which greedily devoured Stowe's preposterous tale of whip-loving, Negro-hating slave masters, making it a 19th-Century bestseller.  So influential was *Uncle Tom's Cabin* in swaying Northern opinion against the South that it has gone down in history as one of the factors that enabled Lincoln to launch his war.  According to Yankee legend, after meeting her in 1862, midway through the North-South conflict, Lincoln himself referred to Stowe as "the little

---

1074. Buckingham, Vol. 2, p. 112.
1075. Stowe admitted as much, which is why Henson later republished his autobiography under the title: *The Memoirs of Uncle Tom*.

woman who made this great war."[1076]

Another literary weapon Lincoln used to his advantage was the book, *The Impending Crisis of the South: How to Meet It*.   Penned by Southern writer Hinton Rowan Helper, and published in 1857, it promoted both abolition and the idea of a violent slave revolt in the South against slave owners and slave traders.  According to Helper, slavery encouraged a single-crop system (cotton), which restricted economic opportunities for poor white non-slave owning families, the majority class in the South.

Roundly approved by Lincoln's Republican Party, Helper's book was seen as an ideal campaign strategy for the election of 1860.  In 1859, it was reprinted as a small digest and some 100,000 copies were distributed throughout the country.

"Helperism" had its intended effect, but it went both ways. Helper's pamphlet gave the North more reason to despise the South, but it also gave the South more reason to want to distance itself from the North.

What Northerners did not seem to realize was that Helper's advocacy of abolition was not based on a desire for racial equality.  He was actually what we would call an emancipationist-racist, a white supremacist who believed in getting rid of slavery because it hurt whites, not blacks.  And in fact, his book endorsed the ideas that whites and blacks should not marry, or even mix, and that all slaves should be "shipped back to Africa."[1077]

Since Lincoln was also an emancipationist-racist and a strong supporter of these same policies, it is little wonder that he endorsed Helper's book.[1078]  The real wonder is that so few questioned that a white supremacist was running for president using a white supremacist's book to promote the idea of the abolition of slavery.

---

1076. Fields, p. 269. As usual, Lincoln refused to take responsibility for his actions; in this case, in initiating war on the South.

1077. See Helper, ICS, passim.

1078. Helper was so Negrophobic that he refused to stay at hotels with black staff or eat at restaurants with black waiters.  In his later years he worked to get a railroad constructed between North America and South America, hoping that it would help rid Southern white society of its "cumbersomely and worthlessly base and black and brown elements in the vile and deleterious forms of human rubbish around them." Helper, OAD, p. 20.  His idea failed and an embittered poverty-stricken Helper committed suicide in Washington, D.C. in 1909.  This was one of the men who Lincoln looked to for support to help him win his first presidential election and launch his illegal and needless war against the South.

Lincoln's capacity for double-dealing was truly nothing short of astonishing. As we will see, "Lincoln's Great Lie" about slavery was not the first, nor would it be the last example of his duplicitous rhetorical skills.

The reality is that by 1860 most of the South had already accepted the demise of slavery, for the Industrial Revolution, with its new "high-tech" gadgets, made slavery economically unsound. In essence it was becoming cheaper now to use machinery and hire a small, paid, trained workforce to run it than to buy, feed, house, and maintain an army of largely uneducated, extremely costly slaves to work the fields. Urbanization also played a role, as more and more families left their farms for higher paying jobs in the city.

Where in 1860 then was the incentive to buy, trade in, and keep slaves? Though studies have shown that slavery was more profitable than ever that year,[1079] for Dixie the institution had lost its luster. It was slowly fading away day by day, month by month, year by year. Indeed, had it not been for Lincoln's interference, it would have soon been gone altogether, for the South, being the founder of the American abolition movement, had been pushing vigorously and steadily toward complete emancipation for some two-hundred years.

And herein lies one of the many reasons we know that for the South the War was not over slavery: no Southerner was about to spill his blood over an institution that had long outlived its time, was becoming evermore socially unacceptable, and was on the verge of complete extinction.

Such sentiments were moved along by several key factors.

Most other Western nations had already abolished slavery (England, for example, banned it in 1840), and the "Age of Enlightenment," which promoted the idea of the "natural rights of man," had swept around the world, making the concept of enslaving humans not only ethically questionable, but spiritually and morally reprehensible.

Another reason slavery was naturally drawing to a close came from the slaves themselves. As the generations passed, they had gradually replaced their black African ways with white American ways. In adopting American society and culture, they also adopted the

---

1079. See Fogel and Engermann, pp. 38-106.

American obsession with freedom.[1080]

And so the erosion of American slavery had already begun centuries earlier, in the hearts and minds of bonded Africans. In this sense, American slavery itself was condemned from the beginning by the very men who had created it: slave traders and slave owners.

In short, though up until 1860 slavery continued to financially benefit the small minority of wealthy Southern plantation owners, it had become so socially unacceptable that overall prosperity was decreasing across Dixie. It was for these reasons that in its new Constitution, the Confederate Congress prohibited slave trading with foreign nations, paving the way for a full ban on the trade within the Confederacy and eventual complete abolition.

It is obvious then that when Lincoln entered office, the South was already well on its way to making slavery illegal; which is one reason we know that she did not fight the North over this issue. In fact, Confederate States like Tennessee banned slavery even before the War ended.

The North, while harboring an extremely small minority of abolitionists, would also have never agreed to send its sons off to fight in a conflict to free slaves. As proof we have a number of Northern abolitionists themselves, such as William Lloyd Garrison, who voted to allow the South to keep slavery and peacefully secede.[1081]

Garrison's view was not entirely altruistic, however. In fact, behind it lay a myriad of reasons why the North, as a whole, did not want to see slavery abolished "prematurely."

As mentioned, in the beginning not only did the North possess more slaves than the South, but Yankees made vast fortunes sending slave ships to Africa, then selling their human cargo at exorbitant prices back in America, both in the North and in the South.

Slave trading was indeed big business for Northerners, and in many areas it was the literal cornerstone of the region's economy. Furthermore, it was these very businessmen, among them the famous "Wall Street Boys," who Lincoln relied on most heavily for financial backing in his bid for the White House in both 1860 and 1864. Not only

---

1080. C. Adams, p. 129.
1081. W. B. Garrison, LNOK, p. 144.

that, "Honest Abe" would come to rely on the profits these men made from Northern slavery to fund his war against the South.[1082]

Many Northerners were also extremely concerned that a flood of freed Southern slaves would take away precious jobs from whites. Not wanting to scare away either his white supporters or his white money-men, on March 4, 1861, during his First Inaugural Address, Lincoln made his position on slavery clear:

> I have no purpose, directly or indirectly, to interfere with the institution of slavery in the States where it exists. I believe I have no lawful right to do so, and I have no inclination to do so.[1083]

How could Lincoln, said to be the "Great Emancipator" and the "True Friend of the Black Man," place money and politics above human rights? Very simply because he had no love for the African race, or of colored people in general. In fact, Lincoln was one of the world's great white supremacists, as he himself made patently clear throughout his political career.

For example, in his reply to Democratic senatorial candidate Stephen Arnold Douglas (1813-1861), on August 21, 1858, at Ottawa, Illinois (one of eight public debates with Douglas), Lincoln stated the following to a packed house:

> I have no purpose to introduce political and social equality between the white and black races. There is a physical difference between the two, which, in my judgement, will probably forever forbid their living together upon the footing of perfect equality, and, inasmuch as it becomes a necessity that there must be a difference, I . . . am in favor of the race to which I belong having the superior position. I have never said anything to the contrary . . .[1084]

One of Lincoln's primary complaints about Douglas was that the Vermonter wanted to open up the new Western territories of the Louisiana Purchase (Louisiana, Iowa, Oklahoma, Missouri, Nebraska, Kansas, Arkansas, the Dakotas, Montana, and parts of Wyoming,

---

1082. See Spooner, NT, No. 6, p. 54; Pollard, LC, p. 154.
1083. Nicolay and Hay, ALCW, Vol. 2, p. 1.
1084. Nicolay and Hay, ALCW, Vol. 1, p. 458.

Minnesota, and Colorado) to slavery.

But Lincoln was not against Douglas on this issue because he was concerned about human rights, because he cared about blacks, or because he was against slavery.  As he himself said several years earlier, in another reply to Douglas at Peoria, Illinois, on October 16, 1854:

> Whether slavery shall go into Nebraska, or other new Territories, is not a matter of exclusive concern to the people who may go there.  The whole nation is interested that the best use shall be made of the Territories.  We want them for homes of free white people.  This cannot be, to any considerable extent, if slavery shall be planted within them.[1085]

Lincoln's secretary of state, William H. Seward, put the matter even more straightforwardly: the reason abolitionists are against the spread of slavery, he declared, was never about concern for the Negro; it was only about concern for the white man.[1086]

Simply put, Lincoln did not want whites in the Louisiana Purchase to have to compete with blacks for jobs and land.  By keeping blacks out in order to create a whites-only region, Lincoln hoped to curry support *and* white votes in the West.  Why would Lincoln want a whites-only preserve?

Like all racists, Lincoln believed his own race to be superior to every other.  Indeed, he considered "all colored people" to be "inferior races," including both Africans and Mexicans, the latter whom he referred to as "greasers"[1087] and "mongrels."[1088]

Lincoln was not alone in his thinking.  His beloved Republican Party (then akin to today's liberal Democrats) was comprised of numerous other white supremacists.  One was his friend Illinois Senator Lyman Trumbull, who stated in no uncertain terms where their party stood on the matter of people of African descent:

> I, for one, am very much disposed to favor the colonization of such free negroes as are willing to go in Central America.  I want to have

---

1085. Nicolay and Hay, ALCW, Vol. 1, p. 197.
1086. Denson, p. 228.
1087. Nicolay and Hay, ALCW, Vol. 1, p. 524; Neely, p. 213.
1088. See e.g., Nicolay and Hay, ALCW, Vol. 1, p. 449.

nothing to do either with the free negro or the slave negro. We,
the Republican party [Lincoln's party], are the white man's party.
[Great applause] We are for free white men, and for making white
labor respectable and honorable, which it never can be when negro
slave labor is brought into competition with it. [Great applause]
       We wish to settle the Territories with free white men,
and we are willing that this negro race should go anywhere that it
can to better its condition, wishing them God speed wherever they
go. We believe it is better for us that they should not be among us.
I believe it will be better for them to go elsewhere.[1089] . . . When
we say that all men are created equal, we do not mean that every
man in organized society has the same rights. We do not tolerate
that in Illinois.[1090]

It was not just his racism that made Lincoln want to prevent
slavery from spreading into the West. As always, he had political
motives as well.

In 18th-Century America, slave-heavy states received
disproportionate representation politically and economically. This is
because it is the states' populations that determine both the number of
congressional seats they are allowed and the distribution of taxes. Thus,
though slaves themselves could not vote and were considered taxable
property, their numbers gave the slave-intensive states in the Democratic
South added electoral votes while superficially magnifying their
representation in Congress.[1091] Northern Republicans were naturally not
happy with the situation.

In 1787, to compensate for this imbalance (and to more properly
enumerate the dispensation of taxes and the apportionment of the
members of the U.S. House of Representatives and the U.S. Electoral
College), Northerners at the U.S. Constitutional Convention pushed
through the Three-Fifths Compromise. It read:

> Representatives and direct Taxes shall be apportioned among the
> several States which may be included within this Union, according
> to their respective Numbers, which shall be determined by adding
> to the whole Number of free Persons, including those bound to

---

1089. Trumbull, p. 13.
1090. *The Congressional Globe*, 36th Congress, 1st Session, p. 58; Carey, p. 181.
1091. By 1860, for example, slaves represented nearly one-third of the South's population.

Service for a Term of Years, and excluding Indians not taxed, three
fifths of all other Persons.[1092]

From then on, only three-fifths of the slave population was to be
counted, so that in each state five slaves were counted as only three
individuals (instead of as five).[1093] Lincoln the white supremacist would
probably have preferred that slaves not be counted at all. But if they
were to be counted, even as three-fifths of a person each, the less in the
West the better.

With hundreds of thousands of slaves already in the Democratic
South, the idea of further extending slavery into the Louisiana Purchase
was sure to weight Congress in favor of the Southern Democrats. If he
was to win, Lincoln could not afford to lose a single electoral vote.[1094]
And so, as America's first sectional presidential candidate (he was
nominated almost solely by Northern liberals), he opposed allowing
slavery to spread into the new Western territories. Not for humanitarian
and ethical reasons, but for personal, racial, and political ones.

YANKEE RACISM
Since Lincoln disliked the idea of living with blacks, held that they were
an inferior race, opposed the spread of slavery for fear of losing the 1860
election, did not want them to have equal rights, mix with or marry
whites, or take away jobs from whites, what then was his solution to the
"Negro problem"?[1095]

As we have seen, Lincoln was an arch proponent of the idea of
"shipping blacks back to Africa," a mid 19th-Century movement called
colonization. The idea was not Lincoln's. He borrowed it from white

---

1092. The Three-Fifths Compromise is part of Article 1, Section 2, Clause 3 of the U.S. Constitution.
1093. After the War, in 1865, the passage of the Thirteenth Amendment to the United States Constitution
abolished slavery, making the Three-Fifths Clause null and void. Three years later, in 1868, the Fourteenth
Amendment (Section 2) replaced Article 1, Section 2, Clause 3, with the following: "Representatives shall
be apportioned . . . counting the whole number of persons in each State . . ." Findlay and Findlay, pp. 20-23,
226-228.
1094. Lincoln predicted he would lose the South, and he was right. Being an anti-South, big government
liberal and atheist, he received no electoral votes from any state in the conservative, small government,
religious South during the 1860 election. Seabrook, AL, pp. 270-274.
1095. It should be noted that throughout America's history, whites like Lincoln have been far from the only
ones opposed to the mixing of the white and black races. From the 1800s into the present day, numerous
black Afrocentric groups and movements have also openly and aggressively promoted the idea of racial
separation.

separatists who preceded him, white separatists like his political idol Henry Clay, who began advancing the colonization concept in 1827. In fact, Clay was one of the founders of the American Colonization Society and remained its president until his death in 1852.[1096]

One of Lincoln's favorite quotes was from Clay:

> There is a moral fitness in the idea of returning to Africa her children, whose ancestors have been torn from her by the ruthless hand of fraud and violence. Transplanted in a foreign land, they will carry back to their native soil the rich fruits of religion, civilization, law, and liberty.[1097]

After he became president, Lincoln pushed even harder to deport all blacks. Midway through his War, in his Annual Address to Congress on December 1, 1862, he said:

> I cannot make it better known than it already is, that I strongly favor colonization.[1098]

When things moved too slowly with his detailed colonization plans, he called a number of freed black leaders to the White House, begging them to take their people back to their native land.[1099] This meeting outraged abolition leaders like William Lloyd Garrison, who fumed at the thought of a white America founded on Lincoln's idea of black colonization. From then on, Garrison began referring to Lincoln as the president of black deportation.[1100]

As always, Lincoln's views on blacks were part racism, part political, but never humanitarian. While he was still a member of the Illinois Legislature, he pushed to have funds set aside for the relocation of all free blacks from his own home state.[1101] During his infamous Copper Union Speech in New York (February 27, 1860), he reasserted

---

1096. Seabrook, L, p. 596; DiLorenzo, RL, pp. 16-17.
1097. Nicolay and Hay, ALCW, Vol. 1, p. 175.
1098. Nicolay and Hay, ALCW, Vol. 2, p. 274.
1099. Hacker, p. 584; Quarles, pp. 146-147. For the full text of Lincoln's racist plea to convince his black guests to leave the U.S., see Seabrook, L, pp. 622-627; Nicolay and Hay, ALCW, Vol. 2, pp. 222-225. See also W. P. Pickett, pp. 317-323.
1100. H. Mayer, p. 531.
1101. Berwanger, p. 5.

his long-held view that blacks should be sent back to Africa in order that "their places be . . . filled up by free white laborers."[1102]

Lincoln's original place of choice for sending American blacks was Africa, as he noted during his debate with Stephen Douglas at Ottawa, Illinois, on August 21, 1858. When pressured to offer his solution to the "Negro problem," Lincoln responded:

> My first impulse would be to free all the slaves, and send them to Liberia—to their own native land.[1103]

As time passed, however, curiously, he changed his mind about Liberia, and began advocating that American blacks might be shipped to Haiti or to the Danish West Indies. While New Englander Caleb Blood Smith, Lincoln's Secretary of the Interior, worked on developing the president's blueprint for colonization,[1104] Republican Senator Samuel Clarke Pomeroy took on the role of supervisor, suggesting that blacks be resettled in a Central American community to be named the "Colony of Linconia."[1105]

Ever the politician, the clever Lincoln knew his anti-black policies would garner him the most votes. Why? Because the North was largely Negrophobic and thus not interested in the abolition of slavery, the plight of the Negro, or human rights for blacks.

Lincoln was not the only politician to see and understand the great anti-abolitionism sweeping the North, or to use it to his advantage: not one of the four political parties who ran a presidential candidate in the 1860 election supported the idea of abolishing slavery, including Lincoln's Republican Party.

Northern politicians had their fingers on the pulse of their

---

1102. Nicolay and Hay, ALCW, Vol. 1, p. 608.
1103. Nicolay and Hay, ALCW, Vol. 1, p. 288.
1104. It is interesting to note that while Smith began his service under Lincoln as an ardent supporter, when war beckoned in 1860 he became dovish and strongly advised his hawkish boss to stay away from Fort Sumter and avoid conflict with the Confederacy at all costs. Unfortunately for the nation, Lincoln ignored him. Smith did have one thing in common with the President, however: racist sentiments. After the start of the War neither Smith or Lincoln showed any interest in allowing blacks to serve in the Union Army. Only when it became militarily expedient, about half way through the War (in 1863), did Lincoln change his mind. Inevitably, as Lincoln's dictatorial radicalism increased, Smith's devotion to him decreased, and in December of 1863 Smith resigned his seat as secretary of the interior. He passed away only months later, on January 7, 1864, never seeing the end of the War he had protested so adamantly against.
1105. Staudenraus, p. 247.

people, and knew well that the vast majority of the Northern public was against the abolition of slavery as well. When Garrison tried to hand out his antislavery newspaper, *The Liberator*, at a Boston abolition meeting, he barely lived to tell about it, and he was burned in effigy all across the Northern states.[1106]

Another New Englander, Prudence Crandall, defied Northern law and opened up a school for blacks, for which she was harassed, arrested, jailed, and finally run out of town.[1107]   One Northern abolitionist, Elijah Lovejoy, was not as lucky as Garrison or Crandall. After destroying his presses and newspaper offices, a Yankee lynch mob brutally killed him.[1108]

With such intense Negrophobia, it is not surprising that the Northern states were the birth place of the ultra-racist Black Codes. The Black Codes were generally meant to restrict the rights and freedoms of blacks and freed slaves, but more specifically they protected largely white (and anti-states' rights) states from blacks migrating across their borders.

Lincoln's home state, Illinois, for instance, had some of the most restrictive and racist Black Codes, not even allowing blacks to live within its boundaries, resulting in by far the most brutal Negro-hating law ever issued in a Northern state.  By not refuting this 1853 ruling, it is clear that Lincoln was supporting it.[1109]

More proof of the North's hostility toward the idea of abolition comes from her military forces.  Halfway through the War, when Lincoln cannily altered the character of the conflict from "preserving the Union" to "freeing the slaves," the Union Army became "demoralized." Why? Because Yankee soldiers were almost all "strongly anti-abolition."

General Joseph Hooker (1814-1879), one of Lincoln's top military commanders,[1110] recorded the reaction of the Union army shortly after his boss finally grudgingly pushed through the Emancipation Proclamation:

---

1106. Lytle, p. 29.
1107. Nye, p. 63; G. W. Williams, HNRA, Vol. 2, p. 151; Garrison and Garrison, Vol. 1, p. 323.
1108. Furnas, pp. 521-522; Buckley, p. 62.
1109. Berwanger, p. 49.
1110. Some say that Hooker allowed his war-time camps to include brothels, which is why his surname has entered popular language as a euphemism for a prostitute: a "hooker." For more on the topic of prostitution see my book, *Aphrodite's Trade: The Hidden History of Prostitution Unveiled*.

> At that time . . . a majority of the officers, especially those high in rank, were hostile to the policy of the Government in the conduct of the war. The emancipation proclamation had been published a short time before, and a large element of the army had taken sides antagonistic to it, declaring that they would never have embarked in the war had they anticipated the action of the Government.[1111]

During the War several Yankee officers tried to emancipate blacks, but were forbidden by anti-abolitionist Lincoln. One of these was the "Pathfinder," General John Charles Frémont (1813-1890), who declared martial law, then unlawfully freed slaves in Missouri. Lincoln rescinded both orders, had the slaves returned to their owners, and relieved Frémont of his command—despite a tearful face-to-face plea from Frémont's famous wife, Jessie Benton (1824-1902).[1112]

In his stern reply to Jessie, Lincoln reiterated his "preservation of the Union" lie while revealing that slavery truly was not the cause, or even one of the causes, of the War: your husband should have left the Negro out of this, he callously told her. This conflict is conducted for the cause of a "great national idea."[1113] As we will see, in the name of political expediency Lincoln would soon go against his own words.

Frémont's successor, General David Hunter (1802-1886), also bucked Lincoln's racism by trying his own hand at emancipation. Hunter's "General Order No. 11" declared all slaves in the Union-held territories of South Carolina, Georgia, and Florida "forever free." Lincoln was not amused and again revoked the proclamation.[1114] But the slavery-hating Hunter continued to disobey the chief executive. When Hunter formed the 1st South Carolina Regiment, made up of blacks he had (illegally) enlisted in that state, Lincoln promptly ordered him to disband the group,[1115] reaffirming that he would not free the slaves until "it shall have become a necessity indispensable to the maintenance of the

1111. Henderson, Vol. 2, p. 411.
1112. W. B. Garrison, LNOK, pp. 136-138. Note: Frémont's wife, my cousin Jessie Ann Benton, was the daughter of the illustrious Democratic (then conservative) Senator and Southern slave owner, "Old Bullion," Thomas Hart Benton (1782-1858), who once owned land in Leiper's Fork, near Franklin, Tennessee.
1113. Donald, L, p. 315. For more on Jessie's confrontation with Lincoln, see Nicolay and Hay, ALCW, Vol. 4, p. 415; Rhodes, Vol. 3, p. 478.
1114. Black, p. 165; Wiley, SN, pp. 296-298; Leech, pp. 305-306.
1115. Confederate leaders, including President Jefferson Davis, were outraged at Hunter's unlawful activities, and sent out an order stating that he was a "felon to be executed if captured."

Government . . ."[1116]

Others in Lincoln's cabinet and military who tried to abolish slavery were also blocked by the white supremacist president, among them Simon Cameron,[1117] John W. Phelps, and Jim Lane.[1118]

BLACK INSURRECTIONS

One reason Lincoln was against abolition early in his presidential career was the very real fear of a black rebellion and race riots. Later he would use this paranoia to try and drive a stake through the heart of the Confederacy. But in 1860 and 1861 he shared the widespread dread, current among both Northerners *and* Southerners, of the "Black Terror":[1119] an uprising of African-American slaves upon their emancipation. After all, between 1805 and 1850 there were some eighty black rebellions in the Caribbean alone.[1120]

In Haiti, for instance, one of the nations to which Lincoln later wanted to ship American blacks, newly freed slaves burned down white-owned homes, farms, and businesses, then raped, tortured, and murdered some 80,000 of their white owners.[1121] The bloodshed was so horrendous during what became known as the Haitian Revolution (in which the goal was to establish black rule),[1122] that in 1802 Napoleon I (1769-1821) moved in with 45,000 troops to restore law and order.

All of Napoleon's men were either killed or driven off the island,[1123] while some 20,000 white Haitians were put to death by bayonet, hanging, burning, and other forms of torture "too horrid to describe," as one contemporary put it.

Haiti's black revolution against white (French) colonization, the first genocide of the modern world, is just one example of the type of

---

1116. Greeley, AC, Vol. 2, p. 246.

1117. Donald, L, p. 363; Leech, p. 155.

1118. Quarles, pp. 113-116.

1119. Nye, p. 18; E. M. Thomas, p. 237.

1120. C. Adams, p. 129.

1121. Crocker, p. 23.

1122. These early successful slave revolts against the French made history in other ways: Haiti is the world's oldest black republic.

1123. Napoleon's crushing defeat by former Haitian slaves made him reconsider the idea of owning and maintaining colonies abroad, which is why he sold the Louisiana Territories to the U.S. in 1803. Little did Napoleon realize that fifty-eight years later, America's Louisiana Purchase would play a major role in launching Lincoln's War Against Southern Independence.

black ethnic cleansing that petrified 19<sup>th</sup>-Century white Americans, making them extremely wary of abolishing slavery.[1124]

If this was not enough to prevent them from freeing their slaves, there were also black uprisings—though insignificant by comparison—breaking out much closer to home. The most infamous of these occurred on August 21 and 22, 1831, when religious fanatic and black slave Nathaniel "Nat" Turner (1800-1831) recruited gangs of black supremacists and black racists, who eagerly roamed the Virginia countryside for two days murdering white families, most of whom were non-slave owners.

Using "quiet" instruments to avoid detection, such as hatchets and knives, psychopath Turner intentionally chose to kill whites in their sleep. As they snuck from house to house in the dead of night, no one was spared, not even women, children, and newborn infants.

Urged on by a solar eclipse (a "supernatural sign from God"), Turner plotted his insurrection, one that would begin with the murder of his own master, Joseph Travers, and his entire family. Why? Travers was known to be a gentle, benevolent, religious man to all, including Turner. Turner himself later admitted that Travers "was to me a kind master, and placed the greatest confidence in me. In fact, I had no cause to complain of his treatment to me."[1125] Unaccountably, on that dark night of August 21, 1831, Turner and his gang went first to the Travers house.

Climbing up a ladder, Turner crawled through a window and let his thugs in through the door. Sneaking into the bedroom of Joseph and his wife, both were quickly slain with axes. Several of the Travers children were then brutally dispatched in their sleep, Turner bragging that "not one of them awoke."[1126]

After the mob left the house, it was realized that they had forgotten about a tiny baby sleeping in its cradle. Turner sent two of his henchmen back to finish the job. As he later coldly testified, "Henry and Will returned and killed it."[1127]

Over the next forty-eight hours some fifty-five whites were

1124. C. Adams, p. 130.
1125. H. Howe, p. 472.
1126. H. Howe, p. 472.
1127. H. Howe, p. 472.

viciously slaughtered[1128] before Turner was captured (cowering in a cave), arrested, tried, and finally hanged on November 11, 1831, in Jerusalem, Virginia.[1129]

Turner did far more damage than good. Instead of forcing the abolition of slavery, the original intention of "the Turner Rebellion," the Virginia legislature voted not only to retain slavery, but to impose new harsher rules on both slaves and free blacks. Fear among whites of another black insurgency made even questioning the institution of slavery a crime.[1130] Little wonder that in 1860 the majority of Northerners, including Lincoln, were against abolition.

Turner was right, of course, in wanting to end slavery. Where he went wrong was in using violence. Though a Christian zealot, he disregarded one of his Savior's most important teachings: according to Jesus, resisting evil only creates more evil.[1131]

THE AMERICAN SYSTEM

Three decades later, atheist and warmonger Lincoln also ignored Jesus' teaching on pacifism. But more importantly, he also disregarded every peaceful and legal solution to resolving the North's disagreements with the South. In opting to use violence to settle these matters, Lincoln became the first president ever to make war on his own people, finally killing, by some estimates, up to three million American

---

1128. The names of the individuals killed by Turner and his men on August 21 and 22, 1831, are as follows: Joseph Travers and wife and three children; Mrs. Elizabeth Turner; Hartwell Prebles; Sarah Newsome; Mrs. P. Reese and son William; Trajan Doyle; Henry Bryant and wife and child, and wife's mother; Mrs. Catherine Whitehead, son Richard and four daughters and grandchild; Salathiel Francis; Nathaniel Francis' overseer and two children; John T. Barrow; George Vaughan; Mrs. Levi Waller and ten children; William Williams, wife and two boys; Mrs. Caswell Worrell and child; Mrs. Rebecca Vaughan; Ann Eliza Vaughan, and son Arthur; Mrs. John K. Williams and child; Mrs. Jacob Williams and three children; Edwin Drury.
1129. For the complete and *true* story of the Nat Turner rebellion, see T. R. Gray, passim.
1130. Though a psychopathic murderer and an overt racist, strangely, Turner continues to be regarded as a romantic and political hero by many blacks around the world. His end was not very heroic, however. After his short but violent life came to a close at the end of the hangman's noose, he was skinned, beheaded, and quartered, his body parts handed out as gruesome souvenirs. Dozens of lives were lost, including Turner's. For what? His death, by strengthening the very institution he was trying to destroy, helped postpone emancipation for decades and turned thousands of white Southern abolitionists into pro-slavery advocates and Negrophobes. As we have seen, slavery was a horror that was coming to a natural end. Unfortunately, like Lincoln thirty years later, Turner showed no interest in abolishing slavery peacefully through the use of compensated manumission, as most other nations around the world had done, or were considering at the time. Instead, both men chose the path of violence, living and dying by the sword, acts that left wounds in the American psyche that will never heal.
1131. Matthew 5:39.

citizens—including both military and non-civilians, white and black, free and bonded.[1132]

In our quest to understand Nathan Bedford Forrest, it is important that we understand Lincoln, the man who initiated the "Civil War," the conflict that both consumed and determined the entire last half of the General's life. Our question is this: what drove Lincoln to such an extreme? What would push him to violate both the Constitution and the Geneva Convention, along with countless civil, social, moral, and religious laws, to achieve his agenda?

While today, without personally examining him we cannot completely understand Lincoln—that is, the psychology of a 19th-Century man who struggled with severe depression, numerous personal tragedies, an unhappy and mentally ill wife, and perhaps Marfan Syndrome—we do know where most of Lincoln's political ideas came from.

From the moment he first heard of the militant Kentucky Whig, Henry Clay, Lincoln became literally obsessed with him, from that day forward modeling many of his own thoughts, beliefs, and actions after him. By his own admission Lincoln worshiped him as both a teacher and leader,[1133] even giving the eulogy at Clay's funeral in 1852, where he compared himself to the deceased Whig and intimated that he would be the one to take up Clay's banner. He is "my *beau ideal* of a statesman, the man for whom I fought all my humble life," the president said of him.[1134]

Curiously, while Clay the "Great Compromiser" was technically against slavery, he was himself a slaver, one who was not only willing to tolerate it, but who was actually strongly opposed to abolition of the institution. As we have seen, Lincoln adopted this view as well.

It was Clay's radical, liberal American System, however, which promoted the ideas of a strong centralized government, a nationalized banking system, modern industrialization, a market-oriented economy, protective tariffs, and internal improvements, that most appealed to Lincoln, and for which he zealously fought the rest of his life. And yet, it was these very ideas, all detrimental to Dixie and detested across the

---

1132. Timothy Manning, personal correspondence.
1133. Ashworth, Vol. 2, p. 212.
1134. Nicolay and Hay, ALCW, Vol. 1, p. 299.

South, which helped sow the seeds of discontent that helped bring about his illegal war.

Lincoln's obsession with implementing Clay's American System, his seeming hatred of Dixie, and the outrageous tariffs he and his liberal predecessors imposed on the South were not the only triggers of the War of 1861. There were also cultural, social, and religious issues.

A NATION PULLED ASUNDER

At the time, Southern culture was largely Celtic, Protestant, family-oriented, rural, and agricultural. Northern culture, on the other hand, was primarily English, Catholic, education-oriented, urban, and technological. The two societies could scarcely have been further apart on the cultural spectrum, adding further fuel to an already highly inflammable situation.

This hatred was not new in 1861. Animosity between Celts and Anglo-Saxons started nearly 1,000 years earlier, when England began invading and dominating the Gaelic lands of Ireland, Wales, and Scotland.

Sadly, this problem continues in the United Kingdom to this day. Northern Ireland, Wales, and Scotland all remain under the rule of the British crown,[1135] and are still struggling for sovereignty in an effort to reestablish home rule under their own independent governments. In Scotland this effort is moving forward under the Scottish National Party,[1136] in Wales under *Plaid Cymru*,[1137] and in Northern Ireland under *Sinn Féin*.[1138]

These three nations, still living under the thumb of their ancient Saxon oppressor, have much in common with the American Confederate States as they existed just prior to Lincoln's election in November 1860.[1139]

It was shortly after this date that South Carolina delegates called

---

1135. The Irish, Welsh, and Scottish are still treated as second-class citizens by some English men and women.
1136. For more information on the Scottish National Party visit their Website: www.snp.org.
1137. For more information on the Welsh National Party, Plaid Cymru, visit their Website: www.plaidcymru.org.
1138. For more information on the Irish National Party, Sinn Féin, visit their Website: www.sinnfein.org.
1139. And in fact, the Irish Republican Army (IRA), as one example, has many commonalities with Forrest and his cavalry.

for a special secession convention. It was clear that with a South-loathing, anti-Constitution Lincoln in the White House, the Southern states would be destroyed, or as the delegation put it:

> The guarantees of the Constitution will then no longer exist; the equal rights of the States will be lost. The Slaveholding States will no longer have the power of self-government or self-protection, and the Federal Government will have become their enemies.[1140]

At the South Carolina convention, held on December 20, the delegates voted unanimously to secede from the Union.

Other Southern states quickly followed. Mississippi seceded on January 9, 1861; Florida on January 10; Alabama on January 11; Georgia on January 19; Louisiana on January 26; Texas on February 1. The Confederate States of America (C.S.A.) was officially formed February 4-9, 1861, at the Confederate States Convention in Montgomery, Alabama.[1141]

After Lincoln took office, on March 4, 1861, and threatened to make war on the South, four more Southern states joined the C.S.A.: Virginia seceded on April 17; Arkansas on May 6; Tennessee on May 7; and North Carolina on May 20.

Two states wavered, but joined later: parts of Missouri seceded on November 2, 1861, and parts of Kentucky seceded on November 20 (the citizens of these states remained divided over their allegiance). This made thirteen Confederate states, revealingly, the same number of American states that originally seceded from Britain in 1775.

As the spring of 1861 approached, the first (and only) president of the newly formed Confederate States of America, Jefferson Davis (1808-1889), and his Congress drew up their Constitution and prepared to move forward with the business of forging a new confederate republic.

## LINCOLN'S TRICKERY IN INITIATING WAR ON THE SOUTH

Beginning in December 1860, while President James Buchanan was still in the White House, the C.S.A.'s "business" as an independent country

---

1140. E. McPherson, PHUSAGR, p. 16.
1141. Denney, p. 25.

began in earnest, starting with the gradual takeover of various U.S. troops, supplies, and properties scattered throughout the South. These included the seizure of Fort Moultrie and Castle Pickney in South Carolina; Fort Palaski in Georgia; Fort Jackson, Fort St. Phillips, Fort Pike, and the New Orleans Custom House in Louisiana; Fort Barrancas, Fort McRae, Fort Pickens, and the Pensacola Navy Yard in Florida; and Little Rock Arsenal in Arkansas. Through all of this Buchanan stood by, wisely refraining from violence, hoping the situation would go away on its own. But such was not to be.

On March 2, 1861, Texas Confederates captured the Federal cutter *Dodge*. This would be the last time the South would be allowed to touch U.S. property unmolested. Two days later, on March 4, a furious and menacing Lincoln was inaugurated. By separating from the Union and capturing Federal properties, the South was interfering with his plan to replace the Founding Father's government with Clay's American System, and he was not happy about it. One way or another, the C.S.A. had to be punished, then brought back into the Union.

Lincoln threatened, tempers simmered, newly forming militias bristled, war brewed.

To show good faith, shortly after Lincoln took office, President Davis sent a Confederate peace commissioner to Washington, D.C., offering to pay for all Federal properties seized in the South. Lincoln would not meet with him. Davis sent another. Again, Lincoln disregarded him, refusing even to recognize the commissioner's presence.

If the Yankee president did not understand the seriousness of the situation, the rest of the world did. France's emperor, Napoleon III, stepped in and generously volunteered to help resolve the growing contention between the North and the South. Incredibly, Lincoln ignored his offer as well.[1142] For he was hell-bent on going to war, and nothing was going to stand in his way. This certainly explains what happened next.

Fort Sumter was a small U.S. garrison on a small island strategically located in Charleston Harbor off the coast of South

---

1142. DiLorenzo, RL, p. 121.

Carolina.[1143] It was one of the last Federal outposts that had not been seized by the Confederacy, and was considered a great prize.

On April 11, 1861, Yankee Major Robert Anderson[1144] and his troops were stationed at Fort Sumter, hoping to keep it in Union hands. As they had been there since December 26, 1860 (six days after South Carolina seceded), it was believed that they were in need of food and provisions. Actually, Confederate General P. G. T. Beauregard had allowed Anderson and his troops to purchase groceries in Charleston up until April 5. The Union soldiers on the island were thus well-stocked with victuals and were in no way "starving," as some Northern newspapers had been telling their eager readers.[1145]

Should the fort be "reprovisioned"? Lincoln claimed so, but his cabinet, including the attorney general and the secretaries of the interior, war, navy, and state, all advised against it. "Abandon Fort Sumter," said Winfield Scott, head of Lincoln's armies. "It's militarily useless to us." Caleb B. Smith, Lincoln's secretary of the interior, agreed. "If you send in provisions it will trigger a civil war."[1146]

What his cabinet did not seem to realize was that this is exactly what Lincoln wanted. And the "starving fort" tale was the very trigger mechanism Lincoln needed to initiate it.

On April 12, against the advice of his own cabinet and the sentiment of most of the Northern people, Lincoln sent a provisions supply ship to Fort Sumter. Accompanying it were several armed warships. Lincoln had meticulously planned out every detail and knew what was about to happen.

Seeing the Federal fleet moving through Charleston harbor toward Fort Sumter, Confederate troops let loose their cannon. For a full thirty-six hours they bombarded the island, expecting at any moment to receive enemy fire. But the expected Yankee response never came. Why? Because Lincoln had ordered them not to. It was all a hoax, one meant to goad the Confederacy into firing the first shot.

---

1143. Fort Sumter is now a national monument and is once again—to the discontentment of pro-South sympathizers everywhere—flying the U.S. flag. For more information on modern Fort Sumter visit the following Website: www.nps.gov/fosu.

1144. Like many in Lincoln's army, Kentucky-born Anderson was pro-slavery.

1145. Tilley, FHLO, pp. 38-47; Meriwether, p. 263.

1146. C. Adams, p. 20.

Shrewd as he was, Lincoln cannot claim credit for the idea of tricking the Confederates; only for perpetrating the fraud.[1147]   It originated with his secretary of the navy, Gideon Welles,[1148] who slyly advised the president that "it is very important that the Rebels strike the first blow in the conflict."[1149]

Lincoln's assistant secretary of the navy, Gustavus Fox, then took Welles' idea and worked out the details of the plan.  Writing to Montgomery Blair (soon to be Lincoln's postmaster general) on February 23, 1861, Fox had said:

> I simply propose three tugs, convoyed by light-draft men-of-war. . . . The first tug to lead in empty, to open their fire.[1150]

Fox's plan never materialized, however, because the Rebels, having been grossly misled and lied to, went ahead and bombed and captured the fort first.  But either way, the end result was still what Lincoln had intended: the South appeared to the world to be the instigator.[1151]  Now the onus of initiating war lay with the Confederacy.

On May 1, 1861, three weeks after his heinous deed at Sumter had been committed, Lincoln acknowledged his devilish connivance in a letter to Fox.  While Fox was disappointed that his and Welles' plan had not succeeded, Lincoln was elated:

> I sincerely regret that the failure of the attempt to provision Fort Sumter should be the source of annoyance to you . . .[1152]
> You and I both anticipated that the cause of the country would be advanced by making the attempt to provision Fort Sumter even if it should fail; and it is no small consolation now to feel that our anticipation is justified in the results.[1153]

What "results?"  The inauguration of a war he so desperately wanted! Even Lincoln's own authorized biographers, John G. Nicolay and John

---

1147. Harwell, p. 344.
1148. Grissom, p. 108.
1149. Scharf, pp. 129-130; Tilley, FHLO, p. 50.
1150. ORA, Ser. 1, Vol. 4, pp. 224-225.
1151. Tilley, FHLO, pp. 50-51.
1152. Tilley, FHLO, p. 51.
1153. Thompson and Wainwright, Vol. 1, p. 44.

Hay, admitted that:

> When the President determined on war, and with the purpose of making it appear that the South was the aggressor, he took measures . . . [1154]

In short, the entire Fort Sumter event was a cleverly calculated conspiracy, as one Northern newspaper described it, to incite the South into firing the first shot. In this way the Confederacy was seen as the aggressor, a hot-headed rebel who had fired on the U.S. flag and tried to prevent food from reaching starving U.S. soldiers. [1155]

On April 14, Anderson, now out of ammunition, surrendered. The Union flag was lowered, and the Confederate flag was raised. Fort Sumter was now official Confederate property.

Amazingly, no one on either side was killed in the melee. But the perception that the South made a "vicious attack" on an unarmed Union supply vessel whipped Northerners into a fever pitch of anti-Dixie hatred. Millions of Northern citizens who, before April 12, had been for peaceful secession or who had been sitting on the fence, now fell squarely in behind Lincoln, demanding retribution against the South for "attacking the U.S."

Lincoln, who had preplanned the entire scheme, wasted no time granting their wish. On April 15, 1861, the day after a humiliated Anderson (a Southerner who had joined the Union ranks and was very much against going to war with Dixie) surrendered Sumter to the South, he issued a proclamation calling for 75,000 U.S. troops to invade the South and crush the "rebellion." [1156] The War was on.

For Forrest, Lincoln's overt act of aggression crossed the line, both literally and figuratively. [1157] Though on February 9, 1861, Forrest's home state of Tennessee had voted to remain squarely in the Union, on May 6, it angrily held another popular referendum on the question of secession. On June 8, by a vote of 108,339 to 47,233, the state at last decided to join the Confederacy. His current state of residence,

---

1154. Ashe, p. 56.
1155. DiLorenzo, RL, pp. 119-121.
1156. Nicolay and Hay, ALCW, Vol. 2, p. 34.
1157. Mathes, p. 23.

Mississippi, had already seceded much earlier, on January 9. Forrest could himself remain neutral no longer.

Lincoln would not give peace a chance, and so Dixie's sons had no choice but to fight. Many Southerners felt just as Forrest did, as he would later say in an 1868 interview:

> I went into the war because my vote had been unable to preserve the peace.[1158]

It was at this flash point in American history, on June 14, 1861, six days after Tennessee joined the Confederacy, that Forrest, along with his youngest brother Jeffrey and his son William, determinedly strode into the local recruiting office in Memphis and enlisted in the Confederate Army.

---

1158. *The United Daughters of the Confederacy* magazine, Vols. 56-57, 1993, p. 22.

# - 1861, Part 2 -
# Forrest Gets Up a Regiment

"I've got no respect for a young man who won't
join the colors." — Nathan Bedford Forrest

## SIDING WITH THE CONFEDERACY

T HOUGH PRIOR TO THE WAR Forrest had actually been a
"strong Union man" who was against Southern secession,
Lincoln's unlawful attack was too much.[1159] A dyed-in-the-wool
Southerner, a fervent states' rights advocate, a free-trader, and a
constitutional conservative,[1160] Forrest was not going to stand by while
Lincoln perverted the Constitution and transformed the government of
the Founding Fathers from a confederate republic into a federate
empire—one of Lincoln's primary goals.

The main problem, however, was financial in nature. Lincoln,
as we have seen, had been pushing for extra high tariffs to be applied
across Dixie, an act that would surely have bankrupted many Southern
businesses. Forrest, always the businessman, saw the South's economy
in jeopardy and knew he had to act. Thus for Southerners like Forrest,
supporting the Confederacy was not just about pride, patriotism, and
politics, it was also a matter of survival.

He wasted no time enlisting in the army that June, at first
serving as a private in Captain Josiah S. White's Tennessee Mounted

1159. Henry, FWMF, p. 29.
1160. Jordan and Pryor, p. 40.

Rifles Company. White's Company constituted Company D in the Sixth Tennessee Battalion (organized on September 7, 1861), later becoming part of the well-known Seventh Tennessee Regiment of Cavalry.[1161]

Seeing the appalling lack of supplies, like many other wealthy Confederates, Forrest outfitted, equipped, clothed, armed, and fed his soldiers wherever and whenever he could, all without any aid from the Confederate government.[1162] In one case, for instance, he advanced his quartermaster and commissary $20,000 from his own "private funds" for Colt's navy pistols, saddles, and other supplies, the equivalent of about $430,000 today.[1163]

His naturally keen grasp of military tactics, along with his elevated socioeconomic status (there were not many multimillionaire privates in the Confederate Army!) and sterling recommendations from the citizens of Memphis, impressed both Governor Isham Greene Harris, Tennessee's only Confederate governor, and Bishop-General Leonidas Polk.

Soon, despite his lack of military training, Forrest won a promotion to colonel. His star continued to rise quickly and by October he was commanding his own regiment, "Forrest's Tennessee Cavalry Battalion."

He was also an excellent recruiter. Hundreds of Tennesseans, young and old, eagerly joined the Confederate army under Forrest's rousing promise that there would be "ample opportunity to kill Yankees."

## FORREST ENLISTS AFRICAN-AMERICANS
Contrary to Yankee myth, Forrest was no respecter of race, which is why he recruited his own slaves as well, naturally seeing them as

---

1161. The Seventh Tennessee Regiment of Cavalry was one of the last groups of Rebels to surrender at the end of the War in May 1865. Wyeth, LGNBF, pp. 23-24.
1162. Mathes, pp. 24, 162. The Confederate States of America never had the funds to properly supply its armies. In particular, while Billy Yank was equipped with the breech-loading rifle, Johnny Reb often had to make do with a shotgun or a squirrel rifle (brought from home), or even the same type of muzzle-loading musket his great-grandfather had used in the Revolutionary War nearly ninety years earlier. That Confederates were proudly fighting America's Second Revolutionary War with the same rifles used in America's First Revolutionary War was an irony not lost on the average Rebel soldier. Wyeth, LGNBF, p. 51.
1163. ORA, Ser. 1, Vol. 31, Pt. 3, p. 789. The Confederate government never repaid Forrest for this $20,000, for it was destroyed by Lincoln. Morton, p. 136.

potential recruits in the South's fight against Northern aggression. This was several years before Lincoln and the U.S. government to the North allowed blacks to enlist in the Union army. But Forrest, as usual, was out in front of everyone else. Believing that the institution of slavery was on its way out he promised his servants their freedom at war's end—no matter which side won and even if slavery continued.[1164]

Throughout Lincoln's illegitimate and needless four-year conflict, as many as 300,000 African-Americans fought courageously for the Confederacy[1165] alongside their European-American brethren (their exact number will never be known because Yankees, like war criminal General Edward Hatch,[1166] specifically targeted Southern courthouses—where records were kept—for burning).[1167] Dixie was, after all, their homeland as well, and the only one they had ever known.

Among them were sixty-five slaves serving under Forrest, forty-five of them belonging to the dashing officer himself.[1168] Of these particular individuals, the General later remarked that at the start of the conflict:

> I said to forty-five colored fellows on my plantation that . . . I was going into the army; that if they would go with me, if we got whipped they would be free anyhow, and that if we succeeded and slavery was perpetuated, if they would act faithfully with me to the end of the war, I would set them free. Eighteen months before the war closed I was satisfied that we were going to be defeated, and I gave these forty-five men, or forty-four of them, their free papers[1169] . . .

---

1164. Browning, p. 10. Irish General Patrick R. Cleburne, "Stonewall of the West," who fought with Forrest (and died at the Battle of Franklin II), promoted this same idea to their president, Jefferson Davis who, at the time, unfortunately and unwisely turned it down. For hundreds of thousands of Southern-born African-Americans were eager to fight against Northern tyranny, a powerful and much-needed force that would have certainly influenced the outcome. On March 18, 1865, however, near the end of the War, Forrest's and Cleburne's wisdom was finally, though only partially, realized. The Confederate Congress gave the go-ahead, and slaves were officially recruited (though emancipation was not at first promised). Sadly, it was far too late. Lee's "surrender" at Appomattox was only weeks away.

1165. Barrow, Segars, and Rosenburg, BC, p. 97.

1166. See e.g., Jordan and Pryor, p. 531.

1167. See e.g., Henry, ATSF, p. 188.

1168. Henry, FWMF, p. 14.

1169. *Report of the Joint Select Committee to Inquire into the Condition of Affairs in the Late Insurrectionary States*, p. 20.

Revealingly, during the War none of Forrest's black soldiers ever tried to flee or join the enemy, and as promised, he granted all of the heroic survivors their liberty. However, as we just saw, he did not wait until the end of the War as he had previously pledged. He abolished slavery in his own cavalry in September 1863 (shortly after the Battle of Chickamauga).[1170] As noted earlier, this was over two years prior to the ratification of the Thirteenth Amendment (on December 6, 1865), which finally halted slavery all across the U.S.

Throughout 1864 Forrest energetically continued his black impressment and enrollment program, as the following example from his headquarters at Okolona, Mississippi (dated August 5, 1864), reveals. Note that Forrest intended to use these particular blacks, not as slave laborers as Lincoln did when he first reluctantly enlisted African-Americans, but as regular armed soldiers:

> . . . all that can be done shall be done in North Mississippi to drive the enemy back. At the same time I have not the force to risk a general engagement, and will resort to all other means in my reach to harass, annoy, and force the enemy back. I have ordered the impressment of negroes for the purpose of fortifying positions, blockading roads and fords upon the rivers, and shall strike him in flank and rear, and oppose him in front to the extent of my ability and fight him at all favorable positions along his line of march.[1171]

None of this is surprising when we consider that Tennessee was from one of the most racially tolerant states in either the CSA or the USA at the time. Indeed, Tennessee became the first state, South or North, to authorize the enlistment of free blacks in its Confederate armies. This occurred in June 1861, one year and three months before the Union officially sanctioned the recruitment of blacks in August, 1862,[1172] and over two years before Lincoln actually began to enlist them (months after he issued his fake Emancipation Proclamation).[1173] That June the Tennessee legislature passed an act allowing the governor to receive into the military service "all male free persons of color, between

1170. Wyeth, TDF, p. xxi.
1171. ORA, Ser. 1, Vol. 39, Pt. 2, p. 756. See also Jordan and Pryor, p. 556.
1172. Jordan, pp. 218, 266.
1173. Nicolay and Hay, ALCW, Vol. 2, p. 288.

the ages of 15 and 50 . . . ."[1174] Tennessee's black soldiers, unlike Lincoln's, were treated, clothed, and fed on an equal basis with Tennessee's white soldiers.[1175]

Contrary to Yankee myth Forrest's black soldiers did not all serve in servile occupations. While some certainly worked as cooks and teamsters (vital jobs that were also performed by thousands of white soldiers), others were in charge of keeping track of the payroll and handing out pay packets.[1176]

We know of at least one enlisted black man by name (there were no doubt others) who served in the General's famed Escort: Polk Preston Arnold. A courageous private riding under the command of Captain J. C. Jackson, Arnold lost his life at the Battle of Harrisburg, Mississippi, on July 17, 1864, after which his wife Caldonia Arnold applied for and received a Confederate pension.[1177]

Another black who served with Forrest was the grandfather of my friend Nelson W. Winbush.[1178] His name was Private Louis Napoleon Nelson, of the Seventh Tennessee Cavalry. Nelson, both a soldier and the only known black Confederate chaplain, was present at such conflicts as the Battles of Vicksburg, Shiloh, Lookout Mountain, Fort Pillow, and Brice's Cross Roads.[1179] A member of the United Confederate Veterans, like most of Forrest's other proud black soldiers, he attended postwar reunions (some thirty-nine of them) and requested that he be buried with his medals.[1180]

According to an African-American soldier who served with Forrest at the Battles of Shiloh and Brice's Cross Roads, the General had seven armed black guards, steadfast soldiers who protected him both day and night.[1181] So serious were they about their occupation that they made up ranks for themselves, Forrest's own body servant being called

1174. ORA, Ser. 4, Vol. 1, p. 409.
1175. Jordan, pp. 218-219.
1176. Bradley, p. 217.
1177. Bradley, p. 219.
1178. Mr. Winbush wrote the Foreword to my bestselling book, *Everything You Were Taught About the Civil War is Wrong, Ask a Southerner!*
1179. Nelson W. Winbush, personal correspondence.
1180. Website: http://scvcamp741.tripod.com/causes/cause2.htm. Confederate pride was passed down through Nelson's African-American family to his descendants, some of whom became members of the Sons of Confederate Veterans, and still belong to this day.
1181. Ashdown and Caudill, pp. 184-185.

the "Gin'ral" by the others.

A story goes that one morning a black "subordinate" roused Forrest out of his sleep at an ungodly hour. After receiving a severe tongue-lashing the chastised soldier was allowed to explain himself. "I was gived otters by the Gin'ral," he stuttered. "What orders?" Forrest bellowed. "That we was to kep dem horns a'silent, and 'stead waken ever'one up at four o'clock sharpish."[1182] Forrest's response to this can only be imagined!

The point here is that if Forrest was a cruel racist, as critics of the South assert, why did he insist on having armed *African-American* guards specifically, and how was he able to sleep peacefully at night in their presence? How indeed.

Some of Forrest's black soldiers have been memorialized. At the town cemetery in Canton, Mississippi, stands a twenty foot obelisk commemorating the black Mississippians who served in "Harvey's Scouts," a partisan unit attached to Forrest's cavalry in 1864.[1183]

Despite such evidence many modern enemies of the South continue to pretend that "no blacks would have ever fought for, with, or under racist Forrest." How then do they explain the following official report, written by Union Lieutenant Colonel John G. Parkhurst after Forrest's successful raid on Murfreesboro July 13, 1862?

> The [Confederate] forces [under Forrest] attacking my camp were the First Regiment Texas Rangers, Colonel [Jack] Wharton,[1184] and a battalion of the First Georgia Rangers, Colonel Morrison, and a large number of citizens of Rutherford County, many of whom had recently taken the oath of allegiance to the United States Government. There were also quite a number of negroes attached to the Texas and Georgia troops, who were armed and equipped, and took part in the several engagements with my forces during the day.[1185]

Thanks to what I call the "Great Yankee Coverup," and the spiteful Yankee habit of burning down Southern courthouses, we will

---

1182. Wiley, SN, p. 140.
1183. Greenberg and Waugh, p. 373.
1184. Colonel Wharton was later an officer in Forrest's Sixth Texas Cavalry. Jordan and Pryor, p. 702.
1185. ORA, Ser. 1, Vol. 16, Pt. 1, p. 805.

never know the identities and histories of most of the African-Americans who served with Forrest. For the sake of posterity, besides those noted above, let us record a few others who *are* known:

- Preston Roberts (head of mess), who was in charge of seventy-five cooks, as well as purchaser of food not provided by the commissary. After the War the United Daughters of the Confederacy awarded Roberts the Southern Cross of Honor.
- Jones Greer (servant of Lieutenant George Cowan).
- Ben Davis (teamster), who applied for a Confederate pension in 1921.
- Nim Wilkes (teamster), who applied for a Confederate pension in 1915.[1186]

Forrest's white soldiers later noted in their writings that the Confederate blacks who served with them were just as happy over their command's victories as the whites were, and just as sad at their losses. After the War Forrest's black soldiers faithfully attended reunions, where they were always met with open arms from everyone present.[1187]

On September 22, 1876, at the Confederate Veterans Reunion of the Seventh Tennessee Cavalry, Forrest's Corps, Colonel William Sanford gave a speech that included the following words:

> And to you, our colored friends . . . we say welcome. We can never forget your faithfulness in the darkest hours of our lives. We tender to you our hearty respect and love, for you never faltered in your duty nor betrayed your trust.[1188]

Forrest himself said of the African-Americans who served under him: "These boys stayed with me, drove my teams, and better Confederates did not live."[1189]

---

1186. Bradley, p. 219.
1187. Heny, ATSF, p. 105.
1188. Website: www.southernheritage411.com/bc.php?nw=037.
1189. Cincinnati *Commercial*, August 28, 1868.

# - 1862 TO 1863 -
# MILITARY EXPLOITS

"I cannot speak in too high terms of the conduct of my whole command." — Nathan Bedford Forrest

## FORREST'S RAID INTO KENTUCKY

FORREST'S MILITARY CAREER ITSELF WAS nothing short of amazing. Indeed, though all true, it reads like a Hollywood movie script for a fantasy action-hero. A few stories will be instructive.

Just a colonel at the time, his first clash with the Yanks was at Sacramento, Kentucky (December 28, 1861). An idea of the ferocity with which he fought here was given by Confederate Major David C. Kelley, who, for the first time, witnessed Forrest in the heat of battle. At first Kelley did not recognize the man who rode up to him:

> Forrest seemed in a desperate mood and very much excited. His face was flushed till it looked like a painted warrior, and his eyes, usually mild in expression, glared like those of a panther about to spring upon its prey. He looked as little like the Forrest of the mess-table as the storm of December resembles the quiet of June.[1190]

Though this was Forrest's initial fight, he was already drawing positive attention from his superiors for his skills and valor on the field

---

1190. Wyeth, LGNBF, p. 32.

of action, as Confederate Brigadier General Charles Clark noted in his official report:

> Report of Brig. Gen. Charles Clark, C. S. Army.
> HEADQUARTERS HOPKINSVILLE, Ky.,
> January 8, 1862.
> LIEUTENANT: I have the honor to transmit herewith, for the information of the major-general, the official report of Col. N. B. Forrest of his brilliant and dashing affair at Sacramento on the 28th ultimo:
>
> The report of Colonel Forrest is a modest recital of one of the most brilliant and successful cavalry engagements which the present war has witnessed, and gives a favorable omen of what that arm of our service will do in future on a more extended scale.
>
> The loss of the enemy, it will be seen, is estimated by Colonel Forrest at 65 killed and 35 wounded and prisoners, and from private and unofficial sources I learn that the number is not overestimated.
>
> Our own loss was but 2 killed, but in the death of Capt. C. E. Meriwether, who fell while gallantly leading his command into action, the country and the service have sustained a loss which I most deeply deplore. A brave and chivalrous gentleman, I esteemed him as one of the very best officers of his rank in the service. Colonel Forrest pays what I doubt not is a well-merited tribute to the gallantry and good conduct of his officers and men generally and specially. For the skill, courage, and energy displayed by Colonel Forrest he is entitled to the highest praise, and I take great pleasure in calling the attention of the general commanding and of the Government to his services. I am assured by officers and men that throughout the entire engagement he was conspicuous for the most daring courage; always in advance of his command. He was at one time engaged in a hand-to-hand conflict with 4 of the enemy, 3 of whom he killed, dismounting and making a prisoner of the fourth.
>
> The other field officers, Lieutenant-Colonel [James W.] Starnes and Major Kelly [Kelley], by their coolness, courage, and promptitude, contributed largely to the success of the day.
> I have the honor to be, lieutenant, respectfully, &c.,
> CHARLES CLARK, Brigadier- General, Commanding.
> Lieut. D. G. WHITE, Acting Assistant Adjutant- General, Bowling Green, Ky.[1191]

---

1191. ORA, Ser. 1, Vol. 7, p. 64.

Of this particular period in Forrest's military career, Major Kelley noted:

> In the short period since its organization, this command found that it was his single will, impervious to argument, appeal, or threat, which was ever to be the governing impulse in their movements. Everything necessary to supply their wants, to make them comfortable, he was quick to do, save to change his plans, to which everything had to bend. New men naturally grumbled, but when the work was done all were reconciled by the pride felt in the achievement.[1192]

Later, Kelley penned the following:

> In his early battles he was so disregardful of the ordinary rules of tactics, so reckless in personal exposure, that I felt sure his career would be short. It seemed certain that whenever he should meet a skilful opponent his command would be utterly cut to pieces. So fierce did his passion become that he was almost equally dangerous to friend or foe, and, as it seemed to some of us, he was too wildly excitable to be capable of judicious command. Later we became aware that excitement neither paralyzed nor misled his magnificent military genius. What had seemed to us the most unreasonable command when given proved, both in its result and his after-explanation of the reasons on which he acted, consummate generalship. His genius in action rose to every emergency; he always did what the enemy least expected him to do, and when defeated, as others would have counted defeat, he was more fertile in resources, more energetic in attack, more resistless in his fiery onset than when the action began. While his desperate bravery and frequent charges were characteristic of his military career, they by no means exhausted his resources.
>
> The manoeuvring of his forces in the presence of the enemy, his messages to opposing commanders, his matchless shrewdness in impressing them with the overwhelming superiority of his forces, and the necessity for surrender, were equally characteristic. The use of his artillery, often thrust forward to the skirmish-line, which would have been madness in an ordinary commander, was vindicated by the splendid results which he won. His common-sense led him at an early date to see that the day was past when a cavalry charge with sabres could be made effective in

---

1192. Wyeth, LGNBF, p. 35.

the presence of infantry.[1193]

Forrest's own official account of the battle (included by General Clark with his own) is of equal interest:

> Report of Col. Nathan B. Forrest, Forrest's Regiment, C. S. Army.
> HOPKINSVILLE, Ky., December 30, 1861.
> Under orders to reconnoiter to the front, especially in the direction of Rochester and Greenville, and if deemed best to continue our observations towards Ramsey, my command left camp Thursday, 26th instant, myself with detachments from Companies A, C, and D, First Lieutenant Crutcher, Captains May and Gould with a detachment of 25 men of Captain Meriwether's company, under his command, Major Kelly [Kelley] , with detachments from Companies E, F, and G, under Lieutenants Hampton, Kance, and Cowan, having been ordered to Greenville to await orders.  Leaving the Greenville road 4 miles from Hopkinsville I moved in the direction of Rochester, until fully satisfied that there were no movements of the enemy in that direction.
> The next day, on reaching the Russellville and Greenville road, I turned towards Greenville, and on Saturday morning formed a junction with a detachment of 40 cavalry from Russellville, under command of Lieutenant-Colonel Starnes and Captain McLemore, who, with Major Kelly, were awaiting my arrival at Greenville.  Colonel Starnes had the day before been at South Carrollton, where he had engaged a party of the enemy, killing 3.
> Hearing nothing still from the enemy, it was determined to extend our march to the vicinity of Rumsey.  The command, about 300 strong, were moved forward in one column, with advance guard under Captain Meriwether and rear under Captain McLemore; the head of the column under my command; the center under Major Kelly, and the rear under Lieutenant-Colonel Starnes. We had moved 8 miles down the Rumsey road when information reached me that the enemy 500 strong had that morning crossed from Calhoun to Rumsey.  My men were ordered to a rapid pace, and as the news of the proximity of the enemy ran down the column it was impossible to repress jubilant and defiant shouts, which reached the height of enthusiasm as the women from the houses waved us forward.  A beautiful young lady [Mollie

---

Morehead], smiling, with untied tresses floating in the breeze, on horseback, met the column just before our advance guard came up with the rear of the enemy, infusing nerve into my arm and kindling knightly chivalry within my heart.

One mile this side the village of Sacramento our advance guard came up with their rear guard, who halted, seemingly in doubt whether we were friends or foes. Taking a Maynard rifle, I fired at them, when they rode off rapidly to their column. The column moved up the hill and formed just over its brow. I ordered up the head of my column, telling my men to hold their fire until within good range. The enemy commenced firing from the time we were within 200 yards of them. When we had moved 120 yards farther I ordered my men to fire. After three rounds I found that my men were not up in sufficient numbers to pursue them with success, and as they showed signs of fight, I ordered the advance to fall back. The enemy at once attempted to flank our left, and moved towards us and appeared greatly animated, supposing we were in retreat. They had moved down over 100 yards and seemed to be forming for a charge, when, the remainder of my men coming up, I dismounted a number of men with Sharp's carbines and Maynard rifles to act as sharpshooters; ordered a flank movement upon the part of Major Kelly and Colonel Starnes upon the right and left, and the detachments from the companies under my command, still mounted, were ordered to charge the enemy's center.

The men sprang to the charge with a shout, while the undergrowth so impeded the flankers that the enemy, broken by the charge and perceiving the movement on their flanks, broke in utter confusion, and, in spite of the efforts of a few officers, commenced a disorderly flight at full speed, in which the officers soon joined. We pressed closely on their rear, only getting an occasional shot, until we reached the village of Sacramento, when, the best mounted men of my companies coming up, there commenced a promiscuous saber slaughter of their rear, which was continued at almost full speed for 2 miles beyond the village, leaving their bleeding and wounded strewn along the whole route. At this point Captain Bacon, and but a little before Captain Burges, were run through with saber thrusts, and Captain Davis thrown from his horse and surrendered as my prisoner, his shoulder being dislocated by the fall. The enemy, without officers, threw down their arms and depended alone upon the speed of their horses. Those of my men whose horses were able to keep up found no difficulty in piercing through every one they came up with, but as my horses were almost run down while theirs were much fresher, I deemed it best to call off the chase, for such it had become, leaving many wounded men hanging to their saddles to prevent their falling from their horses. Returning, we found their dead and wounded in every direction. Those who were able to be moved we placed in wagons. Captains Bacon and Burges were made as comfortable as we could, and applied to the nearest farm house to take care of them.

There were killed on the field and mortally wounded, who have since died, about 65; wounded and taken prisoners, about 35, making their loss about 100. Among their killed were two captains and three lieutenants and several non-commissioned officers.

The fight occurred in the woods; the run was principally along lanes. I have the pleasure of stating that Colonel Starnes and Major Kelly acted in the most noble and chivalrous manner, and, indeed, I can say that Captain Gould, Captain May, Captain Meriwether (who unfortunately fell in front of the engagement), Lieutenant Crutcher, in command of Captain Overton's company; Lieutenant Nance left in command of Captain Hambrick's company; Lieutenant Cowan, in command of Captain Logan's company (he acting as surgeon at the time), and Lieutenant Hampton, in command of Captain Truett's [?] company, with the men under their respective commands are deserving praise for their conduct.

Our loss was Captain Meriwether and Private Terry, of Captain McLemore's company, killed, and 3 privates slightly wounded; 2 from Captain May's and the other from Captain Hambrick's.

We returned to Greenville the night of the fight (Saturday), and from thence started to camp, and arrived last night.

Before closing this report I most respectfully call your attention to the gallant conduct of Lieutenant Bailey, of Captain Gould's company; Private J. W. Ripley, of Captain May's company, and Private J. M. Luxton, also of Captain May's; and Private B. W. Johnson, of Captain Logan's company, and, indeed, many others, whose horses being not quite so fast, did not come immediately under my own observation. Capt. M. B. Logan (who was acting as surgeon on that occasion) deserves praise for his noble conduct throughout the engagement.

All of which is most respectfully submitted.

Respectfully, N. B. FORREST, Colonel, Commanding Forrest Regiment.[1194]

---

1194. ORA, Ser. 1, Vol. 7, pp. 64-66.

Sacramento would be merely a warmup for Forrest's first major conflict: the fight against Grant at the Battle of Fort Donelson, Tennessee, February 11-16, 1862.

## A "GLORIOUS VICTORY" LOST: THE FORT DONELSON DEBACLE

The consequences of the Confederate loss at Fort Donelson would haunt the South not only throughout the War, but into the present day, for this was no ordinary battle. It could even be said that Fort Donelson doomed the Confederate struggle from the beginning. A writer for *Harper's Weekly* called it: "The Beginning of the End."[1195] Wyeth refers to it as "a blow which staggered the Confederacy, and from which it is safe to say it never fully recovered."[1196]

Despite a skirmish which damaged Yankee gunboats and forced a Federal retreat, things looked grim for the Rebels, as Grant's reinforcements were now large enough to nearly encircle the fort. Forrest, however, never one to be discouraged, felt sure that the garrison could be held, especially after he attacked and secured a Yankee artillery battery.

His superiors, Brigadier Generals John Buchanan Floyd, Gideon Johnson Pillow, and Simon Bolivar Buckner, however, did not the see the situation in the same light. Assuming there was no way out, they ordered a surrender of the fort.

At a hurried and frantic war council held between 11:00 PM and midnight on Saturday, February 15, 1862, Forrest argued that the Rebels were not "penned up, surrounded, or whipped," and were thus not yet beaten.[1197] In such a situation he could not and would not give up the fight. Pillow, a soldier very much like Forrest, now sided with the tenacious Tennessean. Floyd and Buckner held their ground, insisting on surrender, as scouts sent out earlier had spied the enemy reinvesting the area.[1198]

In particular Buckner maintained that there was not enough ammunition, for some reason disregarding telegraph communications

---

1195. *Harper's Weekly*, March 1, 1862.
1196. Wyeth, LGNBF, p. 37.
1197. Mathes, pp. 39-40.
1198. Lytle, p. 69.

stating that a steamboat load of ammunition from Clarksville, Tennessee, was heading along the Cumberland River for the fort that very day.[1199]

The meeting was brief. Forrest and his men had not seen the enemy anywhere in the area. Why capitulate then? Enraged at their timidity, Forrest roared: "I did not come here to surrender my command! I would rather my bones bleach on the hillside than go to a Yankee prison!"[1200] He then stormed out (a habit he would repeat many times during his military career), mumbling a litany of caustic expletives. Back at camp he told his men: "We're going out even if we die in the attempt!"[1201]

Unwisely ignoring Forrest's ingenious plan to "whip the Yanks" there and then, Buckner (who thought it his duty to stay with his men and share their fate) remained at the fort with some 12,000 soldiers. Meanwhile, disregarding the order to surrender, Pillow abandoned Forrest and stole away across the Cumberland River on a small boat that night, while Floyd left early the next morning, with two Virginia regiments, on a steamer bound for Nashville.[1202] Of the 15,000 Confederate troops at Fort Donelson, about 1,500 men escaped with these two commanders.[1203]

Forrest, of course, was not the kind of individual to stand by and watch a Confederate garrison surrender. It was simply not in his nature. "Boys," he said determinedly to his soldiers, "these people are talking about surrendering, and I am going out of this place before they do, or bust hell wide open."[1204] His men, cut from the same frontier cloth,

---

1199. The steamboat did, in fact, arrive on the night of February 15, in plenty of time to allow the fight to continue the next day. Wyeth, LGNBF, p. 58. Several more boats, bearing provisions and additional ammunition, arrived around daylight on the 16th.

1200. Mathes, p. 51.

1201. Mathes, p. 40.

1202. Floyd, a former governor of Virginia, had good reason to want to avoid the Yanks. While he was still serving as the U.S. secretary of war under President James Buchanan, it was believed that he had secretly and illegally shipped large stores of government arms to Southern arsenals so that they could later be used by the Confederate states. In reality, this never happened. It was just another myth from the Yankee propaganda book of anti-South fairy tales. Nonetheless, in January 1861 the U.S. Grand Jury indicted Floyd for "treason and conspiracy." With his state, Virginia, having by then seceded, he believed he would be safe in the South. But when he joined the Confederate Army, he once again put himself in harm's way by coming face to face with Yankee soldiers. Eventually, given command of Fort Donelson under General Albert Sidney Johnston (who had led the Utah expedition against the Mormons in 1857), Floyd, still under indictment, remained a wanted man throughout the War; hence his great fear of being captured by the Union.

1203. Wyeth, LGNBF, pp. 69-70.

1204. A. R. Johnson, p. 67.

could not have agreed more with their commander.

And so at about 2:00 AM, on February 16, 1862,[1205] Forrest simply walked out of the fort and into the freshly fallen snow with 500 of his men (and numerous troops from other units),[1206] then crossed the icy ford at Lick Creek toward the safety of Nashville.[1207] They saw no Federal troops during their movement out of Dover that night, and not a single shot was fired[1208]—an event perfectly captured in John Paul Strain's cover painting for my book, *Nathan Bedford Forrest: Southern Hero, American Patriot.*

As the sun rose the next morning, Buckner found himself completely surrounded with no chance of escape. He had little choice but to capitulate to Grant's demand for "unconditional surrender," and in the ensuing Yankee "victory," Grant seized the fort, capturing 12,000 Confederate soldiers.[1209]

To this day Forrest's critics have called him a "coward" for this act. But he was no coward. To the contrary, as we will now show, he was one of the bravest men who ever lived.

Seeing the confusion and rancor among his commanders at Fort Donelson, Forrest simply saw no purpose in surrendering only to face imprisonment (or worse). And though still ready to fight to the death, he felt that retreat was now the wisest alternative. Thus, his movement across the Cumberland avoided the needless wounding, capture, and deaths of hundreds of soldiers, many of them young boys fresh from home.[1210] Later, Forrest was wisely not punished for his "insubordination."[1211]

---

1205. Morton, p. 33.

1206. Wills, p. 64. According to Wyeth the total number of Rebel soldiers who walked out with Forrest numbered 1,500. Wyeth, LGNBF, p. 71.

1207. Lick Creek is a tributary of the Cumberland River, located near the town of Dover, Tennessee. There is still a road in Dover called "Lick Creek Road."

1208. Browning, p. 15.

1209. It was at Fort Doneslon that Grant earned himself the nickname "Unconditional Surrender Grant," and where he was promoted to major general.

1210. Lytle, p. 76.

1211. As mentioned, the unfortunate surrender of Fort Donelson to the Union was an act violently opposed by Forrest. Had Floyd, Pillow, and Buckner listened to their brash subordinate's suggestions, the battle could have been won, perhaps in turn having an affect on the outcome of ensuing conflicts. Forrest did not listen to his superiors either, however, and in doing so saved the lives of hundreds of Confederate soldiers. To this day, the descendants of the men saved by Forrest at Fort Donelson continue to give him thanks for his astute courage and rebellious personality.

Despite Forrest's foresight and bravery, the Confederate surrender at Fort Donelson will go down in history as one of the greatest and most crippling Rebel blunders during the first half of the War. In his wonderful pro-South work *The Lost Cause*, Edward A. Pollard writes:

> The fall of Fort Donelson was the heaviest blow that had yet fallen on the Confederacy. It opened the whole of West Tennessee to Federal occupation, and it developed [aggravated] the crisis which had long existed in the West.[1212]

To begin with, the surrender was indeed needless. Scouts sent out to the area of Lick Creek ford on Saturday night, February 15, saw no Yanks in the vicinity.[1213] When Forrest himself crossed Lick Creek a few hours later, in the early morning hours of the 16th, again no Federal soldiers were seen.[1214]

As hundreds of Rebel troops moved out during the next few hours, according to the official record, none witnessed a single Union soldier anywhere in the region, none met with any opposition; none, in fact, met with a barrier of any kind that would have prevented their escape. One Confederate soldier reported that there were not even any Federal troops in the nearby town of Dover at the time.[1215]

One thing they did see in the hazy, gray morning light, however, were hundreds of fence posts,[1216] all which had, no doubt, been earlier mistaken by Rebel scouts for Yankee pickets or a line of infantry.[1217] Also, nearby were dozens of burning fires which had been misidentified as signs of enormous enemy encampments. In reality, as Forrest and his men discovered, the enemy was not "reinvesting the area," as Floyd's scouts had earlier claimed. These were nothing but the remnants of earlier Federal fires, fanned by the winds and kept alive by a few remaining wounded Union soldiers.[1218]

Here then is conclusive proof that, since the Confederate

---

1212. Pollard, LC, p. 209.
1213. Lytle, pp. 69-70.
1214. Wyeth, LGNBF, pp. 62-63.
1215. Mathes, p. 41.
1216. Wills, p. 65.
1217. Henry, FWMF, p. 59.
1218. Jordan and Pryor, pp. 92-93.

surrender was made "under a delusion,"[1219] it was completely unnecessary. Some 12,000 Rebel soldiers could have been spared capture and gone onto fight, probably successfully, under Rebel General Albert Sidney Johnston at the Battle of Shiloh (April 6-7, 1862).[1220]

Second, the capture of Fort Donelson by the Yanks caused Johnston to relinquish Kentucky and most of Middle and Western Tennessee, all which had been controlled by the Confederacy up until that time. While this had a number of deleterious consequences for the South, one of its main effects was to allow further strengthening of Union control at Nashville (by now a primary Federal nerve center).[1221] As we will see shortly, this was something that would later come back to mortally wound the Confederacy at the close of 1864.[1222]

But there was another even more significant reason that the needless Confederate surrender at Fort Donelson had such a negative impact on the South's chances for success.

## GRANT'S RISE FROM CRIMINAL TO WAR HERO
It is not widely known outside scholarly circles, but as the Battle of Fort Donelson was unfolding, Grant's head was on the chopping block in Washington, D.C. Both his commander-in-chief, Major General Henry Wagner Halleck (1815-1872), and the general-in-chief of the U.S. army,

---

1219. Wyeth, LGNBF, p. 60.

1220. Mathes, pp. 40-41.

1221. During the War for Southern Independence, Nashville was one of the first major Southern cities to be captured by the Yanks, who held it, much to Forrest's irritation, throughout the duration of the War. See Horn, DBN, passim.

1222. An interesting side note: one of the Confederate soldiers present at the Battle of Fort Donelson, where Forrest fought and escaped with distinction, was Lieutenant Colonel Randal William McGavock, a cousin of mine. Randal was captured at this conflict and served four months at the Yankee prison at Fort Warren, George's Island, Boston, Massachusetts (he was later slain at the Battle of Raymond, Mississippi, May 12, 1863). Randal was a first cousin, once removed, to both Hattie McGavock, who married Irishman Lieutenant George Limerick Cowan—one of Forrest's escorts, and Colonel John W. McGavock, whose father, Randal McGavock, built the famous Carnton Plantation (Franklin, Williamson County, Tennessee) in the early 1800s. Colonel John W. McGavock was living at Carnton during Hood's disastrous Battle of Franklin II, November 30, 1864, at which time he turned the sumptuous house and sprawling grounds into a Confederate field hospital for the wounded and dying. Forrest led the cavalry at 2nd Franklin and is said to have stood on the back balcony of Carnton Mansion—the home of the father-in-law of one of his best soldiers— in order to survey the "valley of death" just prior to the onslaught. Forrest gave Hood a number of brilliant tactical suggestions, any which could have averted the murderous outcome at Franklin II. But all were ignored, and Hood went on to finish off the Army of Tennessee at the Battle of Nashville two weeks later, effectively destroying the Confederacy in the Western theater and ending the War, all in two quick strokes. For more on this sad chapter in American history, see Seabrook, TMCP, pp. 323-369.

276 ᴀ Rᴇʙᴇʟ Bᴏʀɴ

General George Brinton McClellan (1826-1885), were chomping at the bit to arrest and imprison Grant. Why?

Grant's superiors were running out of patience with him due to a number of acts of insubordination, including: disobeying orders, withdrawal from his command without leave, and traveling to Nashville without authorization. Of this situation Grant himself later admitted that Halleck had

> ordered that I should be relieved from duty and that an investigation should be made into any charges against me. He even authorized my arrest. Thus in less than two weeks after the victory at Donelson, the two leading generals in the army were in correspondence as to what disposition should be made of me, and in less than three weeks I was virtually in arrest and without a command. [1223]

Relieved of his command by Halleck, but then restored on March 13, 1862, Grant was only a hair's breath away from becoming a felon. What saved him from certain arrest, court martial, and prison?

It was the unnecessary Confederate surrender at Fort Donelson, which handed the Union a complimentary victory. With this one stroke of fortune, Grant, though he had not earned it, became an instant hero in the eyes of the Northern populace, which simultaneously guaranteed him an eternal place in the military hall of fame while lifting the official accusations against him.

Even worse for Dixie, it allowed him to go on commanding throughout the rest of the conflict, during which time he cut the Confederacy in half at Vicksburg and committed countless war crimes (in conjunction with Lincoln and Sherman) that helped insure a Yankee win.

All of this, in turn, transformed Grant into a symbol of the Union victory, quite naturally leading to his eventual election to president of the U.S. in 1868. As President of the nation's second most corrupt administration (after Lincoln), Grant continued to wound and humiliate the South, supporting and maintaining Reconstruction with brute military force.

The fact is, however, that while Halleck and McClellan had

---

1223. U. S. Grant, Vol. 1, p. 327.

legitimate grievances with Grant's insubordinate behavior, his most serious transgression was his extreme negligence in allowing Lick Creek and the surrounding area to be left unguarded throughout the night of Saturday, February 15, and the early morning hours of Sunday, February 16. Considering the feelings of Halleck and McClellan toward Grant at this time, he would have almost certainly been arrested, demoted, and imprisoned had not Floyd, Buckner, and Pillow surrendered Fort Donelson that same day, an act that transformed Grant into an international Yankee celebrity, literally overnight.

With his star rising and with renewed confidence, now backed by both the U.S. government and its people, Grant was able to go on to deliver one ruinous blow after another against the Confederacy, ultimately helping to seal her fate. He even lived to deliver the final humiliation to the South by being the one to receive Lee's surrender at Appomattox three years later. All of this because Forrest's wisdom was ignored by his superiors at Fort Donelson.

Wyeth put the matter in perspective:

> Ten thousand men, armed and ready for battle, should have marched out that night, and, with the boats which arrived in the early morning, three thousand more could have escaped across the river. Grant would have arrived to find the bird had flown. The empty fort and the artillery only would have been his. How changed would have been the pages of history if the plea of Nathan Bedford Forrest had been heeded by Generals Floyd and Buckner![1224]

## FORREST'S FORT DONELSON REPORTS

What follows are Forrest's two complete official reports of the incident (followed up by two "indorsements" attesting to their accuracy). As always, the General's original spelling, punctuation, and formatting have been retained.

> Reports of Col. Nathan B. Forrest, Tennessee Cavalry.
> FEBRUARY —, 1862.
> Having been ordered by Brigadier-General Clark to Fort Donelson from Hopkinsville, I arrived at Fort Donelson on Monday evening,

---

1224. Wyeth, LGNBF, p. 66.

February 10, and finished crossing with my command on Tuesday morning.

On the same afternoon I was ordered, with 300 of my cavalry, to reconnoiter in the direction of Fort Henry. We met about 3 miles from Fort Donelson the enemy's cavalry, supposed to be about 600, and, after a short skirmish, pressing them hard about 6 miles, captured 1 prisoner and mortally wounded several others.

The following morning I was ordered out with my own regiment, three Kentucky companies, viz, Captains Williams, Wilcox, and Hewey's, and Lieutenant-Colonel Gantt's battalion of Tennessee cavalry (the commanding general having signified to me the night before his desire that I should take charge of all the cavalry at the post as brigadier of cavalry.)

I had gone about 2 miles on the road towards Fort Henry when we met the advance of the enemy. My advance guard engaged them, when I sent forward three rifle companies, and after a skirmish they retreated, leaving several dead and wounded. The enemy halted, and, after maneuvering for some time, commenced to move by a parallel road towards the fort. Receiving information of this change, I changed my position from the right to the extreme left of my line of battle, throwing two squadrons of cavalry across the road. As soon as the enemy's advance came in sight I again attacked them vigorously. The enemy were on an elevated ridge, thickly wooded, and, when the attack was made, little else than their cavalry could be seen.

My first squadron as skirmishers, having been dismounted, were hotly engaged with greatly superior numbers. To enable them to withdraw, the second squadron was ordered to charge, hearing which, Major Kelly, by my request, commanding the left (now center) of my line, ordered an advance of the three squadrons under his command. The enemy gave back at the point where the charge was made, and the cavalry wheeling out of the way on their flank opposite Major Kelly, the infantry rose from the ground and poured in at short range a terrific fire of musketry, accompanied by a volley of grape. I was now able to mount and draw off in good order my skirmishers, and, finding the enemy in large force, ordered my cavalry to fall back, no infantry being near to support me. In answer to my couriers from the fort, General Buckner (General G. J. Pillow absent at Cumberland City) now ordered me back within our intrenchments.

This skirmish was from about 9 a. m. to near 2 p. m. We killed during the day a hundred men and wounded several hundred more, which so delayed the advance of the enemy that they did not move to the attack that day, satisfying themselves with planting a few cannon and commencing at long range a slow cannonade.

In the afternoon General Floyd reached the fort, and the whole army, infantry and cavalry, were engaged during the night in throwing up intrenchments, crowning several hills surrounding Dover. The enemy planted their batteries during the night, and commenced a cannonade from their batteries and ten gunboats early on the morning of Thursday. Soon after, our intrenchments were vigorously attacked at all points, and for six hours there was scarcely a cessation of small-arms and artillery. The musketry ceased about 1 p. m., the cannonading continuing until after dark. The gunboats drew off early in the engagement, supposed to be crippled, returning occasionally. The cavalry were but little engaged, acting only as pickets and couriers.

On Friday I was ordered out with the infantry, passing our intrenchments on the left; but after maneuvering a short time and some sharp shooting between the cavalry and the enemy, I was ordered back into the intrenchments. A demand was then made on me for sharpshooters to dislodge the enemy, who were from heights and trees annoying our infantry in the intrenchments, which we accomplished in about two hours, returning to my command about the time the gunboat attack was made on the fort. Of this attack I was an eye-witness, and have never seen a description which did anything like justice to the attack or defense. More determination could not have been exhibited by the attacking party, while more coolness and bravery never was manifested than was seen in our artillerists. Never was there greater anxiety depicted in the face of brave men than during the terrific roar of cannon, relieved ever and anon by the slow but regular report of our one single 10-inch gun. Never were men more jubilant than when the victory crowned the steady bravery of our little fort; old men wept; shout after shout went up; the gunboats driven back; the army was in the best possible spirits, feeling that, relieved of their greatest terror, they could whip any land force that could be brought against them.

During the night I was called into council with the generals commanding, when it was determined to bring on the attack the next morning by again passing our intrenchments and attacking the enemy's right.

In the early gray of the morning I moved to the attack, the cavalry on the left and in the advance. I found the enemy prepared to receive us, and were again engaged with the sharpshooters till our infantry were formed for the attack, the first gun from the enemy killing a horse in my regiment. General B. H. Johnson commanded the left, which now moved to the front. An obstinate fight of two hours ended in the retreat of the enemy. The undergrowth was so thick that I could scarcely press my horses through it. Finding that the flank of the enemy in retreat was exposed across an open field to my front and left, I immediately led my cavalry to the field, but found the ground a marsh, and we were unable to pass it.

The enemy formed in the edge of a second field to our front and right, and flanking the left of our advancing line of infantry. We could not move to flank them, but by maneuvering to their front and right doubtless prevented their attempting a flank movement on our infantry. Finding that our advancing line of infantry would cut them off while the cavalry prevented their flanking us, they commenced a retreat, accompanied by their cavalry, which we could now see in the distance, but not participating during the day in the fight. Our infantry had now driven them near a mile, they doggedly disputing the whole ground, leaving dead and wounded scattered through the woods and fields up in the ravine. The enemy, leaving their third position for the first time, retreated in haste, advancing by a road through a ravine. I here passed our line of infantry with my command in moving to the center.

I charged the enemy's battery of six guns, which had kept several of our regiments in check for several hours, killing and slaughtering a great many of our men. I captured the battery, killing most of the men and horses. I then immediately moved on the flank of the enemy, obstinately maintaining their position. They finally gave way, our infantry and cavalry both charging them at the same time, committing great slaughter. Moving still farther to our right, I found a regiment of our infantry in confusion, which I relieved by charging the enemy to their front. Here 64 of the enemy were found in 40 yards square. General Pillow, coming up, ordered me to charge the enemy in a ravine. I charged by squadrons, filing the first company of each squadron to the right, and the second to the left, on reaching the ravine, firing and falling in the rear of the third squadron until the three squadrons had charged. We here completely routed the enemy, leaving some 200 dead in the hollow, accomplishing what three different regiments had failed to do. Seeing the enemy's battery to our right about to turn on us, I now ordered a charge on this battery, from which we drove the enemy, capturing two guns. Following down the ravine captured the third, which they were endeavoring to carry off, gunners and drivers retreating up the hill. In this charge I killed about 50 sharpshooters, who were supporting the guns. I ordered forward a number of scouts, who, returning, informed me that the enemy, with three guns and three regiments of infantry, were moving up by the road from Fort Henry. We had driven the enemy back without a reverse from the left of our intrenchments to the center, having opened three different roads by which we might have retired if the generals had, as was deemed best in the council the night before, ordered the retreat of the army. Informing General Pillow of the position the enemy had taken, he ordered two new regiments and one of the regiments in the field, with one piece of artillery, to attack the enemy.

The fight here ended about 2.30 p. m. without any change in our relative positions. We were employed the remainder of the evening in gathering up the arms, and assisting in getting off the wounded. I was three times over the battle-field, and late in the evening was 2 miles up the river on the road to the forge. There were none of the enemy in sight when dark came on. Saturday night our troops slept, flushed with victory, and confident they could drive the enemy back to the Tennessee River the next morning.

About 12 o'clock at night I was called in council with the generals, who had under discussion the surrender of the fort. They reported that the enemy had received 11,000 re-enforcements since the fight. They supposed the enemy had returned to the positions they had occupied the day before.

I returned to my quarters and sent out two men, who, going by a road up the bank of the river, returned without seeing any of the enemy, only fires, which I believed to be the old camp fires, and so stated to the generals; the wind, being very high, had fanned them into a blaze.

When I returned General Buckner declared that he could not hold his position. Generals Floyd and Pillow gave up the responsibility of the command to him, and I told them that I neither could nor would surrender my command. General Pillow then said I could cut my way out if I chose to do so, and he and General Floyd agreed to come out with me. I got my command ready and reported at headquarters. General Floyd informed me that General Pillow had left, and that he would go by boat.

I moved out by the road we had gone out the morning before. When about a mile out crossed a deep slough from the river, saddle-skirt deep, and filed into the road to Cumberland Iron Works. I ordered Major Kelly and Adjutant Schuyler to remain at the point where we entered this road with one company, where the enemy's cavalry would attack if they attempted to follow us. They remained until day was dawning. Over 500 cavalry had passed, a company of artillery horses had followed, and a number of men from different regiments, passing over hard-frozen ground. More than two hours had been occupied in passing. Not a gun had been fired at us. Not an enemy had been seen or heard.

The enemy could not have reinvested their former position without traveling a considerable distance and camped upon the dead and dying, as there had been great slaughter upon that portion of the field, and I am clearly of the opinion that two-thirds of our army could have marched out without loss, and that, had we continued the fight the next day, we should have gained a glorious victory, as our troops were in fine spirits, believing we had whipped them, and the roads through which we came were open [i.e., no Federal soldiers] as late as 8 o'clock Sunday morning [the 16th], as many of my men, who came out afterwards, report.

I made a slow march with my exhausted horses to Nashville, Tenn., where we arrived on Tuesday morning [the 18th], and reported myself to General Floyd, who placed me in command of the city on Thursday, at the time of his leaving. I remained in the city until Sunday evening, during which time I was busily engaged with my regiment restoring order to the city and removing public property.

My loss at the battle in killed, wounded, and taken prisoners amounted to between 300 and 400 men. Among the number was Capt. Charles May, who fell at the head of his company while leading a charge.

My regiment charged two batteries, taking nine pieces of artillery, which, with near 4,000 stands of arms, I had taken inside of our lines. I cannot speak too highly of the gallant manner in which my officers and men conducted themselves on that occasion, as well as others that came under my observation, with the exception of Lieutenant-Colonel Gantt, commanding a battalion of Tennessee Cavalry, who failed to fight on Saturday, and refused to bring his men out with my regiment on Sunday morning when ordered to do so.

Respectfully submitted.

N. B. FORREST, Colonel, Commanding Forrest's Regiment of Cavalry.[1225]

MURFREESEOROUGH, TENN., November 7 1862.

Being informed by General Pillow that it is material for the purposes of justice and a proper understanding by the Government of the operations of the army at Donelson that I should make a statement of the result of the conference of general officers on the night of February 14, at which I was present by order of General Floyd, I make the following supplemental report:

---

1225. ORA, Ser. 1, Vol. 7, pp. 383-387.

On that day and the day before a large, fresh force, said to be 20,000 men, had reached the landing below us. At that time we were invested by a force which our information led us to estimate at 30,000. All the officers present felt the necessity of cutting our way out and resuming our communication with General Johnston. It was therefore resolved to give them battle in the open field the next morning.

I understood it to be the ultimate intention to retire from the place if we succeeded in opening our way, but nothing was said about our retreating from the field. No order was given to that effect and no preparation was made for that purpose; no suggestion was made of that character and no such determination arrived at.

On the day of the fight (15ᵗʰ) no artillery was taken from our intrenchments, except, perhaps, one piece late in the evening; no rations were prepared or taken on the field; blankets and knapsacks were left behind; no order of retreat was prescribed; no quartermaster, commissary, or ordnance stores were prepared to accompany a retreat; and, if a retreat had been attempted from the field of fight, it could not have been accomplished. The commands were scattered and mixed in fragments; very many of the men after the middle of the day had gone back into the town, and were around the fires and up and down the river bank. I had again and again during the day sent portions of my command into the intrenchments and had ammunition brought out on horseback.

The day itself was mainly occupied in the active operations of the fight. Soon after the fighting in the field was terminated fighting was begun on our right, in General Buckner's rifle pits, which lasted until about sundown.

In my opinion the pursuit of the enemy could not have been continued longer without coming in contact with a large, fresh force, which, in the scattered and exhausted condition of our troops, we could not have withstood.

The character of the country over which we would have had to retreat from Donelson to Charlotte was excessively poor and broken, and at that time covered with snow and sleet, and could not have furnished a half-day's ration for our force.
N. B. FORREST, Brigadier- General, Commanding Cavalry.[1226]

(Indorsement No. 1.)
I have compared the above copy with the original supplemental report of General Forrest and attest it as a true copy.

---

1226. ORA, Ser. 1, Vol. 7, p. 387.

W. H. HUMPHREYS, Confederate States District Judge.[1227]

(Indorsement No. 2.)

The services detailed in this report having been performed while General Forrest was under my immediate command and General Floyd being out of service and inaccessible and General A. S. Johnston being dead, I transmit the report direct to the War Department, through the Adjutant-General.

GID. J. PILLOW, Brigadier-General, C. S. Army.[1228]

These reports give a fascinating insight into Forrest the soldier, the cavalryman, the officer, and the subordinate. From them we can be assured that had he been head of the army at Donelson instead of only a small cavalry, he would have safely led most of the Confederate soldiers to Nashville, all spared to fight another day.

He had promised the parents of his younger soldiers that he would protect them, not offer them up as sacrificial prisoners to the Yanks.[1229] And he had stuck by his word, even at the risk of being demoted, or worse, being called a coward.[1230] All this after his superiors had surrendered, not to Grant, but to some dying campfires and a line of old picket fencing!

Forrest's men sided with their commander unanimously: it was at the Battle of Fort Donelson that the immortal legend of "I rode with Forrest" began.

## AUDACIOUS FIGHTING AT THE BATTLE OF SHILOH

Tragically, it was only a few weeks later, at the Battle of Shiloh, Tennessee (the Battle of Pittsburg Landing to Yanks), April 6 and 7, 1862, that Forrest met up with Grant again, a disastrous meeting for the Confederates that should have never taken place.[1231]

While Forrest's brilliant and violent rearguard maneuvers at Shiloh eventually forced the Yanks to retreat to Pittsburg Landing, the

---

1227. ORA, Ser. 1, Vol. 7, p. 387.
1228. ORA, Ser. 1, Vol. 7, p. 388.
1229. Jordan and Pryor, p. 91; Lytle, p. 76.
1230. Mathes, pp. 50-51.
1231. Forrest and Grant did not actually meet on the battlefield at Fort Donelson, but they did meet directly on the battlefield at Shiloh, the first and last time this monumental encounter would take place during Lincoln's War. Lytle, p. 84.

Rebs suffered nearly 11,000 casualties and the noble General Albert Sidney Johnston was killed.[1232]   Realizing the hopelessness of the Confederate situation, Rebel General Pierre Gustave Toutant Beauregard wisely retreated to Corinth, Mississippi.

Though the Confederacy was handed another defeat, on April 8, 1862, Forrest used the Battle of Fallen Timbers to introduce an audacious new form of defensive fighting. Galloping his horse out across the middle of the battlefield, he was shot in the side by a Federal soldier. Though the wound was excruciatingly painful (the bullet entered through his pelvis, nearly severing his spine), Forrest ignored the injury.[1233] Instead, he reached down and grabbed the astonished rifleman by the coat, pulled him up onto the back of his horse, and held him behind him as a human shield. The horrified bluecoats dared not fire at the brazen Confederate officer for fear of hitting their own man.

Flying back to the Rebel side through a hail of sizzling lead balls, Forrest escaped the field without further bloodshed, dropping his terrified attacker unharmed to the ground as he raced away. To the true legend of Nathan Bedford Forrest was added a new page that day.[1234]

FORREST'S BIRTHDAY BASH IN MURFREESBORO
Forrest went on to fight in the advance on Vicksburg (late 1862), and at the Battle of Paducah (March 25, 1864), where military reports note that the near superhuman Forrest rode his 2,500-man cavalry one-hundred miles in a mere fifty hours.

On his forty-first birthday, July 13, 1862, Forrest achieved a particularly stunning victory at the Battle of Murfreesboro, Tennessee, where he routed and captured an army twice the size of his own, with poorly armed and equipped men and without artillery, creating a sensation both across the South and the North.[1235]   Despite the unparalleled win, Forrest's commanding officer, General Braxton Bragg, offered no praise, and instead ignored the cavalryman's masterful achievement. This would ruffle anyone's feathers. It certainly ruffled

---

1232. General Johnston bled to death at Peach Orchard, Tennessee, on April 6, 1862, after being shot in the right leg. Thinking it was not serious he had ignored the wound.
1233. Forrest later had the bullet removed—without anesthetics.
1234. Mathes, pp. 59-60.
1235. Wyeth, LGNBF, p. 94.

Forrest's.

Thus began a long and rancorous animosity between the two, and for the most part they remained bitter enemies until the close of the War. Their heated arguments included yelling matches, up-raised fists, and even death threats. Forrest complained bitterly to those who would listen at Richmond. Things got so serious that he was eventually re-assigned to another state by President Jefferson Davis himself, a new command known forever after as "Forrest's Territory."[1236] Fully aware that the bold and aggressive Tennessean was invaluable to the South, Bragg, to his credit, never reported this particular insubordination to his superiors.[1237] But the fight between these two men was far from over.

FORREST AT THE HERMITAGE

On July 21, 1862, Forrest and his men made a one-hour stop at the Hermitage (in what is now Hermitage, Tennessee, a few miles east of Nashville), the former home of the seventh president of the U.S., Andrew Jackson.[1238] Forrest believed that his men needed a short sabbatical, and also that they might be inspired by Jackson's memory—as well as his reputation as a successful military man.[1239]

Forrest himself, no doubt, felt an affinity with Jackson: both were Southerners who had had difficult childhoods on the frontiers of their respective states; both were rough-hewn men with an abundance of pride and little formal education; both were hot-headed, adventurous, and fearless; and both lived by the Wild West's masculine code of honor—particularly when it came to defending women. The two overcame incredible adversity in adulthood as well, going on to attain not only immense success and wealth, but near universal respect as great military men. Forrest's soldiers may have been comparing their leader to "Old Hickory" in just this fashion as the command rode up the grand driveway of the Hermitage that summer day.

As it so happened, there was a large party going on: a first-anniversary celebration of the Confederate victory at the Battle of

---

1236. Morton, p. 132.
1237. Wyeth, LGNBF, p. 266.
1238. Henry, FWMF, p. 92.
1239. Lytle, p. 104.

Manassas I (July 21, 1861).[1240] While his men lounged, Forrest mingled with the elegantly dressed Victorian ladies and gentlemen for about sixty minutes,[1241] no doubt the center of attention, before heading back out on the trail to hunt down and kill Yankees.[1242]

## FORREST TORMENTS THE YANKS
Over the next few days the General frayed many a nerve in Union camps across the Western theater, as the following Yankee reports from the field reveal:

HEADQUARTERS,
Huntsville, July 22, 1862.
General SMITH, Tullahoma:
Forrest is now between Nashville and Murfreesborough and destroyed three bridges 9 miles from Nashville yesterday.
D. C. BUELL.[1243]

TULLAHOMA, July 22, 1862.
Col. J. B. FRY:
I have information this morning, which I consider reliable, as it comes from several independent sources and from our own scouts and several Union citizens, that Forrest started from the neighborhood of McMinnville for Lebanon on Friday with 1,000 men. He was to have been back on Saturday; has not returned. A train took the Twenty-first Kentucky to Murfreesborough. This finishes the movement of troops ordered from this to that point. One of the trains is ordered to carry through the telegraph party, making repairs as they go.
W. S. SMITH, Brigadier-General.[1244]

TULLAHOMA, July 22, 1862.
Col. J. B. FRY:
One of my scouting parties last night captured a morning report of a rebel force encamped near McMinnville; it is addressed to General Forrest, Chapel Hill, which you will perceive lies between Shelbyville and Franklin. The rebel has not had time to advise him

---

1240. Yanks and scallywags refer to this conflict as the Battle of First Bull Run.
1241. Jordan and Pryor, pp. 176-177.
1242. Mathes, p. 70.
1243. ORA, Ser. 1, Vol. 16, Pt. 2, p. 200.
1244. ORA, Ser. 1, Vol. 16, Pt. 2, p. 200.

of its capture. Cannot we catch him there or Shelbyville, where I
think his army is.

W. S. SMITH, General.[1245]


COLUMBIA, July 23, 1862.

Col. J. B. Fry:

A citizen from Marshall County reports Forrest and 600 men
passed through that county going south last night. Colonel Board
marches to this place to-night. Colonel McCook is ordered here
also.

JAS. S. NEGLEY.[1246]


NASHVILLE, July 23, 1862.

Col. J. B. FRY:

Received answers to my two dispatches. Yours this morning were
promptly received, but one sent by me in cipher last night is not
alluded to. Have an apprehension the enemy have an operator
replying in your name, and accordingly send this in cipher,
requesting acknowledgment.

The enemy's [Forrest's] cavalry is not less than 2,000,
and possibly 4,000, and increasing. Bridges on Chattanooga road
near this place destroyed and detachments guarding them killed or
captured; 80 of those of Second Kentucky came in paroled this
morning. A wagon train being sent for Nelson is being followed by
the enemy and will be surely captured; also every detachment from
here to Nelson's outposts. After that Forrest announces that he
will come back to attack the town. Our force being menaced on
the Louisville road, Colonel Boone announces from Gallatin that
Richland, 15 miles beyond, is held by 1,000 rebel cavalry, and
Colonel Boone has detained the train from this place. We cannot
send force from Nashville to guard the trains, and I telegraphed
Boone if well satisfied of enemy at Richland to send the trains back
to town. Also telegraphed Colonel Bruce at Bowling Green to
send to Boyle for instructions and force. He answers that his own
force is 450 men and that it would not be proper to expose the
Bowling Green bridges, as it is evident that the enemy are rising
rapidly to control our communication and perhaps strike Nashville
when they feel strong enough.

Forrest sent a challenge to Miller last night to come out
and fight him. The postmaster sent your mails on the 17th, 20th,
and to-day. Have just received your dispatch stating you had

---

1245. ORA, Ser. 1, Vol. 16, Pt. 2, p. 200.
1246. ORA, Ser. 1, Vol. 16, Pt. 2, pp. 203-204.

information.

W. H. SIDELL, Major.[1247]

HEADQUARTERS DISTRICT OF THE OHIO,
Nashville, July 23, 1862.
Col. J. B. FRY:
Asst. Adjt. Gen., Chief of Staff, Huntsville, Ala.:
Have no knowledge that organized bodies of men re-enforce Forrest, though he boasts of expecting them, so as to get Nashville on Saturday night. [John Hunt] Morgan may possibly join him. I meant individual accessions, as reported by Union men and our men returned paroled after capture and detention—in one day 40 in Lebanon, in another 50 in La Vergne. Colonel Miller can count 200 of whom he has knowledge. On the road many mounted men are seen going toward Forrest, reasonably supposed to be his recruits, and the country people are openly exultant. There is negro testimony that the roads from Knoxville and East Tennessee toward this region are lined with men, seemingly recruits. This is not corroborated. Last night our scouts saw nothing of the enemy within 10 miles. Train started for Louisville this morning presumed all right, though yesterday's did not come in. Nothing heard to-day from Colonel Boone.

W. H. SIDELL, Major, Fifteenth Infantry, Actg. Asst. Adjt. Gen.[1248]

MURFREESBOROUGH, July 26, 1862.
Major-General BUELL:
John Morgan is retreating from Kentucky and will come in at Sparta. I want cavalry, and I want General Jackson, who is now in Nashville, to command it. I have sent repeated orders to Colonel Boone for his regiment to come here at once, and he will neither answer nor does he come. I also ordered one battalion of Wolford's cavalry to march here. I hear nothing of it one way or the other. I can settle this part of the country and stop Morgan and Forrest and be in position to receive any forces from Chattanooga, if I can get my orders obeyed. I have ordered the Thirty-first Indiana, Colonel Cruft, to march here and join its brigade. If Morgan and Forrest get together they will have 3,500 well mounted cavalry. General Manson arrived this morning.

W. NELSON, General.[1249]

1247. ORA, Ser. 1, Vol. 16, Pt. 2, p. 204.
1248. ORA, Ser. 1, Vol. 16, Pt. 2, p. 205.
1249. ORA, Ser. 1, Vol. 16, Pt. 2, p. 213.

## FORREST CUTS GRANT'S COMMUNICATIONS

In the fall of 1862 Forrest was busy putting the fear of God into other Yankee officers, among them General James S. Negley.[1250] After Forrest successfully "demonstrated" against Negley around Nashville, the Yankee officer sent the following field report to his superior General William S. Rosecrans:

> HEADQUARTERS POST, Nashville, Tenn. November 13, 1862.
> Major-General ROSECRANS, Comdg. Fourteenth Army Corps, Dept. of the Cumberland:
> GENERAL: I regret to inform you that the picket officers report the Fourth Ohio Cavalry driven in in great disorder by Forrest, with 1,200 cavalry and six pieces of artillery. Permit me to respectfully suggest extreme caution in operating against Forrest's cavalry. They are between 4,000 and 5,000 strong, are constantly moving, and are always watching for an inferior force and ready to remove from an equal one. . . .
> I have the honor to remain, yours, very truly,
> JAS. S. NEGLEY, Brigadier-General, Commanding Post.[1251]

That winter, around December 20, 1862, Forrest got a chance to harass and annoy General Grant, as the Union officer sourly noted in his memoirs. It was at this time, the future U.S. president wrote, that

> . . . Forrest got on the line of railroad between Jackson, Tenn., and Columbus, Ky., doing much damage to it. This cut me off from all communications with the North for more than two weeks, and that interval elapsed before rations of forage could be issued from stores in the regular way. . . . I determined, therefore, to abandon my campaign into the interior with Columbus as a base, and returned to La Grange and Grand Junction . . .[1252]

## RODERICK THE FALLEN CHARGER

On March 5, 1863, at the Battle of Thompson's Station, Tennessee, Forrest lost his favorite warhorse Roderick. The amazing animal, which had been given to him as a gift by Mr. Cocke of Tennessee, served with

---

1250. Nashville's famous Fort Negley is named after this Union general. Prior to Lincoln's War, the site, once known as St. Cloud Hill, was a popular picnic area for local residents.
1251. ORA, Ser. 1, Vol. 20, Pt. 2, p. 41.
1252. U. S. Grant, Vol. 1, pp. 432-433.

Forrest through a number of conflicts,[1253] and was known to follow him around camp like a hunting dog. The story of Roderick's amazing love for his master, as well as his gallant death on the battlefield at Thompson's Station, is legendary in Middle Tennessee.

During the fighting the horse was wounded in three places, after which Forrest ordered him taken to the rear where he could be cared for by the hostlers. While being attended to, however, Roderick heard his master's voice in the distance as he was commanding another charge against the enemy. The steed's ears immediately perked up and away he sped, taking off so quickly that none of the men could catch him.

The horse easily followed Forrest's booming yell, even over the sound of gunfire, and within moments he was at his side. Unfortunately, after wildly jumping three fences in order to reach his master, Roderick received an additional wound which was now bleeding profusely. Realizing that the horse's end was near, Forrest stroked him affectionately for the last time, as tears flowed down his cheeks. The General ordered Roderick to be buried where he died: on the battlefield at Giddens farm.

Recently a large statue of the famous warhorse was commissioned and after completion was placed at the site of his original interment on that cool March day in 1863. Some 150 years later Roderick is still remembered fondly around Thompson's Station, Spring Hill, and Franklin, Tennessee, and a number of housing developments have been named after him.[1254] Indeed, in honor of the horse's memory the Giddens House itself is now known simply as "Roderick."[1255]

ATTEMPTED MURDER OF FORREST

While Forrest was making the lives of his Yankee adversaries miserable, he was also raising eyebrows—and hackles—among his own subordinates. One of these was Lieutenant Andrew Wills Gould, who held a grudge against the General for an imagined earlier slight made

---

1253. Wyeth, LGNBF, p. 161.

1254. Strangely, though Roderick was a gelding (a castrated male horse), his Thompson's Station statue portrays him as a stallion (an uncastrated male horse).

1255. Logsdon, TATG, pp. 49-50.

against his character.[1256]

On June 13, 1863, with vengeance in his heart, Gould angrily tracked down Forrest and tried to murder him at the quartermaster's office (in the Masonic Building) at Columbia, Tennessee.[1257] Here he cornered his superior in a hallway, then stuck a pistol in his ribs and fired, with every intent to end the General's life there and then.[1258]

Fortunately, the bullet missed the vital organs and only wounded Forrest (above the left hip), who then turned the tables on his attacker: holding down Gould with one hand, he used the other to pry open a small knife with his teeth. Driving the knife into his struggling opponent's chest, Forrest quickly and efficiently ended the scuffle. Gould, screaming in pain, fled the scene. Forrest yelled, "damn it, no one kills me and lives to tell about it!" and took off in pursuit.[1259]

A doctor was called for Forrest, who pronounced the wound serious and ordered the General to the hospital.[1260] But, Forrest yelled, it ain't nothin' but a tiny goddamned ball, so forget about that for now! Go find Gould and take him over to the Nelson House. Accommodate him ever' way possible. And save his life, damn it, no matter what![1261]

By the time the impetuous young officer was found, however, he lay dying.[1262]

For two days Gould struggled for life at the Nelson House Hotel,[1263] while Forrest recuperated a short distance away at the Galloway House.[1264] Realizing that his fate was sealed (Forrest had cut two of his ribs apart, a mortal wound), the boy asked to see Forrest one last time. Leaning over his dying comrade, Forrest wept, asked for forgiveness, and expressed regret. Gould too apologized, then passed

---

1256. Bradley, p. 79. Earlier, Forrest had transferred Gould to another command after the young officer had wrongly abandoned two guns on Sand Mountain. Though not meant personally, Gould took it so. Lytle, p. 181.
1257. Wyeth, LGNBF, pp. 223-224.
1258. Sheppard, p. 119.
1259. Morton, pp. 102-103.
1260. Lytle, p. 181.
1261. Henry, FWM, p. 163.
1262. Sheppard, p. 120.
1263. Lytle, p. 182. Built in 1828, the Nelson House Hotel can still be seen in Columbia on North Main Street across from City Hall. Gould's room was on the left on the second floor (facing the street).
1264. The Galloway House still stands in Columbia. It is located on the southwest corner of West Ninth Street and School Street. Coincidentally, Forrest's room (like Gould's at the Nelson House) was also on the left on the second floor (facing the street).

into the better land.[1265]  An individual at the scene later wrote:

> Forrest wept like a child.  It was the saddest of all the sad incidents of the long and bitter war I witnessed.[1266]

Forrest had acted in self-defense and no charges were filed.[1267] But the tragic episode had a profound emotional effect on the General. There and then a wretched and contrite Forrest vowed that he would never kill another human being, except for Yankees—and then only in defense of the Confederacy.[1268]

## THE BATTLE OF CHICKAMAUGA

By now Forrest and his men had the entire Union brass in a state of panic.  Forrest's uncanny ability to melt into the vast Southern countryside without a trace, only to attack suddenly—and without warning, spooked even the most experienced and hardened military men.  Fear reverberated up and down the Yankee chain of command, going all the way to the top.  On May 27, 1863, an unnerved Lincoln wrote hastily to General Rosecrans: "Where is Forrest's headquarters?"[1269]  The answer, unknown to Lincoln, was: wherever Forrest is at the moment!

While the Federal military brass sweated over Forrest's whereabouts, he was off doing what he did best: fighting Yankees. September 18 through 20, 1863, found him at the Battle of Chickamauga, Georgia.  Early on the morning of the 18th, according to historian John Bowers, the first sight to appear on the misty horizon was the visage of a mysterious and otherworldly figure, dressed in a long white linen duster, bristling with pistols, knives, and sabers.  It was none other than Forrest, the first man on the scene, alert, wild-eyed, looking for Yankee blood to shed.[1270]

Forrest did in fact fire both the first and the last shot at

---

1265. Morton, pp. 103-104.
1266. Wyeth, LGNBF, p. 226.
1267. Forrest recovered quickly from Gould's attack, and led his men into battle a mere twelve days later. Mathes, pp. 130-132.
1268. Mathes, p. 132.
1269. ORA, Ser. 1, Vol. 23, Pt. 2, p. 365.
1270. Bowers, p. 60.

Chickamauga, while scoring numerous crushing blows against the Yanks that helped win the day for the South.[1271]  And the battle was indeed a bloody one, making the name Chickamauga (Cherokee for the "River of Blood") particularly fitting.[1272]

However, to everyone's surprise, the military perfectionist felt that the Confederate victory had been won more by accident than by good soldiering: at a crucial point in the fight, Forrest had asked for reinforcements (to chase down the retreating Yanks).[1273]  But the request was rejected by Bragg (who was then suffering from the delusion that the Rebs had been squarely beaten),[1274] destroying a golden opportunity to take down Rosecrans' army.  To his men Forrest snapped: Why does he bother fighting?[1275]  No wonder, Forrest must have pondered, that Bragg was widely known as the man with the metal heart, a heavy hand, and an empty head.[1276]

Adding to his disgust, Forrest was once more passed over for promotion by Bragg.  This time it went to Joseph "Fightin' Joe" Wheeler, one of the Rebel officers Forrest liked least, and one admittedly far inferior to him on the battlefield.[1277]  Fuming, Forrest turned in his resignation.  But his more sensible superiors would have none of it, and instead promoted him to major general.[1278]

One Rebel officer, General D. H. Hill, who witnessed Forrest on the Chickamauga battlefield, later said:

> I would ask no better fortune, if again placed on a flank, than to have such a vigilant, gallant, and accomplished officer guarding its approaches.[1279]

Indeed, Forrest's stunning tactics at Chickamauga made him more famous than ever across the South.  From that day forward he

---

1271. Wyeth, LGNBF, p. 244.
1272. Lytle, p. 187.
1273. Wills, pp. 140-142.
1274. Lytle, p. 233.
1275. Henry, FWMF, p. 193.
1276. Lytle, p. 113.
1277. In fairness to Wheeler, he had not sought the promotion and would have much preferred to serve under Forrest rather than over him.
1278. Henry, ATSF, p. 42.
1279. Mathes, p. 149.

became one of the most charismatic, legendary, and romantic figures of the War for Southern Independence.[1280]

## FORREST, BRAGG, & WHEELER

There was jealousy among the ambitious men of Jefferson Davis' administration and armies, however, and not everyone was happy that Forrest, a non-West Pointer and a volunteer, was being so rapidly promoted. Nonetheless, being a natural-born commander—one who could lead but could not be led[1281]—the Western frontiersman well earned his rise to the top, overcoming all resistance through his sheer iron will, self-reliance, and military genius.[1282]

On the other hand, Forrest was not happy with many of his superiors either, Bragg in particular. When word of Forrest's negative comments about Bragg's lack of gumption at Chickamauga eventually reached the ears of the latter, Forrest found himself abruptly relieved of his command. Bragg's order, sent through Adjutant General George W. Brent, read:

> HEADQUARTERS ARMY OF TENNESSEE,
> Missionary Ridge, September 28, 1863.
> Brigadier-General FORREST, Near Athens:
> GENERAL: The general commanding desires that you will without delay turn over the troops of your command previously ordered to Major-General Wheeler.
> I am, general, very respectfully,
> GEORGE WM. BRENT, Assistant Adjutant-General.[1283]

Naturally Forrest's loyal band of brothers were infuriated, for they had marched many miles with him, scored many victories under his command, and trusted and loved him deeply.[1284] Forrest was also seething over this latest incident, for this was not the first time, but the third time Bragg had relieved him of his command.[1285]

Worse yet, he was being assigned to serve under one of his least

---

1280. Wyeth, LGNBF, p. 255.
1281. Wyeth, LGNBF, p. 152.
1282. Mathes, p. 33.
1283. ORA, Ser. 1, Vol. 30, Pt. 4, p. 710.
1284. Morton, pp. 132-133.
1285. Mathes, p. 154.

favorite officers: General Wheeler.[1286] A mean-spirited Bragg was fully aware of Forrest's negative feelings toward Wheeler, for after the failed Battle of Dover (or the Battle of Fort Donelson II), Tennessee, February 3, 1863 (at which Wheeler was commander), Forrest had made the now well-known statement to his face: "I will be in my coffin before I will fight again under your command."[1287] Thus Forrest could only take Bragg's order as a personal insult, for that is exactly what it was.[1288]

FORREST GIVES BRAGG A SEVERE DRESSING DOWN
The proud Tennessean could stand it no longer. After receiving Bragg's missive, he "flew into a violent rage," and there and then dictated a letter to his aid-de-camp, Major Charles W. Anderson. According to Anderson:

> The general dictated a letter which I wrote to Bragg, resenting the manner in which he had been treated, and charging the commander of the army in plain, straight language with duplicity and lying, and informing him that he would call at his headquarters in a few days to say to him in person just what he had written. He concluded by saying he desired to shirk no responsibility incurred by the contents of his letter. When Forrest read the letter over and signed it, it was sealed and handed to the courier, and, as he rode away, the general remarked to me, 'Bragg never got such a letter as that before from a brigadier.'[1289]

Two days later, on October 1, 1863, in what for anyone else would have been an act of career suicide, Forrest kept his pledge, riding straight to Bragg's headquarters at Missionary Ridge (Chattanooga, Tennessee) to confront him.[1290] Forrest's Chief Surgeon, Dr. James B. Cowan (Forrest's relative),[1291] who was riding with him, described the

---

1286. Wheeler was one of the few Confederate soldiers who was "allowed" to be buried at Arlington National Cemetery. This was in honor of his service in the war with Spain in 1898. At times during the conflict the Georgia-born officer would forget which war he was in and urge his men to "fight them Yanks!" K. C. Davis, p. 448.

1287. Wyeth, LGNBF, p. 151.

1288. Lytle, p. 235; Wills, p. 102.

1289. Wyeth, LGNBF, p. 264.

1290. Sheppard, p. 132.

1291. Dr. James B. Cowan was the first cousin of Forrest's wife, Mary Ann Montgomery. From my personal family tree.

incident:

I observed as we rode along that the general was silent, which was unusual with him when we were alone. Knowing him so well, I was convinced that something that displeased him greatly had transpired. He wore an expression which I had seen before on some occasions when a storm was brewing. I had known nothing of the letter he had written General Bragg, and was in utter ignorance not only of what was passing in Forrest's mind at this time, but of the object of his visit to the general-in-chief. As we passed the guard in front of General Bragg's tent, I observed that General Forrest did not acknowledge the salute of the sentry, which was so contrary to his custom that I could not but notice it. When we entered the tent, where this officer was alone, General Bragg rose from his seat, spoke to General Forrest, and, advancing, offered him his hand. Refusing to take the proffered hand, and standing stiff and erect before Bragg, Forrest said: 'I am not here to pass civilities or compliments with you, but on other business. You commenced your cowardly and contemptible persecution of me soon after the battle of Shiloh, and you have kept it up ever since. You did it because I reported to Richmond facts, while you reported damn lies. You robbed me of my command in Kentucky and gave it to one of your favorites—men that I armed and equipped from the enemies of our country. In a spirit of revenge and spite, because I would not fawn upon you as others did, you drove me into West Tennessee in the winter of 1862, with a second brigade I had organized, with improper arms and without sufficient ammunition, although I had made repeated applications for the same. You did it to ruin me and my career. When, in spite of all this, I returned with my command, well equipped by captures, you began again your work of spite and persecution, and have kept it up; and now this second brigade, organized and equipped without thanks to you or the government, a brigade which has won a reputation for successful fighting second to none in the army, taking advantage of your position as the commanding general in order to further humiliate me, you have taken these brave men from me. I have stood your meanness as long as I intend to. You have played the part of a damn scoundrel, and are a coward; and if you were any part of a man, I would slap your jaws and force you to resent it. You may as well not issue any more orders to me, for I will not obey them, and I will hold you personally responsible for any further indignities you endeavor to inflict upon me. You have threatened to arrest me for not obeying your orders promptly. I dare you to do it, and I say to you that if you ever again try to interfere with me or cross my path it will be at the peril of your life.'[1292]

Riding away from the scene, Cowan said: "Well, you are in for it now!" But the General countered: "He'll never say a word about it; he'll be the last man to mention it; and, mark my word, he'll take no action in the matter."[1293]

Forrest's prediction came true: Bragg should have court-martialed Forrest, but he did not; nor did he reply to Forrest's earlier letter. He did not even officially report the confrontation at Missionary Ridge, perhaps because he feared for his life (with Forrest a real possibility). It is probable that he simply knew Forrest was right. Bragg also understood Forrest's immense value to the Southern Cause, one to which both men were completely devoted. Either way, Forrest would never serve under Bragg again, which is exactly how they both preferred it.

Forrest's unpleasant encounter with Bragg did come back to haunt him—and in the worst possible way; not only for Forrest, but for the Confederacy itself.

In February 1864 President Davis brought his good friend Bragg to Richmond to serve as his military advisor,[1294] in charge of "the conduct of the military operations in the armies of the Confederacy."[1295] Naturally, during the eight months Bragg spent at the Confederate White House, he used every opportunity to hamper Forrest's military career from behind the scenes (as he did, for example, in April 1864).[1296] He had Davis' ear after all, and being one of the president's favorites, Davis listened to him intently, and with great interest and respect.

Forrest must have at times wondered why he was so often held back from promotion when other less qualified men jumped ahead of him. Tragically, Bragg's personal petty vendetta against Forrest must be counted as one of the many reasons the South lost the War.

Years later Davis had a chance to pour over Forrest's field

1292. Wyeth, LGNBF, pp. 265-266.
1293. Wyeth, LGNBF, p. 266.
1294. Current, TC, s.v. "Bragg, Braxton."
1295. Warner, GG, s.v. "Braxton Bragg."
1296. See Henry, FWMF, p. 270.

reports. It was then and only then that he realized for the first time the true brilliance of the lanky mountaineer he had reined in because of Bragg's wrongheaded, self-serving criticisms. It was Bragg, after all, who went about telling other military brass that Forrest was little more than an unschooled and self-absorbed raider who knew nothing about being a team player.[1297]

Davis would indeed eventually learn how wrong Bragg was, much to his regret. In fact, Davis fled Richmond after Lee's surrender, in great part, because by then he realized that an army formed around Forrest could still save the Confederacy. As Davis records in his brilliant defense of the South, *The Rise and Fall of the Confederate Government*:

> Had the cavalry with which I left Charlotte been associated with a force large enough to inspire hope for the future, instead of being discouraged by the surrender in their rear, it would probably have gone on, and, when united with the forces of [Dabney H.] Maury, Forrest, and [Richard] Taylor, in Alabama and Mississippi, have constituted an army large enough to attract stragglers, and revive the drooping spirits of the country. In the worst view of the case it should have been able to cross the trans-Mississippi Department, and there uniting with the armies of E. K. Smith and [John B.] Magruder to form an army, which in the portion of that country abounding in supplies, and deficient in rivers and railroads, could have continued the war until our enemy, foiled in the purpose of subjugation, should, in accordance with his repeated declaration, have agreed, on the basis of a return to the Union, to acknowledge the Constitutional rights of the States, and by a convention, or quasi-treaty, to guarantee security of person and property. To this hope I persistently clung, and, if our independence could not be achieved, so much, at least, I trusted might be gained.
>
> Those who have endured the horrors of 'reconstruction,' who have, under 'carpet-bag rule,' borne insult, robbery, and imprisonment without legal warrant, can appreciate the value which would have attached to such limited measure of success.
>
> When I left Washington, Georgia, with the small party which has been enumerated, my object was to go to the south far enough to pass below the points reported to be occupied by Federal troops, and then turn to the west, cross the Chattahoochee, and then go on to meet the forces still supposed to be in the field in

---

1297. McWhiney and Hallock, Vol. 2, p. 100.

> Alabama. If, as now seemed probable, there should be no prospect
> of a successful resistance east of the Mississippi, I intended then to
> cross to the trans-Mississippi Department, where I believed
> Generals E. K. Smith and Magruder would continue to uphold our
> cause.[1298]

Sadly for the South, Davis' plan was never to be.[1299] He was captured before he made it out of Georgia.

Eleven years on, in late October 1877, during Forrest's funeral procession in Memphis, Davis and Governor James D. Porter of Tennessee were riding to the cemetery in a carriage together when, as Porter writes:

> . . . Mr. Davis spoke in the highest terms of Forrest's ability as a
> soldier. I remarked: 'History has accorded to General Forrest the
> first place as a cavalry leader in the war between the States, and has
> named him as one of the half-dozen great soldiers of the country.'
> Mr. Davis replied with great earnestness: 'I agree with you. The
> trouble was that the generals commanding in the Southwest never
> appreciated Forrest until it was too late. Their judgment was that
> he was a bold and enterprising partisan raider and rider. I was
> misled by them, and I never knew how to measure him until I read
> his reports of his campaign across the Tennessee River in 1864.
> This induced a study of his earlier reports, and after that I was
> prepared to adopt what you are pleased to name as the judgment of
> history.' In reply I said: 'I cannot comprehend such lack of
> appreciation after he fought the battle at Brice's Cross-Roads in
> June of 1864. That battle was not a cavalry raid nor an accident.
> It was the conception of a man endowed with a genius for war.'
> Mr. Davis replied to this: 'That campaign was not understood at
> Richmond. The impression made upon those in authority was that
> Forrest had made another successful raid, but I saw it all after it was
> too late.'[1300]

Modern history concurs: the Confederate brass misused Forrest. But even if they had not, to this day some believe that there were probably simply too many Braxton Braggs and not enough Nathan

---

1298. J. Davis, Vol. 2, pp. 696-697.
1299. Lytle, p. 357.
1300. Wyeth, LGNBF, p. 634.

Bedford Forrests to drive the Yanks out of the South.[1301]

## FORREST SEEKS A NEW COMMAND & OFFERS A BOLD NEW PLAN

Weeks earlier, on August 9, 1863, Forrest, already anticipating problems with Bragg, had written a letter to Confederate General Samuel Cooper at Richmond, asking for an independent command in West Tennessee or Mississippi. Included in Forrest's missive was a proposal for what was certainly the most outstanding plan by a Confederate officer during the entire conflict: prolong the War—thus exhausting the North—by closing down the Yankees' major supply routes, the Mississippi and Tennessee Rivers.[1302]

By this time most of the Union forces, including those under Grant, were relying strictly on these two waterways for provisions. Had Forrest's proposition (already backed by other important Confederate leaders, such as General Joseph E. Johnston) been taken seriously *and* implemented, it is clear that the outcome of Lincoln's War would have been very different.[1303]

In his 1885 *Memoirs*, Grant himself admitted that a protraction strategy would have won the War:

> I think that [this] . . . policy was the best one that could have been pursued by the whole South—protract the war, which was all that was necessary to enable them to gain recognition in the end. The North was already growing weary . . .[1304] Anything that could have prolonged the war a year beyond the time that it did finally close, would probably have exhausted the North to such an extent that they might then have abandoned the contest and agreed to separation.[1305]

Forrest's original letter to Cooper, which, unfortunately, was to pass through Bragg's hands,[1306] reads:

---

1301. Parks, p. 191.
1302. Sheppard, pp. 306-307.
1303. Wyeth, LGNBF, p. 641.
1304. U. S. Grant, Vol. 2, p. 345.
1305. U. S. Grant, Vol. 2, p. 167.
1306. Lytle, p. 194.

HEADQUARTERS FIRST DIVISION CAVALRY,
Kingston, August 9, 1863.
General S. COOPER, Adjutant-General, Richmond, Va.:
GENERAL,—Prompted by the repeated solicitations of numerous friends and acquaintances resident in west Tennessee and northern Mississippi, also by a desire to serve my country to the best of my ability, and wherever those services can be rendered most available and effective, I respectfully lay before you a proposition which, if approved, will seriously, if not entirely, obstruct the navigation of the Mississippi River, and in sixty days procure a large force now inside the enemy's lines, which without this, or a similar move, cannot be obtained.

The proposition is this: Give me the command of the forces from Vicksburg to Cairo, or, in other words, all the forces I may collect together and organize between those points—say in northern Mississippi, west Tennessee, and those that may join me from Arkansas, Mississippi, and southern Kentucky. I desire to take with me only about four hundred men from my present command—viz., my escort, sixty; McDonald's battalion, one hundred and fifty; the Second Kentucky Cavalry, two hundred and fifty—selected entirely on account of their knowledge of the country in which I propose to operate. In all, say, men and outfit, four hundred men, with long-range guns (Enfield), four three-inch Dahlgren or Parrott guns, with eight number one horses to each gun and caisson, two wagons for the battery, one pack-mule to every ten men, and two hundred rounds of ammunition for small arms and artillery.

I would like to have Captain (W. W.) Carnes, now at Chattanooga, in some portion of General Bragg's army, to command the battery, and, in case he was detached for the expedition, that he be allowed to select his cannoneers, etc. I have resided on the Mississippi for over twenty years, was for many years engaged in buying and selling negroes, and know the country perfectly well between Memphis and Vicksburg, and also am well acquainted with all the prominent planters in that region, as well as above Memphis. I also have officers in my command and on my staff who have rafted timber out of the bottoms, and know every foot of the ground between Commerce and Vicksburg. With the force proposed, and my knowledge of the river- bottoms, as well as the knowledge my men have of the country from Vicksburg up, I am confident we could so move and harass and destroy boats on the river that only boats heavily protected by gunboats would be able to make the passage.

I ask also authority to organize all troops that can be obtained, and that I be promised long-range guns for them as soon as organizations are reported. There are many half-organized regiments, battalions, and companies in northern Mississippi and west Tennessee, but they are without arms and have no way of getting out, and it only requires a little time and a nucleus around which they can form, to organize and put them in the field. I believe that in sixty days I can raise from five to ten thousand men between Vicksburg and Cairo, well mounted and ready for service as soon as provided with guns and ammunition.

In making this proposition, I desire to state that I do so entirely for the good of the service. I believe that I can accomplish all that I propose to do. I have never asked for position, have taken position and performed the duties assigned me, and have never yet suffered my command to be surprised or defeated. I should leave this department with many regrets, as I am well pleased with the officers in my command and with the division serving under me. I shall especially regret parting with my old brigade. It was organized by me, and a record of its past services and present condition will compare favorably with any cavalry command in the service, and nothing but a desire to destroy the enemy's transports and property, and increase the strength of our army, could for a moment induce me voluntarily to part with them. There are thousands of men where I propose to go that I am satisfied will join me, and that rapidly (otherwise they will remain where they are), until all the country bordering on the Mississippi from Cairo down is taken and permanently occupied by our forces.

I am, general, very respectfully, your obedient servant,

N. B. Forrest, Brigadier-General.[1307]

## TYPOGRAPHICAL SHENANIGANS

A week and a half later, a copy of this remarkable letter was given to President Davis, who promptly invited Forrest to Montgomery, Alabama, for a personal interview.[1308] Strangely, by the time the copy arrived, some of the wording in the original version to Cooper had been altered. As can be seen above, in the last paragraph of that version we find the text (italics mine):

I should leave this department with many regrets, as I am well pleased with *the officers in my command* and with the division serving

---

1307. ORA, Ser. 1, Vol. 23, Pt. 2, pp. 955-956; ORA, Ser. 1, Vol. 30, Pt. 4, pp. 508-509.
1308. Morton, p. 131.

under me.[1309]

In the later copy to Davis, however, the words "the officers in my command" were replaced with "the officers in command."[1310]

Was the omission of the word "my" in Davis' copy due to careless copying? Or was it intentional, a sign of Forrest's acute awareness that Bragg was undermining him in Richmond? We will never know. Yet it is obvious that Forrest wanted to increase the odds that his proposition would be warmly received at the Confederate White House, a goal almost impossible with Davis' best friend—and Forrest's worst enemy—General Braxton Bragg advising the Confederate President from the field.[1311]

Not aware of the alteration, or perhaps regarding it as unimportant, after receipt of his copy, the "personal interview" between Davis and Forrest at Montgomery proceeded as planned.[1312] Things went well, but just as Forrest had predicted, his ingenious proposition was postponed, then largely ignored, then later completely vetoed by Davis after having first been read over by Bragg.[1313]

Davis' inevitable dismissal, written in late August 1863, to his secretary of war, James A. Seddon (1815-1880), reads:

> The indorsement of General Bragg indicated the propriety of a postponement. Subsequent events have served to render the proposition more objectionable. Whenever a change of circumstances will permit, the measure may be adopted.
> J. DAVIS.[1314]

That "change of circumstances" never came, of course.

---

**1309.** ORA, Ser. 1, Vol. 23, Pt. 2, p. 956.

**1310.** Lytle, p. 194.

**1311.** Bragg also undermined numerous other Rebel officers, such as Leonidas Polk and Joseph E. Johnston. His sabotage of Johnston was especially troubling as Johnston had supported Bragg when Bragg was his superior. See Lytle, pp. 283-284, 308.

**1312.** Morton, p. 131.

**1313.** Dated August 14, 1863, from Chattanooga, Tennessee, Bragg's duplicitous "endorsement" read: "I know no officer to whom I would sooner assign the duty proposed, than which none is more important, but it would deprive this army of one of its greatest elements of strength to remove General Forrest." ORA, Ser. 1, Vol. 30, Pt. 4, p. 509. This mischievous missive drove the final nail into the coffin of Forrest's brilliant plan to wear down and finally conquer Lincoln and his Yankee invaders.

**1314.** ORA, Ser. 1, Vol. 30, Pt. 4, p. 510.

While Forrest had not helped matters by verbally attacking Bragg at Missionary Ridge, in the end it was Bragg who had caused Davis to "render Forrest's proposition objectionable," for at the time Davis could only see Forrest through Bragg's eyes.[1315] Thus, due to Bragg's vanity and stupidity and Davis' cronyism and short-sightedness, one of the last remaining chances for the Confederacy evaporated into thin air.[1316]

Bragg had got his revenge by preventing Forrest from advancing to the top. But at an enormous cost to the South. Some, like Lytle, literally blame the entire fall of the Confederacy on Davis and Bragg.[1317] Ludwell Johnson called it the biggest mistake of Davis' presidency, perhaps the worst strategical blunder of the entire conflict. For had Forrest's wish been granted, Atlanta would have been spared, and Lincoln would have lost his bid for reelection in 1864. The War would have ended there and then, and the Confederacy would have lived on as a free and independent nation.[1318]

Whatever one's opinion, it is clear that without Forrest at the head of the Army of Tennessee, Dixie had little hope of winning against the meddlesome North and its unscrupulous president.

On October 29, 1863, a few months after this pitiful and unnecessary military soap opera took place, Forrest received a letter from Davis (under Bragg's influence) transferring him to his new field of duty: an independent command in West Tennessee and North Mississippi.[1319]

FORREST GETS UP A CAVALRY & ENLISTS SLAVES
The "unlettered general," as some derogatorily referred to him,[1320] wasted no time in organizing new troops, and by the end of 1863 Forrest had several thousand soldiers under his command, a battle-hardened group of prize soldiers known as "Forrest's Cavalry."

Though, like the Confederate government itself, he had been

---

1315. Henry, FWMF, p. 102.
1316. Lytle, pp. 342-343.
1317. Lytle, p. 395.
1318. L. Johnson, pp. 160-161.
1319. Wyeth, LGNBF, pp. 271-273; Morton, p. 132.
1320. Sheppard, p. 260.

unofficially impressing blacks into his command since the beginning of the War—among them forty-five of his own servants—these had been mainly used as laborers, teamsters, cooks, body servants, and hostlers.[1321] By December 11, 1863, however, we have official proof that Forrest was also enrolling Southern slaves as combatants; that is, as soldiers.[1322] In a letter to Union General Stephen A. Hurlbut,[1323] Union General John D. Stevenson[1324] writes:

> CORINTH, December 11, 1863.
> Major-General HURLBUT,
> Memphis:
> Scouts to-day from Purdy, Eastport, and Tuscumbia Valley. Forrest is conscripting every man capable of bearing arms, and taking all negro men fit for soldiers; at the same time accumulating stores at Jackson.
>     A part of Roddey's command crossed the Tennessee River yesterday, above Eastport, with trains, and have gone down river to Savannah; the rest of his command remains near Tuscumbia. Nothing reported in direction of Okolona.
> JNO. D. STEVENSON, Brigadier-General.[1325]

As mentioned, Forrest had no doubt been enrolling Southern slaves as soldiers long before this time. However, even taking December 1863 as the beginning of his black enlistment, it is important to note that this was just months after Lincoln grudgingly and finally gave his approval for enlisting blacks in the U.S. army—and that only out of "military necessity."[1326]

Additionally, unlike Lincoln's segregated Northern troops,

---

1321. Henry, ATSF, pp. 45-46, 105.

1322. Wyeth, LGNBF, pp. 276-277.

1323. Originally from South Carolina, Yankee officer Hurlbut had a troubled record both during the War—when he upset Lincoln and was nearly arrested for "corrupt practices" (the case was dropped but he was eventually "honorably mustered out"), and after—when he was charged with drunkenness, corruption, "unfortunate management," and using his official position to personally advance himself financially. Warner, s.v. "Stephen Augustus Hurlbut."

1324. Born in Virginia, Stevenson, like Hurlbut, was also a Southerner-turned-Yankee. Warner, s.v. "John Dunlap Stevenson."

1325. ORA, Ser. 1, Vol. 31, Pt. 3, p. 385.

1326. Seabrook, L, pp. 159-161. Though Lincoln's Final Emancipation Proclamation, issued January 1, 1863, officially called for the enlistment of blacks into the Union military for the first time (see Nicolay and Hay, Vol. 2, p. 287), the policy—which Lincoln revealingly called, not a necessary civil rights measure, but a "necessary war measure"—was not put into effect until several months later. Quarles, p. 195.

Forrest's command was racially integrated: white Southerners fought alongside black Southerners, unified in a common purpose (to preserve the Founders' confederate republic and the original Constitution), under a leader they loved and respected, whatever the color of their skin.[1327]

## THE BATTLE OF OKOLONA

Despite the interruption to his military career, Forrest's amazing military conquests continued unabated. These were highlighted by the fact that he was nearly always outnumbered and outgunned by the enemy. On January 12, 1864, for example, an awed Yankee journalist (with the Cincinnati *Commercial*), writing from Memphis, noted that:

> Forrest, with less than four thousand men, has moved right through the Sixteenth Army Corps, has passed within nine miles of Memphis, carried off a hundred wagons, two hundred beef cattle, three thousand conscripts, and innumerable stores; torn up railroad-tracks, destroyed telegraph-wires, burned and sacked towns, run over pickets with a single derringer pistol, . . . and all in the face of ten thousand men.[1328]

And this was just the beginning of 1864!

More sensational successes quickly ensued. On February 22, at the Battle of Okolona, Mississippi,[1329] Forrest relied on the same tactics that Frederick the Great had used in 1757 at Leuthen, Prussia (present-day Poland) and in 1758 at Zorndorf, Prussia (also present-day Poland). The principle difference was that Forrest's attack had not been preplanned or learned from a military manual. He had concocted it literally on the hoof.[1330]

Here with only 2,500 severely under-equipped Rebs, he went up against, and beat, a massive force of 7,000 of the Union's finest cavalrymen—all bearing repeating rifles and pistols, backed up by twenty pieces of artillery. Among them were the much hated Fourth U.S. Cavalry, one of whose members had murdered the beloved Confederate Captain Sam L. Freeman in cold blood in April 1863 (to be

---

1327. Bradley, pp. 22, 215-219.
1328. Jordan and Pryor, pp. 379-380.
1329. Okolona is a Native-American word meaning "Queen of the Prairie."
1330. Lytle, p. 266.

discussed in more detail shortly). With true vengeance in their hearts, Forrest's men fought with particular ferocity that day,[1331] the spirit of which has been perfectly captured by acclaimed military artist John Paul Strain on the cover of this book.[1332]

Though his own brother, Colonel Jeffrey Forrest, along with Colonel James A. Barksdale, both perished in the attack, the General, in fact, routed the Federals, sending them fleeing toward Memphis. Yankee officer Colonel George E. Waring, Jr., writes of the event from the Union perspective:

> The retreat to Memphis was a weary, disheartening, and almost panic-stricken flight, in the greatest disorder and confusion, and through a most difficult country. The First Brigade reached its camping-ground five days after the engagement, with the loss of all its heart and spirit, and nearly fifteen hundred fine cavalry horses. The expedition filled every man connected with it with burning shame, and it gave Forrest the most glorious achievement of his career.[1333]

This honest Yankee gave a fairly forthright account the Battle of Okolona, as is apparent from Forrest's much more detailed official report:

> Ten miles from Pontotoc they [the Yanks] made a last and final effort to check pursuit, and from their preparations, numbers, and advantageous position no doubt indulged the hope of success. They had formed in three lines across a large field on the left of the road, but which a turn in the road made it directly in our front. Their lines were at intervals of several hundred paces, and the rear and second lines longer than the first. As the advance of my column moved up they opened on us with artillery. My ammunition was nearly exhausted, and I knew that if we faltered they would in turn become the attacking party, and that disaster might follow. Many of my men were broken down and exhausted with clambering the hills on foot and fighting almost constantly for the last 9 miles. I determined, therefore, relying upon the bravery and courage of the few men I had up, to advance to the attack. As we moved up, the

1331. Morton, p. 150.
1332. Strain's painting is appropriately entitled: "Vengeance at Okolona."
1333. Wyeth, LGNBF, p. 317.

whole force charged down at a gallop, and I am proud to say that my men did not disappoint me. Standing firm, they repulsed the grandest cavalry charge I ever witnessed. The Second and Seventh Tennessee drove back the advance line, and as it wheeled in retreat poured upon them a destructive fire. Each successive line of the enemy shared the same fate and fled the field in dismay and confusion, and losing another piece of artillery, and leaving it strewn with dead and wounded men and horses.

Half of my command were out of ammunition, the men and horses exhausted and worn down with two days' hard riding and fighting, night was at hand, and further pursuit impossible.

Major-General [Samuel J.] Gholson arrived during the night. His command was small, but comparatively fresh. I ordered him to follow on the next morning and press them across the Tallahatchie. Having received no official report from him, I cannot give any details of his pursuit after them.

Considering the disparity in numbers and equipments, I regard the defeat of this force, consisting as it did of the best cavalry in the Federal army, as a victory of which all engaged in it may justly feel proud. It has given, for a time at least, peace and security to a large scope of rich country whose inhabitants anticipated and expected to be overrun, devastated and laid waste, and its moral effect upon the raw, undisciplined and undrilled troops of this command is in value incalculable. It has inspired them with courage and given them confidence in themselves and their commanders. Although many of them were but recently organized, they fought with a courage and daring worthy of veterans.

I herewith transmit you a list of casualties, which, under all the circumstances, is small, and especially so when compared with that of the enemy.

The killed and wounded of the enemy who fell into our hands amounts to over 100. We captured 6 pieces of artillery, 3 stand of colors, and 162 prisoners. By pressing every horse, buggy, carriage, and vehicle along the road they were enabled to take off all their wounded, except those severely or mortally wounded, and it is but reasonable to suppose amid a low estimate to place their loss in killed, wounded, and missing at 800.

My force in the fight did not exceed 2,500 men, while that of the enemy was twenty-seven regiments of cavalry and mounted infantry, estimated at 7,000 strong.

I regret the loss of some gallant officers. The loss of my brother, Col. J. E. Forrest, is deeply felt by his brigade as well as myself, and it is but just to say that for sobriety, ability, prudence, and bravery he had no superior of his age. Lieutenant-Colonel

Barksdale was also a brave and gallant man, and his loss fell heavily on the regiment he commanded, as it was left now without a field officer.

I desire to testify my appreciation of the skill and ability of Colonels McCulloch, Russell, and Duckworth, commanding brigades. Colonel McCulloch, although wounded on the evening of the 22d, continued in command. Colonel Russell assumed command of Bell's brigade after the injury to Colonel Barteau, and Colonel Duckworth took command of Forrest's brigade after Colonel Forrest fell on the morning of the 22d ultimo.

I have formally congratulated and returned my thanks to the officers and troops of my command for their gallant and meritorious conduct; for their energy, endurance, and courage, and it would afford me pleasure to mention individual instances of daring and dash which came under my own observation but for fear of doing apparent injustice to others who in other parts of the field perhaps did as well.

My escort deserves especial mention: Commanded by Lieut. Thomas S. Tate on the 21$^{st}$, and by its commander, Captain Jackson, on the 22d, its battle-flag was foremost in the fray, sustaining its reputation as one of the best fighting cavalry companies in the service. I also desire to acknowledge, as I have often done before, my indebtedness to Maj. J. P. Strange, my assistant adjutant-general; Capt. Charles W. Anderson, my aide-de-camp, and Lieutenant Tate, assistant inspector-general, for prompt and faithful services rendered in the delivery and execution of all my orders on the field.

All of which is respectfully submitted.

N. B. FORREST, Major-General.[1334]

## GRANT TRIES TO NEGATE FORREST'S ACHIEVEMENT

Years later, Yankee war hero and America's eighteenth president, Ulysses S. Grant, tried to dilute Forrest's achievement at Okolona by spreading disinformation about the condition of the Rebel leader's command. In his *Memoirs* Grant writes:

> Forrest had about 4,000 cavalry with him, composed of thoroughly well-disciplined men, who under so able a leader were very effective. Smith's command was nearly double that of Forrest, but not equal, man to man, for the lack of a successful experience such

---

1334. ORA, Ser. 1, Vol. 32, Pt. 1, pp. 354-355.

as Forrest's men had had. The fact is, troops who have fought a few battles and won, and followed up their victories, improve upon what they were before to an extent that can hardly be counted by percentage. The difference in result is often decisive victory instead of inglorious defeat. This same difference, too, is often due to the way troops are officered, and for the particular kind of warfare which Forrest had carried on neither army could present a more effective officer than he was.[1335]

Pure Yankee folklore.

In truth, a large number of Forrest's men had never experienced battlefield action, and only a small minority, less than 500, had ever fought under Forrest until that day. Thus, as Wyeth pointed out, most of the General's men were far from what Grant called "thoroughly well-disciplined men." Clearly the Federals had the advantage in every respect—yet they still lost to Forrest. Grant, writing years after the War (in 1885) when he had easy access to all military files, should have been ashamed for attempting to falsify the official record of the Battle of Okolona.[1336]

A few weeks later Forrest issued the following circular to his men, immortalizing the truth about the Mississippi fight:

> Columbus, March 11, 1864.
> The major-general commanding desires to return his thanks and acknowledgments to the officers and men of his command for their recent gallant and meritorious conduct in defeating and routing the largest, most carefully selected, and best equipped cavalry and mounted infantry command ever sent into the field by the enemy. And it affords him both pleasure and pride to say that by your ability, unflinching bravery, and endurance, a force three times your own was defeated, routed, demoralized, and driven from the country, his plans frustrated, his ends unaccomplished, and his forces cut to pieces. Thus by your valor and courage you have given safety and security to the homes and firesides of the defenseless and helpless inhabitants of the country, whose grateful acknowledgments are showered upon you and whose prayers daily and nightly ascend to heaven for your future prosperity and success.

1335. U. S. Grant, Vol. 2, pp. 108-109.
1336. Wyeth, LGNBF, p. 321.

The major-general commanding deplores the loss of some of his bravest officers and men. They have fallen in the discharge of their duty as soldiers and patriots, and have yielded up their lives in defense of all that man holds dear. He desires that you cherish their memory, emulate their example, and achieve your independence or perish in the attempt.

In conclusion, the major-general commanding desires to say that all who were engaged may feel justly proud of their participation in a victory so pregnant with disaster to the enemy and so glorious in its results to our cause, and which has delivered a grateful people from that oppression, devastation, and destruction which follows the footsteps of a dastardly and brutal foe.

By your past conduct and heroism he confidently relies upon and predicts your future success in whipping the enemy wherever you meet them.

By command of Major-General Forrest:

J. P. Strange, Assistant Adjutant-General. [1337]

Sherman later confessed, with overt jealousy, that Forrest's clever maneuvers "excited my admiration."[1338] But he could not afford to stand by admiring him for too long. As we will see, because he was a primary threat to Federal stability in the area, Sherman put out an order to "follow Forrest to the death, [even] if it cost 10,000 lives and breaks the Treasury!"

To this end, Sherman sent Brigadier General Samuel D. Sturgis into northern Alabama and Mississippi with the sole purpose of getting rid of that "Hell-hound,"[1339] or more popularly, "that Devil Forrest," as Sherman called him and as he came to be known by Union troops. Sherman even promised to promote Sturgis to major general if he saw to it that Forrest was killed.[1340]

But Sherman, like Forrest's own commanders, far underestimated the charismatic and sharp-witted cavalryman. In what has become known as "the perfect battle" of the War for Southern Independence, Sturgis in particular would pay dearly for his arrogance toward Forrest.

---

1337. ORA, Ser. 1, Vol. 32, Pt. 1, pp. 365-357.
1338. Sherman, Vol. 2, p. 164.
1339. Henry, ATSF, p. 123.
1340. Wyeth, LGNBF, p. 391.

THE BATTLE OF BRICE'S CROSS ROADS

That "perfect battle," the Battle of Brice's Cross Roads, took place near Baldwyn, Mississippi, on June 10, 1864. Here, with a mere 3,200 men, the audacious Forrest went up against, and whipped, Sturgis and 8,500 Union men, forcing the Yanks into a disorderly and humiliating retreat. As always, Forrest used both cunning and trickery, pretending he had a much larger force, to bring down the enemy.

With innate aplomb and stunning brilliance, Forrest commandeered his forces through one spectacular victory after another at Brice's Cross Roads that spring day, finally forcing the weary Federalists into a desperate run for their lives. A master of the offensive who never received an attack but always launched it,[1341] Forrest greatly exaggerated the size of his command, chasing a terrified Sturgis through six counties on a rout that lasted some thirty hours.[1342]

At one point, between skirmishes, Forrest's nearly exhausted men were resting, hoping to hear the welcome order to "retire from the field." Instead their imposing commander approached them on horseback, looking fiery, energetic, and ready to do battle at a moment's notice.[1343] One of Forrest's soldiers, John Milton Hubbard, later recalled the scene:

> Mounted on his big sorrel horse, sabre in hand, sleeves rolled up, his coat lying on the pommel of his saddle, looking the very God of War, the General rode down our line as far as we could see him. I remember his words, which I heard more than once: 'Get up men. I have ordered Bell to charge on the left. When you hear his guns, and the bugle sounds, every man must charge, and we will give them hell!'[1344]

When the "hell" was all over, Forrest had suffered 492 casualties while Sturgis had suffered nearly 2,500.[1345] Sturgis lost a third of his soldiers and all his trains. In return Forrest captured 1,600 prisoners

1341. Wyeth, LGNBF, p. 404.
1342. Henry, ATSF, p. 46.
1343. Lytle, p. 299.
1344. Hubbard, pp. 110-111.
1345. The Brice's Cross Roads National Battlefield Site, six miles west of Baldwyn, Mississippi, memorializes the conflict. See Website: www.nps.gov/brcr/index.htm.

(including sixty officers), sixteen guns, twenty-seven limbers, two colors, 184 animals, 192 wagons, 1,500 stands of arms, and a huge assortment of artillery and ammunition.[1346]

A few weeks later, Sturgis was still quite unaware of Forrest's ruse, as is clear in his official report. Even one of Sturgis' "very intelligent" officers who had been captured by Forrest, believed that the Tennessean had nearly four times as many men as he actually had. Wrote Sturgis dejectedly:

> . . . I need hardly add that it is with feelings of the most profound pain and regret that I find myself called upon to record a defeat and the loss and suffering incident to a reverse at a point so far distant from the base of supplies and re-enforcements. Yet there is some consolation in knowing that . . . [my] army fought nobly while it did fight, and only yielded to overwhelming numbers.
>
> The strength of the enemy [Forrest] is variously estimated by my most intelligent officers at from 15,000 to 20,000 men. A very intelligent sergeant who was captured and remained five days in the hands of the enemy reports the number of the enemy actually engaged to have been 12,000, and that two divisions of infantry were held in reserve.[1347]

If Forrest ever had a chance to read this document, we can be sure he and his 3,200 soldiers had a hearty and well deserved laugh!

A few months later, in a report to his superior, Sherman made pitiful excuses for Sturgis' loss:

> HDQRS. MILITARY DIVISION OF THE MISSISSIPPI,
> In the Field, near Atlanta, August 24, 1864—8 p. m.
> ADJUTANT-GENERAL,
> Washington, D. C.:
> SIR: . . . I do know that misfortunes may befall us all, and these are rendered more likely in wooded countries, with narrow roads and deep mud. [General Sturgis] . . . was dealing with a bold and

---

1346. Sheppard, pp. 190-191. For his failure at Brice's Cross Roads, Samuel D. Sturgis was demoted to the West where he served under U.S. Lieutenant Colonel George Armstrong Custer. On detached duty at the time, he narrowly missed meeting his end at the doomed and infamous Battle of Little Bighorn, Montana, in 1876. His son, Lieutenant James G. Sturgis, however, perished in the conflict. The town of Sturgis, North Dakota (home of the annual Sturgis Motorcycle Rally), is named after Samuel. See Website: www.nps.gov/libi/index.htm.

1347. ORA, Ser. 1, Vol. 39, Pt. 1, p. 95.

daring foe, on fresh horses, familiar with the roads and by-paths, and perfectly unencumbered with trains. I consider a train of wagons reduces a command just one-half for it cannot move without covering its train.

I am, with respect,

W. T. SHERMAN, Major- General, Commanding.[1348]

In his *Memoirs*, Grant saw things a little more realistically:

> Farther west also the troubles were threatening. Some time before, Forrest had met Sturgis in command of some of our cavalry in Mississippi and handled him very roughly, gaining a very great victory over him. This left Forrest free to go almost where he pleased, and to cut the roads in rear of Sherman who was then advancing. Sherman was abundantly able to look after the army that he was immediately with, and all of his military division so long as he could communicate with it; but it was my place to see that he had the means with which to hold his rear. Two divisions under A. J. Smith had been sent to Banks in Louisiana some months before. Sherman ordered these back, with directions to attack Forrest.[1349]

## OFFICIAL UNION REPORTS ON THE BATTLE OF BRICE'S CROSS ROADS

Forrest's outrageous and seemingly improbable victory over the Yanks at Brice's Cross Roads put all of Washington on edge. The "Forrest mill," as Federal officer Colonel Waring referred to it in his book *Whip and Spur*, was continuing to grind up Yankee meat at a fearful rate, and no one seemed able to stop it.[1350]

A baffled Union Secretary of War, Edwin M. Stanton, wrote a sharp note to General Sherman about it, who exploded when he heard the news. First Stanton's missive to Sherman, then a furious Sherman's reply:

> WAR DEPARTMENT, June 14, 1864—12 m.
> Major-General SHERMAN:
> We have just received from General [Cadwallader C.] Washburn

---

1348. ORA, Ser. 1, Vol. 39, Pt. 1, p. 89.
1349. U. S. Grant, Vol. 2, pp. 306-307.
1350. Waring, p. 130.

report of battle between Sturgis and Forrest, in which our forces were defeated with great loss. Washburn estimates our loss at not less than 3,000, and Forrest is in pursuit.
EDWIN M. STANTON,
Secretary of War.[1351]

BIG SHANTY, GA., June 14, 1864—6 p. m.
(Received 11.30 p. m.)
Hon. EDWIN M. STANTON, Secretary of War:
I have just received the news of the defeat of our party sent out from Memphis, whose chief object was to hold Forrest there and keep him off our road. Of course it is to be deplored, but we must prepare for all contingencies. I have ordered A. J. Smith not to go to Mobile, but to go out from Memphis and defeat Forrest at all cost. I know positively that all of Polk's command is here from Mississippi, viz: Loring's and French's divisions and three brigades of cavalry, Ferguson's, Ross', and Starke's. Forrest has only his own cavalry, which had started for North Alabama, and the militia under Gholson. I cannot understand how he could defeat Sturgis with 8,000 men. Our troops must assume the offensive from Memphis.
W. T. SHERMAN, Major- General.[1352]

The next day, after Sherman had had twenty-four hours to think about Forrest and Sturgis, he was, if anything, even more irritated, and he sent off another enraged letter to Stanton. It was in this dispatch that Sherman launched Forrest's now world-famous title, "the devil":

IN THE FIELD, June 15, 1864—6.30 p. m.
(Received 12 p. m.)
Hon. E. M. STANTON,
Washington, D. C.:
I will have the matter of Sturgis critically examined, and, if he be at fault, he shall have no mercy at my hands. I cannot but believe he had troops enough. I know I would have been willing to attempt the same task with that force; but Forrest is the very devil, and I think he has got some of our troops under cower. I have two officers at Memphis that will fight all the time—A. J. Smith and [Joseph A.] Mower. The latter is a young brigadier of fine promise, and I commend him to your notice. I will order them to make up

---

1351. ORA, Ser. 1, Vol. 38, Pt. 4, p. 474.
1352. ORA, Ser. 1, Vol. 38, Pt. 4, p. 474.

a force and go out and follow Forrest to the death, if it cost 10,000 lives and breaks the Treasury. There never will be peace in Tennessee till Forrest is dead. We killed Bishop Polk yesterday, and have made good progress to-day, of which I will make a full report as soon as one of my aides comes from the extreme right flank. General Grant may rest easy that Joe Johnston will not trouble him, if I can help it by labor or thought.
W. T. SHERMAN, Major-General, Commanding.[1353]

The next day, a frustrated Sherman sent off two angry dispatches regarding the incident, one to Union General James B. McPherson and another one to Stanton. Still deeply agitated by Forrest's win, he searched for answers, again pledging to kill Forrest and ruin the South in revenge:

HDQRS. MILITARY DIVISION OF THE MISSISSIPPI,
In the Field, Big Shanty, Ga., June 16, 1864.
Major-General MCPHERSON,
Commanding Department of the Tennessee:
GENERAL: Please direct General Washburn, or one of your inspectors-general, to make close inquiries into the history of the defeat by Forrest of the command of General Sturgis . . . We will not attempt the Mobile trip now, but I wish you to organize as large a force as possible at Memphis, with Generals A. J. Smith or Mower in command, to pursue Forrest on foot, devastating the land over which he has passed or may pass, and make him and the people of Tennessee and Mississippi realize that, although a bold, daring, and successful leader, he will bring ruin and misery on any country where he may pause or tarry. If we do not punish Forrest and the people now, the whole effect of our past conquests will be lost.
I am, W. T. SHERMAN, Major-General, Commanding.[1354]

BIG SHANTY, GA., June 16, 1864.
Hon. EDWIN M. STANTON,
Secretary of War:
I have made the necessary orders through General McPherson to inquire well into the Sturgis matter; also to send as large a force again as he can to get on Forrest's trail, and harass him and the country through which he passes. We must destroy him if possible.

1353. ORA, Ser. 1, Vol. 38, Pt. 4, p. 480.
1354. ORA, Ser. 1, Vol. 39, Pt. 2, p. 123.

Johnston is getting militia from the extreme south to man his extensive lines at Marietta and Atlanta, as well as along the Chattahoochee, which gives him his three corps for maneuvers, and a large force of cavalry, which he designs to use against our communications. It is important that the Gulf fleet, with a small land force, threaten Mobile and the country about Saint Mark's and the mouth of the Appalachicola. Could not the Secretary of the Navy order this, and [Edward R. S.] Canby spare a small force (one brigade) for this purpose?
W. T. SHERMAN, Major-general, Commanding.[1355]

## SHERMAN & LINCOLN PLOT FORREST'S DEATH

On June 24, 1864, Sherman wrote to President Lincoln, informing him of his plans to have Forrest hunted down and murdered like a stray dog:

> NEAR KENESAW, GA., June 24, 1864.
> (Received 2 a. m. 25th.)
> A. LINCOLN,
> President of the United States:
> SIR: I have ordered General A. J. Smith and General Mower from Memphis to pursue and kill Forrest, promising the latter, in case of success, my influence to promote him to a major-general. He is one of the gamest men in our service. Should accident befall me I ask you to favor Mower, if he succeeds in disposing of Forrest.
> W. T. SHERMAN, Major-General.[1356]

Lincoln did not reply, nor did he have to. When rumors of Forrest's death from "lockjaw" surfaced over the next few weeks, Sherman happily wired Washburn:

> HDQRS. MILITARY DIVISION OF THE MISSISSIPPI,
> In the Field, near Atlanta, August 7, 1864.
> General WASHBURN,
> Memphis:
> . . . Is Forrest surely dead? If so, tell General Mower I am pledged to him for his promotion, and if Old Abe don't make good my promise then General Mower may have my place.
> W. T. SHERMAN, Major-General, Commanding.[1357]

---

1355. ORA, Ser. 1, Vol. 39, Pt. 2, p. 123.
1356. ORA, Ser. 1, Vol. 39, Pt. 2, p. 142.
1357. ORA, Ser. 1, Vol. 39, Pt. 2, p. 233.

There is no record of any reply from sly Lincoln, who probably refrained from personal correspondence on this matter to protect himself from later charges of war crimes. His silence, however, can only mean that he had endorsed Sherman's nefarious plot to kill Forrest, for the White House never issued a countermand against it.

Definitive proof, however, comes from two Yankee dispatches, the first from Stanton to Sherman, the second from Sherman to Stanton. By this time it had been discovered that General Joseph A. Mower had only managed to shoot Forrest in the foot, not kill him, and that the great Rebel chieftain was still very much alive.[1358] Nonetheless, from behind closed doors Lincoln approved Mower's promised promotion:

> WASHINGTON, August 12, 1864—11 a. m.
> Major-General SHERMAN:
> I have the pleasure of informing you that your appointment as major-general in the regular army has been ordered to-day, and will be immediately forwarded by mail. General Mower is appointed major-general of volunteers. His appointment will also be transmitted to you.
> EDWIN M. STANTON, Secretary of War.[1359]

Sherman's reply to Secretary of War Stanton:

> NEAR ATLANTA, GA., August 12, 1864—7.30 p. m.
> Hon. E. M. STANTON,
> Secretary of War:
> Please convey to the President my thanks for the honor conferred on me. I would have preferred a delay until the close of the campaign. Also for the commission for General Mower, whose task was to kill Forrest. He only crippled him, but he is a young and game officer. All well.
> W. T. SHERMAN, Major-General.[1360]

## SUMMARIZING BRICE'S CROSS ROADS

Despite the North's many pathetic excuses for their loss against Forrest, the South will always remember the Battle of Brice's Cross Roads as one

1358. Lytle, p. 316.
1359. ORA, Ser. 1, Vol. 38, Pt. 5, p. 471.
1360. ORA, Ser. 1, Vol. 38, Pt. 5, p. 471.

of the greatest, most spectacular events in her history. Tactically speaking, some have called it the most brilliant fight of any war.[1361]

Years later, in 1902, Southerner Captain J. Harvey Mathes wrote one of the best summations of the conflict:

> Forrest could well congratulate his men upon such a remarkable victory over the best troops of the Union army in greatly superior numbers. Away from his immediate superior commander he planned the battle, and it was fought and won in an incredibly short space of time. There was no time or place during the action when he was not outnumbered except at the last, when the retreat began. His forces, although scattered at first and weary from long marches, were brought together and handled with consummate tact and judgment. The general fully grasped the situation, and seized a rare opportunity to win a victory which was without parallel during the war, as conceded by leading generals on both sides. This was doubtless Forrest's greatest achievement from a military standpoint, and the climax of his hard-earned fame.[1362]

## FORREST LEAVES A PATH OF DESTRUCTION & HARRIES THE YANKS

As is obvious, Forrest was by now well adept, and well-known, for striking fear and confusion in the hearts of Yankees. A favorite pastime of his was to overrun undermanned garrisons and outposts.[1363] He was also particularly good at wreaking devastation on the Union supply lines, not only in his home-state, but all across the South.

Throughout Tennessee, for example, he broke apart and tore up railroad tracks, bombed train stations, burned Yankee blockhouses, stockades, and sawmills, dynamited bridges and trestles, destroyed culverts and viaducts, cut telegraph wires, disabled field artillery, fired warehouses, sank supply ships, transport ships, and gunboats, and easily captured Yankee supply trains, depots, and garrisons.[1364]

One of his favorite methods of ruining railroads was to build fires along their length. It required little effort on the part of his men and caused the metal tracks to expand, crack, and buckle, rendering

---

1361. Sheppard, pp. 191-192.
1362. Mathes, pp. 250-251.
1363. Bedwell, p. 55.
1364. Henry, ATSF, pp. 46, 206; Bradley, pp. 118-124; Browning, pp. 23, 25, 27.

them unusable.[1365] And unlike Yankee wrecking crews (who seldom did more than superficial damage to railroads), the destruction heaped upon rail lines by Forrest's men left them completely demolished and irreparable.[1366] In making life wretched for the enemy at every turn, he dispirited the Yanks, bought precious time, and bolstered Southern pride.

What galled Northerners most was Forrest's capture and destruction, in Tennessee, of $6,700,000 (the equivalent of about $91,000,000 today) worth of Yankee machinery, along with a gunboat fleet at Johnsonville. In his official report of the raid, known as the Battle of Johnsonville (November 4-5, 1864), Forrest wrote with barely concealed relish:

HEADQUARTERS FORREST'S CAVALRY CORPS,
Verona, Miss., January 12, 1865.
COLONEL: Continued active service in the field for two months has prevented me from reporting at an earlier day the action of my troops on the expedition along the Tennessee River. I avail myself; however, of the first leisure moment, and have the honor of submitting the following report:

On the 16th of October I ordered Colonel [Tyree H.] Bell to move with his brigade from Corinth and to form a camp at Lavinia. On the 18th Brigadier-General [Abe] Buford was ordered to move with the Kentucky brigade to Lexington for the purpose of watching General [Edward] Hatch, who was reported to be in that direction. I moved from Corinth on the morning of the 19th, with my escort and [Edmund W.] Rucker's brigade, to Jackson, Tenn. At this place I was joined by Brigadier-General [James R.] Chalmers with about 250 men of McCulloch's brigade and 300 of Mabry's brigade, which, with Rucker's brigade, constituted his division. On the 29th I ordered him to proceed to the Tennessee River and there co-operate with Brigadier-General Buford, who was blockading the river at Fort Heiman and Paris Landing. On arriving at the river I found it most effectually blockaded by a judicious disposition of the troops and batteries sent for this purpose.

On the morning of the 29th the steamer *Mazeppa*, with two barges in tow, made her appearance. As she passed the battery

---

1365. Wyeth, LGNBF, p. 120.
1366. Henry, FWMF, p. 112.

at Fort Heiman, supported by Brigadier-General Lyon, she was fired upon by one section of Morton's battery and two 20-pounder Parrott guns. Every shot must have taken effect, as she made for the shore after the third fire and reached the opposite bank in a disabled condition, where she was abandoned by the crew and passengers, who fled to the woods. A hawser was erected on this side of the river and she was towed over, and on being boarded she was found to be heavily loaded with blankets, shoes, clothing, hard bread, &c. While her cargo was being removed to the shore three gun-boats made their appearance, and commenced shelling the men who were engaged in unloading the *Mazeppa*. They were forced to retire, and fearing the boat might be captured Brigadier-General Buford ordered her to be burned.

On the 30th the steamer *Anna* came down the river and succeeded in passing both the upper and lower batteries, but was so disabled that she sunk before she reached Paducah. The *Anna* was followed by two transports (*J. W. Cheeseman*, the *Venus*) and two barges under convoy of gun-boat *Undine*. In attempting to pass my batteries all the boats were disabled. They landed on the opposite side of the river and were abandoned by the crews, who left their dead and wounded. Lieutenant-Colonel Kelley, with two companies of his regiment, was thrown across the river and soon returned to Paris Landing with the boats. The steamer *J. W. Cheeseman* was so disabled that she was ordered, with the two barges, to be burned; the gun-boat was also burned while moving up the river to Johnsonville. The *Venus* was recaptured by the enemy on (November 2,) but was destroyed the next day (November 4) at Johnsonville by my batteries.

On the 1st of November I ordered my command to move in the direction of Johnsonville, which place I reached on the 3d. At this point Colonel Mabry joined General Chalmers with [James C.] Thrall's battery. The wharf at Johnsonville was lined with transports and gun-boats. An immense warehouse presented itself and was represented as being stored with the most valuable supplies, while several acres of the shore were covered with every description of army stores. The fort was situated on a high hill and in a commanding position, and defended by strong works.

All my troops having arrived, I commenced disposing of them with a view of bombarding the enemy. As he commanded the position I designed to occupy, I was necessarily compelled to act with great caution. I planted most of my guns during the night, and while completing the work the next morning my men worked behind ambuscades, which obscured everything from the enemy. Thrall's battery of howitzers was placed in position above Johnsonville, while Morton's and Hudson's batteries were placed nearly opposite and just below town.

I ordered a simultaneous assault to commence at 3 o'clock. All my movements for twenty-four hours had been so secretive the enemy seemed to think I had retired, and for the purpose of making a reconnaissance two gun-boats were lashed together and pushed out just before the attack opened. The bombardment commenced by the section of Morton's battery commanded by Lieutenant Brown. The other batteries joined promptly in the assault. The enemy returned the fire from twenty-eight guns on their gun-boats and fourteen guns on the hill. About fifty guns were thus engaged at the same time, and the firing was terrific. The gun-boats, in fifteen minutes after the engagement commenced, were set on fire, and made rapidly for the shore, where they were both consumed. My batteries next opened upon the transports, and in a short time they were in flames. The immense amount of stores were also set on fire, together with the huge warehouse above time landing. By night the wharf for nearly one mile up and down the river presented one solid sheet of flame. The enemy continued a furious cannonading on my batteries.

Having completed the work designed by the expedition, I moved my command six miles during the night by the light of the enemy's burning property. The roads were almost impassable, and the march to Corinth was slow and toilsome, but I reached there on November 10, after an absence of over two weeks, during which time I captured and destroyed 4 gun-boats, 14 transports, 20 barges, 26 pieces of artillery, $6,700,000 worth of property, and 150 prisoners. Brigadier-General Buford, after supplying his own command, turned over to my chief quartermaster about 9,000 pairs of shoes and 1,000 blankets.

My loss during the entire trip was 2 killed and 9 wounded; that of the enemy will probably reach 500 killed, wounded, and prisoners.

On this expedition my division commanders, Brigadier-Generals Chalmers and Buford, displayed the same prompt observance in obeying orders, the same skill, coolness, and undaunted courage which they have heretofore exhibited, and for which I thank them.

My brigade commanders, Colonels Bell, Rucker, Crossland, and Mabry, are deserving of the highest commendation for their conduct on this as on all former occasions.

Brigadier-General Lyon, who had been assigned to another department, reported to me on this expedition and rendered much valuable service at Johnsonville and Fort Heiman.

To Capt. John W. Morton, acting chief of artillery, and

the brave troops under his command, my thanks are especially due
for their efficiency and gallantry on this expedition. They fired
with a rapidity and accuracy which extorted the commendation of
even the enemy. The rammers were shot from the hands of the
cannoneers, some of whom were nearly buried amid the dirt which
was thrown upon them by the storm of shell which rained upon
them by the enemy's batteries.
All of which is respectfully submitted.
N. B. FORREST, Major-General.[1367]

After the dust had settled, Forrest and Morton went back to
survey the smouldering ruins at Johnsonville. Standing on the west bank
of the Tennessee River, Forrest turned to his chief artillerist and said: If
they'd only give me more men and you more guns, we'd crush Sherman
shore as hell![1368]

Union commanders were both shocked and impressed.
Sherman, of course, was among them. In his report he angrily noted:

> . . . that devil Forrest was down about Johnsonville and was making
> havoc among the gun-boats and transports.[1369]

Grant too was driven to "fits of anger" over Forrest's military
tactics. But he should have been used to all of this by then: two years
earlier, in December 1862, Forrest had destroyed sixty miles of railroad
track connecting Holly Springs, Mississippi, with Columbia, Kentucky,
forcing an infuriated Grant to retreat in despair and disgrace.

THE MOVE TO GET FORREST A LARGER COMMAND
At the time, as Forrest racked up victory after victory, a number of
Confederates went to President Davis in an effort to get the Tennessean
promoted. It was obvious to most by then that Forrest was more than
qualified to command larger forces. Not only that, he was desperately
needed in such a role.

Among those who called for Forrest's advancement were

---

1367. ORA, Ser. 1, Vol. 39, Pt. 1, pp. 870-872.
1368. Lytle, p. 352.
1369. ORA, Ser. 1, Vol. 39, Pt. 3, p. 659.

General Howell Cobb and General Joseph Wheeler.[1370] As early as November 1861, Colonel Samuel Tate had pleaded: "Give Forrest a chance and he will distinguish himself."[1371] Thousands of privates, whose voices were never heard, such as John Milton Hubbard, agreed. The General should be placed at the head of the largest command possible, Hubbard argued.[1372]

Tragically, the two most ardent promoters of this view were two of Davis' least favorite people: General Joseph E. Johnston[1373] and Georgia Governor Joseph E. Brown. On two occasions, in June and July 1864, Johnston had gone to Davis personally, and four times through Bragg (June 3, 12, 16, 26, 1864),[1374] to request that

> an adequate force under the most competent officer in America for such service, General N. B. Forrest, be sent to operate against Sherman's communications.[1375]

Governor Brown made the same plea to Davis, asking the Confederate president to allow Forrest to be in charge of all the cavalry. Both men's requests were repeatedly turned down. Johnston eventually let the matter go, but Brown, boiling mad, sent Davis the following telegraph:

> I regret that you cannot grant my request. I am satisfied that Sherman's escape with his army would be impossible if ten thousand good cavalry under Forrest were thrown in his rear this side of Chattanooga, and his supplies cut off. The whole country expects this, although points of less importance should be for a time overrun in the destruction of Sherman's supplies. Destroy these, and Atlanta is not only safe, but the destruction of the army under Sherman opens Kentucky and Tennessee to us. Your information as to the relative strength of the armies in northern Georgia cannot be from reliable sources. If your mistake should result in the loss of Atlanta, and the capture of other strong points by the enemy in this State, the blow may be fatal to our cause, and

1370. Wyeth, LGNBF, pp. 433-434.
1371. Wyeth, LGNBF, p. 27.
1372. Henry, ATSF, p. 176.
1373. Johnston, like Lee, was an ardent supporter of Forrest's idea of wearing out the North. Lytle, p. 271.
1374. Lytle, p. 307.
1375. Wyeth, LGNBF, p. 432.

remote posterity may have reason to mourn over the error.[1376]

Brown was correct, of course. But Davis did not appreciate having a civilian telling him how to do his job, and let him know about it in a now famous "acid reply."[1377] When it was far too late, the president would come to regret denying Brown's and Johnston's request.

---

1376. Wyeth, LGNBF, p. 433.
1377. See Lytle, p. 307.

# - 1864 -
# FORT PILLOW:
# THE FULL TRUE STORY

"Men, do as I say and I will always lead you to victory." — Nathan Bedford Forrest, to his soldiers prior to the Battle of Fort Pillow

RIGHTING THE ERRORS OF YANKEE MYTHOLOGY

AT THE BATTLE OF FORT Pillow, Tennessee, April 12, 1864, Forrest achieved one of his most stunning triumphs. Sadly, in the ongoing effort to malign Forrest's good name and maintain support for Lincoln's illegal assault on the South, Yankee mythographers quickly invented the story that a racist massacre had taken place.

According to this Dixie-loathing propaganda, Northern blacks (and whites) were allegedly captured, tortured, and crucified, or were gunned down during the act of surrender. Other reports claim that Confederates had buried and burned wounded Union soldiers alive, and that theft of the injured and the dead took place under cover of darkness the night of the battle. One of the more notorious and absurd accusations was that Forrest executed captured Union officer Major William F. Bradford.

Even Lincoln got in on the act: when his constituency began demanding retribution for Forrest's alleged crimes at the fort, the Northern president felt compelled to respond. On April 18, 1864, he made the following public remarks at Baltimore, Maryland, promising retaliation if the scuttlebutt turned out to be true:

A painful rumor—true, I fear—has reached us of the massacre by
the rebel forces at Fort Pillow, in the west end of Tennessee, on
the Mississippi River, of some three hundred colored soldiers and
white officers, who had just been overpowered by their assailants.
. . . We do not to-day know that a colored soldier, or
white officer commanding colored soldiers, has been massacred by
the rebels when made a prisoner. We fear it,—believe it, I may
say,—but we do not know it. To take the life of one of their
prisoners on the assumption that they murder ours, when it is short
of certainty that they do murder ours, might be too serious, too
cruel, a mistake. We are having the Fort Pillow affair thoroughly
investigated; and such investigation will probably show conclusively
how the truth is. If after all that has been said it shall turn out that
there has been no massacre at Fort Pillow, it will be almost safe to
say there has been none, and will be none, elsewhere. If there has
been the massacre of three hundred there, or even the tenth part of
three hundred, it will be conclusively proved; and being so proved,
the retribution shall as surely come. It will be matter of grave
consideration in what exact course to apply the retribution; but in
the supposed case it must come.[1378]

The ridiculous Yankee fables surrounding Fort Pillow were later
enlarged and reenforced by the North's overtly biased Wade-Gooch
Report (issued on May 5, 1864), headed by two extreme radical South-
haters: Senator Benjamin F. Wade and Representative Daniel W. Gooch.
The paper asserted, among other things, that Forrest and his men had
intentionally shot down surrendering pro-Union Tennesseans and former
slaves-turned-soldiers during the battle—even though it was obvious
then as it is now that this was a bald-faced lie: not a single Yank at the
scene ever surrendered.[1379]  With such facts at hand, even many
Northerners admitted that the report was one of the finest examples of
anti-South disinformation and propaganda produced during the War.[1380]

This was the only time during his entire military career that
Forrest was accused of cruelty and inhumane conduct toward
prisoners,[1381] this fact alone making it highly suspect. Because of the
seriousness of these charges, and because his critics maintain that his

---

1378. Nicolay and Hay, ALCW, Vol. 2, pp. 513-514.
1379. Jordan and Pryor, p. 448.
1380. *Ohio Archaeological and Historical Quarterly*, Vol. 48, 1939, p. 40.
1381. Mathes, p. 231.

worst traits (allegedly racism, sadism, and dishonesty) were exhibited here, a detailed examination of this episode will be beneficial in revealing the facts about the General and Fort Pillow.[1382]

## RESISTANCE WAS FUTILE

The truth, from Forrest's own lips, is that if any Union soldiers were killed after the assault, it was only because they continued to shoot *and* resist surrendering.[1383] As he did during most of the conflicts at which he was commander, Forrest had sent out a flag of truce along with a demand of surrender to the enemy at Fort Pillow, with the promise that *all* those captured, both white and black, would be treated as prisoners of war. The purpose? As always, "to prevent the further effusion of blood."[1384] The dispatch read:

> HEADQUARTERS CONFEDERATE CAVALRY, NEAR FORT PILLOW
> April 12, 1864.
> Major [Lionel F.] Booth, Commanding U. S. Forces, Fort Pillow:
> MAJOR: The conduct of the officers and men garrisoning Fort Pillow has been such as to entitle them to being treated as prisoners of war. I demand the unconditional surrender of the entire garrison, promising that you shall be treated as prisoners of war. My men have just received a fresh supply of ammunition, and from their present position can easily assault and capture the fort. Should my demand be refused, I cannot be responsible for the fate of your command.
> Respectfully, N. B. FORREST, Major-General, Commanding.[1385]

Unwisely, the demand was ignored, with the tragic results, as we will explore shortly.

What we have here, however, is proof of Forrest's good and humane intentions at the very start of the conflict.[1386] No acts of cruelty were premeditated or committed. Just a simple and direct plan to

---

1382. Fort Pillow, built by the Confederacy in 1861 to aid in defending the water routes to Memphis, was taken over by the Yankees in 1862. Wills, pp. 179-180.
1383. E. M. Thomas, p. 275.
1384. J. Davis, Vol. 2, pp. 545-546.
1385. ORA, Ser. 1, Vol. 32, Pt. 1, p. 596. See also Jordan and Pryor, p. 431.
1386. Even Yankee officers, such as Captain Lewis M. Hosea, noted that Forrest was always extremely kind when it came to prisoners and the wounded. Gragg, p. 201.

capture the garrison as quickly as possible, with the least amount of fanfare and bloodshed possible. This was the "Forrest method" after all.

Indeed, for the rest of their lives the General and his men would testify under oath that no atrocities occurred, and that

> all allegations to the contrary are mere malicious inventions, started, nurtured, and accredited at a time, and through a sentiment of strong sectional animosity.[1387]

Even those Rebels not with Forrest at Fort Pillow understood what had happened there: it was the result of the irrational and resistant behavior of the Yanks at the fort, despite knowing full well that the garrison would soon be overrun and taken.[1388]

The truth was that the "massacre" legend resulted largely from Northern journalists, or as Forrest himself put it to his men:

> They came forth with threats of vengeance towards you and your commander for the bloody victory of Fort Pillow, made a massacre only by dastardly Yankee reporters.[1389]

Such statements were corroborated by others in the Confederate army. In 1879, Forrest's superior, General Richard Taylor, one of the most respected and fair-minded men of the War on either side, set the record straight. Forrest, wrote Taylor,

> . . . was a tender-hearted, kindly man. The accusations of his enemies that he murdered prisoners at Fort Pillow and elsewhere are absolutely false. The prisoners captured on his expedition into Tennessee . . . were negroes, and he carefully looked after their wants himself, though in rapid movement and fighting much of the time. These negroes told me of Mass Forrest's kindness to them.[1390]

---

1387. Jordan and Pryor, p. 440.
1388. Henry ATSF, p. 157.
1389. ORA, Ser. 1, Vol. 39, Pt. 1, p. 229. Among the "dastardly Yankee reporters" Forrest alludes to were those who worked for pro-Union Southern newspapers, such as the scallywag-run Memphis Bulletin, which helped nurture the "Fort Pillow Massacre" myth in a series of pro-North articles that began on April 13, 1864. Henry, FWMF, p. 266.
1390. R. Taylor, p. 200.

Forrest himself felt strongly enough about the topic that he was willing to give his life for it. During the 1868 presidential campaign, for example, a former Union cavalry officer named Judson Kilpatrick gave a number of public speeches lambasting Forrest for numerous alleged war crimes, among them Fort Pillow, where, the brazen Yankee declared, the Rebel commander had crucified and burned blacks to death.[1391]

Forrest responded as only Forrest could: after calling Kilpatrick several unflattering names, and using the local newspaper to refute the Yankee's claims, he publically challenged him to a duel[1392] (even though dueling was illegal).[1393] After the site, seconds, weapons, and horses had been selected, however, Kilpatrick came to his senses and quickly backed out,[1394] a decision that no doubt greatly prolonged his life.[1395]

The question is why would either Forrest or Kilpatrick have sacrificed their lives over a lie? The answer is that they would not have. For there was no "massacre" at Fort Pillow.

Yet today, many, in particular many Southern blacks and most white liberals, have a deep and abiding hatred for Forrest due to his alleged role at the battle, comparing him to Jack the Ripper, Mussolini, and even Hitler.[1396]

When it comes to Fort Pillow then, who is to be believed, Forrest and his Confederate comrades or a highly biased, South-loathing, Northern media? Let us briefly touch on the highlights of the event, and allow the facts to speak for themselves.

---

1391. Hurst, p. 321.
1392. Browning, p. 101.
1393. Wills, p. 348.
1394. Sheppard, pp. 294-296.
1395. For the full story see Lytle, pp. 378-380.
1396. Ashdown and Caudill, pp. 82-83. Comparing Forrest to Adolf Hitler is the height of irony, of course, for it was not Forrest who was similar to Hitler, it was Lincoln. Both men were socialistic racist dictators who used violence to try and destroy the ideas of states' rights and state sovereignty in their respective countries. Indeed, so enamored was Hitler of Lincoln (not Forrest) that, as we have seen, he lovingly referenced Lincoln's tyrannical ideas in his book *Mein Kampf*. Hitler, Vol. 2, pp. 830-831. Finally, Forrest was a political conservative, the opposite of a socialist. Hitler was the leader of the Nazis, or the National *Socialist* German Workers' Party, as it was more properly known. The phrase "New Deal," a series of economic reform programs instigated during Franklin D. Roosevelt's socialistic administration, was actually borrowed from the socialistic Lincoln administration, when it was coined to describe "Honest Abe's" progressive domestic policies. Seabrook, AL, pp. 491-492.

## THE YANKS' 40 PERCENT DEATH RATE

The Northern press at the time whined that the number of Union soldiers who died in the conflict, 40 percent,[1397] was far above average:[1398] of the 557 Yankee soldiers present (295 whites and 262 blacks), 231 were killed (226 were captured and 100 were wounded).[1399]

Yet, a 40 percent death rate among the enemy is exactly what one would expect of a fort taken by assault, the type of approach used by Forrest and his men at Fort Pillow.[1400] Or to put it another way, as Jordan and Pryor remark: "For a place taken by storm the loss was by no means heavy."[1401]

What is more, throughout the War the mortality rate among black Union soldiers was always 40 percent higher than for white Union soldiers.[1402] This was due in great part to Lincoln's unequal treatment of his black and white soldiers. Black Union soldiers, for example, were given inferior training, weapons, ammunition, and clothing,[1403] and were often used as shock troops, sent into battle first to spare white lives.[1404] Thus the 40 percent figure at Fort Pillow should not be held out as a military anomaly. Rather it was the norm among black Union forces.[1405]

More importantly, many of the blacks among the 40 percent who died at Fort Pillow died *before* the garrison was even attacked by Forrest (who led the main charge at about 11:00 AM),[1406] casualties of his formidable and nationally acclaimed sharpshooters,[1407] whose enfilading fire power completely swept every square foot of terrain in the area that day.[1408]

Yankees at the scene later verified this. In his official report, one

---

1397. Foote, Vol. 3, p. 111.
1398. Mathes, p. 225.
1399. Faust, s.v. "Fort Pillow, Tenn., Battle of."
1400. Henry, FWMF, p. 259.
1401. Jordan and Pryor, p. 444.
1402. Current, TC, s.v. "African Americans in the Confederacy."
1403. See e.g., Quarles, pp. 204-205; ORA, Ser. 3, Vol. 3, pp. 1126-1128.
1404. Cornish, pp. 87, 269.
1405. Lincoln also denied black Union soldiers pensions, bounties, and bonuses, all which were provided to white Union soldiers. See e.g., Leech, p. 312; Current, TC, s.v. "African Americans in the Confederacy."
1406. Wyeth, LGNBF, p. 375.
1407. Eaton, HSC, p. 264; Wyeth, LGNBF, p. 375.
1408. Jordan and Pryor, p. 446.

of these, Union Adjutant Mack J. Leaming, writes:

> At 5.30 o'clock on the morning of the 12ᵗʰ of April, 1864, our pickets were attacked and driven in by the advance of the enemy, under command of General Forrest.[1409] Our garrison immediately opened fire on the advancing rebels from our artillery at the fort, while Companies D and E, of the Thirteenth West Tennessee Cavalry, were deployed as skirmishers, which duty they performed until about 8 a. m., when they were compelled to retire to the fort after considerable loss, in which Lieutenant Barr, of Company D, was killed.
>
> The firing continued without cessation, principally from behind logs, stumps, and under cover of thick underbrush and from high knolls, until about 9 a. m., when the rebels made a general assault on our works, which was successfully repulsed with severe loss to them and but slight loss to our garrison. We, however, suffered pretty severely in the loss of commissioned officers by the unerring aim of the rebel sharpshooters, and among this loss I have to record the name of our post commander Maj. L. F. Booth, who was killed almost instantly by a musket-ball through the breast.[1410]

History is replete with hundreds of examples of real battle massacres that occurred, whose victorious commanders have been lionized not pilloried. Yet Forrest, who led a fair and humane campaign against the Yanks at Fort Pillow, continues to be excoriated.[1411] Why? Because of a blind hatred of the South, along with her heroes and symbols.

But even if a massacre had taken place at Fort Pillow, it would have been justified, for as one writer noted shortly after Lincoln's War:

> Every military man knows that whenever a place is taken by assault under the flag of any nation, many of the defenders are put to death though they throw down their arms and cry for quarter.[1412]

There were numerous other factors that contributed to the 40

---

**1409.** My note: Forrest did not actually arrive until sometime between 9:00 and 11:00 AM—depending on the source—at which time he took over command from General James R. Chalmers.

**1410.** ORA, Ser. 1, Vol. 32, Pt. 1, p. 559.

**1411.** Jordan and Pryor, p. 446.

**1412.** *Blackwood Magazine*, February 1867, p. 187.

percent figure:[1413]
- A poorly designed fort.[1414]
- The loss, early in the fight, of the principle Union commander, the level-headed Major Lionel F. Booth (just mentioned).[1415]
- Booth's replacement by the inexperienced,[1416] weak, cowardly, and vain Union officer Major William F. Bradford.[1417]
- The deaths of most of the commissioned Union officers *before* the Rebels even entered the fort—which left their troops ungoverned for the rest of the fight.[1418]
- The Union defense of an indefensible and strategically unimportant fort[1419] (something no intelligent officer would ever allow).[1420]
- The Yanks' poor plan of defense, which entailed no procedure for surrender.[1421]
- Widespread drunkenness among the Union soldiery,[1422] which caused them to be "crazed" with "fright and intoxication."[1423]
- The Yanks' refusal to surrender.[1424]
- Retreat of the Union garrison without lowering their fort flag.[1425]
- Confusion over the truce.[1426]
- Union-sympathizing Southern civilians in the fort.[1427]
- The "reckless and insane" defense of the fort by a Yankee command that was severely outnumbered and out-officered.[1428]
- A complex topography.[1429]
- Mass Yankee drownings.[1430]

1413. Lytle, p. 279.
1414. Cartmell, p. 146.
1415. Mathes, p. 224.
1416. Wyeth, LGNBF, p. 349.
1417. Sheppard, p. 169; Mathes, p. 221.
1418. Jordan and Pryor, pp. 449, 450.
1419. Ashdown and Caudill, p. 83.
1420. Jordan and Pryor, pp. 445-446.
1421. Henry, FWMF, p. 266.
1422. Lytle, p. 279.
1423. Mathes, p. 227.
1424. Pollard, SHW, Vol. 2, p. 260; Wyeth, LGNBF, pp. 348-349.
1425. Eaton, HSC, p. 264.
1426. Jordan and Pryor, pp. 434-440.
1427. A. Ward, pp. 68, 157-158.
1428. Mathes, p. 227.
1429. Wyeth, LGNBF, pp. 334-337.
1430. Wills, p. 185.

• A lack of promised U.S. naval reinforcement.[1431]

The assertion that Forrest ordered a merciless slaughter of the Yankee garrison then is demonstrably false, for the particulars listed above were all quite beyond his control.[1432] Indeed, it is now known with absolute certainty that he did all he could, not only to forestall any unnecessary violence, but also to check any unnecessary bloodshed.[1433]

Respected British military authority General Viscount Wolseley had this to say on the topic:

> . . . I do not think the fact that about one-half of the small garrison of a place taken by assault, was either killed or wounded, evinced any very unusual bloodthirstiness on the part of the assailants.[1434]

In 1902 many of Forrest's men were still alive and able to comment on the so-called "slaughter" at Fort Pillow on April 12, 1864. According to their testimony concerning the Yankee death toll and other alleged atrocities that day,

> it was not greater than the circumstances justified; . . . none were killed after they surrendered, . . . and no prisoners were killed or mistreated in or out of the fort that day or the next day.[1435]

Forrest himself avowed that no gun was fired and that no Yankee prisoner was injured after the fort was captured.[1436] And even if there had been any atrocities committed, on either side, these would have to be largely attributed to *insania belli* (the "insanity of war"), a terrible but inevitable aspect of all violent conflicts.[1437]

As Jordan and Pryor write, those Yanks who perished at Fort Pillow were

1431. Browning, pp. 54-56; Jordan and Pryor, pp. 437-438.
1432. Eaton, HSC, p. 264.
1433. Foote, Vol. 3, p. 112.
1434. "Lieutenant-General N. B. Forrest: Lord Wolseley's Estimate of the Man and the Soldier," *Southern Historical Society Papers*, Vol. 20, 1892, p. 331 (original from the New Orleans *Picayune*, April 10, 1892).
1435. Mathes, p. 225.
1436. Wyeth, LGNBF, p. 356.
1437. Jordan and Pryor, p. 439. In discussing Fort Pillow pro-North writers only focus on the Union losses. It is important to remember, however, that Forrest also suffered loss of life in his own command: by some counts at least fourteen of his officers and men died, while eighty-six were wounded. Jordan and Pryor, p. 441.

victims, not of unlawful acts of war, as has been so virulently alleged and generally believed at the North, but of an insensate endeavor, as foolishly resolved as feebly executed, to hold a position naturally untenable and badly fortified,—the victims, we may add, in all sincerity, not of a savage ferocity on the part of their late adversaries, but of the imbecility and grievous mismanagement of those weak, incapable officers, whom the fortunes of war unhappily had placed over them.[1438]

## WHERE WAS FORREST DURING THE "MASSACRE"?

The real question is this: was Forrest responsible for any of the purported barbarities that occurred at Fort Pillow?

For one thing, he had been severely injured from a horse falling on him,[1439] and was not even at the front of the lines when the alleged atrocities were said to have taken place. When the fighting momentarily abated, Forrest actually tried to prevent further Yankee deaths by raising a flag of truce, which the enemy duly ignored (indeed, there was never any formal surrender on the part of the Yanks).[1440]

When he finally did arrive at the front (after a five to ten minute ride),[1441] Forrest immediately ordered a cease fire (later attested to by a black U.S. soldier at the scene)[1442] and personally arrested a Rebel soldier who ignored the command.[1443] According to one report, Forrest even killed one of his own men for refusing to give quarter to the enemy.[1444] Clearly, he had gone to extraordinary lengths to prevent any unnecessary bloodshed.[1445]

Forrest was then immediately forced to return to his post in the rear,[1446] some 400 yards back,[1447] because even though a flag of truce was flying,[1448] black Yankee soldiers—many who were inebriated and making

1438. Jordan and Pryor, p. 444.
1439. Mathes, p. 219; Browning, p. 52.
1440. Mathes, pp. 220, 223.
1441. Sheppard, p. 169.
1442. Jordan and Pryor, p. 440.
1443. Wyeth, LGBNF, p. 383.
1444. Ashdown and Caudill, p. 36.
1445. Henry, FWMF, p. 265.
1446. Wills, pp. 185, 186.
1447. Jordan and Pryor, p. 432; Sheppard, p. 167; Wills, pp. 184, 185, 186.
1448. Mathes, p. 227.

vulgar gestures and yelling obscene epithets at the Rebs[1449] (so foul that they cannot be described here)[1450]—were shooting off their rifles in a threatening manner.[1451]

## WHY FORREST ATTACKED FORT PILLOW

One question Forrest's critics never ask is why he attacked this insignificant garrison to begin with.

Forrest's original intention was to shut down the fort and its "nest of outlaws,"[1452] its "lair" of white and black Yankee occupants comprised of scallywag "wretches" and Tennessee Tories, all who had been a menace to West Tennessee.[1453] For some period of time they had been viciously insulting, robbing, raping, despoiling, attacking, and generally preying on the defenseless women, children, and elderly living in the surrounding counties (their sons, brothers, and husbands were all off fighting Lincoln's unlawful invaders).[1454]

Indeed, the U.S.'s own provost marshal records plainly show that at the time Yankee troops were committing untold numbers of "local genocides" across the South, executing hundreds of Southern civilians without trial, deporting thousands of civilians who lived near railroad lines, and routinely raping Southern women. Also revealed in these documents is the fact that Yankee officers were commonly using torture on Southern noncombatants.[1455]

Forrest and his men had another motivation. Like other traditional Southerners, they did not recognize Lincoln's hollow, self-serving, fake Emancipation Proclamation. Why? Because Lincoln only issued it in the South, where he had no legal authority, as Dixie had become an independent nation, the Confederate States of America, in February 1861. (Revealingly, in the North Lincoln left slavery completely intact, "as if this proclamation were not issued," as his edict clearly states.)[1456]

---

1449. Jordan and Pryor, pp. 434, 435.
1450. Wyeth, LGNBF, p. 348.
1451. Lytle, p. 278.
1452. Jordan and Pryor, pp. 422, 424.
1453. Lytle, p. 277.
1454. Mathes, pp. 214-215, 228.
1455. Bradley, pp. 11-12.
1456. Nicolay and Hay, ALCW, Vol. 2, p. 288.

Thus Forrest and his cavalrymen viewed the blacks at Fort Pillow, some 50 percent who were runaway slaves, as "private property" that were by law supposed to be returned to their owners,[1457] as the following field communication from the General to the enemy in the fall of 1864 proves:

HEADQUARTERS FORREST'S CAVALRY,
In the Field, September 24, 1864.
*Officer Commanding U. S. Forces, Athens, Alabama:*
I demand an immediate and unconditional surrender of the entire force and all government stores and property at this post. I have a sufficient force to storm and take your works, and if I am forced to do so the responsibility of the consequences must rest with you. Should you, however, accept the terms, all white soldiers shall be treated as prisoners of war and the negroes returned to their masters. A reply is requested immediately. Respectfully,
N. B. Forrest, Major-General C. 5. Army.[1458]

We will note here that blacks were still considered "contraband" in the North at this time, a dehumanizing term never used by the South for her black servants, and one that proves that most Yankees still viewed blacks as little more than servile pieces of property in 1864. Forrest himself stated that the treatment of captured black soldiers was not a personal matter determined by individual officers, but was decided by the C.S. and the U.S. governments, and was thus out of his hands.[1459]

In short, Forrest's policy concerning captured blacks was, as he so often reiterated, not to kill them, but to "handle them well and return them to their owners . . . ."[1460] As slavery was still protected by both the U.S. Constitution and the C.S. Constitution, this alone was full justification for launching an attack on Fort Pillow.

The fact is that the Union force at the fort had no official business being there: in addition to preying on the local populace, this small group of Yanks had set up a trading post at the site, originally a Confederate fort (and as such the property of the state of Tennessee), for

---

1457. Wyeth, LGNBF, p. 366.
1458. ORA, Ser. 1, Vol. 39, Pt. 1, p. 521.
1459. Ashdown and Caudill, p. 42.
1460. Morton, p. 191.

their own financial gain. Sherman later said that he did not know Federal forces occupied the fort, and that it was not even on his list of garrisons.[1461] Indeed, he had earlier ordered it to be abandoned.[1462] Even Lincoln would have disapproved of a Union military presence there, as it was a waste of valuable government resources.

In 1868 Jordan and Pryor described the situation this way:

> Ever since his advent into West-Tennessee, Forrest had been distressed by well-authenticated instances, repeatedly brought to his notice, of rapine and atrocious outrage upon non-combatants of the country, by the garrison at Fort Pillow. And a delegation of the people of the town of Jackson and surrounding region now waited upon and earnestly besought him to leave a brigade for their protection against this nest of outlaws. According to the information received, the garrison in question consisted of a battalion of whites, commanded by Major Bradford, (a Tennessean,) and a negro battalion under Major Booth, who likewise commanded the post. Many of Bradford's men were known to be deserters from the Confederate army, and the rest were men of the country who entertained a malignant hatred toward Confederate soldiers, their families and friends. Under the pretense of scouring the country for arms and "rebel soldiers," Bradford and his subalterns had traversed the surrounding country with detachments, robbing the people of their horses, mules, beef cattle, beds, plate, wearing apparel, money, and every possible movable article of value, besides venting upon the wives and daughters of Southern soldiers the most opprobrious and obscene epithets, with more than one extreme outrage upon the persons of these victims of their hate and lust.
>
> The families of many of Forrest's men had been thus grievously wronged, despoiled, and insulted, and in one or two cases fearfully outraged, and many of his officers, uniting with the citizens of the country in the petition, begged to be permitted to remain, to shield their families from further molestation. Of course this was impossible; but Forrest determined to employ his present resources for the summary suppression of the evil and grievances complained of, by the surprise, if possible, and capture, at all hazards, of Fort Pillow; and the orders necessary to that end were issued on the 10th of April; Bell's and McCulloch's Brigades, with Walton's Battery—four mountain howitzers—being selected

---

1461. Mathes, p. 214.
1462. Ashdown and Caudill, p. 83.

for the operation.[1463]

Forrest had one other motivation for paying a visit to Fort Pillow: "Uncle Sam's larder." As he noted on April 4, 1864:

> There is a Federal force of 500 or 600 at Fort Pillow, which I shall attend to in a day or two, as they have horses and supplies which we need.[1464]

In summary, when the defenseless people of the region begged Forrest for help, the General, having nothing else pressing at the time and needing provisions and supplies, gladly promised to relieve them of the nefarious invaders. It was for these reasons that Forrest and his men attacked Fort Pillow, not to single out and kill blacks, as anti-South propagandists claim.[1465]

## FALSE CHARGES & YANKEE RACISM

Characteristically, the Yankees labeled Forrest's attack at Fort Pillow a "massacre" and an "assassination." But these were merely the usual scurrilous terms employed—out of jealousy, anger, and frustration—by the North for Confederate successes on the battlefield.[1466] Even historians with no love of the South admit that the Northern media turned the truth into a fictitious tale of wanton cruelty, and that the figures they used were overly and unjustly magnified.[1467]

Besides, "playing the massacre card" was one of the vile hands the Yanks were best at dealing. Indeed, Forrest was far from being the only white Confederate accused of slaughtering blacks. For instance, Union General Cadwallader C. Washburn later slanderously and falsely charged General Stephen Dill Lee with massacring U.S. African-American soldiers at the Battle of Brice's Cross Roads.[1468]

As many Rebels later asserted, both the Union soldiers at the garrison and Lincoln (along with the Northern populace) should have

---

1463. Jordan and Pryor, pp. 422-423.
1464. ORA, Ser. 1, Vol. 32, Pt. 1, p. 609.
1465. Mathes, p. 215.
1466. Pollard, SHW, Vol. 2, p. 261.
1467. Page Smith, p. 320.
1468. Jordan and Pryor, pp. 489-492.

expected what was coming. For, as just mentioned, the Fort Pillow Yanks had been committing outrages on the surrounding noncombatant populace for several months. Forrest and his men, who rightly took these crimes as personal insults, sought only to protect the innocent.[1469] Yankees would have done no less to protect their own.

Of course, one thing that none of the Northern papers reported was that the white and black Union troops stationed at Fort Pillow were segregated,[1470] while Forrest's white and black soldiers at the scene were integrated (segregation of troops was a type of racism unheard of in the Confederate Army, where black and whites fought together, side by side).[1471]

THE FACTS
There is little question that the South won a decisive victory at Fort Pillow, and that a seemingly unusually disproportionate number of Federal soldiers died, many of them African-Americans. The question is why?

The answer that has come down to us today is part fact, part fiction; part emotion, part politics; part Forrest's ingeniousness, part Yankee stupidity. The complete story will never be known.

Nonetheless, we do have some clear facts to work with.

To begin with, a number of the Yankee soldiers, in particular many of the blacks, were thoroughly intoxicated on April 12.[1472] After the battle, countless barrels of whiskey and kegs of beer and ale were found scattered throughout the fort, up and down the works, with tin dippers[1473] and cups tied to them for convenience,[1474] as Forrest and his officers later testified.[1475]

Standing defiantly on the parapets, black U.S. troops taunted, jeered, shouted obscenities, and made obscene gestures at Forrest's men, daring them to attack. In their thoroughly inebriated state they

---

1469. Henry ATSF, p. 158.
1470. A. Ward, pp. 78, 161.
1471. J. C. Perry, pp. 218, 223.
1472. Lytle, p. 279. Many of the black Union soldiers at Fort Pillow were recently freed slaves who were, no doubt, in a celebratory mood that day; hence the over-consumption of alcohol.
1473. Jordan and Pryor, pp. 439-440.
1474. Mathes, p. 227.
1475. Wyeth, LGNBF, p. 350.

apparently felt immortal and refused to obey Forrest's usual command to "surrender or die." Unaware at the time that the Federals were drunk, and observing their staunch resistance, Forrest gave the order to "shoot at everything blue betwixt wind and water until yonder flag comes down."[1476] His soldiers rightfully proceeded to unfurl a galling and murderous fire upon them, and dozens fell.[1477]

This incident only explains some of the Union injuries and deaths, however. In fact, there was another factor behind the hundreds of Yankee casualties, one that can be better understood by examining the enthusiasm with which Forrest's men attacked.

## YANKEE CRIMES AGAINST FORREST'S MEN, RELATIONS, FRIENDS, & NEIGHBORS

Prior to the Battle of Fort Pillow, the Yankee soldiers who manned that garrison (many themselves, like Forrest's men, also from Tennessee) were known to have captured, tortured, and murdered individuals from Forrest's cavalry.

At least seven of Forrest's men died in this manner, though only six are known. We record their names here for posterity: Lieutenant Joseph Stewart, Private John Wilson, Private Samuel Osborn (all three "shot to death"), Private Martin (first name unknown; "shot to death"), Lieutenant Willis Dodds (illegally arrested at his father's house and "put to death by [mutilation and] torture"), and Private Alexander Vale ("shot to death"). The seventh victim, while still alive, was horribly mutilated by Yankees and left to die. Suffering a most appalling death, the details of his unspeakable agonies and numerous wounds are too gruesome to recount here.

These heinous crimes made it into the United States' *Official Records*, there for all to see, read, study, and ponder. One of the primary Yankee villains behind these murders was Colonel Fielding Hurst, sent by another Yankee war criminal, General William Sooy Smith,[1478] to "grub up" West Tennessee. If by "grub up" Smith meant that Hurst should extort, rob, torture, mutilate, and shoot unarmed Confederate

---

1476. Wyeth, LGNBF, pp. 351, 386.

1477. Wyeth, LGNBF, pp. 349-351.

1478. In northeastern Mississippi, for example, Smith and his men robbed and pillaged the people, laying waste the country to the point where it was described as "almost a desert." Lytle, p. 289.

soldiers as well as civilians (even "helpless," physically handicapped children), then Hurst succeeded admirably.

An outraged Forrest ordered one of his officers, Lieutenant-Colonel Wiley M. Reed, to investigate. On March 21, 1864, from his headquarters at Jackson, Forrest wrote to Lieutenant Colonel Thomas M. Jack:

> Numerous reports having reached me of the wanton destruction of property by Col. Fielding Hurst and his regiment of renegade Tennesseans, I ordered Lieut. Col. W. M. Reed to investigate and report upon the same, and herewith transmit you a copy of his report. Have thought it both just and proper to bring these transactions to the notice of the Federal commander at Memphis, and by flag of truce will demand of him the restitution of the money taken from the citizens of Jackson, under a threat from Hurst to burn the town unless the money was forthcoming at an appointed time. Have also demanded that the murderers be delivered up to Confederate authority for punishment, and reply from that officer as to the demand, &c., will be forwarded you as soon as received. Should the Federal commander refuse to accede to the just demands made, I have instructed the officer in charge of the flag to deliver the notice inclosed outlawing Hurst and his command.
> I am, general, very respectfully, your obedient servant,
> N. B. FORREST, Major-General.[1479]

Dated the same day, Reed sent an official report on some of Hurst's crimes to his superior Major John P. Strange:

HEADQUARTERS FORREST'S COMMAND,
Jackson, Tenn., March 21, 1864.
Maj. J. P. STRANGE,
Assistant Adjutant-General:
     MAJOR: Having been appointed by the major-general commanding to investigate the facts of the recent tax levied by Col. Fielding Hurst upon the citizens of this place to indemnify himself and command against damages assessed by the Federal authorities of Memphis in favor of Mrs. Newman, formerly a citizen of Jackson, whose house had been entered and robbed by the Federal soldiery in the summer of 1863, also the facts available in reference

---

1479. ORA, Ser. 1, Vol. 32, Pt. 3, pp. 664-665.

to the murders which have been committed by the enemy upon soldiers and citizens in this part of the State within the past few months, in obedience to instructions I called together a party of citizens, from whom I derived the following facts: About the 7th of February, 1864, Colonel Hurst, with his command, visited Jackson, Tenn., and announced publicly that in consequence of the assessment by the Federal authorities of Memphis, Tenn., against himself and command of damages to the amount of $5,139.25 in favor of Mrs. Newman, formerly a citizen of this place, he was here to demand this amount at once of the citizens, or on refusal or failure promptly to pay said amount into his hands that he would burn the town. Upon application of some of the citizens and the guaranty of 20 of them, five days were granted in which to raise the sum required, to be paid in greenbacks or Kentucky funds. On the 12th of February, 1864, the entire amount, $5,139.25, was paid into the hands of Col. Fielding Hurst by the citizens of Jackson, Tenn.

The murders committed are as follows: Lieut. Willis Dodds, Company F, Colonel Newsom's regiment Tennessee volunteers, Forrest's command, under orders from his commanding officers, collecting his command, was arrested at the residence of his father in Henderson County, Tenn., on or about the 9th of March, 1864, by the command of Colonel Thornburgh, of the Federal army, on their march through this portion of the State eastward, and put to death by torture.

Private Silas Hodges, a scout, acting under orders from Colonel Tansil, states that he saw the body of Lieutenant Dodds very soon after his murder, and that it was most horribly mutilated, the face having been skinned, the nose cut off, the under jaw disjointed, the privates cut off, and the body otherwise barbarously lacerated and most wantonly injured, and that his death was brought about by the most inhuman process of torture.

Private Alex. Vale, Company H, Newsom's regiment Tennessee volunteers, under orders from Colonel Tansil, was arrested and shot to death in Madison County, Tenn., by same command, on or about the 8th March, 1864.

Lieut. Joseph Stewart, Private John Wilson, Private Samuel Osborn, members of Newsom's regiment Tennessee volunteers, while on duty under orders from their commanding officers, were captured by Hurst's command on or about the 15th February, 1864, in McNairy County, Tenn., and about three days thereafter their bodies were found in Haywood County, Tenn., having been shot to death.

On or about the 5th February, 1864, Private Martin, Company—, Wilson's regiment Tennessee volunteers, was captured by same command and was shot to death and the rights of sepulture forbidden while the command remained, some four days. Mr. Lee Doroughty, a citizen of McNairy County, Tenn, a youth about sixteen years of age, deformed and almost helpless, was arrested and wantonly murdered by same command about 1st January, 1864.

I am, major, very respectfully, your obedient servant, W. M. REED, Lieutenant-Colonel, Provisional Army, C. S.[1480]

Forrest had a serious score to settle.[1481] The next day he let it be known among the Yankee brass that if Hurst and his men were ever captured, they would *not* be considered prisoners of war, but rather would be treated as the common criminals they were:

HDQRS. DEPT. OF WEST TENN. AND NORTH MISS.,
In the Field, March 22, 1864.
To whom it may concern:
        Whereas it has come to the knowledge of the major-general commanding that Col. Fielding Hurst, commanding [Sixth] Regiment U. S. [Tennessee Cavalry] Volunteers, has been guilty of wanton extortion upon the citizens of Jackson, Tenn., and other places, guilty of depredations upon private property, guilty of house burning, guilty of murders, both of citizens and soldiers of the Confederate States; and whereas demand has been duly made upon the military authorities of the United States for the surrender of said Col. Fielding Hurst and such officers and men of his command as are guilty of these outrages; and whereas this just demand has been refused by said authorities: I therefore declare the aforesaid Fielding Hurst, and the officers and men of his command, outlaws, and not entitled to be treated as prisoners of war falling into the hands of the forces of the Confederate States.
N. B. FORREST, Major-General, Commanding.[1482]

These were not the first or the last war crimes General Smith would sanction or himself commit. In August of that same year, 1864, as he marched across Mississippi, his unlawful acts against the innocent inhabitants of Oxford spawned the following rebuke from two of Forrest's biographers, Jordan and Pryor:

---

1480. ORA, Ser. 1, Vol. 32, Pt. 1, pp. 118-119.
1481. Wills, p. 173.
1482. ORA, Ser. 1, Vol. 32, Pt. 1, p. 119.

The Federal advance, however, did not enter Oxford until about eight o'clock on the morning of the 22d, but a column of infantry soon followed. The cavalry were speedily and widely scattered through the town, but the infantry were kept in ranks. Up to noon, although there were a number of petty acts of spoliation on the part of individual soldiers, yet no general disposition was shown either to license or commit arson and rapine. The railroad depot was burned in the morning, but, as yet, no private buildings were set on fire. Suddenly, about midday, however, this forbearance ceased. Orders were then given by the Federal commander for the burning of the public buildings and unoccupied houses; and in a little while, to quote the language of a Federal chronicler, 'the public square was surrounded by a canopy of flame; the splendid courthouse was among the buildings destroyed, with other edifices of a public character. In fact, where once stood a handsome little country town, now only remained the blackened skeletons of the houses, and the smouldering ruins that marked the track of war.' In this conflagration were consumed all the principal business houses, with one accidental exception, the two brick hotels of the place, and, of course, the flames speedily spread to several dwellings occupied by women and children, and sick persons, happily rescued, however, from destruction by the exertions of the inhabitants of Oxford.

One occupied mansion, howbeit, was burned to the ground under circumstances which make the act noteworthy in these pages. It will be recollected, Mrs. Thompson's house, several days previously, had been despoiled by the Federal cavalry commander and his men. Major-General Smith now sent an officer of his staff with a detachment to burn it. Mrs. Thompson made a dignified, earnest, but vain appeal that her house might be spared her. Only fifteen minutes were granted for the removal of any articles which she might specially wish to save; but these, as fast as they were brought from the house, in the presence of Federal officers, were ruthlessly stolen from her by the soldiery who clustered around, so that scarcely an article, other than the clothing on her person, escaped fire or pillage.

Up to midday, guards had been set as if to repress pillage; these were withdrawn about that time, and for several hours thereafter Oxford was delivered up to riot and rapacity. Houses on all sides were broken into and despoiled of clothing, bedding, and provisions, which, if not carried off, were maliciously destroyed. Carpets were torn up, curtains cut down, and furniture broken in downright wantonness; and in a number of instances the torch was set to houses thus rifled, and only the exertions of their terrified occupants saved them from destruction. Some subaltern officers were greatly chagrined, and displayed a disposition to restrain their men from acts so disgraceful to their vaunted flag; but no officer of rank was heard to interpose his authority for the suppression of disorder in a place which there had been no effort to defend, nor any conflict in its immediate vicinity. The men, thus assured of the countenance of their commander, set all opposition to their licentiousness at defiance, until five P.M., when they were suddenly withdrawn, and the enemy began their retreat northward so rapidly as to reach Holly Springs by ten A.M., on the next day. So completely, however, had they done their work in Oxford, that its non-combatant inhabitants, mostly women and children, were left absolutely destitute of food until the soldiers' rough rations could be brought up from the Confederate depots south of the Yocona, and distributed among them.[1483]

The looting and burning of homes, along with the torturing and killing of captured prisoners of war is, of course, illegal and immoral, as is torturing and killing noncombatants and civilians. But military and religious law did not prevent Lincoln's forces from engaging in both of these monstrous practices. There was, for instance, the infamous case of Confederate Captain Sam L. Freeman, a much beloved, heavy set Christian officer who was captured at the Battle of Franklin I (April 10, 1863).[1484]

As he was being marched off to prison—prodded along and beaten from all sides by his pitiless Union captors—the weary Rebel leader began to lag behind, stumbling on the path. He was then ordered to run, an impossible task, as he had once again fallen to the ground exhausted.[1485] Instead of helping him to his feet and assisting him along, as required by both international military law and moral ethics, a member of the Fourth U.S. Cavalry rode up to Captain Freeman and shot him in the head at point blank range, killing him instantly.[1486] His body was left unceremoniously on the dusty road where he fell.[1487]

Prior to the shooting Freeman had told the Yank who was about to murder him that he could go no faster, and never once did he resist or

---

1483. Jordan and Pryor, pp. 549-552.
1484. Lytle, pp. 148-149.
1485. Wills, p. 108.
1486. Jordan and Pryor, p. 247.
1487. Morton, p. 88.

try to flee. When Forrest arrived on the scene his eyes were already filled with tears. He took Freeman's cold hand and said "Brave man; none braver!"[1488] Forrest and his soldiers were "stricken with grief" and filled with vengeance, retaining the memory of this horrific event for the remainder of the War.[1489]

Long before the Battle of Fort Pillow, Forrest's men were well aware of the Yankee approach to warfare embodied in such Union officers as Sherman, and the equally hated General Philip Henry Sheridan, who needlessly destroyed Virginia's Shenandoah Valley. As we have seen, according to the U.S. government's own official records, Sherman ordered the burning of homes and the killing of innocent civilians as he lumbered through the Southland.[1490] He even forced captured, unprotected Confederate soldiers to clear their own minefields, an incident that the cocky Yank joyfully recorded in his *Memoirs*:

> . . . the rebels had planted eight-inch shells in the road, with friction-matches to explode them by being trodden on. This was not war, but murder, and it made me very angry. I immediately ordered a lot of rebel prisoners to be brought from the provost-guard, armed with picks and spades, and made them march in close order along the road, so as to explode their own torpedoes, or to discover and dig them up. They begged hard, but I reiterated the order, and could hardly help laughing at their stepping so gingerly along the road, where it was supposed sunken torpedoes might explode at each step, but they found no other torpedoes till near Fort McAllister.[1491]

It is known today that such illicit activities against Confederate soldiers were sanctioned by both Grant and Lincoln, which is hardly surprising since, as the *Official Records* clearly show, both were war criminals themselves.

---

1488. Wyeth, LGNBF, p. 184.
1489. Mathes, p. 107; Sheppard, pp. 99-100.
1490. ORA, Ser. 1, Vol. 39, Pt. 3, p. 494.
1491. Sherman, Vol. 2, p. 194.

## GALVANIZED YANKS, DESERTERS, & TURNCOATS

There were other important factors that influenced the outcome at Fort Pillow. One of the Union commanders at the fort, Major Bradford, along with many of his men, were "galvanized Yanks," or "homemade Yanks"; that is, Southerners who had joined Lincoln's Northern army.[1492] Some of them, according to at least one account, appear to have formerly served under Forrest.[1493] Bradford himself, a practicing lawyer at Dyersburg, Tennessee, was a Middle Tennessee native, the same area Forrest was from.

Adding to the problem for Forrest and his men was the fact that many of Bradford's soldiers were deserters from the Rebel army, nearly all whose families had sided with Jeff Davis and the South.[1494] There were few things worse to the General than a deserter or a turncoat, particularly a Confederate one. As one who had killed deserters from his own ranks,[1495] Forrest definitely would not have been pleased when he heard this news.

It is probable then, if not a dead certainty, that on April 12, 1864, he and his men marched toward Fort Pillow with military law on their minds. For Forrest would have been very much within his rights as a Rebel officer to hunt down Confederate deserters and bring them to justice—as his own commander, General Hood, had ordered him to.[1496]

But there was something else, for Forrest something worse still: the galvanized Yanks from his neighborhood had not joined the North out of any kind of nationalistic pride in the Union. They were at Fort Pillow strictly to partake in the illicit activities of the "lair" of Federal soldiers there: the harassment, molestation, robbery, burglary, mugging, pillaging, rape, and murder of loyal Southerners in the area (mostly women, children, and old men).[1497] Forrest boiled at the mere thought of such treasonous deception.

Is it possible that he may have also attacked Fort Pillow, in part, out of resentment and revenge? While such behavior would not have

---

1492. Watts, s.v. "galvanized Yankee"; Faust, s.v. "Galvanized Yankees."
1493. Wills, p. 192.
1494. Mathes, p. 215.
1495. See e.g., Wyeth, LGNBF, p. 589.
1496. Wyeth, LGNBF, p. 589.
1497. Henry, ATSF, pp. 126, 151.

been officially condoned at Richmond, if he did it is certainly understandable. For Forrest's men the Battle of Fort Pillow was, in some respects, more a local feud than an impersonal fight with strangers. They knew many of the enemy personally, and before the war had been neighbors, even friends. The Yankees' torture and murder of their fellow comrades in arms, along with the growing criminal activities of other Northern troops, and the knowledge of their desertion from the Southern army, no doubt weighed heavily upon their minds that spring day as they approached the garrison.[1498]

COMPLEXITIES & CONFUSION AT FORT PILLOW
There were still other factors that contributed to the disaster at the Tennessee garrison.

There was the difficult and confusing topography surrounding the fort, which itself was situated on an elevated point of land overlooking two bodies of water: the Mississippi River and Cold Creek. Adding to the complexity of the terrain were numerous bluffs, hollows, knolls, gullies, large logs and stumps, steep embankments, overhangs, dense underbrush, muddy river banks, and ravines (one that was 450 feet deep, the height of a forty-five story building).[1499]

We must also mention that there were a series of unexpected events over which Forrest had no control. One example will suffice.

Midway through the conflict a segment of the Yankee troops agreed to surrender and sent up white flags of truce. Only yards away, however, other Federal troops continued to pour canister into the Confederate lines, refusing to give up the struggle.[1500]

About this time, several boats, the *Olive Branch*, the *Hope*, and the *M. R. Cheek* (at least one a Yankee steamer and another a Yankee gunboat—both bristling with soldiers and artillery), chugged toward Fort Pillow's river landing.[1501] Another Yankee gunboat, the *New Era*, already menacingly docked on the river just past the fort, was operating under a prearranged agreement with Yankee General Bradford that if the breastworks were taken by the Rebels, it was to offer assistance by giving

1498. Wyeth, LGNBF, p. 368-369.
1499. Wyeth, LGNBF, pp. 335-337.
1500. Wyeth, LGNBF, p. 354.
1501. Jordan and Pryor, pp. 432-433.

shelter to escaping Union soldiers under a canopy of protective canister.[1502]

The three aforementioned boats, meanwhile, continued to approach the landing, wholly ignoring the white truce flags that were fluttering in the breeze in plain sight: under the rules of military engagement the steamers should have "put about" and moved away.[1503]

Emboldened by the sight of their boats plying toward the fort with promised assistance and reinforcements, those Yanks who had previously agreed to surrender decided to fight on, this time with renewed vigor. The intoxicated blacks in particular—now "indifferent to danger or death"—fought on with insane determination, egged on by the ridiculous Yankee lie that Forrest's men had taken an oath to "automatically kill all captured Negroes."[1504]

Making an already terrible situation even worse, they did not realize, or did not care, that they had left the Union flags of truce flying.[1505] Additionally, a signal flag should have been sent up signifying that a truce was being discussed. The fort, however, never hoisted this particular flag.[1506]

Adding to an already disastrous situation was the fact that, after the breastworks were overrun by the Confederates, the Yankee gunboats, in particular the *New Era*, did not offer either the promised succor or "shower of canister" to cover the fleeing Yanks (in fact, the *New Era* later "disappeared up the river").[1507] As a result, the bewildered, scrambling Union mob, many in a state of drunkenness, threw themselves into either the Mississippi River or Cold Creek and drowned.[1508]

Of course, in the mass confusion that ensued on both sides, Confederate and Federal, more unnecessary injuries and deaths occurred. Had the inebriated blacks alone simply surrendered, most of

---

1502. Jordan and Pryor, pp. 433, 437-438.
1503. Wyeth, LGNBF, pp. 344-345.
1504. Wyeth, LGNBF, p. 385. Actually, it was black U.S. soldiers who had taken an government oath to "give no quarter" to Forrest. Jordan and Pryor, pp. 482, 485-487, 519.
1505. Wyeth, LGNBF, pp. 345-346.
1506. Browning, p. 53.
1507. Jordan and Pryor, p. 442.
1508. Jordan and Pryor, pp. 437-439.

this carnage would have been avoided.[1509]

## DID FORREST KILL WOMEN & CHILDREN AT FORT PILLOW?

What about the detestable accusation against Forrest that he and his men killed innocent civilians, including women and children, who were inside the fort at the time of the attack?

There were indeed male civilians in the garrison at the time, but they had voluntarily elected to stay and fight. As for women and children, however, the *Official Records* make no mention of them. The reason is that they were taken away by boat before the fighting began, as Yankees at the fort themselves testified. One of these, Union surgeon Dr. Charles Fitch, later avowed:

> Early in the morning all of the woman and all of the non-combatants were ordered on to some barges, and were towed by a gunboat up the river to an island before any one was hurt.[1510]

## BURIED ALIVE?

As to the charge that Rebels buried wounded and dying Yankees alive, let us examine this more closely.

Smouldering ruins were extinguished by throwing dirt on them. If a few Union men were partially buried at this time there is a simple and innocent explanation: a number of soldiers, as we have seen, were "dead" drunk, while others simply "played dead" to escape being captured.[1511] It is entirely possible that a few individuals from each of these two categories were "buried." However, their "graves" would have been extremely shallow and they could have gotten up and walked away with little effort, hardly qualifying as being "buried alive."

As for the dead who were interred properly at the scene, the Confederates were not involved, as Federal forces were entirely responsible for burying their own. Actually, far from participating in such outrages, Forrest conscientiously allowed the surviving Yanks to reenter the fort and remove their wounded and bury their dead. The General and his men even helped carry wounded Yanks from the field,

---

1509. Wyeth, LGNBF, p. 355.
1510. *Southern Historical Society Papers*, Vol. 7, 1879, p. 439.
1511. Wyeth, LGNBF, p. 381.

carefully and respectfully placing them in tents and barracks where they could be tended to by their own surgeons.[1512]

As proof that no Yankee was subjected to murderous or even inhumane behavior by the Rebs, we have the fact that many of the injured Federal soldiers, both white *and* black, were actually treated by Forrest's own doctors[1513] under his usual humane order to give attention "to the wounded on both sides."[1514] The official report of Confederate Major Charles W. Anderson, dated February 3, 1864, validates these claims:

> The general says have the salt rolled out, so that it will be safe, and then burn up all the houses at the fort except the one used as hospital. Leave the Federal surgeon and such of the wounded as cannot travel or be moved, and parole them; also parole and leave with them a nurse or two, or slightly wounded men sufficient to wait on them, sending forward all other prisoners and negroes to Jackson immediately.
>
> No negroes will be delivered to their owners on the march; they must all go to Jackson. Leave with the wounded five or six days' supply of provisions and any medicine they may need; the balance of provisions issue to your command.[1515]

BURNED ALIVE?
Another serious charge against Forrest is that *during* the battle he and his men purposefully burned wounded black Yanks alive in their tents and cabins.

First, the "burning incident" occurred the day *after* the battle, April 13. Second, no one was burned alive because all of the wounded had been evacuated by then. The exact series of events were as follows.

On the morning of the 13th, Forrest sent a detail back to the fort under Major Anderson to bury the "overlooked dead" and collect any remaining weapons. A Union gunboat, the *Silver Cloud*, then appeared on the scene and began to fire upon the men.[1516] As there was no longer any reason to guard the fort, and as they were now under attack by a

1512. Wyeth, LGNBF, p. 356.
1513. Jordan and Pryor, p. 442.
1514. Mathes, p. 225.
1515. ORA, Ser. 1, Vol. 32, Pt. 2, p. 664.
1516. Jordan and Pryor, p. 443.

Yankee gunboat on the river, Anderson ordered his men to vacate the area.[1517]

As was the military custom in these situations, upon retreat the enemy's remaining tents and cabins were set ablaze to prevent their contents from being recaptured by the Federals, who were already returning to defend what was left of the fort. The Rebs had no way of knowing this, but there were several dead black soldiers inside the structures, killed during the conflict the day before. Yanks who later came on the scene understandably misunderstood what they saw.[1518] It was this action that gave rise to the patently false rumor that "Forrest had burned black soldiers alive in their tents."[1519] As we will see, Forrest himself was miles away at the time.

## CRUCIFIED YANKS?

Forrest's harshest critics claim that he and his men nailed Union soldiers to wooden beams and tortured them to death. In one case it was alleged that the General nailed a Yank, Lieutenant J. C. Akerstrom, to the side of a house by his clothing and lit him on fire, burning him alive.

Yet, Union testimony itself contradicted these accusations. In the case of Akerstrom, for example, Federal Private John F. Ray later testified that the lieutenant had been killed during the battle, falling dead right in front of him.[1520]

In short, this charge is so patently absurd it scarcely deserves mention. It is false for the same reasons all of the other accusations against Forrest and his men in this chapter are false.[1521]

## DID FORREST MURDER MAJOR BRADFORD?

Charges were later brought against Forrest for the "murder" of Yankee Major William F. Bradford based on the testimony of a Union conscript, who testified that he witnessed the shooting, and that Bradford had been on his knees "begging for his life." But is this story true?

Again the facts turn out to be quite different from Northern

---

1517. Wyeth, LGNBF, p. 358.
1518. Jordan and Pryor, p. 443.
1519. Mathes, p. 226.
1520. Jordan and Pryor, p. 450.
1521. Wyeth, LGNBF, p. 379; Jordan and Pryor, p. 443.

myth.

After capture Bradford was to be paroled to "supervise the burial of his [recently deceased] brother." The night before, giving his word of honor that he would not try to escape, he was placed in a tent under light guard. That evening, however, he slipped out of the tent and into the darkness.[1522] Recaptured, he was now placed under heavy guard.[1523]

The next day, en route to Brownsville, Tennessee, Bradford was being guarded at the rear by five of Forrest's men. Suddenly, he bolted, trying to make another escape. In accordance to military law, he was legally and rightfully shot down, a far cry from being "gunned down in cold blood" under Forrest's order, as pro-North authors claims.[1524]

As Forrest's official report shows below, the General himself, at the front of his command at the time this occurred, did not even hear about Bradford's death until some ten days later.[1525] We will further point out that there were no Confederate officers of any kind involved. This was strictly a "private" matter.[1526]

Yet, if personal vengeance had been wished upon Bradford by Forrest's men, he could have easily been slain during the battle itself. Instead, he was captured and treated with "the utmost consideration and civility." It was his second escape attempt that changed his fate. At that point Forrest's men decided to shoot the war criminal rather than hang him, a difference with little distinction under the circumstances.[1527]

It must also be asked, if Bradford was killed "in cold blood" by Forrest or anyone else, why is there nothing in the *Official Records* pertaining to the arrest, trial, and imprisonment of Bradford's murderers?[1528] Where, in other words, is the evidence?

COMMON THIEVERY?
Finally, there is the accusation that Forrest and his men raided and

---

1522. Lytle, p. 280.
1523. Jordan and Pryor, pp. 440-441.
1524. After arriving at Brownsville Forrest was met by the local townswomen, who thanked him for shutting down Fort Pillow. As a gift of appreciation they had their sewing thimbles melted down, and from them were cast a pair of silver spurs for the General. Lytle, p. 280.
1525. Mathes, p. 228.
1526. Jordan and Pryor, p. 455.
1527. Jordan and Pryor, p. 455.
1528. Wyeth, LGNBF, p. 361.

robbed the fort after dark, stealing valuables from the dead and committing other serious offences.

According to official reports Forrest's *entire* cavalry was well clear of the area by sunset (6:00 PM),[1529] as by that time he had made camp some fifteen miles away[1530] at a farmhouse to the east (on their way back to Jackson, Tennessee).[1531] In fact, Forrest himself left the scene of the battle as soon as it was over that afternoon and never returned. His men soon followed, leaving no Confederates at the fort after dark.[1532]

The nighttime depredations at Fort Pillow can, no doubt, be attributed to one of the many gangs of thugs and ne'er-do-wells that roamed the South at the time, preying on the weak and the defenseless. It was not uncommon to see one of these shameless packs of "hyenas," as Wyeth referred to them, on the smouldering battlefield after a conflict, running from body to body, rifling through the pockets of the wounded and the deceased.[1533]

On March 21, 1864, just weeks before Fort Pillow, Forrest made mention of these gangs in a field report to Lieutenant Colonel Thomas M. Jack:

> The whole of West Tennessee is overrun by bands and squads of robbers, horse thieves and deserters, whose depredations and unlawful appropriations of private property are rapidly and effectually depleting the country.[1534]

## TRUMPED UP CHARGES & FALSE STORIES

Later, Yankee newspapers distorted, exaggerated, and even concocted various events pertaining to Fort Pillow. Why? The usual reason for 19th-Century Yankee yellow journalism: it was another attempt to justify Lincoln's illegal invasion of the South and the Northern hatred of her citizens. Fort Pillow thus became the usual "atrocity story," bloodied up for Northern consumption.

Since the tale of the "massacre" was particularly distasteful to

---

1529. Mathes, p. 226.
1530. Wyeth, LGNBF, p. 384.
1531. Jordan and Pryor, pp. 442-443.
1532. Wyeth, LGNBF, p. 379.
1533. Wyeth, LGNBF, pp. 357-358.
1534. ORA, Ser. 1, Vol. 32, Pt. 3, p. 664.

freed slaves, Lincoln and his government naturally made the most of the trumped-up stories (inciting more discord, racism, and violence), all of which have been handed down to us today as "fact."

But the truth has risen to the surface, despite the North's ongoing attempts to suppress it: later, during the Fort Pillow tribunal, most of the affidavits attesting to Forrest's "butchery" at Fort Pillow, in fact, came from Yankee blacks who were illiterate and could not even sign their own names. As such, the resultant documents were "conflicting and extravagant."[1535] Why? Who wrote out this ridiculous paperwork?

Obviously the incriminating "evidence" was illegally penciled in by South-hating Northern whites who had but one intention: to permanently disgrace Forrest and taint his name.

There is also the fact that at least 23 percent (eighteen out of seventy-eight) of those who testified against Forrest were not eyewitnesses, yet their statements were treated with the same solemnity as those who were actually at the scene. Here we have proof that the U.S. government, which revealingly called its final report on the "massacre" a "war measure," tried to create a case against Forrest out of nothing for the sole purpose of tarnishing his reputation and humiliating the South.[1536] Neither Forrest or any of his subordinates ever ordered a massacre, or even anything illegal. In short, the Union report was anti-South wartime propaganda, pure and simple.[1537]

THE BEGINNING OF THE LIE

Much of the nefarious anti-Forrest mythology concerning Fort Pillow began with Yankee Adjutant Mack J. Leaming, whose official view of an important event during the battle was based on a visual error.

On the afternoon of the 12th, as the four water craft—one Yankee gunboat (the *New Era*) and three steamers (one laden with Yankee troops)—approached to reinforce the fort, Leaming believed Forrest violated the flag of truce. This occurred when the Yankee officer thought he saw Forrest move some of his men into a ravine near the river

---

1535. Mathes, pp. 228, 229.
1536. Wyeth, LGNBF, p. 381.
1537. Sheppard, pp. 171-172.

in order to shell the oncoming boats *while the truce flag was flying*. In his official report Leaming wrote of the supposed incident:

> During the cessation of firing on both sides, in consequence of the flag of truce offered by the enemy, and while the attention of both officers and men was naturally directed to the south side of the fort where the communications were being received and answered, Forrest had resorted to means the most foul and infamous ever adopted in the most barbarous ages of the world for the accomplishment of his design. Here he took occasion to move his troops, partially under cover of a ravine and thick underbrush, into the very position he had been fighting to obtain throughout the entire engagement, up to 3.30 p. m.[1538]

In reality, the Confederates had not just moved into the ravine. They had captured this area much earlier in the day, long before the flag of truce had been raised. What Leaming saw were some of Forrest's troops, under Confederate Colonel C. R. Barteau, moving *out of the ravine they had already occupied* in order to stop the Yankee boats loaded with artillery and infantry from coming ashore. As the Yankees had not signaled their boats to stop and turn around (as they should have done under military regulations regarding truces), Forrest had every right to do whatever was necessary to prevent them from landing.[1539]

Forrest himself vehemently denied Leaming's accusation, as did his other officers, Chalmers, Bell, McCulloch, and Anderson, among many others. What is more, even Yankee officers corroborated Forrest's side of the story. One of these, Union General George F. Shepley, who had been aboard one of the boats (the *Olive Branch*) driving toward the fort, fully backed Forrest and his officers in his report to the U.S. Committee on the Conduct of the War.[1540]

As this document completely exonerates Forrest, it is worth including here.

> Report of Brig. Gen. George F. Shepley, U. S. Army, of Affairs, April 12.

---

1538. ORA, Ser. 1, Vol. 32, Pt. 1, p. 561.
1539. Wyeth, LGNBF, pp. 345-346.
1540. Wyeth, LGNBF, p. 346.

HEADQUARTERS NORFOLK AND PORTSMOUTH
Norfolk, VA May 7, 1864.

SIR: At my own request, having been relieved from duty as military governor of Louisiana and ordered to report for duty to the commanding general of the army, I left New Orleans on the evening of the 6ᵗʰ of April as a passenger in the *Olive Branch*, New Orleans and Saint Louis passenger steamer, not in the service of the Government, but loaded with male and female passengers and cargo of private parties. The steamer was unarmed, and had no troops and no muskets for protection against guerrillas when landing at woodyards and other places.

The boat stopped at Vicksburg, and I went ashore. When I returned to the boat, as she was about leaving, I found that a detachment of a portion of the men of two batteries—one Ohio and one Missouri—belonging to the Seventeenth Army Corps, with the horses, guns, caissons, wagons, tents, and baggage of the two batteries, had been put on board, with orders, as I afterward learned on inquiring, to report to General Brayman at Cairo.

The horses occupied all of the available space, fore and aft, on the sides of the boilers and machinery, which were on deck. The guns, caissons, baggage wagons, tents, garrison and camp equipage were piled up together on the bows, leaving only space for the gang-plank.

The men had no small-arms, so that when the boat landed, as happened in one instance, at a wood-yard where guerrillas had just passed, the pickets thrown out to prevent surprise were necessarily unarmed.

As the boat was approaching, and before it was in sight of Fort Pillow, some females hailed it from the shore, and said the rebels had attacked Fort Pillow and captured two boats on the river, and would take us if we went on.

The captain of the *Olive Branch* said they had probably taken the *Mollie Abel*, which was due there about that time from Saint Louis. He turned his boat, saying he would go back to Memphis.

I objected to going back; stopped the boat below the next point hailed another smaller steamer without passengers, which I saw approaching, and ordered it alongside. I ordered the captain of this boat to cast off the coal barges he had in tow, and take me on board with a section of a battery to go to Fort Pillow. While he was trying to disencumber his boat of the coal barges, another boat, better fitted for the purpose (the [*M. R.*] *Cheek*), hove in sight. Finding that I could get her ready quicker than the other, I had her brought alongside and went aboard myself with Captain Thornton, of my staff, and Captain Williams, the ranking officer of the batteries. Before we could get the guns on board, a steamer with troops hove in sight coining down the river from Fort Pillow. We could not distinguish at first whether they were Union or rebel soldiers.

I asked Captain Pegram, of the *Olive Branch*, if the story of the women turned out to be true and the rebels had the steamer, could his boat sink her. Captain Pegram replied: "Yes, my boat can run right over her." I ordered him to swing out into the stream to be ready for her. When she approached we saw U.S. infantry soldiers on board that had just passed the fort. She kept on going rapidly down with the current, only hailing the *Olive Branch*: "All right up there; you can go by. The gun-boat is lying off the fort." This steamer was the *Liberty*.

We then proceeded up the river in the *Olive Branch*. Near Fort Pillow some stragglers or guerrillas fired from the shore with musketry, aiming at the pilot-house.

I was then in the pilot-house, and, as we kept on, I observed that one of the two other boats I have mentioned, which followed us at some distance, was compelled to put back. The *Olive Branch* kept on to report to the gun-boat on the station.

An officer came off from the gun-boat in a small boat, and said he did not want any boat to stop; ordered us to go on to Cairo, and tell captain (name not recollected) to send him immediately 400 rounds of ammunition. There was no firing at the fort at this time. The Union flag was flying, and after we had passed the fort we could see a "flag of truce" outside the fortifications.

No signal of any kind was made to the boat from the fort or from the shore.

No intimation was given us from the gun-boat, which had the right to order a steamer of this description, other than the order to proceed to Cairo to send down the ammunition.

From the fact that the *Liberty* had just passed down the river from the fort, with troops on board; from her hailing us to go by, and continuing her course down the river without stopping; that no signal was made the *Olive Branch* from the fort on the shore, and no attack was being made on the fort at the time; that the officer of the gun-boat said he did not want any boats to stop, and ordered the captain of the *Olive Branch* to go on and have ammunition sent down to him by first boat, I considered, and now consider, that the captain of the *Olive Branch* was not only justified in going on, but bound to proceed. The *Olive Branch* was incapable of rendering any assistance, being entirely defenseless. If any guns could have been placed in position on the boat, they could not have been elevated to reach sharpshooters on the high, steep bluff outside the fort. A very few sharpshooters from the shore near the fort could have prevented any landing, and have taken the boat. We supposed the object of the rebels was rather to seize a boat to effect a crossing into Arkansas than to capture the fort. We had no means of knowing or suspecting that so strong a position as Fort Pillow had not been properly garrisoned for defense, when it was in constant communication with General Hurlbut at Memphis.

The *Olive Branch* had just left Memphis, General Hurlbut's headquarters, where it had been during the previous night. If it had not been for the appearance of the *Liberty*, I should have attempted a landing at Fort Pillow in the small steamer. If any intimation had been given from the gun-boat, or the shore, I should have landed personally from the *Olive Branch*. The order given to the contrary prevented it.

Coming from New Orleans, and having no knowledge of affairs in that military district, I could not presume that a fort, with uninterrupted water communication above and below, could possibly be without a garrison strong enough to hold it for a few hours.

. . . Captain Thornton, Twelfth Maine Volunteers, a gallant officer, distinguished for his bravery at Ponchatoula, where he was wounded and left in the hands of the enemy, was on board the *Olive Branch*, and will take this communication to the committee. I respectfully ask that he may be thoroughly examined as to all the circumstances. I am conscious that a full examination will show that I rather exceeded than neglected my duty.

I have the honor to be, with great respect, your obedient servant, G. F. SHEPLEY, Brigadier-General, Commanding.

Hon. D. W. Good, Of Committee on Conduct of the War.[1541]

## HOW FORREST HIMSELF CONTRIBUTED TO THE "FORT PILLOW MASSACRE" MYTH

On April 15, 1864, just three days after the fall of Fort Pillow, Forrest sent a short report concerning the battle to Confederate Lieutenant Colonel Thomas M. Jack. It read, in part:

Arrived there on the morning of the 12th and attacked the place with a portion of McCulloch's and Bell's brigades, numbering about 1,500 men, and after a sharp contest captured the garrison and all of its stores. A demand was made for the surrender, which

---

1541. ORA, Ser. 1, Vol. 32, Pt. 1, pp. 572-574.

was refused. The victory was complete, and the loss of the enemy will never be known from the fact that large numbers ran into the river and were shot and drowned. The force was composed of about 500 negroes and 200 white soldiers (Tennessee Tories). The river was dyed with the blood of the slaughtered for 200 yards. There was in the fort a large number of citizens who had fled there to escape the conscript law. Most of these ran into the river and were drowned. The approximate loss was upward of 500 killed, but few of the officers escaping.[1542]

We will recall that Forrest had left the scene of the battle as soon as the Confederate flag was raised above the fort. At the time accurate statistics were not yet available as to how many Yanks had been taken prisoner, how many had been wounded, how many had escaped, or how many had been killed.

As discussed earlier, it was later determined that only 231 of the 557 Yankee soldiers, 40 percent, were killed.[1543] Thus Forrest's assumption, that he and his men had killed nearly 72 percent (i.e., 500 out of 700) of the Union soldiers, was wildly incorrect and greatly overstated.[1544] In this unfortunate manner Forrest himself added fuel to the Northern myth that he had committed heinous war crimes at Fort Pillow.

Forrest's unlucky exaggeration was indeed later used against him by none other than Yankee General Ulysses S. Grant, who, in his *Memoirs*, gleefully repeated Forrest's sentence about the river being "dyed with the blood of the slaughtered."[1545] As the official numbers of the dead were available to Grant at the time he wrote this piece of Northern propaganda (1885), it is obvious that he was intentionally trying to sully Forrest's character.[1546] (This is the same man who Americans, largely Northerners, later voted in as their eighteenth president, and whose face they placed on the U.S. fifty-dollar bill.)

Nonetheless, Grant's ploy worked. Thanks to this single sentence in his *Memoirs*, entirely based on Forrest's own faulty statement,

---

1542. ORA, Ser. 1, Vol. 32, Pt. 1, p. 610.
1543. Henry, FWMF, p. 259.
1544. Wyeth, LGNBF, p. 362.
1545. U. S. Grant, Vol. 1, p. 138.
1546. Wyeth, LGNBF, p. 362.

the belief that a "massacre" took place at Fort Pillow has gone down in history, Yankee history at least, as objective truth. Not only is the Battle of Fort Pillow now routinely referred to as the "Fort Pillow Massacre," a number of extremely venomous, defamatory, anti-Forrest books have been published on this topic as well, further keeping the falsehood alive.

(Let us note here at least one reason why such works are impossible to take seriously: most base their conclusions partly or wholly on the outrageous, farcical, unscientific, highly biased, error-ridden publication, *Fort Pillow Massacre*, printed in the Spring of 1864 by a South-hating U.S. government. Since this work was long ago discredited by Southern historians and scholars, modern anti-Forrest works based on it must also be called into question, if not rejected altogether.)

It did not help matters that Forrest's own official report of the battle got delayed in transit and was not available for public scrutiny until four months afterward.[1547] This 120-day period helped allow ridiculous and damaging innuendo to grow into rumors, rumors into myth, myth into legend, and legend into "fact."


YANKS' PROMISE REVENGE BUT NEVER FOLLOW THROUGH

In Washington, D.C., when Lincoln heard about Forrest's "massacre," he immediately sent word to his Secretary of War, Edwin M. Stanton, to investigate "the alleged butchery of our troops." Stanton then contacted Grant in the field,[1548] passing on Lincoln's edict, which ordered physical reprisal against Forrest and his offending officers—if found guilty.[1549]

Grant bitterly denounced the affair,[1550] writing furiously to Sherman on April 15:

> CULPEPER, VA.,
> April 15, 1864—8 p. m.
> Major-General SHERMAN:
> Forrest must be driven out, but with a proper commander in West Tennessee there is force enough now. Your preparations for the coming campaign must go on, but if it is necessary to detach a

1547. Faust, s.v. "Fort Pillow, Tenn., Battle of."
1548. Foote, Vol. 3, p. 112.
1549. J. M. McPherson, BCF, p. 794.
1550. Woodward, p. 596.

portion of the troops intended for it, detach them and make your campaign with that much fewer men.

Relieve Maj. Gen. S. A. Hurlbut. I can send General Washburn, a sober and energetic officer, to take his place. I can also send you General L. C. Hunt to command District of Columbus. Shall I send Washburn? Does General Hurlbut think if he moves a part of his force after the only enemy within 200 miles of him that the post will run off with the balance of his force?

If our men have been murdered after capture, retaliation must be resorted to promptly.

U. S. GRANT, Lieutenant-General.[1551]

Grant's last sentence clearly illustrates that at the time not even the highest ranking Yankee officers believed that a massacre had taken place, or that Forrest was capable of such an act.[1552]

Most revealingly of this fact, however, is that no retaliation against Forrest ever followed, not by Lincoln, Stanton, Grant, or Sherman, or anyone else for that matter.[1553] And, as they had all well demonstrated throughout the War, these were not men to shrink from exacting retribution on those they deemed worthy.[1554]

While in the South, Lincoln's refusal to avenge Fort Pillow was rightly seen as a further sign of Forrest's innocence, in the North it was taken as just another indication of the president's white supremacist sentiments.[1555] Yet years later, in his memoirs, Sherman sided with Forrest, theorizing (correctly) that Forrest would never have led such a murderous assault as the alleged "massacre" ascribed to him, and was instead no doubt out of both eyesight and earshot at the rear. Wrote Sherman:

> . . . I am told that Forrest personally disclaims any active participation in the assault, and that he stopped the firing as soon as he could. I also take it for granted that Forrest did not lead the assault in person, and consequently that he was to the rear, out of sight if not of hearing at the time, and I was told by hundreds of our men, who were at various times prisoners in Forrest's possession,

---

1551. ORA, Ser. 1, Vol. 32, Pt. 3, p. 366.
1552. Wyeth, LGNBF, p. 382.
1553. Woodward, p. 596; J. M. McPherson, BCF, p. 794; Foote, Vol. 3, p. 112; Wyeth, LGNBF, p. 382.
1554. Henry, FWMF, p. 268.
1555. A. Ward, p. 323.

that he was usually very kind to them.[1556]

Indeed, it was the testimony of both Confederate and Union eyewitnesses on the stand before the investigative committee that proved Forrest's innocence.[1557] One from the latter category, Union Dr. Charles Fitch, said that he had always believed that Forrest never knew anything about any kind of "massacre."[1558]

Another Yankee, the aforementioned Adjutant Mack J. Leaming, agreed, testifying under oath that Forrest was nowhere in sight during the height of the alleged "massacre," and that when the General heard about uncontrolled Rebel shooting he immediately ordered a cease-fire:

> Committee: Did you observe any effort on the part of their officers to suppress the murders?
> Leaming: No, sir; I did not see any where I was first carried; just about dusk, all at once several shots were fired just outside. The cry was: 'They are shooting the darkey soldiers.' I heard an officer ride up and say: 'Stop that firing; arrest that man.' I suppose it was a rebel officer, but I do not know. It was reported to me, at the time, that several darkeys were shot then. An officer who stood by me, a prisoner, said that they had been shooting them, but that the general [Forrest] had had it stopped.[1559]

Yet another Union officer at Fort Pillow, Captain John G. Woodruff, testified that any Negroes killed at the battle "were not killed by General Forrest's orders." Rather, Forrest "stopped the massacre as soon as he was able to do so."[1560] More to the point, Confederate clergyman, David C. Kelley,

> now a minister at Columbia, Tennessee, testifies that a day or two after the fight at Fort Pillow, in a conversation with General Forrest in regard to the colored troops, the general said that he was opposed to the killing of negro troops; that it was his policy to capture all he could and return them to their owners.[1561]

1556. Sherman, Vol. 2, pp. 12-13.
1557. Wyeth, LGNBF, pp. 346-387.
1558. Wills, pp. 189-190.
1559. *Reports of Committees of the Senate of the United States*, p. 40.
1560. ORA, Ser. 1, Vol. 32, Pt. 1, p. 558.
1561. Wyeth, LGNBF, p. 390.

Despite the obvious jaundiced perspective in Fitch's, Woodruff's, and Leaming's statements, they and many others like them left the U.S. government little choice when it came to Forrest's involvement: subsequently he was cleared of all charges of wrongdoing in connection with Fort Pillow, a decree that the modern anti-Forrest movement still refuses to accept.[1562]

## TESTIMONY OF FORREST'S AID-DE-CAMP, MAJOR CHARLES W. ANDERSON

Thirty-four years after Fort Pillow, one of Forrest's officers, Major Charles W. Anderson, who was at the battle with his commander, gave the following sworn affidavit before W. H. Hindman, the Notary Public of Rutherford County, Tennessee, on February 23, 1898:

> I, Charles W. Anderson, of Florence, Rutherford County and State of Tennessee, do solemnly swear that I was at the time Captain of Cavalry and Acting Adjutant-General on the staff of General N. B. Forrest, and was the only member of the staff with him at the capture of Fort Pillow, April 12, 1864. Before the assault on the works I was temporarily placed in command of three companies of dismounted men from McCulloch's brigade, and ordered to take position on the face of the bluff just below the fort, and prevent the landing of steamers (then approaching) during truce.
>
> When Forrest's last and imperative demand for immediate surrender was refused, the general in person ordered me to 'hold my position on the bluff, prevent any escape of the garrison by water, to pour rifle-balls into the open ports of the *New Era* when she went into action, and to fight everything blue betwixt wind and water until yonder flag comes down.'
>
> When driven from the works, the garrison retreated towards the river, with guns in hand, and firing back, and as soon as in view we opened fire on them, and continued it rapidly until the Federal flag came down, when firing was stopped at once, the detachment ordered back to their regiment, and in less than two minutes after the flag came down I joined the general inside of the works.
>
> To the best of my knowledge and belief it did not exceed twenty minutes from the time our bugles sounded for the assault until the fort was in our possession and firing had ceased on every

---

1562. Morton, p. 191; Wills, pp. 187-188.

part of the ground.

I further swear that six cases of rifle ammunition were found on the face of the bluff, in the immediate rear of the fort, with tops removed and ready for immediate distribution and use; also that about two hundred and seventy-five serviceable rifles and carbines were gathered up between the water's edge and the brow of the bluff, where they had been thrown down by the garrison when they found the gunboat *New Era* had deserted them and escape impossible. As my command did the most destructive as well as the very last firing done at Fort Pillow, the testimony of certain witnesses made before a sub-committee of the United States Congress, that a massacre of the garrison took place after capture, is false, and I further swear that to the best of my knowledge and belief the heavy loss in killed and wounded during their retreat was alone due to the incapacity of their commander, the drunken condition of the men, and the fatal agreement with and promise of Captain Marshall of the *New Era* to protect and succor them when driven from the works.

Charles W. Anderson. State of Tennessee, County of Rutherford, February 23, 1898.[1563]

## CONFEDERATE REALITY

The truth about Fort Pillow is that Forrest himself never participated in any of the claimed atrocities. For one thing, he was not present at the front line (when and where these events were supposed to have taken place), and when he did reach it, he ordered his troops to pull back and cease fire. Also, in the midst of battle, when one of his horses was shot out from under him, it fell on Forrest, disabling him for several days after.[1564]

Obviously blameless, at the close of the War, both Federal eyewitnesses and the U.S. government cleared Forrest of all charges.[1565] Despite this, the Fort Pillow debacle and indictments of racism have been affixed to Forrest for fifteen decades.

In reality, Forrest was no respecter of race. He captured or killed all Yanks, whatever their skin color, with the same swift and unerring force. As we will see, he himself said:

---

1563. Wyeth, LGNBF, pp. 386-387.
1564. Forrest lost three horses at Fort Pillow, illustrating the severity of the battle. Wyeth, LGNBF, pp. 342, 606; Jordan and Pryor, p. 429.
1565. Mathes, p. 361.

> . . . I slaughter no man except in open warfare, and . . . my prisoners, both white and black, are turned over to my Government to be dealt with as it may direct.[1566]

Indeed, while forty-five of his own black servants fought in his integrated command at the Battle of Fort Pillow, the white and black Yankee soldiers inside the garrison were segregated—per Lincoln's orders. Forrest was not a racist. He was a Yankeeist.

## FORREST'S OFFICIAL FORT PILLOW REPORT

What follows is General Forrest's full official field report of the Battle of Fort Pillow.

> HEADQUARTERS FORREST'S CAVALRY DEPARTMENT,
> Jackson, Tenn., April 26, 1864.
> COLONEL: I have the honor respectfully to forward you the following report of my engagement with the enemy on the 12th instant at Fort Pillow:
> My command consisted of McCulloch's brigade, of Chalmers' division, and Bell's brigade, of Buford's division, both placed for the expedition under the command of Brig. Gen. James R. Chalmers, who, by a forced march, drove in the enemy's pickets, gained possession of the outer works, and by the time I reached the field, at 10 a. m., had forced the enemy to their main fortifications, situated on the bluff or bank of the Mississippi River at the mouth of Cold Creek. The fort is an earth-work, crescent shaped, is 8 feet in height and 4 feet across the top, surrounded by a ditch 6 feet deep and 12 feet in width, walls sloping to the ditch but perpendicular inside. It was garrisoned by 700 troops with six pieces of field artillery. A deep ravine surrounds the fort, and from the fort to the ravine the ground descends rapidly. Assuming command, I ordered General Chalmers to advance his lines and gain position on the slope, where our men would be perfectly protected from the heavy fire of artillery and musketry, as the enemy could not depress their pieces so as to rake the slopes, nor could they fire on them with small-arms except by mounting the breast-works and exposing themselves to the fire of our sharpshooters, who, under cover of stumps and logs, forced them to keep down inside the works. After several hours hard fighting the desired position was gained, not, however, without

---

1566. ORA, Ser. 1, Vol. 32, Pt. 1, p. 591.

considerable loss. Our main line was now within an average distance of 100 yards from the fort, and extended from Cold Creek, on the right, to the bluff, or bank, of the Mississippi River on the left.

During the entire morning the gun-boat kept up a continued fire in all directions, but without effect, and being confident of my ability to take the fort by assault, and desiring to prevent further loss of life, I sent, under flag of truce, a demand for the unconditional surrender of the garrison, a copy of which demand is hereto appended, marked No. 1, to which I received a reply, marked No. 2. The gun-boat had ceased firing, but the smoke of three other boats ascending the river was in view, the foremost boat apparently crowded with troops, and believing the request for an hour was to gain time for re-enforcements to arrive, and that the desire to consult the officers of the gun-boat was a pretext by which they desired improperly to communicate with her, I at once sent this reply, copy of which is numbered 3, directing Captain [W. A.] Goodman, assistant adjutant-general of Brigadier-General Chalmers, who bore the flag, to remain until he received a reply or until the expiration of the time proposed.

My dispositions had all been made, and my forces were in a position that would enable me to take the fort with less loss than to have withdrawn under fire, and it seemed to me so perfectly apparent to the garrison that such was the case, that I deemed their [capture] without further bloodshed a certainty. After some little delay, seeing a message delivered to Captain Goodman, I rode up myself to where the notes were received and delivered. The answer was handed me, written in pencil on a slip of paper, without envelope, and was, as well as I remember, in these words: "Negotiations will not attain the desired object." As the officers who were in charge of the Federal flag of truce had expressed a doubt as to my presence, and had pronounced the demand a trick, I handed them back the note saying: "I am General Forrest; go back and say to Major Booth that I demand an answer in plain, unmistakable English. Will he fight or surrender?" Returning to my original position, before the expiration of twenty minutes I received a reply, copy of which is marked No. 4.

While these negotiations were pending the steamers from below were rapidly approaching the fort. The foremost was the *Olive Branch*, whose position and movements indicated her intention to land. A few shots fired into her caused her to leave the shore and make for the opposite. One other boat passed up on the far side of the river, the third one turned back.

The time having expired, I directed Brigadier-General Chalmers to prepare for the assault. Bell's brigade occupied the right, with his extreme right resting on Coal Creek. McCulloch's brigade occupied the left, extending from the center to the river. Three companies of his left regiment were placed in an old rifle-pit on the left and almost in the rear of the fort, which had evidently been thrown up for the protection of sharpshooters or riflemen in supporting the water batteries below. On the right a portion of Barteau's regiment, of Bell's brigade, was also under the bluff and in rear of the fort. I dispatched staff officers to Colonels Bell and McCulloch, commanding brigades, to say to them that I should watch with interest the conduct of the troops; that Missourians, Mississippians, and Tennesseans surrounded the works, and I desired to see who would first scale the fort. Fearing the gun-boats and transports might attempt a landing, I directed my aide-de-camp, Capt. Charles W. Anderson, to assume command of the three companies on the left and rear of the fort and hold the position against anything that might come by land or water, but to take no part in the assault on the fort. Everything being ready, the bugle sounded the charge, which was made with a yell, and the works carried without a perceptible halt in any part of the line. As our troops mounted and poured into the fortification the enemy retreated toward the river, arms in hand and firing back, and their colors flying, no doubt expecting the gun-boat to shell us away from the bluff and protect them until they could be taken off or re-enforced. As they descended the bank an enfilading and deadly fire was poured into them by the troops under Captain Anderson, on the left, and Barteau's detachment on the right. Until this fire was opened upon them, at a distance varying from 30 to 100 yards, they were evidently ignorant of any force having gained their rear. The regiments which had stormed and carried the fort also poured a destructive fire into the rear of the retreating and now panic-stricken and almost decimated garrison. Fortunately for those of the enemy who survived this short but desperate struggle, some of our men cut the halyards, and the United States flag, floating from a tall mast in the center of the fort, came down. The forces stationed in the rear of the fort could see the flag, but were too far under the bluff to see the fort, and when the flag descended they ceased firing. But for this, so near were they to the enemy that few, if any, would have survived unhurt another volley. As it was, many rushed into the river and were drowned, and the actual loss of life will perhaps never be known, as there were quite a number of refugee citizens in the fort, many of whom were drowned and several killed in the retreat from the fort. In less than twenty minutes from the time the bugles sounded the charge, firing had ceased, and the work was done. One of the Parrott guns was turned on the gun-boat. She steamed off without replying. She had, as I afterward understood, expended all her ammunition, and was therefore powerless in affording the Federal garrison the aid and protection they doubtless expected of her when they retreated toward the river. Details were made, consisting of the captured Federals and negroes, in charge of their own officers, to collect together and bury the dead, which work continued until dark.

I also directed Captain Anderson to procure a skiff and take with him Captain Young, a captured Federal officer, and deliver to Captain Marshall, of the gun-boat, the message, copy of which is appended and numbered 5. All the boats and skiffs having been taken off by citizens escaping from the fort during the engagement, the message could not be delivered, although every effort was made to induce Captain Marshall to send his boat ashore by raising a white flag, with which Captain Young walked up and down the river in vain signaling her to come in or send out a boat. She finally moved off and disappeared around the bend above the fort. General Chalmers withdrew his forces from the fort before dark and encamped a few miles east of it.

On the morning of the 13th, I again dispatched Captain Anderson to Fort Pillow for the purpose of placing, if possible, the Federal wounded on board their transports, and report to me on his return the condition of affairs at the river. I respectfully refer you to his report, numbered 6.

My loss in the engagement was 20 killed and 60 wounded. That of the enemy unknown. Two hundred and twenty-eight were buried on the evening of the battle, and quite a number were buried the next day by details from the gun-boat fleet.

We captured 6 pieces of artillery, viz., two 10-pounder Parrott guns, two 12-pounder howitzers, and two brass 6-pounder guns, and about 350 stand of small-arms. The balance of the small-arms had been thrown in the river. All the small-arms were picked up where the enemy fell or threw them down. A few were in the fort, the balance scattered from the top of the hill to the water's edge.

We captured 164 Federals, 75 negro troops, and about 40 negro women and children, and after removing everything of value as far as able to do so, the warehouses, tents, &c., were destroyed by fire.

Among our severely wounded is Lieut. Col. Wiley M. Reed, assigned temporarily to the command of the Fifth Mississippi Regiment, who fell severely wounded while leading his regiment. When carried from the field he was supposed to be mortally wounded, but hopes are entertained of his ultimate recovery. He is a brave and gallant officer, a courteous gentleman, and a consistent Christian minister.

I cannot compliment too highly the conduct of Colonels Bell and McCulloch and the officers and men of their brigades, which composed the forces of Brigadier-General Chalmers. They fought with courage and intrepidity, and, without bayonets, assaulted and carried one of the strongest fortifications in the country.

On the 15th, at Brownsville, I received orders which rendered it necessary to send General Chalmers, in command of his own division and Bell's brigade, southward; hence I have no official report from him, but will, as soon as it can be obtained, forward a complete list of our killed and wounded, which has been ordered made out and forwarded at the earliest possible moment.

In closing my report I desire to acknowledge the prompt and energetic action of Brigadier-General Chalmers, commanding the forces around Fort Pillow. His faithful execution of all movements necessary to the successful accomplishment of the object of the expedition entitles him to special mention. He has reason to be proud of the conduct of the officers and men of his command for their gallantry and courage in assaulting and carrying the enemy's work without the assistance of artillery or bayonets.

To my staff, as heretofore, my acknowledgments are due for their prompt and faithful delivery of all orders.

I am, colonel, very respectfully, your obedient servant,

N. B. FORREST, Major- General, Commanding.

[Lieut. Col. THOMAS M. JACK, Assistant Adjutant- General.][1567]

## THE FORT PILLOW PAPERS OF GEN. LEONIDAS POLK

[First indorsement.]

AUGUST 1, 1864.

Respectfully referred to General Cooper, Adjutant and Inspector General.

These papers were found among papers of Lieutenant-General Polk and forwarded by his aide, Lieutenant Gale.

By order of President: WM. PRESTON JOHNSTON, Colonel and Aide-de-Camp.[1568]

## SEDDON'S OFFICIAL LETTER TO PRES. JEFFERSON DAVIS

James A. Seddon was a Confederate secretary of war under President Jefferson Davis, to whom this letter is addressed:

---

**1567**. ORA, Ser. 1, Vol. 32, Pt. 1, pp. 613-617.

**1568**. ORA, Ser. 1, Vol. 32, Pt. 1, p. 617.

[Second indorsement.]
AUGUST 7, 1864.
Respectfully submitted to the President, who will not be surprised to see the groundlessness of the misrepresentations so industriously circulated by our unscrupulous enemies respecting the merciless conduct of our troops on that occasion.
J. A. SEDDON, Secretary.[1569]

## PRES. DAVIS' REPLY TO SEDDON

In his reply to Seddon, President Davis praises Forrest for his behavior at Fort Pillow:

[Third indorsement.]
AUGUST 10, 1864.
SECRETARY OF WAR:
It would be well to have the report and accompanying papers published in refutation of the slanders which have been promulgated by the Government of the enemy in relation to the conduct of our gallant and humane soldiers. Instead of cruelty, General Forrest, it appears, exhibited forbearance and clemency far exceeding the usage of war under like circumstances.
JEFF'N DAVIS. [President of the Confederate States of America][1570]

## FORREST'S OFFICIAL LETTER (1) TO CONFEDERATE GEN. STEPHEN DILL LEE

General Stephen D. Lee, who served with Forrest, was a relative of General Robert E. Lee. Here is a letter Forrest sent to S. D. Lee pertaining to Fort Pillow:

ADDENDA.
HEADQUARTERS FORREST'S CAVALRY,
Tupelo, Miss., May 16, 1864.
Maj. Gen. S. D. LEE,
Demopolis, Ala.:
GENERAL: So much has been said by the Northern press in regard to the engagement at Fort Pillow that, at the suggestion of Colonel Brent and others, I have sent Judge Scruggs down for

---

1569. ORA, Ser. 1, Vol. 32, Pt. 1, p. 617.
1570. ORA, Ser. 1, Vol. 32, Pt. 1, p. 617.

the purpose of conversing with, and procuring the statements of, Captain Young and other Federal officers in regard to the matter. They are survivors of the so-called massacre, and Captain Young, who received and delivered the correspondence relative to the demand for surrender, was also with my aide-de-camp, Captain Anderson, with flag of truce on the day succeeding the capture in delivering the wounded on board the U. S. vessels. I respectfully suggest, therefore, that you furnish Judge Scruggs with such papers as will enable him to make the examination desired, as it may prove important; and inasmuch as the investigating committee appointed by the Federal President have reported, a communication to Confederate authority may be made on the subject, and it is due to my command to place at the command of the War Department all the facts in the premises.

I am, general, very respectfully &c., your obedient servant,
N. B. FORREST, Major-General. [1571]

## FORREST'S OFFICIAL LETTER (2) TO GEN. STEPHEN DILL LEE
Another letter Forrest sent to S. D. Lee concerning Fort Pillow:

HEADQUARTERS FORREST'S CAVALRY,
Tupelo, June 24, 1864.
Maj. Gen. S. D. LEE,
Commanding Department, Meridian:

GENERAL: I have the honor herewith to inclose you copy of letter addressed to Major-General Washburn; also his letter addressed to you or the commanding officer Confederate forces near Tupelo. I have not in anywise compromised you, and leave the answer to General Washburn to yourself, provided you deem it necessary or advisable to communicate with him further. I deemed it due myself and command to say what I have said to him, but did not think it proper to make any communication over your signature.

I also have the honor to inclose you statements of Captain Young, who was captured at Fort Pillow, and you can make such use of them as you may deem necessary. As my official reports are in the hands of the Department at Richmond I did not, nor do I, consider that I have any defense to make, or attempt any refutations of the charges made by General Washburn. The character and tenor of his letter is also so outrageously insulting that but for its importance to my men—not myself—I should not have replied to

---

**1571.** ORA, Ser. 1, Vol. 32, Pt. 1, pp. 617-618.

it at all.

I shall forward you tomorrow a statement of the capture of Fort Pillow, by giving you a copy of communication asked for unofficially by Colonel Brent, assistant adjutant-general, and made by my aide-de-camp, Capt. C. W. Anderson.

I have taken pains, also, in my official report made to Lieutenant-General Polk, to place all the facts in the possession of the Government in order that they might meet any demands made by Federal authority.

Should you, however, think proper to place in the hands of General Washburn the papers sent you upon this subject, you are, of course, at liberty to use them. As for myself, entirely conscious of right, I have no explanations, apologies, or disavowals to make to General Washburn nor to any one else but my Government, through my superior officers.

I am, general, very respectfully, your most obedient servant,

N. B. FORREST, Major-General.[1572]

## OFFICIAL LETTER TO FORREST FROM CONFEDERATE GEN. LEONIDAS POLK

General Polk, a cousin of U.S. President James Knox Polk, sent Forrest a letter regarding his West Tennessee campaign, which included Fort Pillow:

DEMOPOLIS, April 24, 1864.

Major-General FORREST,

Via Tupelo:

Your brilliant campaign in West Tennessee has given me great satisfaction, and entitles you to the thanks of your countrymen. Appropriate orders in writing will be transmitted you immediately. A movement of the enemy up the Yazoo [River] has made it necessary that a division of your troops should move to meet it. I have ordered the brigade with General Chalmers and another from Okolona to move promptly so as to unite and give to General Adams the support he needs. I have also ordered Morton's battery to join them.

L. POLK, Lieutenant-General.[1573]

---

1572. ORA, Ser. 1, Vol. 32, Pt. 1, p. 618.
1573. ORA, Ser. 1, Vol. 32, Pt. 1, p. 619.

## THE CONFEDERATE CONGRESS THANKS FORREST

The Rebel Congress, like General Polk and every other true Confederate, was more than pleased with Forrest's actions at Fort Pillow. In gratitude Congress gave Forrest an official thank you:

> JOINT RESOLUTION of thanks to Maj. Gen. N. B. Forrest and the officers and men of his command, for their campaign in Mississippi, West Tennessee, and Kentucky.
>
> Resolved by the Congress of the Confederate States of America, That the thanks of Congress are eminently due, and are hereby cordially tendered, to Maj. Gen. N. B. Forrest, and the officers and men of his command, for their late brilliant and successful campaign in Mississippi, West Tennessee, and Kentucky—a campaign which has conferred upon its authors fame as enduring as the records of the struggle which they have so brilliantly illustrated.
>
> Approved, May 23, 1864.[1574]

## FORREST RESPONDS TO AN ILL-NATURED YANK

Despite the obvious truth, the General received many unkind, biased, and threatening letters from Yankee officers after Fort Pillow. As mentioned above by Forrest in one of his reports, some of the more caustic missives came from Union General Cadwallader C. Washburn (later to become one of the organizers of the food production company now known as General Mills).[1575]

Forrest's replies to Washburn follow. In them he forcefully describes, and clears up, many of the mysteries surrounding the conflict at the Tennessee garrison:

> HEADQUARTERS FORREST'S CAVALRY,
> Tupelo, June 25 [23], 1864.
> Maj. Gen. C. C. WASHBURN,
> Commanding U. S. Forces, Memphis:
> GENERAL: I have the honor to acknowledge the receipt (per flag of truce) of your letter of 17th instant, addressed to Maj. Gen. S. D. Lee, or officer commanding Confederate forces near Tupelo. I

1574. ORA, Ser. 1, Vol. 32, Pt. 1, p. 619.
1575. Warner, GB, s.v. "Cadwallader Colden Washburn."

have forwarded it to General Lee with a copy of this letter.

I regard your letter as discourteous to the commanding officer of this department, and grossly insulting to myself. You seek by implied threats to intimidate him, and assume the privilege of denouncing me as a murderer and as guilty of the wholesale slaughter of the garrison at Fort Pillow, and found your assertions upon the *ex parte* testimony of your friends, the enemies of myself and country.

I shall not enter into the discussion, therefore, of any of the questions involved nor undertake any refutation of the charges made by you against myself; nevertheless, as a matter of personal privilege alone, I unhesitatingly say that they are unfounded and unwarranted by the facts. But whether these charges are true or false, they, with the question you ask as to whether negro troops when captured will be recognized and treated as prisoners of war, subject to exchange, &c., are matters which the Government of the United States and Confederate States are to decide and adjust, not their subordinate officers.

I regard captured negroes as I do other captured property and not as captured soldiers, but as to how regarded by my Government and the disposition which has been and will hereafter be made of them, I respectfully refer you through the proper channel to the authorities at Richmond. It is not the policy nor the interest of the South to destroy the negro—on the contrary, to preserve and protect him—and all who have surrendered to us have received kind and humane treatment.

Since the war began I have captured many thousand Federal prisoners, and they, including the survivors of the Fort Pillow massacre (black and white), are living witnesses of the fact that with my knowledge or consent, or by my order, not one of them has ever been insulted or in any way maltreated.

You speak of your forbearance in not giving to your negro troops instructions and orders as to the course they should pursue in regard to Confederate soldiers that might fall into their (your) hands, which clearly conveys to my mind two very distinct impressions. The first is that in not giving them instructions and orders you have left the matter entirely to the discretion of the negroes as to how they should dispose of prisoners; second, an implied threat to give such orders as will lead to "consequences too fearful for contemplation." In confirmation of the correctness of the first impression (which your language now fully develops), I refer you most respectfully to my letter from the battle-field of Tishomingo Creek and forwarded you by flag of truce on the 14th instant. As to the second impression, you seem disposed to take into your own hands the settlements which belong to, and can only be settled by, your Government, but if you are prepared to take upon yourself the responsibility of inaugurating a system of warfare contrary to civilized usages, the onus as well as the consequences will be chargeable to yourself.

Deprecating, as I should do, such a state of affairs, determined as I am not to be instrumental in bringing it about, feeling and knowing as I do that I have the approval of my Government, my people, and my own conscience, as to the past, and with the firm belief that I will be sustained by them in my future policy, it is left with you to determine what that policy shall be—whether in accordance with the laws of civilized nations or in violation of them.

I am, general, yours, very respectfully,
N. B. FORREST, Major- General.[1576]

[Inclosure No.2.]
HEADQUARTERS FORREST'S CAVALRY,
In the Field, June 23, 1864.
Maj. Gen. C. C. WASHBURN,
Commanding U. S. Forces, Memphis, Tenn.:
GENERAL: Your communication of the 19th instant is received, in which you say "you are left in doubt as to the course the Confederate Government intends to pursue hereafter in regard to colored troops."

Allow me to say that this is a subject upon which I did not and do not propose to enlighten you. It is a matter to be settled by our Governments through their proper officers, and I respectfully refer you to them for a solution of your doubts. You ask me to state whether "I contemplate either their slaughter or their return to slavery." I answer that I slaughter no man except in open warfare, and that my prisoners, both white and black, are turned over to my Government to be dealt with as it may direct. My Government is in possession of all the facts as regards my official conduct and the operations of my command since I entered the service, and if you desire a proper discussion and decision, I refer you again to the President of the Confederate States.

I would not have you understand, however, that in a matter of so much importance I am indisposed to place at your command and disposal any facts desired, when applied for in a manner becoming an officer holding your rank and position, for it is certainly desirable to every one occupying a public position to be placed right before the world, and there has been no time since the capture of Fort Pillow that I would not have furnished all the facts connected with its capture had they been applied for properly; but now the matter rests with the two Governments. I have, however, for your information, inclosed you copies of the official correspondence between the commanding officers at Fort Pillow and myself; also copies of a statement of Captain Young, the senior officer of that garrison, together with (sufficient) extracts from a report of the affair by my aide-de-camp, Capt. Charles W. Anderson, which I approve and indorse as correct.

As to the death of Major Bradford, I knew nothing of it until eight or ten days after it is said to have occurred. On the 13th (the day after the capture of Fort Pillow) I went to Jackson, and the report that I had of the affair was this: Major Bradford was with other officers sent to the headquarters of Colonel McCulloch, and all the prisoners were in charge of one of McCulloch's regiments. Bradford requested the privilege of attending the burial of his brother, which was granted, he giving his parole to return; instead of returning he changed his clothing and started for Memphis. Some of my men were hunting deserters, and came on Bradford just as he had landed on the south bank of Hatchie, and arrested him. When arrested he claimed to be a Confederate soldier belonging to Bragg's army; that he had been home on furlough, and was then on his way to join his command. As he could show no papers he was believed to be a deserter and was taken to Covington, and not until he was recognized and spoken to by citizens did the guards know that he was Bradford. He was sent by Colonel Duckworth, or taken by him, to Brownsville. All of Chalmers' command went south from Brownsville via La Grange, and as all the other prisoners had been gone some time, and there was no chance for them to catch up and place Bradford with them, he was ordered by Colonel Duckworth or General Chalmers to be sent to me at Jackson. I knew nothing of the matter until eight or ten days afterward. I heard that his body was found near Brownsville. I understand that he attempted to escape, and was shot. If he was improperly killed nothing would afford me more pleasure than to punish the perpetrators to the full extent of the law, and to show you how I regard such transactions I can refer you to my demand upon Major-General Hurlbut (no doubt upon file in your office) for the delivery to Confederate authorities of one Col. Fielding Hurst and others of his regiment, who deliberately took out and killed 7 Confederate soldiers, one of whom they left to die after cutting off his tongue, punching out his eyes, splitting his mouth on each side to his ears, and cutting off his privates.

I have mentioned and given you these facts in order that you may have no further excuse or apology for referring to these matters in connection with myself, and to evince to you my determination to do all in my power to avoid the responsibility of causing the adoption of the policy which you seem determined to press.

In your letter you acknowledge the fact that the negro troops did take an oath on bended knee to show no quarter to my men; and you say further, "you have no doubt they went to the battle-field expecting to be slaughtered," and admit also the probability of their having proclaimed on their line of march that no quarter would be shown us. Such being the case, why do you ask for the disavowal on the part of the commanding general of this department or the Government in regard to the loss of life at Tishomingo Creek? That your troops expected to be slaughtered, appears to me, after the oath they took, to be a very reasonable and natural expectation. Yet you, who sent them out, knowing and now admitting that they had sworn to such a policy, are complaining of atrocities, and demanding acknowledgments and disavowals on the part of the very men you went forth sworn to slay whenever in your power. I will in all candor and truth say to you that I had only heard these things, but did not believe them to be true; at any rate, to the extent of your admission; indeed, I did not attach to them the importance they deserved, nor did I know of the threatened vengeance, as proclaimed along their lines of march, until the contest was over. Had I and my men known it as you admit it, the battle of Tishomingo Creek would have been noted as the bloodiest battle of the war. That you sanctioned this policy is plain, for you say now "that if the negro is treated as a prisoner of war you will receive with pleasure the announcement, and will explain the fact to your colored troops at once, and desire (not order) that they recall the oath; but if they are either to be slaughtered or returned to slavery, let the oath stand."

Your rank forbids a doubt as to the fact that you and every officer and man of your department is identified with this policy and responsible for it, and I shall not permit you, notwithstanding, by your studied language in both your communications, you seek to limit the operations of your unholy scheme and visit its terrible consequences alone upon that ignorant, deluded, but unfortunate people, the negro, whose destruction you are planning in order to accomplish ours. The negroes have our sympathy, and so far as consistent with safety will spare them at the expense of those who are alone responsible for the inauguration of a worse than savage warfare.

Now, in conclusion, I demand a plain, unqualified answer to two questions, and then I have done with further correspondence with you on this subject. This matter must be settled. In battle and on the battle-field, do you intend to slaughter my men who fall into your hands? If you do not intend to do so, will they be treated as prisoners of war? I have over 2,000 of Sturgis' command prisoners, and will hold every officer and private as hostage until I receive your declarations and am satisfied that you carry out in good faith the answers you make, and until I am assured that no Confederate soldier has been foully dealt with from the day of the battle at Tishomingo Creek to this time. It is not yet too late for you to retrace your steps and arrest the storm.

Relying as I do upon that Divine Power which in wisdom disposes of all things; relying also upon the support and approval of my Government and countrymen, and the unflinching bravery and endurance of my troops, and with a consciousness that I have done nothing to produce, but all in my power consistent with honor and the personal safety of myself and command to prevent it, I leave with you the responsibility of bringing about, to use your own language, "a state of affairs too fearful for contemplation."

I am, general, very respectfully, yours, &c.,

N. B. FORREST, Major-General.[1577]

## FORT PILLOW: IN SUMMARY

In the final analysis, if Forrest had truly wanted to "massacre" every last Yankee at Fort Pillow, a mere word from him to his men would have easily accomplished this order in but a short time.[1578] Indeed, a complete capture of the garrison could have been executed by Forrest's sharpshooters alone, without any need for an assault by storm.[1579] The bold fact remains that 60 percent of the Union soldiers survived, hardly what one would call a massacre.[1580]

Actually, Forrest and his soldiers fought in a professional and reasonable manner over an eight-hour period, giving the Yanks plenty of opportunities to either fight their way out or surrender. Forrest should not be blamed because they succeeded at neither. Instead, he should be hailed as a hero for ridding the fort of its "nest" of Yankee bullies, swindlers, bandits, criminals, hustlers, thieves, rapists, sadists, psychopaths, and murderers, or what Forrest called "a motley herd of

---

1577. ORA, Ser. 1, Vol. 32, Pt. 1, pp. 591-593.
1578. Mathes, p. 227.
1579. Jordan and Pryor, p. 446.
1580. Wyeth, LGNBF, p. 367.

negroes, traitors, and Yankees."[1581]

And what about those African-American Yanks who were among the 40 percent who perished? Some estimate their individual casualty rate at about 64 percent.[1582] Why so high compared to the whites?

Careful research proves that they were certainly not the victims of systemized racial butchery inside the fort, as South-haters wildly claim. The reality is that most of them died during the fighting that took place *outside* the fort, under the bluffs and in the surrounding waters. Also, many, being drunk and feeling quite invincible, refused to surrender. These men were shot down in isolated events during the first morning wave of Confederate assaults on the fort, finally perishing near or in the river. Had Forrest and his men been acting out of racial animosity, as Northern myth claims, every single black Union soldier would have died.[1583] Considering the number who survived under the complex conditions at Fort Pillow on April 12, 1864, it would be more accurate to say that the Rebels went out of their way *not* to massacre African-Americans that day.

The Federal investigative committee that later tried to indict Forrest for "war crimes" at the fort had few scruples and a clear anti-Forrest agenda, and was no doubt intended to aid Lincoln's anti-South propaganda efforts.[1584] Naturally it failed in its goal, for it had rested its case on "extravagant," highly dubious, contradictory, inconsistent, obviously erroneous, even inadmissible "evidence"[1585]—much of it hearsay and gross exaggeration,[1586] and most of it collected long after the event occurred;[1587] the "written" testimony of illiterate soldiers; and "eyewitnesses" who were nowhere near the fort during the battle. Indeed, the entire charade was based on the charge that a "slaughter" had occurred "after surrender," a surrender itself that never took place.[1588]

Among the interviews procured during the investigation was one between the Yankee committee members and a black man named Jacob

1581. Wyeth, LGNBF, p. 427.
1582. Browning, p. 56.
1583. Browning, pp. 56-58.
1584. Sheppard, p. 171.
1585. Mathes, pp. 229-231.
1586. Cornish, p. 173.
1587. Sheppard, p. 172.
1588. Lytle, p. 280.

Thomas:

> Committee: Did you see any rebel officers about there when this
> [the "massacre"] was going on?
> Thompson: Yes, sir; old Forrest was one.
> Committee: Did you know Forrest?
> Thompson: Yes, sir; he was a little bit of a man. I had seen him
> before at Jackson.
> Committee: Are you sure he was there when this was going on?
> Thompson: Yes, sir.[1589]

Referring to the enormously powerful, muscularly intimidating, 6 foot, 2 inch Forrest as "a little bit of a man" must have garnered a chuckle, even from the Union committee members! It was, in part, obvious fictitious "testimonies" such as this that finally discredited the groups' investigation.

Additionally, it will be remembered, Forrest, atypically in this case, did not lead the charge at Fort Pillow. Having been injured from a falling horse, he was 400 yards to the rear for much of the conflict, and left the scene of the battle as soon as it was over, long before nightfall. So it would have been virtually impossible for Jacob Thomas, or anyone else, to have seen Forrest anywhere near the fort.

It was more than obvious, even to many Northerners at the time, that the charges against Forrest were absurd, false, and villainous.[1590] Despite leading questions, ignorant "eyewitnesses," and a fully biased court, eventually honest and trustworthy soldiers (from both sides) who were actually at the scene attested to Forrest's innocence, and the U.S. government took him off their list of suspects.[1591] For in the end, not one of the five charges of the committee's report could withstand a detailed examination of the facts.[1592]

For the benefit of history, two of the Yankees who attested to Forrest's innocence deserve special mention. Not surprisingly, both were African-Americans.

---

1589. *Reports of Committees of the Senate of the United States*, p. 30.
1590. See e.g., Wyeth, LGNBF, pp. 346-387.
1591. Jordan and Pryor, pp. 452-453. See also the *Memphis Commercial Appeal*, May 30, 1901; May 17, 1905; May 7, 1988.
1592. Henry, FWMF, p. 260.

The first, a black Union private named Ellis Falls, said that without a doubt Forrest had commanded his men to "stop fighting" when it seemed things were about to get out of control.[1593]  The second, a black Union private named Major Williams, heard a Confederate yell out during the battle that Forrest did *not* want any blacks killed; that they were to be captured and returned to their owners.[1594]

As is typical of Northern myth, Forrest, the inevitable Southern scapegoat, takes the blame for everything that happened at Fort Pillow. But what about the Yanks?  Are none of them to be held accountable? Either Booth or Bradford could have surrendered.  Indeed, under the circumstances (an indefensible fort against an overpowering enemy), they should have.  They had nothing to fear as Forrest had promised to treat all those captured, both white and black, as prisoners of war.[1595]

Confederate Captain W. A. Goodman, who served under General Chalmers, and who was the purveyor of several notes that passed between Forrest and the Yanks at Fort Pillow, later recalled:

> I have no copy . . . of any of the correspondence that ensued, before me, but I am satisfied that my recollection of the substance of the different notes is correct; and I remember the proposition in the first to treat the garrison as prisoners of war, provided they were surrendered, the more clearly because, when the note was handed to me, there was some discussion about it among the officers present, and it was asked whether it was intended to include the negro soldiers as well as the white; to which both General Forrest and General Chalmers replied, that it was so intended; and that if the fort was surrendered, the whole garrison, white and black, should be treated as prisoners of war.  No doubt as to the meaning and scope of this proposition was ever expressed or intimated in any of the notes and conversations which followed it under the flag of truce.[1596]

We must also consider that Bradford allowed his men to drink, become inebriated, and harass and mock the Confederates.  Completely mismanaging his command, he disregarded Forrest's promise to treat

---

1593. *Reports of Committees of the Senate of the United States*, p. 15.
1594. *Reports of Committees of the Senate of the United States*, p. 27.
1595. ORA, Ser. 1, Vol. 32, Pt. 1, p. 596; Jordan and Pryor, p. 431.
1596. Jordan and Pryor, p. 431.

both whites and blacks as prisoners of war, delayed the inevitable surrender, ignored a flag of truce, neglected to wave off approaching Union gunboats, then failed to raise a signal flag that would have told the steamers that a truce was under discussion—a "perfect storm" of factors that could only lead to one thing: the disaster that followed.[1597]

And what about the Union president? Does he not bear some of the responsibility for the deaths of the black Yankees at Fort Pillow? As even Northern abolitionists complained at the time, Lincoln treated black Union soldiers with obvious contempt and racial prejudice, not only referring to them as an inferior race[1598] (using the "n" word)[1599] and segregating them, but also refusing to grant them the protection of citizenship or the right to vote. Why should the soldiers in Forrest's command have been expected to treat them any better?[1600]

Former black servant and sagacious abolitionist, author, and orator, Frederick Douglass, was horrified by the white racism he saw in Lincoln's armies. Searching for the cause, he eventually had to concede that as a fish rots from the head down, the trouble lay with white racist, white supremacist, white separatist, Lincoln himself—the same man who, as we have seen, said: "What I would most desire would be the separation of the white and black races."[1601] Why should Negroes enlist when the U.S. military and you, its commander-in-chief, are so prejudiced against them?, Douglass asked the Yankee president rhetorically.[1602]

While Yankee and New South historians delight in regaling their readers with the fairy tale of the "Fort Pillow Massacre," they conveniently gloss over authentic incidents in which black Union soldiers massacred white Confederate soldiers. One of the more notable of these

1597. See Browning, p. 58.

1598. See e.g., Nicolay and Hay, ALCW, Vol. 1, pp. 289, 370, 457, 458, 469, 539; Basler, ALSW, pp. 400, 402, 403-404; Stern, pp. 492-493; Holzer, pp. 189, 251.

1599. See e.g., Nicolay and Hay, CWAL, Vol. 11, pp. 105-106; Nicolay and Hay, ALCW, Vol. 1, p. 483; Holzer, pp. 22-23, 67, 318, 361.

1600. See e.g., Barrow, Segars, and Rosenburg, BC, p. 4; Mullen, p. 31; L. Johnson, p. 134; *Charlotte Daily Bulletin*, November 13, 1862; *The Liberator*, May 22, 1863; Leech, p. 312; Current, TC, s.v. "African Americans in the Confederacy"; Quarles, pp. 64, 204-205; Faust, s.v. "black soldiers"; Simmons, s.v. "Negro troops"; Page Smith, p. 308; C. Adams, p. 134; Henderson, Vol. 2, p. 411; Cartmell, pp. 144, 145; Alotta, pp. 26-28.

1601. Seabrook, TUAL, p. 91.

1602. *Douglass' Monthly*, March 1863, Vol. 5, p. 802.

occurred at Fort Blakely, Alabama, where, without orders, black Federal troops charged a Rebel stronghold and mercilessly slaughtered surrendering white soldiers. The white Yankee officers in command had little sympathy for their white counterparts from the South, noting the fact that even though the Rebs had tried to surrender, nothing could have saved them from being cut down and slaughtered by "our niggers." Even black leaders, such as Chaplain Henry M. Turner, were horrified by such wanton mass murders.[1603]

## THE SOUTH RESTS HER CASE

In all actuality, Fort Pillow embodies one of the true and great ironies of the "Civil War": while Forrest's name has long been associated with racism and violent atrocities at the battle, it has been repeatedly proven that he and his men were completely innocent of any and all such charges. This is why Forrest could publically state, with a clear conscience, that "I have no explanations, apologies, or disavowals to make . . ." Yet, the Yankee soldiers at Fort Pillow, who committed assaults, burglary, rape, and even murder upon the local citizenry over a period of many months, are held up as paragons of virtue and the "innocent victims of Southern brutality." And they call Southern history a "lie"!

In his letter to President Andrew Johnson after the War, Forrest voiced his final thoughts on the entire matter. As a Confederate soldier and officer, he wrote, I feel completely justified concerning the attack on Fort Pillow. Rational individuals will never be taken in by the leading questions and thoroughly inculcated "witnesses" called forth by the U.S. committee assigned to investigate the battle, Forrest went on to note.[1604]

Millions of Southerners understood and agreed. One of them, William Witherspoon,[1605] one of Forrest's cavalrymen, spoke for many when he wrote in 1910 that the Yankee version of what occurred at Fort Pillow is nothing remotely similar to what actually took place. We Southerners have already expressed more than enough regret,

---

1603. Hurst, pp. 382, 414.
1604. Davison and Foxx, p. 424.
1605. Witherspoon is a relation of my cousin, Louisiana native and Oscar-winning actress Reese Witherspoon. One of Reese's ancestors, Scotsman John Witherspoon, was a signatory of the Declaration of Independence, a document that was near and dear to traditional Southerners like Forrest.

Witherspoon declared, and the truth is that no apology is needed—not now or in the future.[1606]

In 1868, echoing Witherspoon, Jordan and Pryor wrote:

> We submit to the candid and those who are capable of accepting the truth that, in what occurred after the Confederates stormed the trenches, there was neither cruel purpose nor cruel negligence of duty, neither intention nor inadvertence, on the part of General Forrest, whose course, therefore, stands utterly devoid of the essence of rage or wrong.[1607]

In 1866 one of the South's greatest champions, Edward A. Pollard, offered his summary of the battle:

> In the capture of Fort Pillow the list of casualties embraced five hundred out of a garrison of seven hundred; and the enemy entitled the affair "The Fort Pillow Massacre," and Northern newspapers and Congressional committees circulated absurd stories about negro troops being buried alive. The explanation of the unusual proportion of carnage is simple. After the Confederates got into the fort, the Federal flag was not hauled down; there was no surrender; relying upon his gunboats in the river, the enemy evidently expected to annihilate Forrest's forces after they had entered the works; and so the fighting went on to the last extremity. Some of the negro troops, in their cowardice, feigned death, falling to the ground, and were either pricked up by the bayonet, or rolled into the trenches to excite their alarm—to which circumstance is reduced the whole story of "burying negroes alive." Forrest was a hard fighter; he had an immense brain; but he knew but little about grammar and dictionaries. In describing the alarm and bewilderment in Fort Pillow to a superiour officer—who, by the way, has frequently expressed the opinion that Forrest, notwithstanding his defects in literary education, stood second only to Stonewall Jackson as the most remarkable man of the war,—Forrest said: "General, the damned Yankees kept firing horizontally right up into the air."[1608]

An Atlanta newspaper also defended Forrest's actions at Fort

---

1606. Henry, ATSF, p. 125.
1607. Jordan and Pryor, p. 453.
1608. Pollard, LC, p. 499.

Pillow, stating that the General's wartime bravery, which was manifestly apparent on countless bloody fields, will certainly and eventually persuade the world that such a man completely lacks the ability to commit the crimes and atrocities for which he has been unfairly charged.[1609]

In a word, there is not a single shred of incontestable evidence that Forrest was guilty of anything at Fort Pillow,[1610] as even the most scurrilous anti-Forrest supporters must now admit. Yet, since his exact role will never be fully known,[1611] he will forever remain a target of South-haters who feel free to fill in the missing pages with whatever slur, lie, or fable they choose to invent.

All the anti-Forrest vitriol in the world, however, does not make the General guilty. If anything, it only further proves his innocence. As John Allan Wyeth remarked in 1899, the story of the so-called "Fort Pillow massacre"

> was deftly woven out of the exaggerated testimony of two or three of the officers and some of the negroes and whites who were of the garrison, much of which testimony was so self-contradicting as to prove its falsity, and all of which was *ex parte* and inadequate in establishing the trumped-up charges of a violation of the rules governing civilized warfare.
>
> Forrest had become a man of great importance in the mighty struggle the South was making. The opportunity which now presented itself to injure his reputation and blacken his character and that of his men was not to be lost.[1612]

---

1609. Sachsman, Rushing, and Morris, p. 325; Davison and Foxx, p. 424.
1610. Cimprich, p. 83.
1611. Bedwell, p. 66.
1612. Wyeth, LGNBF, p. 371.

# - 1864 -
# SPRING HILL, FRANKLIN II, & NASHVILLE

*"General Hood, if you'll give me one strong division of infantry with my cavalry, I'll agree to flank the Federals from their works within two hours." — Nathan Bedford Forrest, prior to the disastrous Battle of Franklin II*

## A BRILLIANT & MOVING SPEECH

ON JUNE 28, 1864, FORREST gave a stirring address to his men, which included these memorable words:

Soldiers! You have done much, but there is still work for you to do. By prompt obedience to orders and patient endurance you will be enabled to repeat these great achievements. The enemy is again preparing to break through the living wall erected by your noble bosoms and big hearts. In the name and recollection of ruined homes, desolated fields and the bleaching bones of your martyred comrades, you are appealed to again. The smoke of your burning homesteads, the screams of your insulted women, and the cries of starving children will again nerve your strong arms with strength. Your fathers of '76 had much to fight for, but how little and unimportant was their cause compared with yours. They fought not against annihilation, but simply to be independent of a foreign, yet a constitutional and free, government. You are struggling against the most odious of all tyranny, for existence itself, for your property, your homes, your wives, and children, against your own enslavement, against emancipation, confiscation, and subjugation, with all their attendant horrors.[1613]

## FORREST PLEADS FOR A FURLOUGH

After Fort Pillow Forrest went onto fight in a number of other important battles, including Memphis, August 21, 1864, and, as mentioned, Johnsonville, November 4-5, 1864, awing soldiers on both sides whenever he appeared on the battlefield. His very real threat to whip and even shoot cowards (before firing squads) helped maintain strength and order in the Confederate ranks.[1614]

On October 8, 1864, from Cherokee, Alabama, a by now exhausted Forrest sent the following request to his superior General Richard Taylor (son of President Zachary Taylor and President Davis' former brother-in-law):

> HEADQUARTERS FORREST'S CAVALRY,
> Cherokee, October 8, 1864
> Lieut. Gen. R. TAYLOR,
> GENERAL: I have been constantly in the field since 1861, and have spent half the entire time in the saddle. I have never asked for a furlough for over ten days in which to rest and recruit, and except when wounded and unable to leave my bed have had no respite from duty. My strength is failing and it is absolutely necessary that I should have some rest. I left a large estate [Green Grove, at Sunflower Landing] in Mississippi and have never given my private affairs a day's attention at any one time since the war began. . . . I respectfully ask that my two divisions be placed as they originally were under the command of Brigadier-Generals Chalmers and Buford, and that Mabry's brigade be substituted for McCulloch's, which change would in my opinion be satisfactory to all parties. I have captured since I came into this department over 30 pieces of

---

1613. ORA, Ser. 1, Vol. 39, Pt. 1, p. 230. In this speech Forrest speaks out "against emancipation." As this statement is often used to "prove" that Forrest was pro-slavery, let us examine it. Like nearly all Southerners, Forrest was not against emancipation itself. He was against being told when and how to emancipate. The North had allowed itself decades to gradually and peacefully eliminate slavery from its own region—*after* it became unprofitable. All that Forrest and the rest of Dixie asked was that they be allowed the same privilege. Left-wing liberal Lincoln, however, found that pushing Southern emancipation through quickly, and at the tip of a gun barrel, better suited his true agenda: to destroy the idea of states' rights, ship all African-Americans "back to their native land," and install big government in Washington, D.C. The truth of the matter is, as we discuss throughout this book, Forrest did believe in emancipation, which is why he freed many of his slaves *before* the War, the rest *during* the War.

1614. Henry, ATSF, p. 120. During the War for Southern Independence Forrest was definitively known to have shot down and killed a number of Confederate soldiers who fled the battlefield in fear. See e.g., Wyeth, LGNBF, pp. 173, 552.

artillery, fitting up my command with four batteries (in all sixteen guns). They are now scattered, and I desire if possible to get all my command together, and with General Chalmers as senior officer feel that it would be safe to leave the command for a short time, which in my present state of health is absolutely necessary and which you will confer a favor on me by granting as early as consistent with the good of the service.

I am, general, very respectfully, your obedient servant,

N. B. FORREST, Major-General.[1615]

The General was listening to his intuition, which was pleading for rest and relaxation, an attempt by the body to recuperate its spent forces and strengthen its immune system. If only the Confederate brass had listened to his plea as well, for it was at this moment that Forrest's life span hung in the balance: a furlough would lengthen it; a denial would shorten it.

Sadly, and tragically as we will see, Forrest's request was briefly considered, but finally denied.[1616]  Not because it was not taken seriously, but because the Confederacy could simply not afford to operate one day without him, as the following telegraphed message from Sherman to Grant illustrates.

ENEMIES & FRIENDS

Dated October 9, 1864—the day after Forrest sent his letter to Taylor—we find a desperate Sherman finally giving up any hope of keeping his Atlanta-to-Nashville communications open. The culprit? Primarily "that Devil Forrest":

> It will be a physical impossibility to protect the roads, now that Hood, Forrest, and Wheeler, and the whole batch of devils, are turned loose without home or habitation.[1617]

About this time, on November 12, 1864, having by then heard about the reelection of the treasonous, *and* treacherous, liberal Lincoln to a second term (on November 8), Forrest took a few moments to send

---

1615. ORA, Ser. 1, Vol. 39, Pt. 3, p. 807.
1616. Wyeth, LGNBF, p. 516.
1617. ORA, Ser. 1, Vol. 39, Pt. 3, p. 162.

a thank-you note to General Richard Taylor, one of the few Confederate officers the Tennessean actually looked up to and respected. As Wyeth points out, the missive reveals both the deeply personal relationship the two had forged and Forrest's undying devotion to the Confederate Cause:

HEADQUARTERS FORREST'S CAVALRY,
Corinth, November 12, 1864.
Lieut. Gen. R. TAYLOR:
GENERAL: In a few days I will forward you a report of my recent operations on the Tennessee River, together with a report of my expedition to Memphis. These two documents will, I presume, for the present terminate my official connection with you, an event which I deeply deplore. Our intercourse has not been of long duration, but to me it has been most pleasant and agreeable, certainly of such a character as to render our separation a source of regret, but duty calls me elsewhere. I go to share in the toils and, I trust, in the victories of other fields, but in leaving you I shall carry with me a sincere friendship made so by your kindness and official courtesy. I congratulate you on leaving that so much of the territory under your jurisdiction has been rescued from the grasp of the invader. Twelve months ago I entered your department and found the people groaning under the most cruel and merciless oppression. They were despondent and traitors exultant. I leave the department in security and the people hopeful. The unprincipled, uncivilized, and destroying foe has been driven to other fields where the strong arms of patriots are still striving to chastise his atrocities. I know not how long we are to labor for that independence for which we have thus far struggled in vain, but this I do know that I will never weary in defending our cause, which must ultimately triumph. Faith is the duty of the hour. We will succeed. We have only to "work and wait." Be assured, my dear general, that wherever I may go, I shall deeply sympathize in all that concerns your interest and always exult in your success.
With great respect, I am, general, your friend and obedient servant,
N. B. FORREST, Major-General.[1618]

---

1618. ORA, Ser. 1, Vol. 39, Pt. 3, p. 915.

## THE BATTLE OF SPRING HILL: THE FIRST OF A STRING OF CATASTROPHES

In late November 1864 the warrior-celebrity was at the Battle of Spring Hill with the ever controversial John Bell Hood, chief commander of the Army of Tennessee. Forrest had already butted heads with Hood, who had suffered a number of serious war wounds by then: with one leg gone and a paralyzed arm in a sling, the old-fashioned officer had to be lifted and strapped into his saddle.[1619]

It was here, at Spring Hill, Tennessee, on the 29th that Hood allowed some 25,000 Union soldiers to slip past his Confederate forces in the dead of night.[1620] A glaring and tragic military blunder by any definition, it gave the Yanks a full day's head start on the Rebels, allowing them to thoroughly entrench themselves in downtown Franklin the next day without interference.[1621] In that space of time they had made the town essentially invulnerable.[1622]

It is impossible to overstate the consequences that this one mistake cost the South. Wyeth calls it a "failure to take advantage of one of the most brilliant opportunities ever offered a commanding officer."[1623] Had Hood posted guards that night, the 29th, the ill-fated Battle of Franklin II could have been avoided the following day. Thousands of lives would have been spared (on both sides). Nashville would have been recaptured by the Confederates two weeks later, and Hood's Tennessee campaign would have been a success. Instead, Hood's oversight at Spring Hill literally promised to destroy the Confederacy. And it did.

The next morning Hood called a breakfast meeting at Nathaniel F. Cheairs House (now known as Rippavilla Plantation) and, as usual, blamed his subordinates for the debacle.[1624] Forrest, understandably, was outraged and stormed out of the house, with Hood close behind.

---

1619. Hood lost the use of his left arm when it was severely injured at the Battle of Gettysburg, July 2, 1863. At the Battle of Chickamauga, September 18, 1863, Hood's right leg was destroyed by enemy fire and had to be amputated. This, Hood's second major wound during the War, was so serious it was assumed that he would die, and his severed leg was sent with him for burial. Hood, however, survived, much to the detriment, according to many, of the Confederacy.

1620. McDonough and Connelly, pp. 48-55.

1621. Mathes, pp. 310-311.

1622. Sheppard, p. 250.

1623. Wyeth, LGNBF, p. 542.

1624. Logsdon, TATG, pp. 65-66; McDonough and Connelly, pp. 53-55; Brandt, pp. 194-195.

On the front porch Forrest turned to his handicapped superior and growled: "Sir, if you were a whole man I'd whip you to within an inch of yer life!"

## DISASTER AT THE BATTLE OF FRANKLIN II

That day, November 30, Forrest rode a new horse with his men northward up Columbia Pike into Franklin, where he stood on the upper porch at Carnton Mansion to survey the battlefield.[1625]

At Winstead Hill, Hood's observation post, he again quarreled with his superior. This time it was about the Kentuckian's suicidal plan of attack, which would send some 25,000 Confederate soldiers unprotected across a "gentle plateau" called the Plain of Franklin, in full view of a well-entrenched, well-fed, well-rested enemy.[1626] Forrest, like most of the other generals present, preferred a flanking maneuver.[1627] The open flat field, several miles square, had quickly been dubbed the "Valley of Death" by Hood's pessimistic officers.

Hood's soldiers certainly expected the worst. In preparation for their seemingly inevitable funerals, they dressed in their best uniforms and gave their jewelry, watches, photographs, letters, and other valuables to army chaplain James M'Neilly, to be sent home to their families after the battle.[1628]

The hard-headed Hood ignored Forrest's protestations, as well as the more prudent attack strategies of another of the Army of Tennessee's brilliant cavalrymen, "Stonewall of the West," the Irish General Patrick Ronayne Cleburne (1828-1864). Cleburne had suggested moving forward in life-saving columns rather than in death-defying rows. Disgusted with Hood, the Celtic officer turned toward the battlefield and said, "if we are to die, let us die like men."[1629] Cleburne's words could not have been more prophetic.

For his insubordination, some say, an angry Hood sent Cleburne and his men onto the battlefield where the heaviest fighting promised to

1625. Bradley, pp. 212-213. Carnton Mansion (part of Carnton Plantation), built in the early 1800s by my cousins the McGavocks, has its own detailed and incredible Confederate history, which I discuss at length in my books, *The McGavocks of Carnton Plantation: A Southern History*, and *Carnton Plantation Ghost Stories*.
1626. Jordan and Pryor, p. 625.
1627. Wyeth, LGNBF, p. 544.
1628. McDonough and Connelly, p. 156.
1629. Website: www.cleburnes-division.com/CleburneBio.aspx.

take place. This would prove to be a momentous decision for both men. Forrest, no doubt, would have been sent into the same area except that he was placed with half his cavalry to the far right (east), and was thus possibly spared the fate of Cleburne.

Yet, as Yankee General James H. Wilson later noted, dividing Forrest's cavalry into two flanks turned out to be one of Hood's greatest blunders of many that he made on November 30.[1630] It was at Franklin II, Wilson wrote, that

> Hood made a fatal mistake, for it will be observed that he had detached Forrest, with two divisions of his corps, on a side operation, which left him only Chalmers's division to co-operate with the main attack of his infantry [on the western side of the battle]. Had his whole cavalry force advanced against me, it is possible that it would have succeeded in driving us back.[1631]

Without waiting for his artillery to show up (it was still en route from Spring Hill), Hood launched his insane attack against Union General John M. Schofield (1831-1906).[1632] That day, in "five tragic hours," as the 2nd Battle of Franklin has been called, the South lost nearly 2,000 lives, including Cleburne himself and five other generals. Adding to the toll were five wounded generals and one captured,[1633] along with the injury or death of fifty-six regimental commanders.[1634]

In all, the Army of Tennessee wasted some 7,000 of the South's finest (nearly one-fifth of its forces) at Franklin II alone: officially these included 1,750 dead, 4,500 wounded, and 702 taken prisoner,[1635] though some modern Southern historians think these numbers were probably much higher, for these figures do not include those missing in action (many of whom later died), or those only slightly wounded and

1630. Lytle, pp. 359-360.
1631. Wyeth, LGNBF, p. 546; Morton, p. 274.
1632. Lytle, p. 360.
1633. Browning, p. 86.
1634. Debate still rages as to how many of Hood's dead generals were brought to Carnton after the Battle of Franklin II. Theories range from four to six. The six are: Patrick Ronayne Cleburne, States Rights Gist, John Adams, Otho Strahl, Hiram Bronson Granbury, and John Carpenter Carter. Recent research, however, has determined that only four were laid on Carnton's back porch: Cleburne, Adams, Strahl, and Granbury. Seabrook, TMCP, p. 155.
1635. McDonough and Connelly, p. 157.

thus still able to fight and march.[1636] (By comparison the Yanks' losses were "comparatively light":[1637] 189 killed, 1,030 wounded, and 1,104 missing.)[1638]

The Battle of Franklin II, sometimes known as the "Gettysburg of the West," turned out to be the final resting place of the Army of Tennessee, wrote one survivor years later.[1639] Here, as Lytle expressed it, Hood destroyed his own army,[1640] handicapping the Confederacy across the entire Western theater, nearly destroying its heart and soul. Or as Wyeth put it, 2nd Franklin "had broke the spirit of this army."[1641]

Forrest survived, but the South never recovered from the terrible blow. Rebel Private Sam Watkins, who was on the battlefield that day, called it

> the blackest page in the history of the war . . . the finishing stroke to the independence of the Southern Confederacy. . . . Would to God that I had never witnessed such a scene![1642]

Forrest himself sent a note to a Laura Galloway (the daughter of friends William Galloway and Amanda Johnson of Columbia, Tennessee), concerning Franklin II. It read (in the General's usual spelling):

> My compliments to Miss Laura—hoping she may never have to morn over another defete of the Confederate Army.[1643]

## THE BATTLE OF NASHVILLE: DEATH OF THE CONFEDERACY IN THE WESTERN THEATER

Hood would go on to make a number of other spectactularly poor decisions—sealing the Confederacy's fate—including again detaching

---

1636. Thomas Cartwright, personal interview.
1637. Jordan and Pryor, p. 629.
1638. Hansen, p. 566. Confederate historians think these numbers are too small, as well, for in fact the Federals actually had no idea how many of their men perished at Franklin II. Why? Because they struck out for Nashville the night of the battle, November 30, 1864, leaving their dead and wounded on the field. Thomas Cartwright, personal interview.
1639. Sword, CLH, p. 266.
1640. Lytle, p. 359.
1641. Wyeth, LGNBF, p. 561.
1642. Watkins, pp. 208-209.
1643. From Laura Galloway's Autograph Book, courtesy Elizabeth Scott-Whipkey.

Forrest (this time to Murfreesboro)[1644] on December 5, 1864.[1645] If there was one time in Hood's entire career when he should not have sent Forrest away, this was it.[1646] But detach Forrest he did, along with more than half of the army's cavalry,[1647] while he rode on to Nashville without his most aggressive, successful, and sharp-witted officer.[1648] Outnumbered three to one, the outcome against Yankee General George H. "the Rock of Chickamauga" Thomas was predestined from the beginning.

In his book, *The Decisive Battle of Nashville*, Stanley F. Horn calls the conflict a calamitous blunder, noting that it was here, in Music City, December 15-16, 1864, that the fate of the Confederacy was ordained.[1649] While there are numerous reasons for the South's loss at Nashville, certainly one, if not the greatest, of these was sending Forrest thirty-four miles away to Murfreesboro.

## HOOD'S RETREAT

Despite Hood's egregious oversight, Forrest managed to save his superior one last time.

Two weeks after Nashville—where Hood wasted hundreds more of his men—Forrest met up with him one last time, at Columbia, Tennessee.[1650] Here, beginning December 18,[1651] though most of his infantrymen were now barefoot,[1652] he rescued what was left of Hood's dilapidated forces from complete annihilation by protecting the army's rear from attack as it was chased from Nashville all the way to Tupelo, Mississippi.[1653] (This route through Middle Tennessee—the War's last Confederate retreat out of the Volunteer State[1654]—is marked with historical signs today entitled "Hood's Retreat.")[1655]

---

1644. Jordan and Pryor, p. 631.
1645. J. Davis, Vol. 2, p.577; Sheppard, pp. 251-252; Wyeth, LGNBF, p. 548.
1646. Lytle, p. 360.
1647. Sheppard, p. 254.
1648. Mathes, p. 315; Morton, p. 280.
1649. Horn, DBN, p. 166.
1650. Morton, pp. 285, 289.
1651. Jordan and Pryor, p. 645; Morton, p. 290.
1652. Browning, p. 88.
1653. J. Davis, Vol. 2, p. 579; J. M. McPherson, ACW, p. 196.
1654. Mathes, p. 322.
1655. For a full description of Hood's Retreat, see Jordan and Pryor, pp. 639-654.

On January 20, 1865, in his official report, Hood's Nashville nemesis, General Thomas, wrote from Eastport, Mississippi, about Forrest's rearguard service:

> Notwithstanding the many delays to which the command had been subjected, I determined to continue the pursuit of Hood's shattered forces; and for this purpose decided to use General Wilson's cavalry and General Wood's corps of infantry, directing the infantry to move on the pike, whilst the cavalry marched on its either flank across time fields; the remainder of the command, Smith's and Schofield's corps, to move along more leisurely, and to be used as the occasion demanded.
>
> Forrest and his cavalry, and such other detachments as had been sent off from his main army whilst besieging Nashville, had rejoined Hood at Columbia. He had formed a powerful rear guard, made up of detachments from all his organized force, numbering about 4,000 infantry, under General Walthall, and all his available cavalry, under Forrest. With the exception of his rear guard, his [Hood's] army had become a disheartened and disorganized rabble of half-armed and barefooted men, who sought every opportunity to fall out by the wayside and desert their cause to put an end to their sufferings. The rear guard, however, was undaunted and firm, and did its work bravely to the last. [1656]

On December 27 Hood personally acknowledged Forrest as the savior of his army.[1657] Likewise, an article in *Harper's Weekly*, dated May 7, 1864, credited Forrest with "saving General Hood's army from utter destruction." On February 28, 1865, the plucky Confederate officer's impressive tactics earned him another promotion, this time to lieutenant general. At the time of this promotion Forrest was the commander of 10,000 men in three states.[1658]

How different things might have been had Hood not detached Forrest to Murfreesboro, as even the Yanks at Nashville admitted. Wrote Wilson:

> The fortunate absence of Forrest, with a large part of his cavalry, relived the operations of the Federal cavalry from the great peril it

---

1656. ORA, Ser. 1, Vol. 45, Pt. 1, p. 42.
1657. Mathes, p. 330; Wyeth, LGNBF, p. 573.
1658. Browning, p. 90.

would have otherwise incurred.[1659]

Indeed, Spring Hill, Franklin II, and finally Nashville marked the death knell of the Confederate cause in the Western theater.[1660] Forrest, however, believed that Nashville in particular marked the end of the War itself.[1661]

But the Yankees did not get off without loss or injury; not with Forrest in the mix. In their summary of Hood's Tennessee Campaign, Jordan and Pryor write:

> General Forrest completed his passage to the north bank of the Tennessee [River], on the 18th day of November, with not more than 3000 men, and was then placed in chief command of the Confederate cavalry with Hood's army, which, with [William H.] Jackson's Division, numbered 5500 effectives, officers and men. The campaign, with its eventful disasters, lasted 35 days, during which Forrest's Cavalry were incessantly in sharp conflict with the enemy, at a season of singular inclemency. With this force he captured and destroyed 16 block-houses, 20 considerable railroad bridges, more than 30 miles of railroad, of immediate vital importance to the communications of the enemy, 4 locomotives, at least 100 cars, and 100 wagons. He captured as many as 1800 of the enemy, 100,000 rounds of ammunition, 200,000 rations, and 9 pieces of artillery; and brought away 3 pieces of artillery and 10 wagons and teams more than he had carried in, besides many horses, while the aggregate of the killed and wounded of the enemy may be set down at 2000.[1662]

## FORREST'S OFFICIAL REPORTS ON SPRING HILL, FRANKLIN II, MURFREESBORO II, & NASHVILLE

As the dust was still settling over the Nashville fiasco, Forrest wrote out his official reports on the three battles that would alter both Southern and American history.

> Report of Maj. Gen. Nathan B. Forrest, C. S. Army, commanding cavalry, of operations November 16, 1864—January 23, 1865.

1659. Wyeth, LGNBF, p. 554.
1660. Sheppard, p. 260.
1661. Morton, p. 300.
1662. Jordan and Pryor, p. 654.

HEADQUARTERS FORREST'S CAVALRY CORPS,
Verona, Miss., January 24, 1865.

COLONEL: I have the honor to submit the following report of the operations of the troops under my command during the recent movements in Middle Tennessee:

While in West Tennessee I received orders from General Beauregard on the 30th of October, to report without delay to General Hood at Florence, Ala. I was then actively operating against Johnsonville, and so soon as I completed the destruction of the enemy's fleet and stores at that place I commenced moving up the Tennessee River. I halted my command at Perryville with a view of crossing the river at that point, but being without facilities, and the river already high and rising rapidly, I found it impossible to cross over. I succeeded, however, in throwing across a portion of Rucker's brigade, while I moved to Corinth with the balance of my command. My men and horses were much jaded, but I moved at once to Florence and crossed the river on the 16th and 17th of November. On my arrival at Florence I was placed in command of the entire cavalry then with the Army of Tennessee, consisting of Brigadier-General Jackson's division and a portion of Dibrell's brigade, under command of Colonel Biffle, amounting to about 2,000 men, together with three brigades of my former command, making in all about 5,000 cavalry. I bivouacked my command at Shoal Creek until the morning of the 21st, when, in obedience to orders from General Hood, I commenced a forward movement. My command consisted of three divisions—Chalmers', Buford's, and Jackson's. I ordered Brigadier-General Chalmers to advance via West Point, Kelly's Forge, Henryville, and Mount Pleasant. Brigadier-Generals Buford and Jackson were ordered to move up the military road to Lawrenceburg, and thence southeastward in the direction of Pulaski. Both these divisions had several engagements with the enemy, and were almost constantly skirmishing with him, but drove him in every encounter.

At Henryville Brigadier-General Chalmers developed the enemy's cavalry and captured forty-five prisoners. At Fouché Springs the enemy made another stand. I ordered General Chalmers to throw forward Rucker's brigade and to keep up a slight skirmish with the enemy until I could gain his rear. I ordered Lieutenant-Colonel Kelley to move by the left flank and join me in rear of the enemy. Taking my escort with me I moved rapidly to the rear. Lieutenant-Colonel Kelley being prevented from joining me as I had expected, I made the charge upon the enemy with my escort alone, producing a perfect stampede, capturing about 50 prisoners, 20 horses, and 1 ambulance. It was now near night, and I placed my escort in ambush. Colonel Rucker pressed upon the enemy, and as they rushed into the ambuscade my escort fired into them, producing the wildest confusion. I ordered Colonel Rucker to rest his command until 1 a. m., when the march was renewed toward Mount Pleasant, where he captured 35,000 rounds of small-arm ammunition and the guard left in charge of it. Meantime Brigadier-Generals Buford and Jackson had proceeded from Lawrenceburg toward Pulaski and encountered Hatch's division of cavalry at Campbellsville, and routed him after a short but vigorous engagement, in which he lost about 100 prisoners and several in killed and wounded. Most of my troops having reached Columbia on the evening of the 24th I invested the town from Duck River to the extreme north, which position I held until the arrival of the infantry on the morning of the 27th, when I was relieved.

Columbia having been evacuated on the night of [November] the 28th [27th] I was ordered to move across Duck River on the morning of the 28th. Chalmers' division was ordered to cross at Carr's Mill, seven miles above Columbia, Jackson's, at Holland's Ford, while I crossed at Owen's Ford with a portion of Colonel Biffle's regiment. Before leaving Columbia I sent my escort to Shelbyville for the purpose of ascertaining the movements of the enemy and destroying the railroad, and I regret to announce that Captain Jackson was seriously wounded on this expedition. On the night of the 28th I was joined by Chalmers' division about eight miles from Columbia on the Spring Hill and Carr's Mill road. Jackson's division was ordered to proceed to the vicinity of Hurt's Cross Roads on the Lewisburg pike. At 11 o'clock at night I received a dispatch from General Buford informing me that the enemy had made such a stubborn resistance to his crossing that he could not join the command until the morning of the 29th. I ordered General Jackson to move along the Lewisburg pike toward Franklin until he developed the enemy. Brigadier-General Armstrong notified me that he had struck the enemy, when I ordered him not to press too vigorously until I reached his flank with Chalmers' division. The enemy gradually fell back, making resistance only at favorable positions. After waiting a short time for my troops to close up, I moved rapidly toward Spring Hill with my entire command. Two miles from town the enemy's pickets were encountered and heavy skirmishing ensued. I ordered General Armstrong to form his brigade in line of battle. I also ordered a portion of the Kentucky brigade and the Fourteenth Tennessee Regiment, under Colonel White, to form, which being done I ordered a charge upon the enemy, but he was so strongly posted upon the crest of a hill that my troops were compelled to fall back. I then dismounted my entire command amid moved upon the enemy. With a few men I moved to the left on a high hill, where I discovered the enemy hurriedly moving his wagon train up the Franklin pike. I ordered my command to push the enemy's right flank with all possible vigor. At the same time I ordered Brigadier-General Buford to send me a regiment mounted. He sent the Twenty-first Tennessee, Colonel Wilson commanding, which I ordered to charge upon the enemy. Colonel Wilson at the head of his splendid regiment made a gallant charge through an open field. He received three wounds, but refused to leave his command. About this time I received orders from General Hood to hold my position at all hazards, as the advance of his infantry column was only two miles distant and rapidly advancing. I ordered up my command, already dismounted. Colonel Bell's brigade was the first to reach me, when I immediately ordered it to the attack. Major-General Cleburne's division soon arrived, and, after some delay, was formed in line of battle and moved upon the enemy on my left. Colonel Bell reported that he had only four rounds of ammunition to the man when I ordered him to charge the enemy. This order was executed with a promptness and energy amid gallantry which I have never seen excelled. The enemy was driven from his rifle-pits, and fled toward Spring Hill. I then ordered Brigadier-General Jackson to move with his division in the direction of Thompson's Station and there intercept the enemy. He struck the road at Fitzgerald's, four miles from Spring Hill, at 11 o'clock, just as the front of the enemy's column had passed. This attack was a complete surprise, producing much panic and confusion. Brigadier-General Jackson had possession of the pike and fought the enemy until near daylight, but receiving no support, he was compelled to retire, after killing a large number of horses and mules and burning several wagons. Chalmers' and Buford's divisions being out of ammunition, I supplied them from the infantry (my ordnance being still at Columbia), when I ordered Brigadier-General Chalmers to move at daylight on the morning of the 30th to the Carter's Creek turnpike, between Columbia and Spring Hill, and there intercept a column of the enemy reported to be cut off. General Chalmers moved as ordered, but reported to me that the enemy had passed unmolested on the main pike during the night. Buford and Jackson were ordered to move forward with their divisions on the Franklin pike and to attack the enemy. They overtook his rear two miles from where General Jackson had cut his column the night previous and pushed him on to Winstead's Hill, where he was strongly posted. General Stewart's corps arriving upon the ground, I moved with Buford's and Jackson's divisions to the right, my right extending to Harpeth River, and ordered Brigadier-General Chalmers on the left. The enemy retired from Winstead's Hill toward their fortifications at Franklin.

I ordered Brigadier-General Chalmers to advance on the left, which he did, charging and dislodging the enemy from every position he had taken. The enemy was posted on a strong hill on the opposite side of Harpeth River, from which position he was firing upon our troops on the Lewisburg pike. I ordered Brigadier-General Jackson to cross over and drive the enemy from this hill and to protect our right. I ordered Brigadier-General Buford to dismount his command and take position in line of battle on the right of Stewart's corps, covering the ground from the Lewisburg pike to Harpeth River. Skirmishing at once commenced, and Buford's division rapidly advancing drove the enemy across Harpeth River, where he joined the cavalry. Brigadier-General Jackson engaged the united forces of both infantry and cavalry, and held him in check until night, when he threw forward his pickets and retired across Harpeth for the purpose of replenishing his ammunition. The enemy held strong positions commanding all the fords. I ordered Brigadier-General Buford to remount his command and hold himself in readiness for action at a moment's warning. Brigadier-General Jackson's troops being out of ammunition, and my ordnance still in the rear, Captain Vanderford furnished me with the necessary supply.

At daylight on the 1st of December [1864] I moved across Harpeth River and advanced up the Wilson pike, and struck the enemy at Owen's Cross-Roads, in strong force. I ordered Captain Morton to open upon him with his battery. Soon afterward I ordered Brigadier-General Buford to charge, which order he executed by dislodging the enemy and capturing several prisoners. I then moved with Jackson's and Buford's divisions to Brentwood, where I was joined by Brigadier-General Chalmers. Ordering Chalmers to proceed with his division up the Franklin and Hillsborough pike, and to cross over and intercept, if possible, the enemy retreating toward Nashville, I moved with Buford's and Jackson's divisions toward the Nashville pike, and, learning the enemy had reached Nashville, I camped for the night.

On the following morning (the 2d) I ordered Brigadier-General Chalmers to move on the left and to guard the Hillsborough and Hardin pikes, while I proceeded to the right with Buford's and Jackson's divisions and took position in sight of the capitol at Nashville. I ordered Brigadier-General Buford to move with his division across to Mill Creek and to form line of battle near the lunatic asylum on the Murfreesborough pike. Jackson's division was ordered into position so as to cover the Nashville and Mill Creek pike. My command being relieved by the infantry I commenced operating upon the railroad, block-houses, and telegraph lines leading from Nashville to Murfreesborough. I ordered Buford's division on the Nashville and Chattanooga Railroad for the purpose of destroying stockades and block-houses.

On the 3d of December stockade No. 2 surrendered, with 80 prisoners, 10 men killed, and 20 wounded in the attack by Morton's battery. On the day previous, while assaulting stockade No. 2, a train of cars came from Chattanooga loaded with negro troops. The train was captured, but most of the troops made their escape.

On the 4th I ordered Brigadier-General Buford to attack block-house No. 3, but the demand for surrender was complied with, and the garrison of thirty-two men made prisoners. An assault was also ordered on stockade No. 1, on Mill Creek, but the garrison unhesitatingly surrendered. I ordered the destruction of the block-house and two stockades, in which were captured 150 prisoners.

On the morning of the 4th I received orders to move with Buford's and Jackson's divisions to Murfreesborough, and to leave 250 men on the right to picket from the Nashville and Murfreesborough pike to the Cumberland River. Colonel Nixon, of Bell's brigade, was left for this purpose.

On the morning of the 5th I moved, as ordered, toward Murfreesborough. At La Vergne I ordered Brigadier-General Jackson to move on the right of town and invest the fort on the bill, while I moved with Buford's division to block-house No. 4. The usual demand for surrender was sent under flag of truce and a surrender made. The garrison on the hill, consisting of 80 men, 2 pieces of artillery, several wagons, and a considerable supply of stores, also surrendered to Brigadier-General Jackson. A large number of houses, built and occupied by the enemy, were ordered to be burned.

Four miles front La Vergne I formed a junction with Major-General Bate, who had been ordered to report to me with his division for the purpose of operating against Murfreesborough. I ordered Brigadier General Jackson to send a brigade across to the Wilson [Wilkinson] Pike, and moving on both pikes the enemy was driven into his works at Murfreesborough. After ordering General Buford to picket from the Nashville and Murfreesborough to the Lebanon pikes on the left, and Jackson to picket on the right to the Salem pike, I encamped for the night.

The infantry arrived on the morning of [December] the 6th, when I immediately ordered it in line of battle and to move upon the enemy's works. After skirmishing for two hours the enemy ceased firing, and showed no disposition to give battle. I ordered a regiment from Brigadier-General Armstrong's brigade, with which I made a careful reconnaissance of the enemy's position and works. On the evening of the 6th I was re-enforced by Sears' and Palmer's brigades of infantry. I ordered Colonel Palmer in position on the right upon a hill, and to fortify during the night.

On the morning of the 7th I discovered from the position occupied by Colonel Palmer the enemy moving out in strong force on the Salem pike, with infantry, cavalry, and artillery. Being fully satisfied that his object was to make battle, I withdrew my forces to the Wilkinson pike, and formed a new line on a more favorable position. The enemy moved boldly forward, driving in my pickets, when the infantry, with the exception of Smith's brigade, from some cause which I cannot explain, made a shameful retreat, losing two pieces of artillery. I seized the colors of the retreating troops and endeavored to rally them, but they could not be moved by any entreaty or appeal to their patriotism. Major-General Bate did the same thing, but was equally as unsuccessful as myself. I hurriedly sent Major Strange, of my staff, to Brigadier-Generals Armstrong and Ross, of Jackson's division, with orders to say to them that everything depended on their cavalry. They proved themselves equal to the emergency by charging on the enemy, thereby checking his farther advance. I ordered the infantry to retire to Stewart's Creek, while my cavalry encamped during the night at Overall's Creek. The enemy returning to Murfreesborough, I ordered my cavalry to resume its former position.

It is proper to state here that I ordered Brigadier-General Buford to protect my left flank, but he was so remote the order never reached him. While the fight was going on, however, he made a demonstration on Murfreesborough, and succeeded in reaching the center of town, but was soon compelled to retire.

On the 9th General Hood sent to my support Smith's brigade, commanded by Colonel Olmstead, and ordered Bate's division to report back to his headquarters. On the 11th I ordered Brigadier-General Buford to proceed to the Hermitage, and to picket the Cumberland River, so as to prevent any flank movement in that direction. On the 12th I ordered the infantry to destroy the railroad from La Vergne to Murfreesborough, which was most effectually done. Brigadier-General Jackson, who had been previously ordered to operate south of Murfreesborough, captured, on [December] the 13th, a train of seventeen cars and the Sixty-first Illinois Regiment of Infantry, commanded by Lieutenant-Colonel Grass. The train was loaded with supplies of 60,000 rations, sent from Stevenson to Murfreesborongh, all of which were consumed by fire, after which the prisoners, about 200 in number, were sent to the rear.

On the 14th I moved with Colonels Olmstead's and Palmer's brigades across Stone's River and east of

Murfreesborough, with a view of capturing the enemy's forage train, but on the evening of the 15th I received notice from General Hood that a general engagement was then going on at Nashville, and to hold myself in readiness to move at any moment. Accordingly, on the 16th I moved my entire command to the Wilkinson Cross-Roads, at the terminus of the Wilkinson pike, six miles from Murfreesborough. On the night of the 16th one of General Hood's staff officers arrived, informing me of the disaster at Nashville and ordering me to fall back via Shelbyville and Pulaski. I immediately dispatched orders to Brigadier-General Buford to fall back from the Cumberland River, via La Vergne, to the Nashville pike, and to protect my rear until I could move my artillery and wagon train. From this position General Buford was ordered across to the Nashville and Columbia pike, for the purpose of protecting the rear of General Hood's retreating army. My sick, wounded, and wagon train being at Triune, I did not retreat via Shelbyville, but moved in the direction of Lillard's Mills, on Duck River. I ordered Brigadier-General Armstrong to the Nashville and Columbia pike. Most of the infantry under my command were barefooted and in a disabled condition, and being encumbered with several hundred head of hogs and cattle, my march along the almost impassable roads was unavoidably slow. On reaching Duck River at Lillard's Mills I ordered everything to be hurried across, as the stream was rapidly rising. After putting over a part of my wagon train the stream became unfordable. I was therefore compelled to change my direction to Columbia, which place I reached on the evening of the 18th.

On the morning of [December] the 19th the enemy was reported at Rutherford's Creek in strong force. I immediately commenced disposing of my troops for the purpose of preventing his crossing. Everything being across Duck River I was ordered by General Hood to withdraw my command at 3 o'clock, which I did, and went into camp at Columbia. Chalmers' division having been sent to the right, I am unable to state anything from personal knowledge as to his operations from the 3d to the 19th; but I learn from his official report that his line extended from the Hillsborough pike, on the right, across the Hardin and Charlotte pikes to the river, on the left; that he captured two transports laden with horses and mules; that the transports were recaptured, but leaving on his hands 56 prisoners and 197 horses and mules; that the enemy made several attempts with his monitors and gun-boats to silence his river batteries, all of which were unsuccessful; that he maintained a strict blockade of the river and his position until Ector's brigade of infantry fell back; that he prevented Hatch from gaining the rear of our army; and that he was constantly and severely engaged every day while protecting the rear of General Hood's army until he crossed Rutherford's Creek.

On the 20th General Hood, on leaving Columbia, gave me orders to hold the town as long as possible, and when compelled to retire to move in the direction of Florence, Ala., via Pulaski, protecting and guarding his rear. To aid me in this object he ordered Major-General Walthall to report to me with about 1,900 infantry, 400 of whom were unserviceable for want of shoes. The enemy appeared in front of Columbia on the evening of the 20th and commenced a furious shelling upon the town. Under a flag of truce I proceeded to the river and asked an interview with General Hatch, who I informed by verbal communication across the river that there were no Confederate troops in town, and that his shelling would only result in injury to the women and children and his own wounded, after which interview the shelling was discontinued.

The enemy succeeded in crossing Duck River on the morning of the 22d. I at once ordered my troops to fall back in the direction of Pulaski. Brigadier-General Chalmers was ordered on the right down the Bigbyville pike toward Bigbyville. The infantry moved down the main pike from Columbia to Pulaski, the rear protected by both Buford's and Jackson's divisions of cavalry, while a few scouts were thrown out on the left flank. The enemy made his first demonstration on my rear pickets near Warfield's, three miles south of Columbia. He opened upon us with artillery, which forced us to retire farther down the road in a gap made by two high hills on each side of the road; where he was held in check for some time. On the night of the 23d I halted my command at and near Lynnville, in order to hold the enemy in check and to prevent any pressure upon my wagon train and the stock then being driven out.

On the morning of [December] the 24th I ordered the infantry back toward Columbia on the main pike and my cavalry on the right and left flanks. After advancing about three miles the enemy was met, where a severe engagement occurred and the enemy was held in check for two hours. I retreated two miles, where I took position at Richland Creek. Brigadier-General Armstrong was thrown forward in front and General Ross on the right flank. Chalmers and Buford formed a junction, and were ordered on the left flank. Brigadier-General Armstrong was ordered to the support of six pieces of my artillery, which were placed in position immediately on the main pike and on a line with Buford's and Chalmer's divisions and Ross' brigade, of Jackson's division. After severe artillery firing on both sides two pieces of the enemy's artillery were dismounted. The enemy then flanked to the right and left and crossed Richland Creek on my right, with the view of gaining my rear. I immediately ordered Armstrong and Ross, of Jackson's division, to cross the bridge on the main pike and move around and engage the enemy, who were crossing the creek. Both Buford and Chalmers were heavily pressed on the left, and after an engagement of two hours I ordered them to fall back across Richland Creek. I lost 1 killed and 6 wounded in this engagement. The enemy lost heavily. Brigadier-General Buford was wounded in this engagement, and I ordered Brigadier-General Chalmers to assume command of Brigadier-General Buford's division together with his own. I reached Pulaski without further molestation.

On the morning of the 25th, after destroying all the ammunition which could not be removed from Pulaski by General Hood and two trains of cars, I ordered General Jackson to remain in town as long as possible and to destroy the bridge at Richland Creek after everything had passed over. The enemy soon pressed General Jackson, but he held him in check for some time, killing and wounding several before retiring. Seven miles from Pulaski I took position on King's Hill, and awaiting the advance of the enemy, repulsed him, with a loss of 150 killed and wounded, besides capturing many prisoners and one piece of artillery. The enemy made no further demonstrations during the day. I halted my command at Sugar Creek, where it encamped during the night.

On the morning of [December] the 26th the enemy commenced advancing, driving back General Ross' pickets. Owing to the dense fog he could not see the temporary fortifications which the infantry had thrown up and behind which they were secreted. The enemy therefore advanced to within fifty paces of these works, when a volley was opened upon him, causing the wildest confusion. Two mounted regiments of Ross' brigade and Ector's and Granbury's brigades of infantry were ordered to charge upon the discomfited foe, which was done, producing a complete rout. The enemy was pursued for two miles, but showing no disposition to give battle my troops were ordered back. In this engagement he sustained a loss of about 150 in killed and wounded; many prisoners and horses were captured and about 400 horses killed. I held this position for two hours, but the enemy showing no disposition to renew the attack, and fearing he might attempt a flank movement in the dense fog, I resumed the march, after leaving a picket with orders to remain until 4 o'clock. The enemy made no further attack between Sugar Creek and Tennessee River, which stream I crossed on the evening of the 27th of December. The infantry were ordered to report back to their respective corps, and I moved with my cavalry to Corinth.

The campaign was full of trial and suffering, but the troops under my command, both cavalry and infantry, submitted to every hardship with an uncomplaining patriotism; with a single exception, they behaved with commendable gallantry.

From the day I left Florence, on the 21st of November, to the 27th of December my cavalry were engaged every day with the enemy. My loss in killed and wounded has been heavy. I brought out of the campaign three pieces of artillery more than I started with.

My command captured and destroyed 16 block-houses and stockades, 20 bridges, several hundred horses and mules, 20 yoke of oxen, 4 locomotives, and 100 cars and 10 miles of railroad, while I have turned over to the provost-marshal-general about 1,600 prisoners.

To my division commanders—Brigadier-Generals Chalmers, Buford, and Jackson—I take pleasure in acknowledging the promptitude with which they obeyed and executed all orders. If I have failed to do justice in this report it is because they have not furnished me with a detailed report of the operations of their respective commands.

I am also indebted to Major-General Walthall for much valuable service rendered during the retreat from Columbia. He exhibited the highest soldierly qualities. Many of his men were without shoes, but they bore their sufferings without murmur and were ever ready to meet the enemy.

I am again under obligations to my staff for their efficient aid during the campaign.

All of which is respectfully submitted.

N. B. FORREST, Major- General.

Lieut. Col. A. P. MASON, Assistant Adjutant-General.


[Indorsement.]

HEADQUARTERS MILITARY DIVISION OF THE WEST, Charlotte, N. C., February 25, 1865.

Respectfully forwarded to the War Department for its information. General Forrest and his command deserve well of the country for the gallantry, energy, and activity displayed during this severe campaign in Middle Tennessee.

G. T. BEAUREGARD, General.


ADDENDA.

Address of Maj. Gen. N. B. Forrest to his troops.

SOLDIERS: The old campaign is ended, and your commanding general deems this an appropriate occasion to speak of the steadiness, self-denial, and patriotism with which you have borne the hardships of the past year. The marches and labors you have performed during that period will find no parallel in the history of this war.

On the 24th day of December there were 3,000 of you, unorganized and undisciplined, at Jackson, Tenn., only 400 of whom were armed. You were surrounded by 15,000 of the enemy, who were congratulating themselves on your certain capture. You started out with your artillery, wagon trains, and a large number of cattle, which you succeeded in bringing through, since which time you have fought and won the following battles—battles which will enshrine your names in the hearts of your countrymen, and live in history an imperishable monument to your prowess: Jack's Creek, Estenaula, Somerville, Okolona, Union City, Paducah, Fort Pillow, Bolivar, Tishomingo Creek, Harrisburg, Hurricane Creek, Memphis, Athens, Sulphur Springs, Pulaski, Carter's Creek, Columbia, and Johnsonville are the fields upon which you have won fadeless immortality. In the recent campaign in Middle Tennessee you sustained the reputation so nobly won. For twenty-six days, from the time you left Florence, on the 21st of November to the 26th of December you were constantly engaged with the enemy, and endured the hunger, cold, and labor incident to that arduous campaign without murmur. To sum up, in brief, your triumphs during the past year, you have fought fifty battles, killed and captured 16,000 of the enemy, captured 2,000 horses and mules, 67 pieces of artillery, 4 gun-boats, 14 transports, 20 barges, 300 wagons, 50 ambulances, 10,000 stand of small-arms, 40 block-houses, destroyed 36 railroad bridges, 200 miles of railroad, 6 engines, 100 cars, and $15,000,000 worth of property.

In the accomplishment of this great work you were occasionally sustained by other troops, who joined you in the fight, but your regular number never exceeded 5,000, 2,000 of whom have been killed or wounded, while in prisons you have lost about 200.

If your course has been marked by the graves of patriotic heroes who have fallen by your side, it has, at the same time, been more plainly marked by the blood of the invader. While you sympathize with the friends of the fallen, your sorrows should be appeased by the knowledge that they fell as brave men battling for all that makes life worth living for.

Soldiers! you now rest for a short time from your labors. During the respite prepare for future action. Your commanding general is ready to lead you again to the defense of the common cause, and he appeals to you, by a remembrance of the glories of your past career; your desolated homes; your insulted women and suffering children; and, above all, by the memory of your dead comrades, to yield a ready obedience to discipline, and to buckle on your armor anew for the fight. Bring with you the soldier's safest armor—a determination to fight while the enemy pollutes your soil; to fight as long as he denies your rights; to fight until independence shall have been achieved; to fight for home, children, liberty, and all you hold dear. Show to the world the superhuman and sublime spirit with which a people may be inspired when fighting for the inestimable boon of liberty. Be not allured by the siren song of peace, for there can be no peace save upon your separate independent nationality. You can never again unite with those who have murdered your sons, outraged your helpless families, and with demoniac malice wantonly destroyed your property, and now seek to make slaves of you. A proposition of reunion with a people who have avowed their purpose to appropriate the property and to subjugate or annihilate the freemen of the South would stamp with infamy the names of your gallant dead and the living heroes of this war. Be patient, obedient, and earnest, and the day is not far distant when you can return to your homes and live in the full fruition of freemen around the old family altar.

N. B. FORREST, Major-General.

Major-General, Comdg. District of Mississippi and East Louisiana.[1663]

## END OF THE TENNESSEE CAMPAIGN

Hood had destroyed the Army of Tennessee in just thirty-five days.[1664] Thus, after Nashville he resigned in dishonor, and the tattered remains of the Army of Tennessee were taken over by General Richard Taylor,[1665] the son of America's twelfth president, Zachary Taylor.[1666] Hood retired in New Orleans, where he went bankrupt and died, along with his wife, of the yellow fever epidemic that swept through the city in 1879.

President Davis had given Hood a position for which he was not completely qualified, trying, as a wit once remarked, to make out of him what even God Almighty himself could not: a good leader. Davis' single act irreparably damaged Hood and helped bring down the

---

1663. ORA, Ser. 1, Vol. 45, Pt. 1, pp. 751-760.
1664. Lytle, p. 370.
1665. McDonough and Connelly, p. 178.
1666. I am cousins with President Taylor, his son General Richard Taylor, and Richard's sister, Sarah Knox Taylor, the first wife of the Confederacy's only president, Jefferson Davis. Sarah and Jefferson had one child: Jefferson Davis, Jr. (b. about 1834). From the author's personal family tree.

Confederacy.[1667]

## HOW FORREST'S INGENIOUS PLAN COULD HAVE SAVED THE SOUTH

To this day, many have wondered what the outcome of the War for Southern Independence would have been had Forrest been given Hood's position as commander of the Army of Tennessee. Certainly Forrest would have continued to weaken Grant by luring his troops away in an effort to drive him off.[1668] And as he would have never let Sherman take Atlanta, as Hood did,[1669] Lincoln would not have been reelected. It was, after all, the fall of Atlanta that helped get Lincoln into the U.S. White House a second time,[1670] and it was Lincoln's second term that sealed the fate of the South. How?

Lincoln's first election triggered the War to begin with, for, as we have seen, the conservative Constitution-loving South, understandably, could not tolerate an anti-Southern, anti-Constitution, big-government, big-spending liberal in the White House. Up until mid 1864 pessimism had been growing in the North, however, as the new Confederate nation forged its way through victory after victory. All that changed on July 22, 1864, when, thanks to Hood's suicidal (and by now, obsolete) method of frontal attacks, Sherman captured and destroyed Atlanta (Sherman suffered some 6,000 casualties, Hood over 13,000).

Up until that day neither Lincoln's supporters or Lincoln himself believed he had any chance of being reelected over his opponent, Democratic candidate Union General George Brinton McClellan. Why?

By mid1864, as a war-weary North was beginning to lose faith in Lincoln and what appeared to be his failed war, McClellan's party plank, calling for U.S. withdrawal and a quick end to the conflict, became more and more appealing. With Hood's loss and Sherman's momentous win at Atlanta, however, the North, now with renewed hope, reelected Republican (the liberal Democrats of the mid 1800s)

---

**1667.** Sheppard, p. 302. Hood is often cited in modern business courses as the embodiment of the Peter Principle: one who is promoted to a level beyond his or her abilities, capacities, and intelligence.
**1668.** Sheppard, p. 307.
**1669.** Wyeth, TDF, p. xvii.
**1670.** Lytle, p. 331.

candidate Lincoln to a second term in November 1864.[1671]

While Lincoln died at the hands of Northerner John Wilkes Booth only months later, the reelection of his party, which included the South-hating Radicals (that is, minority Yankee abolitionists), assured a continuation of the War into the following year. Unfortunately for the South it did not have enough money, men, weapons, ammunition, food, or clothing to carry itself through another year. As Forrest himself said in early 1865:

> To my mind it is evident that the end is not far off; it will only be a question of time as to when General Lee's lines at Petersburg will be broken, for Grant is wearing him out; with unlimited resources of men and money, he must ultimately force Lee to leave Virginia or surrender. Lee's army will never leave Virginia; they will not follow him out when the time comes, and that will end the war.[1672]

Forrest was right of course. But his plan—which would have thoroughly depleted the energies of both Grant and Sherman, the two primary forces behind the Northern victory—could have prevented all of this. Amazingly, it was all but ignored until it was too late. But for Davis' momentous decision to disregard Forrest, the Confederate States of America would almost certainly exist today alongside the United States of America.

---

1671. Lytle, pp. 271-272.
1672. Wyeth, LGNBF, p. 578.

## - 1865 -
## War's End

"I will share the fate of my men." — Nathan
Bedford Forrest

## THE YANKEE HUNT FOR FORREST CONTINUES

AS THE YEAR 1865 OPENED, fearsome Forrest was still very much on the minds of Yankee officers. Sherman, the Tennessean's arch nemesis, was still promoting his plan to "hunt down and kill Forrest," as he penned in the report to Union General George H. Thomas below. Note in particular the casualness with which Sherman approaches waging total war on the South, along with his complete misunderstanding of the Southern people.

HEADQUARTERS MILITARY DIVISION OF THE MISSISSIPPI,
In the Field, Savannah, Ga., January 21, 1865.
Maj. Gen. GEORGE H. THOMAS,
Commanding Army in the Field, North Alabama, via Nashville:
GENERAL: Before I again dive into the interior and disappear from view, I must give you, in general terms, such instructions as fall within my province as commander of the division. I take it for granted that you now reoccupy in strength the line, of the Tennessee from Chattanooga to Eastport. I suppose Hood to be down about Tuscaloosa and Selma, and that Forrest is again scattered to get horses and men and to divert attention. You should have a small cavalry force of, say, 2,000 men to operate from Knoxville through the mountain pass along the French Broad into North Carolina, to keep up the belief that it is to be followed by a considerable force of infantry. Stoneman could do this, whilst

Gillem merely watches up the Holston. At Chattanooga should be held a good reserve of provisions and forage, and in addition to its garrison a small force that could at short notice relay the railroad to Resaca, prepared to throw provisions down to Rome, on the Coosa. You remember I left the railroad track from Resaca to Kingston and Rome with such a view. Then with an army of 25,000 infantry and all the cavalry you can get, under Wilson, you should move from Decatur and Eastport to some point of concentration about Columbus, Miss., and thence march to Tuscaloosa and Selma, destroying former, gathering horses, mules (wagons to be burned), and doing all the damage possible; burning up Selma, that is the navy-yard, the railroad back toward the Tombigbee, and all iron foundries, mills, and factories. If no considerable army opposes you, you might reach Montgomery and deal with it in like manner, and then at leisure work back along the Selma and Rome road, via Talladega and Blue Mountain, to the Valley of Chattooga, to Rome or La Fayette. I believe such a raid perfectly practicable and easy, and that it will have an excellent effect. It is nonsense to suppose that the people of the South are enraged or united by such movements. They reason very differently. They see in them the sure and inevitable destruction of all their property. They realize that the Confederate armies cannot protect them, and they see in the repetition of such raids the inevitable result of starvation and misery. You should not go south of Selma and Montgomery, because south of that line the country is barren and unproductive. I would like to have Forrest hunted down and killed, but doubt if we can do that yet. Whilst you are thus employed I expect to pass through the center of South and North Carolina, and I suppose Canby will also keep all his forces active and busy. I have already secured Pocotaligo and Grahamville, from which I have firm roads into the interior. We are all well.

Yours, truly, W. T. SHERMAN, Major-General, Commanding. [1673]

Sherman's fear of Forrest at this time was well justified: on January 28, 1865, just seven days after his letter to Thomas, Rebel General Beauregard put Forrest in command of the Cavalry Department of Alabama, Mississippi, East Louisiana, and West Tennessee. [1674] On February 28, as we have seen, Forrest was given what would become his

---

1673. ORA, Ser. 1, Vol. 45, Pt. 2, pp. 621-622.
1674. Wyeth, LGNBF, p. 580.

final promotion, lieutenant-general, after which he rode to West Point, Mississippi, where he established his headquarters.[1675] In late March he moved his troops into Alabama for what would be his final battle in Lincoln's illegal War. He was now in charge of the last body of organized Confederate soldiers in the Western theater.[1676]

Though in his heart he knew the War was already over,[1677] Forrest no doubt felt justified in continuing the fight: Yankee war criminals, like General John Croxton (under orders from General James H. Wilson), were now cruelly, and needlessly, burning down Southern schools, like the University of Alabama.[1678] Such deeds were sure to make any Rebel's blood boil, particularly Forrest's. As he approached the final days of the War for Southern Independence, he had plenty of fight left in him.

FORREST'S LAST STAND

He would need that inner "fight" for his last demonstration against the Yanks, for the Rebel army was by now coming unglued from within.

That spring, on March 18, 1865, Forrest commented on the sad "state of affairs" in Kentucky, Mississippi, and West Tennessee. It was not a pretty picture:

> General Johnson was often reported to have from 1,200 to 1,800 men, was finally wounded and captured, and his men scattered to the four winds. Brigadier-General Lyon then succeeded him and was driven across the Tennessee River into North Alabama, with only a handful of men. Nothing has been added to our army, for while the men flock to and remain with General Johnson or General Lyon as long as they can stay in Kentucky, as soon as the enemy presses and they turn southward the men scatter, and my opinion is that they can never be brought out or organized until we send troops there in sufficient numbers to bring them out by force. So far from gaining any strength for the army, the Kentucky brigade now in my command has only about 300 men in camps (Third, Seventh, and Eighth Kentucky Regiments). They have deserted and attached themselves to the roving bands of guerrillas,

1675. Mathes, p. 334.
1676. Lytle, p. 371.
1677. Wyeth, LGNBF, p. 578.
1678. Browning, p. 91.

jayhawkers, and plunderers who are the natural offspring of authorities given to parties to raise troops within the enemy's lines. The authorities given to would-be colonels, and by them delegated to would-be captains and lieutenants, have created squads of men who are dodging from pillar to post, preying upon the people, robbing them of their horses and other property, to the manifest injury of the country and our cause.

The same state of affairs exists in West Tennessee and along the Mississippi River. The country is filled with deserters and stragglers, who run away and attach themselves to the commands of those who have the authorities referred to. They never organize, report to nobody, are responsible to no one, and exist by plunder and robbery.[1679]

With the Confederate military falling apart in tatters all around him, on April 2, 1865, Forrest went out to land his last blow against Lincoln for God and Dixie.

Here, at the Battle of Selma, Alabama, he was wounded several times, his horse was injured, some of his escort, including Captain Nathan Boone,[1680] were injured, and Forrest killed his thirtieth and last Yankee.[1681] Selma became the only Confederate loss at which he was commander, a loss that occurred primarily because the enemy intercepted one of his couriers—who happened to be carrying several dispatches containing the General's battle plans.[1682] Thus the conflict was fated to be a Union victory even before it began.[1683]

There were other factors at play as well, however: the Yanks at Selma, under the command of General James H. Wilson, possessed some 13,500 men, while Forrest's defense numbered about 3,100 men, with a total of not more than 5,000.[1684]

Adding to the numerical weakness of the Rebels was the fact that Forrest had enlisted "every free, able-bodied male citizen into the ranks." As such, he had to try and control a mixed command of hundreds of untrained young and old greenhorns alongside thousands of war-weary

1679. ORA, Ser. 1, Vol. 49, Pt. 2, pp. 1124-1125.
1680. Nathan Boone is a relative of frontiersman Daniel Boone and modern singer/actor Pat Boone. As an Appalachian-American, I am related to all three.
1681. Bradley, p. 132.
1682. Morton, pp. 309-310; Bedwell, p. 36.
1683. Lytle, p. 375.
1684. Wyeth, LGNBF, p. 614.

vets, a nearly impossible task for even the most talented officer.[1685] As Grant later wrote in his memoirs:

> Wilson moved out with full 12,000 men, well equipped and well armed. He was an energetic officer and accomplished his work rapidly. Forrest was in his front, but with neither his old-time army nor his old-time prestige. He now had principally conscripts. His conscripts were generally old men and boys. He had a few thousand regular cavalry left, but not enough to even retard materially the progress of Wilson's cavalry. Selma fell on the 2d of April, with a large number of prisoners and a large quantity of war material, machine shops, etc., to be disposed of by the victors. Tuscaloosa, Montgomery and West Point fell in quick succession. These were all important points to the enemy by reason of their railroad connections, as depots of supplies, and because of their manufactories of war material. They were fortified or intrenched, and there was considerable fighting before they were captured. Macon surrendered on the 21st of April. Here news was received of the negotiations for the surrender of Johnston's army. Wilson belonged to the military division commanded by Sherman, and of course was bound by his terms. This stopped all fighting.[1686]

Despite this, his first and only military failure, Forrest and a number of his men escaped.[1687] Old Bedford and his "critter company"[1688] may have derived some consolation from the fact that they lost at Selma: with Lee's April 9th surrender at Appomattox only one week away, a Confederate win at the Alabama town would no doubt have entailed a much heavier casualty rate, by then a useless waste of time, energy, and life.[1689]

What Forrest would not liked to have known at the time, however, was the fact that Wilson, the Yankee general who beat him at Selma, would be the same man who would go on to capture President Jefferson Davis on May 10, 1865, at Irwinsville, Georgia,[1690] as he fled Richmond in an effort to reach the Western theater. Davis' plan? He

---

1685. Mathes, p. 346.
1686. U. S. Grant, Vol. 2, p. 521.
1687. Denney, pp. 553-554.
1688. Lytle, p. 235.
1689. Morton, pp. 311-312.
1690. Lytle, p. 375.

had been on his way to meet with Forrest in order to ask him if he would be willing to carry on the struggle for Southern independence.[1691]  Had Forrest beaten Wilson at Selma on April 2, and had Davis made it to Forrest's camp, who knows what might have transpired?[1692]

## ANTI-FORREST MYTH-MAKING

Even as he was losing his last fight, the Yanks were already busy thinking up slanderous lies about the Battle of Selma in order to besmirch Forrest's character and reputation.  One of these appears in the *Official Records*.  The author of this particularly absurd piece of anti-South propaganda is Yankee Dr. F. Salter, "Surgeon, U.S. Volunteers, Medical Director, Cavalry Corps, Military Division of the Mississippi."  Salter wrote:

> Forrest escaped with his escort of 100 men and retreated toward Plantersville.  On his way he came across a party of Federals asleep in a neighboring field under command of Lieutenant Roys, of the Fourth U.S. Cavalry, and Lieutenant Miller.  He charged on them in their sleep, and refusing to listen to their cries of surrender killed or wounded the entire party, numbering twenty-five men.[1693]

Yankee General and Southern turncoat George H. Thomas later repeated this same asinine fable:

> Forrest, who had fled by the Burnsville road, turned across the country to Plantersville, and thence west to Marion, beyond the Cahawba, where he found several of his brigades and the remainder of his artillery, all of which should have reached Selma two days before.  On his way during the night he discovered a scouting party of the Fourth regulars, under Lieutenant Royce, who had gone into camp after night a few miles from Selma, and feeling that he was within the Union lines, had failed to post sentinels.  Forrest fell upon the party with the ferocity of a wild Indian, and killed every man of it.[1694]

---

1691. J. Davis, Vol. 2, pp. 590-591.

1692. Lytle, p. 375.

1693. ORA, Ser. 1, Vol. 49, Pt. 1, p. 406.

1694. Piatt and Boynton, p. 614. As we will see, Forrest and his men did engage in killing Yanks in the days shortly after the fall of Selma. However, these attacks were on Yankee "bummers" who had been robbing and raping their way across the South, and as such were fully justifiable.

Confederate Lieutenant George Limerick Cowan,[1695] loyal member of Forrest's prize Escort, later testified that these tall tales were just that: "wholly untrue."[1696]

## FORREST REFUSES TO LAY DOWN HIS WEAPONS

On April 15, 1865, Forrest was at his new headquarters in Gainesville, Alabama, when the doleful rumors began: Lee had surrendered at Appomattox, Northern newspapers bragged.[1697] It was all over. At least for everyone but the battle-hardened Tennessean.

Though the War had come to an end, Forrest, a natural-born warrior who loved the manly, open-air life of the soldier, could not bear to put his weapons down. There was something in him that could simply not accept defeat or offer capitulation, and for a few days, in vain hope, he considered the story of Lee's surrender nothing more than Yankee disinformation, as his April 25th-general order to his men indicates:

> HEADQUARTERS FORREST'S CAVALRY CORPS,
> In the field, April 25, 1865.
> SOLDIERS: The enemy have originated and sent through our lines various and conflicting dispatches indicating the surrender of General Robert E. Lee and the Army of Northern Virginia. A morbid appetite for news and sensation rumors has magnified a simple flag of truce from Lieutenant General Taylor to General Canby at Mobile into a mission for negotiating the terms of surrender of the troops of his department. Your commanding general desires to say to you that no credence should be given to such reports; nor should they for a moment control the actions or influence the feelings, sentiments, or conduct of the troops of this command. On the contrary, from Southern sources and now published in our papers, it is reported that General Lee has not surrendered; that a cessation of hostilities has been agreed upon between Generals Johnston and Sherman for the purpose of

---

1695. Lt. Cowan, who married Harriet "Hattie" McGavock of Carnton Plantation fame, is buried at Mount Hope Cemetery, Franklin, Tennessee, in the Cowan family plot. Hattie was the daughter of Confederate Col. John W. McGavock and Carrie Winder, the owners of Carnton in Franklin when it was used as a Confederate field hospital beginning November 30, 1864, during the Battle of Franklin II. For more on the McGavocks, one of the South's most fascinating and loyal Confederate clans, see my works, *The McGavocks of Carnton Plantation: A Southern History*, and *Carnton Plantation Ghost Stories: True Tales of the Unexplained From Tennessee's Most Haunted Civil War House!*
1696. Wyeth, LGNBF, p. 609.
1697. Jordan and Pryor, pp. 678-679.

adjusting the difficulties and differences now existing between the
Confederate and the United States of America. Also that since the
evacuation of Richmond and the death of Abraham Lincoln, Grant
has lost in battle and by desertion 100,000 men. As your
commander he further assures you that at this time, above all
others, it is the duty of every man to stand firm at his post and true
to his colors. Your past services, your gallant and heroic conduct
on many victorious fields, forbid the thought that you will ever
ground your arms except with honor. Duty to your country, to
yourselves, and the gallant dead who have fallen in this great
struggle for liberty and independence, demand that every man
should continue to do his whole duty. With undiminished
confidence in your courage and fortitude, and knowing you now
will not disregard the claims of honor, patriotism, and manhood,
and those of the women and children of the country, so long
defended by your strong arms and willing hearts, he announces his
determination to stand by you, stay with you, and lead you to the
end. A few days more will determine the truth or falsity of all the
reports now in circulation. In the meantime let those who are now
absent from their commands for the purpose of mounting
themselves, or otherwise, return without delay. In conclusion, be
firm and unwavering, discharging promptly and faithfully every
duty devolving upon you. Preserve untarnished the reputation you
have so nobly won, and leave results to Him who in wisdom
controls and governs all things.
N. B. FORREST, Lieutenant- General.[1698]

With gossip and confused communications abounding, and with
thousands of Confederates across the South, particularly in always
independent Texas, refusing to surrender, Forrest's position is not
surprising. Even his own troops wanted to continue the fight, though
further west, with the Trans-Mississippi Department.[1699]

Forrest was sorely tempted; that is, until he heard more bad
news. This time it was Rebel General Joseph Eggleston Johnston's
surrender to Sherman[1700] on April 26, at the Bennet House, near

---

**1698.** ORA, Ser. 1, Vol. 49, Pt. 2, pp. 1263-1264.

**1699.** Wyeth, LGNBF, p. 612.

**1700.** Johnston's surrender was monumental: after Lee's surrender at Appomattox Johnston was the
commander of the last large Confederate force in the east.

Durham Station, North Carolina.[1701] Then, a few days later, on April 29, Forrest learned of Taylor's official surrender to Union General Edward Richard Sprigg Canby near Mobile, Alabama.[1702] On May 6, Richmond issued official notice of Lee's surrender.[1703]

The old warrior could no longer ignore the obvious. Though even then, while painfully accepting the defeat of his short-lived nation, he still craved the fight, and briefly considered heading southwest to join in the Mexican Revolution.[1704]

The North had won largely by simple attrition, over a four-year period grinding down the South with nothing more than superior numbers in men and weaponry, and, by now, the support of much of the world. (This global support, however, was not genuine, or voluntary: Lincoln had lied to Europe, for example, about the cause of the War—pretending it was about abolition—while threatening violence on any nation that interfered with his fight against the South or aided the Confederacy.)[1705]

Above all, with the ability to constantly replenish its supplies, the North had time on its side: with far more financial backing than the South, the Yanks could wage war indefinitely (or so Lincoln falsely believed).[1706] While the South, defending her families, homeland, and principles, fought with far more intensity and determination, in the long term she could not sustain itself against such odds. Time, money, and an amoral U.S. president—who ignored both the Constitution and the Geneva Conventions—had, *for the time being*, ended the South's dream of independence and self-determination.

Despite Lee's and Johnston's surrenders, and the entirely hopeless situation across Dixie, Forrest continued to roam the now

---

**1701.** Johnston's death was an ignoble one: in mid February 1891, while serving as a pallbearer at the funeral of his arch-nemesis Sherman, Johnston refused to wear a hat (thinking it unmasculine) and caught a serious cold. He perished ten days later, March 21, 1891, of pneumonia. Sherman beat him after all.
**1702.** Morton, p. 312.
**1703.** Mathes, p. 351.
**1704.** Wyeth, LGNBF, pp. 611-612.
**1705.** For examples of Lincoln's various dire warnings, threats, and promises to wage war on any European nation that impeded his assault on the South, see Owsley, KCD, pp. 309, 315, 331, 350, 359, 399, 401, 402, 408, 411, 423, 425, 436, 440, 446, 453, 464, 507, 510, 516-517, 524, 539-540, 544.
**1706.** See e.g., Nicolay and Hay, ALCW, Vol. 2, p. 614. General Grant, however, knew the truth. In his *Memoirs* he states: "Anything that could have prolonged the war a year beyond the time that it did finally close [April 1865], would probably have exhausted the North to such an extent that they might then have abandoned the contest and agreed to separation." U. S. Grant, Vol. 2, p. 167.

nearly empty battlefields with his men for several months afterward in what President Davis later admiringly called a "show of continued resistance."[1707] The North could not rest easy as long as Forrest was on the prowl, continuing to defy, looking for Yanks to kill.

It was only a final and definitive "summons to surrender," sent to Forrest from Union Brigadier General Edward Hatch on May 3, 1865, that persuaded the diehard commander to finally hang up his famous Navy sixes and double-sided razor-sharp saber.

Forrest's mood at the time was encapsulated during a night ride with his aid-de-camp Major Charles W. Anderson. When they came to a fork in the road Anderson asked, "Which way sir?", to which Forrest replied:

> Either. If one road led to hell and the other to Mexico, I would be indifferent as to which one to take.[1708]

Anderson wisely talked the General out of his despondency, reminding him of his responsibility to be a role model of postwar peace to his men.[1709]

But soon rumors began to circulate that Forrest, at the request of many of his soldiers, was seriously considering founding a colony in Mexico.[1710] Nothing ever came of the wild scheme, however, no doubt in part due to threats from the U.S. government—which promised that he would be considered an "outlaw" if he left the country.[1711]

In the end logic prevailed. A somber Forrest accepted the fate of his nation and submitted to the inevitable. When he was prevailed upon by former Tennessee governor Isham G. Harris and Mississippi governor Charles Clark to remain in the field and continue the fight

---

1707. J. Davis, Vol. 2, p. 693.
1708. Morton, p. 316.
1709. Henry, FWMF, p. 437.
1710. Forrest was, by some accounts, still discussing this notion in February 1868. By then, however, the plan had developed into one that included conquering the entire nation of Mexico in six months with a regiment of 20,000 Southern men! Forrest allegedly even planned to confiscate all of the mines and ensconce himself as "King or President." See Henry, FWMF, pp. 452-453. This was all probably nothing but hearsay—or more likely, a bit of fun on Forrest's part.
1711. Some Confederates, such as Isham G. Harris, actually moved to Mexico for a time, where they were warmly received and given homes and land. Most eventually returned to their beloved Southern states. Morton, pp. 316-317, 319-320.

against the North, Forrest replied acidly:

> Men, you may all do as you please, but I'm a-goin' home. Any man who is in favor of a further prosecution of this war is a fit subject for a lunatic asylum, and ought to be sent there immediately.[1712]

At Gainesville, Alabama, all Confederates were issued certificates of parole, while Forrest, like other Confederate officers, was forced to sign the Yankees' purposefully humiliating "Oath of Allegiance." It read:

> I, the undersigned, prisoner of war, belonging to the Army of the Department of Alabama, Mississippi, and East-Louisiana, having been surrendered by Lieutenant-General R. Taylor, Confederate States Army, commanding said department, to Major-General E. R. S. Canby, United States Army, commanding Army and Division of West-Mississippi, do hereby give my solemn parole of honor that I will not hereafter serve in the armies of the Confederate States, or in any military capacity whatever against the United States of America, or render aid to the enemies of the latter, until properly exchanged in such manner as shall be mutually approved by the respective authorities.[1713]

## FORREST'S FAREWELL TO HIS MEN

Admitting defeat was not in Forrest's blood, nor in his men's. Thus War's end was especially hard for them. For fighting with the General had always made his soldiers cheerfully confident that the South would win. This was in stark contrast to the men in many other Confederate armies, who, understandably in many cases, grew more despairing and fatalistic as the conflict progressed.[1714]

In Gainesville, Alabama, on May 9, he bid farewell to his soldiers as only a man like Forrest could. It is one of the War's most sublime speeches:[1715]

---

1712. Website: http://old.nationalreview.com/hanson/hanson040502.asp.
1713. Jordan and Pryor, p. 680.
1714. Lytle, p. 342.
1715. Forrest's speech was not actually given, but was handed out on flyers. Morton, p. 317.

HEADQUARTERS FORREST'S CAVALRY CORPS,
GAINESVILLE, ALA., MAY 9, 1865.
SOLDIERS, By an agreement made between Lieutenant-General Taylor, commanding the Department of Alabama, Mississippi, and East Louisiana, and Major-General Canby, commanding United States forces, the troops of this department have been surrendered.

I do not think it proper or necessary at this time to refer to causes which have reduced us to this extremity; nor is it now a matter of material consequence to us how such results were brought about. That we are beaten is a self-evident fact, and any further resistance on our part would justly be regarded as the very height of folly and rashness.

The armies of Generals Lee and Johnson having surrendered, you are the last of all the troops of the Confederate States Army east of the Mississippi River to lay down your arms.

The Cause for which you have so long and so manfully struggled, and for which you have braved dangers, endured privations, and sufferings, and made so many sacrifices, is today hopeless. The government which we sought to establish and perpetuate, is at an end. Reason dictates and humanity demands that no more blood be shed. Fully realizing and feeling that such is the case, it is your duty and mine to lay down our arms, submit to the "powers that be," and to aid in restoring peace and establishing law and order throughout the land.

The terms upon which you were surrendered are favorable, and should be satisfactory and acceptable to all. They manifest a spirit of magnanimity and liberality, on the part of the Federal authorities, which should be met, on our part, by a faithful compliance with all the stipulations and conditions therein expressed. As your Commander, I sincerely hope that every officer and soldier of my command will cheerfully obey the orders given, and carry out in good faith all the terms of the cartel.

Those who neglect the terms and refuse to be paroled, may assuredly expect, when arrested, to be sent North and imprisoned. Let those who are absent from their commands, from whatever cause, report at once to this place, or to Jackson, Mississippi; or, if too remote from either, to the nearest United States post or garrison, for parole.

Civil war, such as you have just passed through naturally engenders feelings of animosity, hatred, and revenge. It is our duty to divest ourselves of all such feelings; and as far as it is in our power to do so, to cultivate friendly feelings towards those with whom we have so long contended, and heretofore so widely, but honestly, differed. Neighborhood feuds, personal animosities, and private differences should be blotted out; and, when you return home, a manly, straightforward course of conduct will secure the respect of your enemies. Whatever your responsibilities may be to Government, to society, or to individuals, meet them like men.

The attempt made to establish a separate and independent Confederation has failed; but the consciousness of having done your duty faithfully, and to the end, will, in some measure, repay for the hardships you have undergone.

In bidding you farewell, rest assured that you carry with you my best wishes for your future welfare and happiness. Without, in any way, referring to the merits of the Cause in which we have been engaged, your courage and determination, as exhibited on many hard-fought fields, has elicited the respect and admiration of friend and foe. And I now cheerfully and gratefully acknowledge my indebtedness to the officers and men of my command whose zeal, fidelity and unflinching bravery have been the great source of my past success in arms.

I have never, on the field of battle, sent you where I was unwilling to go myself; nor would I now advise you to a course which I felt myself unwilling to pursue. You have been good soldiers, you can be good citizens. Obey the laws, preserve your honor, and the Government to which you have surrendered can afford to be, and will be, magnanimous.[1716]

Forrest and his men, now paroled and free—after four long years of hardship, blood, glory, tears, sweat, grime, and horror—returned to their families and farms. As there were few train tracks left in the South (thanks in part to Forrest himself), many walked home, some for hundreds of miles through scarred tree-less wastelands with only "Sherman's Sentinels" (lone-standing chimneys) to guide their way. [1717] Forrest, however, managed to find a working railway from Jackson to Memphis. From here he returned to his beloved Mississippi plantation,[1718] Green Grove, 225 miles southward, to begin life anew.[1719]

As he rode westward in his Victorian railroad car, the lonely clickety-clack of the tracks in his ears, the General may have been comforted by a singular fact: in October 1862, at Shelbyville, Tennessee, 105 men had enlisted in his escort. On May 9, 1865, at Gainesville,

---

1716. ORA, Ser. 1, Vol. 49, Pt. 2, pp. 1289-1290.
1717. Grissom, p. 148.
1718. Lytle, p. 378.
1719. Mathes, p. 354.

Alabama, 110 men lay down their arms with their commander. Forrest's Escort had ended with more men that it had begun with, the only known Confederate unit to have achieved such a feat.[1720]

As a New Orleans newspaper would later proudly remark on one of the South's favorite sons: in the whole war no Rebel force had more successes, more miraculous get-aways, more brilliant outcomes with such a small command, as that officered by General Nathan Bedford Forrest.[1721]

---

1720. Bradley, pp. 135, 197.
1721. Ashdown and Caudill, p. 86.

# Part 5

# FORREST IN THE POSTBELLUM WORLD

# - MID TO LATE 1860S -
# POSTBELLUM RECONSTRUCTION

"I went into the army worth a million and a half
dollars. . . . I came out of the war pretty well
wrecked; completely used up, shot all to pieces,
crippled, a beggar." — Nathan Bedford Forrest

## A NEW BEGINNING

FORREST'S DAZZLING MILITARY CAREER WAS now finished
and he re-entered the civilian world. His life, however, was about
to become more colorful and controversial than ever before.

Tragically, as occurred with so many other Southerners, the War
bankrupted the multimillionaire. And so now middle aged, war weary,
suffering from serious wounds, and with little capital, Forrest faced the
daunting and nearly incomprehensible task of starting his life over.
Thanks to Lincoln, for the next ten years the General would live largely
from "hand to mouth."[1722]

Fortunately for his family and the South, the word "impossible"
was not in his vocabulary.[1723] About this time a conciliatory Forrest
remarked: At one time I tried as hard as I could to help the South secede
from the U.S. Now that the War is over, he continued, I can say that it
was a futile venture, and that I am now ready to stand up for the U.S.
government as enthusiastically as I once struggled against it.[1724]

---

1722. Bradley, p. 138.
1723. Jordan and Pryor, p. 208; Morton, p. 62.
1724. W. L. Jones, Vol. 2, p. 174.

Sherman arrogantly predicted that a destitute Forrest would be forced to resort to a life of crime after the War.[1725] Not only was this the last thing a man like Forrest would do, but the former Rebel chieftain actually had much working in his favor, despite his great financial losses.

Among his best assets were his personality, character, and reputation: Forrest had emerged from the War as the most important and popular man in Western Tennessee.[1726] Even his former sworn enemies confirmed this. One of them, Yankee General Edward Hatch (a relative of today's Republican Senator Orrin Hatch of Utah), would later testify before the U.S. Congress that:

> There is no more popular man in West Tennessee to-day than the late rebel General Forrest. The quartermaster of my old regiment is partner with Forrest on a plantation; he said he took the plantation because Forrest is popular, and will take care of him and his interests.[1727]

STARTING OVER

In late May 1865, Forrest left Grenada, Mississippi, with twenty of his former black servants and headed for Sunflower Landing, the site of his beloved 3,000-acre plantation, Green Grove. There, he and his wife Mary Ann set about repairing their lives, so rudely shattered by Lincoln's illicit war. First on the list was cleaning up the mess that resulted from his four-year absence.[1728]

In September 1865, in an effort to bring in immediate cash, he repaired his steam saw mill and began selling a wide variety of lumber.[1729] The rest of that autumn found Forrest harvesting corn while Mary Ann made butter and raised chickens.[1730] Forrest described this period this way: "Immediately after the war, in 1866, I planted."[1731]

About this time he took up farming operations with a new business partner, a former Yankee officer named Major B. E. Diffinbach,

1725. Wills, p. 320.
1726. Henry, FWMF, p. 441.
1727. *Report of the Joint Committee on Reconstruction, at the First Session, Thirty-ninth Congress*, p. 106.
1728. Wyeth, LGNBF, p. 616.
1729. Wills, pp. 320-321.
1730. Henry, FWMF, p. 440.
1731. *Report of the Joint Select Committee to Inquire into the Condition of Affairs in the Late Insurrectionary States*, p. 25.

from Missouri.[1732] He also rented plantations and land to seven other former Union commanders,[1733] who, a hospitable Forrest said, "made my house their home on Sundays."[1734]

The General was obviously not one to hold a grudge, especially if there was money to be made.[1735] And indeed money *was* made: by the end of 1867 Forrest and Diffinbach had managed to turn a sizeable profit, and the General was financially solvent once more.[1736] As before the War, he was helped in attaining this success mainly by blacks, not whites.

## BLACK LABOR AT GREEN GROVE

When he reopened Green Grove many of Forrest's former black servants ("slaves" to Northerners) returned,[1737] as did many of those that he had set free before Lincoln's War,[1738] each one keen to become an employee of the man they had once called "Marse Bedford."[1739] All became loyal and productive postwar workers, bold facts that once again demolish the Yankee myth that he was a sadistic racist. The aforementioned story of Thomas ("Tom") Edwards, one of Forrest's black employees, is revealing here.

When the General tried to prevent Edwards from beating his wife, the man turned on him with an axe. An unarmed Forrest wrenched the weapon from his attacker and buried it in his skull, killing him instantly. The next day a black judge examined the case and found that the General had acted in self-defense, all charges were dropped, and he was applauded by his other black employees for having rid the plantation of a mean, cruel, violent, temperamental, and dangerous individual.[1740]

---

1732. Sheppard, p. 284. Some sources say his name was spelled Diffenbacher, or Diffenbocker, and that he was from Minnesota. See e.g., Henry, FWMF, p. 400.

1733. Ashdown and Caudill, p. 55.

1734. *Report of the Joint Select Committee to Inquire into the Condition of Affairs in the Late Insurrectionary States*, p. 24.

1735. In fact, shortly after the War ended Forrest began welcoming Northerners into the South.

1736. Sheppard, p. 284.

1737. Henry, ATSF, p. 45.

1738. Sheppard, p. 283.

1739. Wyeth, LGNBF, p. 616; Henry, ATSF, p. 127.

1740. Mathes, pp. 359-360. Edwards was known for his cruelty to animals as well. Only weeks prior to his death at Forrest's hands, the freedman had mercilessly beat a mule to death. On another occasion Edwards whipped his wife so badly that a doctor had to be called. Wills, pp. 325-326.

Another indication of the way Forrest was seen by blacks—in complete opposition to the anti-Forrest propaganda of Yankee mythology—was that around this time he offered to let his 200 black employees (all former slaves) out of their work contracts. Only eighteen opted to leave. The other 182 chose to stay on.[1741]

Yankee agents took notice. One, Union General Oliver O. Howard, commissioner of the Freedmen's Bureau, met with Forrest. After examining his plantation's working conditions Howard noted that the former Rebel officer was doing all that he could to be just and equitable in the handling of his African-American employees.[1742] Another, Captain Collis of Connecticut, visited Green Grove, after which he happily reported that General Forrest's management of his farm and black workers was the best he had ever seen, particularly concerning work hours, free time, and overall quality of life.[1743]

Yet curiously, Collis, representing the U.S. government—the same body that had attacked Forrest for "racism" during the War—was also harshly critical of the General for his leniency toward his freed black workers. For one thing, the Yankee government did not approve of Forrest's habit of allowing them to carry guns and knives, both during work and at home.[1744]

Northern military men also expressed grim dissatisfaction when they learned that he was making generous financial advances to his black employees. It was for granting these "injurious indulgences" that the U.S. government eventually ordered Forrest to cease and desist, with the veiled threat of severe repercussions if ignored.[1745] Despite this overt racism from the North, and Forrest's obvious utter lack of prejudice, it is the latter who is routinely pilloried for being a "racial bigot."

FORREST PRESERVES HIS MILITARY RECORD
Since his own Confederate superiors did not always appreciate him during the War, Forrest certainly knew that many in the North never would either, especially since the victor was inevitably going to rewrite

---

1741. Hurst, p. 273.
1742. McFeely, p. 264.
1743. Hurst, p. 274.
1744. Wills, p. 328.
1745. Memphis *Avalanche*, April 10, 1866, p. 2.

history (as the Yankee indeed did). Thus, in September 1866 he began collecting materials, as he wrote to former Rebel General Charles Clark, in an attempt to preserve the truth about his role in the great conflict, before it disappeared.

These papers were to become the foundation for Thomas Jordan and John P. Pryor's seminal work, *The Campaigns of General Nathan Bedford Forrest*. Forrest himself too labored intently on the book, providing the authors with his private papers and granting oral interviews. After its publication the General was very proud of *The Campaigns*, referring to it as the real and true chronicle of his military career.[1746]

## FORREST IS "PARDONED" BY THE U.S. GOVERNMENT

In November 1866 Forrest wrote President Andrew Johnson, asking for "amnesty" for his "treason" against the United States. As Forrest, like all other traditional Southerners, never accepted Lincoln's ridiculous lie that the Confederacy was illegal (actually, it was Lincoln's invasion of the South that was illegal), this was no doubt one of the most difficult tasks the proud Southerner ever undertook.

The humiliation was doubled by the fact that it was not until July 1868, nearly two years later, that the "pardon" was issued. And while amnesty still granted him no political power (harsh Reconstruction laws prohibited Confederate officers from carrying firearms,[1747] and from voting until 1870),[1748] for many Northerners the reprieve helped repair some of the damage done to his image.

As such, in the eyes of some Yankees Forrest had by now become the model U.S. citizen and the very personification of a peace-loving reconstructed Rebel. As the General himself said:

> When the war closed I looked upon it as an act of Providence, and felt that we ought to submit to it quietly; and I have never done or said anything that was contrary to the laws that have been

---

1746. Wills, pp. 353, 342-343.
1747. Martinez, p. 20.
1748. Mathes, p. 358.

enacted.[1749]

Former Union General Frank P. Blair would have concurred. Forrest, Blair said, was the most influential man in all of West Tennessee, one who used his power only for peaceful purposes, spreading friendliness wherever he went. Not only was Forrest among the best soldiers in the Confederacy, but his upstanding attitude and compliant spirit since the end of the War has caused me to regard him more highly than any man I have ever met, Blair went on to comment.[1750]

Forrest was indeed a changed man. In September 1869, at a barbeque near Gadsden, Alabama, he welcomed a group of Yankees from Massachusetts and Connecticut to the South, saying that this was the most honorable moment of his life, for it was a day when he could offer true comradeship to his Yankee brothers from the North. A momentous change has occurred: we are now one people, South and North, Forrest continued, and it is time to meet the new challenge of reuniting the country.[1751]

## BACK TO MEMPHIS

In 1867, after two years at Green Grove, Forrest sold the plantation and returned to Memphis,[1752] where he built a home on the Mississippi River and settled into the more predictable life of husband and townsman. Desperate to increase his income, he became president of a local fire insurance firm.[1753] But the position does not seem to have lasted very long, for soon he began working on an idea he had had for some time: constructing a railroad line from Memphis to Selma, Alabama, in an effort to help rebuild the battered South.[1754] Of this period in his life Forrest remarked:

> I want our country quiet once more, and I want to see our people

1749. Report of the Joint Select Committee to Inquire into the Condition of Affairs in the Late Insurrectionary States, p. 20.
1750. Henry, FWMF, p. 441.
1751. Hurst, p. 332.
1752. Lytle, p. 378; Sheppard, p. 292.
1753. Henry, FWMF, p. 452.
1754. Mathes, p. 361.

united and working together harmoniously.[1755]

Forrest's work resulted in the organization of the Selma, Marion, and Memphis Railroad, of which he became president. One of his associates at the rail company was former Confederate Colonel Edmund Winchester Rucker,[1756] like Forrest, a cousin of the author.[1757]

The new rail endeavor would now enable him to earn a steady living. But it was more than just a business to Forrest. He also wanted to both help Dixie regain her prosperity and mend the enormous wound purposely created by Lincoln between South and North. As he later stated in 1872:

> I said when I started out with my roads that railroads had no politics; that I wanted the assistance of everybody; that railroads were for the general good of the whole country.[1758]

As part of Forrest's plan to aid in the rebuilding of the nation, he hired some 400 blacks to work on his rail lines; not just as laborers, but also as architects, engineers, conductors, and foremen. Though the General was still considered a "racist" by many in the racist North, Southerners knew the truth: after his black employees' one-year contract ran out, all but fifteen returned to continue working for him.[1759]

## FORREST, RECONSTRUCTION, & THE KKK

It is commonly asserted that around this time, in late 1865 or early 1866, Forrest founded the Pulaski Circle or Pulaski Den, or what would soon be given the meaningless name, the Ku Klux Klan.[1760]

The idea that Forrest started the KKK is an absurd fallacy that has been in existence for so long that it is now accepted as fact, not only by many of his modern relatives, but also by countless reputable Civil

---

1755. *Report of the Joint Select Committee to Inquire into the Condition of Affairs in the Late Insurrectionary States*, p. 30.

1756. Wills, p. 366; Hurst, 362.

1757. My 4th great-grandmother is Phoebe Rucker of Orange Co., Virginia, Edmund's 1st cousin.

1758. *Report of the Joint Select Committee to Inquire into the Condition of Affairs in the Late Insurrectionary States*, p. 17.

1759. *Report of the Joint Select Committee to Inquire into the Condition of Affairs in the Late Insurrectionary States*, p. 17.

1760. Henry, FWMF, p. 443.

War authors and scholars. One can even still hear this old chestnut repeated by ignorant tour guides at historic sites across the South. To make matters worse, the Internet-savvy, anti-Forrest crowd has picked up on this falsehood, posting it online where it is now read by people around the globe as a genuine product of "scholarly research."

In actuality, as we will now prove, the organization was initiated by others, while Forrest only became associated with it much later.[1761]

Though it was at first formed as a secret social society for the amusement and recreation of its largely playful, college-age members, when the North began passing a series of vicious and revengeful, anti-South Reconstruction Acts in March 1867, the KKK eventually transformed into a political paramilitary body that sought to maintain law and order throughout the Confederate states during the postwar chaos.[1762]

Packs of scallywags (anti-South Southern opportunists) and carpetbaggers (anti-South Northern opportunists), along with gangs of freed former slaves, were by now roaming the countryside, bribing, intimidating, extorting, pillaging, and even raping, torturing and killing, members of now disarmed and disenfranchised Confederate families.[1763] Thousands of homes were burned down and countless farms, businesses, and lives were lost.[1764] In Chicot County, Arkansas, for example, as Forrest himself observed, "bloodthirsty and riotous blacks" forced whites from their homes, robbed them, then burned their houses down, among "other lawless acts."[1765]

Amidst the smouldering rubble armed Union forces stalked the streets of what was left of Southern towns, enforcing violent military rule upon an already humiliated and subjugated people. It should be noted that Northern military rule was deemed necessary because Yankees widely believed that Lincoln's (unconstitutional) invasion had totally destroyed the South's infrastructure. The South, so the North maintained, would now need to be "reconstructed"—a Yankee euphemism for Northernization.

---

1761. Lytle, p. 382.
1762. Sheppard, pp. 286-287.
1763. Seabrook, NBF, p. 53.
1764. Mathes, p. 371.
1765. Mathes, pp. 368-369.

But such was not the case. The South's infrastructure had not been "completely demolished," as many roads, bridges, railways, telegraph lines, water supplies, courts, stores, farms, markets, and plantations will still functioning. Furthermore, as all Southerners agreed, Dixie should have been left alone to rebuild herself. For many decades, however, the meddlesome North had already proven that it was incapable of minding its own affairs. And so the work of "reconstruction" began in earnest, literally the same day Lee stacked arms at Appomattox.

Lincoln's "Reconstruction" should be more properly called "Deconstruction," for far from being rebuilt, during this period the injured South was further brutalized by the North through abject neglect and vicious exploitation. (As proof we offer the following: in 1860 the bulk of the top ten most affluent states were in the South. Since the end of Lincoln's War in 1865, however, not a single state in Dixie has managed to achieve the national per capita income average. The effects of Lincoln's War are indeed with us still.)[1766]

Thus began twelve additional years of horror, degradation, and sorrow across Dixie, a period I call "America's Reconstruction Holocaust."

As part of "Reconstruction," the South's minority of carpetbaggers, scallywags, and freed slaves were allowed to take over local politics. The new carpetbag-scallywag regime gave the vote to (largely illiterate) freedmen—though only if they agreed to cast their vote for Lincoln and the Republican ticket—while this same right was now denied former Rebel soldiers and their families, intentionally setting the stage for continuing civil, racial, and social unrest between blacks and their former owners. Incredibly, as if being disfranchised of all their civil rights was not enough, noble, brave, honest, and law-abiding Confederate officers, such as Forrest, Longstreet, and Lee, were considered "prisoners on parole," subject to impromptu arrest and imprisonment on charges of "treason" to the U.S. government.[1767]

The new Reconstruction Acts called for a military state to be imposed on Dixie, which the North arrogantly divided into five "military

1766. Bradley, p. 137.
1767. R. E. Lee, Jr., pp. 347-348.

districts," each headed by a Yankee officer and armed militia. Within these five districts local governments were subordinated to the central government in Washington, D.C. (yet another clear violation of the Constitution), which operated under the orders of the occupying Northern officers.[1768]

Though Lincoln was by now dead (shot through the back of the head by a *Northerner*), many of his preposterous and illegal ideas were now implemented, one of which was the "forty acres and a mule" directive: the North would take over (that is, steal) the plantations of former Confederates, divide them into smaller farms, and hand them out freely to former slaves.

Lincoln's new federate democracy (originally intended to be, and to remain, a confederate republic by the Founding Fathers)[1769] added to the abasement by treating white Southerners as vanquished foreigners in their own land, even pushing through the Fourteenth Amendment of the Constitution at gunpoint, completely against the will of the Southern people.[1770] According to the Constitution, the U.S. government was supposed to be protecting the Southern people. Instead, it was oppressing them.[1771] Along with the inevitable political corruption and judicial anarchy brought on by the carpetbag-scallywag regime, the once rich Southland began sinking into unmitigated poverty.[1772]

Surely if there was ever a time for a loyal Southern body of "regulators" to protect the people and their property and maintain the peace, it was now.[1773] Even the U.S. Congress would later accept the creation of the KKK as a logical and understandable Southern reaction to the North's horrid laws, official ineptitude, and general immorality.[1774]

---

**1768.** J. Davis, Vol. 2, p. 732.

**1769.** See Stephens, CV, Vol. 1, pp. 504-505.

**1770.** To this day the Fourteenth Amendment, which was used by Lincoln and his Northern-controlled Congress to replace America's original Republic-style government with a Federal-style government, has still not been legally or formerly ratified. The Confederacy understandably rejected the Fourteenth Amendment, since it transferred power from the individual sovereign states to Lincoln's new all-powerful, highly centralized government in Washington, D.C., the form in which it remains to this day. For more on why the Fourteenth Amendment was condemned across Dixie, see L. Johnson, pp. 241-242; Woods, pp. 86-90; Findlay and Findlay, pp. 228-235; DiLorenzo, RL, pp. 207-208, 211.

**1771.** Lester and Wilson, p. 28.

**1772.** Browning, p. 98.

**1773.** Sheppard, p. 287.

**1774.** *Report of the Joint Select Committee to Inquire into the Condition of Affairs in the Late Insurrectionary States*, pp. 453-454. See also Adams and Sanders, p. 217.

It was thus in this climate of fear and defeat that the Ku Klux Klan was born, in an effort to protect its own.

The Klan's sole purpose at this time was to act as a self-policing, relief-and-aid society for the protection and care of all Southern families, particularly those made homeless and jobless by Lincoln's War.[1775] Forrest himself accurately called it a "protective, political, military organization."[1776] The organization's creed stated plainly that its "objects" were to be an "institution of Chivalry, Humanity, Mercy, and Patriotism," and that its purposes were to

> protect the weak, the innocent, and the defenseless from the indignities, wrongs, and outrages of the lawless, the violent, and the brutal; to relieve the injured and the oppressed; to succor the suffering and unfortunate, and especially the widows and orphans of Confederate soldiers.[1777]

But the "protection" provided by the Klan was not just for whites, it was for blacks as well. For contrary to Northern folklore the original KKK was not an anti-black organization, it was an anti-Yankee organization;[1778] or more specifically, an anti-carpetbagger and anti-scallywag organization. In fact, there were thousands, of black members in this, the original KKK.[1779] We even have evidence that an all-black KKK was in operation in the Nashville area.[1780]

So if not blacks, who was the KKK supposed to protect its members from? In 1872, when asked this same question, Forrest answered, "from anybody."[1781]

Forrest, like so many of his neighbors, was quick to support the

---

1775. Seabrook, TMCP, p. 163.

1776. *Reports of the Committees of the Senate of the United States (for the Second Session of the Forty-second Congress)*, p. 33.

1777. Morton, p. 338.

1778. Morton, p. 343; Horwitz, pp. 200-201.

1779. Lester and Wilson, p. 26; Rogers, p. 34; Browning, p. 103; Hurst, p. 305.

1780. Horn, IE, pp. 362-363. We will note that at one time (1920s-1930s) even the modern KKK—though it has no connection with the original KKK—possessed African-American members, and treated both whites and blacks the same. Terkel, p. 239. In Indiana, for example, after white klansmen decided they wanted to broaden their racial base, they organized a "colored division" whose uniform was white capes, blue masks, and red robes. Blee, p. 169.

1781. *Report of the Joint Select Committee to Inquire into the Condition of Affairs in the Late Insurrectionary States*, p. 23.

fledgling organization, which immediately set up "dens" in various Tennessee towns such as Franklin, Columbia, Shelbyville, and Nashville. With their homes, livelihoods, lives, and very culture at stake, Forrest's decision is not difficult to understand, especially from a 21ˢᵗ-Century perspective. Who today would not want to do all they could to protect the innocent, the weak, the elderly, the widowed, and the orphaned, under the same circumstances?

In a speech at Brownsville, Tennessee, in the summer of 1868, addressing both whites and blacks, Forrest supported any organization that would help guard his people, offer police protection, and maintain the South's constitutional rights: Lincoln's War, he asserted, took everything from us but our honor. It is now time to defend the honor of our spouses, our loved ones, and our region from further depredations.[1782]

Forrest's support, fame, and notoriety lent cachet to the Klan and in 1867, at the Nashville KKK Convention, some say that he was made the first Grand Dragon of the Tennessee chapter. But unfortunately for those making this claim, indisputable evidence for this does not exist.

What is known is that his affiliation with the organization by this time had drawn thousands of new recruits until, at its zenith, the organization had an official membership of nearly 600,000 individuals nationwide.[1783] The South was rising up in pride and defense against an overwhelming occupying force whose publically stated goal was to destroy not only the very heart and soul of Dixie, but also its economic and political power.

Throughout the War Northern interests had been bribing and intimidating blacks to foment violence and insurrection against their former masters, using the Loyal League (or Union League or Black Loyal League, as it was also called), to hide their anti-South activities.[1784] By 1869 the result was an explosion of race riots and racial tensions across the South, particularly in Georgia, where the mugging of white men and the rape of white women by blacks had become commonplace.[1785]

---

1782. Wills, p. 350.
1783. Lester and Wilson, p. 30.
1784. Lester and Wilson, pp. 79-80; Mathes, p. 372; Henry, FWMF, p. 443; Ridley, pp. 649-650.
1785. Lester and Wilson, p. 31.

As anti-white hate crimes by racist blacks peaked, elements of the KKK grew increasingly hostile toward African-Americans (the William Lloyd Garrison-inspired Nat Turner Rebellion of 1831, in which roving gangs of black supremacists and black racists indiscriminately murdered white families, had not yet been forgotten thirty-eight years on).  Out of fear and in retaliation, commensurate harassment and murder of blacks by some KKK members began in earnest.[1786]  Their crimes, however, soon became just as bad as those committed by Northern reconstructionists against the South.[1787]

When this occurred, an indignant Forrest, the Klan's most influential supporter (one who was moving ever closer to fully embracing Christianity), tried to quell "outrages" by both whites *and* blacks.[1788]

This effort having failed, in January 1869 he issued "General Order Number One," which commanded the entire organization to dissolve.[1789]  The KKK, Forrest declared, had become "perverted from its original honorable and patriotic purposes," becoming "injurious instead of subservient to the public peace and public safety for which it was intended."[1790]

Additionally, he noted, it was no longer needed because the KKK had accomplished its main objectives: to overthrow the carpetbag-scallywag regime and restore civilization and power to the South.[1791]  Or as Forrest himself put it, the dissolution of the KKK was necessary because:

> There was no further use for it . . . the country was safe . . . there was no apprehension of any [more] trouble.[1792]

When asked if the KKK had proven beneficial to the South in any way, Forrest replied:

---

1786. Browning, pp. 99-100.

1787. Morton, p. 341.

1788. Ashdown and Caudill, p. 62.

1789. Horn, IE, pp. 356-357.

1790. Morton, p. 342.

1791. Morton, p. 346.

1792. *Report of the Joint Select Committee to Inquire into the Condition of Affairs in the Late Insurrectionary States*, p. 16.

No doubt of it. Since its organization the [Loyal] leagues have quit killing and murdering our people. There were some foolish young men who put masks on their faces and rode over the country frightening negroes; but orders have been issued to stop that, and it has ceased.[1793]

Contrary to Northern anti-South folklore, when Forrest ordered the KKK shut down, he meant just that: according to his own testimony, and probably his own personal order,

three members of the Ku-Klux have been court-martialed and shot for violations of the orders not disturb or molest people.[1794]

This is not the Forrest of Northern myth. It is the Forrest of Southern reality.

Here is the text of "General Order Number One":

Whereas, information of an authentic character has reached these head-quarters that the blacks in the counties of Marshall, Maury, Giles, and Lawrence are organized into military companies, with the avowed determination to make war upon and exterminate the Ku Klux Klan, said blacks are hereby solemnly warned and ordered to desist from further action in such organizations, if they exist.

The G. D. (Grand Dragon) regrets the necessity of such an order. But this Klan shall not be outraged and interfered with by lawless negroes and meaner white men, who do not and never have understood our purpose.

In the first place this Klan is not an institution of violence, lawlessness, and cruelty; it is not lawless; it is not aggressive; it is not military; it is not revolutionary.

It is essentially, originally, and inherently a protective organization; it purposes to execute law instead of resisting it, and to protect all good men, whether white or black, from the outrages and atrocities of bad men of both colors, who have been for the past three years a terror to society, and an injury to us all.

The blacks seem to be impressed with the belief that this Klan is especially their enemy. We are not the enemy of the

---

1793. *Reports of the Committees of the Senate of the United States (for the Second Session of the Forty-second Congress),* p. 34.

1794. *Reports of the Committees of the Senate of the United States (for the Second Session of the Forty-second Congress),* p. 34.

blacks, as long as they behave themselves, make no threats upon us, and do not attack or interfere with us.

But if they make war upon us, they must abide the awful retributions that will follow.

This Klan, while in its peaceful movements and disturbing no one, has been fired into three times. This will not be endured any longer; and if it occurs again, and the parties be discovered, a remorseless vengeance will be wreaked upon them.

We reiterate that we are for peace and law and order. No man, white or black, shall be molested for his political sentiments. This Klan is not a political party; it is not a military party; it is a protective organization, and will never use violence except in resisting violence.

Outrages have been perpetrated by irresponsible parties in the name of this Klan. Should such parties be apprehended, they will be dealt with in a manner to insure us future exemption from such imposition. These impostors have, in some instances, whipped negroes. This is wrong! Wrong! It is denounced by this Klan as it must be by all good and humane men.

The Klan now, as in the past, is prohibited from doing such things. We are striving to protect all good, peaceful, well-disposed, and law-abiding men, whether white or black.

The G. D. deems this order due to the public, due to the Klan, and due to those who are misguided and misinformed.

We therefore request that all newspapers who are friendly to law, and peace, and the public welfare, will publish the same. By order of the G. D., Realm No. 1.[1795]

The consummation of the KKK's aims came when the much reviled, radical liberal, New South, Tennessee Governor William G. Brownlow, resigned to become a U.S. senator. The horrors of "Brownlowism" were finally over. The new governor, DeWitt C. Senter, took office in February 1869, after which he dropped the voting ban against former Confederates, who duly aided him in winning the state election in August 1869.[1796]

Forrest was now free to speak his mind publically without fear of arrest by Brownlow and his henchmen. To whites and blacks everywhere, the General said: Let's get rid of both the Ku Klux Klan *and* the Loyal League. Both are now unnecessary. Let us join together as

---

1795. Ridley, pp. 657-658.
1796. Browning, p. 102.

one nation.[1797]

Forrest was ignored and the Klan continued on under various names (for example, the Constitutional Union Guards, the Pale Faces, the White Brotherhood, the White League, and the Knights of the White Camelia),[1798] reorganizing in 1915 and flourishing into the present day.

## THE DIFFERENCE BETWEEN THE ORIGINAL & MODERN KKK

Let us record here that the original authentic KKK of late 1865 is in no way linked to the KKK of today. The two could not be more opposite in function and purpose. Indeed, it is the height of irony that among Forrest's greatest critics are those who support full civil rights for all people. And yet this was one of the main purposes of the original KKK, the organization to which Forrest belonged.

He detested the intolerance, racism, and violence that later crept into the KKK, which is why he eventually both disassociated himself from it and ordered it to break up and disperse. As such, the original KKK, which lasted a mere three years and four months (December 1865-March 1869) and the modern KKK (post 1915-present) are in no way connected and should not be confused with one another.

Forrest clearly played no role whatsoever in the development of the modern KKK,[1799] and would certainly not be a member if he were alive today. In fact, he would have repudiated such an organization, just as he did in 1869 when violence and racial intolerance began to manifest in the original KKK.

## WAS FORREST THE FOUNDER OF THE KKK?

Now for some plain speaking.

The anti-South movement delights in condemning Forrest for his role as the father and first leader of the Ku Klux Klan.[1800] But in reality neither charge is true. The names of the six men who established the KKK on Christmas Eve 1865, in a haunted house in Pulaski, Tennessee, are legendary and well-known.[1801] They are: J. Calvin Jones, Captain

---

1797. Horn, IE, p. 104.
1798. Morton, pp. 342-343.
1799. Mathes, p. 373.
1800. See, e.g., Highsmith and Landphair, p. 28.
1801. Henry, FWMF, p. 443.

John C. Lester, Richard R. Reed, Captain James R. Crowe, Frank O. McCord, and Captain John B. Kennedy.[1802] As we have seen, Forrest did not begin to associate with the organization until two years later, in 1867. Obviously he could not have been the founder.

FORREST AS "GRAND WIZARD"?

As for the General's alleged role as the grand wizard of the KKK,[1803] even many among the virulent anti-Forrest movement admit that there is no evidence for this other than hearsay and Yankee folklore,[1804] for Klan members never recorded anything on paper,[1805] and as such, no official records exist stating that he was their leader.[1806] Indeed, no Klansman in Forrest's day ever named the grand wizard in public.

John C. Lester, for example, one of the founders of the organization, wrote a complete history of the original KKK and never named him. Forrest's chief of artillery, John W. Morton, also a member of the Klan, penned a detailed account of Forrest, but never once connects him with the leadership of the organization.[1807]

One of Forrest's most important biographers, John Allan Wyeth, authored a 600-page book covering every detail of its subject's

1802. Lester and Wilson, pp. 19-21.

1803. Forrest was said to have been voted in as grand wizard at a meeting in Room 10, in the Maxwell House Hotel (see Morton, p. 344), although there is absolutely no evidence for this assertion. Revealingly, the entry on the Maxwell House Hotel in *The Tennessee Encyclopedia of History and Culture* makes no mention of Forrest, or even of the KKK, in relation to the building, though this seems to be what it was most famous for right up into the present day. Indeed, when the Maxwell House Hotel burned down in 1961, many believed that it was most likely the victim of arson due to its associations with the Klan. Constructed in 1859 (and opening in 1869), the Maxwell House stood on the northeast corner of Fourth Avenue North and Church Street, in downtown Nashville, Tennessee. One of the city's most popular establishments, it was noted for its grand Christmas dinners and the visits of seven U.S. presidents. One of them, Theodore Roosevelt, said that the Maxwell House's coffee was "good to the last drop," which became the famous slogan for America's first blended coffee. Other illustrious guests included Thomas Edison, William F. "Buffalo Bill" Cody, and Henry Ford. Website: http://tennesseeencyclopedia.net/. The Maxwell House Hotel was built by Col. John Overton, Jr. (1821-1898), who named it after his wife Harriet Virginia Maxwell (1831-1899). John's daughter, Martha Overton (1853-1917), married Jacob McGavock Dickinson, Sr. (1851-1928) in Nashville. Jacob served as assistant attorney general under President Stephen Grover Cleveland and secretary of war under President William Howard Taft. Martha's grandfather, Judge John Overton, Sr. (1766-1833) was the owner of Travellers Rest (in Nashville), used as headquarters by Rebel General John Bell Hood between the Battles of Franklin and Nashville in December 1864. The Judge, along with Andrew Jackson and General James Winchester (the grandfather of the author's cousin Confederate Col. Edmund Winchester Rucker), founded the city of Memphis, TN. Seabrook, TMCP, p. 537.

1804. Ashdown and Caudill, p. 60.

1805. Henry, FWMF, pp. 20, 442.

1806. Horn, IE, p. 37.

1807. Henry, FWMF, p. 443.

life, including the KKK period. But again, no mention of Forrest being either the grand wizard or even a member.[1808] Another significant Forrest biographer, Captain J. Harvey Mathes, devotes several pages to the KKK in his work *General Forrest* without directly connecting Old Bedford to the Klan.[1809]

Who then was the head of the original KKK? All we know is that it was not Forrest. What little circumstantial evidence exists indicates that my cousin George Washington Gordon was grand wizard between 1865 and 1869,[1810] as Gordon's own wife later testified.[1811]

At most Forrest may have been some kind of advisor or recruiter, but even this is not known for sure.[1812] Many of the claims that he was grand wizard come from late testimony, primarily from the untrustworthy memories of the Klan's cofounders.[1813] Not even the all-powerful Reconstruction leaders in Washington, D.C., with their secret police force and strong-arm detectives, could find any evidence that Forrest was the organization's leader.[1814]

On June 27, 1871, Forrest himself was put on the witness stand before a highly prejudicial, South-loathing, U.S. governmental investigative committee on Klan activities. The General not only denied being the leader of the KKK, but he also disclaimed even being a member (though he did state that he was "in sympathy" with the Klan and that he had been a member of the Pale Faces, a Mason-like organization). The KKK was nothing more than a defensive body, he rightly asserted, organized to counter the nefarious work of the North's Freedmen's Bureau, Union League, and various Loyal Leagues, all anti-South organizations.[1815]

After a severe grilling the committee sided with Forrest, finding him innocent of all charges in association with the organization,[1816] and

---

1808. Wyeth, LGNBF, p. 619.
1809. Mathes, pp. 370-373.
1810. Gordon was one of the unlucky 702 Rebels captured at the Battle of Franklin II, November 30, 1864.
1811. Wills, p. 336.
1812. Mathes, p. 373.
1813. Ashdown and Caudill, p. 61.
1814. Lytle, p. 385.
1815. *Reports of the Committees of the Senate of the United States (for the Second Session of the Forty-second Congress)*, pp. 22, 33, 34.
1816. Henry, FWMF, p. 448.

concluding that he was not and had never been either the founder of or the first leader of the KKK.[1817] According to the *Report of the House Congressional Committee*, which interviewed Forrest and other former Confederates in 1871 and 1872:

> The statements of these [former Confederate] gentlemen are so full and explicit that comment would only weaken their force. The evidence taken before the committee fully sustains them as to the other States relative to which evidence was heard, and it is only necessary to turn to the records and official documents of the State of Tennessee to show that all General Forrest said about the alarm which prevailed in Tennessee during the administration of Governor [William G.] Brownlow was strictly true. No State was ever reduced to such humiliation and degradation as that unhappy commonwealth during the years Brownlow ruled over her. Her constitution was imposed upon her by a fraction of her people and the people of other States; her legislature, under the dictation of her [pro-North] governor, as early as 1865 began a series of acts of outlawry and oppression which drove her people almost to desperation; whatever was necessary to maintain in power the [Northern] men who had seized the reins of government was ordered and executed with a high hand, and, when necessary, at the point of the bayonet.
>
> An act restricting suffrage was passed, which disfranchised three-fourths of the native population of Middle and West Tennessee; commissioners of registration were appointed and removed at the caprice of the governor; votes of counties by the dozen were rejected when they did not vote as ordered; acts ratifying the illegal edicts of the governor were passed by an obsequious legislature; the men who decided who should and who should not vote, who controlled the registration and elections, were the tools of the governor, when he was himself a candidate.
>
> The sedition law was revived, freedom of speech and of the press was overthrown, and a militia force was organized, which was responsible to the governor alone, composed principally of ignorant and debased men, under the lead of the most unscrupulous [Yankee] partisans, of course. The [carpetbag-scallywag] rulers and their adherents were loud in their professions of loyalty, which simply meant there, as everywhere else, subserviency to the dominant party. Everybody was loyal who voted for and maintained Brownlow and his friends, and everybody was disloyal

1817. Kelly, Michael. "History Tells the Real Story of Forrest," *The Daily News Journal*, December 9, 2006.

who dared to oppose them.[1818]

In the end the U.S. government actually attained at least some understanding of why the South created the KKK, correctly saying that "misgovernment and criminal exploiting of the country by the reconstruction leaders had provoked natural resistance."[1819]

A SUMMARY OF FORREST & THE KKK

When the myth and dross are cleared away, here are the documented facts about Forrest and the Ku Klux Klan:

• Forrest did not form the KKK. It was founded by six men in Pulaski, Tennessee, in December 1865. Forrest was living and working in Memphis at the time. The founders' names are well-known: Captain John C. Lester, Captain John B. Kennedy, Captain James R. Crowe, Richard R. Reed, Frank O. McCord, and J. Calvin Jones.

• Forrest was not even aware of the KKK until late 1866 or early 1867, one to two years after its formation.

• While Forrest was certainly an ardent supporter of the KKK, there is no hard evidence that he was the grand wizard, or even a member.

• It is most probable that George W. Gordon was grand wizard during the short life of the original KKK.

• The rumors that Forrest was the founder and grand wizard of the KKK were started by anti-South advocates shortly after the War in order to humiliate Forrest, his family, and his soldiers. As the original KKK did not keep written records, no one can prove that either of these legends have any truth to them. And in fact, numerous people, including authentic KKK members, testified that they were patently false.

• The trouble-making uninformed Yankee propagandists who started the rumors about Forrest and the KKK were the same ones who

1818. *Report of the Joint Select Committee to Inquire into the Condition of Affairs in the Late Insurrectionary States*, pp. 453-454.
1819. Morton, p. 343.

started the rumor that the original KKK was a racist group.

• As was proven in Forrest's "General Order Number One," the original KKK was not a racist organization. It was a relief-and-aid society, set up to assist war widows, orphans, and Confederate veterans, whatever their skin color. This helps explain why the original KKK had thousands of black members and even an all-black KKK chapter at Nashville.

• During the original KKK years Forrest threatened to shoot any whites who harassed blacks. This warning included both white Northerners and white Southerners.

• In early 1869, when Forrest felt the organization had fulfilled its stated mission (to aid and protect the South and her citizens), he ordered it to be closed down. Thus the original KKK lasted just a little over three years.

• Forrest, or perhaps a leader within the KKK, had several Klan members tried and executed for ignoring Forrest's order.

• In 1871 Forrest was questioned before a U.S. government committee investigating the KKK, where he was found innocent of any misconduct associated with the organization. This fact alone should end any and all disputes concerning Forrest and his relationship with the Klan.

• The modern nationwide KKK that was founded after 1900 has no relation whatsoever with the original KKK of the 1860s. Indeed, they are so completely dissimilar in every way that if the modern KKK had not borrowed the name of the original KKK, no informed individual today would even make any connection between the two.


BANKRUPTCY & AMNESTY

With his finances now in tatters, on February 5, 1868, former multimillionaire Forrest filed a petition for bankruptcy in the U.S. District Court at Memphis. In an attempt to discharge all of his debts, he gave up his property to his creditors. A year later, in the spring of 1869, the discharge was granted.

In the summer of 1868 Forrest was one of forty-nine Southerners chosen to be delegates at the first postwar Democratic National Convention, set in New York City on July 4. As he was by then considered a national celebrity, the General's appearance in Gotham created a sensation, at once both polarizing and controversial.

While some Yankee newspapers unfairly called him the "Butcher of Fort Pillow," other more objective journals treated him with the respect and dignity he deserved. One of these, the New York *Herald*, wrote that it found the General quite charismatic. Representing the finest specimen of the archetypal Southern Rebel, it went on to say, he is a highly rational man and among the greatest of the former Confederacy's reconstructed officers.[1820]

At the convention Forrest supported fellow Democrat and Tennessean, President Andrew Johnson[1821]—until the delegation realized he could not win. Forrest's vote then went to the democratic (i.e., conservative) Governor Horatio Seymour of New York.
Sadly for the nation, former Yankee general and war criminal Ulysses S. Grant—one of the men who tried to hunt down and murder Forrest during the War—went on to win the presidential election that fall, subjecting Americans, both South and North, to two terms of the second most corrupt administration in U.S. history since Lincoln.

While Forrest's support did not help Johnson in his bid to win the presidency, it seems to have helped Forrest himself. On July 17, 1868, he was kindly pardoned by President Johnson for "treason" against the U.S. This was a bitter pill to swallow for any Southerner, in particular a former Confederate officer. But he had little choice if he wanted to remain in the U.S.

A fortunate side effect of Forrest's pardon was that, to a great extent, it helped restore his still tarnished reputation in Yankeedom. Despite this, due to a mean-spirited constitutional amendment, the General and other Southern sympathizers were not allowed to vote until 1870.[1822]

---

1820. Henry, FWMF, p. 454.
1821. Though Johnson was born (in 1808) in North Carolina, he spent most of his adult life in Tennessee, where he served as governor, a senator, a representative, and a military governor (under Lincoln). He married Tennessean Elizabeth McCardle in 1827. Johnson died in the Volunteer State in 1875.
1822. Mathes, p. 358.

## - 1870s -
# FINAL YEARS, DEATH, & BURIAL

"My strength is failin' and it is absolutely
necessary that I should have some rest." —
Nathan Bedford Forrest

### RAILROAD FAILURE & PRESIDENT'S ISLAND

JUST AS FORREST'S ALABAMA RAILROAD scheme was starting
to get off the ground (surveying and grading were already
underway), a wave of yellow fever swept over Memphis and the
Panic of 1873 hit the nation.  With the South still in ruins and investors
closing their pocketbooks, his dream of building a railroad line from
Memphis to Selma collapsed.  As he had committed much of his own
money to the project, Forrest lost a small fortune, leaving him again
nearly penniless.[1823]

After three thankless years as its head executive—during which
more trouble and lawsuits were produced than profits—he resigned on
April 1, 1874, making his donation of $5,000 (payable in his railroad
company's stock)[1824] toward the 1873-founding of Nashville's Vanderbilt
University valueless.[1825]

With his remaining capital the General leased a double log cabin
on a twelve-mile long, 32,000 acre piece of land called President's

---

**1823**. Sheppard, p. 296.
**1824**. Forrest's $5,000 donation to the building of Vanderbilt University in 1873 is today's equivalent of
$90,000.
**1825**. Henry, FWMF, p. 458.

Island,[1826] located in the Mississippi River just south of Memphis.[1827] It would be the last private residence he would ever live in. The largest island on the Mississippi, Forrest hired some 100 white and black convicts (male and female) from Shelby County to work his new 1,300 acre plantation there, an act for which his critics still complain loudly and often.[1828]

What these individuals seem to have forgotten, however, is that this type of "involuntary servitude" was legalized and legitimized by the Northern-created Thirteenth Amendment (one of Lincoln's pet projects). Though it officially ended slavery all across the U.S. for the first time (on December 6, 1865), this act made an exception for convict labor. Thus Forrest was obeying the law in every respect as laid down by the Constitution and one of its Yankee-made amendments.[1829]

We must also bear in mind that the leasing of convict labor was the norm at a time when official workhouses and prisons had not yet been established in the South.[1830] And finally, Forrest's use of convict labor aided not only the state of Tennessee and its citizens (by taking some of the burden for housing these inmates off the backs of taxpayers), but it also helped rehabilitate the felons themselves, who, like most of the General's soldiers during the War, grew from boys into men under his rough, intuitive, no-nonsense tutelage.

After building quarters for his laborers, Forrest settled in with his family and began to give speeches at a variety of Confederate reunions and ceremonies. While his plantation cultivated corn, potatoes, cotton, and millet, Forrest cultivated his own vegetable garden. The famed former Confederate chieftain was once again seen walking the streets of Memphis dressed in the modest and unpretentious postwar garb of a Tennessee farmer.[1831]

---

1826. President's Island takes its name from Old Hickory, President Andrew Jackson, who once owned a small farm there.
1827. Lytle, p. 386.
1828. Mathes, pp. 362-363.
1829. Drescher and Engerman, p. x.
1830. Henry, FWMF, p. 459; Wills, p. 459.
1831. Lytle, p. 386.

## FORREST CONVERTS

As Forrest aged he continued to grow and mature, experiencing the sting of regret for past mistakes and sins. It was at this time that he converted to Christianity, repented, and apologized to all those he had wronged. He became the true "Christian warrior" personified.

His conversion caused something of a stir since he had never been considered the religious type. During the War he had shown great respect for spiritual concerns, asking chaplains to say prayers at meals and on special occasions. He even held church parades for his men and started each morning with prayer in his tent.[1832] But he never attended church himself, much to his wife Mary Ann's dismay.[1833]

All of that changed near the end of his life, however, when one day, November 7, 1875, he was walking down a Memphis street.[1834] As he strode through town, he bumped into Texan Raleigh R. White, a former lieutenant-colonel who had served under him during Lincoln's War.[1835] Forrest, discovering that White had since become a reverend, led the clergyman into the lobby of a nearby bank and asked him to say a prayer on his behalf. The two knelt down in the parlor and Reverend White asked God to bless Forrest and to accept him into his fold.

Shortly thereafter, on November 14, 1875, the General was baptized into his wife's faith, the Cumberland Presbyterian Church of Memphis.[1836] I have turned my life over to Jesus, my Lord and Savior, he later earnestly told Reverend George Stainback, the church's minister.[1837]

Forrest's conversion to Christianity had a profound impact on the old war chief. Among other things, he dropped all of his lawsuits, even though his attorneys assured him that they were winnable and that they would have enabled him to recoup most of his financial losses.[1838] One of his legal advisors, a former Forrest soldier named General John T. Morgan, continued to pressure him to fight for his claims, to which

---

1832. Sheppard, p. 309.
1833. Mathes, p. 373.
1834. Browning, p. 104.
1835. Wills, p. 373.
1836. Mathes, p. 374.
1837. Hurst, p. 378.
1838. Wyeth, LGNBF, p. 623.

Forrest responded:

> General, I am broken in spirit and have not long to live. My life has
> been a battle from the start. It was a fight to achieve a livelihood
> for those dependent upon me in my younger days, and an
> independence for myself when I grew up to manhood, as well as in
> the terrible turmoil of the Civil War. I have seen too much
> violence, and I want to close my days in peace with all the world,
> as I am now at peace with my Maker.[1839]

## FORREST FORGIVES THE NORTH

In the 1870s Forrest officially forgave the North for its many
transgressions, even leading a Confederate ceremony at Elmwood
Cemetery in Memphis on May 30, 1875, to decorate the gravestones of
the Federal dead buried there.

Forrest then issued a public letter, stating that though the South
had fought hard to secede from the U.S. government, it must now accept
its fate as a member of that same political body. After all, Forrest
asserted, this was the government of our fathers, and it will now be the
government of our children.[1840]

## FORREST & BLACK CIVIL RIGHTS

Having shut down the KKK and thoroughly repudiated racial prejudice,
it was at this time that he also became an ardent civil rights advocate,
pushing for equal rights for blacks.[1841] As we have seen, as president of
the Selma, Marion, and Memphis Railroad, the one-time States' Rights
Rebel hired some 400 former slaves to work as conductors, engineers,
foremen, and architects,[1842] jobs still forbidden to blacks in the North at
the time.[1843]

In 1872, when asked if he was ever opposed to Negro suffrage,

---

1839. Wyeth, LGNBF, p. 622.

1840. Hurst, p. 365.

1841. Hurst, p. 11.

1842. *Report of the Joint Select Committee to Inquire into the Condition of Affairs in the Late Insurrectionary States*, p. 17.

1843. As discussed earlier, first-hand reports by both Northerners and Southerners disclose that blacks were treated much more equitably in Dixie than they were in the North, before, during, and after the War.

he gave a resounding "no sir."[1844] Then when asked, "what do you think of negro suffrage?", Forrest replied:

> If the negroes vote to enfranchise us, I do not think I would favor their disenfranchisement. We will stand by those who help us. And here I want you to understand distinctly, I am not an enemy of the negro. We want him here among us; he is the only laboring class we have; and, more than that, I would sooner trust him than the white scalawag or carpet-bagger.[1845]

Earlier, during the original KKK period (1865-1869), Forrest had vowed not to harm blacks, only Radical (i.e., liberal) whites for stirring up trouble between the races. "I have no powder to burn killing negroes," he stated. "I intend to kill the Radicals."[1846]

Later, in the summer of 1868, at Brownsville, Tennessee, Forrest gave a speech to an integrated audience about the dangers facing Dixie from this nefarious left-wing group. I'd like to say a few words to the black men here today, Forrest began. Don't abandon those who brought you up from childhood and cared for you during both sickness and health. It is we who are your true friends. Reject the Loyal Leagues, whose main occupation is deception, and who would turn you against those who have always stood by you.[1847]

The following year, on March 9, 1869, Forrest elaborated on his views of white and black relations in an interview aboard a train with a reporter from the Louisville *Courier-Journal*:

> *Reporter*: The South has been depopulated. What is to be done?
> *Forrest*: I say, let us bring in more blacks. They are the finest workers the South has ever known. I have nothing but kindly feelings toward the freedmen.
> *Reporter*: Where would we find enough Negroes?
> *Forrest*: There are thousands that could be gotten from Africa [where they are already enslaved through tribal warfare]. Why not

---

1844. *Report of the Joint Select Committee to Inquire into the Condition of Affairs in the Late Insurrectionary States*, p. 20.

1845. *Report of the Joint Select Committee to Inquire into the Condition of Affairs in the Late Insurrectionary States*, p. 34.

1846. *Report of the Joint Select Committee to Inquire into the Condition of Affairs in the Late Insurrectionary States*, p. 34.

1847. Kinshasa, p. 55.

use them? My business partners and I have recently brought over about 400 Africans, and they are as good as any workers I've ever known. These talented hardworking men alone are quite capable of rebuilding our entire region.

*Reporter*: What about Yankees or Europeans?

*Forrest*: I welcome them, but they will never come to the South to be mere laborers. This is one of the main reasons I vote to use fresh African labor. If they come to help us revive the South, I promise to protect them with my very life. And if and when the U.S. government finally ends its prejudice against the Negro, it will also support my idea. There is no longer any place, or need, for racial hatred.[1848]

Forrest's racial plan for the future of America, which also included hiring Chinese and Japanese immigrants to help rebuild the South,[1849] was in stark contrast to Lincoln's. As we have seen, until the day he died our sixteenth president was an ardent black colonizationist, one who campaigned ceaselessly to make America white from coast to coast. This was to be accomplished, he repeatedly proclaimed, by shipping as many blacks out of the country as possible, preferably, as he put it, back "to their own native land."[1850]

So enthusiastic was Lincoln to establish American apartheid that both his District of Columbia Emancipation Act (issued April 16, 1862) and his Preliminary Emancipation Proclamation (issued September 22, 1862) called for black colonization.[1851] Settle them anywhere in the world; anywhere but here in the U.S., Lincoln declared.[1852]

Thus while Lincoln was plotting to send all American blacks "back to Africa," Forrest was formulating plans to bring more African blacks to America. Despite these plain facts, according to Yankee myth, civil rights supporter Forrest was a virulent racist while white supremacist Lincoln was the "Great Emancipator" and the "true friend of the black man." Yet it was Forrest, not Lincoln, who said that he had

---

1848. "An Interview with Gen. Forrest," Louisville *Courier-Journal*, March 9, 1869; reprinted in the Memphis *Daily Appeal*, March 12, 1869, and again in the New York *Times*, March 15, 1869. I have paraphrased Forrest's words here while retaining his original meaning. For more on this fascinating interview, see Hurst, p. 330.

1849. Wills, pp. 360-361.

1850. Nicolay and Hay, ALCW, Vol. 1, p. 288.

1851. See Seabrook, L, pp. 599-601, 614-619.

1852. Nicolay and Hay, ALCW, Vol. 2, p. 237.

sympathy for blacks, that he felt a humane kindness toward them, and that he and other Southerners wanted to protect and preserve them, not hurt, destroy, or deport them.[1853]

In August 1874 Forrest revealed that far from being a racist, as the uniformed continue to charge, he cared deeply about all races and colors. That month a number of blacks were killed by white vigilantes, the result of a scuffle between blacks and whites at a barbeque in the town of Trenton, Tennessee. At an "indignation meeting" in Memphis on August 28, Forrest stood up and said publically: If I had the authority to do so, I would arrest and execute the whites who perpetrated this contemptible act.[1854]

Nowhere is Forrest's lack of racism more evident than in another speech he gave, this one in Memphis on July 4, 1875. His audience was the Independent Order of Pole Bearers, a sociopolitical group of black Southerners (and forerunner of the NAACP).[1855] As reported by the unreconstructed Memphis *Daily Avalanche*, July 6, 1875, an African-American woman named Miss Lou Lewis, handed Forrest a bouquet of flowers, "as a token, of reconciliation, an offering of peace and good will." Bowing to the crowd, Forrest said:

> Miss Lewis, ladies and gentlemen—I accept these flowers as a token of reconciliation between the white and colored races of the South. I accept them more particularly, since they come from a lady, for if there is any one on God's great earth who loves the ladies, it is myself.
>
> This is a proud day for me. Having occupied the position I have for thirteen years, and being misunderstood by the colored race, I take this occasion to say that I am your friend. I am here as the representative of the Southern people—one that has been more maligned than any other.[1856] I assure you that everyman who was in the Confederate army is your friend. We were born on the same

---

1853. See e.g., ORA, Ser. I, Vol. 32, Pt. 1, pp. 590, 593.

1854. Hurst, pp. 361, 385.

1855. Browning, p. 103.

1856. In order to sabotage Forrest and arouse Yankee hatred of the South, the North had long portrayed him as a racist, much to his dismay. To a great extent their ploy worked. To this day, to a majority of people—even in the South—Forrest's name is associated with racism. This despite the fact that, as this book has shown, he was, unlike Lincoln and most other Northerners, not truly prejudiced against the African race. To the contrary, he did much to help blacks before and during the War, while working hard to heal the rift between the races afterward.

soil, breathe the same air, live in the same land, and why should we not be brothers and sisters.

When the war broke out I believed it to be my duty to fight for my country, and I did so. I came here with the jeers and sneers of a few white people, who did not think it right. I think it is right, and will do all I can to bring about harmony, peace and unity. I want to elevate every man, and to see you take your places in your shops, stores and offices. I don't propose to say anything about politics, but I want you to do as I do—go to the polls and select the best men to vote for. I feel that you are free men, I am a free man, and we can do as we please.

I came here as a friend, and whenever I can serve any of you I will do so. We have one Union, one flag, one country, therefore let us stand together. Although we differ in color, we should not differ in sentiment.

Many things have been said in regard to myself, and many reports circulated, which may perhaps be believed by some of you, but there are many around me who can contradict them. I have been many times in the heat of battle—oftener, perhaps, than any within the sound of my voice. Men have come to me to ask for quarter, both black and white, and I have shielded them. Do your duty as citizens, and if any are oppressed, I will be your friend. I thank you for the flowers, and assure you that I am with you in heart and hand.[1857]

That same year, 1875, Forrest publically stated that African-Americans should be free to enter any profession they desired, without restriction. This was an idea that went far beyond anything Lincoln and most other Northerners ever espoused. Indeed, having spent most of his life around blacks, Forrest knew better than any Yank that African-Americans possessed the same potentialities as whites. Unlike Lincoln and his other racist compatriots to the North, however, instead of impeding black advancement, the philanthropic, humane, and beneficent Forrest went one step further and actually advocated full civil rights for all races.[1858]

## BLACK PERSECUTION OF FORREST
In a cruel ironic twist, the middle-aged Forrest—who fought so

---

1857. Memphis *Daily Avalanche*, July 6, 1875, p. 1.
1858. Hurst, pp. 385-386.

diligently for black civil rights and who so earnestly supported organizations such as the NAACP-like International Order of Pole Bearers, a man who freed his slaves long before Lincoln did and who integrated his troops while Lincoln segregated his—has long been viciously attacked by blacks.

Comparing him to Hitler and Jack the Ripper, many modern blacks excoriate Forrest for a host of alleged "atrocities" that he never committed, "barbarisms" that are actually inventions of Northern mythologists and Yankee propagandists, most dating from the time of Lincoln's War.

One of the latest and most absurd insults against Forrest's good name comes from the NAACP itself: in 1988 the organization asked the city of Memphis to move Forrest's Equestrian Monument (statue), along with his and his wife's remains, from their present burial site to a more inconspicuous location.[1859] They also insisted that Forrest Park—the area in which he was buried and which was named after him—be renamed.[1860] Why? Forrest was not the enemy of blacks. As we have repeatedly seen, unlike white separatist and white supremacist Lincoln, in real life Forrest was the friend of blacks. He is only their "enemy" in Northern story books and biased Yankee newspaper articles.[1861]

## CHARITY

In his last years, though he himself was no longer wealthy, Forrest gave generously to charities, in particular those dedicated to Confederate veterans, widows, and orphans, donating, in fact, most of his fortune to them.[1862] Indeed, he exhausted most of what was left of his estate supporting the families of his men after the War. (And we will remember that he spent thousands of dollars of his own money outfitting his troops during the War.) He even offered his services as a military

---

1859. Browning, p. 107.

1860. Ashdown and Caudill, p. 180.

1861. Ironically, while the Independent Order of Pole Bearers admired, understood, and respected Forrest (as well as other Confederates), its modern offspring, the NAACP, has today become one of the most intolerant, most ardent anti-Confederate organizations in existence. Responsible for leading numerous crusades in an attempt to besmirch Forrest's name, it has been denounced as a hate group even by many blacks, such as Reverend Jesse Lee Peterson. See Peterson's Brotherhood Organization of a New Destiny (BOND) Website: www.bondinfo.org.

1862. Wyeth, LGNBF, pp. 621, 16.

man to his old nemesis Sherman (who arrogantly turned him down).[1863]

END OF "RECONSTRUCTION"

In the spring of 1877, as Forrest's postwar life was still stabilizing, he and the rest of the South, both white and black, received good news: under the Compromise of 1877, twelve years of "Reconstruction" was now finally coming to an end, thanks to the nation's new president, Rutherford B. Hayes. In his Inaugural Address, March 5, 1887, Hayes said:

> Let me assure my countrymen of the Southern States that it is my earnest desire to regard and promote their truest interests, the interests of the white and of the colored people, both and equally, and to put forth my best efforts in behalf of a civil policy which will forever wipe out in our political affairs the color line, and the distinction between North and South, to the end that we may have, not merely a united North or a united South, but a united country.[1864]

Sticking to his pledge, on April 10, 1877, Hayes pulled all U.S. troops out of South Carolina.[1865] On April 24, 1877, he withdrew them from Louisiana, as well, sounding the death knell for the carpetbag-scallywag regime,[1866] along with Lincoln's ridiculous, illegal, and insulting plan to Northernize the South.[1867]

Hayes then put a stop to the enforcement of the anti-South Fourteenth[1868] and Fifteenth Amendments,[1869] appointed ex-Confederates to various administrative posts,[1870] and in September he toured Dixie, promising reconciliation, solidarity, and *genuine*

---

1863. Hurst, p. 360.

1864. C. R. Williams, Vol. 2, p. 13.

1865. J. H. Franklin, p. 216.

1866. Weintraub, p. 76

1867. Kane, p.217.

1868. In essence the Fourteenth Amendment was an attempt by liberals to supercede the Tenth Amendment, the part of the Bill of Rights that guarantees states' rights. W. S. Powell, p. 145. For more on why the Fourteenth Amendment was condemned across Dixie, see L. Johnson, pp. 241-242; Woods, pp. 86-90; Findlay and Findlay, pp. 228-235; DiLorenzo, RL, pp. 207-208, 211.

1869. Bradley, p. 138. At the time the Fifteenth Amendment was passed, Radical, anti-South, Yankee liberal Thaddeus Stevens, arrogantly said: "I shall vote for this not because of any constitutional right, but because we have the power." Stonebraker, p. 76.

1870. Rosenbaum, s.v. "Hayes, Rutherford Birchard."

reconstruction (as opposed to Lincoln's fake "reconstruction") through a policy of pacification.

Finally, despite opposition within his own party, Hayes made government appointments based on merit rather than party loyalty and political patronage.[1871] One of Hayes' Supreme Court appointments, William B. Woods of Georgia (the first Southerner appointed to the Court since Lincoln's War), spoke for the majority by wisely calling for an end to government efforts to combat the KKK.[1872]

After nearly sixteen years to the day (April 12, 1861 to April 10, 1877)—during which time the South was subjected to an illegal invasion and the social and political upheaval and unnecessary bloodshed that went along with it—Southerners began to retake control of their region. Jubilation was felt in every home across Dixie: "Reconstruction" had utterly failed in its sixteen-year attempt to turn the agricultural South into an exact image of the industrial North.

For freedmen and freedwomen, however, there was no celebration. Lincoln's promise of "forty acres and a mule" turned out to be just another lie:[1873] there were no mules[1874] and most of his so-called "black land giveaways" ultimately went to rich white Northerners.[1875]

HEALTH ISSUES

Forrest had little time, or desire, to celebrate along with the rest of Dixie: he had been having annoying medical problems since the end of the War. But now his health was beginning to deteriorate more rapidly than ever, probably in great part due to overworking in the malarial swamps on President's Island.

In an effort to restore his health he began "taking the waters" at several resorts, one at Hot Springs, Arkansas, and one at Hurricane Springs, Tennessee, both which were said to have special healing qualities.[1876] Neither had any lasting effect.[1877] In the summer of 1877

1871. Parry, s.v. "Hayes, Rutherford B."
1872. DeGregorio, pp. 286, 287.
1873. Mullen, p. 33; Rosenbaum and Brinkley, s.v. "Forty Acres and a Mule."
1874. J. H. Franklin, p. 37.
1875. Thornton and Ekelund, p. 96.
1876. Sheppard, p. 298; Henry, FWMF, p. 460.
1877. Wyeth, LGNBF, p. 623.

Forrest told a good family friend, his former aid-de-camp Major Charles W. Anderson:

> I am not the same man you were with so long and knew so well. I've been leading—trying to lead—another kind of life. Mary has been praying for me night and day for all these years. I reckon it was through her prayers that my life was spared and I was brought safely through so many dangers. I hope I'm a better man now than I was in those days when we were together.[1878]

## FINAL PUBLIC APPEARANCE & SPEECH

Forrest's final public appearance was on September 21, 1877, at a reunion of the Seventh Tennessee Regiment of Cavalry in Memphis (he had enlisted in the regiment as a private sixteen years earlier, on June 14, 1861).[1879] From astride his horse he read the following speech, his last one, to the attentive crowd:

> Soldiers of the Seventh Tennessee Cavalry. Ladies, and Gentlemen: I name the soldiers first because I love them best. I am extremely pleased to meet you here to-day. I love the gallant men with whom I was so intimately connected during the war. You can hardly realize what must pass through a commander's mind when called upon to meet in reunion the brave spirits who, through four years of war and bloodshed, fought fearlessly for a cause that they thought right, and who, even when they foresaw as we did, that the war must soon close in disaster, and that we must all surrender, yet did not quail, but marched to victory in many battles, and fought as boldly and persistently in their last battles as they did in their first. Nor do I forget those many gallant spirits who sleep coldly in death upon the many bloody battle-fields of the late war. I love them too, and honor their memory. I have often been called to the side, on the battle-field, of those who have been struck down, and they would put their arms around my neck, draw me down to them, and kiss me, and say: 'General, I have fought my last battle and will soon be gone. I want you to remember my wife and children and take care of them.' Comrades, I have remembered their wives and little ones, and have taken care of them, and I want everyone of you to remember them too, and join with me in the

---

1878. Wyeth, LGNBF, p. 623.
1879. At the time the Seventh Tennessee was known as White's Tennessee Mounted Rifles. Wyeth, LGNBF, p. 23.

labor of love.

Comrades, through the years of bloodshed and weary marches you were tried and true soldiers. So through the years of peace you have been good citizens, and now that we are again united under the old [U.S.] flag, I love it as I did in the days of my youth, and I feel sure that you love it also. Yes, I love and honor that old flag as much as those who followed it on the other side; and I am sure that I but express your feelings when I say that should occasion offer and our country demand our services, you would as eagerly follow my lead to battle under that proud banner as ever you followed me in our late great war. It has been thought by some that our social reunions were wrong, and that they would be heralded to the North as an evidence that we were again ready to break out into civil war. But I think that they are right and proper, and we will show our countrymen by our conduct and dignity that brave soldiers are always good citizens and law-abiding and loyal people.

Soldiers, I was afraid that I could not be with you to-day, but I could not bear the thought of not meeting with you, and I will always try to meet with you in the future. And I hope that you will continue to meet from year to year, and bring your wives and children with you, and let them, and the children who may come after them, enjoy with you the pleasure of your reunions.[1880]

In late October 1877 Forrest was brought by raft to Memphis, then borne on a litter to the home of his last surviving brother Jesse. Old friends visited, including President Jefferson Davis. Toward the end of the month, on the 26th, the New York *Times* noted that Forrest remained in critical condition, and that, due to chronic diarrhea, he weighed only 100 pounds.[1881]

On October 29, frail, emaciated, and gentle, with "the voice and manner of a woman,"[1882] but still possessing his "blazing eyes" and his fiery Anglo-Celtic spirit, a mellowed, silver-haired, white-bearded Forrest uttered his last coherent words: "Call my wife."[1883]

Fifteen minutes later, at 7:15 PM, he died peacefully from exhaustion, high blood pressure related issues,[1884] the effects of a spinal

1880. Mathes, pp. 374-376.
1881. Elizabeth Scott-Whipkey, personal correspondence.
1882. Wyeth, LGNBF, p. 621.
1883. Henry, ATSF, p. 292.
1884. Bradley, p. 138.

wound (received at the Battle of Shiloh), malaria, chronic dysentery and diarrhea, and complications due to diabetes.[1885] At fifty-six years of age he was still young, even by Victorian standards.

The next day, October 30, his death notice appeared in the local paper, the Memphis *Avalanche*. Forrest met his death with religious composure and complete acceptance, his obituary read in part.[1886]

The following day, October 31, the General's body, dressed in his Confederate uniform, was taken to Elmwood Cemetery in a black hearse pulled by four black horses. There he was buried by his wife Mary Ann (who was to outlive him by sixteen years). President Davis, along with many members of his cabinet, attended the ceremony, and, along with members of Forrest's staff, acted as pallbearers.[1887]

Forrest's Escort, led by Lieutenant George L. Cowan, was followed by the lodge of the Independent Order of Odd Fellows, of which Forrest had been a member.[1888] Also in the funeral procession were a host of other Confederate veterans, carriages, horsemen, firemen, policemen, black convict workers from his plantation, numerous everyday citizens, and a brass band playing the *Dead March*. The entire procession was some three miles long, stretching from Jesse's home all the way to Elmwood.[1889]

After the firing of minute guns and the tolling of the church bells, Reverend George Stainback (the aforementioned pastor from Forrest's church, the Cumberland Presbyterian Church of Memphis) gave the poignant eulogy.

The once headstrong warrior went Home a humbled peacemaker. But not before offering the world one last glimpse of the real Nathan Bedford Forrest: among the 20,000 individuals who attended his funeral the next day to pay their respects to the acclaimed Confederate officer, were thousands of grieving African-Americans, a fact that thoroughly demolishes the Yankee myth that Forrest was a racist who was hated and feared by the blacks of his day.

According to the Memphis *Appeal*, many hundreds of African-

---

1885. Henry, FWMF, p. 459.
1886. Bradley, pp. 141-142.
1887. Mathes, p. 376.
1888. Henry, FWMF, p. 461.
1889. Wills, p. 379.

Americans (of all ages) "flocked" to Forrest's funeral, demonstrating not only a fascination with the General, but "genuine sorrow" over the demise of the celebrated military man. On the morning of October 31 alone, over 500 blacks walked solemnly past Forrest's casket. From them not a single denigrating word was heard. Only adulation and admiration.[1890]

### NATHAN BEDFORD FORREST PARK

On November 11, 1904, the remains of Forrest and his wife Mary Ann (who had passed away in Memphis on January 22, 1893) were reinterred in the Memphis park named after him: Nathan Bedford Forrest Park. They were moved there to be placed beneath a large bronze statue of Forrest, the famous Forrest Equestrian Monument (sculpted by Charles H. Niehaus and cast in Paris, France), which had been set up at the site on April 8, 1904.

On May 16, 1905, some 30,000 people (from seven states) attended the dedication ceremony. The band played *Dixie* as Forrest's eight year-old great-granddaughter, Kathleen Forrest Bradley, unveiled the statue to the public for the first time.

Forrest's impressive equestrian monument still stands. And though it is regularly defaced by the uninformed, it continues to blaze forth in the Memphis sky, a testament to Southern tradition, culture, heritage, individuality, courage, invincibility, and a love of liberty and the original Constitution of the Founding Fathers.

British military man General Viscount Wolseley wrote what many consider the ideal remembrance of the immortal Tennessean:

> Forrest had fought like a knight-errant for the cause he believed to be that of justice and right. No man who drew the sword for his country in that fratricidal struggle deserves better of her; and as long as the chivalrous deeds of her sons find poets to describe them and fair women to sing of them, the name of this gallant general will be remembered with affection and sincere admiration. A man with such a record needs no ancestry.[1891]

---

1890. Memphis *Appeal*, November 1, 1877.
1891. Wyeth, LGNBF, p. 624.

# Part 6

# Forrest:
# A Hero for All Ages

# FOLK HERO:
# TRUE TALES ABOUT OLD BEDFORD

"This is my country. I am hard at work upon my plantation, and carefully observing the obligations of my parole. If the Federal government does not regard it they will be sorry. I shall not go away." — Nathan Bedford Forrest

## CAMPFIRE STORIES

WHILE WE HAVE EXAMINED HIM in great detail, nothing can bring us closer to the real Forrest of Southern history (as opposed to the false Forrest of Northern mythology) than actual accounts of his everyday behavior, actions, thoughts, and words. To that end the following true stories and anecdotes will prove invaluable in our effort to defend the General from a century and a half of slander, lies, ridicule, and hyperbole.

I began hearing many of these tales in my childhood: shared lovingly back and forth infinite times, we eventually grew to know them by heart. Indeed, the main corpus of Forrest stories have been passed around so often, for so long, by so many Southerners, that for the most part their origins are now obscure.

Many of the following accounts were sent to me by loyal Forrest admirers after hearing that I would be including a chapter on "favorite Forrest stories" in this book. For the benefit of the reader, I have tried to find sources for as many of the narratives as possible.[1892]

## FORREST HAS HIS HEAD EXAMINED

In 1854, several years prior to Lincoln's illegal War on the South, Forrest attended a free lecture at a hall in Memphis. The speaker was New York phrenologist Dr. Orson G. Fowler. When the physician finished his talk he asked the audience to select someone for one of his famous phrenological examinations. The first name called out was "Forrest," at which the lanky frontiersman strode quickly up to the stage.

After admiringly inspecting Forrest's head with his fingers Dr. Fowler noted the Tennessean's most predominant traits, saying:

> Here is a man who would have been a Caesar, a Hannibal, or Napoleon if he had had the opportunity. He has all the qualities of a great military genius. If he could not go over the Alps he would go through them.[1893]

The audience applauded thunderously as Forrest walked back to his seat. Little could he have dreamed that in just seven short years the exact characteristics Fowler discovered in the bumps on his cranium would make him a household name.

## FORREST INSTILLS THE FEAR OF GOD IN A YANK

In the summer of 1864 we find an example of the raw terror that nearly every Federal officer and soldier felt toward Forrest, even those who had never fought him, met him, or had even seen him.

Yankee war criminal General Andrew Jackson Smith had just attacked the sleepy town of Oxford, Mississippi, beating and robbing its innocent citizens, then burning their homes to the ground. Hundreds of noncombatant men, women, and children were pointlessly turned into homeless refugees, to wander the streets without food or clothing, by Smith and his soldiers.

The more intelligent Federals among them knew that Forrest

---

1892. Since the following stories are between 135 and 200 years-old, the exact words of the conversations that took place in them cannot be known with certainty. I have thus used poetic license to paraphrase inside quote marks. Indented quotations, however, are exact transcriptions from what may be original, or possibly secondary, sources.
1893. Mathes, p. 21.

was not far behind (he was then in Memphis), and that he would exact his revenge on them for their inhumanity.

One of the Union officers in Oxford at the time, a Captain Cannon, asked Mr. Cook, a local inhabitant, about the Rebel chieftain. "What sort of man is this Forrest?", the Yank inquired rather cavalierly. After proudly describing the General, Cook asked Cannon a question in turn.

"Now that you know who he is, would you be willing to take 100 of your soldiers and fight Forrest with 100 of his own men?"

"Never," came the immediate answer, Cannon's face now white as a sheet. "I wouldn't fight Forrest with any amount of men. I pray to God that I never meet up with him!"[1894]

A YANK SPARES FORREST'S LIFE

On June 4, 1863, several months after the Battle of Franklin I (April 10, 1863), Forrest found himself in "Tennessee's most handsomest town" yet again, once more hunting down Union soldiers who had no business being there.[1895]

Under orders of Union General David Stanley, Yankee troops had recently burned down ten homes in and around Franklin.[1896] The act was cruel, superfluous, and cowardly, and Forrest and his men were not in a generous mood.

Fortunately for Forrest the Yanks were.

From his location Forrest watched as Union Colonel J. P. Baird of the Eighty-fifth Indiana began waving a white signal flag from Franklin's Fort Granger, a Confederate hilltop garrison on the Harpeth River that the Yanks had captured earlier. Baird's flag waving was actually a call for help to his superior stationed at the town of Triune, some fifteen miles to the east.[1897]

Oddly, for one of Forrest's exceptional military acumen, he misidentified the signal as a flag of truce. After ordering his men to cease fire, he rode boldly forward to discuss the terms of surrender.

He was not at first noticed by the bulk of Union troops manning

1894. Henry, ATSF, p. 254.
1895. Strangely, Forrest never wrote out an official report on the Battle of Franklin I. Sheppard, p. 312.
1896. ORA, Ser. 1, Vol. 23, Pt. 1, p. 237.
1897. Wyeth, LGNBF, p. 227.

the fort. At that moment a Federal officer jumped up from behind a row of bushes and whispered loudly: "General Forrest, I know you and I don't want to see you hurt! Go back sir! There is no truce; that is a signal flag!"[1898] Forrest lifted his hat in salute to the kind Yankee, then quickly wheeled his horse around and sped off.[1899]

As he galloped away he turned and gave one last look: there, standing with the gallant Yank who had exempted him from the death penalty, was an entire detachment of Union soldiers, all placidly watching him. They could have let loose a sheet of fire that would have killed Forrest instantly. But all remained quiet stationary observers, nodding silently as Forrest saluted his "magnanimous foe" one last time.[1900]

Why was Forrest's life spared? We cannot be sure. Perhaps it was sheer awe and admiration.

A more realistic possibility: the Union officer at Fort Granger that day was among those the General had captured earlier at Murfreesboro. As Forrest always treated his prisoners humanely, the Federal commander returned the good deed by letting Forrest go.[1901]

## A PRIVATE DISTURBS FORREST

In September 1864, at West Point, Mississippi, Forrest was planning his next move. In his usual intense frame of mind, he began pacing round and round the town's small railroad station, head down, completely lost in profound thought.

This was not the time to disturb the General. But a soldier had a grievance to deliver to his superior that could not wait. Interrupting Forrest every five minutes or so, he was met with the same curt response each time: "Goddamn it, leave me alone private! Not now!"

Working up his courage, the soldier witlessly approached the imposing, not-to-be-trifled-with Forrest once more. Instead of the usual stony reply, however, this time Forrest socked the man solidly in the jaw, knocking him out cold. Without hesitating, Forrest continued to calmly pace the circumference of the little building, nonchalantly

---

1898. Jordan and Pryor, p. 286.
1899. Lytle, p. 183.
1900. Morton, p. 106.
1901. Mathes, pp. 128-129.

stepping over the private's prostrate body each time he came around.

## THE HORSE THAT OUTSMARTED FORREST
Early in the War, while Forrest was still a colonel, he and his men were camped at Hopkinsville, Kentucky.

One morning it was discovered that a horse had slipped its halter and was happily munching away on one of the great piles of horse corn that was stacked in the center of the camp. The owner, a young private, was brought before Forrest and given a lecture on carelessness.

"But," the boy protested vigorously, "my hoss is the smartest hoss around. I swear that there ain't no gear that kin restrain 'im!"

At this, Forrest gave him detailed instructions on how to tie off a halter, and the lad, rolling his eyes, went away lamely promising to follow them to the letter.

The next morning the offending horse was found at the center of camp once again, calmly chewing away at the huge mound of corn. And once again the boy was brought to Forrest for a thorough scolding. This time Forrest threatened to have him arrested for refusal to obey orders.

"But I done jes' as you told me to Colonel," the boy replied innocently enough, "tied 'im up nice and neat. Like I said, that thar hoss cain't be haltered!"

Forrest said that he himself would make sure the horse was tied up properly that night, that way there would be no more problems with the animal.

When dawn broke the next day, however, there was the empty halter hanging from its pole again, and there was the horse back at the corn pile, oblivious to the furor it was creating around camp.

A flustered Forrest brought the boy back into his tent one last time. "I shore didn't mean to embarrass you sir," the young private pled in his defense, "but thar it is. Thar simply ain't no man that kin keep my hoss from gittin' loose if'n he has a mind to."

Still mystified, Forrest crinkled his brow, studied the animal for a moment, then said gravely: "I reckon any horse that hardheaded deserves an extra heapin' of corn now and agin." This was the only time Forrest was ever known to surrender to an adversary.

## A MYSTERIOUS MAN & A BLACK STEED

In 1861, while camped near Randolph, Tennessee, Confederate Private John Milton Hubbard, of the Seventh Tennessee Cavalry, had an unusual experience while out riding near his quarters. As Hubbard told the story years later:

> . . . one day I met a soldier speeding a magnificent black horse along a country road as if for exercise, and the pleasure of being astride of so fine an animal. On closer inspection I saw it was Bedford Forrest, [then] only a private like myself, whom I had known ten years before down in Mississippi. I had occasion afterward to see a good deal of him.[1902]

## A NARROW ESCAPE FROM FORREST'S WRATH

Forrest was not always at the center of the story. Sometimes he was only featured in it.

In April of 1863, on the Columbia Turnpike near Franklin, Tennessee, Forrest was desirous of getting a message to his artillery chief, Captain John W. Morton. A courier by the name of Bob Dalton was chosen and sent off.

Arriving at the rear of Morton's Battery, Dalton asked where Captain Morton could be found. "At the head of the column," responded one of the men. As he rode toward the front, Dalton continued to inquire as to the whereabouts of Captain Morton. "Keep on. He's up front," came the same answer from the gunners.

Arriving at the head of the battery Dalton saw a beardless, skinny youngster leading the column. "If I give this order to that lil' boy, Forrest will shore give me hell!," he exclaimed to one of the men. "That little boy" turned out to be Captain Morton, Forrest's personal friend and prize gunner.

Learning of his mistake, Dalton quickly passed on the order, narrowly escaping a dressing down from the War's most feared cavalryman.[1903]

---

1902. Hubbard, p. 15.
1903. Morton, pp. 88-89.

AN IMPOSSIBLE TACTIC—THAT SUCCEEDED

In January 1863 Forrest and his men found themselves near Clifton, Tennessee, surrounded on at least two sides by advancing Yanks. One of Forrest's subordinates, Colonel Charles Carroll, came running up to his imposing commander in a great state of panic.

As bullets whistled by on every side the terrified officer yelled out: "Sir, we are between two lines of battle. What shall we do?"

Not one to waste time or words, Forrest immediately screamed: "Charge 'em both ways!"

The daring tactic worked and Forrest and his men escaped to fight another day.[1904]

FORREST GENTLY REPRIMANDS AN OLD YANKEE OFFICER

On December 20, 1862, after winning a skirmish against the Yanks at Trenton, Tennessee, Forrest was approached by an elderly Federal officer, Colonel Jacob Fry, who asked about the terms of surrender. "Unconditional," Forrest replied tersely.

At this the old man grimly unsheathed his sword and, with great sadness in his eyes, handed it to Forrest saying: "This has been in my family for forty years."

The Rebel chieftain rolled the saber over in his hands for a few moments, eyeing its decorative markings. Then, suddenly handing it back to Fry, Forrest said: "You may have your sword back sir, as it is important to you. However, I truly hope that when it is next worn, that it will be for a better cause than trying to subjugate your fellow countrymen."[1905]

FORREST TEACHES HIS NEIGHBOR A LESSON

While still living with his mother as a young man, the Forrest family began to have problems with a neighbor. The man's large male ox had developed a propensity for jumping the fence into the Forrests'

---

1904. Wyeth, LGNBF, pp. 135-136.
1905. Jordan and Pryor, p. 201. We will note here that at the Trenton skirmish, Forrest, with a force of a mere 275 men, captured 400 U.S. prisoners (including numerous officers, like Fry), 300 U.S. black laborers, 1,000 horses and mules, thirteen wagons and ambulances, seven caissons, 20,000 rounds of artillery, 400,000 rounds of small-arm ammunition, 100,000 rations, cavalry equipment, clothing, quartermaster stores, soldiers' baggage, and more, all valued at $500,000 (about $11,000,000 in today's currency). Jordan and Pryor, p. 202. Just another day on the battlefield with General Forrest.

cornfield, where it would stuff itself unceasingly while trampling down and destroying yards of precious produce.

Forrest warned his neighbor to restrain the beast or else he would shoot it dead. The man ignored the admonition and promised retribution if a single hair on his animal's head was harmed.

Sure enough, the next morning there was the ox in the Forrests' cornfield. A single shot from his musket ended the beast's career as a corn stealer.

Hearing the blast that took the life of his prize bull, the neighbor jumped the fence himself, and with rifle cocked, ran angrily straight at Forrest. Forrest let loose a well timed and well placed volley that whistled past the man's ear, stopping him dead in his tracks. He had apparently not considered the young man either a threat or a crack shot.

The last thing Forrest saw was his neighbor scurrying hurriedly back over the fence and running up the hill toward his own farm. The Forrests never had a speck of trouble from him or any of his bovine charges ever again.

## FORREST MAKES A YANK QUIT THE ARMY

On December 18, 1862, one day prior to the Battle of Jackson (Tennessee), Forrest crushed a Union cavalry unit being led by lauded Northern atheist Colonel Robert G. Ingersoll.

The Yankee colonel's loss had a dramatic impact on him, one that, in a small way, changed the course of the War.

After his capture, Ingersoll asked to speak to Forrest, a request the General was happy to fulfill. Looking up at Forrest from his seat on the cold ground, the bedraggled and frustrated Yank said: I have always believed that I was a soldier and that I could win any fight. But after being outmaneuvered and caught by you and your men, I've come to realize that I'm not a real soldier at all. I'm not one now, never have been, and never will be.[1906]

As soon as he was able to Ingersoll left the military, never to return.

---

1906. Brooksher and Snider, p. 74.

## HOW FORREST HANDLED SHIRKERS

One thing the indefatigable hardworking Forrest could not stand was laziness. Once, in the fall of 1864, he and his men found themselves poling boats across the Tennessee River. At the front of his own craft Forrest spied a lieutenant standing idly, watching the approaching shoreline.

"Why don't you take an oar and help?" Forrest yelled up to him impatiently.

"I'm an officer," he replied crisply, "and there are plenty of privates to do the work."

This was not the answer Forrest was looking for.

Charging up to the bow, he slapped the sassy lieutenant so hard across the face that he sailed over the side and into the icy water. The other men were ordered to haul him back into the boat with one of the poles. But his pain and humiliation was not over yet.

As the freezing wiseacre was gasping for breath, Forrest bellowed at him: "Now, damn you, grab hold of an oar and get to work. The next time I have to knock you out of the boat, I'll let you drown!"

The foolhardy young man learned a valuable lesson that day, from then on becoming one of Forrest's most indispensable officers—not to mention a first-rate deck hand.[1907]

## FORREST DENIES A FURLOUGH

One of the General's officers decided he needed a furlough, despite the fact that the Confederate army could not spare any men at the time. He had sent an application to Forrest twice requesting leave, and was turned down both times.

Unwisely, the determined captain sent in a third request. When he received the application back he found a note scrawled on the reverse side. In Forrest's own handwriting it read: "I told you twixt goddamn it, know!"

This was the last request the officer ever made to Forrest.[1908]

---

1907. Wyeth, LGNBF, pp. 507-508.
1908. Mathes, p. 383. Translated from the original Forrestese, the note reads: "I told you twice goddamn it, no!"

## FORREST & THE CAPTURED YANKEE UNIFORM

Early morning, August 21, 1864. Forrest's cavalry was galloping toward the town of Memphis on a daring raid against the Federals under General Cadwallader C. Washburn. Washburn was sleeping soundly in a neighborhood house when news came warning of Forrest's approach. The lucky Yankee officer escaped out the back door and fled to a Union occupied fort a half mile away.

Washburn had left in such a hurry, however, he had not had time to get properly dressed. Thus, when Forrest's younger brother, Lieutenant Jesse Forrest, made his way into Washburn's empty bedroom, he was able to "capture" the Union general's uniform.

Excited by his success, Jesse proudly took the trophy to his famous older sibling. The elder Forrest, however, being the Southern gentleman that he was, returned the clothing, with his "personal compliments," to Washburn under a flag of truce. The Northerner must have been quite stunned by this genuine act of Southern hospitality from a man who but a short time earlier had been trying to kill him.

Nonetheless, Washburn was grateful: a few weeks later he had a beautiful Confederate uniform, made by Forrest's Memphis tailor, sent to the General. Forrest proudly wore it throughout the rest of the War.[1909]

Not long afterward, Yankee General Stephen A. Hurlbut commented sarcastically on the incident: I lost my command because I couldn't prevent Forrest from entering West Tennessee. Washburn, however, can't prevent Forrest from entering his bedroom, yet he gets to keep his command![1910]

## FORREST GIVES DESERTERS A NEAR-DEATH EXPERIENCE

In the summer of 1864 General Forrest was headquartered at Oxford, Mississippi. By this time his troops were suffering terribly from deprivations caused by Lincoln's unlawful naval blockade.[1911] As discontent increased, so did desertion rates.

Forrest managed to capture nineteen deserters and had them

---

1909. Wyeth, LGNBF, pp. 474-475.

1910. McIlwaine, p. 141.

1911. Lincoln's blockade was illegal because it violated numerous international laws, including the Treaty of Paris (signed by the U.S.), and later, the Geneva Conventions. See Owsley, KCD, passim.

brought back to Oxford, to be tried and shot. Their mothers, along with numerous important citizens and clergymen, begged the General to let the boys go, but he would have none of it. There was even threat of a mutiny. Still, Forrest was not to be dissuaded. "Discipline must be imposed and the other men taught a lesson," he said sternly.[1912]

The day for their certain punishment came. The doomed youngsters were blindfolded and placed on their coffins, which sat before their freshly dug graves. They were allowed a moment for prayer. Each one firmly believed that he was about to meet his Maker. Rifles were loaded and cocked. It was a terrible moment. All that was left was for the order to "fire!"[1913]

A long pause filled the air. Horror was clearly visible on the faces of the unfortunate prisoners as well as their family members. Many were sobbing uncontrollably.

All of a sudden Forrest rode up and ordered the shooters to lower their weapons. A cheer went up. The nineteen deserters were granted amnesty and allowed to return to the ranks.

Had he planned the reprieve all along, or had the idea come to him in the final seconds? Forrest took the answer to his grave. What we do know is that from then on the desertion rate in Forrest's command fell to zero.[1914]

## A SUBORDINATE TEACHES FORREST A FEW THINGS
During Forrest's raid into West Tennessee in late 1862, an incident occurred that reveals the General's open-mindedness and enthusiasm for learning.

In the midst of a skirmish with the Yanks, Forrest assigned one of his regiments to act as rearguard. With them he placed a section of artillery under the future Rebel lieutenant, Edwin H. Douglas,[1915] who takes up the story from here:

> When our section was ordered to take position and get ready for action, according to the manual of artillery drill we galloped up to

---

1912. Jordan and Pryor, p. 384.
1913. Wyeth, LGNBF, p. 296.
1914. Mathes, p. 172.
1915. Lytle, p. 137.

the position, unlimbered, and the horses were moved obliquely to take their place in the rear of the guns and out of range. The general did not understand the rapid movement of the horses to the rear. Mistaking it for a cowardly runaway on the part of the drivers, he rode up to the man on the lead horse, and, as he struck him over the shoulders with the flat of his sabre, yelled: 'Turn those horses around and get back where you belong, or by God I'll kill you!' The artilleryman answered: 'General, I'm moving in accordance with tactics.' Forrest yelled back at him: 'No you are not; I know how to fight, and you can't run away with the ammunition-chest!'

A few days after[,] I took my book of tactics to the general's tent and showed him that it was necessary for the horses to move off out of range, and offered to give him an exhibition-drill, so that he could see the reasons for such a manoeuvre. This was accepted, and he became greatly interested. In less than a week he had mastered the manual and become an expert among experts in placing a battery and in the use of the guns. I may also add that he was just as prompt and earnest in his apology to the soldier he had wronged as he was in the infliction of what he then believed to be a merited rebuke.[1916]

## FORREST'S APOLOGIZES & SAVES A MAN'S LIFE

In 1870, while president of the Selma, Marion, and Memphis Railroad, Forrest became dissatisfied with one of his contractors, Colonel A. K. Shepherd, and called a meeting with him.

During the encounter Forrest gave Shepherd an ear full, turning the air crimson with words that surely broke the Third Commandment. Outraged at the way his boss had spoken to him, Shepherd challenged Forrest to a duel. Forrest agreed. The day and the weapons (pistols) were chosen, and they parted company.

That night in bed, filled with guilt over his angry behavior toward his contractor, Forrest tossed and turned. The next day he admitted to a friend: "I haven't slept for thinking about the trouble with Shepherd. I feel sure I can kill him, and if I do I will never forgive myself. I am convinced that he was right in resenting the way I talked to him. I am in the wrong, and do not feel satisfied about it."

Forrest could take it no longer. He marched immediately to

---

1916. Wyeth, LGNBF, p. 138.

Shepherd's quarters, where he found the man preparing for the duel. Shoving his hand forward, Forrest smiled and said: "Colonel, I am in the wrong in this affair and I have come to say so." The obviously relieved contractor nodded. The duel was canceled and Shepherd's life was spared.[1917]

## FORREST PUTS A YANKEE DO-GOODER IN HER PLACE
In the summer of 1868 Forrest was staying at a hotel in New York City while attending the Democratic Convention. One morning, after a loud knock on the door, a puritanical woman stormed into his room carrying a Bible and an umbrella. Forrest, having just woken up, was sitting on his bed, his eyes still bleary, his hair uncombed.

"Is it true that you're the famous Confederate General Forrest?" the lady demanded immediately. "And if so, why did you murder those wonderful colored folks at Fort Pillow? I would like an answer right now sir!"

Forrest rose to his full 6 foot, 2 inch height, and towering over the petite Yankee, calmly said: "Why yes ma'am. After killin' all the men and women, I fed them to my men for dinner. The next mornin' I myself ate the babies for breakfast. Best meal I ever had."

With that the woman screamed and ran out through the hall and into the street, never to be heard from again.[1918]

## FORREST'S OPINION OF THE YANKEE OATH OF ALLEGIANCE
In late December 1862 Forrest and his men were near Trenton, Tennessee. Still reveling in their win at the Battle of Jackson on December 19, they were in good spirits and ready for the next fight.

Before leaving the area for Columbus, Kentucky, however, Forrest thought he would give the Yanks one last indication of what he and his men thought of them.

Captain Charles W. Anderson was sent out to gather up all of the Union bonds and Federal oaths of allegiance that had been illegally forced upon the county's kindly citizens. A great pile of paper was amassed and carried to the courthouse yard. Here, it was set ablaze to

---

1917. Wyeth, LGNBF, pp. 618-619.
1918. O'Brien, SLCW, p. 292; Lytle, p. 381.

the merry whoops and hollers of Forrest's men and the local townsfolk.

## BUMMERS GET A TASTE OF FORREST'S BRAND OF JUSTICE
One night, after Selma had been captured by the Yanks on April 2, 1865, Forrest and his men were retreating along the Alabama River when they heard a woman screaming for help.

Flying to her house the General burst in upon four "bummers," degenerate soldiers from Lincoln's armies. They had just pillaged her home of all its valuables and were about to rape three other women who had fled to the house to hide. Forrest wasted no time on formalities. All four of the Yankee criminals were taken outside and immediately shot dead.[1919]

The sight of a house full of lone Southern women (their sons, brothers, and husbands off fighting Lincoln's illicit invaders) being robbed and vilely abused by Federal soldiers so angered Forrest and his men that they promised revenge on any other Northern bandits they found in the area.[1920]

By the end of the evening at least thirty-five Yanks were killed or wounded, including some from the much reviled Fourth U.S. Cavalry—payback for the cold-blooded murder of Captain Sam L. Freeman several years earlier after the Battle of Franklin I. Caught red-handed with their plunder, Forrest made sure they never despoiled another Southern home, or woman.[1921]

Though normally known as the most humane man among humane men, Forrest was not above imparting his own brand of justice on the deserving when necessary—and few were more deserving than the deviants among Lincoln's largely already malicious blue-coated henchmen.

## THE ONE QUESTION YOU NEVER ASK FORREST
During the disastrous Battle of Harrisburg (Mississippi), July 14-15, 1864, the commanding Confederate officer, General Stephen Dill Lee, called a hurried meeting of his general officers. Forrest, who could not

---

1919. Jordan and Pryor, p. 676.
1920. Henry, ATSF, pp. 35-36.
1921. Bradley, p. 133.

tolerate losing a fight, was present, sitting silent in the back, Indian fashion, with arms folded, a disgruntled look on his face.

After much discussion between the officers on plans for the next day, Lee turned to a glum Forrest and asked: "General, we're in a hell of a fix. Anything you'd like to contribute?"

"Just one thing, sir," Forrest replied as politely as he could. "If we continue to rely on yer West Point tactics, we'll never beat the Yanks!"[1922]

Lee, who had learned to see past the brilliant Forrest's occasional sarcastic remarks, immediately turned over "active direction" of the command to his headstrong but "unschooled" officer.[1923]

## HOW FORREST FELT ABOUT YANKEE SOLDIERS BEING IN DIXIE

During the Battle of Fort Pillow, April 12, 1864, Forrest was approached on the battlefield by a surrendering Yankee soldier, a surgeon named Dr. Charles Fitch. In the violent melee Fitch had fled to the General seeking protection as a prisoner of war.

Forrest automatically assumed that the doctor was one of the much detested "Tennessee Yankees" stationed at the fort. So when Fitch told him he was from Iowa, Forrest was genuinely surprised.

"What the hell are you doin' down here then?" he angrily asked the stunned Federal, as minié balls whizzed by their ears. "I'm seriously considerin' killin' you for being down here! You Yanks shoulda stayed at home and minded yer own goddamn business!"

Wisely, Fitch did not respond!

Forrest cooled off, lowered and uncocked his giant Navy six, then ordered the very fortunate doctor to be taken to the rear and put under guard.

## FORREST REWARDS TWO BRAVE CONFEDERATE GIRLS

In April 1863 Forrest was in the midst of chasing down fleeing Yankee General Abel D. Streight and his men. As Forrest and his command were nearing the Black Warrior River in Alabama, they were approached by two seventeen year old girls walking barefoot down a lonely country

---

1922. Walsh, p. 304.
1923. Lytle, p. 315.

road.

On their shoulders they carried rifles. Behind them the pair of teenaged Confederates were leading three horses. In front they were driving three Yankee soldiers, who they had recently placed *hors de combat.*[1924] The fatigued prisoners, all who had willingly surrendered, were quickly turned over to the General's men.

The young farm girls then generously volunteered to join the Rebel army, not realizing the absurdity of their offer. The ever sensitive Forrest quickly grasped the situation and stepped in. Instead of turning them down, he gave them each a beautiful cavalry horse as a gift for "military services already performed."

This did the trick. The proud girls rode off back to their homes on their new equines, beaming from ear to ear.[1925]

## FORREST'S MOM TAKES ON THE YANKS

One need not look far to see where Forrest got his rough-and-tumble approach to life. As they say, the apple never falls far from the tree. According to a friend of the Forrest family:

> My grandmother would often tell us children of the following incident that took place during the War Between the States.
>
> One day Mrs. Mariam Forrest, General Forrest's mother, drove into Memphis in a buggy to get supplies. At the time the city was in the hands of the Federals. Among the things she picked up was a pair of cavalry boots for her young son "Bedford." She put them on so they would not be taken when the buggy was searched.
>
> As she was leaving town she was halted by the Yankee pickets, who told her she would not be allowed to take the boots to her boy. "I reckon I will," she replied implacably.
>
> After quite a lengthy parley of this sort of thing, she told them that while a cow lives or a cow dies, *Bedford had to have his boots*. The Yanks continued to order her to give the brogans up.
>
> Mrs. Forrest could take it no longer. Hopping out of the buggy, she popped up her fists and shouted: 'Yous call yerselves men?! Ya'll just set them thar guns down and come at me one at a time. That's right! I'll whip every last one of yous!'

---

1924. *Hors de combat* is French for "out of the fight"; that is, captured.
1925. Morton, p. 93; Jordan and Pryor, p. 265.

Startled, the Yanks hesitated, looked at each other with a slight smirk, then nodded to the feisty Confederate woman. 'Please calm down Mrs. Forrest,' they implored. 'Get back in your buggy and drive on.'

And with that she was on her way, still wearing 'Bedford's boots.'[1926]

## YANKS CEASE-FIRE WHILE FORREST WEEPS

At the Battle of Okolona (Mississippi), February 22, 1864, the General's favorite (and youngest) brother, his beloved Jeffrey, was gunned down. The shot, which passed through his neck, sliced open the carotid artery and severed his spine, killing him instantly.[1927]

As soon as he was told of the death the General galloped to the site, jumped off his steed, and fell sobbing on the bloody corpse. As he called out the boy's name the rest of Forrest's men, now noticing their chieftain weeping, naturally began to withhold their fire. All became quiet on the Rebel side. Of that moment John Milton Hubbard later wrote: "No more pathetic scene was ever witnessed on any battlefield."[1928]

The Yanks sensed something strange going on across the field, and they too ordered a cease-fire. It is possible, at this point, in the deafening silence that day, that they could actually hear Forrest wailing over his lost youngest brother. Ten minutes of complete silence passed, while both sides watched and waited as the moving spectacle unfolded.[1929]

The General soon regained his composure, kissed the lifeless youngster on the forehead, placed Jeffrey's hat over his face, and asked his adjutant-general Major John P. Strange to take care of the body. Leaping back on his horse, he ordered his German bugler Jacob Gaus to sound the charge, and the fighting started up again as suddenly as it had stopped.[1930]

In the short but fearful scrimmage that ensued, under a hail of

---

1926. Letter paraphrased. Original from Mrs. J. Roane Vineyard (at Forrest City, Arkansas), to Mrs. Norma R. Bridgeforth (at Brinkley, Arkansas); dated May 10, 1939. Letter courtesy Ronny Mangrum.

1927. Wyeth, LGNBF, p. 312.

1928. Hubbard, p. 94.

1929. Jordan and Pryor, p. 396.

1930. Morton, p. 152.

sizzling bullets, Forrest rode straight for the Union position, where he quickly killed three Yanks with his bare hands, the actions, no doubt, of an overwrought, angry, and grief-stricken elder brother.[1931]

Of the incident, one of Forrest's men, Dr. James B. Cowan, later wrote:

> I had just reached the spot where Jeffrey Forrest was lying dead, when Major Strange said to me as I rode up, 'Doctor, hurry after the general; I am afraid he will be killed!' Putting spurs to my horse, I rode rapidly to the front, and in about a mile, as I rounded a short turn in the road, I came upon a scene which made my blood run cold. There in the road was General Forrest with his escort, and a few of the advance-guard of the Forrest brigade, in a hand-to-hand fight to the death, with Federals enough, it seemed to me, to have pulled them from their horses. Horrified at the situation, I turned back down the road to see if help was at hand, and, as good-fortune would have it, the head of McCulloch's brigade was coming in full sweep towards me.[1932]

Raw nerve, and the hand of fate, had spared Forrest's life once again, and he lived to kill over a dozen more Yanks before the War was over.


FORREST ACTS COOLY UNDER PRESSURE

In late June of 1863, near Pelham, Tennessee, Forrest and his escort were riding along a road in an attempt to intercept Yankee Colonel General John T. Wilder. It was raining heavily and the soggy Confederates were wearing large thick oilcloth cloaks for protection against the watery elements, thoroughly masking their identities.

As they rode along they found themselves coming up from behind on a detachment of Union cavalrymen. Also wearing waterproofs, the Yanks had about the same number of men as Forrest.

Forrest lazily eased his horse up alongside one of the Federal soldiers and asked: "What company is this?"

"We're with Wilder's Mounted Infantry," came the answer. "Who you with?", he asked in return.

Knowing all of the Union officers and their commands in the

1931. Mathes, p. 183.
1932. Wyeth, LGNBF, p. 315.

area, Forrest cooly replied, "Company C" (a cavalry regiment under another Yankee officer).

Wilder's soldiers had no idea they were talking to "that Devil Forrest," or even to a Confederate! Falling for the General's ruse, they rode on. Forrest fell behind and was able to attack and kill many of them shortly after.[1933]

## FORREST TAKES AN OFFICER DOWN A PEG

On April 24, 1864, just days after the Battle of Fort Pillow, Forrest and his men caught up with a Yankee wagon train. Once the Union soldiers saw that they had been discovered by the Rebels, they began to lay torch to their own wagons to prevent them from falling into Forrest's hands. Their fear was not misplaced: thanks to Lincoln's illegal naval blockade, Forrest was often forced to depend on "Uncle Sam's larder" (captured Yankee supplies) to feed and outfit his troops.

Wanting to douse the flames as soon as possible, from the rear Forrest quickly sent an order down the line: "Move up in front!" His men responded, but too slowly for his taste. Another order was sent forth, this time with a bit more vigor: "Goddamn it, move up in front!" When even this failed to get his men traveling at the desired velocity Forrest himself decided to go to the head of the line, horse hooves loudly snapping twigs and brush as he angrily rode through the dense woods.

"Can't you see that those damned Yankees are burning my wagons?", he yelled upon reaching the front. "Get off your horses and throw them burning beds off!" This got things moving in double time, as the General was never to be trifled with.

His troops dismounted and were bravely ridding the red-hot wagons of their smouldering beds, when Forrest noticed one of his lieutenants sitting calmly astride his horse. Riding over to his subordinate he asked: "Why are you not helping?"

"Because I'm an officer, of course," came the foolish reply. This was no way to answer a question from Forrest, as the lieutenant came to learn.

Lifting his sword in the air, Forrest bellowed: "I'll officer *you*!"

At that the lieutenant dismounted in a flash and quickly fell to

---

1933. Wyeth, LGNBF, pp. 234-235.

the task of saving the burning wagons.[1934]

He was no slacker. He just needed a small reminder that, lieutenant or not, in Forrest's eyes he was still just one of "the boys."

## FORREST ENLISTS SOME YANKEES
After his successful raid on Murfreesboro, Tennessee, on July 13, 1862 (his forty-first birthday), Forrest found that he had almost as many prisoners as he had soldiers. As he did not have enough guards to watch them all, this was a dangerous situation, one that needed to be remedied as quickly as possible. As always, the impromptu Forrest came up with his own original idea on how to handle it.

Riding out among his captured foe, Forrest made them an offer: if they would volunteer to serve as his drivers, he would free them all to go home when they reached McMinnville. The response was instant and unanimous. One of the prisoners yelled out: "Three cheers for General Forrest!" Out over the Tennessee countryside rang the extraordinary sound of Northern soldiers cheering a Southern officer.

Soon the citizens of McMinnville were greeted by an equally extraordinary sight: a Confederate command with Union drivers riding into town. After their arrival Forrest kept his promise and released all the prisoners.[1935]

## FORREST & A USEFUL YANKEE DUTCHMAN
In the fall of 1864, near Pulaski, Tennessee, Forrest and his men found themselves before a blockhouse full of stubborn Unions troops. The General could have easily blown the log structure to pieces, but as was his usual custom he sent forward a demand for surrender in an attempt to "avoid the effusion of blood."

The Dutch Yankee officer inside sent back an insolent reply in broken English: "You vill please tell Forrest I vill nefer surrender, and to please to get away from here damn qvick, or I vill shoot his damned head from his shoulders off!"

Forrest was not accustomed to being addressed in this manner and, according to one of his men, "he made the atmosphere blue for a

---

1934. Witherspoon, pp. 68-69.
1935. Lytle, pp. 99-100.

while." Then he decided to have a little fun with the impudent Yank. Turning to his artillery chief, he yelled: "Give 'em hell Captain Morton, as hot as you've got it!"[1936]

The first cannon shot boomed, tearing away the top of a log and showering those within with a hail of debris and wood dust, enough to put the fear of God into most men. However, no flag of surrender appeared.

Annoyed, Forrest ordered a second round, this time aimed straight at the log wall. The cannon ball bore into the wood as commanded, this time sending up a fearful rain of logs, sparks, shingles, and planks. Part of the structure collapsed, injuring nine and killing five. This brought the desired effect: a tiny white flag waved feebly from a porthole, and Morton ordered a cease fire.

But Forrest was not finished yet. "No, keep it up John! That was bully. Send in another round!", he shouted enthusiastically.

"But sir," replied Morton, "look yonder: they've hoisted the white flag."

"I don't see nothin'" Forrest responded. "Keep on firin'. It'd take a damn bed sheet to get my attention at this range!"

Morton dutifully sent in another volley of cannon shot, this time nearly leveling the entire blockhouse. At this, a very large white flag appeared outside one of the remaining portholes, waving energetically in the air. Then and only then did Forrest mercifully accept the Yankee's surrender. The Dutchman and his remaining men eagerly poured out of the smoke-filled building, praising God, and Forrest, that their lives had been spared.

The General then put the captured Dutchman to good practical use: sent into other Yankee blockhouses and garrisons with a flag of truce, the officer's description of Forrest's attack was so frightening that most commands surrendered without a shot being fired.[1937]

KING PHILIP

One of Forrest's most famous warhorses, King Philip—known to be able

---

1936. Morton, p. 231.
1937. Morton, pp. 231-232.

to leap any fence,[1938] was a sturdy iron-gray that had been given to the General as a gift from the grateful people of Rome, Georgia (after his stunning win in the "Jackass Raid" against General Abel D. Streight).[1939] Previous to this, the twelve-year old horse had already seen "hard service" at such conflicts as the Battle of Vicksburg (May 18-July 4, 1863).

The recipient of several wounds courtesy of Lincoln's invaders, King Philip, like Forrest, survived the War for Southern Independence. He was afterward retired to bucolic pastures where he lived out his life in peace and comfort. It was said that Forrest's men were just as fond of the old warhorse as they were of the old General himself.[1940]

One of King Philip's more interesting traits was his seeming imitation of his owner: at the sight of any type of blue clothing the animal would become infuriated, lay back his ears, bare its upper teeth, and dash at the unsuspecting owner of the garment.

While, as one can imagine, this behavior was quite disturbing while off the battlefield (after the War, the horse was known to attack police officers in the streets of Memphis),[1941] on the battlefield it was of great benefit to both Forrest and the Confederacy. Here, "the King" would fly at the blue-coated enemy, ears folded back, teeth gnashing, the whites of his eyes showing, as if wanting to trample down every Yank in sight.[1942]

One of the more infamous of these incidents occurred in August 1865, while Forrest was mending fences at his plantation, Green Grove. Confederate Captain James Dinkins takes up the story:

> It was a warm August morning, about ten o'clock. King Philip and the other horses were grazing in the lot, when a company of Federal cavalry rode up to the 'big gate' and halted. They were searching for government cotton, and hearing that the rebel General Forrest lived there, desired to take advantage of the opportunity and see him. King Philip was the same character of

---

1938. Henry, ATSF, p. 263.
1939. Bradley, p. 79. Some say that King Philip was given to Forrest by the people of Huntsville, Alabama (see e.g., Morton, p. 283). See also Lytle, p. 268.
1940. Mathes, p. 185.
1941. Lytle, pp. 268, 388.
1942. Morton, pp. 283-284.

horse that Forrest was man, and seemed to have been made for just such service as he had seen the past two years. His education had been well attended to during that time. He had never come in view of a company of Federals without having to rush at them with all his speed and energy. No doubt it was with him instinctively a thing which he had no power to resist, and, perhaps, no disposition to avoid.

The Federal captain and his company, ignorant of the character of King Philip, and therefore of impending danger, and confident of their ability to defend themselves, opened the gate and rode in. King Philip had by that time, doubtless, forgotten the horrors of war, as he nipped the fresh young grass, and did not discover the presence of the bluecoats until they had entered the lot. He heard the tramp of the horses and looked up, and the old passion, born of education and hard experience, took possession of him. With head and tail in the air, he rushed at the company with his old-time energy, nor did he halt until every man and horse had been driven from the lot. He kicked and fought like a tiger. After the gate had been closed, he galloped along the fence-row, neighing and shaking his head defiantly.

Jerry [Forrest's African-American personal assistant], hearing the noise and seeing the commotion, ran down to the gate and heard dreadful threats against Philip. One of the men, who was severely hurt by a kick, swore he would kill him; but Jerry grasped a fence-rail, and announced that he would defend Philip with his life; and that was the situation when General Forrest and Captain Billy returned home for dinner.

The [Yankee] officer explained the occurrence to the general, who, after King Philip had been put in the stable, invited the whole company in for dinner and rest. Jerry said: 'Twus not King Philip's fault; dem Yankees opened the gate and rid in bedout sayin nuthin to nobody.'

After all had been seated on the gallery and had laughed over the affair, the Federal captain said: 'General [Forrest], I can now account for your success; your negroes fight for you and your horses fight for you.'[1943]

## FORREST GETS SARCASTIC
In early 1865, while at a dinner-party at Marion, Alabama, Forrest found himself seated between a very attractive, demure, young lady on one side, and a loud, chatty, elderly widow on the other.

---

1943. Dinkins, pp. 265-266.

As the latter showered him with reverential compliments, naturally sensitive Forrest was most interested in the pretty girl. Unfortunately for him, the boisterous spinster kept interrupting the pair with bold and even impudent comments.

She eventually got around to a question that seems to have been bothering her for ages. "General, I'm so very curious to know something," the old lady remarked self-importantly, leaning into Forrest. "Your hair is turning grey, yet your beard is still black. Why is that, sir?"

Forrest, trying to kill two birds with one stone, answered slyly: "Why that thar's a mystery ma'am. But some say it's because I work my head more'n I do my mouth."

The shocked Victorian senior took the hint and, with her nose in the air, politely and quickly vacated her seat.

FORREST IS BROUGHT TO HIS SENSES
During the heat of battle at Chickamauga (September 18-20, 1863), one of Forrest's men lost his nerve and made a run for the rear. His eagle-eyed General spotted the fleeing soldier, however, and as it was Forrest's policy to shoot down "cowards," he drew his Navy six-shooter and ordered the man to halt. His command was duly ignored.

Cocking the trigger, he took aim, preparing to make an example of him to his other men. Just as he was about to squeeze off the shot, his aid-de-camp, Major Charles W. Anderson, seeing a senseless tragedy about to unfold, yelled out across the battlefield, "Oh General, think!"

The plea caused Forrest to pause long enough to consider his actions. As the miserable private disappeared into the smoke at the rear, the General turned his gun back on the enemy and once again began firing.[1944]

FORREST & THE CAISSON
One rainy day in the fall of 1864, not far from Tullahoma, Tennessee, Forrest spied a Rebel soldier struggling to move a captured caisson (an ammunition chest) stuck fast in the mud.

The always efficiency-minded Forrest assumed the man was not applying himself to the task properly. Riding up to the unwitting

---

1944. Wyeth, LGNBF, p. 249.

trooper, the General yelled: "Who's in charge here?"

"I am sir. Captain Andrew McGregor!" came the reply from the officer.

Unruffled by this response, Forrest barked: "Then why in the hell don't you do something about that chest? Move that goddamned piece of equipment, *now!*"

McGregor jumped up and shouted: "I shall not be cursed out by anyone, even a superior officer!" With that, he spitefully grabbed a torch, opened the caisson lid, and thrust the flame inside.

Forrest was horrified of course at the sight of a burning brand being shoved into a wooden box filled with gun powder. Putting spurs to his horse, he let out a string of expletives, along with a loud warning to others to vacate the area immediately.

Arriving out of breath at camp, he inquired of his staff: "Who the hell is that lunatic down there? He just tried to blow the two of us up with a caisson full of powder!"

Knowing the box was empty, the staff members let out a hearty laugh; and so did Forrest—once he caught on to the joke. However, after that it was observed that the General never swore at McGregor again.[1945]

## A GENEROUS CITIZEN

In June 1864, shortly after the Battle of Brice's Cross Roads, Forrest set up his headquarters at Guntown, Mississippi. Finding himself in need of mules to clear some nearby railroad tracks of debris, he sent one of his men out to canvas the area.

Some mules were spotted in a local citizen's yard, and the man was asked if they could be hired out for a few hours. "Absolutely, yes sir," came the jaunty reply. "Ole' Forrest can have anything of mine he likes. Except my wife."

## FORREST CONVERTS A CHAPLAIN

During the War Forrest's men captured a Yankee chaplain. Hearing that he was to be taken before the great Confederate warrior, the man shook with fear, certain he would be tortured and killed in the most horrible

---

1945. Morton, pp. 239-240.

manner by one who he had heard was a filthy barbarian, a sadistic murderer, a ruthless Southerner, and a vulgar atheist.

A completely different sight met his eyes when he was shown into the General's tent, however. A gentle, soft-spoken, nattily dressed Forrest warmly greeted the clergyman, showed him to his seat, then asked him if he would like to dine with he and his staff that evening. Perplexed the chaplain replied nervously, "Ah . . . yes sir."

At the supper table Forrest shocked his guest further when he said: "Parson, will you please ask the blessing?" Certain that this was all a charade, he could not conceal his surprise. Forrest assured him that all was well. The prayer was sent up to the heavens, and a pleasant dinner passed with good food and hospitable conversation all round.

As dawn broke the next day, Forrest had the chaplain brought to him once again. "I have no quarrel with noncombatants," he told the dumbfounded man, and ordered that he be escorted through the Confederate lines and allowed to go free.

Just as the joyous preacher turned to leave, Forrest stopped him, and with just a hint of a grin, said: "Parson, I would keep you here to preach for me if you were not needed so much more by the sinners on the other side."[1946]

## FORREST RISKS HIS LIFE TO URGE ON HIS TROOPS

On June 11, 1864, the night after the Battle of Brice's Cross Roads, Forrest and his cavalry were in hot pursuit of Yankee General Samuel D. Sturgis. All of the sudden he came up on a group of his men who had paused at a creek, hesitating to move forward due to what they believed was a large Union rearguard just ahead.

Forrest lit a candle and held it over his head, making himself a perfect target for any Yanks nearby, horrifying his men. As he peered into the darkness, the candle light illuminated a discarded Federal wagon and cannon in the water. Obviously, the enemy was on the run, terrified of being caught by the Wizard of the Saddle and his dreaded escort.

"Come on men," Forrest yelled, leading the way as he drove his horse into the small river. "In a rout like this, ten men are equal to a

---

1946. Wyeth, LGNBF, p. 631.

thousand. They will not stop to fight!"[1947] As we have seen, Forrest was right.

## FORREST GETS A CLOSE SHAVE

In December 1862 Forrest and his men were positioned near Lexington, Tennessee. Outside his tent the General was in deep discussion with his chief of artillery, John W. Morton, when the sound of a sizzling minié ball was heard approaching them.

As it sailed past Morton's face he was aghast to see Forrest's head drop down.

"Are you hurt, sir?!" Morton asked anxiously.

Forrest slowly lifted his head up, not sure himself if he was dead or alive. Taking off his hat, he eyed the large gapping hole in the brim and said: "No. But didn't it come damn close to me?"[1948]

## FORREST, CHEATHAM, & SOUTHERN PRIDE

Toward the end of December 1864, at Columbia, Tennessee, Forrest was about to move his command across the Duck River, when Rebel General Benjamin Franklin "Frank" Cheatham and his men arrived on the scene with the same objective.

Ordinarily a man in Forrest's position would have given way, courteously allowing the other gentleman to cross the river first. But Forrest was no ordinary man. And besides, he and Cheatham had already verbally sparred at the Battle of Shiloh two years earlier (April 6-7, 1862). Thus when the equally feisty Cheatham appeared at the river's edge that day, Forrest was none too happy to see him.

"I'll be crossing first General," he barked at his fellow officer.

"I think not, sir. You are mistaken," Cheatham replied. "I intend to cross now, and will thank you to move out of the way of my troops."

Outraged, Forrest pulled out his pistol, well prepared to shoot Cheatham down rather than let him cross first. Forrest's and Cheatham's men understood, and those near enough to witness the dramatic confrontation also drew their weapons, ready to defend their

---

1947. Mathes, p. 246.
1948. Morton, p. 68.

respective officers.

Just as a fight between the two bull-headed Confederates was about to commence, a calm, clear-headed General Stephen Dill Lee accidentally rode up on the unfolding scene. He immediately ordered that all weapons be holstered and that the two quarreling men apologize. This done, Lee sent Forrest across the Duck first, Cheatham second. What would have certainly been the War's most bizarre and unnecessary bloodbath had been narrowly averted.

## FORREST IN A BUGGY

The General was shot in his right foot at the Battle of Harrisburg, Mississippi (July 14-15, 1864). His most severe wound of the War, he had no choice but to leave the field and go to Tupelo where he could get it properly cared for. Due to the irritated condition of his foot, Forrest was unable to ride a horse and instead had to travel about in a buggy for several weeks.

There are no written records of anyone's impression of the General's "buggy period," but we can be sure there were some snickers at the sight of the tall, powerfully-built, battle-hardened warrior speeding past in a small, dainty, horse-drawn carriage with a pained grimace on his face and his leg propped up on the side rail.[1949]

## FORREST RISES FROM THE DEAD

News of Forrest's wound at Harrisburg spread like wildfire, eventually turning into a rumor that the mighty general had actually died. His men were struck with grief at the mere thought that they had lost their beloved commander.

Hearing the news of his early demise and the negative impact it was having on his troops, Forrest leaped from his sick bed, jumped on his horse, and charged off to his camp, much to the chagrin of his doctors.

As he galloped up and down the line of his soldiers in his shirt sleeves, the mere sight of him brought ear-shattering, joyous cheers. One of the soldiers on the scene that day, C. W. Robertson, later wrote:

The effect produced upon the men by the appearance of General

1949. Mathes, pp. 261, 264, 266.

Forrest is indescribable. They seemed wild with joy at seeing their great leader was still with them.[1950]

## FORREST SUSTAINS A WOUNDED WARHORSE

On September 21, 1863, the day after the Battle of Chickamauga, Forrest and his men were riding north toward Chattanooga, Tennessee, near the town of Rossville, Georgia, when they came upon the rearguard of a Yankee cavalry. Forrest thought it would be fun to give them some hell. There and then he ordered a charge, leading his 400 men, as was his custom, directly down onto the enemy.

Suddenly hearing the Rebel Yell all around them, the stunned Yanks had little time to react, but managed to get off a few shots as they fled away and up the road. In the smoke and din, Forrest's horse was fatally wounded, blood spurting from its neck. Still at full gallop in pursuit of the Federals, the General reached down and stuck his index finger into the gaping hole, which stopped the bleeding. This allowed the courageous steed to carry his master just long enough to clear the field.[1951]

The moment this was accomplished, Forrest took his finger from the wound and dismounted. At that, the animal collapsed to the ground and died.[1952]

## HORSEPLAY AMONG FORREST'S MEN

In March 1865, one month before the end of Lincoln's War, Forrest and his men were stationed at West Point, Mississippi. Due to the ongoing playful shenanigans of many of his troops, the General was finally forced to impose a ban on horse-racing, random weapons-shooting, and other forms of merriment around the camp. Thinking the order was not that serious, however, a number of the men imprudently ignored it.

After spending the evening gleefully unloading their pistols into the air, the rebellious group decided to hold a horse race the next morning. Not only that, they would stage it right in front of Forrest's tent!

Morning came, the quarter-mile course was marked off, and the

1950. Wyeth, LGNBF, pp. 454-455.
1951. Morton, p. 126.
1952. Wyeth, LGNBF, p. 259.

racing began. A great time was had by all, including Forrest himself, who nonchalantly sat in a chair outside his tent betting on the horses with his staff.

The race now over, the happy-go-lucky thrill-seekers galloped up to Forrest's tent, gave him three cheers, and sped off, laughing and whooping, quite sure of their success.

They had not gone far, however, when they were halted by one of Forrest's mounted guard units. All were promptly hauled before the General, who had them arrested, court-martialed, and unmercifully punished.[1953]

## ANOTHER DAY IN THE LIFE OF GENERAL FORREST

During a skirmish in early 1864, Forrest looked across the battlefield and noticed one of his staff officers, Major Thomas S. Tate, involved in hand-to-hand combat with a mounted Yankee officer. Unfortunately for the horseless Tate, his gun was empty, and the Union soldier was now aiming his own loaded revolver down at him.

Forrest, never one to waste time, rode hard up on the scene and with a single sweep of his sword, nearly decapitated the Yank, whose lifeless body instantly dropped to the ground. As he fell, Tate grabbed the revolver out of the dead man's hand and quickly swung himself up into the empty saddle. Without exchanging a single word, or batting an eye, he and Forrest galloped back to the front to rejoin the main fight.[1954]

## MISTAKEN IDENTITY

In December of 1864, as the tattered remains of General John Bell Hood's Army of Tennessee were escaping south toward the Tennessee River, Forrest and his cavalry were acting as rearguard, staving off the pesky Yankees who were in pursuit. Suddenly Forrest heard shots ringing out down the line, the sounds of Union gunboats shelling Hood's pontoon bridge.

Sprinting ahead he came upon a quartermaster and asked him, "Any idear who's shootin' down thar'?"

"No I don't," the grizzled officer replied. "But I reckon it's

---

1953. Mathes, p. 364.
1954. Jordan and Pryor, p. 400.

prolly Ole Forrest. He's the only one fool enough to try an' capture a Yankee gunboat!" (This was no doubt a reference to Forrest's "horse marines" escapade at the Battle of Johnsonville several weeks earlier, November 4-5, 1864.)

Unruffled, the great cavalryman looked his subordinate squarely in the eye and said: "Well, I'm dead certain it ain't 'Ole Forrest.' That's the name the boys call me."

Realizing the gravity of his error, the quartermaster jumped to attention and saluted. Searching for a way out of the corner he had painted himself into, he quickly stammered: "Errr . . . Beg yer pardon there Gen'rl . . . uhhh . . . I didn't recognize ya with yer clean, new uniform and all!"

Forrest took it all in stride, nodded, and spurred his horse on down the road, no doubt smiling to himself.[1955]

## FORREST SAVES A DYING YANK
During the Battle of Okolona (Mississippi) on March 22, 1864, Forrest was riding his horse through a defeated Union camp when he heard the cries of someone in extreme anguish. The pitiful wailing was coming from a Federal army hut with a hospital flag flying over it.

Jumping off his horse the General entered the small hutch only to find a sight of pathetic horror: in the midst of an amputation, a Yankee soldier had been left on the operating table by his surgeon with the saw still stuck in his leg! Forrest quickly grabbed a cloth, soaked it with chloroform, and placed it over the sufferer's nose, then sent for his own surgeon, Dr. James B. Cowan.

The Confederate physician completed the operation. The one-legged Yank made a full recovery, no doubt thankful until his dying day to the compassionate Rebel chieftain who saved him from certain death.[1956]

## FORREST MAKES A YANKEE WAR CRIMINAL DISAPPEAR
Some stories surrounding Forrest are best told by eyewitnesses.

One such drama occurred at the Battle of Murfreesboro, July

---

**1955**. Mathes, pp. 364-365.
**1956**. Jordan and Pryor, p. 398.

13, 1862, a day on which Confederate Captain William Richardson and another Southerner, James Paul, found themselves held prisoners by the Yanks.[1957]

Tossed into the local jail, the guiltless pair were to be executed the following morning for the alleged crime of "spying." Of the incident Richardson writes:

> Just about daylight on the morning of the 13th I was aroused from sleep by my companion Paul, who had caught me by the arm and was shaking me, saying, 'Listen, listen!' I started up, hearing a strange noise like the roar of an approaching storm. We both leaped to our feet and stood upon an empty box, which had been given us in lieu of a chair, and looked out through the small grating of our prison window. The roar grew louder and came nearer, and in a very few seconds we were sure we could discern the clatter of horses' feet upon the hard turnpike. In a moment more there could be no doubt as to the riders of these horses, for on the morning air there came to our ears with heartfelt welcome the famous rebel yell, the battle-cry of the Confederate soldiers. Almost before we could speak the advance-guard of the charging troopers came into sight and rushed by us on the street, some halting in front of the jail.
>
> Within the prison-yard one company of Federal troops had been stationed, and, seeing they were about to be surrounded by the Confederates and that our rescue was sure, several of these soldiers in wicked mood rushed into the passage-way in front of our cell and attempted to shoot us before they ran from the building. We only saved ourselves by running forward and crouching in the corner of the cell by the door, a position upon which they could not bring their guns to bear. Before leaving the jail one of the Federal guards struck a match, and, lighting a bundle of papers, shoved this beneath the flooring of the hall-way where the planks were loose, and to our horror we realized that he was determined to burn us to death before the rescuing-party could break open the door. When the Southern riders reached us the fire was already under good headway, and the jailer had fled with the keys. It seemed as if we were still doomed. The metal doors were heavy, and it was not until some of our men came in with a heavy iron bar that the grating was bent back sufficiently at the lower corner to permit us to be dragged through as we laid flat upon the

1957. Lytle, pp. 95-96.

floor.

At this moment Forrest dashed up and inquired of the officer in charge if he had rescued the prisoners. He said that they were safe, but added that the jail had been set on fire in order to burn them up, and the guard had taken refuge in the court-house. Forrest said, 'Never mind, we'll get them.' I shall never forget the appearance of General Forrest on that occasion; his eyes were flashing as if on fire, his face was deeply flushed, and he seemed in a condition of great excitement. To me he was the ideal of a warrior. While I was talking to him he turned to a crowd of ladies who, frightened almost out of their wits by the terrible uproar that had so suddenly sprung upon them, had rushed out of their homes and into the streets, many of them in their night-clothes. In most respectful yet very earnest terms he told them they must go back to their homes to save themselves from personal injury.

After the fighting had ceased and the Federal prisoners were all brought together, General Forrest came to me and said: 'They tell me these men treated you inhumanly while in jail. Point them out to me.' I told him there was but one man I wished to call his attention to, and that was the one who had set fire to the jail in order to burn us up. Forrest asked me to go along the line with him and point that man out. I did so. A few hours later, when the list of the private [Yankee] soldiers was being called, the name of this man was heard and no one answered; Forrest said, 'Pass on, it's all right.'[1958]

The General had saved two innocent Rebels and ridded the world of one guilty Yank.

## AN UNRECOGNIZED FORREST IS SCOLDED

After a skirmish in late June of 1863, Forrest and his men, then fighting under General Bragg, found themselves retreating into the Cumberland Mountains through the small town of Cowan, Tennessee. Riding along at the rear, Forrest heard a commotion up ahead.[1959]

Drawing closer he saw a woman castigating some of his soldiers for not "whipping back the Yankees." As Forrest himself rode by, the angry Confederate female shook her fist at him and yelled: "Oh you big, cowardly rascal! Why don't you turn and fight like a man, instead of

---

1958. Wyeth, LGNBF, pp. 90-91.
1959. Morton, p. 110.

running like a cur? I wish old Forrest was here. He'd damn well make you fight!" Apparently she did not, or could not, see the officer's stars on his collar.

Wanting to avoid any further abuse, Forrest spurred his horse into a run, laughing out loud as he charged down the road. Later, in retelling the incident, he said: "I would've rather faced Yankee artillery than that fiery dame!"[1960]

## FORREST'S PERSONAL MESSAGE TO HIS MEN

In August of 1864, as Union troops under Yankee General Andrew Jackson Smith were preparing to attack Mississippi, Forrest found himself coming up against nearly insuperable odds: Smith's army, which outnumbered Forrest's four to one, possessed 4,000 cavalry, 10,000 infantry, 3,000 black soldiers, and three regiments from Minnesota. Forrest had about 5,000 men (sixty-five whom were black), with an overt scarcity of officers.[1961]

Sensing his men's trepidation, Forrest sent out a general order that read:

> Whenever you meet the enemy, show fight, no matter how few there are of you or how many of them, show fight. If you run away they will pursue and probably catch you. If you show fight, they will think there are more of you, and will not push you half so hard.[1962]

## FORREST INTIMIDATES A BULLY

In 1868 Forrest, and several other men from Tennessee and Kentucky, were riding a train to New York City. Forrest had been selected to be a delegate to the first postwar Democratic presidential convention there.

On the way the train pulled in and out of numerous nameless Northern towns to pick up and let off passengers. All was normal until the train stopped at one particular depot. It was at this time that the Yankee train conductor ran up to Forrest's friends. A rowdy crowd, hearing that the General was on aboard, had gathered at the station, he

---

1960. Wyeth, LGNBF, pp. 235-236.
1961. Lytle, p. 321.
1962. Wyeth, LGNBF, p. 644.

told them nervously. Among them was a large and well-known ruffian and boxer who was bragging that he was going to drag Forrest off the train and beat him. The conductor did not want any trouble and asked that Forrest stay in his coach until the train pulled away. When Forrest was told about the commotion, he agreed immediately, and sat calmly in his seat.

Unfortunately, the Yankee fighter had other plans. Boarding the train he yelled out, "Where's that damned butcher, Forrest? I want him!" The hooligan was powerfully built, and huge, much larger even than the 6 foot 2 inch Confederate.

Despite the man's menacing size, Forrest was not one to be spoken to disrespectfully. His Southern honor welling up and his eyes blazing, he leaped from his seat and strode aggressively toward the belligerent boxer. Standing now only feet away, he stared directly at his foe and replied resolutely, "I am Forrest. What do you want?"

The man took one look at the General, then turned and fled down the aisle and out of the coach door. Forrest took off after him, calling for him to stop, but the roughneck disappeared into the crowd and then down a side street, his hat flying off in his desperate attempt to get away.

Forrest himself was the first to grasp the humor of the situation, and he let out a great laugh. The crowd was quick to follow, as did the wide-eyed train passengers. Soon the entire throng was bent over in side-splitting guffaws.

By the time the train pulled away from the station, Forrest, having won over the Yankee mob, was standing on the car's back platform, cordially waving to the crowd amidst raucous cheers and applause.[1963]

FORREST WHIPS A COWARD
In late February 1864 Brigadier-General James R. Chalmers had only recently joined Forrest's command. He had, of course, heard many spectacular stories about his superior, but had never seen him in action.

---

[1963]. Duke, pp. 348-349. After arriving in New York, Forrest was so besieged by interested and adoring crowds that he could not go anywhere without attracting undue attention. Lytle, p. 381. How ironic that today so many New Yorkers revile this same man.

Extremely curious to know if the legends were true, he did not have to wait long to find out.

In a clash with Yanks near Ellis' Bridge, Mississippi, the two were galloping their horses directly into the line of enemy fire, when an incident occurred that aptly illustrates the manner in which Forrest maintained discipline among his men. The occurrence also reveals the intense interest the North took in Forrest, as well as the sense of humor of at least one Yankee journalist. Of the episode, Chalmers writes:

> We had proceeded not more than a hundred yards in the direction of the skirmishers when I noticed, coming at full tilt towards us from that direction a Confederate soldier, who, dismounted and hatless, had thrown away his gun and everything else that could impede his rapid flight to the rear. He was badly demoralized and evidently panic-stricken. As he approached General Forrest, the latter checked up his horse, dismounted quickly, threw the bridle-reins to the orderly who accompanied him, and, rushing at the demoralized soldier, seized him by the collar, threw him down, dragged him to the side of the road, and, picking up a piece of brush that was convenient, proceeded to give him one of the worst thrashings I have ever seen a human being get. The terror and surprise of the frightened Confederate at this unexpected turn in affairs, at a point where he thought he had reached safety, were as great as to me they were laughable. He offered no resistance, and was wise in this discretion, for the general was one of the most powerful men I ever saw, and could easily have whipped him in a free-for-all encounter.
>
> At last he turned him loose, faced him again in the direction of his comrades, and thundered at him: 'Now—damn you, go back to the front and fight: you might as well be killed there as here, for if you ever run away again you will not get off so easy.' It is unnecessary to say that the poor fellow marched back and took his place in line, a wiser if not a braver man. The news of this incident spread rapidly through the command and even through the Southern army, and, almost as soon, it appeared in one of the Northern periodicals of this time, which came out in illustrated form, and was entitled, 'Forrest breaking in a conscript.'[1964]

---

1964. Wyeth, LGNBF, pp. 302-303; Morton, pp. 148-149.

## FORREST DISCOURAGES AN ADMIRER

In 1864 Forrest was on a Mississippi train with some of his staff. Seated alone at the rear of one of the cars, the General, with eyes closed, was deep in thought, planning out his next move. All of the seats around him had been purposefully cleared so that no one would try to sit near him.

Though his men knew enough not to disturb the him, his admirers did not. One of these, a female on the train, asked if she could sit with Forrest and chat. The staff gave her a resounding "no," carefully explaining why he should not be interrupted at this time.

The woman refused to accept this advice, and pressed on toward the back of the coach. Again, she was stopped. Again she was warned, this time more emphatically. Again she declined to heed the ominous caution.

Approaching Forrest, she called out a happy "hello!" Without opening his eyes, Forrest let loose a ferocious growl, so loud it could be heard above the din of the train. The woman flew back down the aisle as fast as she could, emitting screams of terror all the way.[1965]

## FORREST BECOMES A YANKEE OFFICER

During Forrest's Tupelo, Mississippi, expedition in July 1864, the General and one of his officers, Lieutenant Samuel Donelson, were riding one night through a dark woods in an effort to pinpoint the location of a Union army camp.

Soon they found themselves among a group of Yankee teamsters at the rear of the encampment caring for their equine charges. As it was evening, no one could tell that there were two Rebels in their midst, one of them the most feared Confederate fighter of the War!

Making careful observations of the camp's position, the two turned to quietly ride away into the night when they were suddenly ordered to stop by several Yankee pickets. Without missing a beat, Forrest rode immediately and aggressively up to the two men and, feigning offense *and* a Northern accent, scolded the baffled pair, yelling: "What do you mean by halting your commanding officer?!"

There was no reply from the chastened "subordinate," of course, and Forrest and Donelson rode on. By the time the Yankee sentries

---

1965. Lytle, p. 328.

figured out that they had been hoodwinked, the two Rebel officers had disappeared into the inky darkness.[1966]

---

**1966**. Wyeth, LGNBF, p. 440.

# MILITARY HERO:
# RIDING WITH THE
# WIZARD OF THE SADDLE

*"Whenever you see anything blue, shoot at it,
and do all you can to keep up the skeer!" —
Nathan Bedford Forrest*

INNATE SOLDIER

TO THIS DAY NATHAN BEDFORD Forrest is hailed by many as
the paragon of Southern manhood and the archetypal Confederate
officer by which all other soldiers—past, present, and
future—will forever be measured; not just in the U.S., but around the
world.

Widely known as "the greatest revolutionary leader" in the
Confederacy, of him General Dabney H. Maury once remarked:
"General Forrest was a born soldier as men are born poets."[1967] General
Joseph E. Johnston noted:

> Had he the advantages of a thorough military education and training
> he would have been the great central figure of the war.[1968]

Truly an "untutored military genius," as he has been called,
Forrest is considered by many to be the most innovative and outstanding

---

**1967**. Maury, p. 224.
**1968**. Wyeth, LGNBF, p. 653.

American cavalryman to have ever lived. Indeed, his natural leadership, his ability to improvise quickly on the field of action, his seemingly psychic capacity for reading the mind of the enemy,[1969] and his intrinsic sense of military tactics while disregarding all military rules knew no equal.[1970] All this from a man who, unlike most of his colleagues, possessed no law degree and never attended West Point—or any military school for that matter.

The reason behind this was as simple as Forrest's approach to warfare: his tactician was "Old Common Sense," not an army manual,[1971] for according to him, book learning is of little use on the battlefield when bullets are whizzing by your head.[1972]

Of the "low-born and uneducated" Forrest, Wolseley writes:

> A man with such a record needs no ancestry, and his history proves that a general with such a heart and such a military genius as he possessed, can win battles without education.[1973]

Like the true individualist he was, however, the largely self-taught Forrest was proud of his background. "I ain't no graduate of West Point and never rubbed my back up against any college," he often bragged to friends.

Forrest had a right to boast. The West Point approach to warfare (called "West Pointism" by Forrest's men) was to fight one's command by detail, while holding back a large reserve (one-half to two-thirds), with the main objective being to maintain territory and avoid being beaten. Forrest, "the negative of a West Pointer," as Captain John W. Morton called him, did the opposite, often ignoring army regulations and even disobeying superiors whenever the situation called for it.[1974]

In what I term "Forrestism" (the General's approach to warfare), he sent everyone into battle at once with no concept of defeat whatsoever. (Indeed the word surrender was in neither his vocabulary

---

1969. Mathes, p. 101; Wyeth, LGNBF, p. 154.
1970. Parks, p. 186.
1971. Henry ATSF, p. 135.
1972. Black, p. 193.
1973. "Lieutenant-General N. B. Forrest: Lord Wolseley's Estimate of the Man and the Soldier," *Southern Historical Society Papers*, Vol. 20, 1892, p. 334 (original from the New Orleans *Picayune*, April 10, 1892).
1974. Morton, pp. 12, 13.

or his *manual of arms.*)[1975]

His primary objective? To drive the enemy out, chase him down, then capture or kill him. As we have seen, even Grant later admitted that Forrest's approach—which essentially wasted the North's time and drained her energy and resources—was the only one that would have allowed the South to win.[1976]

An insubordinate man who was unwilling to tolerate insubordination,[1977] Forrest was an authentic rebel—*a rebel born*, not just regionally, but socially and psychologically. Being a true nonconformist, he despised military formalities and the idea of "fightin' accordin' to the rules," and he never tried to hide his profound disdain for schooled military men, and in particular "West Pinters," as he disparagingly referred to them. Whether they were Yankee West Pinters or Rebel West Pinters, it made no difference: he disliked both with the same intensity, and as such frequently butted heads with both.

Still, he held special contempt for Union West Pointers. After trouncing dozens of them in battle (among them Generals Hatch, Benjamin Grierson, William Sooy Smith, and Sturgis), the crack military man who never once cracked open a military manual had this to say on the subject:

> Whenever I met one of them fellers that fit by note, I generally whipped hell out of him before he got his tune pitched.[1978]

While this was true, at the same time it must be admitted that Forrest could have benefitted from a stint at West Point. How? Not only would it have given him a more well-rounded idea of the science of war (only improving his already amazing powers of leadership), but undoubtedly he would have been promoted sooner and more often, for President Davis, like nearly all of Forrest's other superiors, had an overt bias toward West Pointers.[1979]

The General's deficiency in the area of formal military schooling

1975. Henry, ATSF, p. 99.
1976. U. S. Grant, Vol. 2, pp. 167, 345.
1977. Morton, p. 13.
1978. Morton, pp. 12-13.
1979. Mathes, p. 171.

did have a positive side, however: it meant that he was not tied to older, often antiquated military concepts, views that held back other more traditional officers, old-fashioned men like Hood, who preferred—and continued to use (much to the South's detriment)—tactics and strategies that were already out-of-date by the middle of the War.

## MILITARY INNOVATOR

Forrest, who proudly never imitated anyone, possessed enough unorthodox military habits to fill a small volume.

Among them were the unrestrained recklessness with which he approached battle, his near-total disregard for following the orders of his superiors, his seeming total indifference for his own life, and the sharpening of his saber to a razor's edge (on both sides of the blade)[1980] and wearing it on his right side[1981] (Forrest later banned the saber from his command as a valueless nuisance).[1982]

Throughout the War he also grew and wore his hair long, in the Cavalier style (perhaps to enhance his fearsome "wild man" image), and seldom used field glasses (binoculars), usually preferring the naked eye for observation, even over great distances.[1983] To ensure the element of surprise, one of his greatest strategies, he never disclosed his plans to anyone but his closest associates until just before battle.[1984]

While fighting he would often send out small forces (usually two companies) to harass and wear down the enemy, which allowed the rest of his soldiers to recuperate.[1985] And he always entered each conflict fully intending to win, as if each might be the deciding battle of the

---

1980. Concerning sharpening of the saber, military regulation specified that the blade be sharpened only a short distance from the point, and that it not be sharpened too finely. These precautions were believed necessary in case one accidentally struck a fellow Reb on the field of action. Forrest, however, an expert swordsman, focused his concern on the killing of Yanks and disregarded the rule. Thus he sharpened his swords to a razor's edge on both sides of the blade, and along its full length. Wyeth, LGNBF, p. 50.

1981. Military regulation stipulated that one's saber be used in the right hand, which necessitated that it hang on the left side. Some say that Forrest, being a "south paw," ignored the rule and wore his saber on his right side. Some claim, however, that he was ambidextrous (Wyeth, LGNBF, p. 629) and, while wearing his saber on his left side, freely transferred it back and forth—from left to right hand and back—during battle as the situation required. Mathes, p. 95.

1982. Morton, p. 12.

1983. Wyeth, LGNBF, pp. 45, 646.

1984. Mathes, p. 198.

1985. Wills, p. 112.

War.[1986]

So adept was the ever alert Forrest at hiding, dodging, attacking, and maneuvering, as well as using the element of surprise, that he was sometimes able to overcome the enemy without a shot being fired. One such instance occurred at Union City, Tennessee, on December 23, 1862, when he captured 106 Yanks without a single gun being discharged.[1987]

Other times soldiers reported to him for duty freshly released from the hospital or as newly exchanged prisoners of war, always without weapons. Operating on the principle that an unarmed soldier was better than no soldier at all (for this made his effective fighting force look larger), Forrest sent these men right into battle, even if their only weapon was the Rebel Yell (which helped intimidate the enemy, he rightly asserted). To those who hesitated at what they perceived as sheer madness, Forrest had this to say:

> Just follow along here, we'll have a fight presently, and then you can git plenty of guns and ammunition from the Yankees.[1988]

Forrest, always the inveterate gambler, sometimes won his conflicts in other even more imaginative ways. In Tennessee in the fall of 1864, for instance, he persuaded a sixty-five man Yankee command to surrender using nothing more than a small vial of "Greek fire" (an inextinguishable incendiary device composed of saltpeter, sulfur, niter, naphtha, oil, and resins). Similar to today's Molotov cocktail or petrol bomb, Forrest threw the bottle against an oak stump as an example of its devastating power. The horrifying effects of the rapidly spreading blaze caused the Federals to instantly relinquish any hope of victory.[1989]

One of the General's more fascinating war strategies was managing to make the enemy believe that he was "everywhere at once." Fighting without reserves, he and his entire command would sweep in from all sides simultaneously, giving the impression of both an

---

**1986.** Lytle, p. 311.
**1987.** Wyeth, LGNBF, p. 119.
**1988.** D. M. Bower, "Concerning Commanders," *Journal of the United Service Institution of India*, United Service Institution of India, Vol. 27, 1898, p. 103.
**1989.** Jordan and Pryor, p. 577.

overpowering force, unearthly ubiquity, and supernatural omnipresence. In the fall of 1864, for example, a discombobulated Sherman, confused and irritated over Forrest's most recent victories, sent Grant the following field report:

> Rome, GA., November 1, 1864—9 a.m.
> Lieut. Gen. U. S. GRANT,
> Comdg. Armies of the United States, City Point, Va.:
> As you foresaw, and as Jeff. Davis threatened, the enemy is now in the full tide of execution of his grand plan to destroy my communications and defeat this army. His infantry, about 30,000, with Wheeler's and Roddey's cavalry, from 7,000 to 10,000, are now in the neighborhood of Tuscumbia and Florence, and the water being low is able to cross at will. Forrest seems to be scattered from Eastport to Jackson, Paris, and the lower Tennessee, and General Thomas reports the capture by him of a gun-boat and five transports. . . .[1990]

"Swift to decide" (he had a mercurial mind)[1991] and seemingly always one step ahead of his foe (his reconnaissance system was superb), one of the more famous Yankee officers once said of the General: "It is impossible to know his whereabouts at any given moment. Yet he seems to know everything about us, where we are at all times; even our hypothetical plans."[1992]

Many of Forrest's soldiers, being country boys and farmers, knew well how to handle the enemy in such circumstances. "Our guards are gathered up by [Forrest] . . . as easily as he would herd cattle," General Don Carlos Buell bitterly complained in an 1862 field report.[1993]

Even though he had never had a single day of military schooling, Forrest instantly knew the strategy needed in every situation. Tossing out the chalkboard used by other officers to chart out their next move, he conceived his battle plans instantly and on the spot, using nothing more than his innate genius for tactical warfare. Then, targeting the enemy's weakest position, he would strike like lightning from every angle with an impact so swift, so unerring, and so resolute, that the

---

1990. ORA, Ser. 1, Vol. 39, Pt. 3, p. 576.
1991. Jordan and Pryor, p. 683.
1992. Henry, ATSF, p. 43. My paraphrasal.
1993. ORA, Ser. 1, Vol. 16, Pt. 2, p. 340.

outcome was usually a foregone conclusion.[1994]

The Confederate armies were always short on food and supplies, in great part because of Lincoln's illegal blockade. However, Forrest seldom worried about such minor details, for he always knew he could procure rations, arms, and clothing for his men directly from what he called "Uncle Sam's larder." How? By winning every battle and skirmish. Afterward, his men were free to take all the supplies and food they needed from the captured and the dead. Forrest even encouraged this method of providing for his troops, saying that not only was a change of diet good for his men (the Confederacy's rations were said to be rather bland), but that the Union's rations were of a greater variety than the Confederacy's, and thus healthier.[1995]

We will note that despite his unorthodox manner of supplying his command, Forrest, unlike Lincoln and most of his Union officers, was strongly against plundering (looting, robbery, and pillaging), and any soldier caught committing this offense was shot where he stood.

FORREST & HORSES
With his own built-in horse sense, Forrest knew how to use horses to their best advantage: because the equine species has much greater senses of sight, smell, and hearing than humans, he was always careful to watch for changes in their behavior.

Once, while searching for Yanks near Hog Mountain, Alabama, in the spring of 1863, his horse stopped abruptly in the middle of the road. A less intuitive and experienced horseman would have simply spurred the animal on. But Forrest knew immediately that something was amiss, and that this could possibly indicate that Union troops were near. Scouts sent out soon returned with confirmation of the horse's signal, and Forrest was able to score another victory for the Confederacy.[1996]

Of Forrest's knowledge of both the equine and the human species, Colonel David C. Kelley wrote: The General was innately knowledgeable about men and horses, on the manner in which to treat

---

1994. Morton, pp. 16-17.
1995. Henry, ATSF, pp. 94-95, 126.
1996. Wyeth, LGNBF, p. 203.

them, their level of endurance, even the time needed for convalescence.[1997]

## FORREST'S LOVE OF THE FIGHT

Coolheaded under fire[1998] and always ready to face the same risks he asked his men to face, he—quite unlike many other commanders—led most of his charges, even in the most hazardous situations, actually preferring to be where the "hottest" fighting was taking place.[1999] In essence, he *led* his men rather than *send* them. This is not surprising: Forrest considered skirmishing and fighting a form of "fun."[2000]

Even serious battlefield injuries did not dampen his love of physical combat. Shortly after being shot near the spine at the Battle of Shiloh (April 6-7, 1862), he wrote to a friend that he could not wait for the next fight to come along—the bigger the better.[2001]

Like Alexander the Great, Forrest's love of one-on-one warfare excited his men's confidence and enthusiasm, inspiring them to the levels of bravery and valor necessary for a small cavalry to overcome and crush much larger forces.[2002] And because he usually fought when, where, and how he chose instead of the enemy, and because no one ever knew exactly what his next move was,[2003] "that Devil Forrest" came to be dreaded by all Union officers.[2004]

He also used "rough handling" by the Yanks to inspire his troops. Dirty fighting by the enemy only served to infuriate the General, who passed on his "we'll-git-even-with-'em" attitude to his soldiers, helping to increase everyone's bloodlust to fever pitch.[2005] As Mathes writes:

> Perhaps no leader in the civil war threw himself, his staff, and escort oftener into the thickest of the many fights in which they were engaged.[2006]

---

1997. Lytle, p. 312.
1998. Browning, p. 32.
1999. Wyeth, LGNBF, p. 646.
2000. Henry, ATSF, pp. xiii, 134-135, 113.
2001. Hurst, p. 96.
2002. Jordan and Pryor, p. 683.
2003. Parks, pp. 190-191.
2004. Wyeth, LGNBF, p. 83.
2005. Wyeth, LGNBF, pp. 153-154.
2006. Mathes, p. 354.

## FORREST'S MEN

Most of Forrest's men, in fact, were cut from the same cloth he was. Many, like the Tennessee mountaineers among his soldiers, were considered the most hard-boiled, wildest, most uncontrollable, most reckless men in the South, ruffians who simply loved to fight for the sake of fighting.

Having never known any restrictions, they were careless, undisciplined, and indifferent to dress, speech, military rules, even their own lives. Thus the cause for which they fought was of little consequence to them. They simply wanted to follow Forrest, live in the open air, and do battle.[2007]

## THE SOLDIER'S LIFE

Of course this suited Forrest—a Tennessee mountaineer himself—perfectly well, for like them he saw military rituals such as drilling, marching, maneuvers, saluting, and standing at attention as a useless strain on both men and horses.[2008] He simply loved the soldier's life and living out-of-doors, and would have no doubt joined the Confederate cavalry even without the promise of pay or glory.

An enthusiast of "desperate chances," of lightening-fast surprise attacks (he never waited to be attacked),[2009] and dashing offensive maneuvers (such as quickly and violently cutting off an enemy's rearguard), Forrest introduced the "hit-and-run" guerilla tactic and the idea of blitzkrieg warfare, both still employed by modern armies.

A master of the double-sided flanking maneuver[2010] (his "hit 'em on the end!" yell was well-known to his troops), he also promoted the use of the mounted saber assault, as well as the "raiding" approach while maneuvering against the enemy. Using his artillery as the picket line baffled and overwhelmed the enemy, while his often dismounted cavalry might have been more aptly called a mounted infantry,[2011] since he normally fought his troops on foot, using his horses mainly for fast and

---

2007. Morton, p. 142.
2008. Morton, p. 12.
2009. Black, p. 198.
2010. At times Forrest liked to split his command in half, attacking the enemy's two flanks at the same time.
2011. Mathes, p. 253.

efficient transport of his men.[2012]

Another interesting eccentricity of the General was that in battle he "stood up" in his stirrups, never touching the saddle. While this certainly endangered his life (by presenting a larger target), at the same time it exhibited a startling and imposing figure to both his men and the enemy: the lithe, huge, 6 foot, 2 inch Tennessean looked a foot taller than he already was,[2013] adding to what his men called the frightening impression of his appearance on the battlefield.[2014] This alarming image certainly struck fear in the hearts of those Yanks unlucky enough to meet him on the field of action, such as those at the General's first major conflict, the Battle of Sacramento (December 28, 1861).

Though Forrest was perhaps best known for his aggressive orders to "move up!" and "show fight!",[2015] sometimes retreat was indeed the better part of valor, a reality even the never-back-down, hit-'em-while-you-can Forrest was keenly aware of. As such, he was not averse to a masterly exit—like the one he performed at Fort Donelson—in order to save human lives, horse flesh, weaponry, and ammunition. This strategy came in especially handy while he was in Middle Tennessee on October 13, 1864.

Pursued by Union forces, he pushed his men deep into the wilderness and hid, not even allowing fires to be lit, despite the frigid weather. When the danger had passed, the General snuck several thousand men and their horses across the icy Tennessee River to safety. If he had hesitated even twenty-four hours Forrest probably would not have survived the War, let alone that day: at the time, a stunning 30,000 Yankee troops—under the command of Union Generals Cadwallader C. Washburn, James B. Steedman, Gordon Granger, George H. Thomas, Joseph D. Webster, Andrew Jackson Smith, John Croxton, and Lovell H. Rousseau—had been diverted from the Georgia campaign and ordered to hit the area from every direction in an attempt to track Forrest down and kill him. By sheer toughness, canniness, and smarts, he once again avoided capture, and possibly much worse.[2016]

---

2012. Wyeth, LGNBF, pp. 35, 648.
2013. Wyeth, LGNBF, p. 308.
2014. Henry, ATSF, p. xii.
2015. Jordan and Pryor, p. 429; Wyeth, LGNBF, pp. 308-309, 644.
2016. Mathes, p. 293.

Many, of course, assumed that Forrest had a charmed life, the only rational explanation for how he managed to survive so many of these types of harrowing incidents. However, the General himself described his life as "a battle from the start,"[2017] and attributed his good luck to his wife's and his mother's prayers.[2018] Both were very religious and prayed for years for Forrest's conversion and salvation, prayers that were answered only toward the end of his short life.

## FORREST'S COMMAND OF THE ENGLISH LANGUAGE

Forrest's enemies claim he was "illiterate." However, this view only reveals their illiteracy, not Forrest's: his "uneducated" vocabulary turns out to be the beautiful, traditional border idiom of his time and place, not a deficiency in brain power,[2019] while his writing (despite the occasional phonetic spelling) was always articulate, unadorned, and candid.[2020]

In truth, Forrest was a genius with little formal schooling. Thus, though uneducated by formal standards, he could not only read and write, but he was highly knowledgeable in numerous areas, the very definition of "literate."[2021]

Indeed, not only was he known to be a natural-born orator, but his command of the English language was often said to be "eloquent and impressive."[2022] His official military reports reflect these abilities: they were not composed by his subordinates, as Northern myth asserts, but were exact replicas of his own words, all which he carefully dictated to staff members, usually Major Charles W. Anderson. If Anderson misspelled a word, or even forgot a punctuation mark, Forrest was quick to catch it. Pointing at the offending mistake he would drawl solemnly, "that thar ain't got the right pitch."[2023]

---

**2017**. Wyeth, LGNBF, p. 622.

**2018**. Mathes, p. 373.

**2019**. Lytle, p. 373.

**2020**. Henry, FWMF, p. 14.

**2021**. Based on the facts of Forrest's life story and the thousands of observations of his contemporaries, there is no question that Forrest's IQ was over 140, the number at which the genius category begins. Scientists reckon that less than one-quarter of 1 percent of the population falls into this elite group.

**2022**. Wyeth, LGNBF, pp. 573-574.

**2023**. Wyeth, LGNBF, p. 426.

## OBSESSIVE-COMPULSIVE FORREST

Forrest was a stickler for cleanliness, neatness, and detail,[2024] and probably possessed what we today would call an obsessive-compulsive personality.  As such, he subjected every inch of his soldiers' accouterments, from their saddlebags to their weaponry, to a rigid daily inspection, making sure everything was up to snuff.  His men learned quickly that they were personally responsible for keeping themselves, their horses, and their weapons clean at all times, and ready for action.[2025]

Forrest indeed took the idea of personal responsibility very seriously, holding both himself and his men to a high standard in this regard.  When he was in the wrong, he could readily admit it.  When one of his soldiers was in the wrong, he meted out the necessary punishment there and then, often attending to the discipline personally.[2026]

Though he and his cavalrymen generally scoffed at traditional forms of military punishment, Forrest's own brand of discipline served he and his troops very well: in the entire four years of Lincoln's War he only lost one battle (Selma) at which he was the commanding officer (and this was mainly because one of his dispatches was intercepted by the enemy).  This is a much higher success rate than for most of those officers who were schooled at West Point.

## FORREST'S RECONNAISSANCE SYSTEM

Uniquely, Forrest, ever the alert, wary, practical man of action,[2027] relied heavily on his vedettes and outpost detachments, which he maintained far in front of his primary command.[2028]

Also of vital importance to him was his advance system of scouts, who fanned out across the countryside in every direction, returning with invaluable intelligence on the position of the enemy.[2029]  This had the added benefit of preventing surprise attacks and ambushes.

---

2024. Lytle, p. 312.
2025. Parks, p. 169.
2026. Morton, p. 142.
2027. Jordan and Pryor, p. 217.
2028. Wyeth, LGNBF, p. 435.
2029. Mathes, p. 269.

## FORREST THE HIDER

Able to literally know when an ambush was coming,[2030] the General was also a good hider, and was known on occasion to conceal his entire command in the brush within 2,100 feet (700 yards) of the enemy as it trundled by, completely unaware that thousands of Rebels and their horses were lurking quietly under cover just feet away.[2031]

In the sweltering summer of 1862, in Tennessee, for example, Yankee Brigadier General William Nelson was ordered to track Forrest down. With 3,000 men, he went in pursuit of the wily Confederate. But each time Nelson got near, Forrest would simply slip his command off into the brush next to the road. After several days of this Nelson gave up, bitterly complaining that chasing Forrest and his men, "mounted on race horses," and in such "hot weather," is a "hopeless task."[2032]

## FORREST'S MILITARY RULES

Though not a "West Pinter," naturally aggressive Forrest had his own set of military rules, forged in earlier days as a child and young man struggling for survival on America's tough and unforgiving Western frontier.[2033]

One of these rules was that in close-quarter combat, once a gun was fired it was not be reloaded, but instead was to be used as a club.[2034] And when a gun was fired, every shot had to count. Forrest considered wastage of any kind (bullets, time, energy) one of the greatest sins a soldier could make.[2035]

He also promoted the very un-West Point-like idea that Southern territory was not to be occupied by Confederate forces, but rather, as we have seen, Yankee forces were to be denied Southern territory. It was just such concepts, strategies, and tactics (which I call "Forrestisms") that gave him the edge over his more militarily-schooled comrades.

---

2030. Lytle, p. 169.
2031. Wyeth, LGNBF, p. 101.
2032. ORA, Ser. 1, Vol. 16, Pt. 2, p. 234.
2033. Browning, p. 29.
2034. Wyeth, LGNBF, p. 407.
2035. Parks, p. 170.

## FORREST & GUNS

Speaking of guns and bullets, Forrest, like most frontiersmen, had a true love and respect for weapons. After all, they not only helped feed the family, they helped protect them as well. Thus guns played a central role in frontier life and the Second Amendment was highly valued.

As a Confederate officer Forrest brought along his obsession with firearms, with orders for his men to always keep their weapons clean and serviceable. Naturally he chose to equip his men with the most efficient guns possible. These were the Navy six-shooter and the short Enfield (a regular Enfield with the barrel shortened).

After discovering that his men often accidently shot away their ramrods during the heat of battle, he had the ramrods attached to the rifles, thereby assuring that he would have ample firepower in any situation. Another indication of how he viewed instruments of war can be found in his custom of reverently burying discarded or inoperable guns, as he did during his victory over Streight in May 1863.[2036]

## FORREST'S APPROACH TO WARFARE

Forrest's calling card was as elegant as it was simple: fighting instinctively, he always did what the enemy least expected him to do.[2037] This usually involved arriving early in order to startle an unprepared enemy, then galloping at full speed into the heart of the fight, where "the soldiers who made him famous"[2038]—his elite, highly mobile strike force made up of prize riders known as Forrest's Escort—would surround the Yanks before they could react.[2039]

Combining the light mobility of the cavalry with the heavy knock down power of the infantry,[2040] his "riflemen on horseback" would then hit their flanks and rear hard, call their bluff (by greatly exaggerating the numbers of his troops and artillery), use artillery in advance of his line like shotguns (by pulling his cannon right up into the face of the

---

**2036**. Lytle, pp. 304, 161.
**2037**. Wyeth, LGNBF, pp. 35, 288.
**2038**. Mathes, p. v.
**2039**. Bradley, pp. 9, 13. Forrest's Escort, the pride of the Confederacy, is today understandably nearly as famous as he is.
**2040**. Henry, FWMF, p. 462.

enemy),[2041] then offer the famed Forrest surrender-or-die "truce." Few Yankee officers dared refuse the General's generous but bone-chilling five-minute offer to relinquish their weapons "in order to prevent the further effusion of blood."[2042]

This terrifying message was used to excellent effect at the Battle of Murfreesboro, July 13, 1862, where a respectful Forrest had it sent by courier to Yankee Colonel H. C. Lester and his Minnesota troops. It read:

> MURFREESBOROUGH, July 13, 1862.
> COLONEL: I must demand an unconditional surrender of your force as prisoners of war, or I will have every man put to the sword. You are aware of the overpowering force I have at my command, and this demand is made to prevent the effusion of blood.
> I am, colonel, very respectfully, your obedient servant,
> N. B. FORREST, Brigadier-General of Cavalry, C. S. Army.[2043]

One of the General's men later wrote of what it was like "ridin' with Forrest": Though we belonged to the "lowly" cavalry, because it was Forrest's cavalry we experienced respect from every level of the military. Wherever we went, he noted, we caused a sensation; whoever we met, they treated us liked champions.[2044]

Just serving under Forrest then, in any capacity, elevated one to superior status in the eyes of both other Confederates and the enemy.

## A RUGGED & RESTLESS COMMANDER

A tough, stern, and sometimes cheerless task master, General Forrest was not always easy to be around: as a disciplinarian, journalist Lafcadio Hearn wrote, his men often feared him more than the Yankee.[2045]

Forrest did indeed demand absolute obedience, particularly on difficult missions. The result was that there were no cowards, slackers, or idlers in his command. To the contrary, nearly every man in Forrest's

---

2041. Wyeth, LGNBF, p. 648.
2042. Mathes, p. 199.
2043. ORA, Ser. 1, Vol. 16, Pt. 1, p. 805.
2044. Henry, FWMF, p. 16.
2045. Ramage, p. 107.

line was himself "a Forrest," equipped with much of the same courage, discipline, toughness, and bottled up fury as their commander.[2046]

Restless by nature, the Anglo-Celtic leader could not remain encamped for long,[2047] and quite unique among the military brass, he cared little or nothing about time, the weather, or road conditions. Thus his order to "mount up" could occur at any moment day or night, in blasting heat, frigid winds, rain, ice, or snow.[2048]

Often, instead of establishing winter quarters, Forrest would continue to hunt for Yankees in the freezing temperatures,[2049] not even letting his men light fires for warmth (since these might give away their position).[2050] One of his men later noted: Whenever the General told us to git some rest, we did, for we never knew when our next break might come.[2051]

Another of Forrest's soldiers wrote that no matter what time it was, no matter what the season, he never tired. He seemed to be everywhere at once, attacking the enemy out of the blue without warning from all directions. Forrest was no mere soldier. He was a deity of war.[2052]

Like the true war-god that he was, Forrest detested "ornamental officers" (those who hung about doing nothing, only adding a cachet of importance to their superior) and did not allow them on his staff. Additionally, all those who served under Forrest, even anyone who happened into his camp on official business (for example, attachés, clerks, and couriers), were expected to, on a moment's notice, pick up a gun and be prepared to go into battle with him.[2053]

## ADMIRAL FORREST

Unlike his more buttoned up, over-educated West Point associates, the General—"never at a loss for resources in the most sudden

---

2046. Henry, ASTF, p. 97.
2047. Morton, p. 13.
2048. Henry ATSF, p. 149.
2049. Browning, pp. 11-12.
2050. Lytle, p. 339.
2051. Parks, p. 179.
2052. Lytle, p. 313.
2053. Mathes, p. 357.

emergencies"[2054]—had an extremely open, improvisational mind when it came to "fightin' and killin' Yanks."

An instance of this occurred in August 1964. While fighting the enemy in Mississippi, he ordered his men to make a river bridge out of telegraph poles. The men, however, complained that they had no method of getting them to the ferry for transport. "You certainly do," countered their commander. "Horse tails! Braid 'em and attach the poles to 'em!," he yelled. The bridge was soon constructed and Forrest and his men crossed over without problem.[2055]

The ever innovative Forrest was also not above turning his cavalrymen into marines when the situation called for it. This actually happened on October 30, 1864, when he and his men captured a Union gunboat, the *Undine*, and two transports, the *J. W. Cheeseman* and the *Venus*, on the Tennessee River near Fort Henry.[2056] The *Undine*, with two of Forrest's impressive 20-pounder Parrott guns transferred over to it, became his flagship.[2057]

As the gunboat fleet chugged along the Tennessee River, Confederate flags billowed beautifully in the wind from their mastheads, the first ones seen on that body of water since 1862. Throngs of fellow Southerners eagerly crowded the shores to cheer on what quickly came to be called Forrest's "Horse Marines," the first known cavalry to ever man gunboats.[2058] The resourceful General's "brilliant career" as admiral of the "Forrest Fleet" ended when both ships were finally scuttled under enemy fire five days later on November 3.[2059]

Due to what Scottish historian Thomas Carlyle called an "interior talent for war,"[2060] Forrest has garnered fans from around the world. One of these, British General Viscount Wolseley, wrote:

> . . . he was a man of quick resolves and prompt execution, of inexhaustible resource, and of ready and clever expedients. He had

---

**2054.** Jordan and Pryor, p. 684.
**2055.** Lytle, p. 322.
**2056.** Denney, pp. 482,483.
**2057.** Wyeth, LGNBF, pp. 523-524.
**2058.** Morton, p. 249.
**2059.** Mathes, pp. 300-301; Morton, pp. 250-251. For a detailed account of the entire "Horse Marines" episode, see Jordan and Pryor, pp. 593-599.
**2060.** Jordan and Pryor, p. 234.

all the best instincts of the soldier, and his natural military genius was balanced by sound judgment. He always knew what he wanted, and consequently there was no weakness or uncertainty in his views or intentions, nor in the orders he gave to have these intentions carried out. There was never any languor in that determined heart, nor weariness in that iron body. Panic and fear fled and hid at his approach, and the sound of his cheer gave courage to the weakest heart.[2061]

## ONE OF "THE BOYS"

Despite his reputation as a dour and tough-as-leather commander, Forrest—at his core, a farmer who was born and died in a log cabin—was highly approachable by either a private or a fellow officer, for he laid little stock in ceremony and military etiquette.[2062] As a prewar civilian Forrest had been uncontrived, easy going, and sociable, often walking about in his shirt sleeves. This informality was something that, to a great extent, he carried into the military.[2063]

As such, he allowed his soldiers to retain their essentially Wild West character rather than force them to conform to what he regarded as highfalutin military regulations. Irregulars by nature, his troops were made up mainly of gritty farm boys and rough-and-tumble frontiersman, just like Forrest himself. Naturally, he accepted them as they were, giving them great freedom of expression, even allowing them to dress and wear their hair and beards however they liked (much to the consternation of his superiors).[2064]

Forrest, in fact, commanded his men much like an older brother, with an intense personal and protective attachment to them. This was quite unlike other Rebel officers, such as Bragg, who was well-known for controlling his troops with icy, impersonal orders taken directly from military manuals. Truly, as has been said of Forrest, under his tutelage, the everyday soldier became something more. He became a great warrior in his own right.[2065]

Forrest also had a funny bone and was not afraid to use it. As

---

2061. Wyeth, LGNBF, p. 123.
2062. Morton, p. 142.
2063. Henry, ATSF, p. 179.
2064. Henry, ATSF, p. 38.
2065. Lytle, pp. 149, 313.

such, he was not above laughing heartily with his troops at a well-timed joke. He also loved a good game of checkers, as well as a host of sports, which he played with enthusiasm, when time permitted, with his men. These included pitching quoits, jumping, racing, and playing marbles. Obviously, from this we can see that though he demanded respect from his soldiers, he did not place himself above them. Instead, like Napoleon I, he shared the hazards and difficulties of his subordinates, even sleeping on the ground alongside them and eating the same food they did when necessary.[2066]

Between the arduous marching, camping, and fighting, there was always time for a "heap o' fun," as Forrest referred to it. In the winter of 1863, at Jackson, Mississippi, for instance, he set aside an entire evening for raucous "celebratin', feastin', and square dancin'." The local women cooked a sumptuous banquet, replete with whiskey-soaked eggnog. The town square was cleared, bonfires lit, and the fiddlers were tuned up. Forrest, his men, and the townsfolk joined together in a great square dance of frivolity and merriment that lasted well into the early morning hours.[2067] (There are no records describing the intense, indomitable Forrest as he cut loose and danced the *Virginia Reel*, but we can be sure that it would have been a sight few would ever forget.)

All of this, of course, only endeared his soldiers to their General all the more. Second only to General Robert E. Lee, Forrest was in fact adored by his men, who would do anything he asked, on or off the battlefield.[2068] So widespread was Forrest's reputation as a great Rebel leader that deserters from other Confederate commands were often only willing to reenter the military if they could serve under him.[2069]

Most of Forrest's "boys" were enlisted behind enemy lines (that is, in Yankee-occupied Southern territory), making every Southerner a target of suspicious Yanks who had become paranoid hearing tales of the General's incredible, almost supernatural, feats. The always impudent, South-hating Sherman—who, like Grant, both feared and respected Forrest—had plenty to say on the subject. Of Forrest and his effect on the Union armies, the obviously exasperated Yankee general said:

---

2066. Mathes, pp. 364, 366.
2067. Lytle, p. 251.
2068. Bedwell, p. 35.
2069. Jordan and Pryor, pp. 460-461.

It is none of our business to protect a people that has sent all its youth, and arms, and horses, and all that is of any account to war against us. Forrest may cavort about that country as much as he pleases. Every conscript they now catch will cost a good man to watch. The cavalry movement in Mississippi was designed by Joe Johnston to delay my march, and he signally failed. I have made my junction, and all you need to do is to protect the interests and property of the United States. The people have done all the harm they can, so let them reap the consequences.[2070]

## FORREST THE TRICKSTER

Using captured flour and coffee to free stuck wagon wheels from muddy roads gives us an inkling of Forrest's true on-the-spot inventiveness and craftiness.[2071] However, he saved his biggest and best tricks for the Yankees themselves.

Though he seldom had more than 5,000 men under his command (the most he had at one time was 15,000),[2072] one of his best known gimmicks was to over-exaggerate the numbers of his forces. This was, no doubt, a carryover from his youth, at which time he excelled at such games as "brag and bluff"[2073] and various mule-swapping pranks. After all, Forrest correctly figured, if the enemy merely believes he is out manned then it is not necessary to actually have a superior force, for the battle is already half won.[2074] This psychological sleight of hand maddened the Yanks, emboldened Forrest's soldiers, and endlessly delighted the Southern people.

Smarter and quicker than any Yankee,[2075] one of Forrest's favorite methods of accomplishing this was to spread a number of his more rhythmically adept men out across a wide area and beat upon captured kettledrums.[2076] This gave the Yanks the impression that he had, in addition to his large dauntless cavalry, an enormous infantry force under his command,[2077] on the field and ready to do battle.[2078] At other

---

2070. ORA, Ser. 1, Vol. 31, Pt. 3, p. 187.
2071. Hurst, p. 110.
2072. Henry, ATSF, p. ix.
2073. Wyeth, LGNBF, pp. 108-109.
2074. Lytle, pp. 101, 102.
2075. Sheppard, p. 306.
2076. Wyeth, LGNBF, p. 109.
2077. Jordan and Pryor, pp. 198-199.
2078. Mathes, p. 85.

times he would simply order his bugler, Gaus, to blow the call for his men to form a circle. "I will often have need of this maneuver," he once laconically understated it to a fellow officer, "as it will be necessary from time to time for me to show more men than I actually have on the field."[2079]

But Forrest—who was often aided on the battlefield by his brother Captain William "Bill" Forrest's famous "Forty Scouts"[2080] (better known as the Independents)[2081]—had numerous other methods of achieving the same effect. One of those for which he was most famous required nothing more than the quick rearrangement of his men, such as when he made his usual 4,500-man force appear like a 10,000-man army at Athens, Alabama, in late September 1864.

Prior to surrender the Yankee officer in charge asked to inspect Forrest's troop strength and cannon power, to which Forrest immediately agreed. What the Union commander did not realize was that Forrest, who assumed the inspection would take place, had already dismounted a large portion of his cavalrymen so that they appeared to be infantrymen. After the Yank had reviewed their numbers and passed on into another section, Forrest had those same men run to a new position, mount their horses, and present themselves as cavalrymen. Adding to the psychological impact was the movement of the same artillery pieces from position to position. In this way Forrest was able to present an overwhelming force, and the unsuspecting enemy conceded defeat.[2082]

In another similar case, in Estenaula, Tennessee, in December 1863, Forrest divided up his small units and sent them out against the Yanks with orders for each to act as if it were his entire army. Under a frigid night sky his men used the cover of darkness to their advantage by spreading out into a wide, single, frontal line, while yelling commands to brigades behind them that did not exist. To up the effect Forrest's men drove their horses through a cornfield full of dried up stalks. The

---

2079. Wyeth, LGNBF, p. 640.
2080. Wyeth, LGNBF, pp. 196, 471.
2081. Bill Forrest's Independents were an irregular force of about forty men who served unofficially under General Forrest during his campaigns into Mississippi and West Tennessee. The Independents received no pay from the Confederate government, but instead lived by foraging off the enemy, and also friends when necessary. This was true Confederate faithfulness and commitment, and to this day we in the South salute them. Wyeth, LGNBF, p. 124.
2082. Wyeth, LGNBF, p. 492.

ear-shattering sounds of the brittle vegetation breaking under the horses' hooves magnified what was actually a puny sixty-five man unit into what sounded like an overwhelmingly huge Confederate force. The ploy worked: some 600 Union soldiers fled for their lives before Forrest's tiny command.[2083]

One of the better examples of this particular artifice, one that might most accurately be called "the dismounting and remounting trick," occurred in December 1862 when Forrest, with only 2,500 men (and of those only 1,500 effective), deluded the Yanks into thinking he had as many as 20,000 men![2084] The Union field report of Brigadier-General Jeremiah C. Sullivan captures the aura of mayhem Forrest created around the Yanks at the time:

> JACKSON, December 18, 1862—7.10 p. m.
> My cavalry was whipped at Lexington to-day. Colonel Ingersoll taken prisoner and section of artillery captured. The enemy [Forrest] are reported to be from 10,000 to 20,000 and still crossing the river. They are now within 6 miles of my outposts. I will try and find their number by daylight.
> JER. C. SULLIVAN, Brigadier-General.[2085]

Of these types of deceptive shenanigans, Forrest's chief of artillery, Captain John W. Morton, wrote:

> A stratagem successfully practiced by this bold raider, with the assistance of his trusty scouts, consisted in spreading greatly exaggerated reports of the strength of his force. No device for creating this impression was too insignificant to be called into play. The constant beating of kettledrums, the lighting and tending of numerous fires, moving pieces of artillery from one point to another, the dismounting of cavalry and parading them as infantry—nothing was overlooked. Again and again these tactics were successfully employed.[2086]

Forrest would often send his entire force into battle at one time.

---

2083. Wyeth, LGNBF, pp. 284-285.
2084. Morton, pp. 49-50.
2085. ORA, Ser. 1, Vol. 17, Pt. 1, p. 551.
2086. Morton, p. 49.

This startled the enemy, of course. But more importantly, the Yanks assumed that he still had many more soldiers in reserve,[2087] making them more likely to surrender on the spot.

Forrest's men also often resorted to the use of "Quaker guns": logs painted black then mounted on ordinary wagons drawn by mules. An old wooden box mounted on another wagon, serving as the "caisson," completed the ruse. When Yanks spied these "weapons" from afar they were certain Forrest possessed large numbers of cannon, and either fled or capitulated there and then.[2088]

At night Forrest was able to confuse Lincoln's soldiers by building long lines of unnecessary and unused campfires. This fooled the Yanks into believing that a large Confederate force was camped in the area, ready to strike. During daytime conflicts he would make a detachment look as if it were the advance guard of a division. Shortly after, the real advance guard would attack, along with strikes on the enemy from various unexpected quarters. This "magnification" caused great confusion while creating an impression of overwhelming Confederate strength.[2089]

As mentioned, on occasion the General would send unarmed men into battle (his troops were nearly always under-equipped throughout the War).[2090] Naturally many balked at the seemingly insane order, at which Forrest barked: "Get in line and advance on the enemy with the rest! I want to make as big a show as possible!" In every case this performance succeeded.[2091]

One of his favorite and most productive deceptions was to simply release Yankee prisoners who, unbeknownst to themselves, had been inculcated with hours of disinformation about Forrest's numbers, strength, and location. Another was to dress a detachment of his men in blue overcoats and send them out at night to reconnoiter amidst the enemy.[2092]

---

2087. Mathes, p. 354.
2088. Mathes, p. 199.
2089. Mathes, p. 206.
2090. D. M. Bower, "Concerning Commanders," *Journal of the United Service Institution of India*, United Service Institution of India, Vol. 27, 1898, p. 103.
2091. Wyeth, LGNBF, p. 135.
2092. Lytle, p. 83.

Forrest was very fond of capturing Yankee telegraph offices and intercepting their dispatches,[2093] as he did at Spring Hill, Tennessee, on October 1, 1864. He would then send back misleading "Union" dispatches using the names of nonexistent Confederate officers.[2094] By spreading disinformation about his troops' strength, locations, and movements among the Federal military, he was able to buy valuable time, increasing the odds for the South.[2095] At other times he simply tapped Union telegraph lines, gathering vital intelligence that he was able to use against the enemy.[2096]

On March 4, 1864, for example, a flustered and confused Yankee General William Sooy Smith wrote from Nashville that:

> Exaggerated reports of Forrest's strength reached me constantly, and it was reported that Lee was about to re-enforce him with a portion or the whole of his command.[2097]

All of this was patently false. These were merely rumors that Forrest himself had set in motion![2098]

In a similar vein, Forrest would send some of his most devoted men into Yankee camps pretending to be deserters. Enthusiastically welcomed by the unsuspecting Union troops, they would willingly offer detailed intelligence on Forrest's numbers, whereabouts, and plans—all of it erroneous. At the same time, these same men would gather important information from the Yanks, bringing it back to Forrest, who advantageously used the data to further harass and destroy Lincoln's henchmen.[2099]

An official Union report on September 12, 1863, provides an example of this particular ploy. One of Forrest's fake "deserters," a "J. C. Hopkins," had fled to the Federal camp where he regaled the naive Yanks with tall tales of Forrest's engagements and troop movements. Note the crafty soldier's statements about the high level of

---

2093. Jordan and Pryor, p. 575.
2094. Mathes, p. 291.
2095. Wyeth, LGNBF, p. 299.
2096. Wyeth, LGNBF, p. 504.
2097. ORA, Ser. 1, Vol. 32, Pt. 1, pp. 256-257.
2098. Wyeth, LGNBF, pp. 299-300.
2099. Wyeth, LGNBF, pp. 239, 241-242.

"dissatisfaction" among Forrest's men, and their increasing desire to desert and join the Union army.

> SEPTEMBER [12], 1863.
> Statement of [Confederate] J. C. Hopkins, General Forrest's escort: I left my command on the night of the 10th instant at Pea Vine Church, 16 miles from this place. Forrest has command of the cavalry on the right wing of the army. I think he has about 5,000 mounted men. He went down the La Fayette road yesterday toward La Fayette. He had some light artillery with him. Fighting had been going on along the road near Gordon's Mills from 12 o'clock noon of yesterday until about dark. The Union army had been driving us all the time. I think we had fallen back about 5 miles. I was not in the fight. I heard we had several wounded. I was in the woods and waited until our forces fell back. When the Federals came up I surrendered, and delivered my arms to a sergeant of Anderson Cavalry. I saw General Armstrong's brigade (rebel) and one battalion of McDonald's cavalry engaged on our side. I do not know that we had any more troops engaged. The rebels fell back after the firing ceased in the direction of La Fayette. The soldiers are generally very much dissatisfied. From what I know I think most of the men would desert if they had an opportunity. Many of them are hiding out, and waiting for the advance of the Federal army.
> (Received Headquarters Department of the Cumberland, September 12, 1863.)[2100]

As not one word in this report is true, it must have been several weeks before the susceptible Yanks figured out the full extent of Forrest's clever gimmick.

Another favored trick: at night Forrest and his men would purposefully ride slowly up into the rear of a Union cavalry, pretending to be Yanks. After engaging some of the unsuspecting bluecoats in idle conversation, the Feds would drop back and ride casually along with the unperceived Rebels. Often the bluecoats would complain about Forrest, much to the delight of the General and his soldiers. At that point, out would come Forrest's famous "Navy sixes," which his men would cock in the ears of the Federals. It was then announced: "You are now with Forrest's men. Hand over your arms and roll off that horse." This

---

2100. ORA, Ser. 1, Vol. 30, Pt. 3, p. 563.

deception was extremely successful and many a Union soldier was captured in this way.[2101]

Another example of the General's "brag and bluffs" occurred on September 24, 1864, at Athens, Alabama, where he had yet another Federal garrison in his sights. After he got his men into position he sent the Yankee commander the following sobering letter:

> HEADQUARTERS FORREST'S CAVALRY,
> In the Field, September 24, 1864.
> Officer Commanding U. S. Forces, Athens, Ala.:
> I demand an immediate and unconditional surrender of the entire force and all Government stores and property at this post. I have a sufficient force to storm and take your works, and if I am forced to so the responsibility of the consequences must rest with you. Should you, however, accept the terms, all white soldiers shall be treated as prisoners of war and the negroes returned to their masters. A reply is requested immediately.
> Respectfully, N. B. FORREST, Major-General, C. S. Army.[2102]

Forrest's "offer" was declined, but he was not dissuaded from his goal to capture the post. Instead, he immediately arranged a meeting with the Union officer in command, Colonel Wallace Campbell. In person Forrest made another offer, inviting Campbell to inspect his troops in order to prove that he had an overwhelming force, one quite big enough to take the garrison.

Unconvinced, the colonel accepted the invitation, and promptly rode up and down the lines, carefully scrutinizing Forrest's forces. Assured that Forrest had at least 8,000 men on the ground—far more than necessary to capture the post—Campbell quickly surrendered his comparatively tiny force of 1,400 soldiers.

What he did not realize was that Forrest had skillfully and cunningly arranged his men so that they appeared to be twice their actual size: dismounted cavalry pretended to be infantry, then mounted again moments later out of view to reappear as cavalry. Meantime, horse-holders at the rear were brought up to appear as another body of infantry, while the same artillery was circled around and around.

---

2101. Henry, ATSF, pp. 128-129.
2102. ORA, Ser. 1, Vol. 39, Pt. 1, p. 521.

Campbell's report reveals that he believed Forrest had some 224 guns and as many as 12,000 men on the field that day. In reality, Forrest had only eight guns and around 4,500 soldiers.[2103]

## AGGRESSIVE & MOBILE

Naturally aggressive and always the attacking party (he met every charge with a counter advance), Forrest never missed an opportunity to fight Yankees, even getting his men up between 2:00 and 4:00 in the morning in order to increase his odds.[2104]

Though a highly skilled swordsman, he preferred his men use the revolver rather than the saber.[2105] Nonetheless, he was not averse to using a sword himself when need be. The only objection his superiors had was that, against army regulations, he sharpened both the entire length *and* the top and the bottom edges of his sabers to a razor's edge (in order to expedite the dispatch of the enemy).[2106]

Forrest helped develop and refine Alexander the Great's idea of mobilized guerilla warfare, turning the hit-and-run cavalry attack of earlier wars into a literal art form.[2107] This tactic, a great contribution to military science (his fighting forces were not called the "winged infantry," "lightening infantry," and "flying cavalry" for nothing),[2108] was as simple as it was effective: using mounted infantry,[2109] an army was relentlessly chased, harassed, and attacked until it either surrendered or was killed off. For as Forrest firmly believed, the best time to whip an enemy is when he is on the run.[2110] In fact, trying to flee from Forrest only made him want to give chase all the more, just as a running jack rabbit stimulates a cougar's attack reflex.

A frontier hunter from early childhood—one who stalked his prey for days then killed it—the General was a master of this particular tactic, a precursor of our modern day Commandos and Rangers.[2111] An

---

2103. Mathes, pp. 286-287; Lytle, pp. 332-333.
2104. Mathes, p. 241.
2105. Henry, ATSF, pp. 24-25.
2106. Wyeth, LGNBF, p. 50.
2107. Henry, FWMF, pp. 472, 9-10.
2108. ORA, Ser. 1, Vol. 32, Pt. 1, p. 302.
2109. Denney, p. 16.
2110. Lytle, p. 231.
2111. Henry, FWMF, p. 16.

outstanding example was his battle with Yankee General Abel D. Streight, a fight that Forrest was assisted in by a young patriotic Confederate girl.

## THE STORY OF EMMA SANSOM & GEN. STREIGHT

On April 29, 1863, hearing from his scouts that Streight was nearby, Forrest and his men hurried out of the town of Courtland, Lawrence County, Alabama, in a bitter rain.

On April 30, at Day's Gap (the summit of Sand Mountain),[2112] Forrest caught up with Colonel Abel D. Streight's rearguard and a battle ensued. Forrest's gave his usual general order: "Shoot at anythin' blue, and keep up the skeer!"[2113] Streight managed to repel the Confederates long enough to get away.[2114] But, vastly underestimating his wily pursuer, Streight did not realize that there was no escape from the relentless and deadly Forrest.

The tenacious Tennessean nipped at Streight's heels almost unceasingly for several more days (once riding steadily for forty-four out of forty-eight hours), engaging the Yanks in numerous skirmishes, gradually grinding them down.[2115]

On May 2, at Black Creek, on the road between Blountsville and Gadsden, Alabama, Forrest found that Streight had crossed the only bridge in the area and burned it behind him. While Forrest was pondering his next move he came upon a young lass named Emma Sansom, who told him of a "lost ford" downstream.[2116] The Yanks had taken all of her family's horses, but she would be happy to lead him to it. With no time to lose and bullets flying around them, Forrest pulled the youngster up onto his saddle and sped away with her guiding him.[2117]

---

2112. Day's Gap is in what is now Cullman County, Alabama.

2113. Morton, p. 196; Wyeth, LGNBF, p. 198; Mathes, p. 116.

2114. Though the Battle of Day's Gap is considered a Union victory by most military scholars, I would beg to differ, especially considering what followed over the next several days.

2115. Wyeth, LGNBF, pp. 204-205. Some of the skirmishes between Forrest and Streight that surrounded the Battle of Day's Gap were fought at Crooked Creek, Hog Mountain, Blountsville, Black Warrior River, Black Creek, the Bethsadia Community, Ryan's Creek, and Blount's Plantation.

2116. The Sansoms were one of the vast majority of Southern families, over 96 percent, who did not own slaves.

2117. Some of the Yankee bullets actually passed through little Emma's skirt, but she was unharmed. She put herself in further danger when, wishing to protect the General, she stood up and waved her bonnet at the Union boys in an attempt to get them to cease fire. The trick worked. The Yanks not only immediately stopped firing, they waved their own hats in the air and gave three raucous cheers. This gave Forrest and

Locating the shallow river crossing, the Southern celebrity quickly took Emma home and dropped her off with her stunned and speechless mother—but not before they both had been shot at numerous more times.[2118]

In gratitude Forrest gave Emma a horse and asked her to mail him a lock of her hair. Then, before resuming the chase, he left a thank you note for her at her house, etched in pencil on the leaf of one of his field notebooks.[2119] It read:

> Hed Quaters in Sadle, May 2, 1863
> My highest regardes to Miss Ema Sansom for hir gallant conduct while my posse was skirmishing with the Federals a cross Black Creek near Gadsden Allabama.
> N. B. Forrest, Brig. Genl. Comding N. Ala.[2120]

Emma's brave assistance saved Forrest at least three hours,[2121] valuable time that brought him to within breathing distance of the enemy, unbeknownst to Streight.[2122]

Horrified to discover Forrest now just behind him, Streight and his troops rode "like the wind," but all for nought. Because of Forrest's unrelenting pursuit, Streight's men and their horses had not eaten or slept for several days. All were nearly out of steam.

On May 3, 1863, near Cedar Bluff, Alabama, Forrest sent a flag of truce forward. Frazzled and depressed, Streight finally stopped and

---

Emma just enough time to make their escape. After the War the governor of Alabama presented Emma with land and a gold medal for her bravery in serving the Confederate Cause. Jordan and Pryor, p. 269.

2118. Jordan and Pryor, p. 265.

2119. Mathes, p. 121.

2120. Wyeth, LGNBF, pp. 212-213.

2121. It was widely believed among the Yanks that the Confederates had fabricated the story of Emma Sansom, and that it was nothing but a wild Southern yarn. See Henry, ASTF, pp. 229, 232. It is little wonder that they thought this: Northerners made up hundreds of stories about Forrest themselves. I can attest that the story is true, however, for I descend from the Sansoms. See following footnote.

2122. Though her surname is spelled Sanson in early Forrest biographies, this is inaccurate. The correct spelling is Sansom, as corroborated by family members and court records. Emma Sansom was born June 2, 1847, in Social Circle, Walton County, Georgia. The daughter of Micajah Cades Sansom, Jr. of Rutherford City, North Carolina, and Permelia B. Vann of Burk, Georgia, Emma married Christopher Bullard Johnson on October 29, 1864, and had at least eight known children, the first born being named Mattie Forrest Johnson. Emma passed away on August 9, 1900, in Little Mound, Texas, where she was buried. An inscription on the family monument reads: "E.S.J. Girl heroine who piloted Gen. Forrest across Black Creek and enabled him to capture Col. Strait." Emma's grandfather was Micajah Cades Sansom, Sr. of Virginia. I descend from the Virginia Sansoms: my great-grandmother is a Sansom from Wayne Co., West Virginia.

asked to speak with Forrest face to face. Meeting in a nearby woods the exasperated Yankee officer told Forrest: "I will not surrender unless I know your force is equal to mine."

That very second Forrest's artillery just happened to pass within sight of the pair. Cunningly, he had previously ordered the section to move in a slow wide circle to make it appear as if new cannons and batteries were constantly arriving on the scene.[2123] Streight was horrified.

"In the name of God man, how many guns have you got?" he asked incredulously.

"Wall, that's fifteen I've counted so far, sir," Forrest replied nonchalantly, chewing on a long piece of grass. Then for added effect: "Reckon that's all that has kept up."

With no inkling that in reality Forrest had only two cannon, was almost out of ammunition, and that he had few men left in fighting condition, Streight hesitated nervously.[2124]

Sensing his enemy's indecisiveness, the crafty Rebel insisted: "I've got enough to whip ya out of yer boots Colonel."

Streight still looked doubtful, at which point Forrest yelled to his bugler Gaus: "Sound to mount!"

That was it. An exhausted and humiliated Streight and his 1,740 men immediately capitulated to the General and his little 400-man force,[2125] there and then earning him the title, "Wizard of the Saddle." The audacious Rebel had saved yet another Southern town (Rome, Georgia) and her railway lines from certain capture.

A generous and kindly Forrest gave the Yanks permission to keep their sidearms and baggage, and offered them drinks. He then allowed Streight to address his men and give three cheers for the Union (we can be sure that if captured, Forrest and his men would not have been allowed the same courtesies).[2126]

Forrest later spoke of the moment of surrender. "After ordering my men to take possession of the enemy's arms," he said, "the jinx was

2123. Jordan and Pryor, p. 273.
2124. Parks, p. 184.
2125. Bradley, p. 78.
2126. Jordan and Pryor, p. 275.

up"[2127]:

> When Streight saw they were barely four hundred, he did rear!
> Demanded to have his arms back and that we should fight it out.
> I just laughed at him and patted him on the shoulder, and said, 'Ah,
> Colonel, all is fair in love and war, you know.'[2128]

Confederate Major Charles W. Anderson one-upped Forrest in the humor department. After the surrender, he noticed a glum Streight pouting over the deception that had led to his downfall. A double humiliation came when the crest-fallen Yank officer heard that Forrest's men were already calling the affair the "Jackass Raid."[2129] According to Southern lore, Anderson walked over to Streight, put his arm around his shoulder, and said: "Cheer up, Colonel. This is not the first time a bluff has beat a straight!"

Forrest had marched and fought for five days and nights, traversing some 150 miles of mountainous terrain nearly non-stop. "Braggin' and bluffin'" the whole way, he captured an entire Yankee command nearly four times the size of his own.[2130]

Classic Forrest.

Bragg cheerfully reported to his superiors at Richmond:

> TULLAHOMA, May 5, 1863.
> On May 3, between Gadsden and Rome, after five days and nights of fighting and marching, General Forrest captured Colonel Streight and his whole command, about 1,600, with rifles, horses, &c.
> BRAXTON BRAGG.[2131]

Here we have the embodiment of the "shock and awe" approach to fighting, used today by America's modern military. Forrest, ahead of his time, was employing the maneuver 150 years ago.

Little wonder that the General's capture of Streight has been

---

2127. My paraphrasal.
2128. Lanier, Vol. 4, p. 282.
2129. Black, p. 136.
2130. Wyeth, LGNBF, pp. 218-220.
2131. ORA, Ser. 1, Vol. 23, Pt. 1, p. 294.

called "one of the most remarkable performances known to warfare,"[2132] or that the Confederate Congress expressed gratitude to Forrest for the victory. The official document reads:

> *Thanks of the Confederate Congress to General Nathan B. Forrest and the officers and men of his command.*
>
> *Resolved by the Congress of the Confederate States of America*, That the thanks of Congress are again due, and are hereby tendered, to General N. B. Forrest and the officers and men of his command, for meritorious service in the field, and especially for the daring, skill, and perseverance exhibited in the pursuit and capture of the largely superior forces of the enemy, near Rome, Ga., in May last; for gallant conduct at Chickamauga, and for his recent brilliant services in West Tennessee.
> Approved February 17, 1864.[2133]

## AN UNAPPRECIATED MILITARY GENIUS

Unfortunately, the genius behind such feats was not fully recognized by Forrest's superiors until after the War, as the writings of both President Jefferson Davis and General Robert E. Lee reveal. Over the past century and a half, many have noted, for example, that had Forrest replaced Hood as the commander of the Army of Tennessee before the Battle of Atlanta (July 22-September 1, 1864), the outcome of the War for Southern Independence might have been quite different.[2134]

Strange that, at the time, the Union seems to have appreciated Forrest's brilliance sooner and more often than his own commanders. Sherman, for instance, was in awe of Forrest,[2135] while Grant named him "the ablest cavalry general in the South,"[2136] sentiments echoed by thousands of professional soldiers into the present day.

---

2132. Only days after Streight's capture, the grateful residents of nearby Rome, Georgia, set aside May 6 as a day of tribute to Forrest. After presenting him with a powerful new horse (he had lost several chasing Streight), a festive barbeque was planned. Unfortunately, Forrest was quickly called away on a new mission against the Yanks and could not attend. Wyeth, LGNBF, pp. 220-222; Mathes, p. 126.

2133. ORA, Ser. 1, Vol. 23, Pt. 1, p. 295.

2134. Many believe that one of the Confederacy's weakest links was President Davis himself, who often chose friends over more qualified strangers for important cabinet and military positions (cronyism), and who preferred West Pointers over the less educated (favoritism). In fact, Davis, himself a graduate of West Point, never offered a major command position to any non-West Pointer, effectively eliminating Forrest from the running, a fact that will be forever lamented by many in the South. See Wyeth, LGNBF, pp. 162-163, 220.

2135. Gragg, p. 199.

2136. U. S. Grant, Vol. 2, p. 346.

After the War, here is what Sherman told one of Forrest's officers, General Frank C. Armstrong:

> After all, I think Forrest was the most remarkable man our Civil War produced on either side. To my mind he was the most remarkable in many ways. In the first place, he was uneducated, while Jackson and Sheridan and other brilliant leaders were soldiers by profession. He had never read a military book in his life, knew nothing about tactics, could not even drill a company, but he had a genius for strategy which was original, and to me incomprehensible. There was no theory or art of war by which I could calculate with any degree of certainty what Forrest was up to. He seemed always to know what I was doing or intended to do, while I am free to confess I could never tell or form any satisfactory idea of what he was trying to accomplish.[2137]

Forrest, comfortable on horseback from birth and rightfully nicknamed the "Wizard of the Saddle,"[2138] was the only individual, Confederate or Union, to rise from private to lieutenant general during the War; that is, he was the only enlisted man to make it to the rank of general.[2139] In fact, he was one of only twenty-four Confederates who attained this rank, twenty of them West Point graduates, the other three all experienced military men. Forrest was the only one among this elite group of twenty-four who lacked a military educational background, making his ascent to the top all the more astonishing.[2140]

Forrest never spent a single night in a Yankee wartime prison until he finally surrendered at Gainesville, Alabama, and after the War he was never indicted or arrested, despite the numerous charges brought against him: now grudging admirers of him, former Union officers—such as Grant, Sherman, Sheridan, Winfield S. Hancock, John

---

2137. Wyeth, LGNBF, p. 635.

2138. While Forrest's title as the Wizard of the Saddle was well earned, he was of course far from being the only Confederate who had mastered the horse. Johnny Reb came mainly from rural areas and lived and worked on farms his entire life, making familiarity with the horse second nature. Billy Yank, in contrast, came primarily from industrialized urban areas in the North, where he had less direct contact with the equine race. Additionally, the Rebels used their horses quite differently, forming them into massive tactical forces, as opposed to the Federalists, who assembled their horses into smaller groups used mainly for reconnaissance and patrolling. In a word, as most would now agree, the Confederate cavalry was vastly superior to the Union cavalry.

2139. Henry, FWMF, p. 10.

2140. Browning, p. 105.

M. Schofield, George H. Thomas, George Stoneman, and Judson Kilpatrick—refused to engage in postbellum retribution, and instead heaped praise upon him at every opportunity.[2141]

It is also said that during the four years of Lincoln's illegal war, Forrest never lost a battle which he commanded—until Selma, and until then he had been the only Rebel commander in the Western theater who had never been defeated;[2142] that twenty-nine horses were shot out from under him[2143] (Forrest himself claimed that thirty-nine horses were killed while he was riding them);[2144] that he was shot at 179 times; that he was seriously wounded four times;[2145] that he killed thirty Union soldiers and wounded hundreds more; that he seized and destroyed millions of dollars worth of Yankee supplies; and finally, that he captured, in total, some 31,000 prisoners. At one time or another, nearly 50,000 Confederate soldiers came under Forrest's command, including some 100 organizations, such as regiments, battalions, and batteries.[2146] Impressive statistics for a non-military military man from any time period!

General Richard Taylor noted in his book *Destruction and Reconstruction*:

> I doubt if any commander since the days of the lion-hearted Richard killed as many enemies with his own hand as Forrest.[2147]

Forrest's approach to fighting was certainly rudimentary, but it was extremely effective. After letting loose the famed Rebel Yell, he would give his favorite charge command, "Come on boys!"—much beloved by his men, and one of the keys to his success as a Confederate officer. His other favorite commands were, "Forward men, and mix with 'em!" and "Give 'em hell!"—both always sure to motivate his

---

2141. Mathes, p. 361.
2142. Lytle, p. 327.
2143. Bradley, p. 10. A horse-lover his entire life, the horrid and painful deaths of his many noble steeds during the War was, no doubt, particularly difficult for Forrest.
2144. W. B. Garrison, CWC, p. 75.
2145. Henry, FWMF, p. 17.
2146. Henry, ATSF, pp. 216, ix. As Forrest was constantly being transferred and organizing new regiments, only a few men served with him from the start of the War to its finish. Two such individuals were Major John P. Strange and Major Gilbert V. Rambaut, two of the most fortunate men in the South. Henry, ATSF, pp. ix-xi.
2147. R. Taylor, p. 200.

troops.[2148]  Viewing active duty as "training," and the enemy (not the Confederate government) as his main source of supplies, Forrest's army was one of the most efficiently run military bodies in the history of war.

In his mind winning came down to a simple, rustic formula: "get there first with the most men."[2149]  (Forrest asserted that he could beat anyone if he managed to get in the first punch.)[2150]  And believing that one could not fight and win without loss, he was the strongest proponent of his own now famous axiom: "war means fightin', and fightin' means killin'."[2151]

Once when asked how he managed to win all of his battles, he replied: I always decide when, where, who, and how to fight.[2152]  This approach allowed Forrest to consistently win against much larger forces, proving, to the Southern people at least, that the Confederate military's main defense problem was not it soldiers, but its generals.[2153]

But Forrest, known as one of the "big guns" by Confederate soldiers,[2154] was not just an expert at cutting down Yanks in battle. Being a Southern gentleman he was also known for sparing their lives when occasion demanded it.  Forrest held special admiration for those Federal soldiers who displayed outstanding courage on the field of action, and was rightly acclaimed for his mercy, sensitivity, and respect in such cases.

An example of this occurred at the Battle of Thompson's Station, March 5, 1863.  Here several Union officers surrendered to Forrest, who allowed the men to keep both their mounts and their pistols.[2155] According to the Yankees' official report of the conflict:

> The bravery of the little band surrounded and captured was so conspicuous as to elicit the applause of the enemy himself [i.e., General Forrest], and we are informed that Colonels [John] Coburn and Gilbert, and Major [W. R.] Shafter, of the Nineteenth Michigan, were permitted on this account to retain their horses and

2148. R. Taylor, p. 200.
2149. Wyeth, LGNBF, p. 33.
2150. Henry, ATSF, p. 120.
2151. Wyeth, LGNBF, pp. 50-51.
2152. Henry, ATSF, p. 57.
2153. Lytle, p. 174.
2154. Watkins, p. 124.
2155. Mathes, p. 103.

side-arms.[2156]

Reverend Major David C. Kelley, one of Forrest's most detail oriented observers, later wrote of some of the General's more spectacular traits:

> In his early battles he was so disregardful of the ordinary rules of tactics, so reckless in personal exposure, that I felt sure his career would be short. It seemed certain that whenever he should meet a skilful opponent his command would be utterly cut to pieces. So fierce did his passion become that he was almost equally dangerous to friend or foe, and, as it seemed to some of us, he was too wildly excitable to be capable of judicious command. Later we became aware that excitement neither paralyzed nor misled his magnificent military genius. What had seemed to us the most unreasonable command when given proved, both in its result and his after-explanation of the reasons on which he acted, consummate generalship. His genius in action rose to every emergency; he always did what the enemy least expected him to do, and when defeated, as others would have counted defeat, he was more fertile in resources, more energetic in attack, more resistless in his fiery onset than when the action began. While his desperate bravery and frequent charges were characteristic of his military career, they by no means exhausted his resources. The manœuvring of his forces in the presence of the enemy, his messages to opposing commanders, his matchless shrewdness in impressing them with the overwhelming superiority of his forces, and the necessity for surrender, were equally characteristic. The use of his artillery, often thrust forward to the skirmish-line, which would have been madness in an ordinary commander, was vindicated by the splendid results which he won. His common-sense led him at an early date to see that the day was past when a cavalry charge with sabers could be made effective in the presence of infantry.[2157]

In reading the U.S. government's *Official Records*, one is struck by how many dispatches, orders, and letters contain references to Forrest, an officer whose authority and command were never considered large or important at Richmond. Obviously, the Yankees were quite obsessed with the General! I have counted some 5,597 mentions of his

---

2156. ORA, Ser. 1, Vo. 23, Pt. 1, p. 84.
2157. Wyeth, LGNBF, pp. 35-36.

name in the *Official Records of the Union and Confederate Armies*. Series 1, Volume 39, Part 2, alone has 594 references to Forrest, spanning a mere seven-month period between May 1864 and November 1864.

So highly venerated is Forrest today among those who understand and know the real man, that his very name is synonymous with heroism, brilliance, and inventiveness. After eagerly studying Forrest's "campaigns and tactics," early 20th-Century British cavalry officers decided he was the greatest of the cavalry leaders in the Western world.[2158] There is some evidence that Forrest's methods may have been used at such World War I conflicts as the First Battle of Ypres.[2159]

Of him Lord Garnet Joseph Wolseley, Commander-in-Chief of the British Army, said:

> Panic found no resting place in that calm brain of his, and no danger, no risks appalled that dauntless spirit. Inspired with true military instincts, he was, most verily, nature's soldier.[2160]

His commission was, as one of his own men later noted, acknowledged not only by President Davis, but by God himself—as every one of his men was well aware.[2161]

Little wonder that a century and a half later Forrest's strategies, tactics, tricks, and techniques are still taught at military schools around the world; that his methods and ideas have influenced both modern warfare and modern business practices; that so many Southern parents name their sons after him; and that schools, local parks, State parks, cemeteries, businesses, monuments, golf courses, apartment complexes, libraries, office buildings, housing projects, and subdivisions across America are named after him. Indeed, entire cities (Forrest City, Arkansas)[2162] and counties (Forrest County, Mississippi)[2163] have been named after him.[2164]

---

2158. *Tennessee Historical Quarterly*, Vol. 4, 1945, p. 188.
2159. Ashdown and Caudill, pp. xix-xx.
2160. "Lieutenant-General N. B. Forrest: Lord Wolseley's Estimate of the Man and the Soldier," *Southern Historical Society Papers*, Vol. 20, 1892, p. 326 (original from the New Orleans *Picayune*, April 10, 1892).
2161. Lytle, p. 313.
2162. See Website: www.forrestcity-ar.com.
2163. See Website: www.forrestcountyms.us.
2164. Seabrook, NBF, p. 72.

Neither is it a surprise that he has appeared (or is mentioned) in various television series (e.g., *I'll Fly Away*), comic books (e.g., *It Really Happened*), and films (e.g., *Last Stand at Saber River*), or that authors and writers from William Faulkner, Shelby Foote, Howard Bahr, and John Grisham, to O. Henry, Harry Turtledove, Robert Penn Warren, and Winston Groom have incorporated Forrest into their stories or used him as a template for their fictional figures.

Groom's literary and cinematic character "Forrest Gump" alone has made Forrest a household name around the world, and when the General was defended by Shelby Foote in Ken Burns' 11-hour PBS series, *The Civil War*,[2165] some 40,000,000 Americans were watching.[2166]

---

2165. Burns' documentary has been widely, and rightly, condemned by traditional Southerners as overtly pro-North.

2166. Mississippian Faulkner was particularly fond of Forrest: he mentions or features the General in eight of his stories and essays and in nine of his novels. See Ashdown and Caudill, pp. 188-191.

# CONFEDERATE HERO: SPIRITUAL COMFORTER OF THE SOUTHERN PEOPLE

"What I desire most of you, my son, is never to
gamble or swear. These are baneful vices." —
Nathan Bedford Forrest, to his son Willie

PARAGON OF THE AMERICAN DREAM

THOSE WHO WOULD CONDEMN FORREST are ill-informed.
For in him we have the epitome of the American Dream; an
exemplar who, against nearly insurmountable odds, rose above
the limitations of dire indigence, disease, and a large father-less family to
become a self-made multimillionaire, and one of the most prosperous
men in the South, all before the age of forty.

Along the way, amazingly, the self-taught individualist literally
pulled himself up by his own boot straps, transforming himself from an
impoverished, impetuous rustic, into a wealthy, sophisticated
humanitarian, all with less than six months of formal education.

Raised in a Eurocentric America that often viewed African slaves
as little more than human livestock, he instead saw them as people,
invaluable servants to be treated humanely and respectfully. Freeing all
of his slaves before and during the War, afterward he happily hired them
back as paid employees and fought for racial equality, stating that it is not
necessary for there to be a battle between people of different colors.
"Let us all work together. In that way our entire nation will flourish," he

said repeatedly.[2167] Seeking to repopulate the South with blacks, he often remarked on the warm feelings he felt toward them. He even had a detailed plan on how to procure laborers from both Africa and China.

After giving four years of his life to Lincoln's unconstitutional war on the South, he survived serious war wounds and countless business failures and bankruptcies. He then built his fortunes back up again, invested in rebuilding the ruined South, and was elected to numerous official positions, in spite of a large coterie of bigots arrayed against him.

Though his Celtic temper, gambling, and proclivity for profane cursing often got the best of him, the gallant cavalryman eventually subdued them, channeling his reckless energies into more constructive social and spiritual pursuits.

## A MAN OF TRUE GRIT, CHARACTER, & NOBILITY

Of royal European blood, Forrest had many admirable traits, among them gumption, drive, ambition, perseverance, and the refusal to accept defeat. He never gave in when he believed he was in the right, and was known to approach desperate situations with a cool and calculating head.

Never a quitter, he always finished what he started, no matter how difficult the road ahead. An innate leader, he inspired and motivated all those around him, often even his enemies, with his composed but forceful presence. And yet he was capable of deep sympathy, compassion, and tenderness, such as was displayed in his great love for children.

A seemingly simple man outwardly, he was actually an exceptionally complex person whose thoughtful and calm exterior hid an indefatigable physical energy and a mercurial mind that knew no rest. Indeed, Forrest never seemed to grow tired and seldom slept, and, as one of his officers said of him, was, in fact, "more like that of a piece of powerful steam machinery than a human being."

Though many think of "Old Bedford," as he was sometimes called, as a grave and solemn figure, as we have seen, in truth he loved a good laugh and had a wonderful lively sense of humor. During the War, Yankee General James Harrison Wilson happened to meet Forrest during a truce. Like so many others, Wilson came away from this brief

---

2167. My paraphrasal.

and unexpected encounter with nothing but awe and admiration for the dyed-in-the-wool Southern gentleman.

According to Wilson, as he and his men were about to depart Forrest's camp,

> the General took my hand in his own . . . and holding it in a cordial grasp, said in a friendly and courteous manner, 'Don't git too far away from your command when you come down into this country—some of our boys may pick you up.[2168]

Forrest, said to be fearsome toward his enemies and faithful to his family and friends, was indeed a good and trusted friend to all who knew him. This despite being betrayed, taken advantage of, and verbally and even physically attacked on numerous occasions.

And for his role in trying to preserve Southern law and order, Southern culture, and Southern pride during the horrors of Reconstruction, he became forever acknowledged as the "spiritual comforter" of his people.[2169] One of Forrest's staff members, Colonel Matthew C. Galloway, later wrote that Forrest was a productive and admired citizen of every town he lived in, was unpretentious and plain-speaking, and possessed an unflagging spirit and a generous soul.

FORREST'S HUMBLE SIDE
Indeed, contrary to Yankee myth that the General was an arrogant and selfish man, he was actually known to be quite modest, humble, and charitable, particularly when the situation warranted.

On one occasion, for example, after Forrest's superb capture of

---

2168. Gragg, p. 201.

2169. The term "spiritual comforter" was applied to Forrest by Southern author and poet Andrew Nelson Lytle (see Lytle, p. 390). Born in Murfreesboro, Tennessee, Lytle was one of the original founders of the Fugitive Poets, a group that in turn founded the *Southern Agrarian Movement* (1920s-1930s), which advanced the idea that the South should reject Northern industrialization and instead continue to maintain itself as an agriculturally based society. This idea was already losing ground before Lincoln's War due to the Industrial Revolution and Eli Whitney's invention of the cotton gin in the late 1700s. In the 1860s Lincoln aided in the process of destroying the South's agrarian nature by imposing Northernization on the South (one of his stated goals). As a result, much to the dismay of most traditional Southerners, Dixie has been growing more industrial and less agricultural with each passing year. An agrarian myself, I continue to promote the idea that closeness with Nature, love of the land, preservation of our wild and green spaces, and above all farming, remain our greatest bulwark against the insidious corrosion of human life by industrialism and modernism in all their many seductive forms.

Streight in the spring of 1863, his superior General Bragg called him into his headquarters, where he was received with "unusual warmth" (as we have seen, the two had often quarreled bitterly). At the brief meeting Bragg suggested to Forrest that he be promoted to major-general and placed in command of the cavalry of the army. The great Nathan Bedford Forrest, by now a national celebrity and a household name around the world, humbly declined the offer, suggesting someone else instead. On another occasion, when Forrest's men captured trophies while fighting Yanks, he sent them back to the enemy, "with the compliments of General Forrest."

## MILITARY MAN PAR EXCELLENCE

Then there is Forrest's military record itself, which is nothing short of astonishing; especially for someone who, unlike most other officers, never attended military school. And though his independent spirit and brashness sometimes prevented promotion, on the field of action his native brilliance and absolute fearlessness awed both his superiors and his enemies.

His love and respect for his troops inspired thousands to fight faithfully for the Southern Cause under his stouthearted leadership. Many would echo the words of Confederate General Pierre Gustave Toutant Beauregard, who once said, "Forrest's capacity for war seemed only to be limited by the opportunities for its display."[2170] Little wonder that so many today, like his own soldiers, never tire of talking about him.

## A BENEVOLENT & FAITHFUL FAMILY MAN

Forrest proved to be an excellent father, a devoted family man, and an industrious provider, as well as a faithful lifelong husband. Indeed, unlike the vast majority of men then as today, he married but one time, for as one of the General's early biographers, Captain Eric William Sheppard, noted, Forrest only loved once in his entire life, and after that never even glanced at another woman.[2171]

A man of ceaseless generosity, from the moment he began to

---

2170. B. A. C. Emerson, p. 116.
2171. The adult divorce rate in Western countries is now about 60 percent (75 percent among teens); that is, three out of five modern Western marriages come to an end, and usually within the first four years.

earn his own money in his teens until his death at age fifty-six,[2172] he gave free-heartedly to family members, friends, and charities.

## A TRUE CHRISTIAN WARRIOR
His final and most important engagement took place on his own inner battlefield, where he conquered his greatest foe and was born again, becoming a "new creature in Christ." His life thus reminds us that being a Christian is about mercy, forgiveness, and transformation; in other words, spiritual growth. Is this not the Christian ideal, the epitome of Christian redemption?

Those who denounce him would do well to consider the words of the Savior he worshiped (John 8:7). For "that Devil Forrest" turns out to be neither a demon or a deity. Just a man. But not just any man.

## THE SOUTH'S SIR WILLIAM WALLACE
To traditional Southerners and lovers of liberty everywhere, Nathan Bedford Forrest remains—along with Robert E. Lee and Stonewall Jackson—one of the three brilliant stars of the Confederate Trinity. His glory is thus fixed in the heavens for all time, beaming, defiant, and immutable. To the South, he was, and still is, what Sir William Wallace is to the Scots.

For those who disagree with this estimation, it must still be admitted that, whatever one thinks of him, Forrest was a rare American original, an honest-to-God American patriot, and a hellbent-for-leather American hero and legend. He will thus always be an integral part of our nation's heritage and a major player on the stage of world history.

---

2172. Why did Forrest die at the young age of fifty-six? In my opinion, this question has never been adequately addressed. Forrest was a robust, powerful, athletic individual who never smoked or drank, and who possessed great mental and physical strength, well into his forties. Could diabetes and his other minor health complications alone kill such an individual? Certainly. But is it possible that there were other less obvious factors that led to the onset of this specific disease? Living in the open for four years, not to mention the intensity with which he fought against the North during the War, would have contributed to weakening his immune system and thus his overall health. He also endured tremendous stress, perhaps, it might be said, far more than the average person. Not only did the War place great strain on him, but he struggled for decades through countless financial difficulties, numerous court battles, physical and psychological fights, and the hatred, abuse, and misunderstanding of others (mainly Northerners). Forrest was also left-handed, something that has been linked (though not conclusively) to a shortened life span by some scientists. (Interestingly, Wyeth called Forrest's left-handedness a "sinister preference," one developed in childhood.) Did any of these things help send Forrest to an early grave? It is a fascinating question, one that future researchers will hopefully one day undertake to answer.

By any standard, in any time or place, this makes him an extraordinary person, one to be revered not reviled; emulated, not castigated; commended, not condemned. For he is not just a figure of Southern history, he is part of our theology: part mythic, part legendary, part reality, just the way we Southerners like our heroes. If the North can idolize men like Lincoln, Grant, Sherman, and Sheridan, all—as the *Official Records* clearly show—war criminals, why is the South not allowed to idolize Forrest, a decent, hard-working, intrepid, and honorable man?

IMMORTAL, INFINITE, ETERNAL FORREST

As they did in the 19th Century, his ill-informed, 21st-Century critics are still making up slanderous stories about him; his unenlightened enemies are still trying to blot out his memory; ignorant South-haters are still trying to tarnish his name. All to no avail.

Not even the almighty Grant or Sherman were able to permanently defile Forrest's character (let alone find him and kill him). The living embodiment of rugged individualism in a world of conformity, perseverance in the face of adversity, self-reliance among a people growing evermore socialistic, and traditional values in a nation of progressive liberalism, he continues to be honored, even worshiped, by millions of people of all races, colors, creeds, religions, and nationalities, from around the globe.

It is true that those who like Forrest best are those who know him best, and that those who like him least are those who know him least. Indeed, while liberals, socialists, the politically correct, and others from among the uninformed continue to denounce Forrest, historians, scholars, and others who have taken the time to examine his life in detail come away respecting him, admiring him, acquitting him of all evildoing.

"The magic name of Forrest will truly," as Wolseley said, "always be remembered with love, devotion, awe, and respect in all of the Southern states."[2173] For, like the immortal archetypal hero of ancient legend that he represents, Forrest will ride his warhorse through the pages of history for all eternity; ageless, timeless, glorious, invincible.

---

2173. My paraphrasal.

Minor Meriwether captured the essence of the man in 1877. "Forrest is eternal," said the former Confederate transportation engineer, "and his image, words, daring, deeds, ingeniousness, and heroism will continue to live on in the hearts and minds of all true patriots, whatever their allegiance, nationality, or race."[2174]

The words imprinted on Forrest's Equestrian statue in Memphis sum up the traditional Southern view of the General perfectly:

Those hoof beats die not upon fame's crimsoned sod,
But will ring through her song and her story;
He fought like a titan and struck like a god,
And his dust is our ashes of glory.[2175]

---

2174. My paraphrasal.
2175. Written by Mrs. Virginia Frazer Boyle. B. A. C. Emerson, p. 317.

# APPENDICES

# APPENDIX A

# OFFICERS UNDER FORREST

*A List of Forrest's Regular Staff Officers*

Major John P. Strange: assistant adjutant-general
Major Charles W. Anderson: aide-de-camp and assistant inspector-general
Major Gilbert Vincent Rambaut: chief commissary
Major George Dashiell: chief paymaster
Major Charles S. Severson: chief quartermaster
Major A. Warren: quartermaster
Major Richard M. Mason: quartermaster
Captain Matthew C. Galloway: aide-de-camp[2176]
Captain William Montgomery "Willie" Forrest (the General's only son): aide-de-camp
Dr. James B. Cowan: chief surgeon
Captain John G. Mann: chief engineer
Captain Charles S. Hill: chief of ordnance
Lieutenant Samuel Donelson: aide-de-camp[2177]

---

2176. In some records his surname is spelled Gallaway.
2177. Jordan and Pryor, p. 685; Mathes, pp. 355-356.

# FORREST'S ENGAGEMENTS

*- Includes Battles, Skirmishes, & Raids -*

November 1861-February 1862: raids from Hopkinsville, KY

December 28, 1861: Battle of Sacramento, KY

February 11-15, 1862: Ft. Henry, TN

February 11-16, 1862: Battle of Fort Donelson, Dover, TN

February 18-22, 1862: Nashville, TN

April 6-7, 1862: Battle of Shiloh, TN (Pittsburg Landing to Yanks)

July 13, 1862: Battle of Murfreesboro, TN

July 13-August 30, 1862: Middle TN and KY

December 10, 1862-January 6, 1863: West TN

December 18, 1862: Battle of Lexington, TN

December 31, 1862: Battle of Parker's Crossroads, TN

February 3, 1863: Battle of Dover (or Battle of Fort Donelson II), TN

March 5, 1863: Battle of Thompson's Station, TN

March 25, 1863: Battle of Brentwood, TN

April 10, 1863: Battle of Franklin I, TN

April 30, 1863: Battle of Day's Gap (Sand Mountain), AL

June 4, 1863: Triune, TN

June 10, 1863: Triune, TN

June 27, 1863: Rearguard, Tullahoma, TN

June 30, 1863: Cowan Pass-Chattanooga, TN

September 18-20, 1863: Battle of Chickamauga, GA

December 1-29, 1863: West TN

February 21, 1864: Battle of West Point, MS

February 22, 1864: Battle of Okolona, MS

March 15-May 5, 1864: West TN

March 25, 1864: Battle of Paducah, KY

April 8, 1862: Battle of Fallen Timbers, TN

April 12, 1864: Battle of Fort Pillow, TN

June 10, 1864: Battle of Brice's Cross Roads, MS

June 11, 1864: Battle of Tallahatchie, MS

June 11, 1864: Battle of Ripley, MS

July 14-15, 1864: Battle of Tupelo (Harrisburg), MS

July 15, 1864: Battle of Old Town Creek, MS

August 16, 1864: Battle of Hurricane Creek, MS

August 21, 1864: Forrest's Raid on Memphis, TN

September 21-October 6, 1864: Northern AL-Middle TN

September 25, 1864: Battle of Sulphur Branch Trestle, Elkmont, AL

September 27, 1864: Battle of Pulaski, TN

October 16-November 16, 1864: West TN

November 3-5, 1864: Battle of Johnsonville, TN

November 24-29, 1864: Battle of Columbia, TN

November 29, 1864: Battle of Spring Hill, TN

November 30, 1864: Battle of Franklin II, TN

December 15-16, 1865: Battle of Nashville (not present at actual battle, but defended the rearguard of the Army of Tennessee on its retreat south through TN, from Dec. 19 on)

December 25, 1864: Anthony's Hill, TN

December 26, 1864: Sugar Creek, TN

April 2, 1865: Battle of Selma, AL (Forrest's only loss as commander)

May 9, 1865: surrender at Gainesville, AL

## APPENDIX C

# A FORREST LIFE CALENDER

## Tracking the Movements of Nathan Bedford Forrest

*- From Birth to Death -*

The following list traces Forrest's movements throughout his life, painstakingly researched by the author. Military buffs will recognize the important battles at which Forrest was present (he was often at the location of a battle days before, and after, it began).

Some of the dates and places are open to question, as even many Forrest scholars disagree on the actual facts. Indeed, it is not always clear, even from the *Official Records*, where Forrest was on any given day. Hence, there are some large gaps in the time line of his life where his exact location is uncertain. In such cases I use "about," "mid," "late," "end of," "early," etc.

To make matters more difficult, some of the towns Forrest once inhabited or visited no longer exist, and many of the counties he was in have been since divided, redrawn, and their names changed.

Then there is Forrest's mercurial restless mind, as well as his instinct to ride fast and swiftly to elude the enemy. (He always moved quickly—one of the elements essential to his many successful engagements on the battlefield.) Thus, on some days he was in more than one city or location at a time. In some instances he was even in more than one state on a single day—and this was on horseback!

Another problem in deciphering Forrest's whereabouts at any given moment was his use of military trickery. During Lincoln's War, one of his favorite ploys was to send one of his escorts over to the Yankee side, pretending to be a deserter. Once the trickster had won the Federals' confidence, he would feed them detailed disinformation on where Forrest was located (he was actually miles away from the spot eagerly described), throwing them off his trail sometimes for days or weeks. While this ruse worked wonderfully (by confusing the enemy and buying time), it has made things much more complicated for modern day Forrest scholars and researchers.

Where large gaps exist after 1859 it is probably safe to say that he was either at his family home Green Grove Plantation at Sunflower Landing, in Coahoma County, Mississippi, or doing business in Memphis, Tennessee. It was in these two locations that he spent the majority of his life.

## 1821: BIRTH

July 13, 1821: Forrest born near what is now Chapel Hill, Bedford Co. (now Marshall Co.), TN.

1823: Monroe Doctrine issued.

1825: Erie Canal completed.

1830: First steam locomotive built in the U.S. (by Peter Cooper).

1831: The reaper invented (by Cyrus McCormick). In Boston, MA, William Lloyd Garrison begins publishing his South-bashing abolitionist newspaper, *The Liberator*, which, for the first time, criminalized both slavery and slave owners and traders. Garrison's disingenuous paper inspired the black racist Nat Turner Rebellion (that same year), and pushed for immediate emancipation in the South, though the North had given itself decades to abolish slavery (and only after it became unprofitable). These factors naturally made Dixie defensive and ended all possibility of settling South-North differences amicably. In this way, Garrison and *The Liberator* were two of the primary catalysts responsible for lighting the flames that led to Lincoln's War.

### 1834: CHILDHOOD YEARS

1833: Forrest's father, William Forrest, moves his family to Tippah Co., MS (near what used to be the town of Salem).

1836: American settlers finally arrive in Oregon.

### 1837: TEEN YEARS

1837: Forrest's father, William Forrest, dies in Tippah Co., MS.

### 1841: YOUNG ADULT YEARS

1841: One of Forrest's brothers (born in 1836, name unknown) dies.

1841: Forrest at New Orleans, LA (en route to TX).

1841: Forrest at Houston, TX (to fight in the Texas Revolution).

1841: Forrest in Tippah Co., MS (near what used to be the town of Salem).

### 1842: ADULT LIFE

Fall 1842: Forrest, now 21, leaves home permanently.

1842: Forrest moves to Hernando, DeSoto Co., MS, and begins working for his uncle, Jonathan Forrest.

### 1843

December 28, 1843: In Marshall, MS, Forrest's mother Mariam remarries to Joseph Luxton, Sr.

### 1845: EARLY WORK YEARS & MARRIAGE

1845: Forrest's twin sister, Fanny Forrest, dies.

March 11, 1845: Forrest's uncle, Jonathan Forrest, murdered (Forrest singlehandedly kills two of the assailants and seriously injures the other two).

Sometime after March 11, 1845: Forrest is made sheriff (constable) of the town of Hernando and Coroner of DeSoto Co., MS, by grateful citizens.

April 25, 1845: Forrest marries high society Southern belle, Mary Ann Montgomery (a relative of Sam Houston), at Hernando, MS.

## 1846 : A SON

September 26, 1846: Forrest's first of two children born: William Montgomery "Willie" Forrest (named after Forrest's father William).

1846: Sewing machine invented (by Elias Howe).

1846-1848: Mexican War.

## 1847

1847: Forrest becomes a member of the Independent Order of Odd Fellows.

Sometime in 1847 (?): Forrest sets up a brick yard business.

## 1848

About 1848: Forrest opens a stage line connecting Hernando, MS, to Memphis, TN.

1848: Gold discovered in California.

## 1849: A DAUGHTER

1849: Forrest's second of two children born: Frances Ann "Fanny" Forrest (named after Forrest's twin sister Fanny).

1849: Forrest loses everything he has earned up to this point when an unscrupulous businessman legally (though unethically) withdraws all of Forrest's savings from his bank account.

## 1850: HERNANDO

1850: Forrest still living in Hernando, MS.

## 1852: MEMPHIS & SLAVERY

Early 1852: Forrest moves his family to Memphis, TN.

Sometime in 1852: Forrest forms a business partnership called "Forrest and Jones," which only lasts one year.

Spring 1852: Forrest at Galveston and Houston, TX (on slave trading business).

By November 1852: Forrest has begun to buy and sell black slaves.

1852: Harriet Beecher Stowe's absurd fiction, *Uncle Tom's Cabin*, is published.

## 1853

January 1853: Forrest at Lexington, KY.

Sometime in 1853: Forrest becomes the junior partner of a Memphis slave trader named Byrd Hill.

## 1854

February 1, 1854: Forrest begins buying real estate in Memphis.

June 26, 1854: Forrest's daughter, Frances Ann "Fanny" Forrest, dies at six years of age of flux (dysentery).

## 1855

Early 1855: In Memphis Forrest forms a business partnership with Josiah Maples.

## 1857

June 1857: Forrest stands up to a mob of 3,000 angry townspeople to save a local ruffian (John Able) from being illegally lynched.

## 1858

1858: By this year Forrest is a multimillionaire.

April 1858: Forrest at Covington, TN.

June 27, 1858: Due to his gallantry in saving the life of John Able, Forrest is elected alderman of the city of Memphis for the first time. This was to be the only political office ever held by him.

After July 1, 1858: In Memphis, TN, Forrest is made head of Memphis' Finance Committee.

October 16, 1858: Forrest buys 1,900 acres of cotton land in Coahoma, Co., MS.

Sometime in 1858: Forrest opens up a slave trading business in Vicksburg, MS.

1858-1860: Forrest makes many trips from Memphis, TN, to Vicksburg, MS.

1858: The Lincoln-Douglas Debates are held, an ill omen of things to come. White supremacist Lincoln assures his Northern audiences that he has no interest in abolishing slavery and that his plans include shipping all American blacks "back to their native land."

### 1859

Sometime in 1859: Forrest becomes a large-scale cotton planter at his plantation Green Grove, at Sunflower Landing, in Coahoma Co., MS.

June 1859: Forrest renominated Memphis alderman.

About June 1859: As alderman, Forrest sets up Memphis' first paid fire department.

By July 1, 1859: Reelected Memphis alderman.

About July 21, 1859: Resigns as Memphis alderman.

September 8, 1859: Forrest agrees to take up the office of alderman of Memphis once again.

October 1859: Psychopath-abolitionist John Brown seizes the government arsenal at Harper's Ferry, VA, another forewarning of dark days ahead for the South.

Before the end of 1859: Forrest sells his last commercial slave and closes both his slave business and his real estate business.

### 1860

Late June 1860: Forrest reelected third time as alderman of Memphis, TN.

Mid July 1860: Forrest resigns a second time as alderman of Memphis, TN.

August 14, 1860: Forrest appointed by the Shelby Co. (Memphis) Democratic Association to help with an enormous public meeting hosted by fiery Southern secessionist William L. Yancy.

November 6, 1860: Anti-South, big-government liberal, Abraham Lincoln, elected president of the U.S.

Close of 1860: Forrest's slave trading business comes to a complete and final end.

### 1861: LINCOLN'S WAR

February 4-9, 1861: The Confederate States Convention is held at Montgomery, Alabama; here the C.S.A. is created, her Constitution is adopted, and her president (Jefferson Davis) and vice president (Alexander H. Stephens) are elected. The South is now a legally formed sovereign republic, separate from the U.S.

April 12-14, 1861: Lincoln tricks the Confederacy into firing the first shot at the Battle of Fort Sumter, intentionally launching the War for Southern Independence.

June 14, 1861: At Memphis, TN, Forrest enlists in the Confederate army as a private in White's Tennessee Mounted Rifles, and begins his stunning military career.

June 20, 1861: Forrest at Randolph, TN.

July 10, 1861: Forrest promoted to lieutenant colonel due to pressure put on Governor Isham G. Harris by grateful Memphis townspeople.

July 20, 1861: Using his own money, Forrest outfits his men, buying some 500 Colt's navy pistols, 100 saddles, and more.

August 1, 1861: Forrest at Memphis, TN.

October 1861: Forrest at Dover, TN.

November 4, 1861: Forrest at Fort Donelson, TN.

November 5, 1861: Forrest at Canton Landing, KY.

November 21, 1861: Forrest at Hopkinsville, KY.

November 24, 1861: Forrest at Greenville, KY.

About November 26, 1861: Forrest at Caseyville, KY.

About November 29, 1861: Forrest at Marion, KY.

Early December, 1861: Forrest at Hopkinsville, KY.

December 26, 1861: Forrest at Henderson, KY.

December 28, 1861: Forrest at Sacramento, KY (his first battle).

## 1862: LINCOLN'S WAR

January 1862: Whereabouts unknown (perhaps Sacramento, KY).

February 7, 1862: Forrest at Fort Donelson, TN (battle).

February 9, 1862: Forrest at Dover, TN.

February 16-18, 1862: Forrest at Nashville, TN, where he quells a riot over the fall of Fort Donelson.

February 23, 1862: Forrest at Murfreesboro, TN (Nashville captured by the Yanks).

February 25, 1862: Forrest at Huntsville, AL.

February 25, 1862: The fall of Nashville, TN: Yanks take over and occupy the city for the rest of the War, a devastating blow to the Confederacy.

March 10, 1862: Forrest promoted to colonel.

March 16, 1862: Forrest at Burnsville, MS.

March 16, 1862: Forrest at Iuka, MS.

April 2, 1862: Forrest at Shiloh, TN (battle).

April 8, 1862: Forrest at Fallen Timbers, TN (battle).

April 9, 1862: Forrest near Monterey, TN.

Mid to late-April 1862: Forrest at Corinth, MS.

Mid to late-April 1862: Forrest at Memphis, TN.

May 1862: Forrest at Corinth, MS.

June 18, 1862: Forrest at Chattanooga, TN.

June 19, 1862: Forrest at Chattanooga, TN.

July 9, 1862: Forrest at Chattanooga, TN.

July 10, 1862: Forrest at Altamont, TN.

July 11-12, 1862: Forrest at McMinnville, TN.

July 12, 1862: Forrest at Woodbury, TN.

July 13, 1862: Forrest at Murfreesboro, TN (battle).

July 13, 1862: Forrest at Readyville, TN, that night.

July 14-17, 1862: Forrest at McMinnville, TN.

July 20, 1862: Forrest at Lebanon, TN.

July 21, 1862: Forrest at the Hermitage, Andrew Jackson's home; also at Antioch, TN; promoted to brigadier general.

July 27, 1862: Forrest at Manchester, TN.

July 30, 1862: Forrest at Sparta, TN.

August 10, 1862: Forrest at McMinnville, TN.

August 11, 1862: Forrest at Knoxville, TN.

August 15, 1862: Forrest at Murfreesboro, TN.

August 28, 1862: Forrest at Woodbury, TN.

End of August 1862: Forrest at McMinnville, TN.

Early September 1862: Forrest at Lebanon, TN.

Early September 1862: Forrest at Tyree Springs, TN.

September 3, 1862: Forrest at Sparta, TN.

September 6, 1862: Forrest at Cumberland River, near Gallatin, TN.

September 8, 1862: Forrest in southern KY.

September, 2nd week, 1862: Forrest at Franklin, KY.

September 10, 1862: Forrest at Glasgow, KY.

September 17, 1862: Forrest at Munfordville, KY.

September 22, 1862: Lincoln issues his Preliminary Emancipation Proclamation, urging Congress to back his plan to deport blacks and colonize them outside the U.S. (preferably in Africa, but also possibly the Carribean, or South America).

September, 3rd week, 1862: Forrest at Elizabethtown and Bardstown, KY.

October, 1st week, 1862: Forrest at Murfreesboro, TN.

November 15, 1862: Forrest at Murfreesboro, TN.

November 20, 1862: Forrest at Tullahoma, TN.

Early December 1862: Forrest at Columbia, TN.

December 6, 1862: Forrest at Columbia, TN.

December 10, 1862: Forrest at Columbia, TN.

December 15, 1862: Forrest at Clifton, TN.

December 18, 1862: Forrest at Wright's Island, TN River, TN.

December 18, 1862: Forrest at Beech Creek, near Lexington, TN (battle).

December 19, 1862: Forrest at Jackson, TN (battle).

December 20, 1862: Forrest at Spring Creek, TN.

December 20, 1862: Forrest at Trenton, TN.

December 21, 1862: Forrest at Rutherford, TN.

December 22, 1862: Forrest at Obion River (crossing), TN.

December 23, 1862: Forrest at Union City, TN.

December 23, 1862: Forrest on TN-KY border.

December 23-25, 1862: Forrest at Moscow, KY.

December 26, 1862: Forrest at Obion River, North Fork, TN.

December 26, 1862: Forrest at Dresden, TN.

December 27, 1862: Forrest at McKenzie, TN.

December 28, 1862: Forrest at McLemoresville, TN.

December 29, 1862: Forrest at the Obion River, TN.

About December 30, 1862: Forrest at McKenzie, TN.

December 31, 1862 (day): Forrest at Parker's Crossroads, TN (battle).

December 31, 1862 (night): Forrest at Lexington, TN.

## 1863: LINCOLN'S WAR

January 1, 1863: Forrest at Tennessee River crossing, Clifton, TN.

January 1, 1863: Lincoln issues his fake, illegal, and pointless Final Emancipation Proclamation, which frees no slaves in the South while allowing slavery to continue in the North. The toothless "war measure" rightfully angers and disgusts abolitionists, Southerners, Christians, Europeans, blacks, and members of his own cabinet.

January 3, 1863: Forrest at Yellow Furnace (TN?).

Early January 1863: Forrest at Mount Pleasant, TN.

Mid January 1863: Forrest at Columbia, TN.

February 2, 1863: Forrest at Palmyra, TN.

February 3, 1863: Forrest at Fort Doneslon, Dover, TN (battle).

February 4, 1863: Forrest at Centerville, Duck River crossing, TN.

February 17, 1863: Forrest at Columbia, TN.

March 5, 1863: Forrest at Thompson's Station, TN (battle).

March 5, 1863: Forrest at Spring Hill, TN.

March, 2nd week, 1863: Forrest at Columbia, TN.

March 11, 1863: Forrest at Rutherford Creek, Maury Co., TN.

About March 13, 1863: Forrest at Columbia, TN.

March 15, 1863: Forrest at Spring Hill, TN.

March 25, 1863: Forrest at Brentwood, TN (battle).

March 25-April 9, 1863: Forrest between Spring Hill and Franklin, TN.

April 10, 1863: Forrest at Franklin, TN (battle).

April 10, 1863: Forrest at Spring Hill, TN.

April 27, 1863: Forrest at Town Creek, AL.

April 28, 1863: Forrest at Moulton, AL.

April 28-29, 1863: Forrest at Courtland, AL.

April 30, 1863: Forrest at Day's Gap (Sand Mountain), AL (battle).

April 30, 1863: Forrest at Hog Mountain, AL.

May 1, 1863: Forrest at Blountsville, AL.

May 1, 1863: First vote of thanks (of four) given to Forrest by Confederate Congress.

May 1, 1863: Forrest at Black Warrior River, AL.

May 2, 1863: Forrest at Big Will's Creek, AL.

May 2, 1863: Forrest at Black Creek (near Gasden), AL (met Emma Sansom).

May 2, 1863: Forrest at Gasden, AL.

May 2, 1863: Forrest at Turkeytown, AL.

May 3, 1863: Forrest at Cedar Bluff, AL.

May 3, 1863: Forrest at Gaylesville, AL.

May 3, 1863: Forrest at Lawrence, AL.

May 3, 1863: Forrest at Rome, GA.

May 7, 1863: Forrest at Gasden, AL.

May, 2nd week, 1863: Forrest at Guntersville, AL.

May, 2nd week, 1863: Forrest at Huntsville, AL.

May 16, 1863: Forrest at Spring Hill, TN.

June 4, 1863: Forrest at Triune, TN.

June 5, 1863: Forrest at Spring Hill, TN.

June 10, 1863: Forrest at Triune, TN.

June 10, 1863: Forrest at Spring Hill, TN.

June 13, 1863: Forrest wounded by Rebel Lt. Andrew W. Gould at Columbia, TN.

June 27, 1863: Forrest at Shelbyville, TN.

June 28, 1863: Forrest at Tullahoma, TN.

Late June 1863: Forrest near Pelham, TN.

Late June 1863: Forrest in Cumberland Mountains, near Cowan, TN.

Summer 1863 (exact date unknown): "Forrest's Homecoming"; the General returns to his boyhood home in Chapel Hill for a recruitment barbeque, at which he seeks to enlist boys from the local populace for his depleted cavalry.

July 27, 1863: Forrest at Chattanooga, TN.

August 9, 1863: Forrest at Kingston, TN.

Late August 1863: Forrest possibly at Dalton, GA.

September, 1st week, 1863: Forrest in northwestern GA.

September 6, 1863: Forrest at Ringgold, GA.

Around September 7, 1863: Forrest at Rome, GA.

September 8, 1863: Forrest at Alpine, GA.

September 10, 1863: Forrest at Ringgold, GA.

September 11, 1863: Forrest at Tunnel Hill, GA.

September 18, 1863: Forrest at Chickamauga, GA (battle).

September 21, 1863: Forrest at Rossville, GA.

September 24, 1863: Forrest near Chattanooga and Loudon, TN.

About September 26, 1863: Forrest at Missionary Ridge, TN.

September 26, 1863: Forrest at Charleston, MS.

September 26, 1863: Forrest at Philadelphia, MS.

September 30, 1863: Forrest at Ringgold, GA.

September 30, 1863: Forrest at Missionary Ridge, TN.

Late September-early October, 1863: Forrest at La Grange, GA, on a ten-day leave to visit his wife Mary Ann (he had not seen her for eighteen months).

Late October 1863: Whereabouts unknown, possibly at Ringgold, GA, or Atlanta, GA.

Fall, 1863: Forrest attempts to resign his commission as a brigadier-general. Realizing he is too important to the Confederacy, President Jefferson Davis refuses to accept Forrest's resignation. He then invites Forrest to meet with him.

Sometime between October and November 1863: Forrest at Montgomery, AL, where he meets with President Davis. At the meeting, described as "a long and satisfactory conference," Forrest is transferred to a new command in north Mississippi and west

Tennessee.

November 7, 1863: Forrest at Atlanta, GA.

Early to mid November 1863: Forrest crosses through AL.

November 15-16, 1863: Forrest at Okolona, MS.

November 25, 1863: Forrest at Okolona, MS.

December 4, 1863: Forrest at Memphis, TN; promoted to major-general (some records say this occurred on December 13).

December 6, 1863: Forrest at Jackson, TN.

December 23, 1863: Forrest at Bolivar, TN.

December 23, 1863: Forrest at Clover Creek, TN.

December 24, 1863: Forrest at Estenaula, TN.

About December 24, 1863: Forrest at Newcastle, TN.

December 25, 1863: Forrest at Somerville, TN.

December 27, 1863: Forrest at Lafayette, TN.

December 28, 1863: Forrest at Collierville, TN.

December 28, 1863: Forrest at Jackson, TN.

December 29, 1863: Forrest at Holly Springs, MS.

## 1864: LINCOLN'S WAR

January 1, 1864: Forrest at Como, MS.

January 13, 1864: Forrest at Meridian, MS.

February 12, 1864: Forrest at Oxford, MS.

About February 16, 1864: Forrest at Grenada, MS.

February 17, 1864: Second vote of thanks (of four) given to Forrest by Confederate Congress.

February 18, 1864: Forrest at Starkville, MS.

February 20, 1864: Forrest at Ellis's Bridge, MS.

February 20, 1864: Forrest at Sakatonchee Creek, MS.

February 21, 1864: Forrest at Ellis's Bridge, MS.

February 22, 1864: Forrest at Okolona, MS (battle).

February 22, 1864: Forrest's brother, Brig. Gen. Jeffrey Forrest, killed at Battle of Okolona, MS.

February 26, 1864: Forrest at Starkville, MS.

Late February 1864: Forrest at Demopolis, AL.

March 17, 1864: Forrest at Tupelo, MS.

March 20, 1864: Forrest at Jackson, TN.

March 22, 1864: Forrest at Trenton, TN.

March 26, 1864: Forrest at Paducah, KY.

April 4, 1864: Forrest at Jackson, TN.

April 12, 1864: Forrest at Fort Pillow, TN (battle).

April 13, 1864: Forrest at Jackson, TN.

April 13, 1864: Forrest's brother, Lt. Col. Aaron Forrest (CSA), dies.

May 5, 1864: Forrest at Ripley, MS.

May 23, 1864: Third vote of thanks (of four) given to Forrest by Confederate Congress.

May 29, 1864: Forrest at Tupelo, MS.

June 1, 1864: Forrest at Tupelo, MS.

June 3, 1864: Forrest at Russellville, AL.

June 6, 1864: Forrest at Tupelo, MS.

June 9, 1864: Forrest at Booneville, MS.

June 10, 1864: Forrest at Brice's Cross Roads, MS (battle).

June 11, 1864: Ripley, MS.

June 11, 1864: Forrest rests with his staff and escort at the house of his maternal uncle, Orrin Beck, near one of his childhood homes, Salem, MS.

June 14, 1864: Forrest at Brice's Cross Roads, MS.

July 2, 1864: Forrest at Tupelo, MS.

July 4, 1864: Forrest at Harrisburg, MS.

July 14-15, 1864: Forrest at Harrisburg, MS (battle).

Late June, 1864: Forrest at Guntown, MS.

Early August 1864: Forrest at Pontotoc, MS.

August 8-18, 1864: Forrest at Oxford, MS.

August 20, 1864: Forrest at Senatobia, MS, near the Hichahala River.

August 20, 1864: Forrest at Hernando, MS.

August 21, 1864: Forrest at Memphis, TN (raid). For his success here Forrest was ridiculously and revengefully indicted by the Circuit Court of the U.S. for the District of West Tennessee, for "treason."

August 21, 1864: Forrest at Hernando, MS.

August 22, 1864: Forrest at Panola, MS.

September 4, 1864: Forrest at Meridian, MS.

September 16, 1864: Forrest at Verona, MS.

Probably September 17, 1864: Forrest at West Point, MS.

September 18-21, 1864: Forrest at Cherokee, AL.

September 20, 1864: Forrest at Tuscumbia, AL.

September 23-24, 1864: Forrest at Athens, AL (battle).

September 25, 1864: Forrest at Sulphur Springs, AL (battle).

September 27, 1864: Forrest at Pulaski, TN.

September 28, 1864: Forrest at Fayetteville, TN.

September 29, 1864: Forrest at Elkton, TN.

September 29, 1864: Forrest at Mulberry, TN.

September 30, 1864: Forrest at Lewisburg, TN.

October 1, 1864: Forrest at Spring Hill, TN.

October 2, 1864: Forrest at Mt. Pleasant, TN.

October 3, 1864: Forrest at Lawrenceburg, TN.

October 5, 1864: Forrest at Florence, AL.

October 6, 1864: Forrest at Cherokee, AL.

October 12, 1864: Forrest at Corinth, AL.

October 19, 1864: Forrest at Corinth, AL.

October 21, 1864: Forrest at Jackson, TN.

October 28, 1864: Forrest at Ft. Heiman, TN.

October 29, 1864: Forrest at Paris Landing, TN.

October 31, 1864: Forrest at Ft. Heiman, TN.

November 3, 1864: Forrest at Johnsonville, TN.

November 4, 1864: Forrest at Johnsonville, TN.

November 6, 1864: Forrest at Perryville, TN; Beauregard orders Forrest to join Hood in Middle, TN; Forrest is given command of all the cavalry of the Army of TN.

November 10, 1864: Forrest at Corinth, MS.

November 12, 1864: Forrest at Corinth, MS.

November 15, 1864: Forrest at Iuka, MS.

November 16, 1864: Forrest at Cherokee, MS.

November 17, 1864: Forrest assumes command of all the cavalry of the Army of TN.

November 18, 1864: Forrest at Florence, AL (joins up with Hood).

November 18, 1864: Forrest at Shoal Creek, AL.

November 22, 1864: Forrest at Fouche Springs, TN.

November 23, 1864: Forrest at Henryville, TN.

November 24-29, 1864: Forrest at Columbia, TN (battle).

November 29, 1864: Forrest at Spring Hill, TN (battle).

November 30, 1864: Forrest at Franklin, TN (battle).

December 1, 1864: Forrest at Wilson's Crossroads, TN.

December 2, 1864: Forrest at Nashville, TN.

December 5, 1864: Forrest at Lavergne, TN.

December 6, 1864: Forrest at Murfreesboro, TN.

December 6, 1864: Fourth vote of thanks (of four) given to Forrest by Confederate Congress.

December 14, 1864: Forrest at Murfreesboro, TN.

(December 15-16, 1864: Battle of Nashville, TN, Forrest not present).

(December 17, 1864: Battle of Franklin III, TN, Forrest not present).

December 18, 1864: Forrest at Columbia, TN.

December 19, 1864: Forrest rejoins Hood at Columbia, TN.

December 24, 1864: Forrest at Richland Creek, TN.

December 24, 1864: Forrest near Pulaski, TN.

December 25, 1864: Forrest at King's Hill, TN.

December 25, 1864: Forrest at Anthony's Hill, TN (battle).

December 25, 1864: Forrest at Sugar Creek, TN.

December 27, 1864: Forrest at TN River, at Bainbridge, AL.

December 27, 1864: Forrest at Corinth, MS.

## 1865: WAR ENDS & THE RETURN HOME

January 28, 1865: Forrest at Verona, MS.

Early to mid February 1865: Whereabouts unknown; probably in northwestern MS.

February 23-24, 1865: Forrest at Rienzi, MS.

March 1-18, 1865: Forrest at West Point, MS.

March 2, 1865: Forrest promoted to lieutenant general (highest rank, but one). Some records say he attained this rank on February 25 or 28, 1865. He is now in charge of 10,000 men, covering three states.

March 18, 1865: Although hundreds of thousands of Southern blacks had been fighting unofficially for the Confederacy from day one, it was on this date that the Confederate Congress passed legislation allowing blacks to officially fight for the Confederacy.

March 29, 1865: Forrest at Selma, AL.

March 30, 1865: Forrest at Scottsville, TN.

March 31, 1865: Forrest at Centerville, AL.

April 1, 1865: Forrest at Randolph, AL.

April 1, 1865: Forrest at Plantersville, AL.

April 2, 1865: Forrest at Selma, AL (battle).

April 3, 1865: Forrest at Plantersville, AL.

April 4, 1865: Forrest at Marion, AL.

April 8, 1865: Forrest at Cahaba, AL.

April 9, 1865: Lee surrenders at Appomattox, VA.

April 14, 1865: Lincoln shot and mortally wounded by Northerner John Wilkes Booth in Washington, D.C.

April 15, 1865: Lincoln dies. Forrest at Gainesville, AL.

March 18, 1865: Forrest at West Point, MS (Forrest's headquarters).

May 3, 1865: Forrest officially (and finally) accepts the defeat of the Confederacy (his men were among the last to surrender in the Western theater).

May 4, 1865: Forrest at Meridian, MS; gives unofficial farewell speech to his troops.

May 9, 1865: Forrest at Gainesville, AL (final surrender).

About May 9, 1865: Forrest's official farewell speech handed out to troops as flyers.


## MID 1865: CIVILIAN LIFE BEGINS AGAIN

May 25, 1865: Forrest returns to his plantation Green Grove, at Sunflower Landing, in Coahoma Co., MS.

December 6, 1865: Thirteenth Amendment ratified, finally abolishing slavery across the entire U.S. Note that this, the official end of American slavery, occurred eight months *after* Lincoln died, revealing the true nature of his "war measure," the Final Emancipation Proclamation.

December 24, 1865: First version of the KKK (then called the "Pulaski Circle") unofficially formed in Pulaski, TN, by six men (not to be confused with the modern KKK, with which it has no connection).


## 1866: KKK YEARS

April 3, 1866: Forrest at Green Grove, Sunflower Landing, Coahoma Co., MS.

June 5, 1866: Official forming of the original KKK.

Fall 1866: Forrest at Nashville, TN; he openly supports KKK (some say he joined at this time, but there is no definitive evidence for this and Forrest himself denied it).

September 3, 1866: After this date the indictment against Forrest for "treason" against the U.S. due to his raid on Memphis (August 21, 1864), is dropped.

November, 1866: Forrest at Little Rock, AR.

December 29, 1866: Forrest at New Orleans, LA.

## 1867

1867: U.S. purchases Alaska.

1867: Forrest joins the Pale Faces, a Mason-like organization.

April 1867: Forrest at Nashville, TN; some say he was elected grand wizard of KKK at this time, but there is no concrete evidence for this assertion.

June 1867: Forrest at Hurricane Springs, TN.

June 5, 1867: First official anniversary of the original KKK.

December 15, 1867: Forrest's mother, Mariam Beck, dies in Navasota, TX, after stepping on a rusty nail while disembarking from a buggy.

## 1868: RAILROADING & BANKRUPTCY

Early 1868: Forrest elected President of Memphis, Okolona, and Selma Railroad.

February 5, 1868: Forrest files for bankruptcy in Memphis, TN.

Early March 1868: Forrest at Atlanta, GA.

May 13, 1868: Forrest at Nashville, TN.

June 9, 1868: Forrest at Nashville, TN; he is elected and sent here as a Democratic delegate to the Nashville State Convention.

Late June 1868: Forrest at New York, NY.

July 4, 1868: In New York City, delegate Forrest attends the first postwar Democratic National Convention, creating a sensation.

July 17, 1868: Forrest pardoned by President Andrew Johnson for "treason" against the U.S.

August 1, 1868: Forrest at Nashville, TN; he is elected chairman of the Council of Peace, a futile but valiant effort by Southerners to reduce the unnecessary brutality of so-called "Reconstruction."

August 11, 1868: Forrest at Brownsville, TN.

August 28, 1868: Forrest at Memphis, TN.

November 9, 1868: Forrest elected President and Director of Memphis and Selma Railroad.

## 1869: END OF KKK

Sometime in 1869: Forrest disbands the original KKK locally in TN.

January 25, 1869: Forrest orders the KKK to "entirely abolish and destroy" its masks and costumes.

Early February 1869: Forrest somewhere in NC.

Before March 1869: Forrest is said to have resigned as grand wizard of the KKK about this time, but, as mentioned, there is no irrefutable evidence that he ever occupied that position.

March 3, 1869: Forrest at Memphis, TN.

About March 10, 1869: Forrest at Jackson, MS.

March 14, 1869: Forrest orders the entire national KKK organization to disband.

March 25, 1869: Forrest at Mobile, AL.

May 1, 1869: Forrest at Memphis, TN.

July 1869: Forrest at Memphis, TN.

September 1869: Forrest at Gadsden, AL.

September 1869: Forrest forms a business partnership in Memphis with Edmund W. Rucker, who had led Rucker's Brigade during Hood's Nashville Campaign; Forrest and Rucker's partnership lasts until 1874.

## 1871

1871: Forrest's brother, Captain William Hezekiah "Bill" Forrest (CSA), dies.

June 27, 1871: Forrest at Washington, D.C.; appears before U.S. governmental committee investigating the KKK, where he is rigorously grilled and exonerated.

## 1872

Day unknown: Nathan Bedford Forrest, II, the General's grandson, born in Oxford, MS, to William Montgomery Forrest and Jane Taylor Cook.

## 1873: BUSINESS TRIPS

1873: Forrest leases a double log cabin and 1,300 acres on President's Island (south of Memphis on the Mississippi River) and moves there with his wife Mary Ann.

January 1873: Forrest at Detroit, MI.

February 1873: Forrest at New York, NY.

March 25, 1873: Forrest at Memphis, TN.

April 25, 1873: Forrest at Memphis, TN.

September 8, 1873: Forrest at New York, NY.

December 1873: Forrest volunteers to fight under Sherman (then in command of the U.S. Army) in an expected war with Spain (Sherman graciously turns him down).

## 1874: MORE POLITICS

1874: Forrest threatens to kill any whites who kill blacks.

Late March 1874: Forrest resigns as president and director of Memphis and Selma Railroad.

August 28, 1874: Forrest at Memphis, TN.

## 1875: CHRISTIANITY & CIVIL RIGHTS

1875: Forrest publically calls for equality for all blacks.

January 1875: Forrest at Nashville, TN.

April 1875: Forrest at Memphis, TN.

May 8, 1875: Forrest's five-year contract with Shelby County (TN) for the hire of prison laborers begins.

May 24, 1875: Forrest at Memphis, TN.

May 30, 1875: Forrest at Elmwood Cemetery, Memphis, TN.

July 5, 1875: Forrest at Memphis, TN; invited by an all-black group to give a speech at their gathering.

August 1875: Forrest becomes a Christian in Memphis, TN.

November 14, 1875: Forrest at Memphis, TN.

## 1876: ILLNESS & POLITICS

1876: Forrest contracts diabetes.

1876: Forrest's brother, John Nathaniel Forrest, dies.

1876: Forrest elected chairman of the Democratic party's Shelby County Executive Committee.

Spring 1876: Forrest at his home farming on President's Island, Memphis, TN.

May 5, 1876: Forrest at his home on President's Island, Memphis, TN.

September 1876: Forrest at Covington, TN.

September 1876: Forrest gives one of his last, perhaps his final, public speech (before the Seventh Tennessee Cavalry).

## 1877: FINAL DAYS

1877: Twelve years of "Reconstruction" ends when a rational U.S. leader, our eighteenth president, Rutherford B. Hayes, finally pulls U.S. troops out of South Carolina and Louisiana. The population of the U.S. is 46,710,000, and there are now thirty-eight states in the Union (several of them created illegally by Lincoln during his administration).

April 1877: Forrest at Hot Springs, AR (for health rehabilitation).

May 5, 1877: Forrest at Hot Springs, AR (for health rehabilitation).

July 1877: Forrest at Nashville, TN.

July 1877: Forrest drops all his lawsuits (against his attorney's advice).

July 4, 1877: Forrest at Hurricane Springs, TN (at a health resort, for health rehabilitation).

July 27, 1877: Forrest at Hurricane Springs, TN. Here, on this day, was held the first reunion of Forrest's Escort and Staff. The group came to be called the Veterans Association.

About August 28, 1877: Forrest at Bailey Springs, AR.

September 15, 1877: Forrest at Bailey Springs, AR.

October 2, 1877: Forrest at Memphis, TN, at his brother Jesse's home.

Mid October 1877: Forrest back home at President's Island, Memphis, TN.

Late October 1877: Forrest at Memphis, TN; deathly ill, he is taken back to the home of his brother Jesse.

## 1877: DEATH & BURIAL

October 29, 1877, about 7:00 PM: Memphis, TN, at age fifty-six, Forrest dies at his brother Jesse Forrest's home due to complications from diabetes, an old war wound, and general exhaustion and debilitation.

October 31 (Halloween), 1877: Forrest is buried at Elmwood Cemetery, Memphis, TN.

## 1890

December 14, 1890: Forrest's brother, Jesse Anderson Forrest, dies.

## 1893

January 22, 1893: Forrest's wife, Mary Ann, dies in Memphis, TN.

## 1904

November 11, 1904: The earthly remains of Forrest and his wife are reintered in the Memphis park named after him: Nathan Bedford Forrest Park.

## 1905

April 7, 1905: Nathan Bedford Forrest, III, the General's great-grandson, born in Memphis, TN, to Nathan Bedford Forrest, II, and Mattie Patton.

May 16, 1905: A dedication ceremony is held for the unveiling of the famous Forrest Equestrian Monument at Forrest Park in Memphis. Some 30,000 people from seven states attend.

## 1908

February 8, 1908: Forrest's only son, Captain William M. "Billie" Forrest, dies in Memphis, TN, while attending a play about the KKK called *The Clansman* (adapted from the novel by Thomas Dixon, Jr.). He is said to have passed away at the exact moment an actor playing his famous father walked out onto the stage.

## 1921

1921: The Tennessee legislature proclaims Forrest's birthday, July 13, a legal holiday. (As early as 1958 Forrest's birthday began to go unobserved in Tennessee, and the day is no longer recognized as an official holiday.)

## 1931

March 13, 1931: Forrest's grandson, Nathan Bedford Forrest, II (son of Forrest's son Willie), dies in FL (some say in Oxford, MS).

## 1942

June 13, 1942: Forrest's great-grandson, Nathan Bedford Forrest, III (son of Nathan Bedford Forrest II), dies while fighting in World War II, at Kiel, Germany, ending the Nathan Bedford Forrest line; Forrest III is buried at Arlington National Cemetery.

# FORREST THE MOON-CHILD

*An Astrological Profile*

## Lochlainn Seabrook

Whether one embraces astrology as a legitimate science or not, without question it can sometimes serve as a useful tool in understanding an individual's inner character and nature.[2178] With an open mind, let us apply it then to Forrest in an effort to get closer to who he really was.

Birth date: July 13, 1821[2179]
Birth place: Chapel Hill, Bedford (now Marshall) Co., Tennessee
Birth time: unknown (chart set at noon)

These aspects give Forrest the following natal horoscope:

SUN ☉ IN CANCER ♋ - General Forrest was born under the Sun sign Cancer, whose symbol is the *crab*, the archetypal animal with a hard exterior and a soft interior (Forrest was widely recognized as a tough guy with a heart of gold). Best known for both its claw-like tenacity (Forrest never gave up) and its moodiness (he was extremely temperamental), Cancer is a *feminine* sign (Forrest was known to be kind and tender-hearted; in his gentler moments, almost childlike, even womanly), ruled by the *Moon* (symbol of emotion), the element *water* (symbol of flux and fluidity), and the quality known to astrologers as *cardinal* (indicating changeability). This makes those born in mid July the most hypersensitive, mercurial, erratic, and irritable of all the Sun signs (Forrest's detractors often criticize him for these very characteristics).

---

2178. Despite the anti-astrology attitude found in most modern Christian denominations today, ancient Christians, as well as the early Jews (the Israelites), evinced a strong interest in the subject, as the Bible's many references to sun signs, star signs, the Zodiac, and various astrological figures and symbols reveals. Some examples: Genesis 1:14-15; Malachi 4:2; Luke 21:25; Matthew 24:3; Revelation 12:1.
2179. Other men of note born on July 13: Julius Caesar, Patrick Stewart, Harrison Ford, Jack Kemp.

The astrological crab is cold-blooded, of course, with an innate ability for squirming its way out of trouble (Forrest was well-known both for his unemotional approach to killing Yanks, and for his innate ability to extricate himself from military and legal problems). Moon-children are also very interested in neatness, fashion, and their appearance (Forrest, though from poverty, later had a well-deserved reputation for cleanliness, a dapper image, and a smart cavalier hair style, all much remarked on by both Victorian ladies and gentlemen).

Cancers, the "mothers" of the Zodiac, are considered highly maternal, affectionate, caring, dedicated (Forrest, who married once and for life, markedly displayed these traits during childhood toward his family, with his soldiers during the War, and lastly in old age toward veterans, widows, and orphans), loyal, and home-loving (Forrest ardently loved both his family home and his home country, Dixie), with a strong affection for women and children (Forrest considered himself their personal champion).

Indeed, by all accounts he was normally even-tempered, soft, gentle, even feminine and motherly, "like a woman," as some depicted him. Revealingly, his soldiers often saw him more as a mother-figure than as a father-figure, as he flitted from man to man, fussing over every detail of their gear, horses, clothing, and weaponry.

Insightful, imaginative, security-conscious, cautious, tenacious, possessive (Forrest was exactly so on the battlefield), materialistic, and good at making money (he was a multimillionaire by the age of forty), they are also prone to melancholy and fits of anger (Forrest had frequent bouts with depression and throughout his life he constantly fought to restrain his quick temper).

Cancers are adept at climbing the ladder of success, reaching positions of authority and prestige with ease (Forrest was the only soldier in either the Confederate or the Yankee armies to rise from the rank of private to lieutenant-general; he was also the founder and president of numerous businesses). The ultimate home-bodies, Cancers are generous and enjoy providing materially for their families and loved ones (Forrest built, bought, and sold numerous houses, and gave generously to family members and charities until the day he died).

The Moon-child is also a staunch traditionalist (Forrest was what we would now call a paleoconservative, one who believed strongly in the original, pre-Lincoln Constitution and first U.S., pre-Lincoln government formed by the Founding Fathers), who honors ancestors, loves antiques, and doing things the old-fashioned way (throughout his life, though he was rich enough to do otherwise, Forrest remained loyal to his humble yeoman roots).

While Cancers have many positive traits, on the negative side they are mainly known for their overly sensitive nature. They are easily hurt and offended, even when nothing of the sort is intended, and they never forget an unkind word or criticism (Forrest was often in a state of indignity over some insult, whether real or imagined, a Cancerian character flaw that actually prevented him from scaling to even greater heights on the ladder of success).

Above all, the Moon-child is devoted, lending his entire being to every task or project, no matter how big or small (Forrest literally gave all of his time, energy, and money—indeed, his entire estate and fortune—to his family and to the Confederate cause).

LIBRA RISING ♎ - Libra on the Ascendant makes one charming, energetic, polite, sincere, friendly, and eager to please. But Libra's symbol is the scales, so imbalance can occur, causing the opposite traits to emerge. Thus this aspect can cause one to sometimes be unpleasant, listless, rude, superficial, hostile, and rebellious.

Physically attractive, or at least possessed of an appealing personality, those with Libra Rising are obsessed with their appearance, dress impeccably, and will often spend inordinate amounts of time in front of the mirror preening and fussing. Love of luxury, art, literature, music, and the finer things in life generally, Libra on the Ascendant makes one a natural flatterer, highly sociable, gracious, diplomatic, and cooperative.

MOON ☽ IN CAPRICORN ♑ - Moon Caps are reliable, old-fashioned, emotionally buttoned up, self-reliant, and obedient, and feel best when they are in control of money, business, family, and home.

MERCURY ☿ IN LEO ♌ - Leo Mercurys are the natural show-offs of the Zodiac. While they are confident, strong-willed, and good communicators, they can also be conceited braggarts, who form their opinions quickly—usually in favor of themselves!

VENUS ♀ IN LEO ♌ - Venus Leos are flamboyant, dramatic, warm, loving, and giving, but they can also be vain and demanding. They like being revered and are drawn to others who, like themselves, have big personalities.

MARS ♂ IN GEMINI ♊ - The Gemini Mars is high-strung, restless, and impatient, and can be assertive, even aggressive, when talking.

JUPITER ♃ IN ARIES ♈ - The Aries Jupiter is independent, intense, and headstrong, and sees life as a series of sporting contests that he must win in order to expand and grow.

SATURN ♄ IN ARIES ♈ - The Aries Saturn is impulsive, but possesses a sense of self-discipline that usually enables him to control his intense and aggressive energies.

URANUS ♅ IN CAPRICORN ♑ - The Capricorn Uranus is tightly wound and eccentric, but is also an ingenious business person, one who will seek to perfect society through work and politics.

NEPTUNE ♆ IN CAPRICORN ♑ - The Capricorn Neptune vacillates between religion and materialism, and is dignified, traditional, and conservative.

PLUTO ♀ IN PISCES ♓ - The Pisces Pluto is understanding and accepting, and is willing to make great sacrifices for whatever he believes most strongly in.

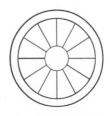

# A FORREST FAMILY TREE

### Eleven generations, from James Forrest, earliest known Forrest ancestor

## COPYRIGHT © LOCHLAINN SEABROOK

GENEALOGICAL MATERIAL FROM THE PERSONAL FAMILY TREES OF
LOCHLAINN SEABROOK AND GENE INGRAM

KEY:
b: born
m: married
d: died
abt: about
+ (cross): *after* a name indicates descent from European royalty

*Direct Line of Descent from James Forrest to Nathan Bedford Forrest, III*

1 James Forrest (Forrester?) b: Abt. 1625 in England? (or Scotland?)
Number of children: ?
...+Alice _____? b: Abt. 1627 in England? m: Abt. 1650 Number of
    children: ?

..2 John Forrest (Forrester?) b: Abt. 1653 in Henrico, VA d: 05 Dec
    1715 Number of children: 3.
........+Mary _____? b: Abt. 1657 in Henrico, VA m: Abt. 1689 in
    Henrico, VA m: Abt. 1689 in Henrico, VA Number of
    children: 3.

...3 James Forrest, Forrester, Sr. b: 1700 in Orange Co., NC d: 05
    Sep 1755 in Orange Co., NC Number of children: 5.
......+Ann Ashley b: Bet. 1700 - 1704 in Orange Co., NC d: 1775 m:
    Abt. 1724 in Orange Co., NC m: Abt. 1724 in Orange Co.,
    NC Number of children: 5 Father: Joseph Ashley; Mother:
    _____ _____?

....4 William Forrest b: Bet. 1720 - 1726 in Orange Co., NC d: 08
Aug 1777 Number of children: 7.

........+Lavinia (Lovisa, Louisa) Gresham, Greshum b: 1731 in VA or
Orange Co., NC d: 1778 m: 1749 in VA m: 1749 in VA
Number of children: 7.

.....5 Shadrack (or Shadrach) Forrest b: Bet. 1740 - 1757 in Western
VA, or Orange Co., NC d: 1820 in Bedford Co., TN
Number of children: 5.

..........+Jane (Jaene) Ledbetter b: Bet. 1744 - 1758 in VA, or
Sumner, TN d: Abt. 1806 in Sumner Co., TN m: Bet. 1766 -
1776 in Orange Co., NC m: Bet. 1766 - 1776 in Orange Co.,
NC Number of children: 5 Father: Henry Ledbetter, Rev.;
Mother: Edy Clark.

......6  Nathan Forrest b: 28 Oct 1776 in Orange Co., NC d: 15 Jan
1827 in Tippah Co., MS Number of children: 15.

............+Nancy Shepherd Baugh,+ b: 16 Apr 1781 in Orange, NC
d: Aft. 1821 in TN m: 14 Jan 1799 in Orange, NC m: 14 Jan
1799 in Orange, NC Number of children: 15 Father: Josiah
Hatcher Baugh, Baw+; Mother: Milly Shepherd, Sheperd.

.......7 William Forrest, I,+ (Nathan Bedford Forrest's father) b: 06
Jul 1801 in NC d: 1837 in Salem, Tippah Co., MS (Salem no
longer exists) Number of children: 11.

..............+Mariam Beck (Nathan Bedford Forrest's mother); her
first name is also sometimes spelled Miriam; b: 1802 in Caney
Springs, Bedford Co., TN or SC? d: unknown, probably
summer of 1868 (some say 1867), in Navasota, Grimes Co.,
TX (where she is buried); m: 1820 in Chapel Hill, (now
Marshall Co.) or the Duck River area, Bedford Co., TN
Number of children: 15 Father: John Emasy Beck; Mother:
Francis Watts.

........8 NATHAN BEDFORD FORREST, I,+ Lt. Gen. CSA, twin,
b: 13 Jul 1821 in the Duck River area of Chapel Hill, Bedford
Co. (now Marshall Co.), TN d: 29 Oct 1877 of diabetes and

other health complications, Memphis, Shelby Co., TN;
Number of children: 2.

..............+Mary Ann Montgomery; b: 24 Oct 1826 in Franklin,
Williamson Co., TN d: 22 Jan 1893 in Memphis, Shelby Co.,
TN m: 25 Sep 1845 in Hernando, DeSoto Co., MS (some
sources state that the marriage took place April 25, 1845)
Number of children: 2; Father: William H. Montgomery;
Mother: Elizabeth McCroskey "Betsy" Cowan.

.........9 William Montgomery "Willie" Forrest, Capt. CSA+ b: 26
Sep 1846 in Hernando, MS       d: 08 Feb 1908 in Memphis,
Shelby Co., TN Number of children: 4.

.................+Jane Taylor Cook b: 03 Feb 1847 in MS d: 16 Nov
1882 m: 1868 m: 1868 Number of children: 4.

.........9 Frances Ann "Fanny" Forrest; b: 1848 in Hernando, MS; died
27 June 1854.

..........10 Nathan Bedford Forrest, II,+ b: 1872 in Oxford, MS; d:
13 Mar 1931 in White Springs, FL Number of children: 4.

....................+Mattie Patton b: Abt. 1874 Number of children: 4.

...........11 Nathan Bedford Forrest, III, Brig. Gen.,+ b: 07 Apr 1905
in Memphis, Shelby Co., TN; d: 13 June 1942, killed in
action, Kiel, Germany, World War II.

.....................+Frances Brassler, b: abt. 1907.

# A MONTGOMERY FAMILY TREE

Six generations, from James Montgomery,
earliest known Montgomery ancestor

## COPYRIGHT © LOCHLAINN SEABROOK

GENEALOGICAL MATERIAL FROM THE PERSONAL FAMILY TREES OF
LOCHLAINN SEABROOK AND GENE INGRAM

KEY:
b: born
m: married
d: died
abt: about
+ (cross): *after* a name indicates descent from European royalty

*Direct Line of Descent from James Montgomery to Mary Ann Montgomery*[2180]

1 James Montgomery (1685 - ) B: 1685 in (Donegal?) Ulster
　　　Province, Ireland, M: 1719 in Ulster Province, Ireland.
...+Ann _____? (1689 - ) B: 1689 in Ulster, Ireland, M: 1719 in
　　　Ulster Province, Ireland.

..2 John Montgomery (1724 - 1795) B: 1724 in Ulster Province,
　　　Ireland, M: 02 Jul 1738 in Eart Twp, Lancaster, PA, D: Abt.
　　　1795 in VA
....+Esther Houston (1724 - ) B: 1724 in Ireland, M: 02 Jul 1738 in
　　　Eart Twp, Lancaster, PA, D: Rockbridge Co., VA.

...3 James P. Montgomery (1740 - 1811) B: Abt. 1740 in Eart
　　　Township, Lancaster, PA, M: 1765 in Augusta, VA, D: Abt.
　　　1811 in Blount, TN
......+Margaret Weir (1746 - ) B: Abt. 1746 in Lancaster, PA, M:

---

2180. Mary Ann's ancestors, no doubt, are connected to the royal Montgomerys of Scotland, and even earlier, those of Normandy, France. Genealogical researchers, however, have not been able to make a definitive connection yet.

1765 in Augusta, VA.

.... 4 Hugh Montgomery (1770 - 1841) B: 1770 in New Providence,
       Augusta, VA, M: Abt. 1789 in VA, D: 1841 in Cowan, TN.
........+Susan Cowan (1774 - ) B: 1774 in Franklin, Williamson Co.,
       TN, M: Abt. 1789 in VA, D: Blount, TN.

.....5 William H. Montgomery (1792 - 1829) B: 1792 in Blount Co.,
       TN, M: Abt. 1821 in TN?, D: Oct 1829 in Cowan, TN
..........+Elizabeth McCroskey "Betsy" Cowan (1802 - )—2nd wife of
       William H. Montgomery; B: Abt. 1802 in Blount Co., TN,
       M: Abt. 1821 in TN?

......6 Mary Ann Montgomery (1826 - 1893) B: 24 Oct 1826 in
       Franklin Co., TN (some say Franklin, Williamson Co., TN),
       M: Sept. 25, 1845 in Hernando, DeSoto Co., MS (some
       sources state that the marriage took place April 25, 1845), D:
       22 Jan 1893 in Memphis, Shelby Co., TN.
............+NATHAN BEDFORD FORREST+ (1821 - 1877) B: 13
       Jul 1821 in Duck River, Bedford Co. (now Marshall Co.),
       TN, M: 25 Sep 1845 in Hernando, DeSoto Co., MS (some
       sources state that the marriage took place April 25, 1845), D:
       29 Oct 1877 in of diabetes, Memphis, Shelby Co., TN. (For
       male descendants, see Forrest Family Tree, Appendix E.)

# A Description of the Forrest Equestrian Monument at Memphis, Tennessee

By Bettie Alder Calhoun Emerson, 1911

## MEMPHIS, TENN.
### EQUESTRIAN STATUE OF FORREST

The height of the entire monument is 22 feet. The height of the bronze figure is 9 feet, and it weighs ninety-five hundred pounds. The cost of the structure approximates thirty-three thousand dollars.

In Forrest Park, Memphis, Tenn., surrounded by fifteen thousand spectators, at 2.30 P. M. on May 16 little Miss Kathleen Bradley pulled the cord that released the veil from the magnificent equestrian statue of her illustrious great-grandfather, Lieutenant-General Nathan Bedford Forrest. There was a momentary silence as the imposing grandeur of this colossal bronze figure of the great "Wizard of the Saddle" and his steed met the gaze of the expectant crowd, then a wild cheer broke from hundreds of his old surviving followers clustered around the base and was enthusiastically taken up by the vast multitude.

The idea of erecting a monument to General Forrest was first projected in 1886, but it was not until 1891 that it took definite shape and a monument association was organized for this purpose. On November 18, 1900, the design was accepted and the order was given to the sculptor, Charles H. Niehaus. The designer of the base was Mr. B. C. Alsup, and it is built of Tennessee marble. The statue, which was made in Europe, arrived in Memphis on April 16, and was placed on its base a day or two later.

The unveiling of the monument was attended with elaborate ceremonies. In the big parade were most of the surviving staff officers of General Forrest, his general officers, and many of his old veterans who rode with him from 1861 to 1865. Judge J. P. Young, who was one of Forrest's old troopers, was master of ceremonies. In opening the proceedings he said in part:

No one who did not ride with Forrest can have so keen an appreciation of the personal qualities of the man as those who were actually under his direct command, and who, from daily, hourly observation, witnessed his fertility of resource, his vehemence in battle and his soulful tenderness toward the stricken soldier, whether friend or foe. But it was no holiday parade. It cost something to ride with Forrest. It meant days and nights of sleepless toil and motion. It meant countless miles under a burning sun in the choking dust. It meant limitless leagues across icy wastes, with a blanket of snow at night for a covering. It meant to run down and destroy miles of freighted supply trains, to burn depots of stores, to scale the parapets of redoubts, and to plunge, mounted, into the seeming vortex of hell, lighted with the fires of a myriad rifles and scores of belching guns.

> "It meant to meet death face to face like a drillmaster, to look into his dread eyes, to toy with the horrid trappings of his trade, to scorn the deadly chill of his breath, and to turn away unscathed or sink into the oblivion of his eternal embrace."

Of the many eloquent tributes paid to the great soldier that day, one of the most significant was that spoken by [Yankee] Colonel C. A. Stanton, of the 3d Iowa Cavalry, 1861- 1865, who for two years was directly opposed to General Forrest. He realized Forrest's methods of war at Brice's Cross Roads, Ripley, Harrisburg, Old Town Creek, Tallahatchie, and Hurricane Creek.

The spectacle of an officer who had fought in the Federal army delivering an address at the unveiling of a Confederate monument was an interesting one, and when Colonel Stanton was introduced the applause was most generous. Colonel Stanton said in part:

> "During the war between the States I served four years in the Federal army, and what I learned then prompts what I now shall say. My knowledge of General Forrest's military career was acquired while for a part of two years with the Federal forces that were directly opposed to him and his command.

> "General Forrest possessed the characteristic traits of the successful soldier; his personal bravery was without limit; his resources

seemed to be endless, and his decisions, like Napoleon's, were instantaneous; he was aggressive, masterful, resolute, and self-reliant in the most perilous emergency; he was comprehensive in his grasp of every situation, supremely confident in himself and in his men, and inspired by his presence and example his soldiers fought as desperately as did Hannibal's fierce cavalry at Canne or the trained veterans of Caesar's Tenth Legion at Pharsalia. I think the battle at Brice's Cross Roads in June, 1864, was one of the best illustrations of General Forrest's daring courage, his ability in a critical moment to decide swiftly, his relentless vigor of action, and his intuitive perception of the time and place to strike fierce, stunning blows which fell like thunderbolts upon his enemy and won for him in this battle an overwhelming victory over an opposing force which greatly outnumbered his command.

"Impartial history has given General Forrest high rank as one of the greatest cavalry leaders of modern times. No American, North or South, now seeks to lessen the measure of his fame, and no one can speak of him without, remembrance of the men who served with him and whose soldierly qualities made it possible for him to win his wonderful victories. No military leader was ever supported by more faithful, gallant, and daring subordinate officers. It has been truly said that 'the spirit of the cavalier which was found in the Southern armies was combined with the steadfastness of Cromwell's Ironsides,' and it is equally true that no soldiers, ever met more promptly every demand made upon them; no soldiers ever faced the enemies' blazing guns more fearlessly or performed greater feats of valor than did the veterans of Forrest's regiments in battles which were as hard-fought as Marathon or Philippi.

"The men who wore the gray from 1861 to

1865 still treasure the memories of those heroic days; but through all the years since that time they have contributed their full share to the advancement and prosperity of our common country, and to-day the nation has no truer friends than the ex-Confederate soldiers of the South.

"The war of 1861-1865 was a mighty conflict which stands without a parallel in the annals of time. Shiloh, Stone's River, Franklin, Chickamauga, and Gettysburg are names made sacred by the deeds done there and by the dead who lie there side by side in common graves, where the gray cloth and the blue have faded into dust alike.

"This monument is history in bronze; it illustrates an eventful era in our national history; it commemorates General Forrest's fame and it represents all the gallant soldiers of his command; it attests the splendid courage which won triumphant victories and did not fail when reverses came; it stands for heroic deeds which are now the proud heritage of all American citizens. It is eminently fitting that this figure should stand here within the borders of the Volunteer State, whose soldiers have marched and fought 'from valley's depth to mountain height and from inland rivers to the sea,' in every war in the history of our republic, with a valor which has helped to make the name and fame of the American soldier immortal."

Mr. Niehaus, the sculptor, is an artist of national reputation, and has a long list of statues and monuments to his credit. The Forrest monument is one of his best.

There is always a peculiar interest that attaches to the making of a statue, and to no one part of it more than to the models. The General Forrest statue, being equestrian, had two models—a man and a horse. The man, though a professional model, is as much *sui generis* as the character he simulated; a Prussian cavalry officer, a fire-eater and a superb horseman, he fitted the part so well that it became a matter of diplomacy to keep the peace while he was posing, for he seemed to have a good American chip on his shoulder all the time.

The horse that posed for the statue was the fourth one selected, all the others being abandoned after a trial of months. The handsome animal who held the job, however, is a full brother of Lord Derby, and of the distinguished Mambrino Chief pedigree. He is jet black, full of spirit, and yet docile, and was easily taught to hold required positions by tips of carrots, apples and sugar.

He also posed for the statue of St. Louis at the Louisiana Purchase Exposition, and is now (1905) doing duty for a statue that is to go on Riverside Drive when completed. His name is "Commander," and he was purchased especially for the General Forrest model.

Fortunately for the artist, the tailor who made General Forrest's clothes had kept his measurements, and it not only enabled a uniform to be made accurately, but furnished accurate measurements that cannot always be obtained from photographs and uncertain testimony. An actual replica of his sword was made and the horse's trappings were copied from originals.[2181]

2181. B. A. C. Emerson, pp. 313-319.

# EDWARD A. POLLARD'S
# DESCRIPTION OF GENERAL FORREST

## - 1867 -

In appearance Gen. Forrest is a remarkable man; a perfect model of human symmetry and strength, with an endurance, it was said, that could wear out any trooper that served under him. He is about six feet high; his dark, piercing, hazel-eyes are full of expression, scintillating when excited, and at times playing with a passionate vengeance terrible to behold. The iron-gray hair covers a brain of wonderful breadth; the finely-cut features betoken native cultivation; the lithe form indicates great physical power and activity. He can have, too, his gentle moods, when the clear metallic voice that so often rang out the battle-charge sinks to tones of winning tenderness, and pleads the cause of the affections.

His military career was a succession of brilliant victories, the details of which would make a volume of romance. By no manner of means a favourite of commanding Generals, or of the government—for he was jealous and sullen under authority, and sometimes had fierce fits of obstinacy—he extorted their applause, and wrenched commission after commission from their unwilling hands, until he had won the wreath of Lieutenant-General, which had never been bestowed upon any other than regularly educated West Point soldiers. Without the advantages of learning, he exhibited a remarkable originality in the conduct of the war, and was the practical author of one of the most important reforms in the service. It was this uneducated man who, above all others, divined the true uses of cavalry in the war, and gave it a new and terrible power. The improvements in modern warfare may be said to have annihilated the uses of cavalry as an arm of attack to be employed against infantry formations. Six hundred Scots Greys rode against the Russian rifles at Balaklava, and of that gallant corps only one hundred and sixty returned from the charge. The infantry line, or square, engages the cavalry column of attack as far as it can be distinctly descried, and it is annihilated before it has reached the point-blank range of the smooth-bore musket. This important fact was fully recognized and acted upon by Forrest, and he aimed to make his mounted troops a body of swift infantry centaurs. The immemorial sabre was almost entirely discarded, and the long-range carbine, or rifle, and navy revolver, usurped its place. It was this change that confounded the enemy, converted the operations of Forrest's cavalry from mere raids to more important service, and made it a practicable and formidable arm on the regular field of battle.

Gen. Forrest had none of that polish which the popular imagination usually ascribes to the chivalric hero. His education was wofully deficient, and his extreme illiterate condition almost surpasses belief. He was the coarse Western man, ungrammatical whenever he opened his mouth, guilty of slang and solecism, but full of the generous fire of conflict, alive with every instinct of chivalry, and with an enthusiasm as simple as that of a boy. He had an immense brain; he was named by a distinguished Confederate General as the most wonderful man of the war, next to Stonewall Jackson; he was quite as peripatetic; he fought through four States in the war; and his quickness of movement and strike in battle gained for him the title of "War Eagle of the West." Forrest never refused an open fight; he disdained ambuscades and surprises; his orders against guerillas who might stray from his command to such dishonourable service, were even more severe than those of the enemy. He once offered a reward for the apprehension of a step-brother, because of his reported unauthorized depredations as a guerilla. Fair-play was the jewel of the man. When in the last periods of the war, [Union General James Harrison] Wilson, with a largely superiour force, chose to harass and weaken him without a battle, Forrest, tired of the game of strategy, sent him word: "If you will come out, I'll give you a fair field, and a square fight, the longest pole to take the persimmon." In this coarse language there is yet something severely and undeniably chivalric.

His prowess in the war was almost marvellous. He was wounded four times and had twenty-nine horses shot under him. He is reported to have said—"I have with my own hand killed a man for every horse I lost in the war, and I was a horse ahead at its close. At Selma, I killed two Yankees, and jumped my horse over a wagon, and got away. My provost-marshal's book will show that I have taken 31,000 prisoners during the war!" The Great Cavalryman "fought for blood." Simple in his conversation, sometimes as full of boisterous humour as a school-boy when relating his exploits, he was yet volcanic in his wrath, and in the gloom of his aroused passions his dearest friends dared not approach him. There is something terrible in such a character, and yet sublime, when the passions are intelligent and not merely exhibitions of temper. Forrest was the incarnation of vengeance in the war, but there was not a trait of personal malice in his record. He was the fierce combatant for the cause of right, the champion with the vizor up, and the blazing countenance fighting to the point of death. His passions were the inspirations of a great contest, not the fume of low personal animosities. The great events of 1861 found him leading an obscure and amiable life, called out an unconscious greatness, touched a hidden enthusiasm, and suddenly raised from this simple man the apparition of a new glory and a new flame in the war.[2182]

---

2182. Pollard, LHL, pp. 758-760.

General Forrest's equestrian statue, Memphis, Tennessee, 1905. From Emerson's *Historic Southern Monuments: Representative Memorials of the Heroic Dead of the Southern Confederacy.*

# ILLUSTRATIONS

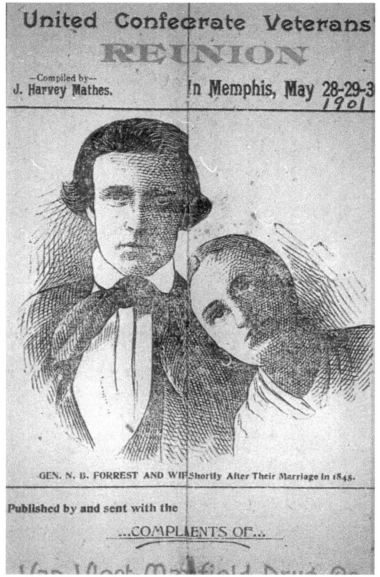

A woodcut of Nathan Bedford Forrest and his wife Mary Ann Montgomery shortly after their marriage in 1845. The future General was twenty-four years old, Mary was nineteen. Photo copyright © from the "Forrest Family Photo Album" of Col. Gene Ingram.

Nathan Bedford Forrest as Memphis alderman, 1850, at age twenty-eight or twenty-nine. One of the earliest known photos of the General. Photo copyright © from the "Forrest Family Photo Album" of Col. Gene Ingram.

Mrs. Nathan Bedford Forrest (Mary Ann Montgomery) and their son William M. "Willie" Forrest, in 1847. William was about one year old in this picture, his mother Mary was twenty-one. Mary was born Oct. 24, 1826, in Tennessee; she died Jan. 22, 1893, in Memphis, Tennessee. Photo copyright © from the "Forrest Family Photo Album" of Col. Gene Ingram.

Gen. Nathan Bedford Forrest's children: William M. "Willie" Forrest, born Sept. 26, 1846, in Hernando, Mississippi; and Frances Ann "Fanny" Forrest, born in 1849, in Hernando, Mississippi. Photo from 1854. William was eight, Frances was five. Sadly, Frances died of dysentery shortly after this picture was taken. Photo copyright © from the "Forrest Family Photo Album" of Col. Gene Ingram.

Col. Nathan Bedford Forrest at age forty-one, 3rd Tennessee Cavalry, Spring 1862. Photo copyright © from the "Forrest Family Photo Album" of Col. Gene Ingram.

Brig. Gen. Nathan Bedford Forrest, 1863, age forty-one or forty-two. Image copyright © from the "Forrest Family Photo Album" of Col. Gene Ingram.

Brig. Gen. Nathan Bedford Forrest, mid 1863, age forty-two. Image copyright © from the "Forrest Family Photo Album" of Col. Gene Ingram.

Maj. Gen. Nathan Bedford Forrest, December 1863, age forty-two. Photo copyright © from the "Forrest Family Photo Album" of Col. Gene Ingram.

Maj. Gen. Nathan Bedford Forrest, late 1863. Photo copyright © from the "Forrest Family Photo Album" of Col. Gene Ingram.

Lt. Gen. Nathan Bedford Forrest, pose #1, March 1865. Photo copyright © from the "Forrest Family Photo Album" of Col. Gene Ingram.

Lt. Gen. Nathan Bedford Forrest, the now famous pose #2, March 1865, age forty-three. Photo copyright © from the "Forrest Family Photo Album" of Col. Gene Ingram.

Last military photo of Lt. Gen. Nathan Bedford Forrest, age forty-three. Photo copyright © from the "Forrest Family Photo Album" of Col. Gene Ingram.

Nathan Bedford Forrest after Lincoln's War, 1865, age forty-four or forty-five. Photo copyright © from the "Forrest Family Photo Album" of Col. Gene Ingram.

Photo of Nathan Bedford Forrest taken in 1868 for the Jordan and Pryor book, *The Campaigns of General Nathan Bedford Forrest and of Forrest's Cavalry*. He was forty-six or forty-seven years of age. Photo copyright © from the "Forrest Family Photo Album" of Col. Gene Ingram.

Nathan Bedford Forrest at the 1868 Democratic Convention in New York City, New York, held July 4-9. Forrest was forty-six, just a few weeks shy of his forty-seventh birthday. His appearance created a sensation, with New Yorkers crowding around him in awe and numerous positive writeups appearing in the local papers. Photo copyright © from the "Forrest Family Photo Album" of Col. Gene Ingram.

Nathan Bedford Forrest in 1873, age fifty-one or fifty-two.  Photo copyright © from the "Forrest Family Photo Album" of Col. Gene Ingram.

Nathan Bedford Forrest in 1875, at age fifty-three or fifty-four, just two years before his death in 1877.  Photo copyright © from the "Forrest Family Photo Album" of Col. Gene Ingram.

Left: Lt. Samuel Donelson; Right: Capt. William M. Forrest, son of Nathan Bedford Forrest; photo taken after Lincoln's War, entitled: "startin' to Ole Miss." Photo copyright © from the "Forrest Family Photo Album" of Col. Gene Ingram.

William M. "Willie" Forrest, son of Nathan Bedford Forrest, upon graduation from Ole Miss. Photo copyright © from the "Forrest Family Photo Album" of Col. Gene Ingram.

William M. "Willie" Forrest, son of Nathan Bedford Forrest, in 1905, age fifty-nine. Photo copyright © from the "Forrest Family Photo Album" of Col. Gene Ingram.

Brig. Gen. Jeffrey E. Forrest, youngest brother of Gen. Nathan Bedford Forrest. Jeffrey was born in 1837 at Tippah, Mississippi. He was killed by Yankee fire at the Battle of Okolona, February 22, 1864, at age twenty-seven. John Paul Strain's cover painting on this book illustrates his older brother's response. Photo copyright © from the "Forrest Family Photo Album" of Col. Gene Ingram.

Jesse Forrest, brother of Gen. Nathan Bedford Forrest. Jesse was born April 8, 1829, at Chapel Hill, Tennessee. General Forrest died at Jesse's home in Memphis on October 29, 1877. Photo copyright © from the "Forrest Family Photo Album" of Col. Gene Ingram.

Nathan Bedford Forrest, II, in 1914, at age forty-two; son of William M. Forrest, grandson of Gen. Nathan Bedford Forrest. N.B. Forrest, II was born in 1872 at Oxford, Mississippi. Photo copyright © from the "Forrest Family Photo Album" of Col. Gene Ingram.

Brig. Gen. Nathan Bedford Forrest, III, in his late thirties or early forties; son of Nathan Bedford Forrest, II, great-grandson of Gen. Nathan Bedford Forrest. N.B. Forrest, III was born April 7, 1905, in Memphis, Tennessee. He was killed in action during World War II at Kiel, Germany. Photo copyright © from the "Forrest Family Photo Album" of Col. Gene Ingram.

Cultural sign, Franklin, Tennessee. Forrest would be elated to witness our modern
dedication to preserving the history of the War for Southern Independence—and battles
such as Franklin II, that had such an impact on his life and that of every Southerner. Photo
© Lochlainn Seabrook.

This pole, flying the twelve star
Forrest Cavalry Corps Confederate
Battle Flag, was donated to the
Forrest Boyhood Home through the
generosity and efforts of
CHRISTOPHER LOWE
RICHARD HAMBLEN
JOHN PAYSINGER

Plaque at the front gate of Forrest's Boyhood Home. Photo copyright © Lochlainn
Seabrook.

Shed behind Forrest's Boyhood Home. Photo copyright © Lochlainn Seabrook.

Rear side view of Forrest's Boyhood Home. Photo copyright © Lochlainn Seabrook.

Front view of Forrest's Boyhood Home, Chapel Hill, Tennessee, with our beautiful Confederate Battle Flag unfurled. Photo copyright © Lochlainn Seabrook.

Closeup of one of the many Forrest monuments in Chapel Hill, Tennessee. This one marks the spot of his birthplace and birth home, the latter which no longer exists. Photo copyright © Lochlainn Seabrook.

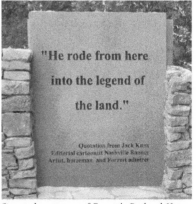

"He rode from here into the legend of the land."

Quotation from Jack Knox
Editorial cartoonist Nashville Banner
Artist, horseman, and Forrest admirer

Sign at the entrance of Forrest's Boyhood Home, Chapel Hill, Tennessee. Photo copyright © Lochlainn Seabrook.

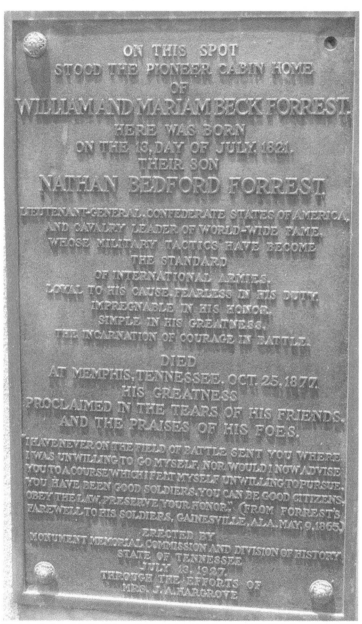

Monument plaque at site of Forrest's parents' original home, and his birthplace, Chapel Hill, Tennessee. Photo copyright © Lochlainn Seabrook.

Part of beautiful Chapel Hill, Tennessee, as it looks today. Photo copyright © Lochlainn Seabrook.

One of the many American businesses named after Forrest. This one is in Chapel Hill, Tennessee. Photo copyright © Lochlainn Seabrook.

One of many street signs in Chapel Hill named after General Forrest. Photo copyright © Lochlainn Seabrook.

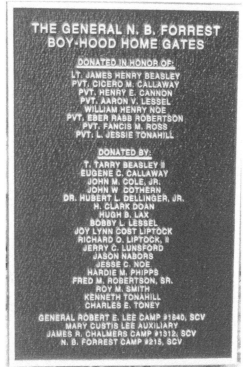

THE GENERAL N. B. FORREST
BOY-HOOD HOME GATES

DONATED IN HONOR OF:
LT. JAMES HENRY BEASLEY
PVT. CICERO M. CALLAWAY
PVT. HENRY E. CANNON
PVT. AARON V. LESSEL
WILLIAM HENRY NOE
PVT. EBER RABB ROBERTSON
PVT. FANCIS M. ROSS
PVT. L. JESSIE TONAHILL

DONATED BY:
T. TARRY BEASLEY II
EUGENE C. CALLAWAY
JOHN M. COLE, JR.
JOHN W. COTHERN
DR. HUBERT L. DELLINGER, JR.
H. CLARK DOAN
HUGH B. LAX
BOBBY L. LESSEL
JOY LYNN COST LIPTOCK
RICHARD O. LIPTOCK, II
JERRY C. LUNSFORD
JASON NABORS
JESSE C. NOE
HARDIE M. PHIPPS
FRED M. ROBERTSON, SR.
ROY M. SMITH
KENNETH TONAHILL
CHARLES E. TONEY

GENERAL ROBERT E. LEE CAMP #1640, SCV
MARY CUSTIS LEE AUXILIARY
JAMES R. CHALMERS CAMP #1312, SCV
N. B. FORREST CAMP #215, SCV

Plaque at the entrance of Forrest's Boyhood Home, Chapel Hill, Tennessee. Photo copyright © Lochlainn Seabrook.

Oaklands Mansion, Murfreesboro, Tennessee. Forrest skirmished here with Union forces on July 13, 1862, the General's forty-first birthday. Forrest subdued the Yanks, chalking up another victory for the Wizard of the Saddle and the Confederacy. The home is dear to traditional Southerners for another reason: President Jefferson Davis stayed at Oaklands during his visit with the Army of Tennessee in late 1862. Photo copyright © Lochlainn Seabrook.

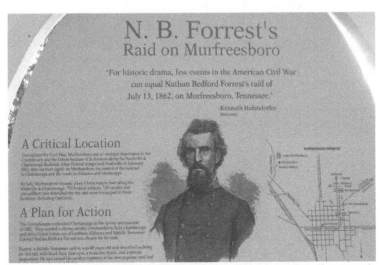

Sign at Oaklands Mansion describing Forrest's Murfreesboro Raid, July 13, 1862. Photo copyright © Lochlainn Seabrook.

## A Birthday Raid

July 13 was Forrest's birthday. The day before the raid, he told the troops he wanted to celebrate his birthday in Murfreesboro. He then gave the command for an all-night ride to Murfreesboro. The brigade reached Woodbury about 11 p.m. and advanced on Murfreesboro via the Readyville Pike.

Forrest and his men slipped into town in the early morning darkness on July 13, riding up East Main Street. One division veered off to attack the Pennsylvania and Michigan forces at Oaklands, while the other proceeded with Forrest to the courthouse and town square.

At approximately 4:30 a.m., the Maney family and the Union forces at Oaklands were awakened by the sounds of guns, shouts, bugles, drums and Rebel yells. Some surprised Union soldiers fell back over the fence separating the camp from the Maneys' yard while others sought shelter behind the trees.

The Union troops at Oaklands collected themselves and offered stiff resistance, driving the Confederates back toward Lascassas Pike by 8 a.m. Col. Duffield, was seriously wounded and carried into Oaklands mansion.

According to Maney family history, the children of Lewis and Adeline Maney viewed the fighting from the mansion's front windows. Relative Augusta Pickard Maney said in a late 1960s interview that Adeline told her "how she had to pull the children away from the windows and put them to bed during the battle... They'd run from one window to the other. It lasted till daybreak and she was exhausted when it was over."

While the battle raged at Oaklands, Forrest and his men attacked and captured the courthouse and city jail and released many citizen prisoners inside.

Another plaque at Oaklands Mansion describing Forrest's Murfreesboro Raid. Photo copyright © Lochlainn Seabrook.

## A Rapid Surrender

Around noon Forrest proceeded to Oaklands where he found the 9th Michigan guarding their camp and resting from the morning's fighting. Forrest attacked, subdued them and sent a communication under flag of truce by one of his aides to Duffield. It read:

*"Colonel- I must demand an unconditional surrender of your forces as prisoners of war, or I will have every man put to the sword. You are aware of the overpowering force I have at my command and this demand is made to prevent the further effusion of blood. I am, Colonel,*
*Your obedient servant,*
*N. B. Forrest, C.S.A."*

Forrest soon received word of Duffield's surrender, which is belied to have taken place inside the mansion around 1 p.m. Duffield remained at Oaklands for another month to recover.

Forrest then demanded the surrender of the 3rd Minnesota Infantry. He allowed the regiment's commander, Colonel Henry C. Lester, to ride to Oaklands to confer with Duffield. During the trip across town, Forrest's men gave Lester the impression of a much larger force by lining as many troops as possible along the route through town. Lester subsequently surrendered around 3 p.m..

The battle, which resulted in relatively few casualties, ended with the remaining Union soldiers being taken prisoner for a short time. Forrest was promoted to brigadier general on July 21, 1862, eight days after his "birthday raid."

Union forces soon reoccupied Murfreesboro and remained there until September. The Confederates held the city until their retreat after the Battle of Stones River in early January 1863. Murfreesboro remained under Federal control for the rest of the war.

A third plaque at Oaklands Mansion concerning Forrest's Murfreesboro Raid. Photo copyright © Lochlainn Seabrook.

Site of the Spring Hill Battlefield as it looked in 2006 when this photo was taken.  Photo copyright © Lochlainn Seabrook.

Sign at the site of the Battle of Spring Hill, Tennessee, where Forrest played a major role.  The area is today threatened with development. Photo copyright © Lochlainn Seabrook.

Historical marker, Spring Hill, Tennessee, describing Forrest's role at the Battle of Spring Hill, Nov. 29, 1864, one day before the Confederate disaster at Franklin. Photo copyright © Lochlainn Seabrook.

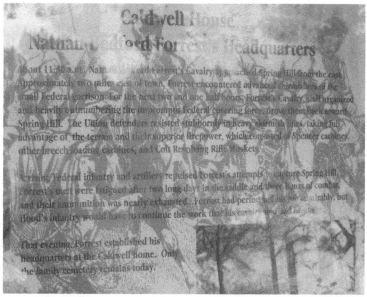

Historical sign at the location of the Caldwell House, Spring Hill, Tennessee, Forrest's headquarters after the Battle of Spring Hill. Photo copyright © Lochlainn Seabrook.

The Caldwell House, Spring Hill, Tennessee, from an old photo. The house no longer exists, but the Caldwell Family Cemetery has been preserved at the site. Photo copyright © Lochlainn Seabrook.

The gravestone of Dr. St. Clair F. Caldwell (1793-1856), Caldwell Family Cemetery, Spring Hill, Tennessee. Dr. Caldwell was a resident of the Caldwell House, site of Forrest's headquarters after the Battle of Spring Hill. His wife, Mary Moore Pointer (1809-1873), was the daughter of Henry Pointer. The Pointers of Virginia married into many local Middle Tennessee clans, including descendants of the McGavocks, Hardings, Cheairs, Figuers, and Perkins families. Photo copyright © Lochlainn Seabrook.

McCutcheons Creek, Spring Hill, Tennessee. Forrest and his men fought around and near this body of water—and no doubt crossed it a number of times—during the Battle of Spring Hill. Photo copyright © Lochlainn Seabrook.

Historical marker, Thompson's Station, Tennessee, describing the Battle of Thompson's Station, March 5, 1863, at which Forrest played an important role. Photo copyright © Lochlainn Seabrook.

Historical marker on Columbia Ave., Franklin, Tennessee, commemorating
events shortly after the Battle of Spring Hill and one day before the debacle
at the Battle of Franklin II, Nov. 30, 1864. Forrest is mentioned. Photo
copyright © Lochlainn Seabrook.

Confederate Gen. John Bell Hood, another
cousin of the author. Hood was Forrest's
superior during the Nashville Campaign in the
latter half of 1864. The two often quarreled,
hampering Confederate effectiveness. Photo
from Ridley's *Battles and Sketches of the Army of
Tennessee*.

Street sign, Franklin, Tennessee,
honoring our Confederate heritage.
Unenlightened non-Southerners, as
well as many Southerners themselves,
wrongly associate the word
"Confederate" with slavery, and are
busy trying to get all traces of this
word removed from the South.
However, as has been shown
throughout this book, it was not the
South but the North (Massachusetts,
to be exact) that was responsible for
legalizing both the American slave
trade and American slavery.
Furthermore, the Confederacy banned
the slave trade before the U.S. did.
Photo copyright © Lochlainn
Seabrook.

Abraham Lincoln, the so-called "Great Emancipator" and America's sixteenth president, the man directly responsible for all of the needless horrors, violence, death, and destruction of the "Civil War." The meddlesome, warmongering, big-government, liberal Yankee was well-known in his day, even by his own party members and friends, as a white racist, white supremacist, and white separatist, one who greatly delayed abolition and fought his entire adult life to have all African-Americans deported out of the U.S. "What I would most desire," he declared in a speech at Springfield, Illinois, on July 17, 1858, "would be the separation of the white and black races." When his goal of black colonization began to lose public support in the North, Lincoln came out publicly for corralling African-Americans into a U.S. state specially set aside for "blacks only" (this bizarre racist idea never went anywhere either, for obvious reasons). Such statements prompted the sagacious black civil rights leader, Frederick Douglass, to rightly describe "Honest Abe's" policies toward African-Americans as lacking "the genuine spark of humanity." "Stinkin' Lincoln," as he was known to 19th-Century Southerners, is also still remembered here in Dixie as an arch anti-Constitutionalist and incorrigible war criminal, who, as the *Official Records* plainly show, sanctioned Sherman's villainous plan to hunt down Forrest and murder him like a rabid animal. Traditional Southerners will never forget: here, Lincoln's name, reputation, presidency, and face will be forever marked with Southern blood, guilt, shame, repugnance, horror, and disgrace. Image from the cover of the author's book, *Abraham Lincoln: The Southern View*. Photo courtesy Library of Congress.

Outskirts of Franklin, Tennessee. Forrest rode along this road, Columbia Pike (today known as Columbia Ave.), passing by these very hills and farmlands on his way north (toward the right) from the Battle of Spring Hill to the Battle of Franklin II on the morning of Nov. 30, 1864. At the time the pike was, of course, a small dirt and gravel roadway. Photo copyright © Lochlainn Seabrook.

Personal handwritten note from Forrest to Laura Galloway, of Columbia, Tennessee, shortly after the Battle of Franklin II. It reads: "My compliments to Miss Laura - hoping she may never have to morn over another defete of the Confederate army. N.B. Forrest, Maj. Genl." From Laura Galloway's Autograph Book, courtesy Elizabeth Scott-Whipkey.

Entrance to the McGavock Confederate Cemetery, Franklin, Tennessee. The nearly 1,500 Rebel soldiers who died at the Battle of Franklin II are buried here. Photo copyright © Lochlainn Seabrook.

Historical marker, McGavock Confederate Cemetery, Franklin, Tennessee. To the left of the sign, famous Carnton Plantation can been seen in the distance. Forrest and the author are both relatives of John McGavock. Photo copyright © Lochlainn Seabrook.

McGavock Confederate Cemetery, located on the grounds of Carnton Plantation. This burial ground, the largest privately owned military cemetery in the U.S., has become a holy site to traditional Southerners, many whose kin and ancestors died at the Battle of Franklin II on Nov. 30, 1864, fighting courageously against Yankee tyranny. The author has relations buried here, one of the better known being John Byars Womack (1839-1864), also a cousin of country artist Lee Ann Womack. Photo copyright © Lochlainn Seabrook.

Another view of the McGavock Confederate Cemetery. By some accounts Forrest was lucky not to have ended up here. It was, in part, Hood's order assigning Forrest to the eastern flank of the battle that may have spared his life, for the "hottest fightin'" took place several miles to the west, near the Carter House. The cemetery is today owned by the Confederate Cemetery Corporation, which includes members of the United Daughters of the Confederacy. The grounds are maintained by the Sons of Confederate Veterans, of which the author is a member. Photo copyright © Lochlainn Seabrook.

Stone marker at McGavock Confederate Cemetery commemorating the 230 Tennesseans who perished at the Battle of Franklin II. Forrest was familiar with many of these fearless boys and men, particular the numerous Rebel officers who died. Photo Copyright © Lochlainn Seabrook.

Grave marker at the McGavock Confederate Cemetery for the 225 unknown Rebel soldiers who gave their lives at Franklin II, Nov. 30, 1864. Photo copyright © Lochlainn Seabrook.

Statue of Roderick—one of General Forrest's most intelligent and most courageous steeds—Roderick Place, Thompson's Station, Tennessee. The monument, which marks the animal's grave site, commemorates Roderick's tragic death at the Battle of Thompson's Station, March 5, 1863. The Confederates won that day, but the General lost his favorite horse. (Curiously, though a gelding, Roderick has been portrayed here as a stallion.) Photo copyright © Lochlainn Seabrook.

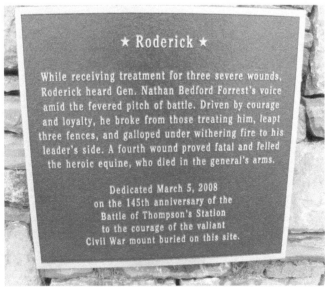

Plaque at the base of Roderick's gravestone monument. Photo copyright © Lochlainn Seabrook.

Another view of Roderick's grave site, Thompson's Station, Tennessee. Photo copyright © Lochlainn Seabrook.

Roderick statue from the rear side. Photo copyright © Lochlainn Seabrook.

Housing development in Franklin, Tennessee, named after Forrest's horse. Roderick Square is located within a large community called Forrest Crossing. The entire complex is situated just yards from where the General made his famous crossing of the Harpeth River during the Battle of Franklin II, Nov. 30, 1864. Photo copyright © Lochlainn Seabrook.

Closeup of Forrest Crossing sign at left, showing the bridge now located at where Forrest is believed to have forded the Harpeth River. Photo copyright © Lochlainn Seabrook.

Road marker, Franklin, Tennessee. Middle Tennessee is famous for its rich Civil War heritage, as well as for its numerous historic houses and battlefield sites. Forrest played a major role in the area's 19th-Century history. Photo copyright © Lochlainn Seabrook.

Street sign, Franklin, Tennessee. Note the top sign, taken from the General's middle name. "Bedford" was given to him by his parents at birth, named for the Tennessee county he was born in. Photo copyright © Lochlainn Seabrook.

Another section of Forrest Crossing, Franklin, Tennessee. Forrest lovers and fans of the Confederacy enjoy seeing the General's name around town. Photo copyright © Lochlainn Seabrook.

Cultural sign, Franklin, Tennessee, this one marking the northwestern border of the Battle of Franklin II. Photo copyright © Lochlainn Seabrook.

Long distance photo of Forrest Crossing, Harpeth River, Franklin, Tennessee. Photo copyright © Lochlainn Seabrook.

Closeup of the Forrest Crossing area, Harpeth River, Franklin, Tennessee. Photo copyright © Lochlainn Seabrook.

Wide closeup of Forrest Crossing area, Harpeth River, Franklin, Tennessee. The ford is today surrounded by a golf course, also named after Forrest. Note the Franklin Hills on the horizon. The center of the fighting at Franklin II was fought several miles north of this spot (to the right). Photo copyright © Lochlainn Seabrook.

Forrest's famous equestrian statue, Forrest Park, Memphis, Tennessee. The monument—which is regularly defaced by the uninformed—marks Forrest's burial spot and is a sacred shrine to traditional Southerners, and to lovers of liberty everywhere. Photo courtesy of Lanny Medlin.

*Inscription on the monument:*

NATHAN BEDFORD FORREST
1821-1877

1904: ERECTED BY HIS COUNTRYMEN IN HONOR
OF THE MILITARY GENIUS OF
LIEUTENANT-GENERAL NATHAN BEDFORD FORREST,
CONFEDERATE STATES ARMY, 1861-1865.

Because of what the General stood for, pro-Forrest sentiment can be found in all fifty states and among all races, classes, and nationalities. Photo copyright © Lochlainn Seabrook.

Forrest School, Chapel Hill, Tennessee, named after one of its most famous citizens. Photo copyright © Lochlainn Seabrook.

Forrest's Boyhood Home, Chapel Hill, Tennessee. Photo copyright © Lochlainn Seabrook.

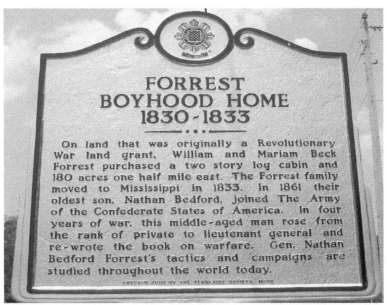

FORREST
BOYHOOD HOME
1830-1833

On land that was originally a Revolutionary War land grant, William and Mariam Beck Forrest purchased a two story log cabin and 180 acres one half mile east. The Forrest family moved to Mississippi in 1833. In 1861 their oldest son, Nathan Bedford, joined The Army of the Confederate States of America. In four years of war, this middle-aged man rose from the rank of private to lieutenant general and re-wrote the book on warfare. Gen. Nathan Bedford Forrest's tactics and campaigns are studied throughout the world today.

ERECTED 2008 BY THE TENNESSEE SOCIETY, MOSB

Historical marker at the entrance of Forrest's Boyhood Home, Chapel Hill, Tennessee. Photo copyright © Lochlainn Seabrook.

One of several Forrest monuments in Chapel Hill, Tennessee. This one marks the site of the General's birth. The original rustic log home of his parents, William Forrest and Mariam Beck, has long since disappeared. Unlike many other Southern towns where the carpetbag-scallywag mindset and political correctness have taken over, the people of Chapel Hill proudly fly the Confederate Battle Flag (left of monument) and the Bonnie Blue Flag (right of monument). Abraham Lincoln tried to destroy these beautiful symbols of Jeffersonianism, but failed. To this day uneducated South-haters continue the Yankee president's attempt to besmirch our emblems and denigrate our region. Chapel Hill, Forrest's birthplace, is to be applauded for standing strong and honoring both the Truth and Southern heritage. Photo copyright © Lochlainn Seabrook.

Another Forrest monument, another Confederate Battle Flag, Chapel Hill, Tennessee. Photo copyright © Lochlainn Seabrook.

Part of Chapel Hill, Tennessee, today. Photo copyright © Lochlainn Seabrook.

As the Lincoln-Douglas Debates of 1858 reveal, Lincoln was what we today would call a white supremacist, a white separatist, and a white racist. Forrest, though a 19th-Century European-American, was quite the opposite. Forrest, for example, enlisted blacks in his units from the beginning of the War, over two years before Lincoln reluctantly allowed black enrollment in the Union army. Photo courtesy Library of Congress.

Virginia servants ("slaves" to Yanks), circa 1862. Despite the claims of pro-North authors, Forrest was well-known during his lifetime for his respectful and humane treatment of both free and bonded blacks. And while Lincoln spent his entire adult life trying to figure out how install American apartheid and rid the U.S. of its African-American population, Forrest sought to incorporate blacks into everyday life, grant them equal rights, and bring new African immigrants into the country to help rebuild the South. Photo courtesy Library of Congress.

One of the many Forrest street signs in his hometown, Chapel Hill, Tennessee. If he were alive today, the humble but dignified frontiersman would be deeply moved by such displays. Photo copyright © Lochlainn Seabrook.

President Andrew Johnson of Tennessee. After Lincoln's War, in the Summer of1868, Johnson "pardoned" Forrest for the crime of "treason" against the U.S. government. For Forrest, and the entire South, it was just another slap in the face. However, the General used it as an opportunity to resuscitate his career and mend his public image, tarnished by Lincoln's Yankee propaganda machine. Photo courtesy Library of Congress.

A closeup of Forrest's most famous photo, showing him in his forties during Lincoln's War. Note the fire in his eyes, a mysterious penetrating inner light often commented on by friends and foe alike. At the young age of fifty-six the General's "Celtic spark" was finally only extinguished by exhaustion and diabetes. He gave everything, including his health, indeed his very life, to the Southern Cause (self-determination), and to fighting the intrusive North's arrogance, aggression, and despotism.

One of dozens of street signs dedicated to Forrest around Nashville. This one is in Franklin, site of three bloody battles (April 10, 1863; Nov. 30, 1864; and Dec. 17, 1864). Forrest fought gallantly at the first two, and only missed the third because Hood had inexplicably sent him to Murfreesboro. Southerners still talk about "what might have been" had the General been on the field at Nashville, Dec. 15-16, 1864. Photo copyright © Lochlainn Seabrook.

White Hall, Spring Hill, Tennessee, built by Dr. Aaron White in 1844. Forrest and his men stopped here on the morning of November 30, 1864, on their way to the Battle of Franklin II, where they were fed by the White family and their neighbors. The house was used as a field hospital after the battle. In 1863 Confederate General Earl Van Dorn used White Hall as his original Spring Hill headquarters. His trysts with local married girl Jessie (McKissack) Peters at the house were the cause of much gossip and the Whites asked him to leave. Van Dorn moved his headquarters down the street to Ferguson Hall, where he was killed shortly thereafter by Jessie's jealous husband, Dr. George B. Peters. To this day the house is considered haunted.

Rippavilla Plantation, Spring Hill, Tennessee. Forrest and Gen. John Bell Hood argued here at breakfast on the morning of Nov. 30, 1864, just prior to the disastrous Battle of Franklin II. Photo copyright © Lochlainn Seabrook.

Historical marker, Murfreesboro, Tennessee, commemorating Forrest's successful raid on the Union-occupied town, July 13, 1862. Born July 13, 1821, he humorously referred to the victory as "my forty-first birthday present." Here, the General captured $500,000 worth of Yankee supplies, today's equivalent of about $10,500,000. If the South had had just a few more Forrests, Lincoln and his Yankee invaders would have been crushed, and 150 million Southerners would today be living in peaceful independence, security, and prosperity. Photo copyright © Lochlainn Seabrook.

Battle of Nashville Monument, Nashville, Tennessee, commemorating the conflict of Dec. 15-16, 1864. Illogically, Hood sent Forrest to Murfreesboro prior to the battle, a move that cost the Army of Tennessee its life. Hood's men were only kept from total extinction by Forrest, who regrouped with him a few days later at Columbia, Tennessee, where he aggressively and successfully guarded the army's rear during its southward retreat. Photo copyright © Lochlainn Seabrook.

Second Lt. George Limerick Cowan, of Forrest's Escort, c. 1862. George was related to Gen. Forrest's wife, Mary Ann Montgomery, whose mother was Elizabeth Cowan of Blount Co., Tennessee. George married Harriet Young "Hattie" McGavock, whose grandfather, Randal McGavock, built famous Carnton Plantation in the early 1800s at Franklin, Tennessee. George and Hattie lived across the road from Carnton in a house called "Windermere." In later years George was made recording secretary of the Veterans Association, which first met July 27, 1877, at Hurricane Springs, Tennessee. The organization began as a sort of reunion between Forrest and his old Escort and staff. Forrest passed away a mere three months later. George, along with Hattie, is buried at Mt. Hope Cemetery, in the Cowan Family Plot in Franklin. The author is cousins with both the McGavocks and the Montgomerys. Photo courtesy Dr. Michael R. Bradley, author of *Nathan Bedford Forrest's Escort and Staff*.

First Lt. Nathan Boone, of Forrest's Escort Company. Boone served in several different positions in the Veterans Association, including vice president and treasurer. The author is cousins with Nathan, and with his kinsmen: famed frontiersman Daniel Boone and modern singer/actor Pat Boone. Photo taken between 1885 and 1910. Courtesy Dr. Michael R. Bradley.

Thomas Cheatham Little, of Forrest's Escort. Little was elected chaplain of the Veterans Association in 1887. Photo probably taken in 1900 at Nashville, Tennessee, at the meeting of the United Confederate Veterans, the forerunner of today's Sons of Confederate Veterans. Photo courtesy Dr. Michael R. Bradley.

This illustration, from 1868, provides further evidence that—contrary to Northern myth—the focus of the original KKK was not on blacks, but on carpetbaggers, treacherous Northern whites who came South after Lincoln's War in order to prey on the ravaged region. We do not know if Forrest ever saw this image, but if he did he would have heartily approved of it.

Grant, like nearly every other Yankee officer, was both alarmed and awed by Forrest's ingenious seemingly supernatural tactics on the field of action, and after the War he grudgingly praised the Confederate chieftain in his *Memoirs*.

Confederate reunion of "Forrest Vets," taken at Booneville, Lincoln Co., Tennessee, in either 1889 or 1903, at one of two reunions. Photo courtesy Dr. Michael R. Bradley.

Reunion of Forrest's Escort, Lynchburg, Tennessee, date unknown (probably 1890s), names of individuals unknown. Note the three black Confederate soldiers in the back row—one far left, two far right (one holding a Confederate flag aloft)—just a few of the dozens of African-Americans who fought loyally alongside Forrest; just three of as many as 300,000 who donned Confederate gray to defend the South against Northern dictatorship.

Members of Forrest's Escort and Staff. From left to right: Col. David C. Kelley (seated left); Forrest's son, Capt. William M. "Willie" Forrest (standing left); Dr. James B. Cowan (seated middle); Capt. John W. Morton (standing right); Maj. Charles W. Anderson (seated right). Photo probably taken in 1905, at Memphis, Tennessee. Photo courtesy Dr. Michael R. Bradley.

Forrest's cavalry raid on his adopted hometown, Memphis, Tennessee, August 21, 1864, as portrayed in this sketch that appeared in the September 10, 1864, edition of *Harper's Weekly*. Forrest's two favorite battle cries were: "Forward men, and mix with 'em!" and "keep the skeer on 'em!"

Forrest's Boyhood Home, front view, Chapel Hill, Tennessee. Forrest was not born here (his birthplace home, a few miles distant, disappeared in the 1800s), but he did live at this residence from the ages of nine to twelve (1830-1833), after which his father William moved the family to Mississippi. The two-floor section on the left of the photo was not part of the original structure but was added later. Forrest and his brothers slept in the second floor room, over the living room area. After the Forrests moved out in 1833 the home was occupied by various families until the 1950s, when it was finally abandoned and fell into disrepair. In 1997 the dilapidated house was purchased from the state of Tennessee by the International Sons of Confederate Veterans. Today it is maintained by the Tennessee Division of the SCV, which is in the process of restoring the home, along with the grounds and outbuildings. Thanks to their hard work, and the generous donations of supporters, the Forrest Boyhood Home will be preserved for future generations. Plans include a visitor's center, museum store, and guided tours. Photo copyright © Lochlainn Seabrook.

Lotz House, Franklin, Tennessee. Once a private family residence, the Lotz House is located across the street from the Carter House (see next page), near what was the center of the fighting during the calamitous Battle of Franklin II. Forrest, leading his cavalry on the opposite side of the conflict, was thus probably spared the horrible fate of dozens of Rebels, including a number of generals, who died within sight of the now famous home—shot down by Yankees who had illegally invaded the town of Franklin. The Lotz family fled to the Carter House for safety during the conflict. The red flag hanging from the front upper balcony indicates that the home was used as a field hospital during Franklin II. Photo copyright © Lochlainn Seabrook.

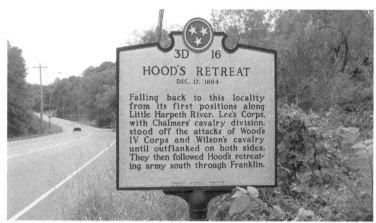

Historical marker in Brentwood, Tennessee, commemorating Hood's Retreat southward, back to the town of Franklin, after the humiliating Rebel defeat at the Battle of Nashville, Dec. 15-16, 1864. Hood had strangely, and unwisely, detached Forrest to Murfreesboro just prior to the conflict, depriving himself of his most able warrior at a time when he needed him most. The result was another Confederate disaster and "Hood's Retreat." Signs marking the ignoble flight line the roadways of Middle Tennessee for miles, from Nashville all the way to the state's southern border. Photo copyright © Lochlainn Seabrook.

Carter House, Columbia Ave., Franklin, Tennessee, located near the epicenter of the fighting at the Battle of Franklin II, Nov. 30, 1864. A number of Confederate generals were gunned down in the area, six of them eventually dying of their wounds (including the incomparable "Stonewall of the West," Patrick R. Cleburne). Bullet holes are still visible in some of the structures on the property. While the all-important Carter House was on the west side of the battle, bewilderingly Hood once again hurt the Confederacy by sending his best officer, Forrest, to harass Yanks around the Harpeth River several miles away on the east side of town. Tragically, nearly 1,500 Rebel soldiers died at Franklin II. Forrest survived—possibly, and ironically, in part because of Hood's mistake. Photo copyright © Lochlainn Seabrook.

Downtown Franklin, Tennessee, today, still looking very much like it did during the Battle of Franklin II, Nov. 30, 1864. Forrest, born in Chapel Hill, a mere thirty-five miles to the southeast, was very familiar with these buildings and streets: he spent much of his time in Franklin and fought in two of the three conflicts here, the Battles of Franklin I and II (he was in Murfreesboro during Franklin III). Photo copyright © Lochlainn Seabrook.

Another view of Old Franklin center, looking down Main Street from the Confederate Monument. Photo copyright © Lochlainn Seabrook.

Confederate Monument, Franklin, Tennessee, commemorating the Battle of Franklin II, the Rebels (including Forrest) who fought here, and the nearly 1,500 Confederate soldiers who perished trying to preserve the original Constitution, states' rights, and Southern honor. Due to ignorance, a carpetbag-scallywag mentality, and pressure from local PC thought police, the town prohibits the exhibition of Confederate flags at the site—presumably because the flag is associated by the ill-informed with slavery. Ironically, the town itself is named after one of America's most famous slave owners: Benjamin Franklin. Photo copyright © Lochlainn Seabrook.

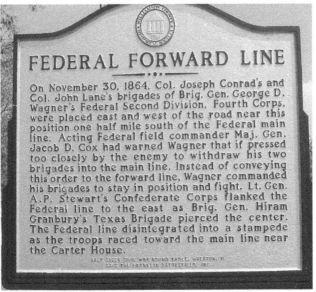

FEDERAL FORWARD LINE

On November 30, 1864, Col. Joseph Conrad's and
Col. John Lane's brigades of Brig. Gen. George D.
Wagner's Federal Second Division, Fourth Corps,
were placed east and west of the road near this
position one half mile south of the Federal main
line. Acting Federal field commander Maj. Gen.
Jacob D. Cox had warned Wagner that if pressed
too closely by the enemy to withdraw his two
brigades into the main line. Instead of conveying
this order to the forward line, Wagner commanded
his brigades to stay in position and fight. Lt. Gen.
A.P. Stewart's Confederate Corps flanked the
Federal line to the east as Brig. Gen. Hiram
Granbury's Texas Brigade pierced the center.
The Federal line disintegrated into a stampede
as the troops raced toward the main line near
the Carter House.

Historical marker, Franklin, Tennessee, describing Yankee activities during the Battle
of Franklin II, just south of the Carter House on Columbia Ave. Photo copyright ©
Lochlainn Seabrook.

3D  26

HARPETH ACADEMY

1.4 miles west, and north of the
road, this boys' school commenced
operations in 1811 under Rev. Gideon
Blackburn, noted Presbyterian missionary. James Hervey Otey, later
first Episcopal bishop of Tennessee,
succeeded him in 1821. In 1825, the
school moved into Franklin, closing
in 1863 when Federal troops destroyed
the buildings.

Historical marker, Franklin, Tennessee, commemorating
Yankee atrocities, probably at the Battle of Franklin I, April
10, 1863. Forrest fought in this conflict, as he did at
Franklin II, Nov. 30, 1864. He was not present at the Battle
of Franklin III on December 17, 1864, however, as Hood
had detached him to Murfreesboro, thirty miles to the east.
Sadly for the good people of Franklin, all three conflicts
were won by the Union. Photo copyright © Lochlainn
Seabrook.

Harpeth River, Franklin, Tennessee. Forrest forded this shallow body of water with his men numerous times during the Battle of Franklin II, Nov. 30, 1864. One of these fords is still called "Forrest Crossing." The river, however, proved to be a benefit to Yankee General John Schofield and his troops (who burned the bridges as they crossed northward toward Nashville), and a hindrance to Confederate General John Bell Hood and his infantrymen. Today the Harpeth is used for more recreational purposes, such as fishing and canoeing. Photo copyright © Lochlainn Seabrook.

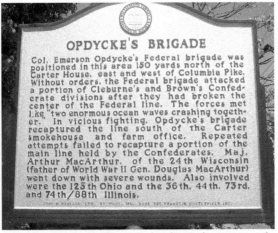

Historical marker, Franklin, Tennessee, describing Yankee activity near the
Carter House during the Battle of Franklin II. As the sign notes, General
Douglas MacArthur's father was present, fighting for Lincoln. Armed men
from Wisconsin, Ohio, and Illinois had no business whatsoever traveling
south and invading the town of Franklin: Tennessee was part of a legally
formed sovereign nation, the C.S.A., at the time. Photo copyright ©
Lochlainn Seabrook.

Historical marker, Franklin, Tennessee, in front of the
Carter House, Yankee headquarters during the Battle of
Franklin II. Capt. Carter's first name has been misspelled.
The correct spelling is Theodrick. The twenty-four year
old Confederate officer fell within yards of his family's
home. He was picked up off the battlefield and carried to
the house where he died on Dec. 2 from his wounds,
surrounded by his grieving family. Better known locally as
"Tod" Carter, his name has become legendary in Franklin,
and his tragic story is still told in these parts as if it
happened yesterday. Photo copyright © Lochlainn
Seabrook.

Carnton Plantation, Franklin, Tennessee, front view. Built in the early 1800s by the author's cousins, the McGavock family of Virginia, the 10,000 square foot mansion became one of the forty-four field hospitals set up around town during the Battle of Franklin II. Hundreds of Confederate soldiers were operated on, and hundreds died inside Carnton's walls (Rebel blood is still visible on some of the floors). Confederate troops marched nearby Carnton's yards on their way to the conflict (in the photo above the eastern flank of Hood's army was positioned to the back right), whose epicenter was about a mile away to the northwest (straight back as the camera is facing) near the Carter House. Hood had ordered Forrest to the east (to the right in the photo), where the dauntless Tennessean and his cavalrymen spent the afternoon cutting down Yankee foreign invaders around the Harpeth River. Today Carnton looks almost nothing like it did when the McGavocks took up residence in their new home for the first time in 1826: the front and back porches had not yet been added, and the yards were then full of enormous trees, fruit orchards, and vegetable and flower gardens. Also missing today are the plantation's dozens of outbuildings and farm structures. These would have included the estate's greenhouse, numerous barns, stables, a five-bay carriage house, horse paddocks, corrals, and servant's quarters. The property Carnton sits on, originally owned by the Cherokee, was part of a Revolutionary War grant given to the author's cousin Randal McGavock (1766-1843), Carnton's founder and Nashville's eleventh mayor. Randal's brother, surveyor David McGavock, drew up the boundaries for Davidson County, Tennessee. Many streets, schools, and businesses around Middle Tennessee have been named after the McGavocks, a noble Confederate family who once entertained men like Andrew Jackson, James Polk, Felix Grundy, and Sam Houston (a relative of Forrest's wife, Mary Ann Montgomery) at Carnton Plantation. For more on this fascinating family and their historic home, see the author's book *The McGavocks of Carnton Plantation: A Southern History*. Photo copyright © Lochlainn Seabrook.

Carnton Plantation, Franklin, Tennessee, rear view. Though Carnton is now known for her back porch, this structure was not part of the original mansion. It was added by the founder's son and author's cousin, John W. McGavock, in the 1840s as part of the Greek Revival that was sweeping the South at the time. Forrest stood on the upper floor of this porch prior to the Battle of Franklin II, using it as an observation deck. Note the sloping "ghost" roof line on the left side of the house where the kitchen once stood. This particular structure, a small wooden house built around 1811, was blown away during a tornado in 1909 and never rebuilt. Thanks to liberal Lincoln and his unconstitutional war on the conservative South and states' rights, Carnton Plantation has a horrifically bloody history, and has thus long been a site of tremendous paranormal activity. For more on this aspect of Carnton, see the author's book *Carnton Plantation Ghost Stories*. Photo copyright © Lochlainn Seabrook.

Servants' quarters ("slave house" to Yanks), Carnton Plantation, Franklin, Tennessee. At one point there were some one dozen field servants' homes on the property. Made of logs these have long since disappeared leaving only this one brick house, the abode of the McGavocks' house servants. The house was divided in half, with one servant family living on each side (the two front doors are still visible at the second floor level). The basement (see windows below the staircases) was used as a workshop for building and repairing furniture and other household items. The brick walls on the structure are original; the roof and wooden stairs are modern restorations. Behind the house runs McGavock's Creek, used by Victorians for swimming, fishing, washing, bathing, and "refrigerating" perishable foods. Though today we rightly bemoan the existence of slavery, it should be remembered that black servants who lived in brick homes like this one were far better off than many free blacks, and even many free whites, who lived in the area at the time. Indeed, the home above, still standing after nearly 200 years, is superior in square footage, comfort, beauty, and craftsmanship to many modern homes found in Franklin today. Photo copyright © Lochlainn Seabrook.

Another of the author's cousins, Caroline "Carrie" (Winder) McGavock (1829-1905), from Louisiana. Carrie was the wife of Confederate Col. John W. McGavock (right), owners of Carnton Plantation during the Battle of Franklin II. Carrie was known as the "Good Samaritan of Williamson County" for her Christian ways and many charitable deeds, such as taking in orphans. Despite this, because she was a conservative and a Confederate, many modern-day writers, as they do with Forrest, continue to slander her name and fabricate lies about her. Photo from Ridley's *Battles and Sketches of the Army of Tennessee*.

Grainy newspaper photo of Confederate Col. John W. McGavock (1815-1893), husband of Carrie Winder (left) and owner of Carnton Plantation during Franklin II. Col. McGavock was a proud member of the United Confederate Veterans (UCV), the forerunner of today's multiracial organization, Sons of Confederate Veterans (SCV). Though they were Democrats, John and his family were what we would today call conservative-libertarians. It is probable that Forrest, also a die-hard conservative, attended one or more of the many Confederate political rallies held in "McGavock's Grove," located at Carnton. John certainly knew Forrest: he allowed the General to use the back porch of Carnton as an observation deck prior to Franklin II. Photo courtesy Williamson County Public Library.

Historical marker at the entrance of the McGavock Family Cemetery, located on the grounds of Carnton Plantation, Franklin, Tennessee. Forrest was distantly related to the McGavocks, though we can be sure that neither he nor the McGavocks were aware of this fact. Photo copyright © Lochlainn Seabrook.

Sign at the entrance of Carnton Plantation, Franklin, Tennessee. Photo copyright © Lochlainn Seabrook.

Sign at Winstead Hill, Confederate Memorial Park, Franklin, Tennessee. Photo copyright © Lochlainn Seabrook.

Winstead Hill, Franklin, Tennessee, site of Confederate General John Bell Hood's observation post during the Battle of Franklin II, Nov. 30, 1864. Forrest met with and, as often occurred, probably argued with Hood here before riding off into battle. Photo copyright © Lochlainn Seabrook.

Monument at Winstead Hill, Franklin, Tennessee, commemorating Freeman's Battery of Forrest's Artillery, which was captured at the Battle of Franklin I, April 10, 1863. Like the other two battles at Franklin, the first was won by the Yanks. Photo copyright © Lochlainn Seabrook.

## BRIGADIER'S WALK

The sense of pride, honor and integrity of the everyday fighting man of the Army of Tennessee made the brilliant careers of these five Brigadier Generals possible. Largely non-slave owning, these brave men of the Army of Tennessee followed Adams, Carter, Strahl, Gist and Granbury across the fields to your right into certain death that November afternoon. Please pause for a moment of respect to their memory!

Sign at "Brigadier's Walk," Winstead Hill, Confederate Memorial Park, Franklin, Tennessee. Photo copyright © Lochlainn Seabrook.

# WINSTEAD HILL

## ⟶⟶OBSERVATION POST⟵⟵

### BATTLE OF FRANKLIN

#### WED. NOVEMBER 30, 1864

"The line advanced at 4 p.m.
with orders to drive
the enemy into or across
the Big Harpeth River . . . .
Never did troops
fight more gallantly"

#### Gen. JOHN BELL HOOD

ARMY OF TENNESSEE
CONFEDERATE STATES of AMERICA

Sign at Winstead Hill, Franklin, Tennessee. Photo copyright © Lochlainn Seabrook.

STATES RIGHTS GIST

The Tragedy of Franklin quite possibly may have been
averted had this scholarly South Carolina Blue Blood
been given the promotion to division command that
his service record warranted. Completely reorganizing
the state of South Carolina's Militia, this South Carolina
College graduate made sure his home state was ready
when Lincoln was elected. Taking command of Barnard
Bee's Brigade after Bee's death at First Manassas, Gist
was promoted to Brigadier General on March 20, 1862.
He fought gallantly at Chickamauga, Chattanooga, and in
the Atlanta Campaign. As the Brigade assembled in front
of Franklin on November 30, 1864, it was still smarting
(the 24th SC in particular) from the lack of initiative that
had deprived it of victory the night before at Spring Hill.
The Brigade, made up of The 46th, 65th & 2nd Battalion
Georgia Sharpshooters, and the 16th and Crack 24th
South Carolina slammed into the 72nd Illinois & 111th
Ohio causing the 72nd to "Break and Run". Having his
horse shot from under him, Gist sprinted for the locust
abatis in his front. Advancing to within a few yards of
the abatis, Gist went down with a bullet in the chest. He
died the next morning at The Harrison House. He was
buried, first in a private cemetery in Franklin, then and
finally, at the Trinity Episcopal Church in Columbia,
South Carolina.

Stone commemoration marker of Confederate General States Right Gist, at "Brigadier's Walk,"
Winstead Hill, Franklin, Tennessee. Gist, who died at Franklin II, was well-known to Forrest, for the
two had fought earlier together at the Battle of Chickamauga. States Rights was the 1st cousin of William
Henry Gist (1807-1874), governor of South Carolina (1858-1860). William signed South Carolina's
"Ordinance of Secession," marking the separation of the first Southern state from the United States of
America and the beginning of the formation of the Confederate States of America. Photo copyright ©
Lochlainn Seabrook.

A view of the Plain of Franklin, as seen from Hood's vantage point on Winstead Hill, just south of the town of Franklin, Tennessee. The road running diagonally across the middle of the photo, from lower right to upper left, is Columbia Ave. (known then as Columbia Pike), the route taken by a large portion of the Army of Tennessee (CSA) as it marched northward toward Franklin center (out of frame, upper left) on Nov. 30, 1864, after the fiasco at Spring Hill the day before. Franklin II was fought primarily on the Franklin Plain, though the center of the conflict ended up taking place northward near the Carter House (to the left, not visible here). Forrest and his men were to the east (upper right, out of frame), a few miles away, marauding along the Harpeth River. The stone markers (bottom right) commemorate some of the famous generals (e.g., Cleburne, Gist, Strahl, etc.) who perished at Franklin II. As this was—thanks to Hood—one of the Confederacy's most disastrous, bloody, unnecessary, foolish, and ill-conceived Rebel attacks of the entire war, Forrest was fortunate indeed not to have his own stone marker here today. For the location of Winstead Hill, Carnton Plantation, Carter House, and other important sites mentioned in this book regarding the Battle of Franklin II, see the map on the following page. Photo copyright © Lochlainn Seabrook.

Cannon, Winstead Hill, Franklin, Tennessee. Photo copyright © Lochlainn Seabrook

Map of the Battle of Franklin II, drawn by the author; from the author's book, *Carnton Plantation Ghost Stories*. Note position of Forrest and his men (bottom right), far from the "hottest" fighting, which occurred around the Carters' cotton gin (upper center). Drawing copyright © Lochlainn Seabrook.

The Carter family cotton gin house, site of the most intense combat during Franklin II, Nov. 30, 1864. Located about 300 feet east of what is now the corner of Columbia Ave. and Cleburne Street, it disappeared long ago. Today a small memorial park stands at the corner in remembrance of that fateful day. Drawing from Ridley's *Battles and Sketches of the Army of Tennessee*.

Historical marker at the site of the Carter family's cotton gin, Franklin, Tennessee, epicenter of the Battle of Franklin II. Photo copyright © Lochlainn Seabrook.

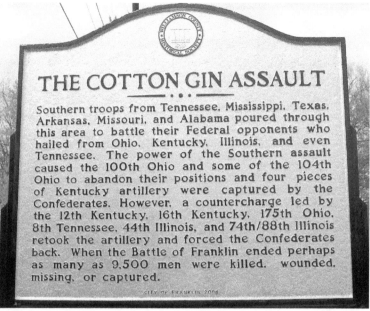

## THE COTTON GIN ASSAULT

Southern troops from Tennessee, Mississippi, Texas, Arkansas, Missouri, and Alabama poured through this area to battle their Federal opponents who hailed from Ohio, Kentucky, Illinois, and even Tennessee. The power of the Southern assault caused the 100th Ohio and some of the 104th Ohio to abandon their positions and four pieces of Kentucky artillery were captured by the Confederates. However, a countercharge led by the 12th Kentucky, 16th Kentucky, 175th Ohio, 8th Tennessee, 44th Illinois, and 74th/88th Illinois retook the artillery and forced the Confederates back. When the Battle of Franklin ended perhaps as many as 9,500 men were killed, wounded, missing, or captured.

CITY OF FRANKLIN 2008

Historical marker, Carter cotton gin memorial park, Franklin, Tennessee. Photo copyright © Lochlainn Seabrook.

Historical marker, Franklin, Tennessee, marking one of the lines of Yankee breastworks (chest-high trenches) during Franklin II. "Forrest's Cavalry" is mentioned. Photo copyright © Lochlainn Seabrook.

SAMUEL WINSTEAD (1778 - 1851)

Samuel Winstead, a native of Virginia, came here in 1799. At his death, his $34,000 estate included several tracts of land and 78 slaves. His will granted freedom and passage to Liberia for all his slaves upon the death of his wife. At Susannah's death in 1862, questions arose as her will attempted to leave the slaves to her 2nd husband, Jeremiah Stephenson. With the Civil War came emancipation and the Winstead slaves never went to Africa. After years in local court, the Tennessee Supreme Court ruled on the issue in 1870 granting the Winstead ex-slaves their $26,900 portion of the estate. Luckily, the escrow had been invested in U. S. bonds and the beneficiaries received $364.25 each. Winstead is buried here along with several members of the John McKinney family, who owned the property prior to 1814.

(Continued on other side)
WILLIAMSON COUNTY HISTORICAL SOCIETY 2005

Yankee-slanted historical marker, Franklin, Tennessee, commemorating Sam Winstead, after whom Winstead Hill was named. Mentioned here are the statements that "with the Civil War came emancipation," and that because of this Winstead's slaves were not deported to Liberia. This is, of course, pure Yankee disinformation and Northern myth, as we discussed in Part 2 of this book. First, emancipation did not automatically "come with the War," since the War was not about slavery to begin with. It came only after white racist Lincoln succumbed to years of pressure from abolitionists, *and* when he discovered that he was running out of white enlistees. Second, if Lincoln had not been assassinated shortly after the end of his War, Winstead's servants would have almost certainly been "sent back to Liberia, to their own native land," as the white separatist president publically phrased it on August 21, 1858. For he was one of the nation's leading proponents of American apartheid and black colonization, pushing for black deportation right up until the day he died—as Yankee General Benjamin F. Butler and others later testified. The truth is that it was not white Southerners who supported black colonization; it was white Northerners, like Lincoln. Indeed, the American Colonization Society (ACS) was founded by white Yankees decades before the "Civil War," while Lincoln himself was a manager of the Illinois chapter of the ACS. In contrast, in the postbellum period General Forrest fought for black civil rights while promoting the immigration of new Africans to aid in the rebuilding of the South, the very region that Lincoln had tried to destroy and de-Africanize. That signs like this are allowed in the South shows the extent to which political correctness and pro-North propaganda have permeated Dixie. Photo copyright © Lochlainn Seabrook.

The Harrison House, Franklin, Tennessee. Today privately owned, the antebellum home has significant ties to the War for Southern Independence. Photo copyright © Lochlainn Seabrook.

Historical marker at the Harrison House, Franklin, Tennessee. Photo copyright © Lochlainn Seabrook.

Stan Dalton as General Nathan Bedford Forrest, Forrest Boyhood Home, Forrest Home Fundraiser 2009, Chapel Hill, Tennessee. Photo copyright © Lochlainn Seabrook.

Dalton as Forrest, standing on the front porch of the Forrest Boyhood Home. Photo copyright © Lochlainn Seabrook.

Another photo of Dalton as Forrest.  Photo copyright © Lochlainn Seabrook.

Reenactment of Forrest encampment, Forrest Boyhood Home, Forrest Home Fundraiser 2009, Chapel Hill, Tennessee. Photo copyright © Lochlainn Seabrook.

Yankee arse-kicker, Forrest Boyhood Home, Forrest Home Fundraiser 2009, Chapel Hill, Tennessee. Photo copyright © Lochlainn Seabrook.

Reenactment of Forrest and some of his staff, Forrest Boyhood Home, Forrest Home Fundraiser 2009, Chapel Hill, Tennessee. The General is on the far left. Photo copyright © Lochlainn Seabrook.

Forrest's cavalry horses, Forrest Boyhood Home, Forrest Home Fundraiser 2009, Chapel Hill, Tennessee. Photo copyright © Lochlainn Seabrook.

Reenactment of Forrest's father's smithy, Forrest Boyhood Home, Forrest Home Fundraiser 2009, Chapel Hill, Tennessee. Photo copyright © Lochlainn Seabrook.

Front porch of the Forrest Boyhood Home, Chapel Hill, Tennessee. Photo copyright © Lochlainn Seabrook.

Interior room of the Forrest Boyhood Home, undergoing restoration. Photo copyright © Lochlainn Seabrook.

Another interior downstairs room of the Forrest Boyhood Home undergoing restoration. Photo copyright © Lochlainn Seabrook.

Staircase leading from the first floor to the second floor, Forrest Boyhood Home. Photo copyright © Lochlainn Seabrook.

View looking out one of the back windows of the Forrest Boyhood Home. As a child the General would have been very familiar with this view. Note the encroaching modern subdivision at the back of the property. Photo copyright © Lochlainn Seabrook.

Upstairs of the Forrest Boyhood Home. It is undergoing restoration and some of the workers' tools and supplies can be seen. Forrest and his brothers used this space as their bedroom. Photo copyright © Lochlainn Seabrook.

View of the Forrest Boyhood Home's chimney.  Photo copyright © Lochlainn Seabrook.

Entrance at the back of the house to the space beneath the Forrest Boyhood Home. The room was probably used for storage, in particular, perishable foods. Photo copyright © Lochlainn Seabrook.

View of the back of the Forrest Boyhood Home, Chapel Hill, Tennessee. Photo copyright © Lochlainn Seabrook.

View from the back of the property looking toward one of the outbuildings and the main house. Photo copyright © Lochlainn Seabrook.

It is not known what significance is attached to this small mysterious stone rectangle located in the backyard of the Forrest Boyhood Home. The dog, named Honky, is a friend of the author's. Photo copyright © Lochlainn Seabrook.

One of the back windows of the Forrest Boyhood Home. The original brick foundation is clearly visible. Photo copyright © Lochlainn Seabrook.

Long distance view of the Forrest Boyhood Home. Photo copyright © Lochlainn Seabrook.

What may be the remnants of a chicken coop at the Forrest Boyhood Home. It is being held together with nylon fabric until restoration begins. Photo copyright © Lochlainn Seabrook.

A crib log barn, Forrest Boyhood Home, probably once used to hold corn or hay. Photo copyright © Lochlainn Seabrook.

Closeup of one of the Forrest Boyhood Home's outbuildings, showing details of the original timber and architectural design from the early 1800s. Photo copyright © Lochlainn Seabrook.

Side view of the Forrest Boyhood Home. Photo copyright © Lochlainn Seabrook.

Entrance to a cave on the property of the Forrest Boyhood Home, a favorite haunt for young Forrest and his childhood playmates. Photo copyright © Lochlainn Seabrook.

Very large and ancient tree near the front yard of the Forrest Boyhood Home. As it is between 150 and 200 years old, young Forrest no doubt spent much time climbing it. Photo copyright © Lochlainn Seabrook.

Sign at the Forrest Boyhood Home. Photo copyright © Lochlainn Seabrook.

Another view of the front of the Forrest Boyhood Home, Chapel Hill, Tennessee. Photo copyright © Lochlainn Seabrook.

Sign out front of the Forrest School, Chapel Hill, Tennessee. The General's name is prominently displayed. Photo copyright © Lochlainn Seabrook.

Roadside banner, Chapel Hill, Tennessee. Photo copyright © Lochlainn Seabrook.

Historical marker at Fort Granger, Franklin, Tennessee. On June 4, 1863, Forrest was nearly killed here by Yankee troops. His life was spared due to the gratitude of a Union officer he had once treated kindly as a prisoner. If this particular officer had wanted everlasting fame, he could have easily acquired it by killing the Wizard of the Saddle there and then. That he did not proves that Forrest was not the monster so commonly portrayed by Northern myth. Photo copyright © Lochlainn Seabrook.

Jefferson Davis, first and only president of the Confederate States of America, later lamented not putting Forrest to better use. Despite his faults and errors (some which led to the South's downfall), Davis was an honorable, brave, patriotic, and dignified man who will always be loved by traditional Southerners. The author celebrates the Rebel leader in his book *The Quotable Jefferson Davis*. Photo courtesy Library of Congress.

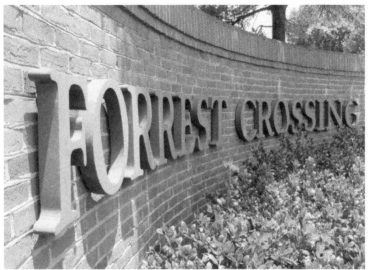

Sign at an area in Franklin, Tennessee, known as Forrest Crossing, named after a nearby spot on the Harpeth River where General Forrest forded his cavalry during the Battle of Franklin II, Nov. 30, 1864. Photo copyright © Lochlainn Seabrook.

Riverside Plantation, Franklin, Tennessee, owned by the author's cousin James Randal McGavock, and his wife Lousia C. Chenault, in the mid 1800s. James was the brother of Confederate Col. John W. McGavock, the owner of Carnton Plantation—where Forrest used the back upper porch to survey the battlefield prior to Franklin II. Forrest was a distant cousin of both James and John McGavock. Photo copyright © Lochlainn Seabrook.

Gravestone of 2nd Lt. George Limerick Cowan, of Forrest's Escort. Cowan family plot, Mt. Hope Cemetery, Franklin, Tennessee. Cowan married Harriet "Hattie" McGavock, of Carnton Plantation. Their little brown house, "Windermere," can still be seen near the foot of Carnton's driveway. Photo copyright © Lochlainn Seabrook.

Sign at Winstead Hill, Franklin, Tennessee, site of Gen. John Bell Hood's observation post during the Battle of Franklin II. The road in this photo is Columbia Ave., which Forrest and his men rode down (from right to left) on their way to the conflict. Photo copyright © Lochlainn Seabrook.

The Hermitage, home of President Andrew Jackson, Hermitage, Tennessee. On July 21, 1862, Forrest and his men paused here to enjoy an anniversary party being held in honor of the Confederate victory at the Battle of Manassas I. Photo copyright © Lochlainn Seabrook.

Burial site of President Andrew Jackson, the Hermitage, which Forrest may have visited while at the plantation in July 1862. Forrest and Jackson had much in common, from their homespun backgrounds, temperaments, and bravery, to their lack of schooling, self-made success, and superb leadership qualities. Photo copyright © Lochlainn Seabrook.

Sign marking the site of the Duck River, at Columbia, Tennessee. Forrest was very familiar with this body of water: not only did he cross over it countless times during his military career, he grew up near it in Chapel Hill, and no doubt swam and fished in it innumerable times. Photo copyright © Lochlainn Seabrook.

Galloway House, Columbia, Tennessee, site of Forrest's headquarters in 1863. After his bloody near fatal fight with Confederate Lt. Andrew W. Gould, the General came here to recover. Photo copyright © Lochlainn Seabrook.

The room Forrest ran to after he had been shot by Gould is in the upper right hand side of this photo (second floor, behind the tree branch). Photo copyright © Lochlainn Seabrook.

The Nelson House Hotel, Columbia, Tennessee. After being stabbed by Forrest, who had acted in self-defense, Lt. Gould fled to this hotel, where he was cared for by a physician for several days. The wound, however, proved fatal, and Gould passed away in the second-floor room on the right side of the building. Photo copyright © Lochlainn Seabrook.

Sign at the front of the Nelson House Hotel, Photo copyright © Lochlainn Seabrook.

Sign out front of the Galloway house. Photo copyright © Lochlainn Seabrook.

Another view of the Nelson House, the site of Gould's death. Photo copyright © Lochlainn Seabrook.

Front lobby of the Nelson House Hotel, now undergoing renovation. Photo copyright © Lochlainn Seabrook.

Forrest family crest with the family's Latin motto, *Vivunt dum Virent*: "They live as long as they (the trees) are green." Note the tree at the top and the leafy motif, symbolically representing a forest; that is, the endurance of the Forrest family members. Photo courtesy *Tennessee Soldiers Photo Project*, Roderick, Forrest's War Horse Camp 2072, SCV.

"In 1608 there came to Jamestown, Virginia, with Captain Newport, one Thomas Forrest, with his wife, and his wife's maid, Anne Buras. Mrs. Forrest was the first English gentlewoman to come to America, and her maid was the first English woman to marry in America. Thomas Forrest was the uncle of Sir Anthony Forrest, and both were members of the Second London Company for the colonization of Virginia.

"The Forrest family is a very ancient one in England. There were two parent branches of the Forrest stock—one at Troutbeck, County Westmoreland; and the other in their own manor house at Morborne, County Huntingdon, England. How long they had been settled at Morborne is unknown, but it was an old family when the Forrest coat-armor 'argent, a chevron between three hinds' heads erased gules; crest, three oak trees all proper,' was recorded in the Herald's College of England, which was in the times of Miles Forrest, who died in 1558 and was in occupation of the old home and a purchaser of adjoining church lands when the monasteries were dissolved by Henry VIII. During Cromwell's 'reign of terror' in Henry's days, Father John Forrest, an observant friar, was burned as a heretic, for denying the King's supremacy in the church. He is celebrated in Foxe's *Acts and Monuments* and recorded in the family genealogy as the 'Blessed John.'

"It was to this branch of the Forrest family that Thomas Forrest, founder of the Virginia and Maryland families, belonged. The American family, founded by Thomas Forrest through his son Peter and the five sons of the latter, has contributed many useful citizens to our republic and, in the person of Gen. Nathan Bedford Forrest, one of the greatest soldiers of any age." — From the book *Makers of America* (1915)

**General Nathan Bedford Forrest Family Silver Service**

93. Mrs. Gen. Forrest (Mary Ann Montgomery Forrest) – 5 piece antebellum silver coffee service, each piece engraved, "M" for "Montgomery," her maiden name, given to her and Gen. Forrest by her mother and father upon their death The silver service is marked "Superior Silver Company" and each piece including tray is marked with identical serial #4091. A superb showpiece, the actual silver service used by General Forrest and his family in their home in Memphis and recently purchased from their descendants. A unique as well as a once in a lifetime opportunity to own the silver service that was used by and belonged to the foremost cavalry officer in American History (five pieces all marked with identical serial numbers – accompanied by letter of provenance from the Forrest family). . . . . . . . . . . . . . . . . . . . . . . . . . . . . . . . . . . . . . . . . . . . . . . . . . . . . . . . . . . . . . . .12,500.

Silver coffee service belonging to General Forrest and his wife, for sale for $12,500.  Photo courtesy *Tennessee Soldiers Photo Project*, Roderick, Forrest's War Horse Camp 2072, SCV.

Collage of old Forrest images.  Photo courtesy *Tennessee Soldiers Photo Project*, Roderick, Forrest's War Horse Camp 2072, SCV.

Tennessee vehicle license plate bearing the name Bedford, for Bedford County. In keeping with a long Southern naming tradition (of naming children after geographical places), the General's parents gave him "Bedford" as his middle name. The area where Forrest was born, however, has since been repartitioned and is now part of Marshall County.

Mississippi vehicle license plate bearing the name Forrest, the county which proudly named itself after the General.

Letter from J. Roane Vineyard to Norma R. Bridgeforth, dated May 10, 1939, containing a story about Mrs. Forrest (the General's mother, Mariam Beck). Photo courtesy *Tennessee Soldiers Photo Project*, Roderick, Forrest's War Horse Camp 2072, SCV.

Signs at the entrance to Franklin, Tennessee, the town where General Forrest spent much of his military career fighting for the Southern Cause: to preserve state sovereignty as promised in the original Constitution (Tenth Amendment), and prevent it from being overturned by liberal Lincoln and his nosey Yankee invaders. Photo copyright © Lochlainn Seabrook.

Prewar military school photo of Andrew Willis Gould, who later tried to kill his commander General Forrest at Columbia, Tennessee, over a personal misunderstanding. Gould lost his life in the attempt. Photo courtesy Cumberland University Library, Lebanon, Tennessee.

Street named after General Forrest, Franklin, Tennessee. Photo copyright © Lochlainn Seabrook.

Golf course named after General Forrest, Franklin, Tennessee. Photo copyright © Lochlainn Seabrook.

Another street named after Forrest, Franklin, Tennessee. Photo copyright © Lochlainn Seabrook.

FORREST'S "STOMPIN' GROUNDS"
- 1821-1877 -

The General spent his entire life in the encircled area (Tennessee, Mississippi, Kentucky, Alabama, Georgia, and Louisiana), venturing outside it only rarely for business and politics (Arkansas, Texas, North Carolina, Michigan, and New York).

Cultural sign, Franklin, Tennessee. The Carter House stood at the epicenter of the fighting during the Battle of Franklin II—at which Forrest was present. Carnton Plantation served as a Confederate field hospital during the conflict. The General used Carnton's back upper portico as an observation deck prior to the opening volley. Photo copyright © Lochlainn Seabrook

Colonel William Asa Dawson, one of Forrest's "boat captains" during the General's short marine career at Johnsonville (Dawson was in charge of the steamer *Undine*). He was killed near Columbia, Tennessee, in Nov. 1864. Photo courtesy Ronny Mangrum Collection.

A well-armed Byrd Troutt. He served with the Seventh and the Second Cavalries under Forrest. He died July 3, 1862. Photo courtesy Tim Heath, SCV, Lebanon, Tennessee.

James P. Travis and his wife Nannie. James fought with the Third Cavalry under Forrest throughout the entire War. Photo courtesy *Tennessee Soldiers Photo Project*, Roderick, Forrest's War Horse Camp 2072, SCV.

Col. James Welbourne Starnes of Forrest's Fourth Tennessee Cavalry. Starnes was killed at Tullahoma, Tennessee, in 1863 by a sniper's bullet. Photo courtesy *Tennessee Soldiers Photo Project*, Roderick, Forrest's War Horse Camp 2072, SCV.

Captain James Chesley Cundiff, a member of Forrest's staff and the Fourth Tennessee Cavalry. Photo courtesy Mr. Boots Nix, Forrest Boyhood Home Caretaker, Chapel Hill, Tennessee.

Captain William S. McLemore of Forrest's Fourth Tennessee Cavalry. Photo courtesy *Tennessee Soldiers Photo Project*, Roderick, Forrest's War Horse Camp 2072, SCV.

John G. Ballentine, an Irishman with Forrest's Seventh Cavalry. Photo courtesy Miss Sallie Bruster, UDC, Pulaski, Tennessee.

Sherwood Green Jenkins of Nolensville, Tennessee. Served under Forrest with Col. James W. Starnes in the Fourth Tennessee Cavalry and was part of President Jefferson Davis' escort after the War. Photo courtesy Robert Clary, Roderick, Forrest's War Horse Camp 2072, SCV.

Captain Thomas Fern Perkins, of Forrest's Eleventh Tennessee Cavalry. Perkins was one of the "Immortal 600," a group of Confederate officers that were imprisoned at various Union forts during the fall and winter of 1864-1865. Their Yankee captors subjected Perkins and his comrades to various forms of cruel treatment and torture, all against the Geneva Conventions: placed in cold damp cells they were denied warm clothing and firewood, and intentionally put on "starvation diets" consisting of moldy cornmeal and soured pickles. In August 1864 the Confederate prisoners were transferred from Fort Delaware (Pea Patch Island, Delaware) to Morris Island, South Carolina. Here they were forced into a cramped stockade that was located in front of Yankee artillery, where they were used as human shields. For forty-five days the men were subjected to the ferocious shelling of Confederate forces, after which the survivors were removed to Fort Pulaski (near Savannah, Georgia). Before it was all over at least forty-three died, lives needlessly sacrificed to Lincoln's lust for power and the barbarity of the Yankee. These brave Rebel officers will always be remembered here in the South as the "Immortal 600" for remaining loyal to the Confederacy and for refusing to take the Union's unconstitutional "Oath of Allegiance." Captain Perkins survived his time as an involuntary "guest" of the Yankees, and after the War returned to his home in Williamson County, Tennessee. Photo courtesy *Tennessee Soldiers Photo Project*, Roderick, Forrest's War Horse Camp 2072, SCV.

Graduation photo of John L. Bell of Cumberland University, before joining Forrest's command. He rose up the ranks, eventually serving as a 1st Lt. and inspector general under General Tyree H. Bell, Bell's Brigade, Buford's Division, Forrest's Cavalry. The young lieutenant was killed at the Battle of Brice's Cross Roads, June 10, 1864. Photo courtesy Cumberland University Library, Lebanon, Tennessee.

Henry H. Smith was a member of General Forrest's staff and was with his commander on the day of the Gould affair, June 13, 1863. After Lieutenant Andrew Wills Gould shot Forrest in a fit of rage at the Masonic Building in Columbia, Tennessee, he was stabbed in turn by Forrest. Gould then fled, running past Smith, who tried to grab him by his coat. Gould slipped away, Smith tearing the young officer's lapel. Photo courtesy *Tennessee Soldiers Photo Project*, Roderick, Forrest's War Horse Camp 2072, SCV.

Assistant Surgeon James Mark Hanner, of Morton's Battery under Forrest. Photo courtesy Mary Ella Burke, Franklin, Tennessee.

Private Thomas M. Turner. Served in Company B, Fourth Tennessee Cavalry under Forrest. Photo courtesy Peggy Dillard, Nashville, Tennessee.

Redding Jones of Forrest's Eleventh TN Cavalry under Col. D. W. Holman. Photo courtesy Ronny Mangrum Collection.

Seven of the estimated 300,000 to 1,000,000 (depending on how one defines the term "soldier") Southern blacks who donned Confederate gray and fought for the Southern Cause. A massive Northern coverup of the truth has meant that the facts about America's courageous black Confederate soldiers have been left out of our history books. Photo Library of Congress.

Two of the sixty-five African-Americans who served with Forrest throughout the War for Southern Independence. Left: Marshall Thompson; Right: Louis Napoleon Nelson. Photo from the October 1930 Confederate Reunion at Nashville, Tennessee. Private Nelson, the only known black Confederate chaplain, served at the Battles of Shiloh and Brice's Cross Roads, among many others. An attendee of dozens of postwar reunions, at his own request he was buried with his Confederate medals. Like many other enlightened men of color, Nelson's grandson, Nelson W. Winbush, is today a beloved and well respected member of the Sons of Confederate Veterans (SCV), exposing the anti-South myth that the SCV is a racist organization. Nelson wrote the Foreword to the author's bestselling book, *Everything You Were Taught About the Civil War is Wrong, Ask a Southerner!* Photo courtesy Ronny Mangrum Collection.

The author's third cousin, Edmund Winchester Rucker (1835-1924), commander of Rucker's Brigade (Chalmer's Division, Forrest's Cavalry), which was organized in September 1864. Rucker fought with Forrest at the disastrous Battle of Franklin II (Nov. 30, 1864), and lost his left arm two weeks later at the Battle of Nashville (Dec. 15-16, 1864). The two were close friends and went into the railroad business together after the War (1869-1874). I am the fourth great-grandson of Phoebe Rucker, who was the first cousin of Colonel Rucker. His 1924 obituary reads: "The death of Gen. E. W. Rucker, at his home in Birmingham, Ala, on the night of Sunday, April 13, 1924, takes another from the fast-dwindling list of gallant Confederate leaders and one of the patriotic upbuilders of the South since the war. He had reached the advanced age of eighty-eight years, but was still an outstanding figure in the business and social life of that city. After the war, and before removing from his native Tennessee, he built a forty-mile stretch of the Memphis and Little Rock Railroad. Later he was president of the Salem, Marion and Memphis Railroad following his removal to Birmingham, and had also been prominently connected with large manufacturing interests in that city. Edmund Winchester Rucker was born July 22, 1835, at Murfreesboro, Tenn., the son of Edmund and Louisa Winchester Rucker, and a grandson of Gen. James Winchester." General Winchester was a pioneer, an officer in the War of 1812, and a co-founder of the city of Memphis, Tennessee. His home, Cragfont, can still be seen at Castalian Springs, TN. Photo courtesy Ronny Mangrum Collection.

"Our Heroes and Our Flags," lithograph printed about 1896, promoting Confederate heritage and pride. Forrest was not included, but many of his superiors were. In the center are full-length portraits of (left to right) Stonewall Jackson, Pierre Gustave Toutant Beauregard, and Robert E. Lee. These three men are surrounded by four different Confederate flags. Starting at the top center and going counterclockwise, the surrounding outer busts are: Jefferson Davis, Pierre Gustave Toutant Beauregard, Braxton Bragg, John Bell Hood, Ambrose Powell Hill, James Longstreet, John Brown Gordon, Wade Hampton, Albert Sidney Johnston, John Hunt Morgan, Edmund Kirby Smith, Joseph Eggleston Johnston, James Ewell Brown "Jeb" Stuart, William Joseph Hardee, Leonidas Polk, Sterling Price, Stonewall Jackson, and Alexander Hamilton Stephens. Photo courtesy Library of Congress.

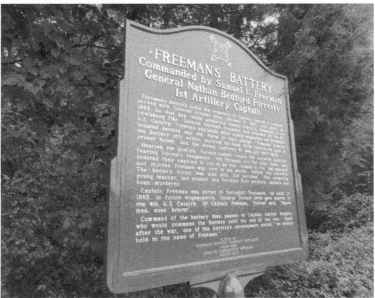

Historical marker, Forrest Boyhood Home, Chapel Hill, Tennessee. Photo copyright © Lochlainn Seabrook.

A multiracial group of Southern belles, Forrest Boyhood Home, Chapel Hill, Tennessee, at the Forrest Boyhood Home Fundraiser, Summer 2011. Contrary to anti-South mythology, Southern girls and women of all races, backgrounds, and nationalities played a huge, vital, and often unrecognized role in the War for Southern Independence—resorting to everything from hand making uniforms and holding bake sales (to raise money for Confederate regiments) to cutting their hair short and disguising themselves as men so they could fight on the front lines with their husbands, brothers, and fathers. While Lincoln completely ignored both Yankee females and the women's movement (which was raging across the North at the time), Southern men happily and lovingly gave credit to their female counterparts for their heroic contributions to the Southern war effort. President Jefferson Davis, for example, opened his celebrated book, *The Rise and Fall of the Confederate Government*, with these words: "To the Women of the Confederacy. . . whose patriotism will teach their children to emulate the deeds of our revolutionary sires these pages are dedicated by their countryman." Photo copyright © Lochlainn Seabrook.

Emma Sansom (1847-1900) of Social Circle, Georgia. Emma gained honor and fame for leading Forrest to a hidden ford on Black Creek following the Battle of Day's Gap near Gadsden, Alabama, in the Spring of 1863. During the escapade she and the General came under fire and almost lost their lives. In honor of Emma's bravery the people of Gadsden erected a monument and the local high school was named after her. Image from Ridley's *Battles and Sketches of the Army of Tennessee*.

Alfred H. D. Perkins, of Forrest's Seventh Cavalry.  Photo courtesy Williamson County Archives.

A number of luminaries attended Chapel Hill's Forrest Boyhood Fundraiser in the summer of 2011, including Tennessee Senator Bill Ketron (standing, fourth from right) of Murfreesboro. A Republican, Ketron represents District 13, which includes Lincoln, Marshall, Maury, and part of Rutherford Counties. Photo copyright © Lochlainn Seabrook.

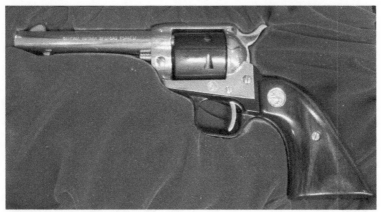

The rare "Colt Frontier Scout" .22 caliber revolver, this one a commemorative issue to General Nathan Bedford Forrest, as noted on the barrel. This particular gun was only made in the year 1969, during which just 3,000 were produced. Gun and case (below) courtesy the Franklin Gun Shop, Franklin, Tennessee. Photo copyright © Lochlainn Seabrook.

Gun case for the commemorative Forrest revolver above, with the General's image and name on the front. Photo copyright © Lochlainn Seabrook.

Forrest's home in Hernando, Mississippi, early 1840s. Image from Mathes' *General Forrest*.

Forrest's signature.

Major David C. Kelley (left) and Forrest (right) at the Battle of Fort Donelson. Image from Wyeth's *Life of General Nathan Bedford Forrest*.

The author's cousin Confederate General Gideon J. Pillow (1806-1878) was second in command at Fort Donelson. During the conflict he sided with Forrest against Generals John B. Floyd and Simon B. Buckner, and was later relieved of duty. Image from Phelan's *School History of Tennessee*.

One of the many drawings of General Forrest, this one from Phelan's *School History of Tennessee.*

Reverend William Mentzel Forrest, a well-known cousin of the General. Born in Baltimore, Maryland in 1868, he was a professor of note at the University of Virginia. Photo from Johnson's *Makers of America.*

Confederate Major George Dashiell, Forrest's chief paymaster. Image from Dinkins' *1861 to 1865, By an Old Johnnie.*

General Forrest's staff. From top center moving clockwise: John P. Strange, William M. Forrest, Charles S. Severson, James B. Cowan, John W. Morton, Gilbert V. Rambaut, Charles W. Anderson. Center: Matthew C. Calloway. Image from Jordan and Pryor's *The Campaigns of Lieut.-Gen. N.B. Forrest*.

Confederate General James R. Chalmers (1831-1898).
Chalmers served, at times acrimoniously, under Forrest as
a division commander throughout Hood's 1864 Tennessee
Campaign. Image from Jordan and Pryor's *The Campaigns of
Lieut.-Gen. N.B. Forrest.*

Confederate General William H. "Red" Jackson (1835-1903). In
Feb. 1865 he was put in command of all the Tennessee cavalry in
Forrest's department. In 1868 Jackson married the author's
cousin Selene Harding of Belle Meade Plantation in Nashville.
Image from Jordan and Pryor's *The Campaigns of Lieut.-Gen. N.B.
Forrest.*

Frederick Douglass (1818-1895), author, lecturer, abolitionist leader, and former *Northern* slave. Speaking for millions of 19th-Century blacks, on April 14, 1876, Douglass gave a public speech at Washington, D.C., informing the world as to what African-Americans really thought of Abraham Lincoln. Correctly calling him a racial bigot whose only true interests were the white race and blocking the *extension* of slavery, Douglass declared: "In Lincoln's interests, in his associations, in his habits of thought, and in his prejudices . . . he was preeminently the white man's president. . . . He was neither our man or our model. . . . Our race was not the special object of his consideration." Douglass could not have made such comments about General Forrest. Photo courtesy Library of Congress.

Historical marker, Columbia, Tennessee. Photo copyright © Lochlainn Seabrook.

A sketch of Nathan Bedford Forrest "in early life."  Image from Mathes' *General Forrest*.

Forrest and his men captured and piloted several Union boats like these for several days during the General's "horse marines" period in the Fall of 1864. With Confederate flags flying proudly from Union mastheads, it was the only time in Lincoln's War in which a cavalry became a navy. Image from *Battles and Leaders of the Civil War.*

Forrest's cavalry taking down another Yankee battery. Image from Wyeth's *Life of General Nathan Bedford Forrest.*

Lieutenant Nat Baxter, Jr., of Freeman's Battery, a company that served with distinction in Forrest's artillery during numerous engagements. Image from Wyeth's *Life of General Nathan Bedford Forrest*.

# BY TELEGRAPH.

## DAY DISPATCHES.

### Gen. Forrest Tenders His Services.

MEMPHIS, December 9.—Gen. N. B. Forrest, in view of possible war with Spain, made a formal tender of his services to Gen. Sherman, who, writing a characteristic letter to Gen. Forrest, said he had sent the letter to the War Department with this endorsement:

"Respectfully referred to the Secretary of War for file. Among the hundreds of offers that come to me, I deem this worthy of a place among the archives to wait coming events. I regard N. B. Forrest as one of the most extraordinary men developed by our civil war, and were it left to me, in the event of war requiring cavalry, I would unhesitatingly accept his services and give him a prominent place. I believe now he would fight against our national enemies as vehemently as he did against us, and that is saying enough."

[Signed] "W. T. SHERMAN."

General Sherman don't believe there will be war. Neither government wants war.

From the *Macon Telegraph and Messenger*, Dec. 9, 1873. Note Sherman's comments about Forrest.

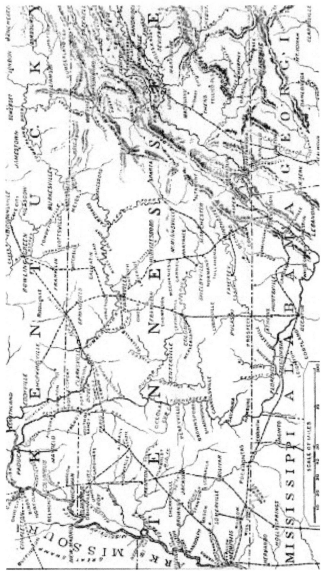

A map of Tennessee showing the area of some of Forrest's military operations around the Volunteer State. Image from Wyeth's *Life of General Nathan Bedford Forrest*.

Confederate General Simon B. Buckner (1823-1914), who surrendered to Grant at the Battle of Fort Donelson against the advice of Forrest. Image from *Battles and Leaders of the Civil War*.

The death of one of Forrest's many warhorses. Image from Wyeth's *Life of General Nathan Bedford Forrest*.

The waterfront at Fort Pillow as it might have looked to Forrest and his troops April 12, 1864, at the start of the notorious battle. Image from *Battles and Leaders of the Civil War*.

For years Yankee war criminal General William T. Sherman (above) tried to find and kill Forrest. Naturally, all of his attempts ended in failure. After Lincoln's War, like Grant, Sherman had little choice but to compliment the Confederate chieftain for his audacity and agility on the battlefield. Image from Gibson's *A School History of the United States of America*.

Six important Confederate commanders. Forrest served with Bragg and Hood amidst a series of rancorous interpersonal incidents. One wonders what might have transpired had he served under the ingenious and magnanimous Lee. Image from Gibson's *A School History of the United States of America*.

Forrest leading one of his many terrifying cavalry attacks against the Yanks. The General's reputation for fearlessness and aggression was widely known, causing some Union regiments to immediately surrender upon hearing that his troops were bearing down on their position. Image from Wyeth's *Life of General Nathan Bedford Forrest*.

# BIBLIOGRAPHY

Abbott, John Stevens Cabot. *The Life of General Ulysses S. Grant*. Boston, MA: B. B. Russell, 1868.

Adams, Charles. *When in the Course of Human Events: Arguing the Case for Southern Secession*. Lanham, MD: Rowman and Littlefield, 2000.

Adams, Francis D., and Barry Sanders. *Alienable Rights: The Exclusion of African Americans in a White Man's Land, 1619-2000*. 2003. New York, NY: Perennial, 2004 ed.

Adams, Henry (ed.). *Documents Relating to New-England Federalism, 1800-1815*. Boston, MA: Little, Brown, and Co., 1877.

——. *The Education of Henry Adams: An Autobiography*. Boston, MA: Houghton Mifflin Co., 1918.

Adams, Nehemiah, Rev. *A South-side View of Slavery: Three Months at the South, in 1854*. Boston, MA: T. R. Marvin, 1855.

Alexander, William T. *History of the Colored Race in America*. Kansas City, MO: Palmetto Publishing, 1887.

Alotta, Robert I. *Civil War Justice: Union Army Executions Under Lincoln*. Shippensburg, PA: White Mane, 1989.

*An Appeal From the Colored Men of Philadelphia to the President of the United States*. N.p.: Philadelphia, PA, 1862.

Anderson, John Q. (ed.). *Brokenburn: The Journal of Kate Stone, 1861-1868*. 1955. Baton Rouge, LA: Louisiana State University Press, 1995 ed.

Andrews, Sidney. *The South Since the War: As Shown by Fourteen Weeks of Travel and Observation*. Boston, MA: Ticknor and Fields, 1866.

Annunzio, Frank (chairman). *The Capitol: A Pictorial History of the Capitol and of the Congress*. Washington D.C.: U.S. Joint Committee on Printing, 9th ed., 1983.

Anonymous. *Life of John C. Calhoun: Presenting a Condensed History of Political Events, From 1811 to 1843*. New York, NY: Harper and Brothers, 1843.

Arnold, Isaac Newton. *The History of Abraham Lincoln, and the Overthrow of Slavery*. Chicago, IL: Clarke and Co., 1866.

Ashdown Paul, and Edward Caudill. *The Myth of Nathan Bedford Forrest*. 2005. Lanham, MD: Rowman and Littlefield, 2006 ed.

Ashe, Captain Samuel A'Court. *A Southern View of the Invasion of the Southern States and War of 1861-1865*. 1935. Crawfordville, GA: Ruffin Flag Company, 1938 ed.

Ashworth, John. *Slavery, Capitalism, and Politics in the Antebellum Republic*. 2 vols. New York, NY: Cambridge University Press, 2007.

Astor, Gerald. *The Right to Fight: A History of African Americans in the Military*. Cambridge, MA: Da Capo, 2001.

Bailey, Anne C. *African Voices of the Atlantic Slave Trade: Beyond the Silence and the Shame*. Boston, MA: Beacon Press, 2005.

Bailey, Hugh C. *Hinton Rowan Helper: Abolitionist-Racist*. Tuscaloosa, AL: University of Alabama Press, 1965.

Bailyn, Bernard, Robert Dallek, David Brion Davis, David Herbert Donald, John L. Thomas, and Gordon S. Wood. *The Great Republic: A History of the American People*. 1977. Lexington, MA: D. C. Heath and Co., 1992 ed.

Baker, George E. (ed.). *The Works of William H. Seward*. 5 vols. 1861. Boston, MA: Houghton, Mifflin and Co., 1888 ed.

Bancroft, Frederic. *The Life of William H. Seward*. 2 vols. New York, NY: Harper and Brothers, 1900.

——. *Slave-Trading in the Old South*. Baltimore, MD: J. H. Furst, 1931.

Bancroft, Frederic, and William A. Dunning (eds.). *The Reminiscences of Carl Schurz*. 3 vols. New York, NY: McClure Co., 1909.

Barnes, Gilbert H., and Dwight L. Dumond (eds.). *Letters of Theodore Dwight Weld, Angelina Grimké Weld and Sarah Grimké, 1822-1844*. 2 vols. New York, NY: D. Appleton-Century Co., 1934.

Barney, William L. *Flawed Victory: A New Perspective on the Civil War*. New York, NY: Praeger Publishers, 1975.

Barrow, Charles Kelly, J. H. Segars, and R. B. Rosenburg (eds.). *Black Confederates*. 1995. Gretna, LA: Pelican Publishing Co., 2001 ed.

——. *Forgotten Confederates: An Anthology About Black Southerners*. Saint Petersburg, FL: Southern Heritage Press, 1997.

Barton, William E. *The Soul of Abraham Lincoln*. New York, NY: George H. Doran, 1920.

Basler, Roy Prentice (ed.). *Abraham Lincoln: His Speeches and Writings*. 1946. New York, NY: Da Capo Press, 2001 ed.

—— (ed.). *The Collected Works of Abraham Lincoln*. 9 vols. New Brunswick, NJ: Rutgers University Press, 1953.

Bateman, William O. *Political and Constitutional Law of the United States of America*. St. Louis, MO: G. I. Jones and Co., 1876.

Beard, Charles A., and Mary R. Beard. *The Rise of American Civilization*. 1927. New York, NY: MacMillan, 1930 ed.

Beard, Charles A., and Birl E. Schultz. *Documents on the State-Wide Initiative, Referendum and Recall*. New York, NY: Macmillan, 1912.

Bearss, Edwin C. *Forrest at Brice's Cross Roads*. Dayton, OH: Morningside Bookshop, 1979.

Beck, Glenn. *Glenn Beck's Common Sense: The Case Against an Out-of-Control Government, Inspired by Thomas Paine*. New York, NY: Threshold, 2009.

Bedwell, Randall (ed.). *May I Quote You, General Forrest? Observations and Utterances from the South's Great Generals*. Nashville, TN: Cumberland House, 1997.

Bell, Madison Smartt. *Devil's Dream: A Novel About Nathan Bedford Forrest*. New York, NY: Pantheon, 2009.

Bennett, Lerone. *Forced into Glory: Abraham Lincoln's White Dream*. Chicago, IL: Johnson Publishing Co., 2000.

Benton, Thomas Hart. *Thirty Years View; or A History of the Working of the American Government for Thirty Years, From 1820 to 1850*. 2 vols. New York, NY: D. Appleton and Co., 1854.

Bergh, Albert Ellery (ed.). *The Writings of Thomas Jefferson*. 20 vols. Washington, D.C.: Thomas Jefferson Memorial Association of the U.S., 1905.

Bernhard, Winfred E. A. *Political Parties in American History* (Vol. 1: 1789-1828). New York, NY: G. P. Putnams' Sons, 1973.

Berry, Wendell. *The Unsettling of America: Culture and Agriculture*. San Francisco, CA: Sierra Club Books, 1996.

Berwanger, Eugene H. *The Frontier Against Slavery: Western Anti-Negro Prejudice and the Slavery Extension Controversy*. 1967. Urbana, IL: University of Illinois Press, 1971, ed.

Beschloss, Michael R. *Presidential Courage: Brave Leaders and How They Changed America, 1789-1989*. New York, NY: Simon and Schuster, 2007.

Beveridge, Albert Jeremiah. *Abraham Lincoln: 1809-1858*. 2 vols. Boston, MA: Houghton Mifflin, 1928.

Black, Col. Robert W. *Cavalry Raids of the Civil War*. Mechanicsburg, PA: Stackpole Books, 2004.

Blackerby, Hubert R. *Blacks in Blue and Gray*. New Orleans, LA: Portals Press, 1979.

Blandin, Isabella Margaret Elizabeth. *History of Higher Education of Women of the South, Prior to 1860*. New York, NY: Neale Publishing Co., 1909.

Blassingame, John W. *The Slave Community: Plantation Life in the Antebellum South*. 1972. New York, NY: Oxford University Press, 1974 ed.

Bledsoe, Albert Taylor. *An Essay on Liberty and Slavery*. Philadelphia, PA: J. B. Lippincott and Co., 1856.

——. *A Theodicy; or a Vindication of the Divine Glory, as Manifested in the Constitution and Government of the Moral World*. New York, NY: Carlton and Porter, 1856.

——. *Is Davis a Traitor; or Was Secession a Constitutional Right Previous to the War of 1861?* Richmond, VA: Hermitage Press, Inc., 1907.

Blee, Kathleen M. *Women of the Klan: Racism and Gender in the 1920s*. 1991. Berkeley, CA: University of California Press, 1992 ed.

Blight, David W. *Frederick Douglass' Civil War: Keeping Faith in Jubilee*. 1989. Baton Rouge, LA: Louisiana State University Press, 1991 ed.

Bliss, William Dwight Porter (ed.). *The Encyclopedia of Social Reform*. New York, NY: Funk and Wagnalls, 1897.

Boatner, Mark Mayo. *The Civil War Dictionary*. 1959. New York, NY: David McKay Co., Inc., 1988 ed.

Bode, Carl, and Malcolm Cowley (eds.). *The Portable Emerson*. 1941. Harmondsworth, UK: Penguin, 1981 ed.

Boorstin, Daniel J. *The Discoverers: A History of Man's Search to Know His World and Himself*. 1983. New

York, NY: Vintage, 1985 ed.

Bowen, Catherine Drinker. *John Adams and the American Revolution*. 1949. New York, NY: Grosset and Dunlap, 1977 ed.

Bowers, John. *Chickamauga and Chattanooga: The Battles that Doomed the Confederacy*. New York, NY: HarperCollins, 1994.

Bowman, John S. *The Civil War Day by Day: An Illustrated Almanac of America's Bloodiest War*. 1989. New York, NY: Dorset Press, 1990 ed.

——. *Encyclopedia of the Civil War* (ed.). 1992. North Dighton, MA: JG Press, 2001 ed.

Bowman, Virginia McDaniel. *Historic Williamson County: Old Homes and Sites*. 1971. Franklin, TN: Territorial Press, 1989 ed.

Bradford, James C. (ed.). *Atlas of American Military History*. New York, NY: Oxford University Press, 2003.

Bradford, Ned (ed.). *Battles and Leaders of the Civil War* (1-vol. ed.). New York, NY: Appleton-Century-Crofts, 1956.

Bradley, Michael R. *Nathan Bedford Forrest's Escort and Staff*. Gretna, LA: Pelican Publishing Co., 2006.

Bradshaw, Wayne. *The Civil War Diary of William R. Dyer: A Member of Forrest's Escort*. Charleston, SC: BookSurge, 2009.

Brady, Cyrus Townsend. *Three Daughters of the Confederacy*. New York, NY: G. W. Dillingham, 1905.

Brady, James S. (ed.). *Ronald Reagan: A Man True to His Word - A Portrait of the 40th President of the United States In His Own Words*. Washington, D.C.: National Federation of Republican Women, 1984.

Brandt, Robert S. *Touring the Middle Tennessee Backroads*. 1995. Winston-Salem, NC: John F. Blair, 2005 ed.

Brent, Linda. *The Deeper Wrong; or Incidents in the Life of a Slave Girl, Written by Herself*. London, UK: W. Tweedie, 1862.

Brinkley, Alan. *The Unfinished Nation: A Concise History of the American People*. 1993. Boston, MA: McGraw-Hill, 2000 ed.

Brockett, Linus Pierpont. *The Life and Times of Abraham Lincoln, Sixteenth President of the United States*. Philadelphia, PA: Bradley and Co., 1865.

Brooks, Gertrude Zeth. *First Ladies of the White House*. Chicago, IL: Charles Hallberg and Co., 1969.

Brooksher, William R., and David K. Snider. *Glory at a Gallop: Tales of the Confederate Cavalry*. 1993. Gretna, LA: Pelican Publishing Co., 2002 ed.

Brown, Dee. *Bury My Heart at Wounded Knee: An Indian History of the American West*. 1970. New York, NY: Owl Books, 1991 ed.

Brown, Rita Mae. *High Hearts*. New York, NY: Bantam, 1987.

Brown, William Wells. *The Black Man: His Antecedents, His Genius, and His Achievements*. New York, NY: Thomas Hamilton, 1863.

Browne, Ray B., and Lawrence A. Kreiser, Jr. *The Civil War and Reconstruction*. Westport, CT: Greenwood Publishing, 2003.

Browning, Robert, M., Jr. *Forrest: The Confederacy's Relentless Warrior*. Dulles, VA: Brassey's, Inc., 2004.

Bruce, Philip Alexander. *The Plantation Negro As a Freeman*. New York, NY: G. P. Putnam's Sons, 1889.

Brunner, Borgna (ed.). *The Time Almanac* (1999). Boston, MA: Information Please, 1998.

Bryan, William Jennings. *The Commoner Condensed*. New York, NY: Abbey Press, 1902.

Buchanan, James. *The Works of James Buchanan*. 12 vols. Philadelphia, PA: J. B. Lippincott Co., 1911.

Buchanan, Patrick J. *A Republic, Not an Empire: Reclaiming America's Destiny*. Washington, D.C.: Regnery, 1999.

Buckingham, James Silk. *The Slave States of America*. 2 vols. London, UK: Fisher, Son, and Co., 1842.

Buckley, Gail. *American Patriots: The Story of Blacks in the Military from the Revolution to Desert Storm*. New York, NY: Random House, 2001.

Bultman, Bethany. *Redneck Heaven: Portrait of a Vanishing Culture*. New York, NY: Bantam, 1996.

Burke, John. *Burke's Peerage: Genealogical and Heraldic History of the Baronetage and Knightage* (104th ed.). 1826. London, UK: Waterlow and Sons, 1967 ed.

Burlingame, Michael. *The Inner World of Abraham Lincoln*. Champaign, IL: University of Illinois Press, 1997.

Burns, James MacGregor, and Jack Walter Peltason. *Government by the People: The Dynamics of American National, State, and Local Government*. 1952. Englewood Cliffs, NJ: Prentice-Hall, 1964 ed.

Burns, James MacGregor, Jack Walter Peltason, Thomas E. Cronin, David B. Magleby, and David M. O'Brien. *Government By the People* (National Version, 2001-2002 ed.). 1952. Upper Saddle River, NJ: Prentice Hall, 2002 ed.

Burton, Robert. *The Anatomy of Melancholy.* 3 vols. 1621. London, UK: George Bell and Sons, 1896 ed.

Bushnell, Horace. *The Census and Slavery, Thanksgiving Discourse, Delivered in the Chapel at Clifton Springs, New York, November 29, 1860.* Hartford, CT: L. E. Hunt, 1860.

Butler, Benjamin Franklin. *Butler's Book (Autobiography and Personal Reminiscences of Major-General Benjamin F. Butler: A Review of His Legal, Political, and Military Career).* Boston, MA: A. M. Thayer and Co., 1892.

Butler, Lindley S., and Alan D. Watson (eds.). *The North Carolina Experience: An Interpretive and Documentary History.* Chapel Hill, NC: University of North Carolina Press, 1984.

Calvert, Thomas H. *The Federal Statutes Annotated.* 10 vols. Northport, NY: Edward Thompson, 1905.

Campbell, Joseph (with Bill Moyers). *The Power of Myth.* New York, NY: Doubleday, 1988.

Cannon, Devereaux D., Jr. *The Flags of the Confederacy: An Illustrated History.* Memphis, TN: St. Luke's Press, 1988.

Carey, Matthew, Jr. (ed.). *The Democratic Speaker's Hand-Book.* Cincinnati, OH: Miami Print and Publishing Co., 1868.

Carlton, Frank Tracy. *Organized Labor in America.* New York, NY: D. Appleton and Co., 1920.

Carlyon, Richard. *A Guide to the Gods: An Essential Guide to World Mythology.* New York, NY: Quill, 1981.

Carpenter, Stephen D. *Logic of History: Five Hundred Political Texts, Being Concentrated Extracts of Abolitionism.* Madison, WI: Stephen D. Carpenter, 1864.

Cartmell, Donald. *Civil War 101.* New York, NY: Gramercy, 2001.

Cash, W. J. *The Mind of the South.* 1941. New York, NY: Vintage, 1969 ed.

Catton, Bruce. *The Coming Fury* (Vol. 1). 1961. New York, NY: Washington Square Press, 1967 ed.

——. *Terrible Swift Sword* (Vol. 2). 1963. New York, NY: Pocket Books, 1967 ed.

——. *A Stillness at Appomattox* (Vol. 3). 1953. New York, NY: Pocket Books, 1966 ed.

Celeste, Sister Mary. *The Old World's Gifts to the New.* 1932. Long Prairie, MN: Neumann Press, 1999 ed.

Chambers, Robert (ed.). *The Book of Days: A Miscellany of Popular Antiquities in Connection with the Calender.* 2 vols. London, UK: W. & R. Chambers, 1883.

Channing, Steven A. *Confederate Ordeal: The Southern Home Front.* 1984. Morristown, NJ: Time-Life Books, 1989 ed.

Chesnut, Mary. *A Diary From Dixie: As Written by Mary Boykin Chesnut, Wife of James Chesnut, Jr., United States Senator from South Carolina, 1859-1861, and afterward an Aide to Jefferson Davis and a Brigadier-General in the Confederate Army.* (Isabella D. Martin and Myrta Lockett Avary, eds.). New York, NY: D. Appleton and Co., 1905 ed.

——. *Mary Chesnut's Civil War.* 1860-1865 (Woodward, Comer Vann, ed.). New Haven, CT: Yale University Press, 1981 ed.

Chodes, John. *Destroying the Republic: Jabez Curry and the Re-Education of the Old South.* New York, NY: Algora, 2005.

Christian, George L. *Abraham Lincoln: An Address Delivered Before R. E. Lee Camp, No. 1 Confederate Veterans at Richmond, VA, October 29, 1909.* Richmond, VA: L. H. Jenkins, 1909.

Cimprich, John. *Fort Pillow, a Civil War Massacre, and Public Memory.* Baton Rouge, LA: Louisiana State University Press, 2005.

Cisco, Walter Brian. *War Crimes Against Southern Civilians.* Gretna, LA: Pelican Publishing Co., 2007.

*Civil War Book of Lists.* 1993. Edison, NJ: Castle Books, 2004 ed.

Civil War Society, The. *Civil War Battles: An Illustrated Encyclopedia.* 1997. New York, NY: Gramercy, 1999 ed.

Cluskey, Michael W. (ed.). *The Political Text-Book, or Encyclopedia.* Philadelphia, PA: Jas. B. Smith, 1859 ed.

Cmiel, Kenneth. *Democratic Eloquence: The Fight Over Popular Speech in Nineteenth-Century America.* Berkeley, CA: University of California Press, 1990.

Coe, Joseph. *The True American.* Concord, NH: I. S. Boyd, 1840.

Coffin, Charles Carleton. *Abraham Lincoln.* New York, NY: Harper and Brothers, 1893.

Coit, Margaret L. *John C. Calhoun: American Portrait.* Boston, MA: Sentry, 1950.

Collier, Christopher, and James Lincoln Collier. *Decision in Philadelphia: The Constitutional Convention of*

*1787*. 1986. New York, NY: Ballantine, 1987 ed.

Collins, Elizabeth. *Memories of the Southern States*. Taunton, UK: J. Barnicott, 1865.

Collins, John A. (ed.). *The Anti-Slavery Picknick: A Collection of Speeches, Poems, Dialogues and Songs Intended for Use in Schools and Anti-Slavery Meetings*. Boston, MA: H. W. Williams, 1842.

Commager, Henry Steele, and Erik Bruun (eds.). *The Civil War Archive: The History of the Civil War in Documents*. 1950. New York, NY: Black Dog and Leventhal, 1973 ed.

Conner, Frank. *The South Under Siege, 1830-2000: A History of the Relations Between the North and the South*. Newnan, GA: Collards Publishing Co., 2002.

Conway, Moncure Daniel. *Testimonies Concerning Slavery*. London, UK: Chapman and Hall, 1865.

Cooke, Alistair. *Alistair Cooke's America*. 1973. New York, NY: Alfred A. Knopf, 1984 ed.

Cooke, John Esten. *A Life of General Robert E. Lee*. New York, NY: D. Appleton and Co., 1871.

Cooper, William J., Jr. *Jefferson Davis, American*. New York, NY: Vintage Books, 2000.

——. (ed.). *Jefferson Davis: The Essential Writings*. New York, NY: Random House, 2003.

Cornish, Dudley Taylor. *The Sable Arm: Black Troops in the Union Army, 1861-1865*. 1956. Lawrence, KS: University Press of Kansas, 1987 ed.

Cottrell, Steve. *Civil War in Tennessee*. Gretna, LA: Pelican Publishing Co., 2001.

Cozzens, Peter. *This Terrible Sound: The Battle of Chickamauga*. Champaign, IL: University of Illinois Press, 1996.

Crallé, Richard Kenner. (ed.). *The Works of John C. Calhoun*. 6 vols. New York: NY: D. Appleton and Co., 1853-1888.

Craven, John J. *Prison Life of Jefferson Davis*. New York: NY: Carelton, 1866.

Crawford, Samuel Wylie. *The Genesis of the Civil War: The Story of Sumter, 1860-1861*. New York, NY: Charles L. Webster and Co., 1887.

Crocker, H. W., III. *The Politically Incorrect Guide to the Civil War*. Washington, D.C.: Regnery, 2008.

Cromie, Alice Hamilton. *A Tour Guide to the Civil War: The Complete State-by-State Guide to Battlegrounds, Landmarks, Museums, Relics, and Sites*. 1964. Nashville, TN: Rutledge Hill Press, 1990 ed.

Cromwell, John Wesley. *The Negro in American History: Men and Women Eminent in the Evolution of the American of African Descent*. Washington, D.C.: American Negro Academy, 1914.

Crutchfield, James A. *Franklin: A Photographic Recollection*. 2 vols. Franklin, TN: Canaday Enterprises, 1996.

Crutchfield, James A., and Robert Holladay. *Franklin: Tennessee's Handsomest Town*. Franklin, TN: Hillsboro Press, 1999.

Cummins, Joseph. *Anything For a Vote: Dirty Tricks, Cheap Shots, and October Surprises in U.S. Presidential Campaigns*. Philadelphia, PA: Quirk, 2007.

Current, Richard N. *The Lincoln Nobody Knows*. 1958. New York, NY: Hill and Wang, 1963 ed.

——. (ed.). *The Confederacy (Information Now Encyclopedia)*. 1993. New York, NY: Macmillan, 1998 ed.

Currotto, William F. *Wizard of the Saddle: Nathan Bedford Forrest*. N.p.: Patchwork Books, 1996.

Curry, Leonard P. *Blueprint for Modern America: Nonmilitary Legislation of the First Civil War Congress*. Nashville, TN: Vanderbilt University Press, 1968.

Curti, Merle, Willard Thorpe, and Carlos Baker (eds.). *American Issues: The Social Record*. 1941. Chicago, IL: J. B. Lippincott, 1960 ed.

Curtin, Philip D. *The Rise and Fall of the Plantation Complex: Essays in Atlantic History*. 1990. Cambridge, UK: Cambridge University Press, 1999 ed.

Curtis, George Ticknor. *Life of James Buchanan: Fifteenth President of the United States*. 2 vols. New York, NY: Harper and Brothers, 1883.

Curtis, William Eleroy. *Abraham Lincoln*. Philadelphia, PA: J. B. Lippincott Co., 1902.

Cushman, Horatio Bardwell. *History of the Choctaw, Chickasaw and Natchez Indians*. Greenville, TX: Headlight Printing House, 1899.

Custer, George Armstrong. *Wild Life on the Plains and Horrors of Indian Warfare*. St. Louis, MO: Excelsior Publishing, 1891.

Dabney, Robert Lewis. *A Defense of Virginia and the South*. Dahlonega, GA: Confederate Reprint Co., 1999.

Daniel, John M. *The Richmond Examiner During the War*. New York, NY: John M. Daniel, 1868.

Daniel, John W. *Life and Reminiscences of Jefferson Davis by Distinguished Men of His Time*. Baltimore, MD: R. H. Woodward, and Co., 1890.

Darwin, Charles. *On the Origin of Species By Means of Natural Selection*. London, UK: John Murray, 1866.

Daugherty, James. *Abraham Lincoln*. 1943. New York, NY: Scholastic Book Services, 1966 ed.

Davenport, Robert R. *Roots of the Rich and Famous: Real Cases of Unlikely Lineage*. Dallas, TX: Taylor Publishing Co., 1998.

Davidson, Basil. *The African Slave Trade*. 1961. Boston, MA: Back Bay Books, 1980 ed.

Davis, Jefferson. *The Rise and Fall of the Confederate Government*. 2 vols. New York, NY: D. Appleton and Co., 1881.

Davis, Kenneth C. *Don't Know Much About the Civil War: Everything You Need to Know About America's Greatest Conflict But Never Learned*. 1996. New York, NY: HarperCollins, 1997 ed.

Davis, Michael. *The Image of Lincoln in the South*. Knoxville, TN: University of Tennessee Press, 1971.

Davis, William C. *Jefferson Davis: The Man and His Hour*. New York, NY: HarperCollins, 1991.

——. *An Honorable Defeat: The Last Days of the Confederate Government*. New York, NY: Harcourt, 2001.

——. *Look Away: A History of the Confederate States of America*. 2002. New York, NY: Free Press, 2003 ed.

Davison, Eddy W., and Daniel Foxx. *Nathan Bedford Forrest: In Search of the Enigma*. Gretna, LA: Pelican Publishing Co., 2007.

Dawson, Sarah Morgan. *A Confederate Girl's Diary*. London, UK: William Heinemann, 1913.

Dean, Henry Clay. *Crimes of the Civil War, and Curse of the Funding System*. Baltimore, MD: William T. Smithson, 1869.

De Angelis, Gina. *It Happened in Washington, D.C.* Guilford, CT: The Globe Pequot Press, 2004.

DeCaro, Louis A., Jr. *Fire From the Midst of You: A Religious Life of John Brown*. New York, NY: New York University Press, 2002.

Deems, Edward Mark. *Holy-Days and Holidays: A Treasury of Historical Material, Sermons in Full and Brief, Suggestive Thoughts, and Poetry*. New York, NY: Funk and Wagnalls, 1902.

De Forest, John William. *A Volunteer's Adventures: A Union Captain's Record of the Civil War*. 1946. North Haven, CT: Archon, 1970 ed.

Delbanco, Andrew. *The Portable Abraham Lincoln*. New York, NY: Penguin, 1992.

Deloria, Vine, Jr. *Custer Died for Your Sins: An Indian Manifesto*. 1969. New York, NY: Avon, 1973 ed.

Denney, Robert E. *The Civil War Years: A Day-by-Day Chronicle of the Life of a Nation*. 1992. New York, NY: Sterling Publishing, 1994 ed.

Denson, John V. (ed.). *Reassessing the Presidency: The Rise of the Executive System and the Decline of Freedom*. Auburn, AL: Mises Institute, 2001.

DeRosa, Marshall L. *The Confederate Constitution of 1861: An Inquiry Into American Constitutionalism*. Columbia, MO: University of Missouri Press, 1991.

Diamond, Jared. *Guns, Germs, and Steel: The Fate of Human Societies*. 1997. New York, NY: W. W. Norton, 1999 ed.

Dicey, Edward. *Six Months in the Federal States*. 2 vols. London, UK: Macmillan and Co., 1863.

DiLorenzo, Thomas J. "The Great Centralizer: Abraham Lincoln and the War Between the States." *The Independent Review*, Vol. 3, No. 2, Fall 1998, pp. 243-271.

——. *The Real Lincoln: A New Look at Abraham Lincoln, His Agenda, and an Unnecessary War*. Three Rivers, MI: Three Rivers Press, 2003.

——. *Lincoln Unmasked: What You're Not Supposed to Know About Dishonest Abe*. New York, NY: Crown Forum, 2006.

——. *Hamilton's Curse: How Jefferson's Archenemy Betrayed the American Revolution—and What It Means for America Today*. New York, NY: Crown Forum, 2008.

Dinkins, James. *1861 to 1865, By an Old Johnnie: Personal Recollections and Experiences in the Confederate Army*. Cincinnati, OH: Robert Clarke, 1897.

Doddridge, Joseph. *Notes on the Settlement and Indian Wars of the Western Parts of Virginia and Pennsylvania, From 1763 to 1783, Inclusive*. Albany, NY: Joel Munsell, 1876.

Donald, David Herbert. *Lincoln Reconsidered: Essays on the Civil War Era*. 1947. New York, NY: Vintage, 1989 ed.

——. (ed.). *Why the North Won the Civil War*. 1960. New York, NY: Collier, 1962 ed.

——. *Lincoln*. New York, NY: Simon and Schuster, 1995.

Dorward, David. *Scottish Surnames: A Guide to the Family Names of Scotland*. Glasgow, Scotland: HarperCollins, 1995.

Douglas, Henry Kyd. *I Rode With Stonewall: The War Experiences of the Youngest Member of Jackson's Staff*.

1940. Chapel Hill, NC: University of North Carolina Press, 1968 ed.

Douglass, Frederick. *Narrative of the Life of Frederick Douglass: An American Slave*. 1845. New York, NY: Signet, 1997 ed.

——. *The Life and Times of Frederick Douglass, From 1817 to 1882*. London, UK: Christian Age Office, 1882.

Drescher, Seymour, and Stanley L. Engerman (eds.). *A Historical Guide to World Slavery*. New York, NY: Oxford University Press, 1998.

DuBose, John Witherspoon. *General Joseph Wheeler and the Army of Tennessee*. New York, NY: Neale Publishing Co., 1912.

Duff, Mountstuart E. Grant. *Notes From a Diary, 1851-1872*. 2 vols. London, UK: John Murray, 1897.

Duke, Basil W. *Reminiscences of General Basil W. Duke, C.S.A.* New York, NY: Doubleday, Page and Co., 1911.

Dunbar, Rowland (ed.). *Jefferson Davis, Constitutionalist: His Letters, Papers, and Speeches*. 10 vols. Jackson, MS: Mississippi Department of Archives and History, 1923.

Durden, Robert F. *The Gray and the Black: The Confederate Debate on Emancipation*. Baton Rouge, LA: Louisiana State University Press, 1972.

Early, Jubal A. *A Memoir of the Last Year of the War for Independence in the Confederate States of America*. Lynchburg, VA: Charles W. Button, 1867.

Eaton, Clement. *A History of the Southern Confederacy*. 1945. New York, NY: Free Press, 1966 ed.

——. *Jefferson Davis*. New York, NY: Free Press, 1977.

Eaton, John, and Ethel Osgood Mason. *Grant, Lincoln and the Freedmen: Reminiscences of the Civil War, With Special Reference to the Work of the Contrabands and Freedmen of the Mississippi Valley*. New York, NY: Longmans, Green, and Co., 1907.

Eckert, Allan W. *The Frontiersman: A Narrative*. Boston, MA: Little, Brown and Co., 1967.

Edmonds, Franklin Spencer. *Ulysses S. Grant*. Philadelphia, PA: George W. Jacobs and Co., 1915.

Elliot, Jonathan. *The Debates in the Several State Conventions on the Adoption of the Federal Constitution, As Recommended by the General Convention at Philadelphia in 1787*. 5 vols. Philadelphia, PA: J. B. Lippincott, 1891.

Elliott, E. N. *Cotton is King, and Pro-Slavery Arguments: Comprising the Writings of Hammond, Harper, Christy, Stringfellow, Hodge, Bledsoe, and Cartwright, on this Important Subject*. Augusta, GA: Pritchard, Abbott and Loomis, 1860.

Ellis, Joseph J. *American Sphinx: The Character of Thomas Jefferson*. 1996. New York, NY: Vintage, 1998 ed.

——. *Founding Brothers: The Revolutionary Generation*. 2000. New York, NY: Vintage, 2002 ed.

Emerson, Bettie Alder Calhoun. *Historic Southern Monuments: Representative Memorials of the Heroic Dead of the Southern Confederacy*. New York, NY: Neale Publishing Co., 1911.

Emerson, Ralph Waldo. *The Complete Works of Ralph Waldo Emerson*. 12 vols. 1878. Boston, MA: Houghton, Mifflin and Co., 1904 ed.

——. *Journals of Ralph Waldo Emerson*. 10 vols. Edward Waldo Emerson and Waldo Emerson Forbes, eds. Boston, MA: Houghton, Mifflin and Co., 1910.

——. *The Journals and Miscellaneous Notebooks of Ralph Waldo Emerson*. 16 vols. Cambridge, MA: Belknap Press, 1975.

Emison, John Avery. *Lincoln Über Alles: Dictatorship Comes to America*. Gretna, LA: Pelican Publishing Co., 2009.

*Encyclopedia Britannica: A New Survey of Universal Knowledge*. 1768. Chicago, IL/London, UK: Encyclopedia Britannica, 1955 ed.

Escott, Paul D. (ed.). *North Carolinians in the Era of the Civil War and Reconstruction*. Chapel Hill, NC: University of North Carolina Press, 2008.

Evans, Clement Anselm (ed.). *Confederate Military History*. 12 vols. Atlanta, GA: Confederate Publishing Co., 1899.

Evans, Eli N. *Judah P. Benjamin: The Jewish Confederate*. 1988. New York, NY: Free Press, 1989 ed.

Evans, Lawrence B. (ed.). *Writings of George Washington*. New York, NY: G. P. Putnam's Sons, 1908.

Farrar, Victor John. *The Annexation of Russian America to the United States*. Washington D.C.: W. F. Roberts, 1937.

Farrow, Anne, Joel Lang, and Jennifer Frank. *Complicity: How the North Promoted, Prolonged, and Profited from Slavery*. New York, NY: Ballantine, 2005.

Faulkner, William. *The Unvanquished*. 1934. New York, NY: Vintage, 1966 ed.

Faust, Patricia L. (ed.). *Historical Times Illustrated Encyclopedia of the Civil War*. New York, NY: Harper and Row, 1986.

Fay, Edwin Hedge. *This Infernal War: The Confederate Letters of Edwin H. Fay*. Austin, TX: University of Texas Press, 1958.

Fehrenbacher, Don E. (ed.). *Abraham Lincoln: A Documentary Portrait Through His Speeches and Writings*. New York, NY: Signet, 1964.

——. *Abraham Lincoln: Speeches and Writings, 1859-1865*. New York, NY: Library of America, 1989.

Fields, Annie (ed.) *Life and Letters of Harriet Beecher Stowe*. Cambridge, MA: Riverside Press, 1897.

Findlay, Bruce, and Esther Findlay. *Your Rugged Constitution: How America's House of Freedom is Planned and Built*. 1950. Stanford, CA: Stanford University Press, 1951 ed.

Finkelman, Paul. *Dred Scott v. Sanford: A Brief History With Documents*. Boston, MA: Bedford Books, 1997.

Fisher, John E. *They Rode With Forrest and Wheeler: A Chronicle of Five Tennessee Brothers' Service in the Confederate Western Cavalry*. Jefferson, NC: McFarland and Co., 1995.

Fite, Emerson David. *Social and Industrial Conditions in the North During the Civil War*. New York, NY: Macmillan, 1910.

——. *The Presidential Election of 1860*. New York, NY: MacMillan, 1911.

Fleming, Walter Lynwood. *Civil War and Reconstruction in Alabama*. New York, NY: Macmillan, 1905.

Flood, Charles Bracelen. *1864: Lincoln At the Gates of History*. New York, NY: Simon and Schuster, 2009.

Fogel, Robert William. *Without Consent or Contract: The Rise and Fall of American Slavery*. New York, NY: W. W. Norton, 1989.

Fogel, Robert William, and Stanley L. Engerman. *Time on the Cross: The Economics of American Negro Slavery*. Boston, MA: Little, Brown, and Co., 1974.

Foley, John P. (ed.). *The Jeffersonian Cyclopedia*. New York, NY: Funk and Wagnalls, 1900.

Foner, Eric. *Free Soil, Free Labor, Free Men: The Ideology of the Republican Party Before the Civil War*. New York, NY: Oxford University Press, 1970.

——. *Reconstruction: America's Unfinished Revolution, 1863-1877*. 1988. New York, NY: Harper and Row, 1989 ed.

Foner, Philip S., and Robert James Branham (eds.). *Lift Every Voice: African American Oratory, 1787-1900*. Tuscaloosa, AL: University of Alabama Press, 1998.

Foote, Shelby. *The Civil War: A Narrative, Fort Sumter to Perryville, Vol. I*. 1958. New York, NY: Vintage, 1986, ed.

——. *The Civil War: A Narrative, Fredericksburg to Meridian, Vol. II*. 1963. New York, NY: Vintage, 1986, ed.

——. *The Civil War: A Narrative, Red River to Appomattox, Vol. III*. 1974. New York, NY: Vintage, 1986, ed.

Ford, Paul Leicester (ed.). *The Works of Thomas Jefferson*. 12 vols. New York, NY: G. P. Putnam's Sons, 1904.

Ford, Worthington Chauncey (ed.). *A Cycle of Adams Letters*. 2 vols. Boston, MA: Houghton Mifflin, 1920.

Forman, S. E. *The Life and Writings of Thomas Jefferson*. Indianapolis, IN: Bowen-Merrill, 1900.

Förster, Stig, and Jörg Nagler (eds.). *On the Road to Total War: The American Civil War and the German Wars of Unification, 1861-1871*. 1997. Cambridge, UK: Cambridge University Press, 2002 ed.

Foster, John W. *A Century of American Diplomacy*. Boston, MA: Houghton, Mifflin and Co., 1901.

Fowler, John D. *The Confederate Experience Reader: Selected Documents and Essays*. New York, NY: Routledge, 2007.

Fowler, William Chauncey. *The Sectional Controversy; or Passages in the Political History of the United States, Including the Causes of the War Between the Sections*. New York, NY: Charles Scribner, 1864.

Fox-Genovese, Elizabeth. *Within the Plantation Household: Black and White Women of the Old South (Gender and American Culture)*. Chapel Hill, NC: University of North Carolina Press, 1988.

Fox, Gustavus Vasa. *Confidential Correspondence of Gustavus Vasa Fox, Assistant Secretary of the Navy, 1861-1865* (Vol. 1). 1918. New York, NY: Naval History Society, 1920 ed.

Franklin, Benjamin. *The Complete Works of Benjamin Franklin*. 10 vols. New York, NY: G. P. Putnam's Sons, 1887.

Franklin, John Hope. *Reconstruction After the Civil War*. Chicago, IL: University of Chicago Press, 1961.

Fremantle, Arthur James. *Three Months in the Southern States, April-June, 1863*. New York, NY: John

Bradburn, 1864.

Friedman, Saul S. *Jews and the American Slave Trade*. New Brunswick, NJ: Transaction, 2000.

Fuchs, Richard L. *An Unerring Fire: The Massacre at Fort Pillow*. Madison, NJ: Fairleigh Dickinson University Press, 1994.

Furguson, Ernest B. *Freedom Rising: Washington in the Civil War*. 2004. New York, NY: Vintage, 2005 ed.

Furnas, J. C. *The Americans: A Social History of the United States, 1587-1914*. New York, NY: G. P. Putnam's Sons, 1969.

Garland, Hugh A. *The Life of John Randolph of Roanoke*. New York, NY: D. Appleton and Co., 1874.

Garraty, John A. (ed.). *Historical Viewpoints: Notable Articles From American Heritage* (Vol. 1 to 1877). 1970. New York, NY: Harper and Row, 1979 ed.

Garraty, John A., and Robert A. McCaughey. *A Short History of the American Nation*. 1966. New York, NY: HarperCollins, 1989 ed.

Garrett, William Robertson, and Robert Ambrose Halley. *The Civil War From a Southern Standpoint*. Philadelphia, PA: George Barrie and Sons, 1905.

Garrison, Webb B. *Civil War Trivia and Fact Book*. Nashville, TN: Rutledge Hill Press, 1992.

——. *The Lincoln No One Knows: The Mysterious Man Who Ran the Civil War*. Nashville, TN: Rutledge Hill Press, 1993.

——. *Civil War Curiosities: Strange Stories, Oddities, Events, and Coincidences*. Nashville, TN: Rutledge Hill Press, 1994.

——. *The Amazing Civil War*. Nashville, TN: Rutledge Hill Press, 1998.

Garrison, Wendell Phillips, and Francis Jackson Garrison. *William Lloyd Garrison, 1805-1879*. 4 vols. New York, NY: Century Co., 1889.

Garrison, William Lloyd. *Thoughts on African Colonization*. Boston, MA: Garrison and Knapp, 1832.

Gates, Henry Louis, Jr. (ed.) *The Classic Slave Narratives*. New York, NY: Mentor, 1987.

Gauss, John. *Black Flag! Black Flag!: The Battle at Fort Pillow*. Lanham, MD: University Press of America, 2003.

Genovese, Eugene D. *Roll, Jordan, Roll: The World the Slaves Made*. New York, NY: Pantheon, 1974.

Gentry, Claude. *General Nathan Bedford Forrest: The Boy and the Man*. Macon, GA: Magnolia, 1972.

Gerster, Patrick, and Nicholas Cords (eds.). *Myth and Southern History*. 2 vols. 1974. Champaign, IL: University of Illinois Press, 1989 ed.

Gibson, John W. *A School History of the United States of America*. 1897. Chicago, IL: A. Flanagan Co., 1913 ed.

Golay, Michael. *A Ruined Land: The End of the Civil War*. New York, NY: John Wiley and Sons, 1999.

Goodman, Nathan G. (ed.). *A Benjamin Franklin Reader*. New York, NY: Thomas Y. Crowell Co., 1945.

Gordon, Armistead Churchill. *Figures From American History: Jefferson Davis*. New York, NY: Charles Scribner's Sons, 1918.

Gower, Herschel, and Jack Allen (eds.). *Pen and Sword: The Life and Journals of Randal W. McGavock*. Nashville, TN: Tennessee Historical Commission, 1959.

Gragg, Rod. *The Illustrated Confederate Reader: Extraordinary Eyewitness Accounts by the Civil War's Southern Soldiers and Civilians*. New York, NY: Gramercy Books, 1989.

Graham, John Remington. *A Constitutional History of Secession*. Gretna, LA: Pelican Publishing Co., 2003.

——. *Blood Money: The Civil War and the Federal Reserve*. Gretna, LA: Pelican Publishing Co., 2006.

Grant, Arthur James. *Greece in the Age of Pericles*. London, UK: John Murray, 1893.

Grant, Michael, and John Hazel. *Who's Who in Classical Mythology*. 1973. New York, NY: Oxford University Press, 1993 ed.

Grant, Ulysses Simpson. *Personal Memoirs of U. S. Grant*. 2 vols. 1885-1886. New York, NY: Charles L. Webster and Co., 1886.

Gray, Robert, Rev. (compiler). *The McGavock Family: A Genealogical History of James McGavock and His Descendants, from 1760 to 1903*. Richmond, VA: W. E. Jones, 1903.

Gray, Thomas R. *The Confessions of Nat Turner: The Leader of the Late Insurrection in Southampton, Virginia*. Richmond, VA: Thomas R. Gray, 1831.

Greeley, Horace (ed.). *The Writings of Cassius Marcellus Clay*. New York, NY: Harper and Brothers, 1848.

——. *A History of the Struggle for Slavery Extension or Restriction in the United States From the Declaration of Independence to the Present Day*. New York, NY: Dix, Edwards and Co., 1856.

——. *The American Conflict: A History of the Great Rebellion in the United States, 1861-1865*. 2 vols. Hartford,

CT: O. D. Case and Co., 1867.

Green, Constance McLaughlin. *Eli Whitney and the Birth of American Technology*. Boston, MA: Little, Brown, and Company, 1956.

——. *Washington: A History of the Capital, 1800-1950*. 1962. Princeton, NJ: Princeton University Press, 1976 ed.

Greenberg, Martin H., and Charles G. Waugh (eds.). *The Price of Freedom: Slavery and the Civil War—Vol. One, The Demise of Slavery*. Nashville, TN: Cumberland House, 2000.

Greene, Lorenzo Johnston. *The Negro in Colonial New England, 1620-1776*. New York, NY: Columbia University Press, 1942.

Greenhow, Rose O'Neal. *My Imprisonment and the First Year of Abolition Rule at Washington*. London, UK: Richard Bentley, 1863.

Grimsley, Mark. *The Hard Hand of War: Union Military Policy Toward Southern Civilians, 1861-1865*. 1995. Cambridge, UK: Cambridge University Press, 1997 ed.

Grissom, Michael Andrew. *Southern By the Grace of God*. 1988. Gretna, LA: Pelican Publishing Co., 1995 ed.

Groom, Winston. *Shrouds of Glory - From Atlanta to Nashville: The Last Great Campaign of the Civil War*. New York, NY: Grove Press, 1995.

Guelzo, Allen C. *Abraham Lincoln As a Man of Ideas*. Carbondale, IL: Southern Illinois University Press, 2009.

Gwatkin, H. M., and J. P. Whitney (eds.). *The Cambridge Medieval History, Vol. 2: The Rise of the Saracens and the Foundation of the Western Empire*. New York, NY: Macmillan, 1913.

Hacker, Louis Morton. *The Shaping of the American Tradition*. New York, NY: Columbia University Press, 1947.

Hafendorfer, Kenneth A. *Nathan Bedford Forrest: The Distant Storm - The Murfreesboro Raid of July 13, 1862*. Louisville, KY: KH Press, 1997.

Hall, B. C., and C. T. Wood. *The South: A Two-step Odyssey on the Backroads of the Enchanted Land*. New York, NY: Touchstone, 1996.

Hall, Kermit L. (ed). *The Oxford Companion to the Supreme Court of the United States*. New York, NY: Oxford University Press, 1992.

Hamblin, Ken. *Pick a Better Country: An Unassuming Colored Guy Speaks His Mind About America*. New York, NY: Touchstone, 1997.

Hamilton, Alexander, James Madison, and John Jay. *The Federalist Papers*. New York, NY: Signet Classics, 2003.

Hamilton, Neil A. *Rebels and Renegades: A Chronology of Social and Political Dissent in the United States*. New York, NY: Routledge, 2002.

Hannity, Sean. *Let Freedom Ring: Winning the War of Liberty Over Liberalism*. New York, NY: HarperCollins, 2002.

Hansen, Harry. *The Civil War: A History*. 1961. Harmondsworth, UK: Mentor, 1991 ed.

Harding, Samuel Bannister. *The Contest Over the Ratification of the Federal Constitution in the State of Massachusetts*. New York, NY: Longmans, Green, and Co., 1896.

Harper, William, James Henry Hammond, William Gilmore Simms, and Thomas Roderick Dew. *The Pro-Slavery Argument, As Maintained by the Most Distinguished Writers of the Southern States*. Charleston, SC: Walker, Richards and Co., 1852.

Harrell, David Edwin, Jr., Edwin S. Gaustad, John B. Boles, Sally Foreman Griffith, Randall M. Miller, and Randall B. Woods. *Unto a Good Land: A History of the American People*. Grand Rapids, MI: William B. Eerdmans, 2005.

Harris, Joel Chandler. *Stories of Georgia*. New York, NY: American Book Co., 1896.

Harris, Norman Dwight. *The History of Negro Servitude in Illinois*. Chicago, IL: A. C. McClurg and Co., 1904.

Hartje, Robert G. *Van Dorn: The Life and Time of a Confederate General*. Nashville, TN: Vanderbilt University Press, 2007.

Hartzell, Josiah. *The Genesis of the Republican Party*. Canton, OH: (n.p.), 1890.

Harwell, Richard B. (ed.). *The Confederate Reader: How the South Saw the War*. 1957. Mineola, NY: Dover, 1989 ed.

Hawthorne, Julian (ed.). *Orations of American Orators*. 2 vols. New York, NY: Colonial Press, 1900.

Hawthorne, Julian, James Schouler, and Elisha Benjamin Andrews. *United States, From the Discovery of the North American Continent Up to the Present Time*. 9 vols. New York, NY: Co-operative Publication Society, 1894.

Hawthorne, Nathaniel. *The Works of Nathaniel Hawthorne*. 15 vols. 1850. Boston, MA: Houghton, Mifflin and Co., 1888 ed.

Haygood, Atticus G. *Our Brother in Black: His Freedom and His Future*. Nashville, TN: M. E. Church, 1896.

Hedrick, Joan D. (ed.). *The Oxford Harriet Beecher Stowe Reader*. New York, NY: Oxford University Press, 1999.

Helper, Hinton Rowan. *The Impending Crisis of the South: How to Meet It*. New York, NY: A. B. Burdick, 1860.

——. *Compendium of the Impending Crisis of the South*. New York, NY: A. B. Burdick, 1860.

——. *Nojoque: A Question for a Continent*. New York, NY: George W. Carleton, 1867.

——. *The Negroes in Negroland: The Negroes in America; and Negroes Generally*. New York, NY: George W. Carlton, 1868.

——. *Oddments of Andean Diplomacy and Other Oddments*. St. Louis, MO: W. S. Bryan, 1879.

Henderson, George Francis Robert. *Stonewall Jackson and the American Civil War*. 2 vols. London, UK: Longmans, Green, and Co., 1919.

Henry, Robert Selph. *The Story of the Confederacy*. 1931. New York, NY: Konecky and Konecky, 1999 ed.

——. (ed.). *As They Saw Forrest: Some Recollections and Comments of Contemporaries*. 1956. Wilmington, NC: Broadfoot Publishing Co., 1991 ed.

——. *First with the Most: Forrest*. New York, NY: Konecky and Konecky, 1992.

Henson, Josiah. *Father Henson's Story of His Own Life*. Boston, MA: John P. Jewett and Co., 1858.

Herndon, William H., and Jesse W. Weik. *Abraham Lincoln: The True Story of a Great Life*. 2 vols. New York, NY: D. Appleton and Co., 1892.

Hervey, Anthony. *Why I Wave the Confederate Flag, Written by a Black Man: The End of Niggerism and the Welfare State*. Oxford, UK: Trafford Publishing, 2006.

Hey, David. *The Oxford Guide to Family History*. Oxford, UK: Oxford University Press, 1993.

Hickey, William. *The Constitution of the United States*. Philadelphia, PA: T. K. and P. G. Collins, 1853.

Highsmith, Carol M. and Ted Landphair. *Civil War Battlefields and Landmarks: A Photographic Tour*. New York, NY: Random House, 2003.

Hills, Parker. *A Study in Warfighting: Nathan Bedford Forrest and the Battle of Brice's Crossroads*. Saline, MI: McNaughton and Gunn, 1996.

Hinkle, Don. *Embattled Banner: A Reasonable Defense of the Confederate Battle Flag*. Paducah, KY: Turner Publishing Co., 1997.

Hitler, Adolf. *Mein Kampf*. 2 vols. 1925, 1926. New York: NY: Reynal and Hitchcock, 1941 English translation ed.

Hofstadter, Richard. *The American Political Tradition, and the Men Who Made It*. New York, NY: Knopf, 1948.

Holland, Jesse J. *Black Men Built the Capitol: Discovering African-American History in and Around Washington, D.C.* Guilford, CT: The Globe Pequot Press, 2007.

Holland, Josiah Gilbert. *The Life of Abraham Lincoln*. Springfield, MA: Gurdon Bill, 1866.

Holland, Rupert Sargent (ed.). *Letters and Diary of Laura M. Towne: Written From the Sea Islands of South Carolina, 1862-1884*. Cambridge, MA: Riverside Press, 1912.

Holzer, Harold (ed.). *The Lincoln-Douglas Debates: The First Complete, Unexpurgated Text*. 1993. Bronx, NY: Fordham University Press, 2004 ed.

Hood, John Bell. *Advance and Retreat: Personal Experiences in the United States and Confederate States Armies*. New Orleans, LA: G. T. Beauregard, 1880.

Horn, Stanley F. *Invisible Empire: The Story of the Ku Klux Klan, 1866-1871*. 1939. Montclair, NJ: Patterson Smith, 1969 ed.

——. *The Decisive Battle of Nashville*. 1956. Baton Rouge, LA: Louisiana State University Press, 1991 ed.

Horwitz, Tony. *Confederates in the Attic: Dispatches from the Unfinished Civil War*. 1998. New York, NY: Vintage, 1999 ed.

Howe, Henry. *Historical Collections of Virginia*. Charleston, SC: William R. Babcock, 1852.

Howe, M. A. DeWolfe (ed.). *Home Letters of General Sherman*. New York, NY: Charles Scribner's Sons,

1909.

Hubbard, John Milton. *Notes of a Private.* St. Louis, MO: Nixon-Jones, 1911.

Hughes, Nathaniel Cheairs, Jr. *Brigadier General Tyree H. Bell, C.S.A.: Forrest's Fighting Lieutenant.* Knoxville, TN: University of Tennessee Press, 2004.

Hurmence, Belinda (ed.). *Before Freedom, When I Can Just Remember: Twenty-seven Oral Histories of Former South Carolina Slaves.* 1989. Winston-Salem, NC: John F. Blair, 2002 ed.

Hunt, John Gabriel (ed.). *The Essential Abraham Lincoln.* Avenel, NJ: Portland House, 1993.

Hurst, Jack. *Nathan Bedford Forrest: A Biography.* 1993. New York, NY: Vintage, 1994 ed.

Ingersoll, Thomas G., and Robert E. O'Connor. *Politics and Structure: Essential of American national Government.* North Scituate, MA: Duxbury Press, 1979.

Isaacson, Walter (ed.). *Profiles in Leadership: Historians on the Elusive Quality of Greatness.* New York, NY: W. W. Norton and Co., 2010.

Jahoda, Gloria. *The Trail of Tears: The Story of the American Indian Removals, 1813-1855.* 1975. New York, NY: Wings Book, 1995 ed.

Jefferson, Thomas. *Notes on the State of Virginia.* Boston, MA: H. Sprague, 1802.

——. *Thomas Jefferson's Farm Book.* (Edwin Morris Betts, ed.). Charlottesville, VA: Thomas Jefferson Memorial Foundation, 1999.

Jenkins, John S. *The Life of James Knox Polk, Late President of the United States.* Auburn, NY: James M. Alden, 1850.

Jensen, Merrill. *The New Nation: A History of the United States During the Confederation, 1781-1789.* New York, NY: Vintage, 1950.

——. *The Articles of Confederation: An Interpretation of the Social-Constitutional History of the American Revolution, 1774-1781.* Madison, WI: University of Wisconsin Press, 1959.

Jimerson, Randall C. *The Private Civil War: Popular Thought During the Sectional Conflict.* Baton Rouge, LA: Louisiana State University Press, 1988.

Johannsen, Robert Walter. *Lincoln, the South, and Slavery: The Political Dimension.* Baton Rouge, LA: Louisiana State University Press, 1991.

Johnson, Adam Rankin. *The Partisan Rangers of the Confederate States Army.* Louisville, KY: George G. Fetter, 1904.

Johnson, B. F. (pub.). *Makers of America: Biographies of Leading Men of Thought and Action* (Vol. 1). Washington, D.C.: B. F. Johnson, 1915.

Johnson, Benjamin Heber. *Making of the American West: People and Perspectives.* Santa Barbara, CA: ABC-Clio, 2007.

Johnson, Clint. *The Politically Incorrect Guide to the South (and Why It Will Rise Again).* Washington, D.C.: Regnery, 2006.

Johnson, Ludwell H. *North Against South: The American Iliad, 1848-1877.* 1978. Columbia, SC: Foundation for American Education, 1993 ed.

Johnson, Michael, and James L. Roark. *Black Masters: A Free Family of Color in the Old South.* New York, NY: W.W. Norton, 1984.

Johnson, Oliver. *William Lloyd Garrison and His Times.* 1879. Boston, MA: Houghton Mifflin and Co., 1881 ed.

Johnson, Robert Underwood (ed.). *Battles and Leaders of the Civil War.* 4 vols. New York, NY: The Century Co., 1884-1888.

Johnson, Thomas Cary. *The Life and Letters of Robert Lewis Dabney.* Richmond, VA: Presbyterian Committee of Publication, 1903.

Jones, John William. *Personal Reminiscences, Anecdotes, and Letters of Gen. Robert E. Lee.* New York, NY: D. Appleton and Co., 1874.

——. *The Davis Memorial Volume; Or Our Dead President, Jefferson Davis and the World's Tribute to His Memory.* Richmond, VA: B. F. Johnson, 1889.

Jones, Wilmer L. *Generals in Blue and Gray.* 2 vols. Westport, CT: Praeger, 2004.

Jordan, Ervin L. *Black Confederates and Afro-Yankees in Civil War Virginia.* Charlottesville, VA: University Press of Virginia, 1995.

Jordan, Thomas, and John P. Pryor. *The Campaigns of General Nathan Bedford Forrest and of Forrest's Cavalry.* New Orleans, LA: Blelock and Co., 1868.

Julian, George Washington. *Speeches on Political Questions*. New York, NY: Hurd and Houghton, 1872.

Kane, Joseph Nathan. *Facts About the Presidents: A Compilation of Biographical and Historical Data*. 1959. New York, NY: Ace, 1976 ed.

Katcher, Philip. *The Civil War Source Book*. 1992. New York, NY: Facts on File, 1995 ed.

——. *Brassey's Almanac: The American Civil War*. London, UK: Brassey's, 2003.

Kautz, August Valentine. *Customs of Service for Non-Commissioned Officers and Soldiers (as Derived from Law and Regulations and Practised in the Army of the United States)*. Philadelphia, PA: J. B. Lippincott and Co., 1864.

Keckley, Elizabeth. *Behind the Scenes, or Thirty Years a Slave, and Four Years in the White House*. New York, NY: G. W. Carlton and Co., 1868.

Kelly, Alfred H., Winfred A. Harbison, and Herman Belz. *The American Constitution: Its Origins and Development* (Vol. 2). 1965. New York, NY: W.W. Norton, 1991 ed.

Kennedy, James Ronald, and Walter Donald Kennedy. *The South Was Right!* Gretna, LA: Pelican Publishing Co., 1994.

Kennedy, Walter Donald. *Myths of American Slavery*. Gretna, LA: Pelican Publishing Co., 2003.

Kennett, Lee B. *Sherman: A Soldier's Life*. 2001. New York, NY: HarperCollins, 2002 ed.

Kettell, Thomas Prentice. *History of the Great Rebellion*. Hartford, CT: L. Stebbins, 1865.

Kinder, Hermann, and Werner Hilgemann. *The Anchor Atlas of World History: From the French Revolution to the American Bicentennial*. 2 vols. Garden City, NY: Anchor, 1978.

King, Charles R. (ed.). *The Life and Correspondence of Rufus King*. 6 vols. New York, NY: G. P. Putnam's Sons, 1897.

King, Edward. *The Great South: A Record of Journeys*. Hartford, CT: American Publishing Co., 1875.

Kinshasa, Kwando Mbiassi. *Black Resistance to the Ku Klux Klan in the Wake of the Civil War*. Jefferson, NC: McFarland and Co., 2006.

Kirkland, Edward Chase. *The Peacemakers of 1864*. New York, NY: Macmillan, 1927.

Knox, Thomas Wallace. *Camp-Fire and Cotton-Field: Southern Adventure in Time of War - Life With the Union Armies, and Residence on a Louisiana Plantation*. New York, NY: Blelock and Co., 1865.

Ladnier, Dr. Gene. *General Nathan Bedford Forrest on Fame's Eternal Battlefield*. Charleston, SC: BookSurge, 2001.

Kuypers, Jim A., and Andrew King (eds.). *Twentieth-Century Roots of Rhetorical Studies*. Westport, CT: Praeger, 2001.

Lamon, Ward Hill. *The Life of Abraham Lincoln: From His Birth to His Inauguration as President*. Boston, MA: James R. Osgood and Co., 1872.

——. *Recollections of Abraham Lincoln: 1847-1865*. Chicago, IL: A. C. McClurg and Co., 1895.

Lang, J. Stephen. *The Complete Book of Confederate Trivia*. Shippensburg, PA: Burd Street Press, 1996.

Lanier, Robert S. (ed.). *The Photographic History of the Civil War*. 10 vols. New York, NY: Review of Reviews Co., 1911.

Lanning, Michael Lee. *The African-American Soldier: From Crispus Attucks to Colin Powell*. 1997. New York, NY: Citadel Press, 2004 ed.

Lawrence, William. *Life of Amos A. Lawrence*. Boston, MA: Houghton, Mifflin, and Co., 1899.

Lee, Robert E., Jr. *Recollections and Letters of General Robert E. Lee*. New York, NY: Doubleday, Page and Co., 1904.

Leech, Margaret. *Reveille in Washington, 1860-1865*. 1941. Alexandria, VA: Time-Life Books, 1980 ed.

Leeming, David Adams. *The World of Myth: An Anthology*. 1990. Oxford, UK: Oxford University Press, 1992 ed.

Lemay, J. A. Leo, and P. M. Zall (eds.). *Benjamin Franklin's Autobiography: An Authoritative Text, Backgrounds, Criticism*. 1791. New York, NY: W. W. Norton and Co., Inc., 1986 ed.

Lemire, Elise. *Black Walden: Slavery and Its Aftermath in Concord, Massachusetts*. Philadelphia, PA: University of Pennsylvania Press, 2009.

Lester, Charles Edwards. *Life and Public Services of Charles Sumner*. New York, NY: U.S. Publishing Co., 1874.

Lester, John C., and D. L. Wilson. *Ku Klux Klan: Its Origin, Growth, and Disbandment*. 1884. New York, NY: Neale Publishing, 1905 ed.

LeVert, Suzanne. *The Civil War Society's Encyclopedia of the Civil War*. New York, NY: Wings Books, 1997.

Levin, Mark R. *Liberty and Tyranny: A Conservative Manifesto*. New York, NY: Threshold, 2009.

Lewis, Lloyd. *Myths After Lincoln*. 1929. New York, NY: The Press of the Reader's Club, 1941 ed.

Lincoln, Abraham. *The Autobiography of Abraham Lincoln* (selected from *Complete Works of Abraham Lincoln*, 1894, by John G. Nicolay and John Hay). New York, NY: Francis D. Tandy Co., 1905.

Lincoln, Abraham, and Stephen A. Douglas. *Political Debates Between Abraham Lincoln and Stephen A. Douglas*. Cleveland, OH: Burrows Brothers Co., 1894.

Lind, Michael (ed.). *Hamilton's Republic: Readings in the American Democratic Nationalist Tradition*. New York, NY: Free Press, 1997.

Litwack, Leon F. *North of Slavery: The Negro in the Free States, 1790-1860*. Chicago, IL: University of Chicago Press, 1961.

——. *Been in the Storm So Long: The Aftermath of Slavery*. New York, NY: Vintage, 1980.

Livermore, Thomas L. *Numbers and Losses in the Civil War in America, 1861-65*. 1900. Carlisle, PA: John Kallmann, 1996 ed.

Livingstone, William. *Livingstone's History of the Republican Party*. 2 vols. Detroit, MI: William Livingstone, 1900.

Locke, John. *Two Treatises of Government* (Mark Goldie, ed.). 1924. London, UK: Everyman, 1998 ed.

Lodge, Henry Cabot (ed.). *The Works of Alexander Hamilton*. 12 vols. New York, NY: G. P. Putnam's Sons, 1904.

Logsdon, David R. (ed.). *Eyewitnesses at the Battle of Franklin*. 1988. Nashville, TN: Kettle Mills Press, 2000 ed.

——. *Tennessee Antebellum Trail Guidebook*. Nashville, TN: Kettle Mills Press, 1995.

Long, Everette Beach, and Barbara Long. *The Civil War Day by Day: An Almanac, 1861-1865*. 1971. New York, NY: Da Capo Press, 1985 ed.

Losson, Christopher. *Tennessee's Forgotten Warriors: Frank Cheatham and His Confederate Division*. Knoxville, TN: University of Tennessee Press, 1989.

Lott, Stanley K. *The Truth About American Slavery*. 2004. Clearwater, SC: Eastern Digital Resources, 2005 ed.

Lowry, Don. *Dark and Cruel War: The Decisive Months of the Civil War, September-December 1864*. New York, NY: Hippocrene, 1993.

Lubbock, Francis Richard. *Six Decades in Texas, or Memoirs of Francis Richard Lubbock, Governor of Texas in War-Time, 1861-1863*. 1899. Austin, TX: Ben C. Jones, 1900 ed.

Lytle, Andrew Nelson. *Bedford Forrest and His Critter Company*. New York, NY: G. P. Putnam's Sons, 1931.

MacDonald, William. *Select Documents Illustrative of the History of the United States 1776-1861*. New York, NY: Macmillan, 1897.

Mackay, Charles. *Life and Liberty in America, or Sketches of a Tour in the United States and Canada in 1857-58*. New York, NY: Harper and Brothers, 1859.

MacLysaght, Edward. *The Surnames of Ireland*. 1985. Dublin, Ireland: Irish Academic Press, 1999 ed.

Madison, James. *Letters and Other Writings of James Madison, Fourth President of the United States*. 4 vols. Philadelphia, PA: J. B. Lippincott and Co., 1865.

Maihafer, Harry J. *War of Words; Abraham Lincoln and the Civil War Press*. Dulles, VA: Brassey's, 2001.

Main, Jackson Turner. *The Anti-Federalists: Critics of the Constitution, 1781-1788*. 1961. New York, NY: W. W. Norton and Co., 1974 ed.

Mandel, Bernard. *Labor, Free and Slave: Workingmen and the Anti-Slavery Movement in the United States*. New York, NY: Associated Authors, 1955.

Maness, Lonnie E. *An Untutored Genius: The Military Career of General Nathan Bedford Forrest*. Oxford, MS: Guild Bindery, 1990.

Manning, Timothy D., Sr. (ed.) *Lincoln Reconsidered: Conference Reader*. High Point, NC: Heritage Foundation Press, 2006.

Marten, James. *The Children's Civil War*. Chapel Hill, NC: University of North Carolina Press, 1998.

Martin, Iain C. *The Quotable American Civil War*. Guilford, CT: Lyons Press, 2008.

Martinez, James Michael. *Carpetbaggers, Cavalry, and the Ku Klux Klan: Exposing the Invisible Empire During Reconstruction*. Lanham, MD: Rowman and Littlefield, 2007.

Martineau, Harriet. *Retrospect of Western Travel*. 3 vols. London, UK: Saunders and Otley, 1838.

Masur, Louis P. *The Real War Will Never Get In the Books: Selections From Writers During the Civil War*. New York, NY: Oxford University Press, 1993.

Mathes, Capt. J. Harvey. *General Forrest*. New York, NY: D. Appleton and Co., 1902.

Maury, Dabney Herndon. *Recollections of a Virginian in the Mexican, Indian, and Civil Wars*. New York, NY: Charles Scribner's Sons, 1894.

Mayer, David N. *The Constitutional Thought of Thomas Jefferson*. Charlottesville, VA: University of Virginia Press, 1995.

Mayer, Henry. *All on Fire: William Lloyd Garrison and the Abolition of Slavery*. New York, NY: St. Martin's Press, 1998.

McAfee, Ward M. *Citizen Lincoln*. Hauppauge, NY: Nova History Publications, 2004.

McCabe, James Dabney. *Our Martyred President: The Life and Public Services of Gen. James A. Garfield, Twentieth President of the United States*. Philadelphia, PA: National Publishing Co., 1881.

McClure, Alexander Kelly. *Abraham Lincoln and Men of War-Times: Some Personal Recollections of War and Politics During the Lincoln Administration*. Philadelphia, PA: Times Publishing Co., 1892.

——. *Our Presidents and How We Make Them*. New York, NY: Harper and Brothers, 1900.

McCullough, David. *John Adams*. New York, NY: Touchstone, 2001.

McDonald, Forrest. *States' Rights and the Union: Imperium in Imperio, 1776-1876*. Lawrence, KS: University Press of Kansas, 2000.

McDonough, James Lee. *Shiloh—In Hell Before Night*. Knoxville, TN: University of Tennessee Press, 1977.

McDonough, James Lee, and Thomas L. Connelly. *Five Tragic Hours: The Battle of Franklin*. 1983. Knoxville, TN: University of Tennessee Press, 2001 ed.

McElroy, Robert. *Jefferson Davis: The Unreal and the Real*. 1937. New York, NY: Smithmark, 1995 ed.

McFeely, William S. *Yankee Stepfather: General O. O. Howard and the Freedmen - The Story of a Civil War Promise to Former Slaves Made—and Broken*. 1968. New York, NY: W. W. Norton, 1994.

McGehee, Jacob Owen. *Causes That Led to the War Between the States*. Atlanta, GA: A. B. Caldwell, 1915.

McGuire, Hunter, and George L. Christian. *The Confederate Cause and Conduct in the War Between the States*. Richmond, VA: L. H. Jenkins, 1907.

McHenry, George. *The Cotton Trade: Its Bearing Upon the Prosperity of Great Britain and Commerce of the American Republics, Considered in Connection with the System of Negro Slavery in the Confederate States*. London, UK: Saunders, Otley, and Co., 1863.

McIlwaine, Shields. *Memphis Down in Dixie*. New York, NY: E. P. Dutton, 1848.

McKissack, Patricia C., and Frederick McKissack. *Sojourner Truth: Ain't I a Woman?* New York: NY: Scholastic, 1992.

McManus, Edgar J. *A History of Negro Slavery in New York*. Syracuse, NY: Syracuse University Press, 1966.

——. *Black Bondage in the North*. Syracuse, NY: Syracuse University Press, 1973.

McMaster, John Bach. *Our House Divided: A History of the People of the United States During Lincoln's Administration*. 1927. New York, NY: Premier, 1961 ed.

McMurry, Richard M. *John Bell Hood and the War for Southern Independence*. 1982. Lincoln, NE: University of Nebraska Press, 1992 ed.

McPherson, Edward. *The Political History of the United States of America, During the Great Rebellion (From November 6, 1860, to July 4, 1864)*. Washington, D.C.: Philp and Solomons, 1864.

——. *The Political History of the United States of America, During the Period of Reconstruction, (From April 15, 1865, to July 15, 1870,) Including a Classified Summary of the Legislation of the Thirty-ninth,*

*Fortieth, and Forty-first Congresses.* Washington, D.C.: Solomons and Chapman, 1875.

McPherson, James M. *The Struggle for Equality: Abolitionists and the Negro in the Civil War and Reconstruction.* 1964. Princeton, NJ: Princeton University Press, 1992 ed.

——. *The Negro's Civil War: How American Negroes Felt and Acted During the War for the Union.* 1965. Chicago, IL: University of Illinois Press, 1982 ed.

——. *Battle Cry of Freedom: The Civil War Era.* Oxford, UK: Oxford University Press, 2003.

——. *The Atlas of the Civil War.* Philadelphia, PA: Courage Books, 2005.

McPherson, James M., and the staff of the *New York Times. The Most Fearful Ordeal: Original Coverage of the Civil War by Writers and Reporters of the New York Times.* New York, NY: St. Martin's Press, 2004.

McWhiney, Grady, and Judith Lee Hallock. *Braxton Bragg and Confederate Defeat.* 2 vols. Tuscaloosa, AL: University of Alabama Press, 1991.

McWhiney, Grady, and Perry D. Jamieson. *Attack and Die: Civil War Military Tactics and the Southern Heritage.* Tuscaloosa, AL: University of Alabama Press, 1982.

Melish, Joanne Pope. *Disowning Slavery: Gradual Emancipation and 'Race' in New England 1780-1860.* Ithaca, NY: Cornell University Press, 1998.

Meltzer, Milton. *Slavery: A World History.* 2 vols. in 1. 1971. New York, NY: Da Capo Press, 1993 ed.

Mencken, Henry Louis. *Prejudices: Fifth Series.* New York, NY: Knopf, 1926.

Meriwether, Elizabeth Avery. *Facts and Falsehoods Concerning the War on the South, 1861-1865.* (Originally written under the pseudonym "George Edmonds".) Memphis, TN: A. R. Taylor, 1904.

*Message of the President of the United States and Accompanying Documents to the Two Houses of Congress at the Commencement of the Third Session of the 40$^{th}$ Congress.* Washington, D.C.: Government Printing Office, 1868.

Miller, Francis Trevelyan. *Portrait Life of Lincoln.* Springfield, MA: Patriot Publishing Co., 1910.

Miller, John Chester. *The Wolf By the Ears: Thomas Jefferson and Slavery.* 1977. Charlottesville, VA: University Press of Virginia, 1994 ed.

Miller, Marion Mills (ed.). *Great Debates in American History.* 14 vols. New York, NY: Current Literature, 1913.

Miller, Nathan. *Star-Spangled Men: America's Ten Worst Presidents.* New York, NY: Touchstone, 1998.

Mills, A. D. *Oxford Dictionary of English Place-names.* 1991. Oxford, UK: Oxford University Press, 1998 ed.

Minor, Charles Landon Carter. *The Real Lincoln: From the Testimony of His Contemporaries.* Richmond, VA: Everett Waddey Co., 1904.

Mirabello, Mark. *Handbook for Rebels and Outlaws.* Oxford, UK: Mandrake of Oxford, 2009.

Mish, Frederick C. (ed.). *Webster's Ninth New Collegiate Dictionary.* Springfield, MA: Merriam-Webster, 1984.

Mitchell, Margaret. *Gone With the Wind.* 1936. New York, NY: Avon, 1973 ed.

Mitgang, Herbert (ed.). *Lincoln As They Saw Him.* 1956. New York, NY: Collier, 1962 ed.

Mode, Robert L. (ed.). *Nashville: Its Character in a Changing America.* Nashville, TN: Vanderbilt University, 1981.

Montgomery, David Henry. *The Student's American History.* 1897. Boston, MA: Ginn and Co., 1905 ed.

Moore, Frank (ed.). *The Rebellion Record: A Diary of American Events.* 12 vols. New York, NY: G. P. Putnam, 1861.

Moore, George Henry. *Notes on the History of Slavery in Massachusetts.* New York, NY: D. Appleton and Co., 1866.

Morgan, Sarah. *The Civil War Diary of a Southern Woman* (Charles East, ed.). Originally published as *A Confederate Girl's Diary* in 1913. New York, NY: Touchstone, 1992 ed.

Morris, Thomas D. *Free Men All: The Personal Liberty Laws of the North, 1780-1861.* Baltimore, MD: John Hopkins University Press, 1974.

Morton, John Watson. *The Artillery of Nathan Bedford Forrest's Cavalry.* Nashville, TN: The M. E.

Church, 1909.

Moses, John. *Illinois: Historical and Statistical, Comprising the Essential Facts of Its Planting and Growth as a Province, County, Territory, and State* (Vol. 2). Chicago, IL: Fergus Printing Co., 1892.

Mullen, Robert W. *Blacks in America's Wars: The Shift in Attitudes from the Revolutionary War to Vietnam.* 1973. New York, NY: Pathfinder, 1991 ed.

Munford, Beverly Bland. *Virginia's Attitude Toward Slavery and Secession.* 1909. Richmond, VA: L. H. Jenkins, 1914 ed.

Murphy, Jim. *A Savage Thunder: Antietam and the Bloody Road to Freedom.* New York, NY: Margaret K. McElderry, 2009.

Napolitano, Andrew P. *The Constitution in Exile: How the Federal Government has Seized Power by Rewriting the Supreme Law of the Land.* Nashville, TN: Nelson Current, 2006.

Neely, Mark E., Jr. *The Fate of Liberty: Abraham Lincoln and Civil Liberties.* New York, NY: Oxford University Press, 1991.

Neilson, William Allan (ed.). *Webster's Biographical Dictionary.* Springfield, MA: G. and C. Merriam Co., 1943.

Neufeldt, Victoria (ed.). *Webster's New World Dictionary of American English* (3rd college edition). 1970. New York, NY: Prentice Hall, 1994 ed.

Nevins, Allan. *The Evening Post: A Century of Journalism.* New York, NY: Boni and Liveright, 1922.

Nicolay, John G., and John Hay (eds.). *Abraham Lincoln: A History.* 10 vols. New York, NY: The Century Co., 1890.

——. *Complete Works of Abraham Lincoln.* 12 vols. 1894. New York, NY: Francis D. Tandy Co., 1905 ed.

——. *Abraham Lincoln: Complete Works.* 12 vols. 1894. New York, NY: The Century Co., 1907 ed.

Nivola, Pietro S., and David H. Rosenbloom (eds.). *Classic Readings in American Politics.* New York, NY: St. Martin's Press, 1986.

Norwood, Thomas Manson. *A True Vindication of the South.* Savannah, GA: Citizens and Southern Bank, 1917.

Nye, Russel B. *William Lloyd Garrison and the Humanitarian Reformers.* Boston, MA: Little, Brown and Co., 1955.

Oates, Stephen B. *Abraham Lincoln: The Man Behind the Myths.* New York, NY: Meridian, 1984.

——. *The Approaching Fury: Voices of the Storm, 1820-1861.* New York, NY: Harper Perennial, 1998.

O'Brien, Cormac. *Secret Lives of the U.S. Presidents: What Your Teachers Never Told You About the Men of the White House.* Philadelphia, PA: Quirk, 2004.

——. *Secret Lives of the Civil War: What Your teachers Never Told You About the War Between the States.* Philadelphia, PA: Quirk, 2007.

Oglesby, Thaddeus K. *Some Truths of History: A Vindication of the South Against the Encyclopedia Britannica and Other Maligners.* Atlanta, GA: Byrd Printing, 1903.

Olmsted, Frederick Law. *A Journey in the Seaboard Slave States, With Remarks on Their Economy.* New York, NY: Dix and Edwards, 1856.

——. *A Journey Through Texas; or a Saddle-Trip on the Western Frontier.* New York, NY: Dix and Edwards, 1857.

——. *A Journey in the Back Country.* New York, NY: Mason Brothers, 1860.

——. *The Cotton Kingdom: A Traveler's Observations on Cotton and Slavery in the American Slave States.* 2 vols. London, UK: Sampson Low, Son, and Co., 1862.

Olson, Ted (ed.). *CrossRoads: A Southern Culture Annual.* Macon, GA: Mercer University Press, 2004.

ORA (full title: *The War of the Rebellion: A Compilation of the Official Records of the Union and Confederate Armies.* (Multiple volumes.) Washington, D.C.: Government Printing Office, 1880.

ORN (full title: *Official Records of the Union and Confederate Navies in the War of the Rebellion*). (Multiple volumes.) Washington, D.C.: Government Printing Office, 1894.

Owsley, Frank Lawrence. *King Cotton Diplomacy: Foreign Relations of the Confederate States of America.* 1931. Chicago, IL: University of Chicago Press, 1959 ed.

Page, Thomas Nelson. *Robert E. Lee, Man and Soldier.* New York, NY: Charles Scribner's Sons, 1911.

Palin, Sarah. *Going Rogue: An American Life.* New York, NY: HarperCollins, 2009.

Parker, Bowdoin S. (ed.). *What One Grand Army Post Has Accomplished: History of Edward W. Kinsley Post, No. 113*. Norwood, MA: Norwood, Press, 1913.

Parks, Aileen Wells. *Bedford Forrest: Horseback Boy*. 1952. Indianapolis, IN: Bobbs-Merrill Co., 1963 ed.

Parrish, T. Michael. *Richard Taylor: Soldier Prince of Dixie*. Chapel Hill, NC: University of North Carolina Press, 1992.

Parry, Melanie (ed.). *Chambers Biographical Dictionary*. 1897. Edinburgh, Scotland: Chambers Harrap, 1998 ed.

Patrick, Rembert W. *Jefferson Davis and His Cabinet*. Baton Rouge, LA: Louisiana State University Press, 1944.

Pearson, Henry Greenleaf. *The Life of John A. Andrew, Governor of Massachusetts, 1861-1865*. 2 vols. Boston, MA: Houghton, Mifflin and Co., 1904.

Perry, James M. *Touched With Fire: Five Presidents and the Civil War Battles That Made Them*. New York, NY: Public Affairs, 2003.

Perry, John C. *Myths and Realities of American Slavery: The True History of Slavery in America*. Shippenburg, PA: Burd Street Press, 2002.

Perry, Mark. *Lift Up Thy Voice: The Grimké Family's Journey From Slaveholders to Civil Rights Leaders*. New York, NY: Penguin, 2001.

Peter, Laurence J., and Raymond Hull *The Peter Principle: Why Things Always Go Wrong*. New York, NY: William Morrow and Co., 1969.

Peterson, Merrill D. (ed.). *James Madison, A Biography in His Own Words*. (First published posthumously in 1840.) New York, NY: Harper and Row, 1974 ed.

——. *Thomas Jefferson: Writings, Autobiography, A Summary View of the Rights of British America, Notes on the State of Virginia, Public Papers, Addresses, Messages and Replies, Miscellany, Letters*. New York, NY: Literary Classics, 1984.

Peterson, Paul R. *Quantrill of Missouri: The Making of a Guerilla Warrior, The Man, the Myth, the Soldier*. Nashville, TN: Cumberland House, 2003.

Phelan, James. *School History of Tennessee*. Philadelphia, PA: E. H. Butler and Co., 1889.

Phillips, Michael. *White Metropolis: Race, Ethnicity, and Religion in Dallas, 1841-2001*. Austin, TX: University of Texas Press, 2006.

Phillips, Robert S. (ed.). *Funk and Wagnalls New Encyclopedia*. 1971. New York, NY: Funk and Wagnalls, 1979 ed.

Phillips, Ulrich Bonnell. *American Negro Slavery: A Survey of the Supply, Employment and Control of Negro Labor as Determined by the Plantation Régime*. New York, NY: D. Appleton and Co., 1929.

Phillips, Wendell. *Speeches, Letters, and Lectures*. Boston, MA: Lee and Shepard, 1884.

Piatt, Donn. *Memories of the Men Who Saved the Union*. New York, NY: Belford, Clarke, and Co., 1887.

Piatt, Donn, and Henry V. Boynton. *General George H. Thomas: A Critical Biography*. Cincinnati, OH: Robert Clarke and Co., 1893.

Pickett, George E. *The Heart of a Soldier: As Revealed in the Intimate Letters of General George E. Pickett, CSA*. 1908. New York, NY: Seth Moyle, 1913 ed.

Pickett, William Passmore. *The Negro Problem: Abraham Lincoln's Solution*. New York, NY: G. P. Putnam's Sons, 1909.

Pike, James Shepherd. *The Prostrate State: South Carolina Under Negro Government*. New York, NY: D. Appleton and Co., 1874.

Pollard, Edward A. *Southern History of the War*. 2 vols in 1. New York, NY: Charles B. Richardson, 1866.

——. *The Lost Cause*. 1867. Chicago, IL: E. B. Treat, 1890 ed.

——. *Lee and His Lieutenants: Comprising the Early Life, Public Services, and Campaigns of General Robert E. Lee and His Companions in Arms*. New York, NY: E. B. Treat, 1867.

——. *The Lost Cause Regained*. New York, NY: G. W. Carlton and Co., 1868.

——. *Life of Jefferson Davis, With a Secret History of the Southern Confederacy, Gathered "Behind the Scenes in Richmond."* Philadelphia, PA: National Publishing Co., 1869.

Post, Lydia Minturn (ed.). *Soldiers' Letters, From Camp, Battlefield and Prison*. New York, NY: Bunce and

Huntington, 1865.

Potter, David M. *The Impending Crisis: 1848-1861*. New York, NY: Harper and Row, 1976.

Powell, Edward Payson. *Nullification and Secession in the United States: A History of the Six Attempts During the First Century of the Republic*. New York, NY: G. P. Putnam's Sons, 1897.

Powell, William S. *North Carolina: A History*. 1977. Chapel Hill, NC: University of North Carolina Press, 1988 ed.

Pratt, Harry E. *Concerning Mr. Lincoln: As He Appeared to Letter Writers of His Time*. Springfield, IL: The Abraham Lincoln Association, 1944.

Pritchard, Russ A., Jr. *Civil War Weapons and Equipment*. Guilford, CT: Lyons Press, 2003.

Putnam, Samuel Porter. *400 Years of Free Thought*. New York, NY: Truth Seeker Co., 1894.

Quarles, Benjamin. *The Negro in the Civil War*. 1953. Cambridge, MA: Da Capo Press, 1988 ed.

Rable, George C. *The Confederate Republic: A Revolution Against Politics*. Chapel Hill, NC: University of North Carolina Press, 1994.

Ramage, James A. *Rebel Raider: The Life of General John Hunt Morgan*. Lexington, KY: University Press of Kentucky, 1986.

Randall, James Garfield. *Lincoln: The Liberal Statesman*. New York, NY: Dodd, Mead and Co., 1947.

Randall, James Garfield, and Richard N. Current. *Lincoln the President: Last Full Measure*. 1955. Urbana, IL: University of Illinois Press, 2000 ed.

Randolph, Thomas Jefferson (ed.). *Memoir, Correspondence, and Miscellanies, from the Papers of Thomas Jefferson* (Vol. 3). Charlottesville, VA: F. Carr and Co., 1829.

Ransom, Roger L. *Conflict and Compromise: The Political Economy of Slavery, Emancipation, and the American Civil War*. Cambridge, UK: Cambridge University Press, 1989.

Rawle, William. *A View of the Constitution of the United States of America*. Philadelphia, PA: Philip H. Nicklin, 1829.

Reaney, P. H., and R. M. Wilson. *A Dictionary of English Surnames*. 1958. Oxford, UK: Oxford University Press, 1997 ed.

Reid, Richard M. *Freedom for Themselves: North Carolina's Black Soldiers in the Era of the Civil War*. Chapel Hill, NC: University of North Carolina Press, 2008.

Remsburg, John B. *Abraham Lincoln: Was He a Christian?* New York, NY: The Truth Seeker Co., 1893.

*Reports of Committees of the Senate of the United States (for the Thirty-eighth Congress)*. Washington, D.C.: Government Printing Office, 1864.

*Report of the Joint Committee on Reconstruction (at the First Session, Thirty-ninth Congress)*. Washington, D.C.: Government Printing Office, 1866.

*Report of the Joint Select Committee to Inquire into the Condition of Affairs in the Late Insurrectionary States*. Washington, D.C.: Government Printing Office, 1872.

*Reports of Committees of the Senate of the United States (for the Second Session of the Forty-second Congress)*. Washington, D.C.: Government Printing Office, 1872.

Reuter, Edward Byron. *The Mulatto in the United States*. Boston, MA: Gorham Press, 1918.

Rhodes, James Ford. *History of the United States from the Compromise of 1850 to the Final Restoration of Home Rule at the South in 1877*. 7 vols. 1895. New York, NY: Macmillan, 1907 ed.

Rice, Allen Thorndike (ed.). *The North American Review*, Vol. 227. New York, NY: D. Appleton and Co., 1879.

——. *Reminiscences of Abraham Lincoln, by Distinguished Men of His Time*. New York, NY: North American Review, 1888.

Richardson, James D. (ed.). *A Compilation of the Messages and Papers of the Confederacy*. 2 vols. Nashville, TN: United States Publishing Co., 1905.

Ridley, Bromfield Lewis. *Battles and Sketches of the Army of Tennessee*. Mexico, MO: Missouri Printing and Publishing Co., 1906.

Riley, Franklin Lafayette (ed.). *Publications of the Mississippi Historical Society*. Oxford, MS: The Mississippi Historical Society, 1902.

——. *General Robert E. Lee After Appomattox*. New York, NY: MacMillan Co., 1922.

Riley, Russell Lowell. *The Presidency and the Politics of Racial Inequality*. New York, NY: Columbia University Press, 1999.

Rives, John (ed.). *Abridgement of the Debates of Congress: From 1789 to 1856* (Vol. 13). New York, NY: D. Appleton and Co., 1860.

Roberts, Paul M. *United States History: Review Text.* 1966. New York, NY: Amsco School Publications, Inc., 1970 ed.

Robertson, James I., Jr. *Soldiers Blue and Gray.* 1988. Columbia, SC: University of South Carolina Press, 1998 ed.

Robuck, J. E. *My Own Personal Experience and Observation as a Soldier in the Confederate Army During the Civil War, 1861-1865.* N.p: Leslie Print and Publishing Co., 1911.

Rogers, Joel Augustus. *The Ku Klux Spirit.* 1923. Baltimore, MD: Black Classic Press, 1980 ed.

——. *Africa's Gift to America: The Afro-American in the Making and Saving of the United States.* St. Petersburg, FL: Helga M. Rogers, 1961.

Rosenbaum, Robert A. (ed.) *The New American Desk Encyclopedia.* 1977. New York, NY: Signet, 1989 ed.

Rosenbaum, Robert A., and Douglas Brinkley (eds.). *The Penguin Encyclopedia of American History.* New York, NY: Viking, 2003.

Rothschild, Alonzo. *"Honest Abe": A Study in Integrity Based on the Early Life of Abraham Lincoln.* Boston, MA: Houghton Mifflin Co., 1917.

Rouse, Adelaide Louise (ed.). *National Documents: State Papers So Arranged as to Illustrate the Growth of Our Country From 1606 to the Present Day.* New York, NY: Unit Book Publishing Co., 1906.

Rowland, Dunbar (ed.). *Jefferson Davis, Constitutionalist: His Letters, Papers, and Speeches.* 10 vols. Jackson, MS: Mississippi Department of Archives and History,1923.

Rozwenc, Edwin Charles (ed.). *The Causes of the American Civil War.* 1961. Lexington, MA: D. C. Heath and Co., 1972 ed.

Russell, Charles Wells (ed.). *The Memoirs of Colonel John S. Mosby.* Boston, MA: Little, Brown, and Co., 1917.

Rutherford, Mildred Lewis. *Four Addresses.* Birmingham, AL: The Mildred Rutherford Historical Circle, 1916.

——. *A True Estimate of Abraham Lincoln and Vindication of the South.* N.p., n.d.

——. *Truths of History: A Historical Perspective of the Civil War From the Southern Viewpoint.* Confederate Reprint Co., 1920.

——. *The South Must Have Her Rightful Place In History.* Athens, GA, 1923.

Rutland, Robert Allen. *The Birth of the Bill of Rights, 1776-1791.* 1955. Boston, MA: Northeastern University Press, 1991 ed.

Sachsman, David B., S. Kittrell Rushing, and Roy Morris, Jr. (eds.). *Words at War: The Civil War and American Journalism.* West Lafayette, IN: Purdue University Press, 2008.

Salley, Alexander Samuel, Jr. *South Carolina Troops in Confederate Service.* 2 vols. Columbia, SC: R. L. Bryan, 1913 and 1914.

Salzberger, Ronald P., and Mary C. Turck (eds.). *Reparations For Slavery: A Reader.* Lanham, MD: Rowman and Littlefield, 2004.

Sandburg, Carl. *Storm Over the Land: A Profile of the Civil War.* 1939. Old Saybrook, CT: Konecky and Konecky, 1942 ed.

——. *Abraham Lincoln: The War Years.* 4 vols. New York, NY: Harcourt, Brace and World, 1939.

Sargent, F. W. *England, the United States, and the Southern Confederacy.* London, UK: Sampson Low, Son, and Co., 1863.

Scarlett, James D. *Tartans of Scotland.* 1972. Cambridge, UK: The Lutterworth Press, 1996 ed.

Scharf, John Thomas. *History of the Confederate Navy, From Its Organization to the Surrender of Its Last Vessel.* Albany, NY: Joseph McDonough, 1894.

Schauffler, Robert Haven. *Our American Holidays: Lincoln's Birthday - A Comprehensive View of Lincoln as Given in the Most Noteworthy Essays, Orations and Poems, in Fiction and in Lincoln's Own Writings.* 1909. New York, NY: Moffat, Yard and Co., 1916 ed.

Schlüter, Herman. *Lincoln, Labor and Slavery: A Chapter from the Social History of America.* New York, NY: Socialist Literature Co., 1913.

Schurz, Carl. *Life of Henry Clay.* 2 vols. 1887. Boston, MA: Houghton, Mifflin and Co., 1899 ed.

Schwartz, Barry. *Abraham Lincoln and the Forge of National Memory*. Chicago, IL: University of Chicago Press, 2000.

Scott, Emmett J., and Lyman Beecher Stowe. *Booker T. Washington: Builder of a Civilization*. Garden City, NY: Doubleday, Page, and Co., 1916.

Scott, James Brown. *James Madison's Notes of Debates in the Federal Convention of 1787, and Their Relation to a More Perfect Society of Nations*. New York, NY: Oxford University Press, 1918.

Scott, Otto J. *The Secret Six: John Brown and the Abolitionist Movement*. New York, NY: New York Times Books, 1979.

Scruggs, Mike. *The Un-Civil War: Truths Your Teacher Never Told You*. Hendersonville, NC: Tribune Papers, 2007.

Seabrook, Lochlainn. *Aphrodite's Trade: The Hidden History of Prostitution Unveiled*. 1993. Franklin, TN: Sea Raven Press, 2011 ed.

——. *Britannia Rules: Goddess-Worship in Ancient Anglo-Celtic Society - An Academic Look at the United Kingdom's Matricentric Spiritual Past*. 1999. Franklin, TN: Sea Raven Press, 2010 ed.

——. *The Caudills: An Etymological, Ethnological, and Genealogical Study - Exploring the Name and National Origins of a European-American Family*. 2003. Franklin, TN: Sea Raven Press, 2010 ed.

——. *Carnton Plantation Ghost Stories: True Tales of the Unexplained From Tennessee's Most Haunted Civil War House!* 2005. Franklin, TN: Sea Raven Press, 2010 ed.

——. *Nathan Bedford Forrest: Southern Hero, American Patriot: Honoring a Confederate Hero and the Old South*. 2007. Franklin, TN: Sea Raven Press, 2010 ed.

——. *Abraham Lincoln: The Southern View - Demythologizing America's Sixteenth President*. 2007. Franklin, TN: Sea Raven Press, 2010 ed.

——. *The McGavocks of Carnton Plantation: A Southern History - Celebrating One of Dixie's Most Noble Confederate Families and Their Tennessee Home*. 2008. Franklin, TN: Sea Raven Press, 2011 ed.

——. *Everything You Were Taught About the Civil War is Wrong, Ask a Southerner! - Correcting the Errors of Yankee "History."* Franklin, TN: Sea Raven Press, 2010.

——. *Lincolnology: The Real Abraham Lincoln Revealed in His Own Words - A Study of Lincoln's Suppressed, Misinterpreted, and Forgotten Writings and Speeches*. Franklin, TN: Sea Raven Press, 2011.

——. *The Quotable Jefferson Davis: Selections From the Writings and Speeches of the Confederacy's First President*. Franklin, TN: Sea Raven Press, 2011.

——. *The Unquotable Abraham Lincoln: The President's Quotes They Don't Want You to Know!* Franklin, TN: Sea Raven Press, 2011.

——. *The Quotable Robert E. Lee: Selections From the Writings and Speeches of the South's Most Beloved Civil War General*. 2011. Franklin, TN: Sea Raven Press, 2014 ed.

——. *The Constitution of the Confederate States of America Explained: A Clause-by-Clause Study of the South's Magna Carta*. Franklin, TN: Sea Raven Press, 2012.

——. *The Old Rebel: Robert E. Lee As He Was Seen By His Contemporaries*. Franklin, TN: Sea Raven Press, 2012.

——. *The Quotable Nathan Bedford Forrest: Selections From the Writings and Speeches of the Confederacy's Most Brilliant Cavalryman*. Franklin, TN: Sea Raven Press, 2012 Sesquicentennial Civil War Edition.

——. *The Quotable Stonewall Jackson: Selections From the Writings and Speeches of the South's Most Famous General*. Franklin, TN: Sea Raven Press, 2012.

——. *Honest Jeff and Dishonest Abe: A Southern Children's Guide to the Civil War*. Franklin, TN: Sea Raven Press, 2012.

——. *Give 'Em Hell Boys! The Complete Military Correspondence of Nathan Bedford Forrest*. Franklin, TN: Sea Raven Press, 2012 Sesquicentennial Civil War Edition.

——. *The Great Impersonator: 99 Reasons to Dislike Abraham Lincoln*. Franklin, TN: Sea Raven Press, 2012.

——. *Forrest! 99 Reasons to Love Nathan Bedford Forrest*. Franklin, TN: Sea Raven Press, 2012 Sesquicentennial Civil War Edition.

——. *The Quotable Nathan Bedford Forrest: Selections From the Writings and Speeches of the Confederacy's Most Brilliant Cavalryman*. Franklin, TN: Sea Raven Press, 2012 Sesquicentennial Civil War

Edition.

——. *Encyclopedia of the Battle of Franklin: A Comprehensive Guide to the Conflict That Changed the Civil War*. Franklin, TN: Sea Raven Press, 2012 Sesquicentennial Civil War Edition.

——. *The Quotable Alexander H. Stephens: Selections From the Writings and Speeches of the Confederacy's First Vice President*. Franklin, TN: Sea Raven Press, 2013.

——. *The Alexander H. Stephens Reader: Excerpts From the Works of a Confederate Founding Father*. Franklin, TN: Sea Raven Press, 2013.

——. *Saddle, Sword, and Gun: A Biography of Nathan Bedford Forrest For Teens*. Franklin, TN: Sea Raven Press, 2013 Sesquicentennial Civil War Edition.

——. *The Articles of Confederation Explained: A Clause-by-Clause Study of America's First Constitution*. Franklin, TN: Sea Raven Press, 2014.

——. *Give This Book to a Yankee: A Southern Guide to the Civil War For Northerners*. Franklin, TN: Sea Raven Press, 2014.

——. *Slavery 101: Amazing Facts You Never Knew About America's "Peculiar Institution."* Franklin, TN: Sea Raven Press, 2015.

——. *Everything You Were Taught About American Slavery War is Wrong, Ask a Southerner!* Franklin, TN: Sea Raven Press, 2015.

——. *Confederacy 101: Amazing Facts You Never Knew About America's Oldest Political Tradition*. Franklin, TN: Sea Raven Press, 2015.

——. *The Great Yankee Coverup: What the North Doesn't Want You to Know About Lincoln's War!* Franklin, TN: Sea Raven Press, 2015.

——. *Confederate Blood and Treasure: An Interview With Lochlainn Seabrook*. Franklin, TN: Sea Raven Press, 2015.

——. *Confederate Flag Facts*. Franklin, TN: Sea Raven Press, 2015.

Segars, J. H., and Charles Kelly Barrow. *Black Southerners in Confederate Armies: A Collection of Historical Accounts*. Atlanta, GA: Southern Lion Books, 2001.

Seligmann, Herbert J. *The Negro Faces America*. New York, NY: Harper and Brothers, 1920.

Semmes, Admiral Ralph. *Service Afloat, or the Remarkable Career of the Confederate Cruisers Sumter and Alabama During the War Between the States*. London, UK: Sampson Low, Marston, Searle, and Rivington, 1887.

Sewall, Samuel. *Diary of Samuel Sewall*. 3 vols. Boston, MA: The Society, 1879.

Sewell, Richard H. *John P. Hale and the Politics of Abolition*. Cambridge, MA: Harvard University Press, 1965.

Shenkman, Richard, and Kurt Edward Reiger. *One-Night Stands with American History: Odd, Amusing, and Little-Known Incidents*. 1980. New York, NY: Perennial, 2003 ed.

Sheppard, Eric William. *Bedford Forrest, The Confederacy's Greatest Cavalryman*. 1930. Dayton, OH: Morningside House, 1981 ed.

Sherman, William Tecumseh. *Memoirs of General William T. Sherman*. 2 vols. 1875. New York, NY: D. Appleton and Co., 1891 ed.

Sherrill, Samuel W. *Heroes in Gray*. Nashville, TN: Claude J. Bell, 1909.

Shorto, Russell. *Thomas Jefferson and the American Ideal*. Hauppauge, NY: Barron's, 1987.

Shotwell, Walter G. *Life of Charles Sumner*. New York, NY: Thomas Y. Crowell and Co., 1910.

Shillington, Kevin. *History of Africa*. 1989. New York, NY: St. Martin's Press, 1994 ed.

Siepel, Kevin H. *Rebel: The Life and Times of John Singleton Mosby*. New York, NY: St. Martin's Press, 1983.

Simkins, Francis Butler. *A History of the South*. New York, NY: Random House, 1972.

Simmons, Henry E. *A Concise Encyclopedia of the Civil War*. New York, NY: Bonanza Books, 1965.

Simpson, Lewis P. (ed.). *I'll Take My Stand: The South and the Agrarian Tradition*. 1930. Baton Rouge, LA: University of Louisiana Press, 1977 ed.

Skeat, Rev. W. Walter. *An Etymological Dictionary of the English Language*. New York, NY: Macmillan and Co., 1882.

Slotkin, Richard. *No Quarter: The Battle of the Crater, 1864*. New York, NY: Random House, 2009.

Smelser, Marshall. *American Colonial and Revolutionary History*. 1950. New York, NY: Barnes and

Noble, 1966 ed.

——. *The Democratic Republic, 1801-1815*. New York, NY: Harper and Row, 1968.

Smith, Hedrick. *Reagan: The Man, The President*. Oxford, UK: Pergamon Press, 1980.

Smith, John David (ed.). *Black Soldiers in Blue: African American Troops in the Civil War Era*. Chapel Hill, NC: University of North Carolina Press, 2002.

Smith, Mark M. (ed.). *The Old South*. Oxford, UK: Blackwell Publishers, 2001.

Smith, Page. *Trial by Fire: A People's History of the Civil War and Reconstruction*. New York, NY: McGraw-Hill, 1982.

Smith, Philip D., Jr. *Tartan for Me!: Suggested Tartan for 13,695 Scottish, Scotch-Irish, Irish and North American Names with Lists of Clan, Family, and District Tartans*. Bruceton, WV: Scotpress, 1990.

Smucker, Samuel M. *The Life and Times of Thomas Jefferson*. Philadelphia, PA: J. W. Bradley, 1859.

Sobel, Robert (ed.). *Biographical Directory of the United States Executive Branch, 1774-1898*. Westport, CT: Greenwood Press, 1990.

Sorrel, Gilbert Moxley. *Recollections of a Confederate Staff Officer*. New York, NY: Neale Publishing Co., 1905.

Spaeth, Harold J., and Edward Conrad Smith. *The Constitution of the United States*. 1936. New York, NY: HarperCollins, 1991 ed.

Spooner, Lysander. *No Treason* (only Numbers 1, 2, and 6 were published). Boston, MA: Lysander Spooner, 1867-1870.

Stampp, Kenneth M. *The Peculiar Institution: Slavery in the Antebellum South*. New York, NY: Vintage, 1956.

Stanford, Peter Thomas. *The Tragedy of the Negro in America*. Boston, MA: Peter Thomas Stanford, 1898.

Stanton, Elizabeth Cady, Susan B. Anthony, and Matilda Joslyn Gage (eds.). *History of Woman Suffrage*. 2 vols. New York, NY: Fowler and Wells, 1881.

Starnes, H. Gerald. *Forrest's Forgotten Horse Brigadier*. Westminster, MD: Heritage Books, 1995.

Starr, John W., Jr. *Lincoln and the Railroads: A Biographical Study*. New York, NY: Dodd, Mead and Co., 1927.

Staudenraus, P. J. *The African Colonization Movement, 1816-1865*. New York, NY: Columbia University Press, 1961.

Stebbins, Rufus Phineas. *An Historical Address Delivered At the Centennial Celebration of the Incorporation of the Town of Wilbraham, June 15, 1863*. Boston, MA: George C. Rand and Avery, 1864.

Stedman, Edmund Clarence, and Ellen Mackay Hutchinson (eds.). *A Library of American Literature From the Earliest Settlement to the Present Time*. 10 vols. New York, NY: Charles L. Webster and Co., 1888.

Steele, Joel Dorman, and Esther Baker Steele. *Barnes' Popular History of the United States of America*. New York, NY: A. S. Barnes and Co., 1904.

Stein, Ben, and Phil DeMuth. *How To Ruin the United States of America*. Carlsbad, CA: New Beginnings Press, 2008.

Steiner, Lewis Henry. *Report of Lewis H. Steiner: Inspector of the Sanitary Commission, Containing a Diary Kept During the Rebel Occupation of Frederick, MD, September, 1862*. New York, NY: Anson D. F. Randolph, 1862.

Stephens, Alexander Hamilton. *Speech of Mr. Stephens, of Georgia, on the War and Taxation*. Washington, D.C.: J & G. Gideon, 1848.

——. *A Constitutional View of the Late War Between the States; Its Causes, Character, Conduct and Results*. 2 vols. Philadelphia, PA: National Publishing, Co., 1870.

——. *Recollections of Alexander H. Stephens: His Diary Kept When a Prisoner at Fort Warren, Boston Harbour, 1865*. New York, NY: Doubleday, Page, and Co., 1910.

Stephenson, Nathaniel Wright. *Abraham Lincoln and the Union: A Chronicle of the Embattled North*. New Haven, CT: Yale University Press, 1918.

——. *Lincoln: An Account of His Personal Life, Especially of Its Springs of Action as Revealed and Deepened by the Ordeal of War*. Indianapolis, IN: Bobbs-Merrill, 1922.

Stern, Philip Van Doren (ed.). *The Life and Writings of Abraham Lincoln*. 1940. New York, NY: Modern Library, 2000 ed.

Stonebraker, J. Clarence. *The Unwritten South: Cause, Progress and Results of the Civil War - Relics of Hidden Truth After Forty Years*. Seventh ed., n.p., 1908.

Strain, John Paul. *Witness to the Civil War: The Art of John Paul Strain*. Philadelphia, PA: Courage, 2002.

Strode, Hudson. *Jefferson Davis: American Patriot*. 3 vols. New York, NY: Harcourt, Brace and World, 1955, 1959, 1964.

Sturge, Joseph. *A Visit to the United States in 1841*. London, UK: Hamilton, Adams, and Co., 1842.

Summers, Mark W. *The Plundering Generation: Corruption and the Crisis of the Union, 1849-1861*. New York, NY: Oxford University Press, 1988.

Sumner, Charles. *The Crime Against Kansas: The Apologies for the Crime - The True Remedy*. Boston, MA: John P. Jewett, 1856.

Sword, Wiley. *The Confederacy's Last Hurrah: Spring Hill, Franklin, and Nashville*. New York, NY: HarperCollins, 1992.

——. *Southern Invincibility: A History of the Confederate Heart*. New York, NY: St. Martin's Press, 1999.

Tarbell, Ida Minerva. *The Life of Abraham Lincoln*. 4 vols. New York, NY: Lincoln History Society, 1895-1900.

Taylor, Richard. *Destruction and Reconstruction: Personal Experiences of the Late War in the United States*. New York, NY: D. Appleton, 1879.

Taylor, Susie King. *Reminiscences of My Life in Camp With the 33$^{rd}$ United States Colored Troops Late 1$^{st}$ S. C. Volunteers*. Boston, MA: Susie King Taylor, 1902.

Terkel, Studs. *Hard Times: An Oral History of the Great Depression*. New York, NY: Avon, 1970.

*Testimony Taken By the Joint Select Committee to Inquire Into the Condition of Affairs in the Late Insurrectionary States*. 13 vols. Washington, D.C.: Government Printing Office, 1872.

Thackeray, William Makepeace. *Roundabout Papers*. Boston, MA: Estes and Lauriat, 1883.

Thatcher, Marshall P. *A Hundred Battles in the West: St. Louis to Atlanta, 1861-1865*. Detroit, MI: Marshall P. Thatcher, 1884.

*The Congressional Globe, Containing Sketches of the Debates and Proceedings of the First Session of the Twenty-Eighth Congress* (Vol. 13). Washington, D.C.: The Globe, 1844.

*The Great Issue to be Decided in November Next: Shall the Constitution and the Union Stand or Fall, Shall Sectionalism Triumph?* Washington, D.C.: National Democratic Executive Committee, 1860.

*The National Almanac and Annual Record for the Year 1863*. Philadelphia, PA: George W. Childs, 1863.

*The Oxford English Dictionary*. Compact edition, 2 vols. 1928. Oxford, UK: Oxford University Press, 1979 ed.

*The Reports of the Committees (of the United States for the Second Session of the Forty-Second Congress, 1871-1872)*. Washington, D.C.: Government Printing Office, 1872.

Thomas, Emory M. *The Confederate Nation: 1861-1865*. New York, NY: Harper and Row, 1979.

Thomas, Gabriel. *An Account of Pennsylvania and West New Jersey*. 1698. Cleveland, OH: Burrows Brothers Co., 1903 ed.

Thompson, Neal. *Driving With the Devil: Southern Moonshine, Detroit Wheels, and the Birth of NASCAR*. Three Rivers, MI: Three Rivers Press, 2006.

Thompson, Frank Charles (ed.). *The Thompson Chain Reference Bible* (King James Version). 1908. Indianapolis, IN: B. B. Kirkbride Bible Co., 1964 ed.

Thompson, Robert Means, and Richard Wainwright (eds.). *Confidential Correspondence of Gustavus Vasa Fox, Assistant Secretary of the Navy, 1861-1865*. 2 vols. 1918. New York, NY: Naval History Society, 1920 ed.

Thorndike, Rachel Sherman (ed.). *The Sherman Letters*. New York, NY: Charles Scribner's Sons, 1894.

Thornton, Brian. *101 Things You Didn't Know About Lincoln: Loves and Losses, Political Power Plays, White House Hauntings*. Avon, MA: Adams Media, 2006.

Thornton, Gordon. *The Southern Nation: The New Rise of the Old South*. Gretna, LA: Pelican Publishing Co., 2000.

Thornton, John. *Africa and Africans in the Making of the Atlantic World, 1400-1800*. 1992. Cambridge,

UK: Cambridge University Press, 1999 ed.

Thornton, Mark, and Robert B. Ekelund, Jr. *Tariffs, Blockades, and Inflation: The Economics of the Civil War.* Wilmington, DE: Scholarly Resources, 2004.

Tilley, John Shipley. *Lincoln Takes Command.* 1941. Nashville, TN: Bill Coats Limited, 1991 ed.

——. *Facts the Historians Leave Out: A Confederate Primer.* 1951. Nashville, TN: Bill Coats Limited, 1999 ed.

Tocqueville, Alexis de. *Democracy in America.* 2 vols. 1836. New York, NY: D. Appleton and Co., 1904 ed.

Tourgée, Albion Winegar. *A Fool's Errand By One of the Fools.* London, UK: George Routledge and Sons, 1883.

Traupman, John C. *The New College Latin and English Dictionary.* 1966. New York, NY: Bantam, 1988 ed.

Trumbull, Lyman. *Speech of Honorable Lyman Trumbull, of Illinois, at a Mass Meeting in Chicago, August 7, 1858.* Washington, D.C.: Buell and Blanchard, 1858.

Truth, Sojourner. *Narrative of Sojourner Truth.* 1850. Mineola, NY: Dover, 1997 ed.

Turtledove, Harry. *The Guns of the South.* New York, NY: Del Rey, 1992.

Tyler, Lyon Gardiner. *The Letters and Times of the Tylers.* 3 vols. Williamsburg, VA: N.P., 1896.

——. *Propaganda in History.* Richmond, VA: Richmond Press, 1920.

——. *The Gray Book: A Confederate Catechism.* Columbia, TN: Gray Book Committee, SCV, 1935.

Upshur, Abel Parker. *A Brief Enquiry Into the True Nature and Character of Our Federal Government.* Philadelphia, PA: John Campbell, 1863.

Vallandigham, Clement Laird. *Speeches, Arguments, Addresses, and Letters of Clement L. Vallandigham.* New York, NY: J. Walter and Co., 1864.

Van Deusen, Glyndon Garlock. *William Henry Seward.* New York, NY: Oxford University Press, 1967.

Voegeli, Victor Jacque. *Free But Not Equal: The Midwest and the Negro During the Civil War.* Chicago, IL: University of Chicago Press, 1967.

Wade, Wyn Craig. *The Fiery Cross: The Ku Klux Klan in America.* 1987. New York, NY: Touchstone, 1988 ed.

Walker, Barbara G. *The Woman's Encyclopedia of Myths and Secrets.* New York, NY: Harper and Row, 1983.

Wallcut, R. F. (pub.). *Southern Hatred of the American Government, the People of the North, and Free Institutions.* Boston, MA: R. F. Wallcut, 1862.

Wallechinsky, David, Irving Wallace, and Amy Wallace. *The People's Almanac Presents The Book of Lists.* New York, NY: Morrow, 1977.

Walsh, George. *"Those Damn Horse Soldiers": True Tales of the Civil War Cavalry.* New York, NY: Forge, 2006.

Ward, Andrew. *River Run Red: The Fort Pillow Massacre in the American Civil War.* New York, NY: Viking, 2005.

Ward, John William. *Andrew Jackson: Symbol for an Age.* 1953. Oxford, UK: Oxford University Press, 1973 ed.

Waring, George Edward, Jr. *Whip and Spur.* New York, NY: Doubleday and McClure, 1897.

Warner, Ezra J. *Generals in Gray: Lives of the Confederate Commanders.* 1959. Baton Rouge, LA: Louisiana State University Press, 1989 ed.

——. *Generals in Blue: Lives of the Union Commanders.* 1964. Baton Rouge, LA: Louisiana State University Press, 2006 ed.

Warren, Robert Penn. *John Brown: The Making of a Martyr.* New York, NY: Payson and Clarke, 1929.

——. *Who Speaks for the Negro?* New York, NY: Random House, 1965.

Washington, Booker T. *Up From Slavery: An Autobiography.* 1901. Garden City, NY: Doubleday, Page and Co., 1919 ed.

Washington, Henry Augustine. *The Writings of Thomas Jefferson.* 9 vols. New York, NY: H. W. Derby, 1861.

Watkins, Samuel Rush. *"Company Aytch," Maury Grays, First Tennessee Regiment; or, A Side Show of the Big*

*Show*. 1882. Chattanooga, TN: Times Printing Co., 1900 ed.

Watts, Peter. *A Dictionary of the Old West*. 1977. New York, NY: Promontory Press, 1987 ed.

Waugh, John C. *Surviving the Confederacy: Rebellion, Ruin, and Recovery - Roger and Sara Pryor During the Civil War*. New York, NY: Harcourt, 2002.

Way, George, and Romilly Squire. *Scottish Clan and Family Encyclopedia*. 1994. Glasgow, Scotland: HarperCollins.

Welles, Gideon. *Diary of Gideon Welles, Secretary of the Navy Under Lincoln and Johnson* (Vol. 1). Boston, MA: Houghton Mifflin, 1911.

Weintraub, Max. *The Blue Book of American History*. New York, NY: Regents Publishing Co., 1960.

White, Charles Langdon, Edwin Jay Foscue, and Tom Lee McKnight. *Regional Geography of Anglo-America*. 1943. Englewood Cliffs, NJ: Prentice-Hall, 1985 ed.

White, Henry Alexander. *Robert E. Lee and the Southern Confederacy, 1807-1870*. New York, NY: G. P. Putnam's Sons, 1897.

White, Robert H. *Messages of the Governors of Tennessee, 1857-1869*. 10 vols. Nashville, TN: Tennessee Historical Commission, 1959.

White, Suzanne. *The New Astrology*. 1986. New York, NY: St. Martin's Press.

Whitman, Walt. *Leaves of Grass*. 1855. New York, NY: Modern Library, 1921 ed.

——. *Complete Prose Works*. Boston, MA: Small, Maynard, and Co., 1901.

Wilbur, Henry Watson. *President Lincoln's Attitude Towards Slavery and Emancipation: With a Review of Events Before and Since the Civil War*. Philadelphia, PA: W. H. Jenkins, 1914.

Wilder, Craig Steven. *A Covenant With Color: Race and Social Power in Brooklyn*. New York, NY: Columbia University Press, 2000.

Wiley, Bell Irvin. *Southern Negroes: 1861-1865*. 1938. New Haven, CT: Yale University Press, 1969 ed.

——. *The Life of Johnny Reb: The Common Soldier of the Confederacy*. 1943. Baton Rouge, LA: Louisiana State University Press, 1978 ed.

——. *The Plain People of the Confederacy*. 1943. Columbia, SC: University of South Carolina, 2000 ed.

——. *The Life of Billy Yank: The Common Soldier of the Union*. 1952. Baton Rouge, LA: Louisiana State University Press, 2001 ed.

Wilkens, J. Steven. *America: The First 350 Years*. Monroe, LA: Covenant Publications, 1998.

Willett, Robert L. *The Lightning Mule Brigade: Abel Streight's 1863 Raid into Alabama*. Carmel, IN: Guild Press, 1999.

Williams, Charles Richard. *The Life of Rutherford Birchard Hayes, Nineteenth President of the United States*. 2 vols. Boston, MA: Houghton Mifflin Co., 1914.

Williams, George Washington. *History of the Negro Race in America: From 1619 to 1880, Negroes as Slaves, as Soldiers, and as Citizens*. New York, NY: G. P. Putnam's Sons, 1885.

——. *A History of the Negro Troops in the War of the Rebellion 1861-1865*. New York, NY: Harper and Brothers, 1888.

Williams, James. *The South Vindicated*. London, UK: Longman, Green, Longman, Roberts, and Green, 1862.

Wills, Brian Steel. *The Confederacy's Greatest Cavalryman: Nathan Bedford Forrest*. Lawrence, KS: University Press of Kansas, 1992.

Wilson, Charles Reagan, and William Ferris. *Encyclopedia of Southern Culture* (Vol. 1). New York, NY: Anchor, 1989.

Wilson, Clyde N. *Why the South Will Survive: Fifteen Southerners Look at Their Region a Half Century After I'll Take My Stand*. Athens, GA: University of Georgia Press, 1981.

——. (ed.) *The Essential Calhoun: Selections From Writings, Speeches, and Letters*. New Brunswick, NJ: Transaction Publishers, 1991.

——. *A Defender of Southern Conservatism: M.E. Bradford and His Achievements*. Columbia, MO: University of Missouri Press, 1999.

——. *From Union to Empire: Essays in the Jeffersonian Tradition*. Columbia, SC: The Foundation for American Education, 2003.

——. *Defending Dixie: Essays in Southern History and Culture*. Columbia, SC: The Foundation for

American Education, 2005.

Wilson, Henry. *History of the Rise and Fall of the Slave Power in America*. 3 vols. Boston, MA: James R. Osgood and Co., 1877.

Wilson, Joseph Thomas. *The Black Phalanx: A History of the Negro Soldiers of the United States in the Wars of 1775-1812, 1861-'65*. Hartford, CT: American Publishing Co., 1890.

Wilson, Woodrow. *Division and Reunion: 1829-1889*. 1893. New York, NY: Longmans, Green, and Co., 1908 ed.

——. *A History of the American People*. 5 vols. 1902. New York, NY: Harper and Brothers, 1918 ed.

Witherspoon, William. *Reminiscences of a Scout, Spy and Soldier of Forrest's Cavalry*. Jackson, TN: McCowat Mercer Printing Co., 1910.

Wood, W. J. *Civil War Generalship: The Art of Command*. 1997. New York, NY: Da Capo Press, 2000 ed.

Woodard, Komozi. *A Nation Within a Nation: Amiri Baraka (LeRoi Jones) and Black Power Politics*. Chapel Hill, NC: University of North Carolina Press, 1999.

Woodburn, James Albert. *The Life of Thaddeus Stevens*. Indianapolis, IN: Bobbs-Merrill, 1913.

Woods, Thomas E., Jr. *The Politically Incorrect Guide to American History*. Washington D.C.: Regnery, 2004.

Woodson, Carter G. (ed.). *The Journal of Negro History* (Vol. 4). Lancaster, PA: Association for the Study of Negro Life and History, 1919.

Woodward, William E. *Meet General Grant*. 1928. New York, NY: Liveright Publishing, 1946 ed.

Woodworth, Steven E. *Jefferson Davis and His Generals: The Failure of Confederate Command in the West*. Lawrence, KS: University Press of Kansas, 1990.

Wright, John D. *The Language of the Civil War*. Westport, CT: Oryx, 2001.

Wyeth, John Allan. *Life of General Nathan Bedford Forrest*. New York, NY: Harper and Brothers, 1899.

——. *That Devil Forrest* (redacted modern version of Wyeth's *Life of General Nathan Bedford Forrest*). 1959. Baton Rouge, LA: Louisiana State University Press, 1989 ed.

Young, Bennett Henderson. *Confederate Wizards of the Saddle*. 1914. Lanham, MD: J. S. Sanders and Co., 1999 ed.

Young, John Russell. *Around the World With General Grant*. 2 vols. New York, NY: American News Co., 1879.

Zaehner, R. C. (ed.) *Encyclopedia of the World's Religions*. 1959. New York, NY: Barnes and Noble, 1997 ed.

Zall, Paul M. (ed.). *Lincoln on Lincoln*. Lexington, KY: University Press of Kentucky, 1999.

Zavodnyik, Peter. *The Age of Strict Construction: A History of the Growth of Federal Power, 1789-1861*. Washington, D.C.: Catholic University of America Press, 2007.

Zinn, Howard. *A People's History of the United States: 1492-Present*. 1980. New York, NY: HarperCollins, 1995.

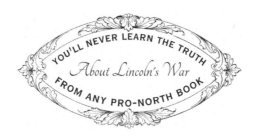

YOU'LL NEVER LEARN THE TRUTH *About Lincoln's War* FROM ANY PRO-NORTH BOOK

# I RIDE WITH FORREST

# INDEX

bummers, Yankee, 420
Burns, Ken, 65, 546
Burras, Anne, 175
Butler, Andrew P., 816
Butler, Benjamin F., 156, 213
C.S.A., 127, 212, 229, 251, 252, 565, 753, 758
Caesar, Julius, 472, 581, 592
calender, of Forrest's life, 560
Calhoun, John C., 86
California, 563, 748, 750
Calvin, John, 86
Cameron, Simon, 106, 246
Campbell, Joseph, 74, 815
Campbell, Wallace, 534
Canada, 49, 175, 751, 760
Canby, Edward R. S., 318, 416, 421, 423, 425, 426
Caney Spring Creek, 173
Caney Springs, Tennessee, 172
Cannon, Captain, 473
Cape Fear (film), 65
capitalism, 5, 747
capture of Nashville, 566
Caribbean, 246
Carlyle, Thomas, 525
Carnes, W. W., 302
Carnton, 2, 18-20, 215, 275, 394, 395, 421, 767
Carnton Mansion, 18, 394
Carnton Plantation, 2, 18-20, 215, 275, 394, 421, 767
Carnton Plantation Ghost Stories (Seabrook), 394, 421
carpetbag rule, 161, 299, 462
carpetbaggers, 161, 438, 439, 761
carpetbag-scallywag regime, 439, 440, 443, 462
Carroll, Charles, 477
Carson, Martha, 816
Carter, John C., 395
Carter, Theodrick "Tod", 816
Carter's Creek, 402, 410
Cartwright, Thomas, 396
Cash, Johnny, 816
Cash, W. J., 40, 62, 63
Castle Pickney, 252
Catharine, slave girl, 205
Catherine the Great, 86
Catton, Bruce, 77
Caucasian, 119, 120
Caudill, Benjamin E., 15, 815
Caudill, Edward, 73
Caudill's Army, 15, 815
cavalrymen, 15, 42, 338, 386, 394, 488, 520, 525, 529
Cedar Bluff, Alabama, 537
Celtic blood, 176
Central America, 137, 239, 243
central government, 5, 64, 440
Chalmers, James R., 321-323, 333, 358, 368, 369, 371, 372, 375, 379, 384, 390, 391, 395, 400, 402, 403, 406-409, 505
Chamberlain, F. W., 199

# MEET THE AUTHOR

**LOCHLAINN SEABROOK,** winner of the prestigious Jefferson Davis Historical Gold Medal for his "masterpiece," *A Rebel Born: A Defense of Nathan Bedford Forrest*, is an unreconstructed Southern historian, award-winning author, Civil War scholar, and traditional Southern Agrarian of Scottish, English, Irish, Dutch, Welsh, German, and Italian extraction. An encyclopedist, lexicographer, musician, artist, graphic designer, genealogist, and photographer, as well as an award-winning poet, songwriter, and screenwriter, he has a 40 year background in historical nonfiction writing and is a member of the Sons of Confederate Veterans, the Civil War Trust, and the National Grange.

Due to similarities in their writing styles, ideas, and literary works, Seabrook is often referred to as the "new Shelby Foote," the "Southern Joseph Campbell," and the "American Robert Graves" (his English cousin).

The grandson of an Appalachian coal-mining family, Seabrook is a seventh-generation Kentuckian, co-chair of the Jent/Gent Family Committee (Kentucky), founder and director of the Blakeney Family Tree Project, and a board member of the Friends of Colonel Benjamin E. Caudill. Seabrook's literary works have been endorsed by leading authorities, museum curators, award-winning historians, bestselling authors, celebrities, noted scientists, well respected educators, TV show hosts and producers, renowned military artists, esteemed Southern organizations, and distinguished academicians from around the world.

COPYRIGHT ©
SEA RAVEN PRESS

Lochlainn Seabrook, Forrest scholar & author of eight books & a screenplay on his cousin General Forrest.

Seabrook has authored over 45 popular adult books on the American Civil War, American and international slavery, the U.S. Confederacy (1781), the Southern Confederacy (1861), religion, theology and thealogy, Jesus, the Bible, the Apocrypha, the Law of Attraction, alternative health, spirituality, ghost stories, the paranormal, ufology, social issues, and cross-cultural studies of the family and marriage. His Confederate biographies, pro-South studies, genealogical monographs, family histories, military encyclopedias, self-help guides, and etymological dictionaries have received wide acclaim.

Seabrook's eight children's books include a Southern guide to the Civil War, a biography of Nathan Bedford Forrest, a dictionary of religion and myth, a rewriting of the King Arthur legend (which reinstates the original pre-Christian motifs), two bedtime stories for preschoolers, a naturalist's guidebook to owls, a worldwide look at the family, and an examination of the Near-Death Experience.

Of blue-blooded Southern stock through his Kentucky, Tennessee, Virginia, West Virginia, and North Carolina ancestors, he is a direct descendant of European royalty via his 6th great-grandfather, the Earl of Oxford, after which London's famous Harley Street is named. Among his celebrated male Celtic ancestors is Robert the Bruce, King of Scotland, Seabrook's 22nd great-grandfather. The 21st great-grandson of Edward I "Longshanks" Plantagenet), King of England, Seabrook is a thirteenth-generation Southerner through his descent from the colonists of Jamestown, Virginia (1607).

The 2nd, 3rd, and 4th great-grandson of dozens of Confederate soldiers, one of his closest connections to Lincoln's War is through his 3rd great-grandfather, Elias Jent, Sr., who fought for the Confederacy in the Thirteenth Cavalry Kentucky under Seabrook's 2nd cousin, Colonel Benjamin E. Caudill. The Thirteenth, also known as "Caudill's Army," fought in numerous conflicts, including the Battles of Saltville, Gladsville, Mill Cliff, Poor Fork, Whitesburg, and Leatherwood.

Seabrook is a descendant of the families of Alexander H. Stephens, John Singleton Mosby, and Edmund Winchester Rucker, and is related to the following Confederates and other 19th-Century luminaries: Robert E. Lee, Stephen Dill Lee, Stonewall Jackson, Nathan Bedford Forrest, James Longstreet, John Hunt Morgan, Jeb Stuart, P. G. T. Beauregard (designed the Confederate Battle Flag), George W. Gordon, John Bell Hood, Alexander Peter Stewart, Arthur M. Manigault, Joseph Manigault, Charles Scott Venable, Thornton A. Washington, John A. Washington, Abraham Buford, Edmund W. Pettus, Theodrick "Tod" Carter, John B. Womack, John H. Winder, Gideon J. Pillow, States Rights Gist, Henry R. Jackson, John Lawton Seabrook, John C. Breckinridge, Leonidas Polk, Zachary Taylor, Sarah Knox Taylor (first wife of Jefferson Davis), Richard Taylor, Davy Crockett, Daniel Boone, Meriwether Lewis (of the Lewis and Clark Expedition) Andrew Jackson, James K. Polk, Abram Poindexter Maury (founder of Franklin, TN), William Giles Harding, Zebulon Vance, Thomas Jefferson, Edmund Jennings Randolph, George Wythe Randolph (grandson of Jefferson), Felix K. Zollicoffer, Fitzhugh Lee, Nathaniel F. Cheairs, Jesse James, Frank James, Robert Brank Vance, Charles Sidney Winder, John W. McGavock, Caroline E. (Winder) McGavock, David Harding McGavock, Lysander

(Photo © Lochlainn Seabrook)

McGavock, James Randal McGavock, Randal William McGavock, Francis McGavock, Emily McGavock, William Henry F. Lee, Lucius E. Polk, Minor Meriwether (husband of noted pro-South author Elizabeth Avery Meriwether), Ellen Bourne Tynes (wife of Forrest's chief of artillery, Captain John W. Morton), South Carolina Senators Preston Smith Brooks and Andrew Pickens Butler, and famed South Carolina diarist Mary Chesnut.

Seabrook's modern day cousins include: Patrick J. Buchanan (conservative author), Cindy Crawford (model), Shelby Lee Adams (Letcher County, Kentucky, portrait photographer), Bertram Thomas Combs (Kentucky's fiftieth governor), Edith Bolling (wife of President Woodrow Wilson), and actors Robert Duvall, Reese Witherspoon, Lee Marvin, Rebecca Gayheart, Andy Griffith, and Tom Cruise.

Seabrook's screenplay, *A Rebel Born*, based on his book of the same name, has been signed with acclaimed filmmaker Christopher Forbes (of Forbes Film). It is now in pre-production, and is set for release in 2016 as a full-length feature film. This will be the first movie ever made of Nathan Bedford Forrest's life story, and as a historically accurate project written from the Southern perspective, is destined to be one of the most talked about Civil War films of all time.

Born with music in his blood, Seabrook is an award-winning, multi-genre, BMI-Nashville songwriter and lyricist who has composed some 3,000 songs (250 albums), and whose original music has been heard in film (*A Rebel Born, Cowgirls 'n Angels*) and on TV and radio worldwide. A musician, producer, multi-instrumentalist, and renown performer—whose keyboard work has been variously compared to pianists from Hargus Robbins and Vince Guaraldi to Elton John and Leonard Bernstein—Seabrook has opened for groups such as the Earl Scruggs Review, Ted Nugent, and Bob Seger, and has performed privately for such public figures as President Ronald Reagan, Burt Reynolds, Loni Anderson, and Senator Edward W. Brooke. Seabrook's cousins in the music business include: Johnny Cash, Elvis Presley, Billy Ray and Miley Cyrus, Patty Loveless, Tim McGraw, Lee Ann Womack, Dolly Parton, Pat Boone, Naomi, Wynonna, and Ashley Judd, Ricky Skaggs, the Sunshine Sisters, Martha Carson, and Chet Atkins.

Seabrook, a libertarian, lives with his wife and family in historic Middle Tennessee, the heart of Forrest country and the Confederacy, where his conservative Southern ancestors fought valiantly against Liberal Lincoln and the progressive North in defense of Jeffersonianism, constitutional government, and personal liberty.

# MEET THE COVER ARTIST

For over 30 years American artist JOHN PAUL STRAIN has been amazing art collectors with his unique talent of capturing moments in time from the early days of the American Frontier, the glory and pageantry of the American Civil War, to contemporary scenic and romantic locations across the world. From the early age of twenty-one, Mr. Strain's paintings were represented by Trailside Galleries, America's most prestigious western art gallery. For fifteen years his beautiful landscapes, wild life paintings, and depictions of Indian life were represented by most every major western art gallery and top art auctions in the United States.

In 1991 Mr. Strain broadened his subjects to include historical art of the American Civil War. During the next seventeen years he focused his work on the world of daring horseback raids and epic battles with great armies and leaders, capturing and preserving a unique era in history. Over a period of years, Mr. Strain became known as America's leading historical artist, with over fifty magazine covers featuring his paintings.

His work is featured in books, movies, and film. Mr. Strain's book, *A Witness to the Civil War*, released in November 2002, was a best seller for his publisher and quickly sold out of its first printing. The book is unusual among art books in that it is written by the artist. The Scholastic Resources Company purchased over 3,000 copies of the edition for school libraries across the US. His newest book was released in 2009.

Strain's paintings have helped to raise funds for many historical restoration projects and battlefield preservation organizations. The National Park Service uses his images in their publications and at battlefield sites. A number of historical private institutions have on site displays featuring his work such as General JEB Stuart's home and estate, and General Jubal Early's boyhood home.

Mr. Strain and his paintings were also featured on the television shows of C-Span's Washington Journal, The History Channel, and Extreme Makeover Home Edition. Throughout his career he has won many awards for his art. Reproductions of his work have won numerous first place awards and "Best of Show" honors, such as the PICA Awards, The Printing Industry of the Carolinas, and just recently at the PIAG 2008 Awards in Georgia, he won the Top Gold Award for his painting "New Year's Wish," and Best Of Category Giclée for "Fire In the Sky."

Strain is also a featured artist for internationally know collector art companies the Bradford Exchange and the Franklin Mint, where he has created a Civil War Chess Set, several limited edition plate series, sculptures, and many other collectable items featuring his paintings. Mr. Strain has also completed a number of commissioned works for the United States Army, which are on permanent display at Fort Leavenworth, Kansas, Fort McNair, Washington, D.C., and the battlefield visitor's center at Normandy, France.

Today, Mr. Strain's original paintings can be found in many noted museums such as the Museum of Fredericksburg, South Georgia Relics Museum, and at Thomas Jefferson's home, Monticello. His work is included in many private fine art collections, corporate collections, and is owned by dignitaries such as United States Senators, Congressmen and a number of State Governors.

## JOHNPAULSTRAIN.COM

"Surviving members of Forrest's staff." Clockwise, beginning at the upper right: George Dashiel, William M. Forrest (the General's son), James B. Cowan, Charles W. Anderson, John W. Morton, and Samuel Donelson. Forrest, of course, is in the middle. Image from Ridley's *Battles and Sketches of the Army of Tennessee*.

# THE FORREST HOME FUND

## Help Preserve the

# NATHAN BEDFORD FORREST BOYHOOD HOME

## CHAPEL HILL, TENNESSEE

PHOTO © LOCHLAINN SEABROOK

If you'd like to help maintain this unique historical landmark and aid in the ongoing restoration process and the building of a visitor's center, if you're interested in donating your time, energy, or supplies, or if you or your company would like to sponsor this project, please mail your correspondence or contribution to:

## ★ The Forrest Home Fund ★

C/O SONS OF CONFEDERATE VETERANS
PO BOX 59
COLUMBIA, TN 38402-0059

". . . his dust is our ashes of glory." Photo copyright © Lochlainn Seabrook.